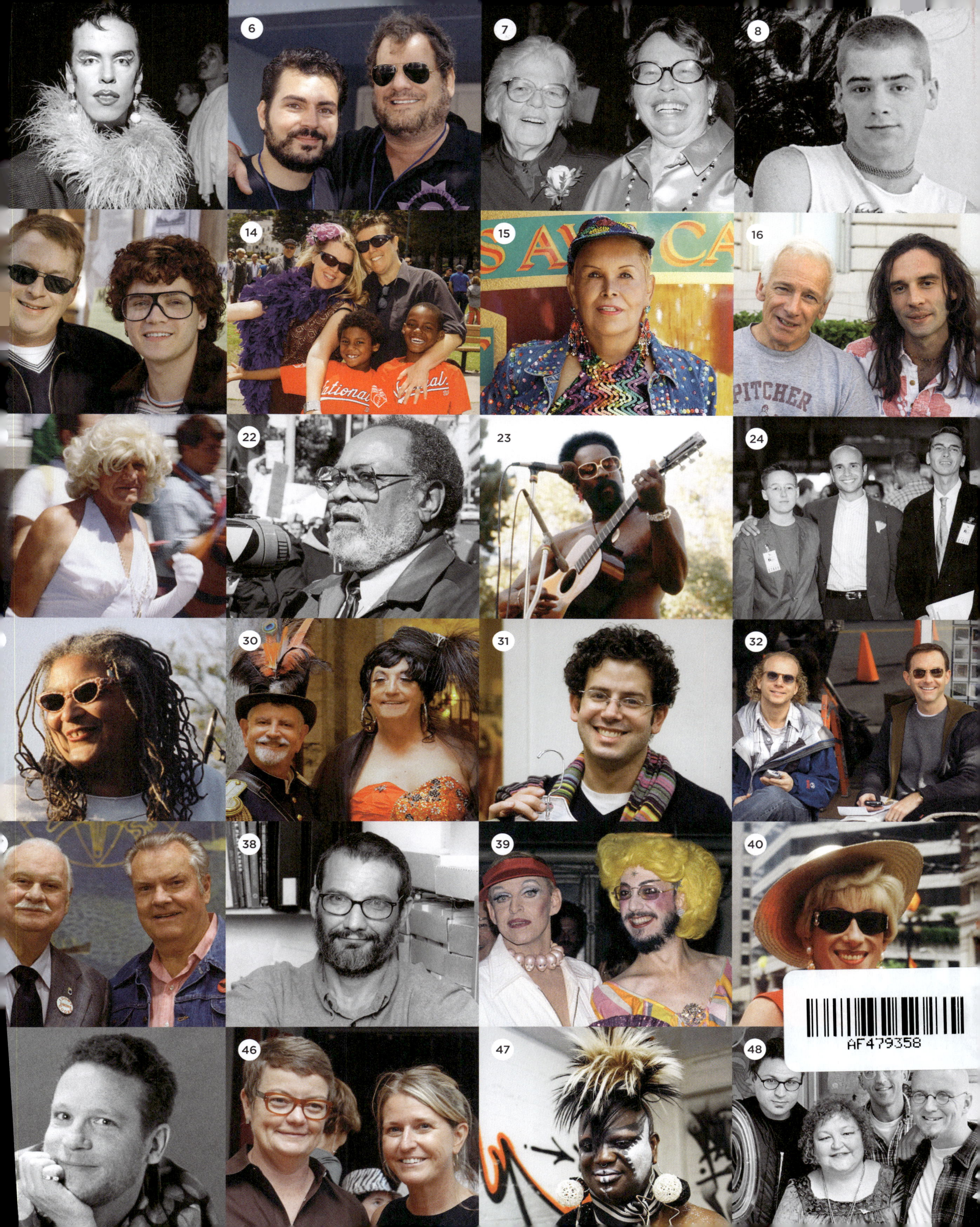
6
7
8
14
15
16
PITCHER
22
23
24
30
31
32
38
39
40
AF479358
46
47
48

And out of what one sees and hears and out
Of what one feels, who could have thought to make
So many selves, so many sensuous worlds,
As if the air, the mid-day air, was swarming
With the metaphysical changes that occur,
Merely in living as and where we live.

- *Wallace Stevens (1944)*

LGBT
San Francisco

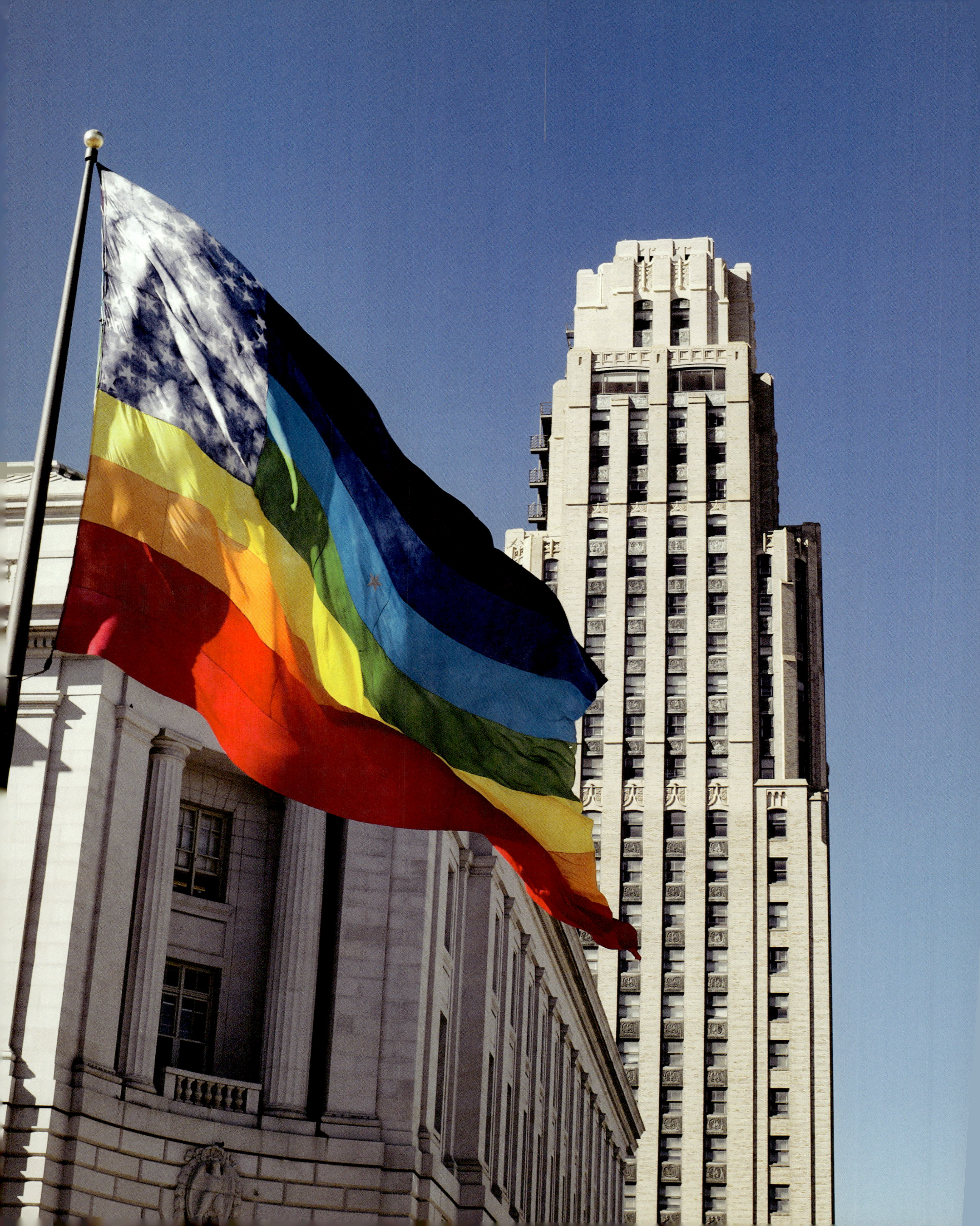

LGBT
San Francisco

THE DANIEL NICOLETTA PHOTOGRAPHS

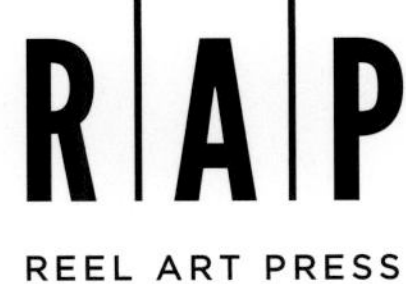

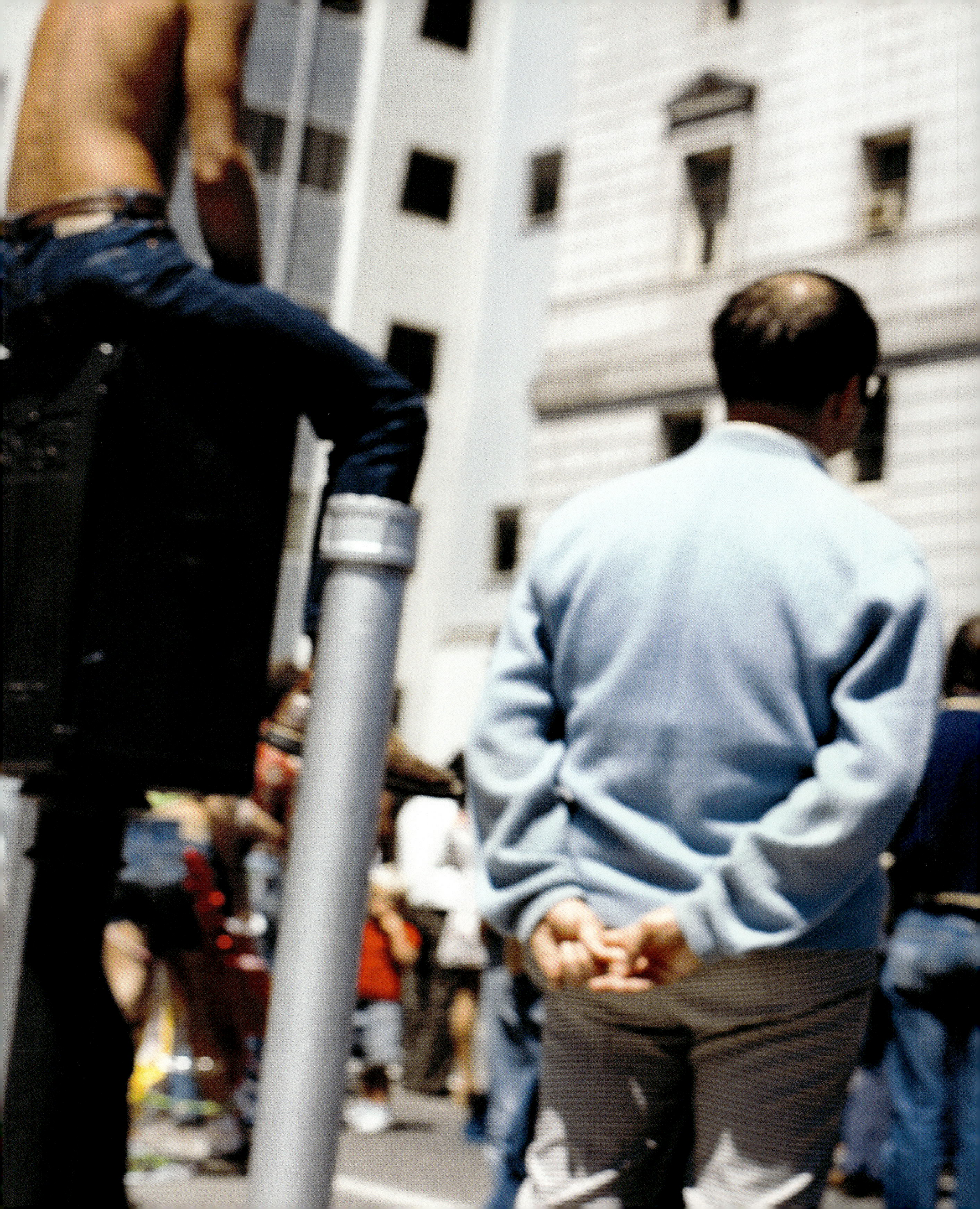

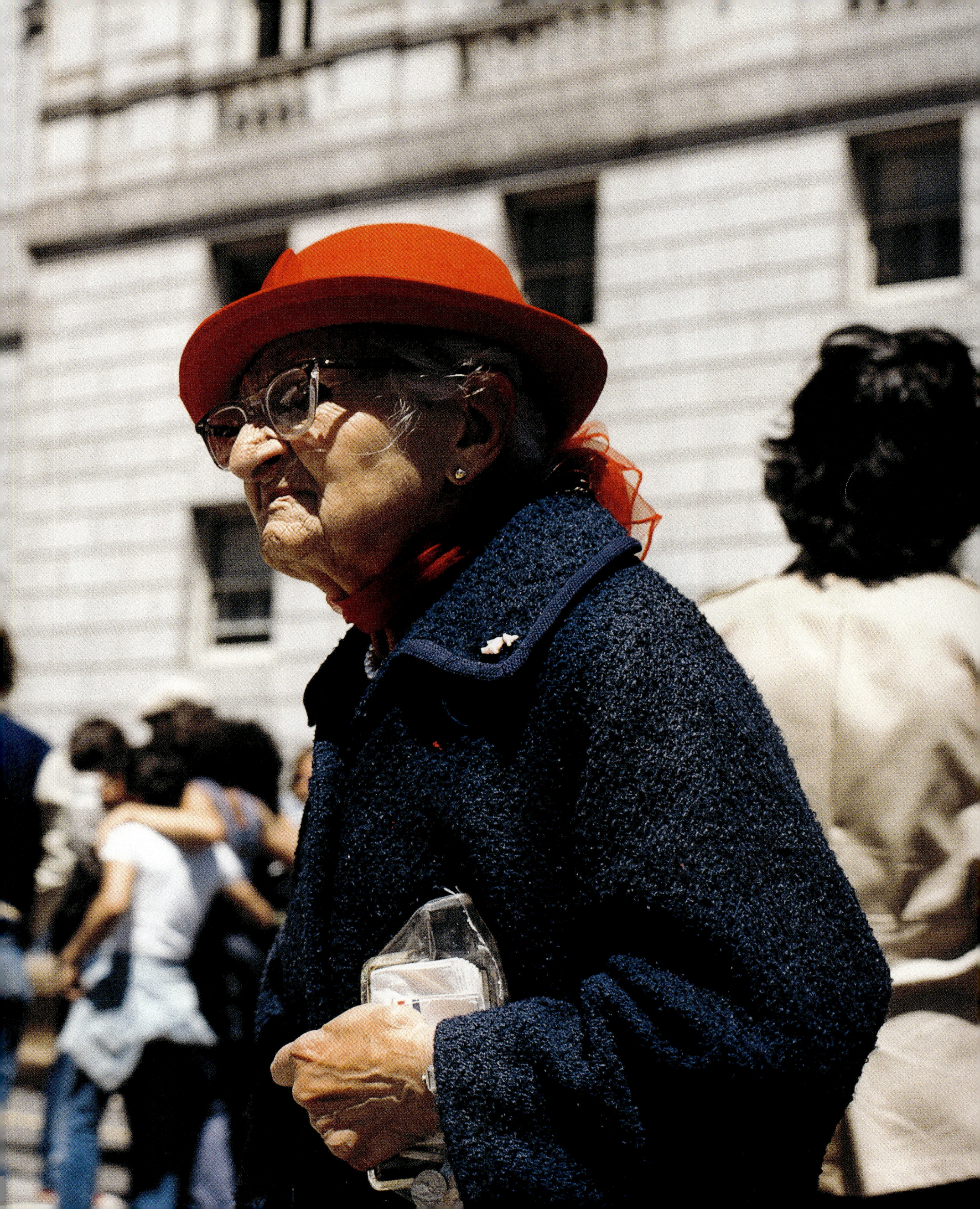

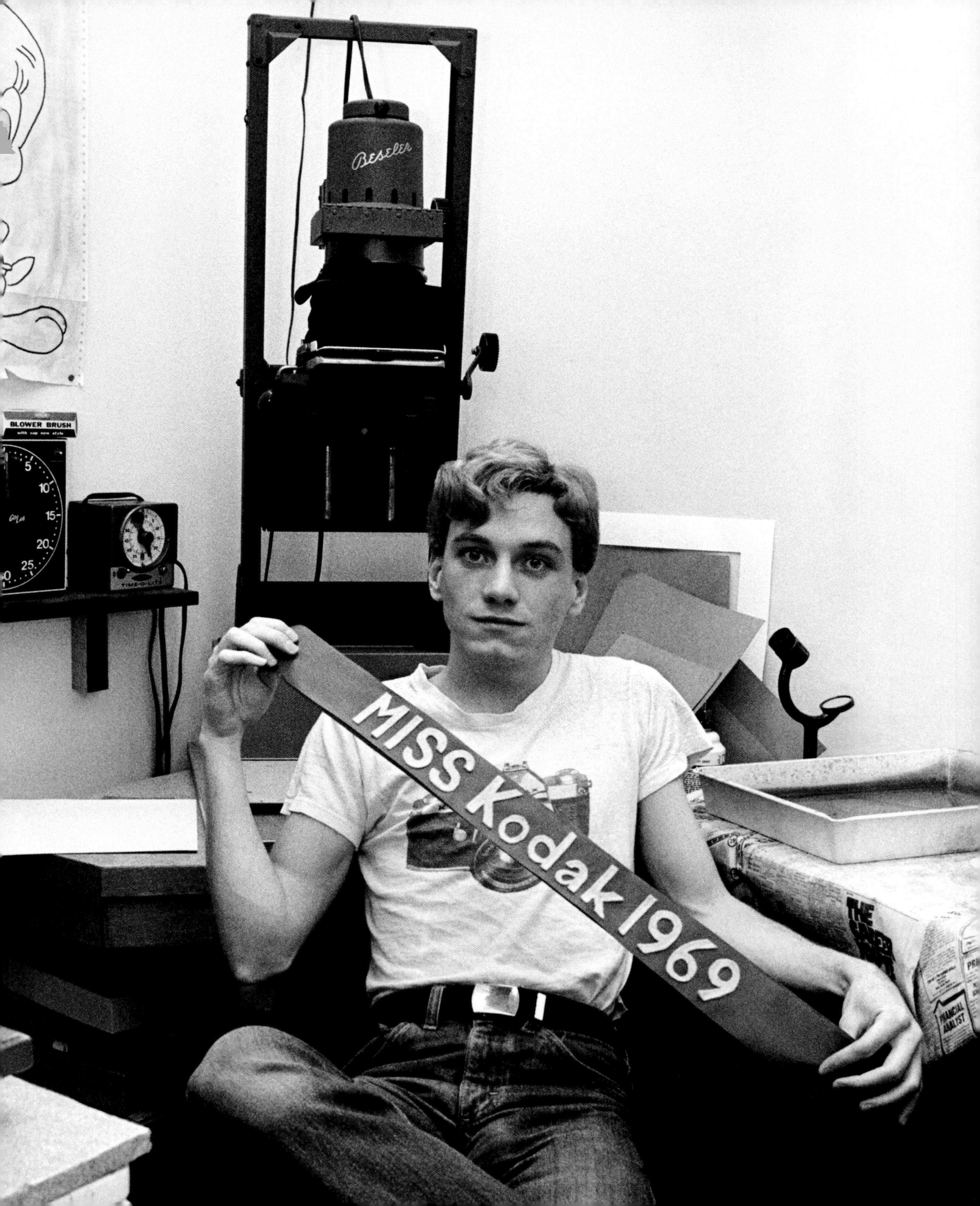
Beseler
BLOWER BRUSH
MISS Kodak 1969

PHOTOGRAPHS
DANIEL NICOLETTA

FOREWORD
GUS VAN SANT

INTRODUCTION
CHUCK MOBLEY

EDITOR
TONY NOURMAND

ART DIRECTION
JOAKIM OLSSON

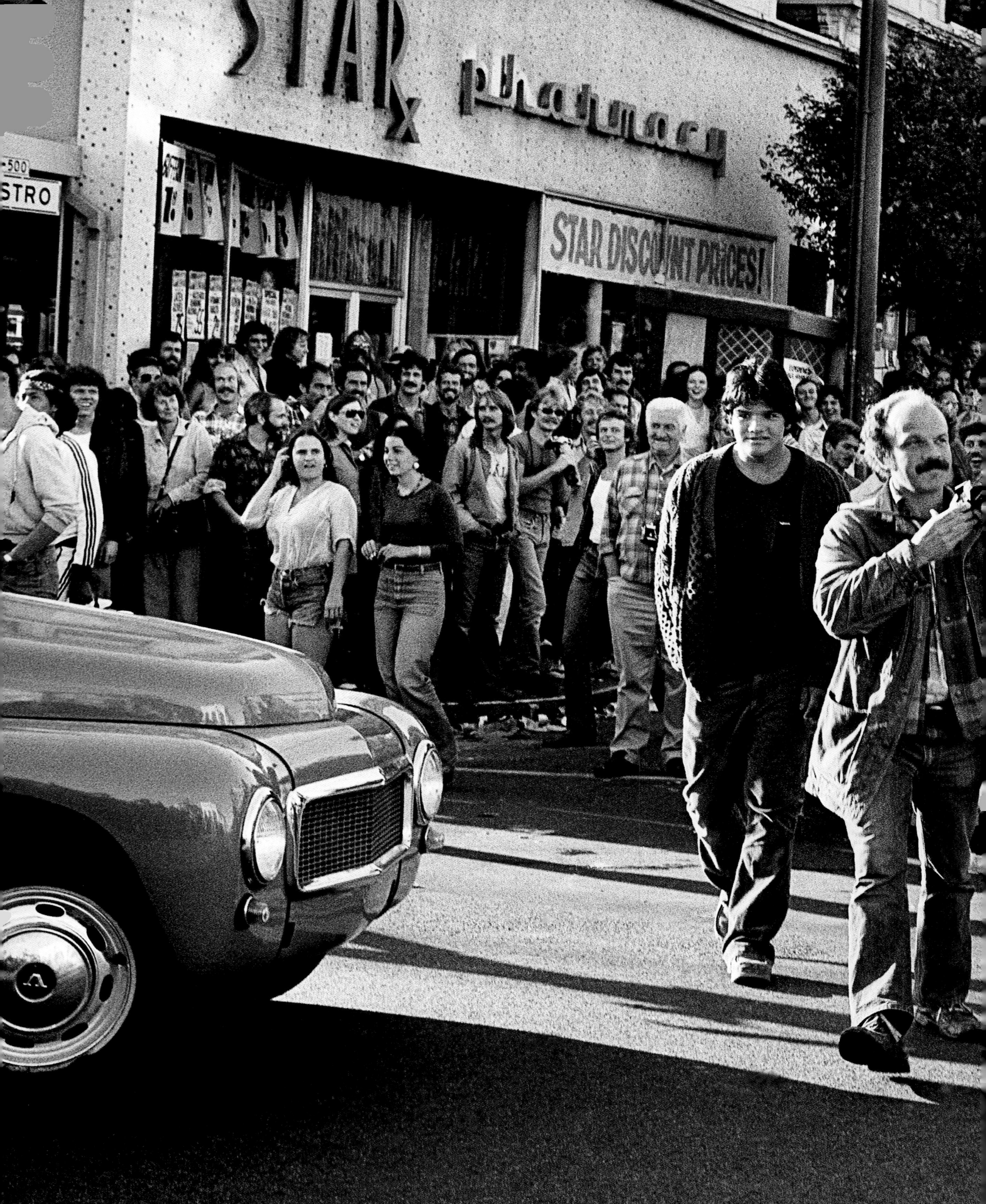
STAR
pharmacy
STAR DISCOUNT PRICES!
STRO
500

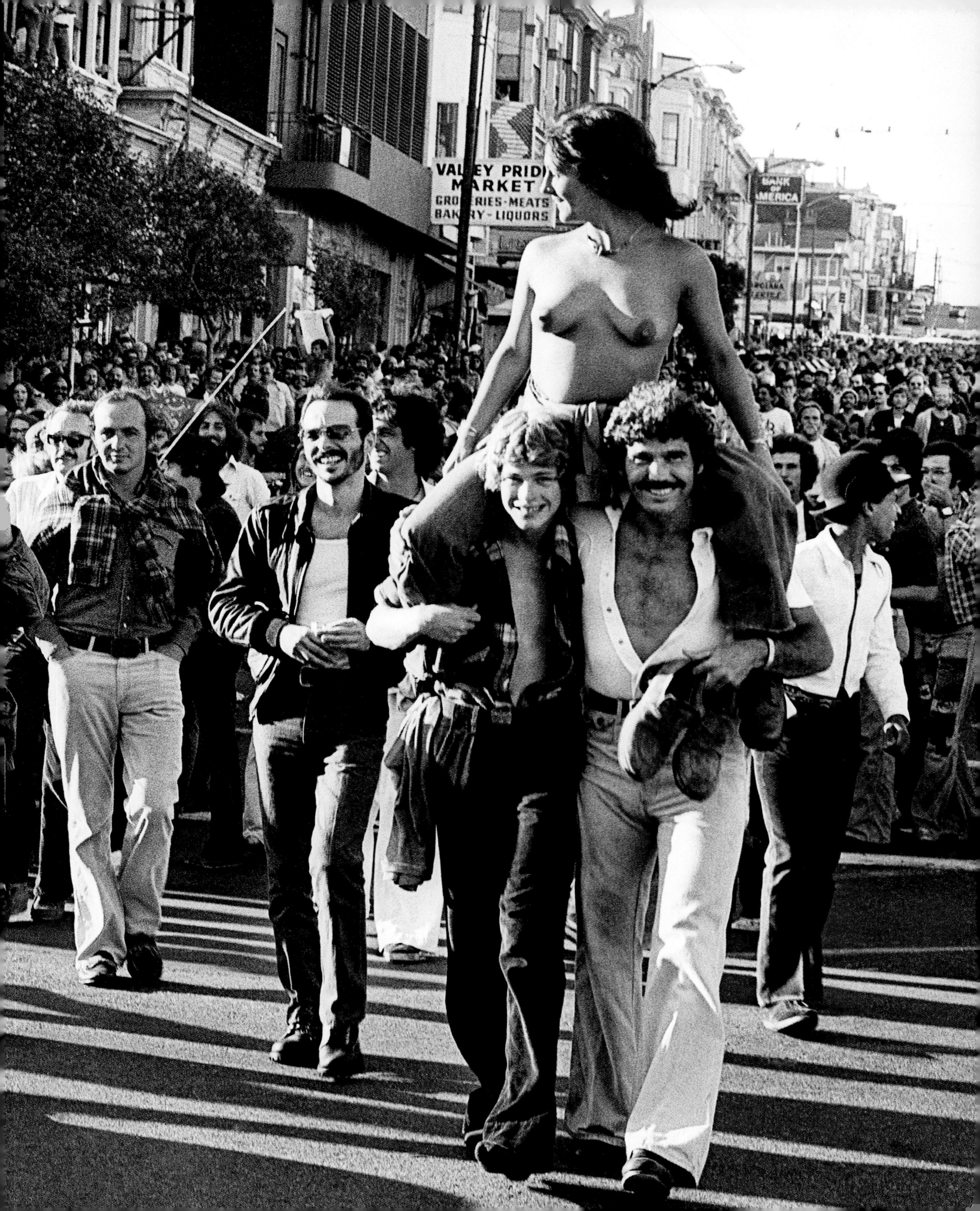
VALLEY PRIDE
MARKET
GROCERIES-MEATS
BAKERY-LIQUORS
BANK
OF
AMERICA

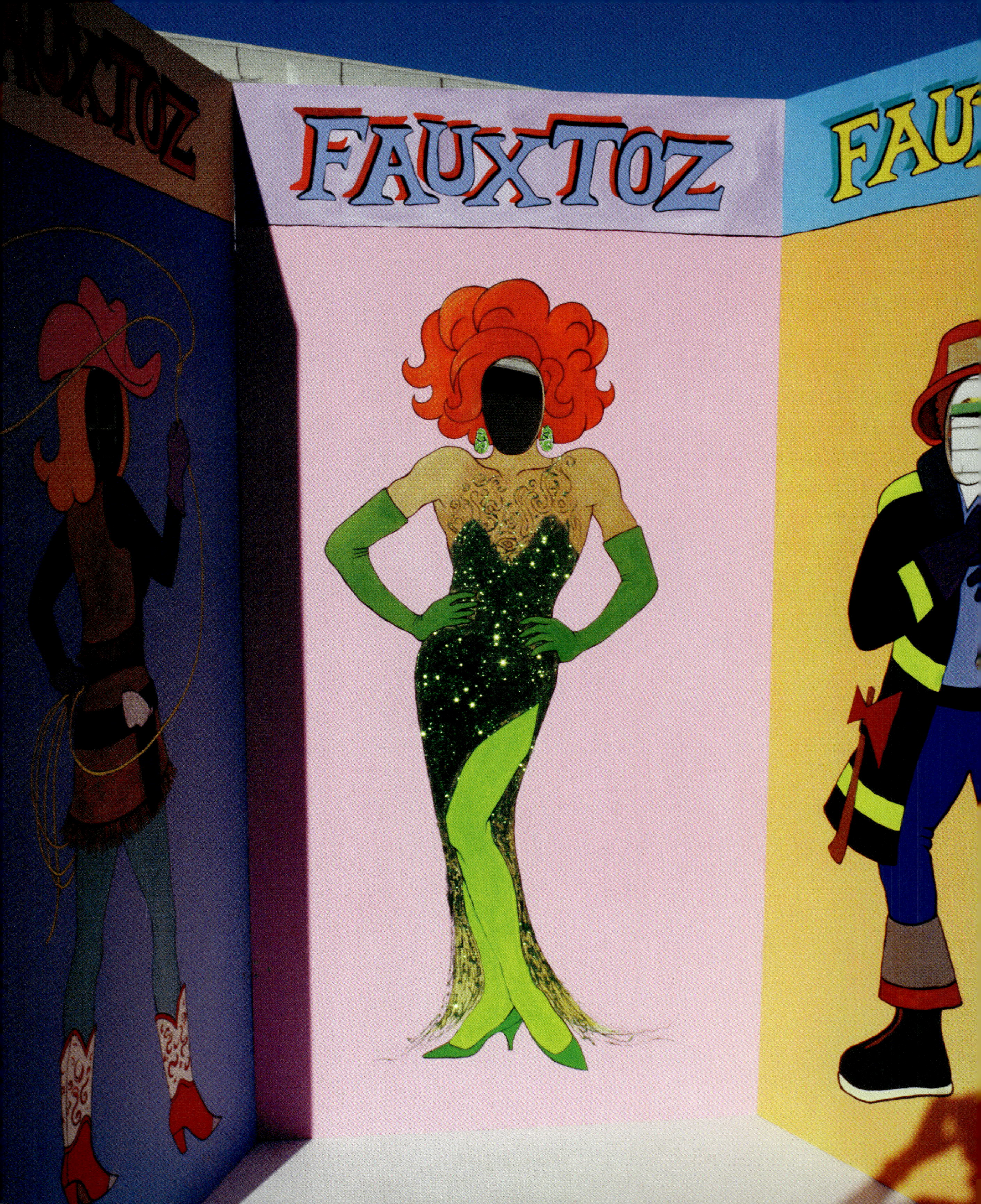
FAUXTOZ

CONTENTS

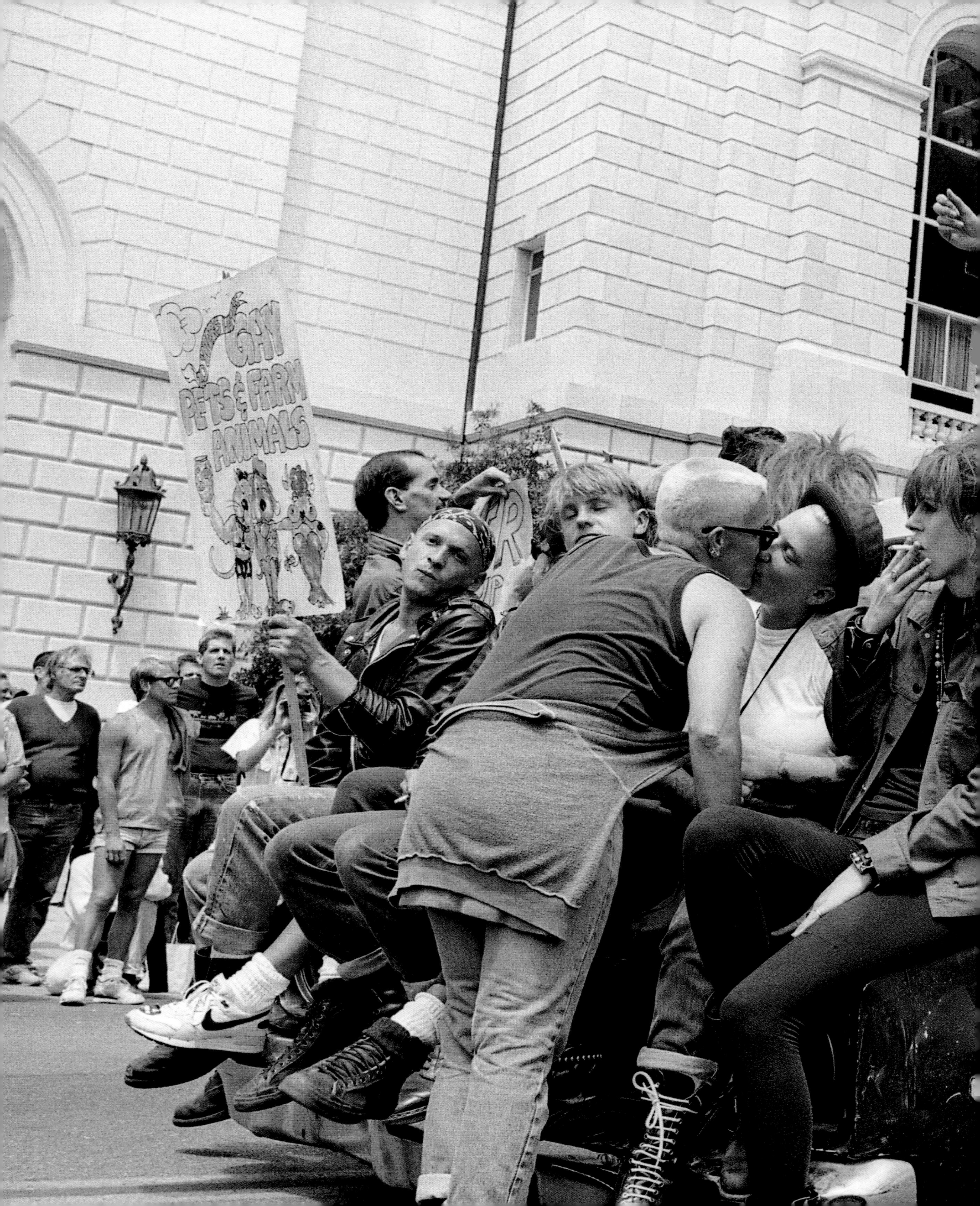
GAY
PETS & FARM
ANIMALS

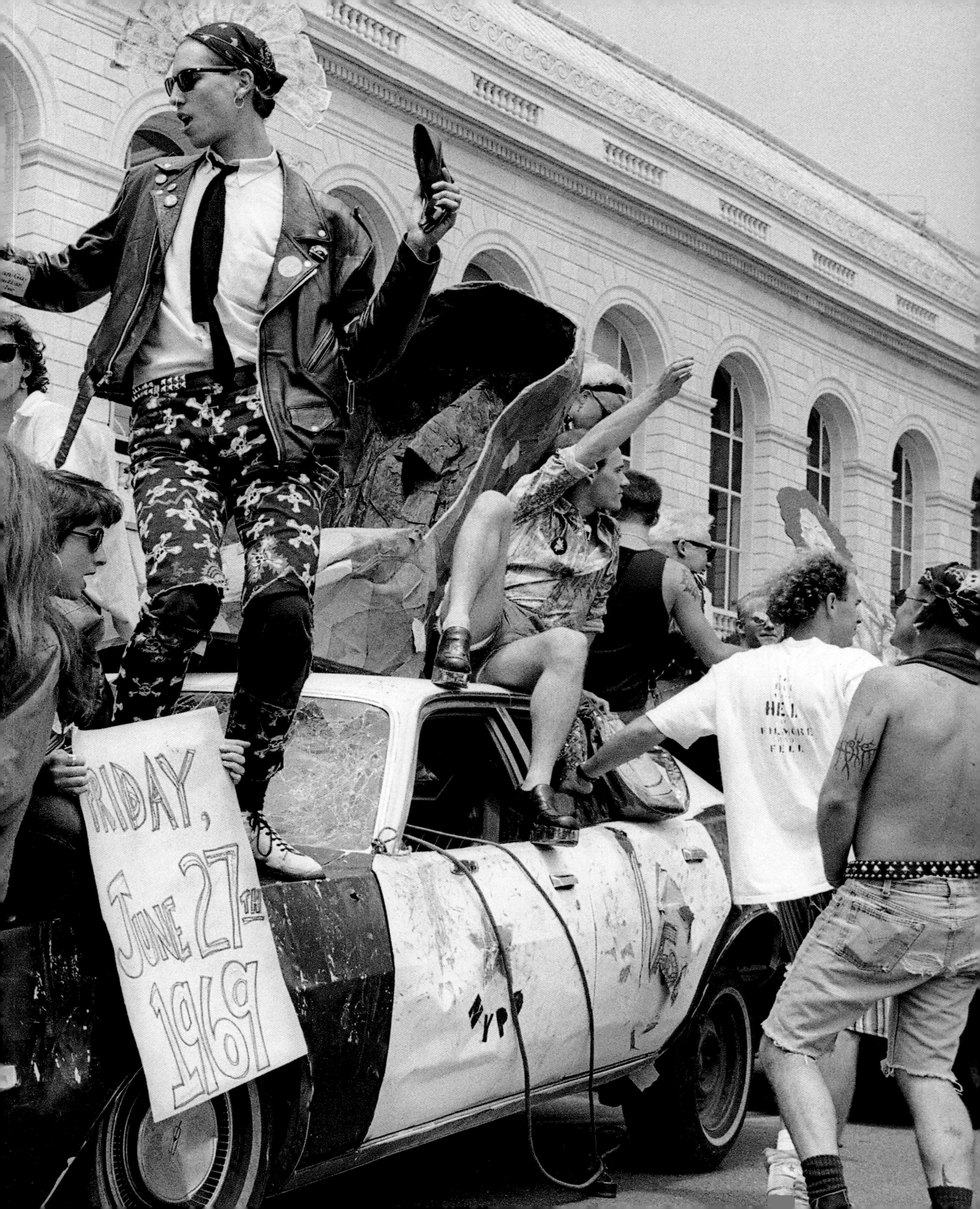
RIDAY,
JUNE 27TH
1969
NYPD

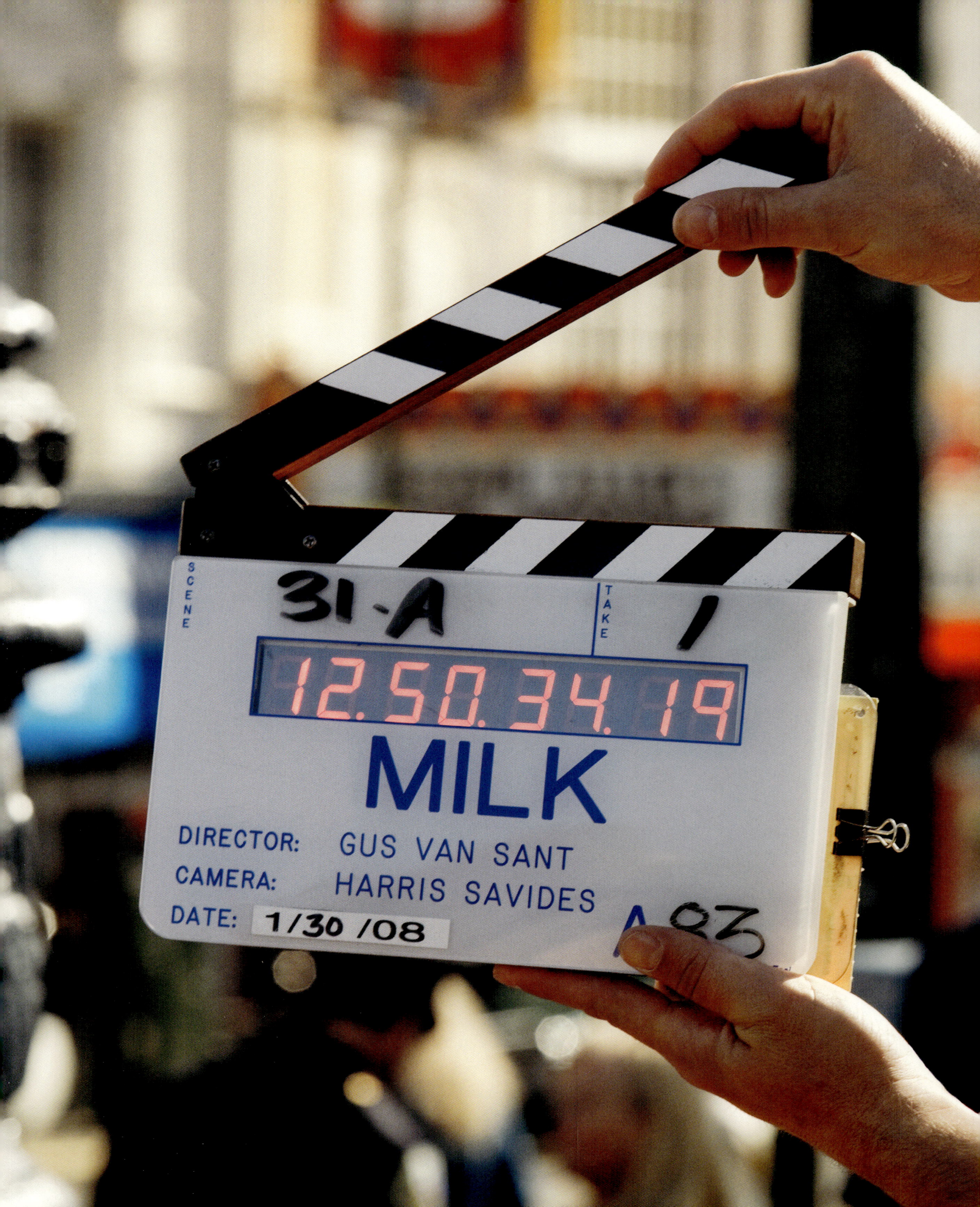
SCENE
31-A
TAKE
1
12.50.34.19
MILK
DIRECTOR: GUS VAN SANT
CAMERA: HARRIS SAVIDES
DATE: 1/30/08
A83

FOREWORD

I saw Danny's work for the first time in the early 1990s. He has an enormous collection of photographs, taken over the past 40 years. Some are iconic photos of Harvey Milk and many are portraits of a shared circle of friends—some of whom were key players in events I was researching in 2008 for our film, *Milk*.

Danny's photographs were a vital resource to the formation of *Milk*. They were examples of the real people and places and influenced our vision for the film in innumerable ways. Danny worked as a photographer on the film as a way to document what we were doing and also advise us on the historical aspects. He helped the actors with details of their characters and the art department regarding visuals, and assisted me with specifics about the time or about Harvey's life.

Danny's photos are a treasured artistic record of the people who initiated a movement from within their own neighborhood, and the work links that exuberant time to the larger history of LGBT people. This book is a very welcome addition to our enduring collective memory.

Gus Van Sant

Milk; January 30, 2008.

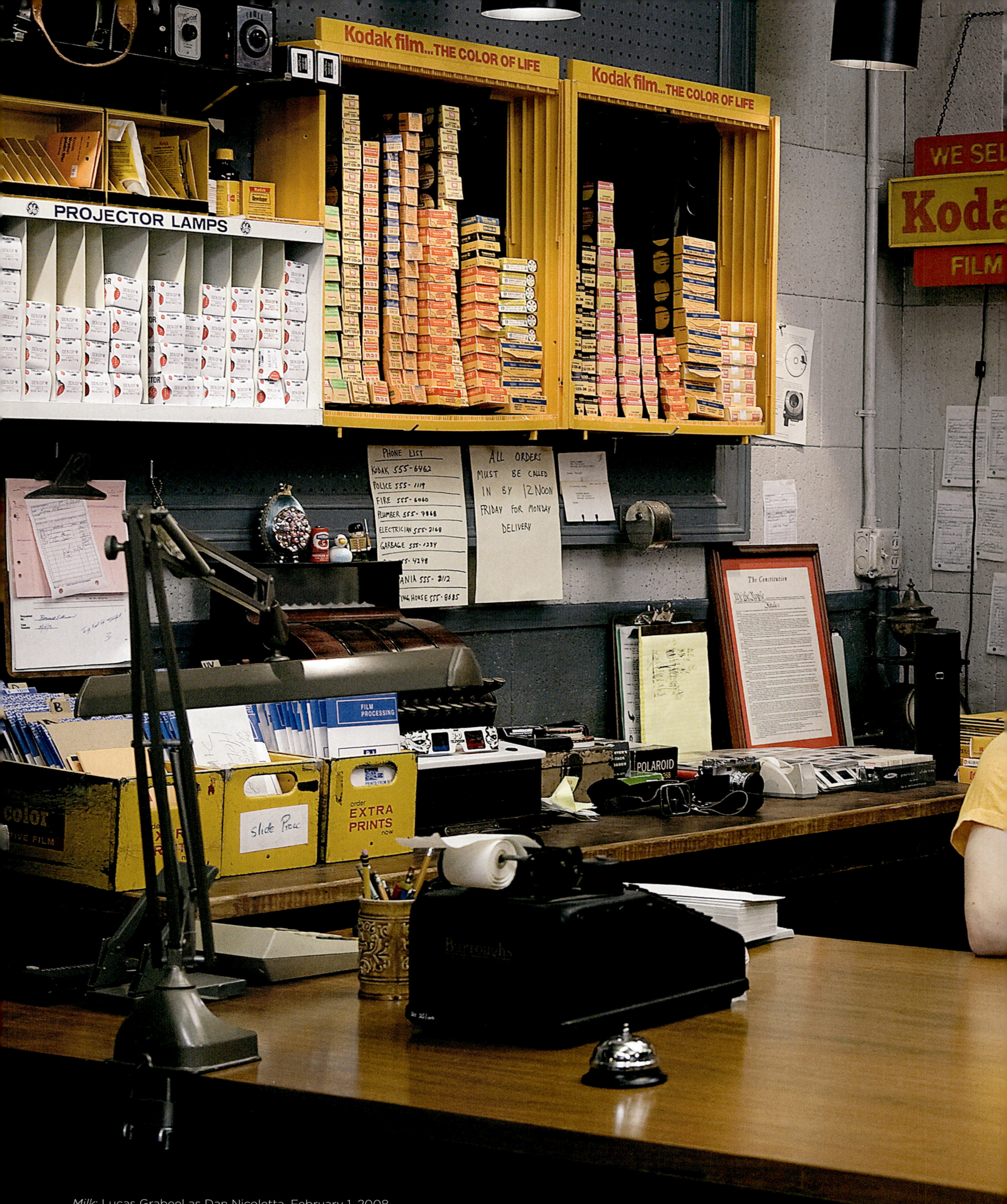

Milk: Lucas Grabeel as Dan Nicoletta, February 1, 2008

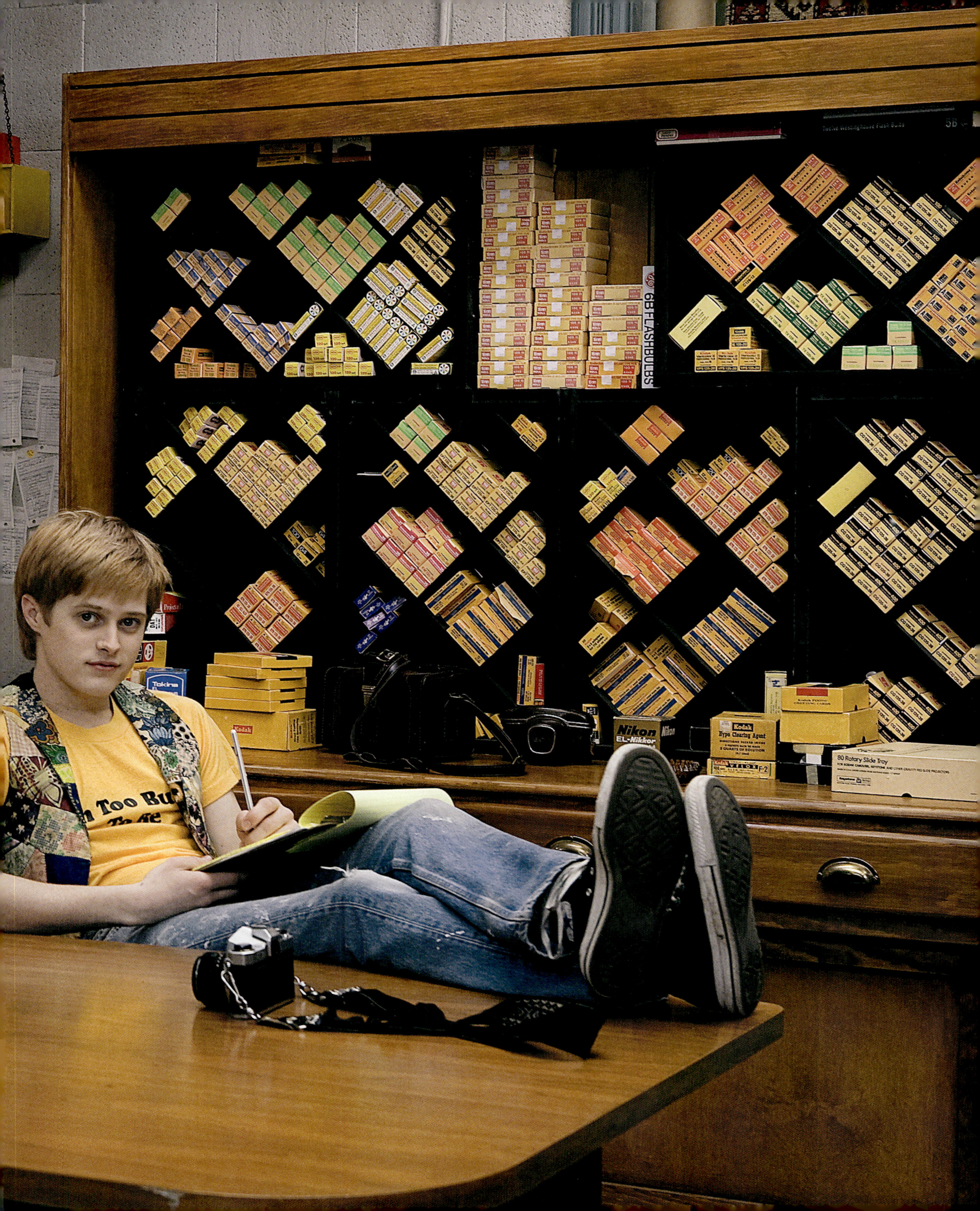

6B-FLASHBULBS
Tokina
Kodak
Nikon
EL-Nikkor
Kodak
Hypo Clearing Agent
80 Rotary Slide Tray

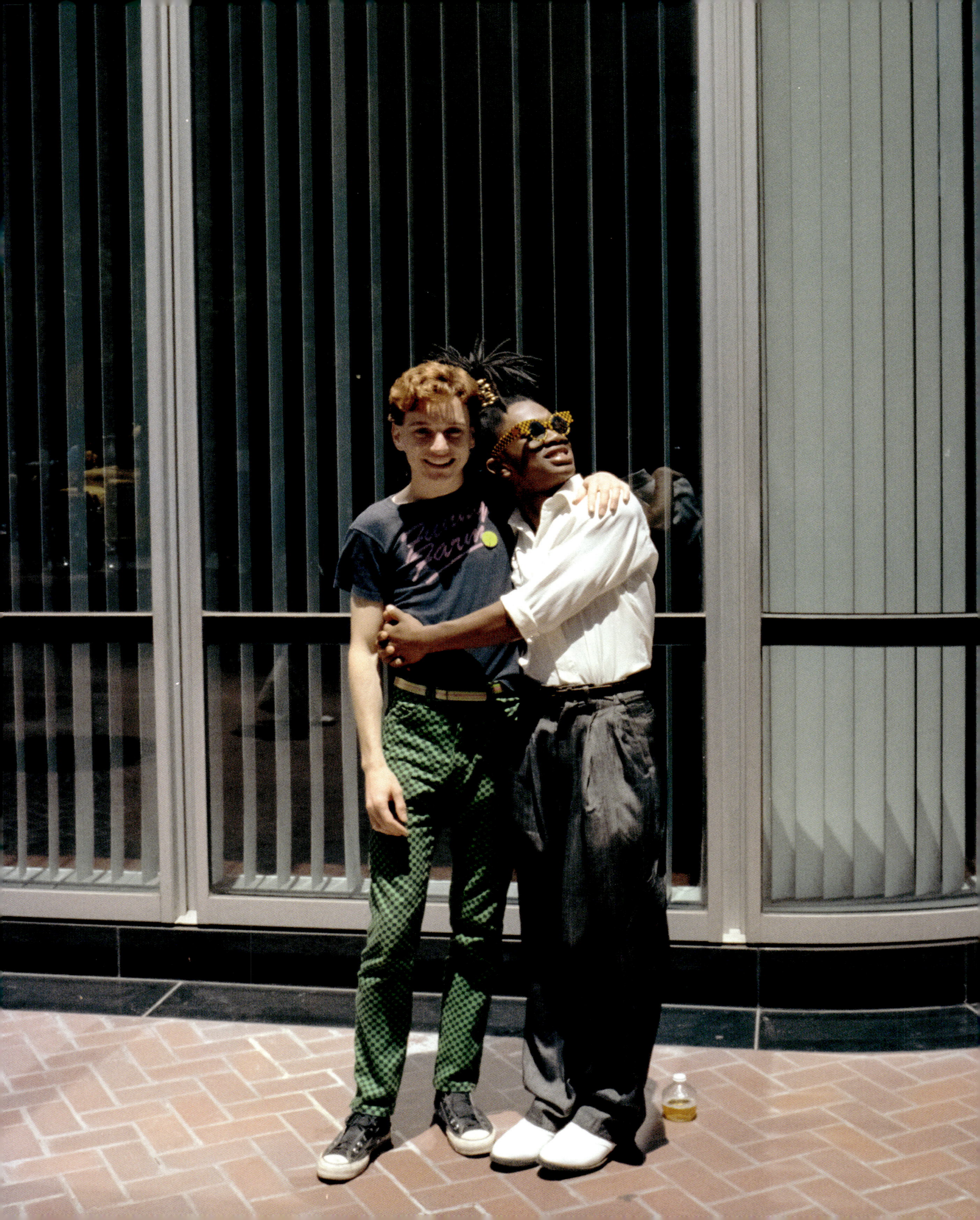

THERE IS NO SHELTER IN THE ARTS:

AN INTRODUCTION TO THE LIFE AND TIMES OF DANNY NICOLETTA

On April 21, 2014 the United States Postal Service announced that a postage stamp honoring Harvey Milk would be issued the following month. The image depicted on the stamp was derived from Daniel Nicoletta's 1977 portrait of a clearly ebullient Milk standing in front of his shop, Castro Camera, prior to his election to the San Francisco Board of Supervisors. A little more than a year after Nicoletta's portrait, Milk would be assassinated in his office at City Hall. The national honor bestowed by issue of a postage stamp marked the end of a kind of long dénouement: at least for those who, like Nicoletta, were closest to Milk and therefore informally charged with securing his legacy and enshrining his achievements into the official instruments of history and institutional memory. As if to add a kind of punctuation mark to this historical moment, in 2014 Nicoletta left San Francisco after 40 years and moved to rural Oregon, leaving behind the places and many of the people who occupy this monograph.[1]

Born on December 23, 1954 in New York City, Nicoletta spent his childhood in exurban Utica, New York. His initial interest in the arts was filmmaking. He received a Kodak Teenage Movie Award at age 17 before leaving New York to attend college: first for a year at Kansas City Art Institute, followed by another year at California College of Arts and Crafts in Oakland, where he would complete his core curriculum. In August of 1974 he moved to San Francisco's Castro neighborhood and began working at Harvey Milk's camera shop. By 1975 he was working as an intern for Crawford Barton, then a staff photographer for the national LGBT-interest magazine *The Advocate*. While his college career was interrupted by a pragmatic response to his fortuitous circumstance—he was at the very nucleus of significant historical change—his informal education continued unbound by the confines of a classroom and expanded to encompass the development of his political and social consciousness.

Nicoletta's move to the Castro was not only an initiation into politics, but also served as his entrée to a thriving, almost utopian, bohemian subculture. In December 1974, he and a group of artists known as the Eureka Valley Artists Coalition staged a four-day video festival in the back room of Castro Camera. The success of which would lead to his being one of many involved in the founding of the San Francisco International LGBT Film Festival in February 1977. In addition, during his short-lived foray into photojournalism, he worked for the LGBT community newspaper *Bay Area Reporter* (known to locals as the *B.A.R.*), photographing drag ball fundraising events, live theater, and performance art programs, receiving $15 per photograph (the equivalent of approximately $50 in 2017).

Entering his 30s and exhausted from the constant demands of political and social engagement, Nicoletta moved to the Sunset District of San Francisco to live with his partner, attorney Michael Pinatelli, and completed his undergraduate studies at San Francisco State University. During this time he was also absorbed in the practical work

Dan Nicoletta and LZ Love, June 27, 1982.

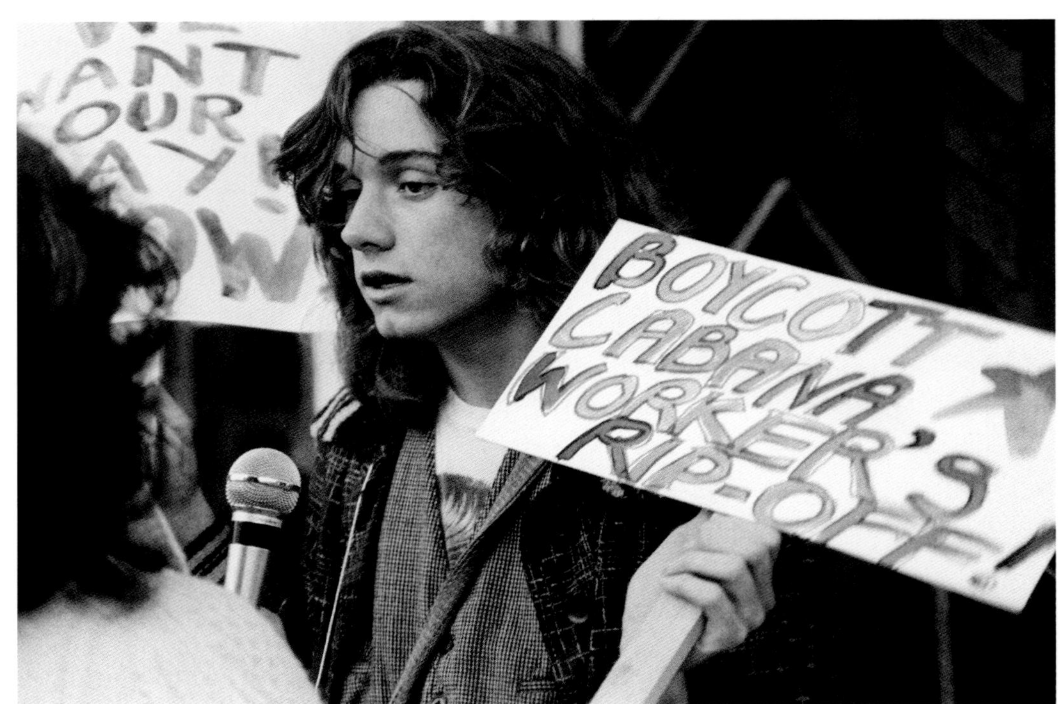

of securing a home for Harvey Milk's archive and caring for friends. The shock of Milk's assassination and fury at the lenient conviction and sentencing of his murderer had barely subsided when San Francisco's LGBT community was faced with the onslaught of yet another tragedy: the HIV/AIDS epidemic. Though he had begun exploring studio portraiture in his photographic practice, he still took to the streets during the height of the epidemic in the 1980s and 1990s to document the activism and memorials that were taking place in a climate of cold public indifference.

The turn of the century would find Nicoletta's life and work coming full circle when he was invited to serve as actor, consultant, and set photographer for the on-location production of Gus Van Sant's 2008 feature film, *Milk*. It is clear that his many years of photographing on chaotic San Francisco streets and his studio practice served him well on set. It was there that he produced some of his most striking work. His moody portrait of actor Josh Brolin in the role of Milk's assassin is saturated in menace and pathos, and one of the most arresting photographs in his oeuvre is his portrait of actor Lucas Grabeel—an actor who is playing a younger version of Nicoletta in the same physical location where he once worked 30 years prior—which serves as a kind of meta-referential self-portrait. Just as a time-based medium such as film is in many ways a representation of life becoming archival, Nicoletta's photographs can be understood similarly. A photographer's lifetime's work is essentially the creation of an archive.[2]

Nicoletta's generation, popularly known as the Baby Boomers, was the beneficiary of many things, not the least of which was the largess of an enormously prosperous post-war America. As the middle-class expanded at a furious rate, so did affordable postsecondary education. In the 20-year period between 1960 and 1980 the existence of both public and private two- and four-year colleges and universities grew by a third and enrollment doubled.[3] Also during this time, a proliferation of college-level photography

Dan Nicoletta picketing against non payment of wages with fellow employees of Castro Cabana Restaurant, circa February 1975.

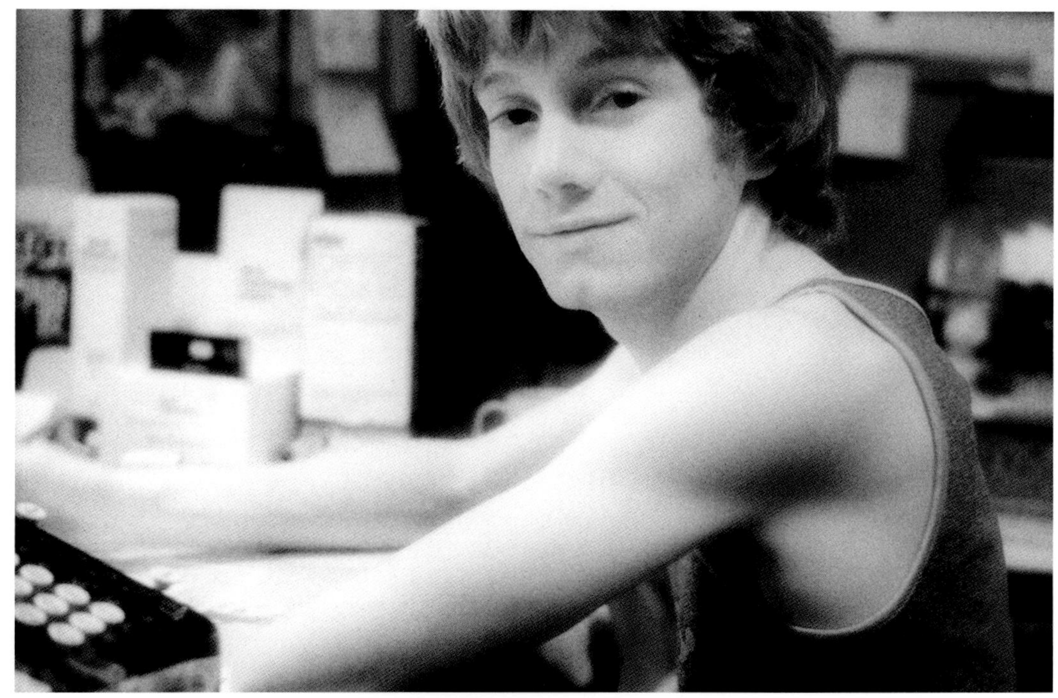

courses also surged.[4] This can, in part, be traced to the technological advances of the time that made prodigious amounts of inexpensive photographic equipment accessible.[5] The popularity of photography in academia can also be linked to the fact that there was just as much need for historical and theoretical education in the medium as there was for technical training. By the middle of the 20th century, the daily life of most Americans was permeated and mediated by images unlike any other time in human history and, after more than 100 years, photography's consequential history had begun to form.[6]

His generation would also inherit a multitude of social movements that would serve to advance massive change in American culture in the final decades of the last century. Perhaps not surprisingly, much of this change was generated in the country's major cities. The migration of white middle- and working-class families from urban centers to suburbs (more commonly known as "white flight") during the 1950s through the 1970s offered an opportunity for historically marginalized LGBT and artist communities to flourish.

Finally, and inarguably, the most horrific thing that his generation would have to face was a plague of devastating proportions; of which the LGBT community would endure the lion's share of unimaginable suffering and grief. Many who had participated in the gay rights movement in the decades prior would not live to share the benefits of their hard won battles to change discriminatory laws or witness the profound cultural shift in attitudes toward those self-identifying as LGBT.

When examining a photographer's life's work retrospectively, it is important to consider the hierarchical structure of photography's historiography as it relates to both the larger art world and the viability of careers in the arts. The "art world," much like the "real world," is not a meritocracy; rather, it is a plutocracy. In the most general terms, those with the means to collect will collect any object that falls under the rubric of "art." It is often in the interest of those holding collections of objects that these objects

Dan Nicoletta by Harvey Milk, fall 1976.

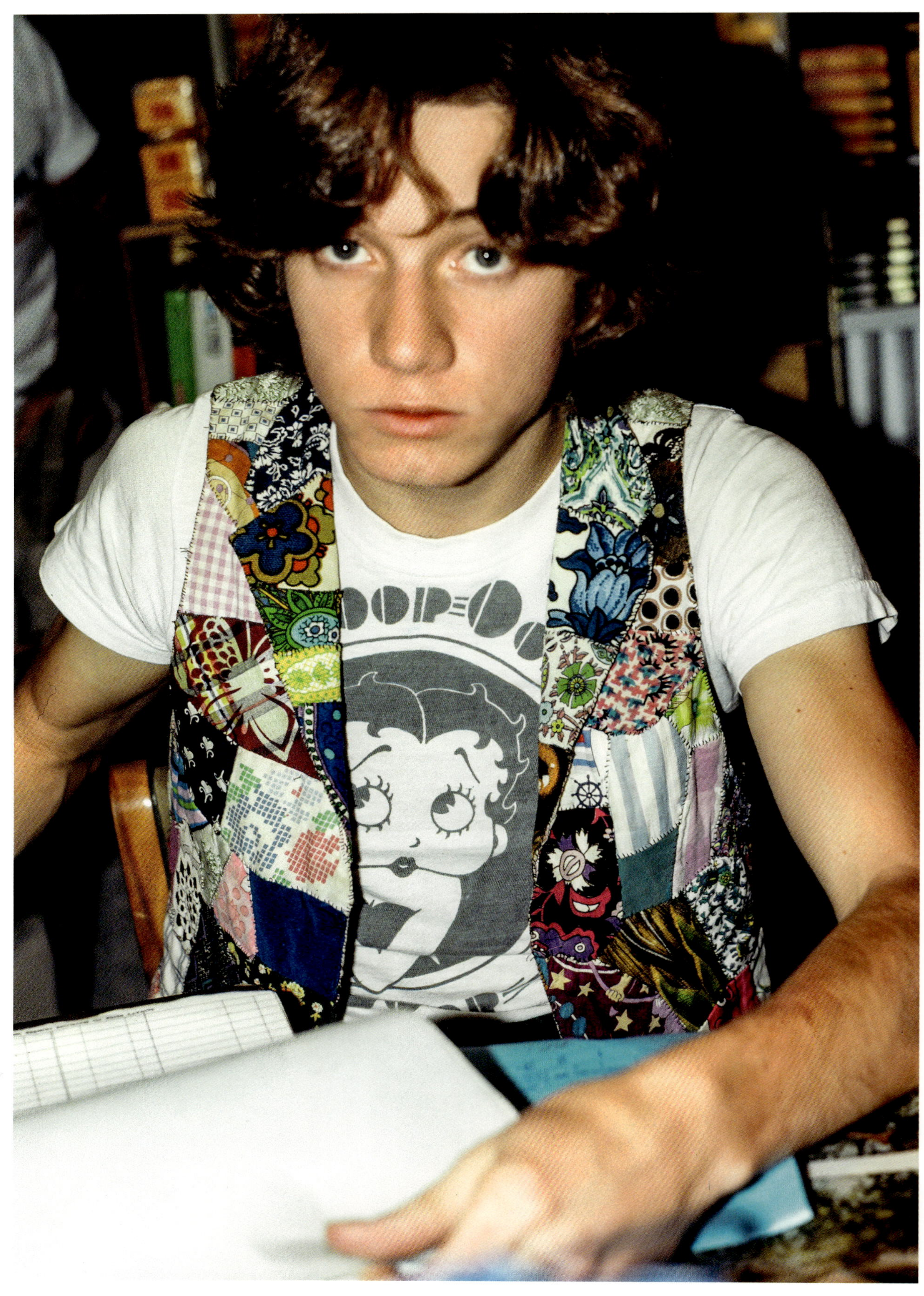

Dan Nicoletta at Castro Camera, 1975.

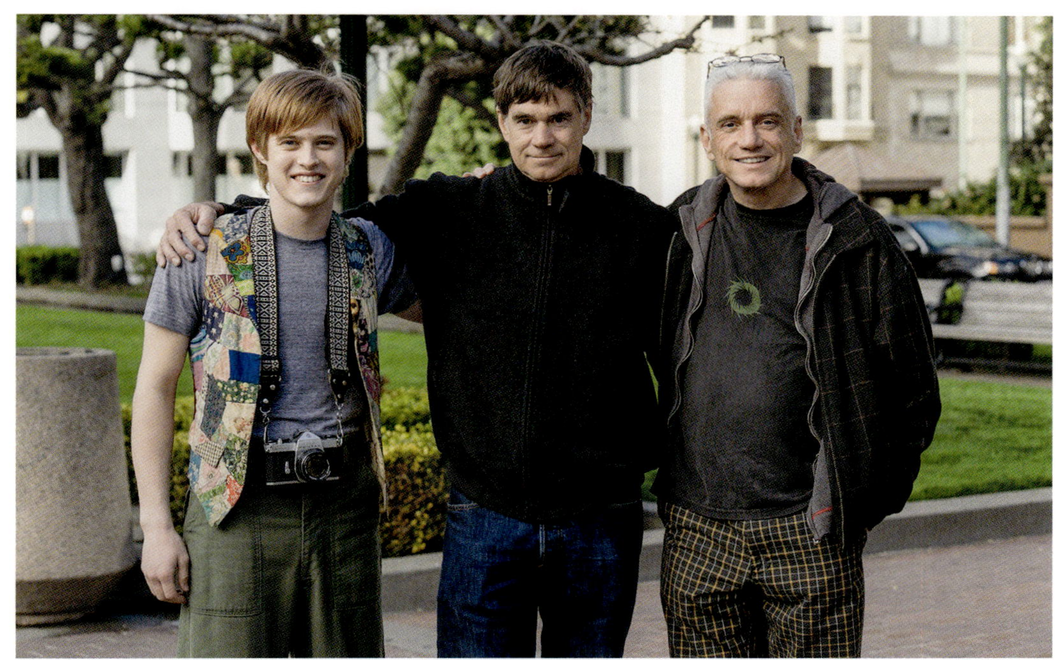

be classified as "high art" and therefore worthy of collection. One way to achieve this is via institutions, by serving on boards of trustees and accession committees. While efforts to legitimize photography as an art form extend as far back as the 19th century, it wasn't until 1940 that New York's Museum of Modern Art, after seven years of collecting photography, became the first museum to establish a Department of Photography. Ergo the museum (MoMA and all who followed suit), as the dominant public institution in the arts, was charged with the responsibility of justifying photography as a medium worthy of collection and preservation. It follows, then, that discriminate, sometimes insidious, systems of categorization and corresponding values would be employed when faced with the task of assembling the medium's canon.[7]

Despite the increased level of interest and scrutiny of the medium, the 1970s market for contemporary "fine art photography" was still an indeterminate one and most career photographers worked as either tenure track professors or in commercial enterprises such as advertising, editorial, or portrait photography. Those that could navigate the murky waters of the art world and find a gallery that would represent their work most often supplemented their income through commissioned portraiture as well as through any of the above listed endeavors. Though notable advances in the use of the medium vis-à-vis its merging with other media and genres (e.g. painting and conceptual art) took place in the 1960s and 1970s, it was not until the 1980s that the gatekeepers of the much larger "art world" began to take serious notice of photography. In short, the world of "fine art photography" was a ghetto.

Perhaps part of the problem was that for too many years, attempts to define what kind of photography could be interpreted as "art" were based on a conservative set of dogmatic (some would say tyrannical) formalist aesthetic criteria that were established during the height of modernism in the middle part of the 20th century. While the ubiquity of the 35mm camera in the 1960s ushered in a new generation of photographers

Lucas Grabeel, Gus Van Sant and Dan Nicoletta on the set of *Milk*, March 14, 2008.

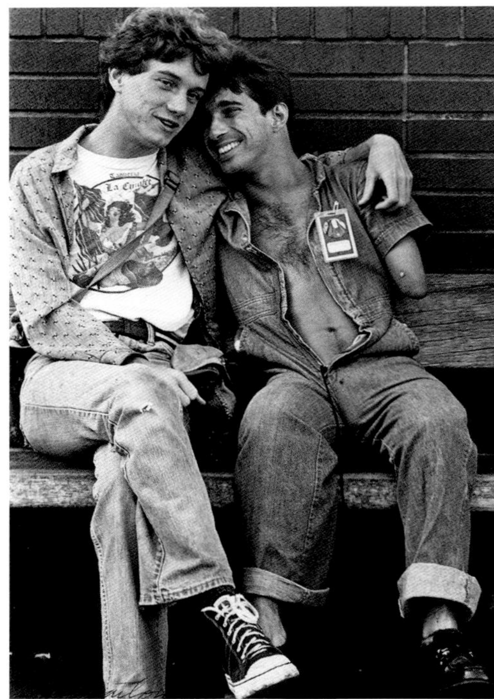
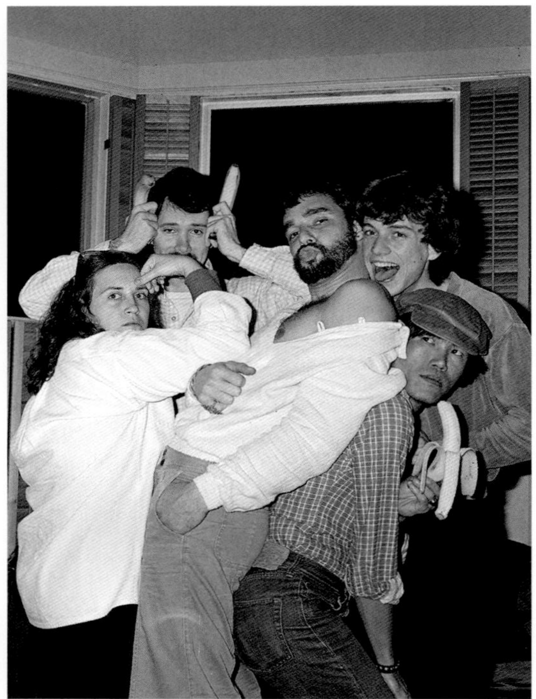

whose work was less formal and more aesthetically aligned with vernacular (or everyday snapshot) photography, critical assessments of this work at the time issued denials of any corollary between the personal and political. Instead this work, categorized as "street photography," would be enveloped in simplistic interpretations of it as ostensibly nothing more than a material manifestation of lighthearted people watching. (How else could it be included in a museum?)[8] Unless the photographs were from an earlier era (or Europe), the more somber (e.g. politically freighted) "social documentary photography" and "photojournalism" belonged in newspapers and magazines. Likewise, color photography was considered, at best, a kind of historical anomaly more appropriately suited for the editorial and advertising industries.

Given this needlessly convoluted scenario, it is hard to place a photographer like Nicoletta into the discreet preciosity of any one genre. Rather, his work seems to function as an archival whole. Further, lacking any kind of self-censorship, photographs like Nicoletta's "Protest rally against the Pope's visit to San Francisco, 1987" (p.195) and "Anti-censorship demonstration and time capsule burial at the San Francisco Arts Commission Gallery, 1990" (p.223) were unlikely to be exhibited or published by a conservative arts establishment in the 1980s or 1990s. The grave political subject matter is not buried under layers of abstract meaning in an opaque conceptual rendering. Instead the graphic signs of the protestors reside in the foreground—entirely legible—not outside the photograph's frame. However disconcerting or unbelievable, it remains an entirely radical act to create works like these in spite of the institutional forces of coercion and conformity. This is one of Nicoletta's great achievements. He has understood that the job of the photographer or artist is to not simply be a mindless intermediary clicking the buttons of an apparatus but to create and present images that are not redundant.[9]

Mercifully, art scholars in the 1970s and 1980s began to parse through the meaning of

(Left) Dan Nicoletta and Dennis Morin, circa 1978. *(Right)* Gay Freedom Photo Archives group self portrait at Dan's apartment, March 3, 1978. Sandy Dimitrios-Maurice, Rink, Glenn Meisenheimer (Cookie), Dan Nicoletta and Efren Convento-Ramirez.

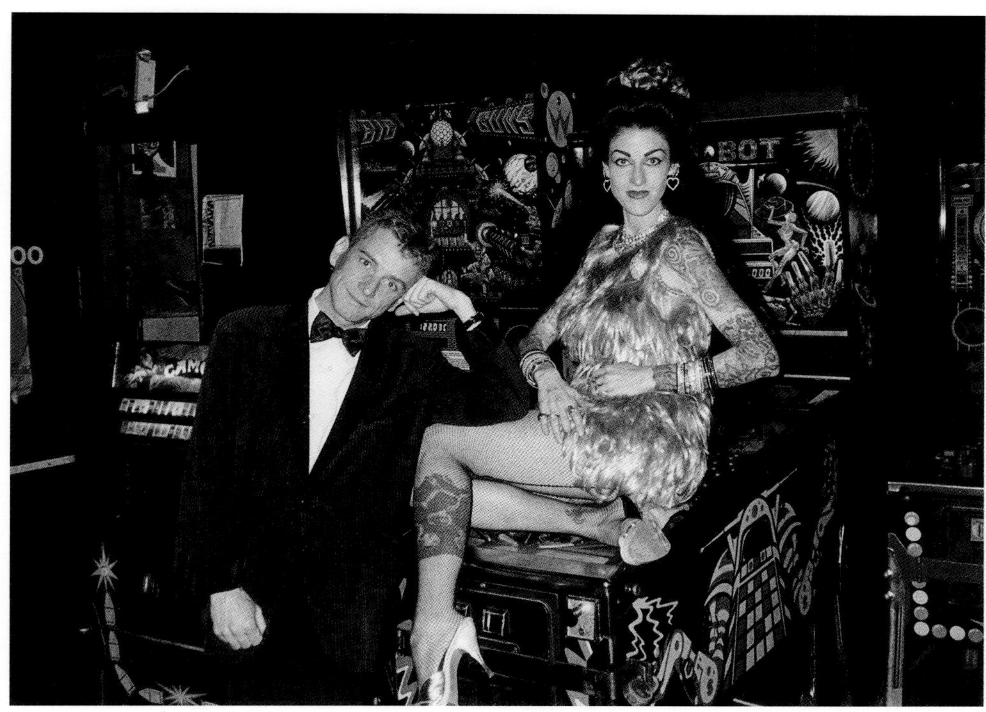

photography and the vagaries of its many genres. Their theoretical research opened up new ways to consider photography's function outside the narrow worldview and political mechanizations of the institutionalized art world and its markets. Given the medium's inextricable ties to memory, it is fitting that much philosophical work in this area in the last 40 years focused on photography's relationship to history and the writing of history. To generalize, it was accepted that both the photographer's era and experience in the world were as meaningful as the content of any photograph they might produce and any assessment of their work should include a critical evaluation of all events and discourses that may have been happening at the time.[10] In essence, moving forward, there would no longer be any shelter in the arts.[11] If, as author Janet Malcolm has perceptively noted, "memory functions as a ruthless editor of God's long-winded truth," then photography, and those bearing the critical skill to articulate its function and meaning, may very well be the court stenographers.[12]

Perhaps it is helpful to remember that the majority of the people depicted in Nicoletta's photographs—especially in the years prior to the digital deluge—did not necessarily grow up surrounded by the kind of imagery found in this book. Everything that they were experiencing—the politics, the love, the parties, their activism, their artistic endeavors, and the community that they were creating—was entirely new. They were making it up as they went along; they weren't simply mimicking what they had grown up seeing in films and photographs. All the while, Nicoletta was there alongside them, quietly building a sustained practice out of what was essentially a collective enterprise: the life and times around him. Ultimately, his photographs defy the bounds of hierarchical genres by being situated within a much larger and more important framework. Their value lies in their inerrant service to the history of the LGBT movement in 20th century America; forming an invaluable chronicle of a specific time and place. And, most especially: the people who created it.

Chuck Mobley

Above: Dan Nicoletta and Carmel Strelein, Tippi's Prom at The EndUp bar, 1991.
Overleaf: Spontaneous memorial to Robert Hillsborough, a victim of an anti-gay murder, June 26, 1978.

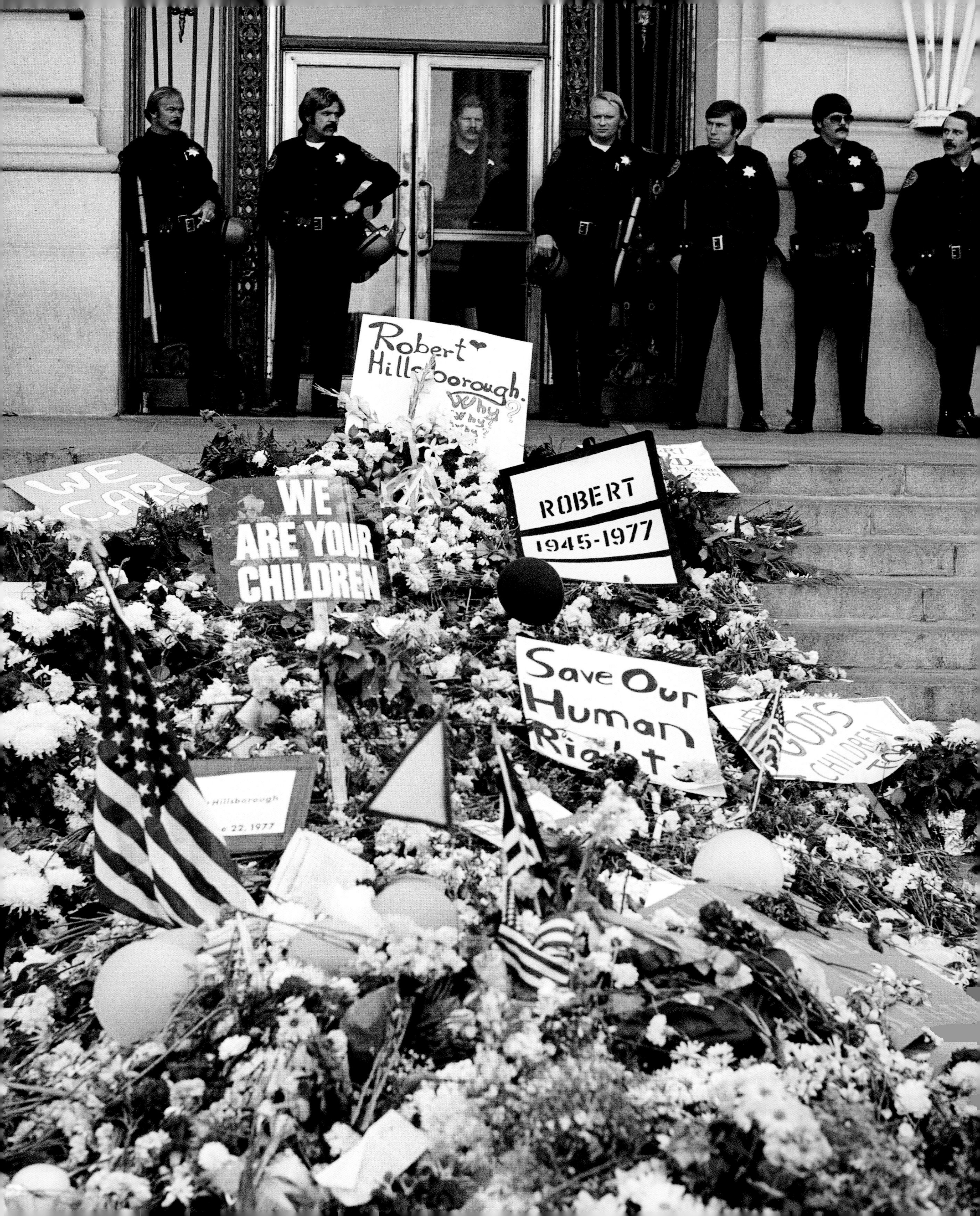
Robert
Hillsborough.
Why?
WE CARE
WE ARE YOUR CHILDREN
ROBERT
1945-1977
Save Our Human Rights
GOD'S CHILDREN TOO

MILK & HONEY

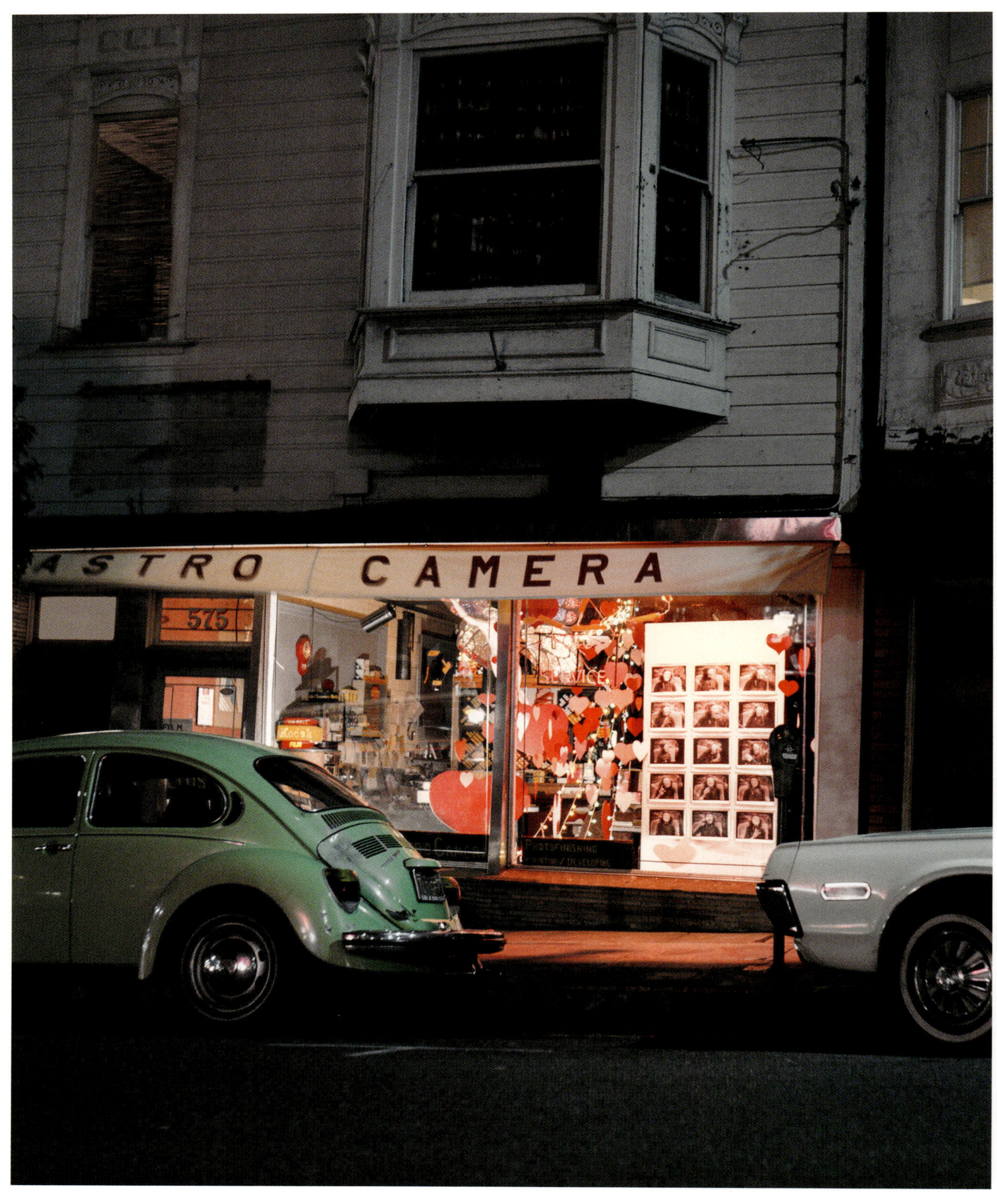

Above: Larry Piet's Valentine's art installation, Castro Camera, February 1977.
Opposite: Vandalized Castro Camera window, June 1977. The display was of the anti-gay propaganda generated by Anita Bryant's crusade to repeal gay rights protections in Dade County, Florida.

THE WORST OF MIAMI

Child pornography: Sickness for sale

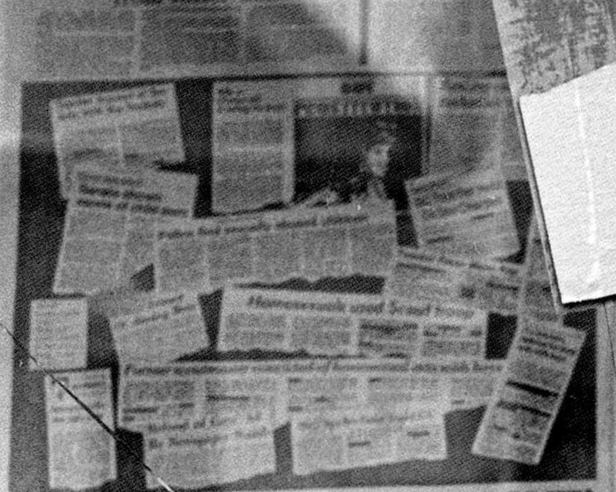

THERE IS NO 'HUMAN RIGHT' TO CORRUPT OUR CHILDREN

Vote FOR repeal of Metro's dangerous homosexual ordinance June 7!

LEST WE FORGET

VOTE FOR REPEAL

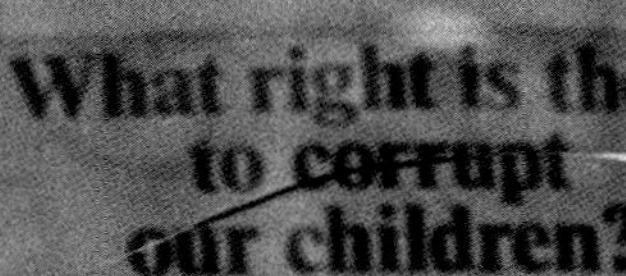

VOTE FOR REPEAL JUNE 7th

Would you want a homosexual "Big Brother" for your fatherless boy?

Here's what happened in Minneapolis:

ENDORSE THE STAND OF SAVE OUR CHILDREN, INC.
AND WE RECOMMEND ON JUNE 7, THAT ALL VOTERS

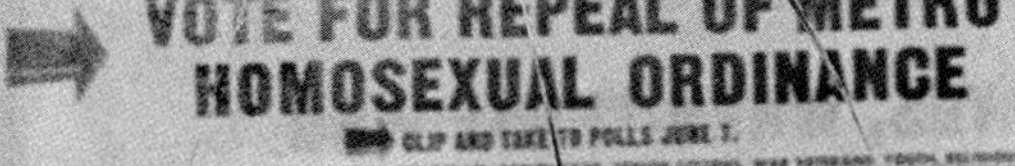

CLIP AND TAKE TO POLLS JUNE 7.

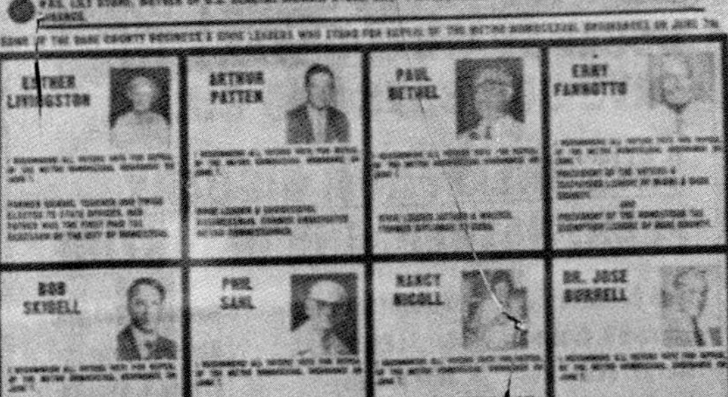

Misguided ordinance will force even religious schools to hire homosexuals

WE ACCEPT ANY INDIVIDUAL — WE DO NOT ACCEPT HOMOSEXUALITY AS AN APPROVED LIFESTYLE

YOUR VOTE FOR REPEAL NEXT TUESDAY IS VITAL

WHY VOTE FOR

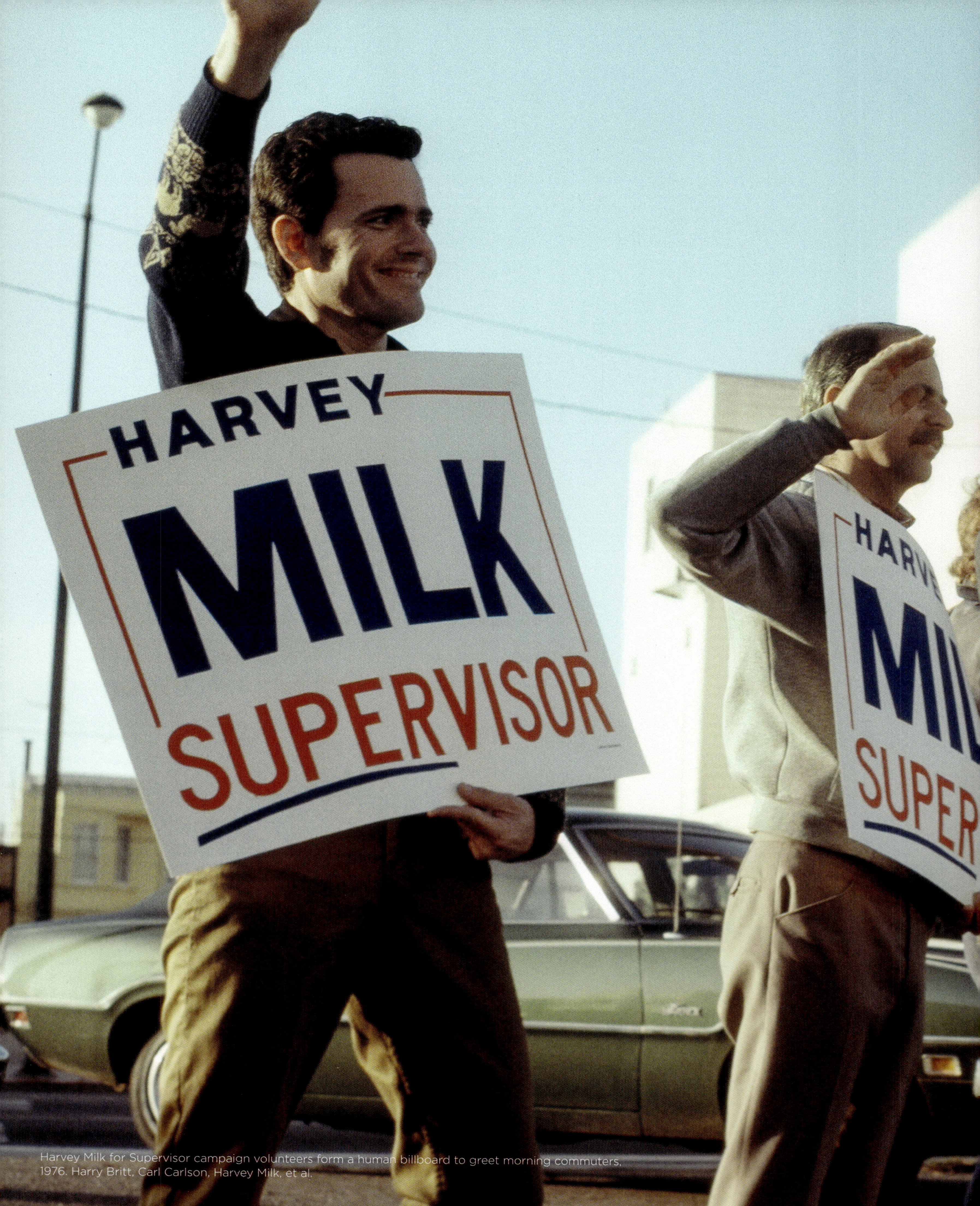

Harvey Milk for Supervisor campaign volunteers form a human billboard to greet morning commuters, 1976. Harry Britt, Carl Carlson, Harvey Milk, et al.

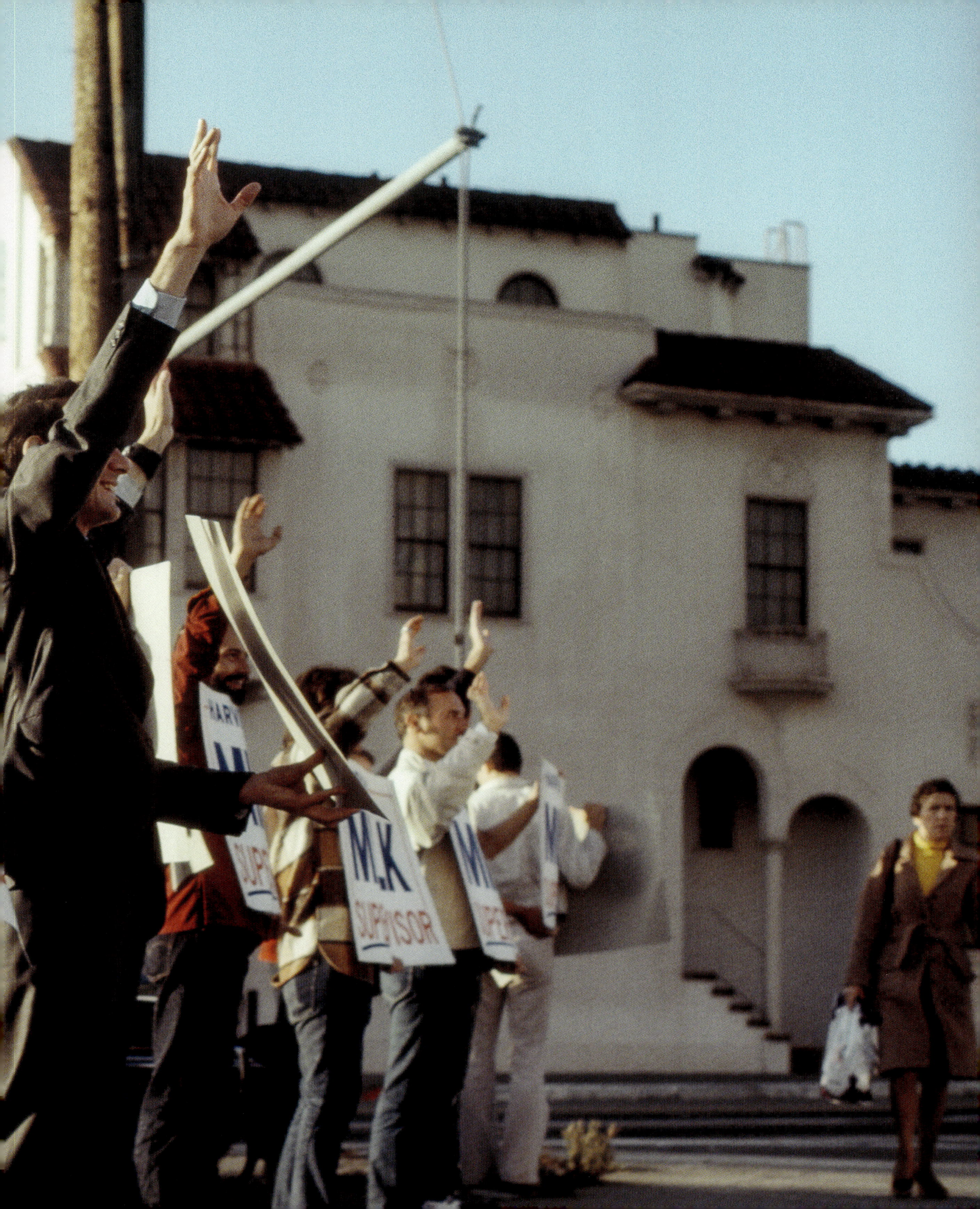

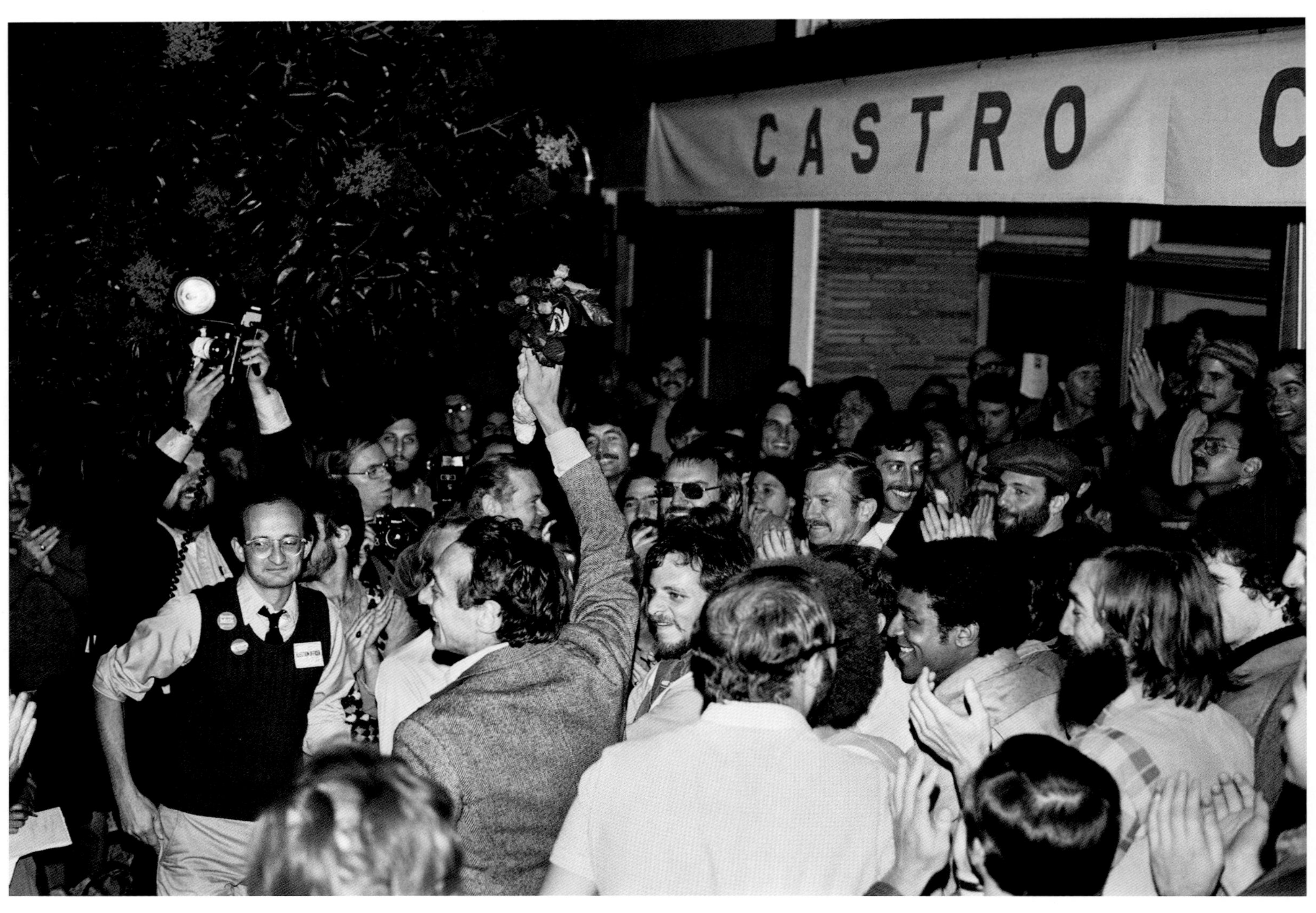

Supervisor Harvey Milk's election night victory party at Castro Camera, November 8, 1977.

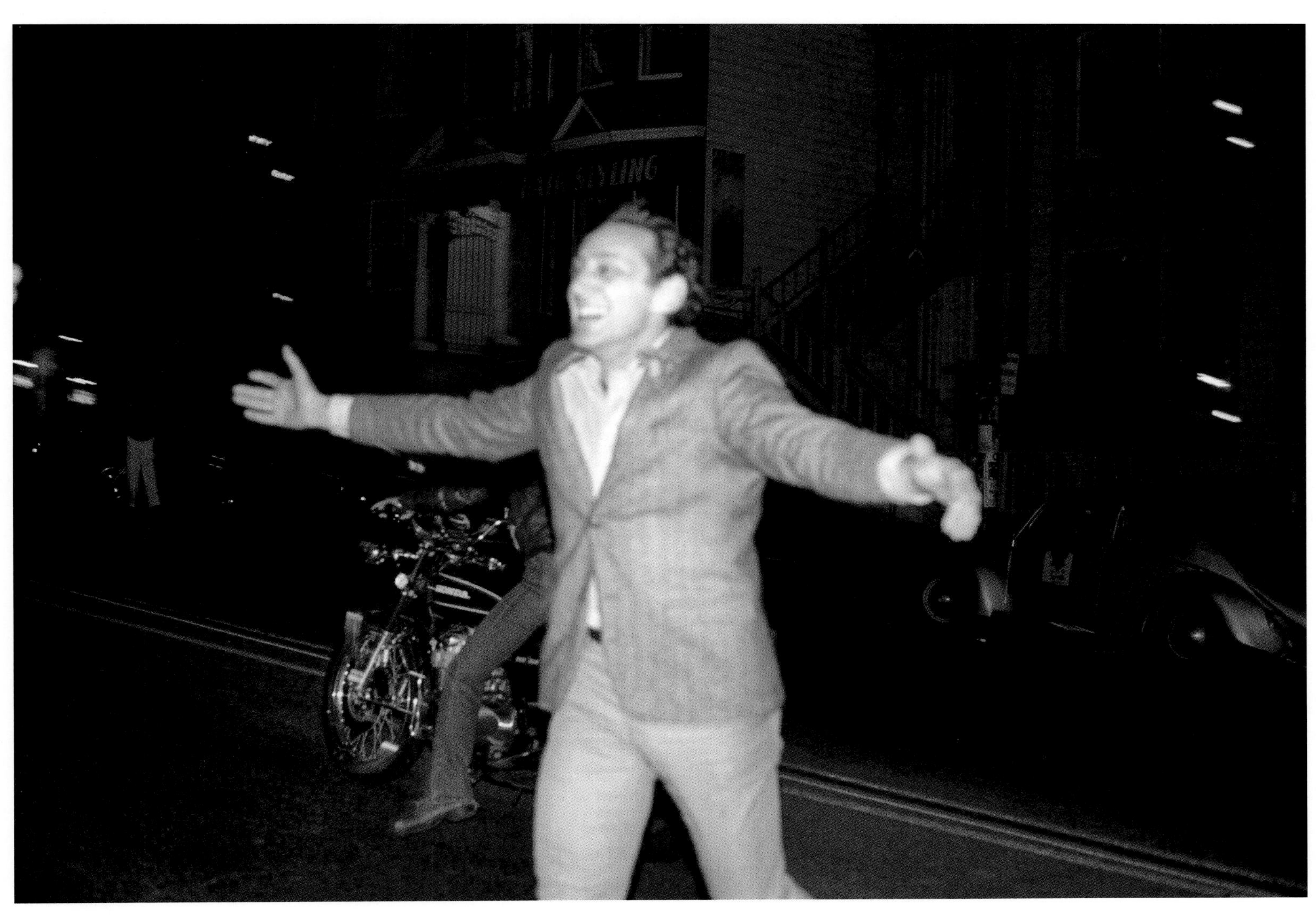

Harvey runs towards supporters on the street at Castro Camera on election night.

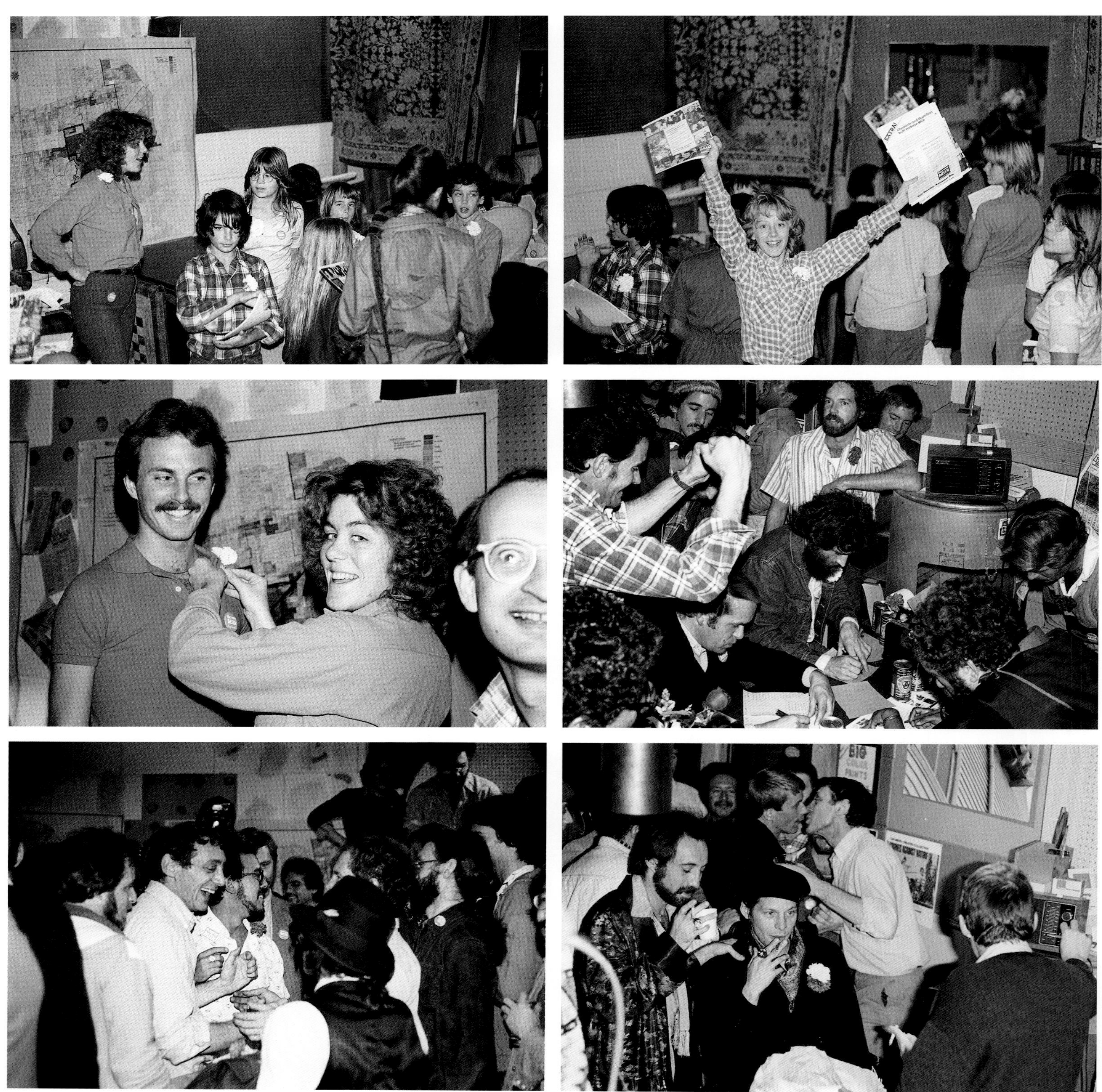

(Clockwise from top left) student group touring Harvey's election headquarters at Castro Camera on election day (two photos); Harry Britt, Wayne Friday, David Weissman, Bill Kraus, Alan French and others huddle at the front counter of Castro Camera to listen to the radio broadcast of favorable voter returns; election night victory party (two photos); Dick Pabich, Anne Kronenberg and Jim Rivaldo on election day.

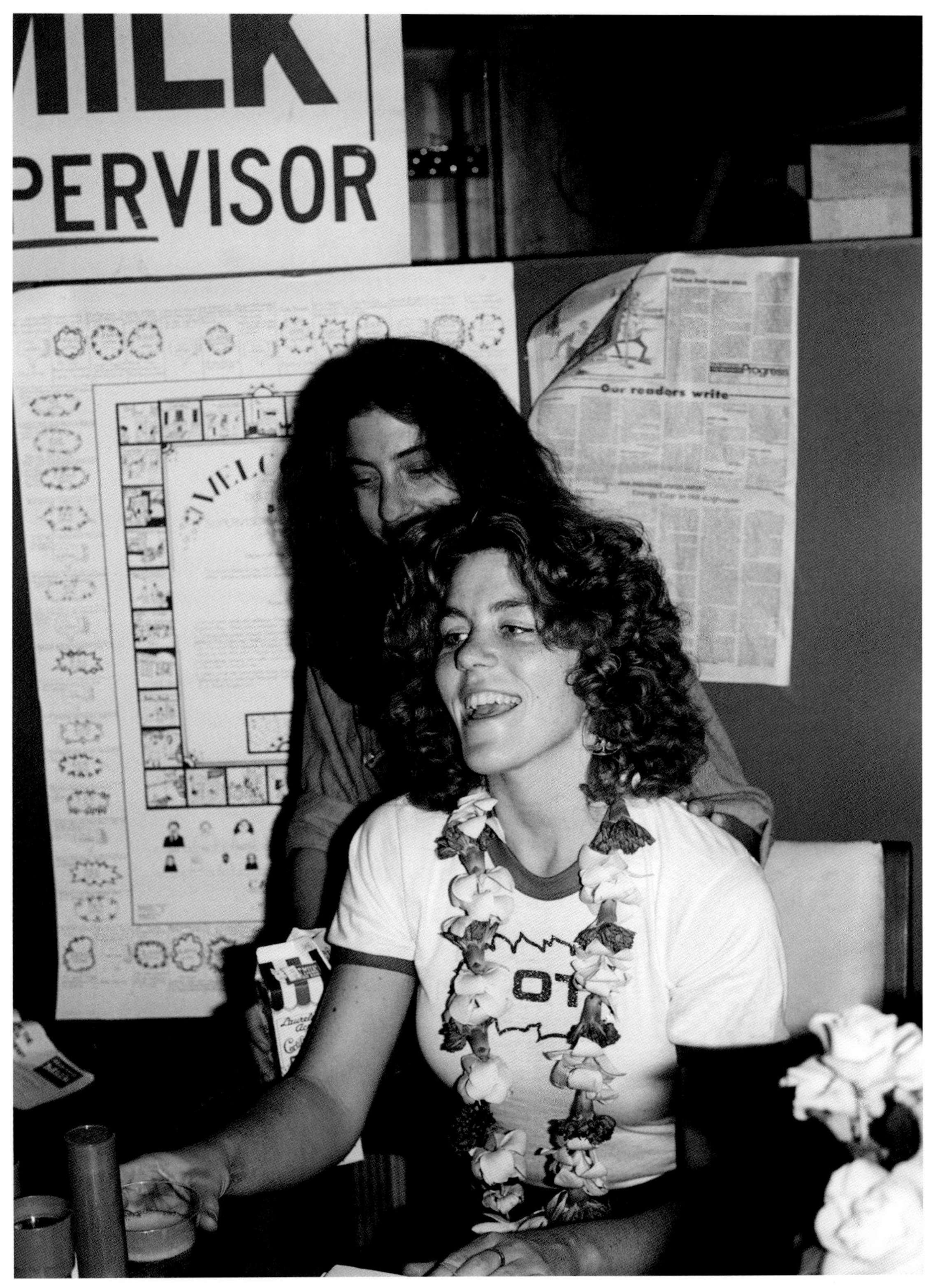

Above: Anne Kronenberg and Joyce Garay at the Camera Store on election day.
Overleaf: SF LGBT Pride Parade, June 26, 1978. Administrative Assistant Anne Kronenberg and recently elected Supervisor Harvey Milk.

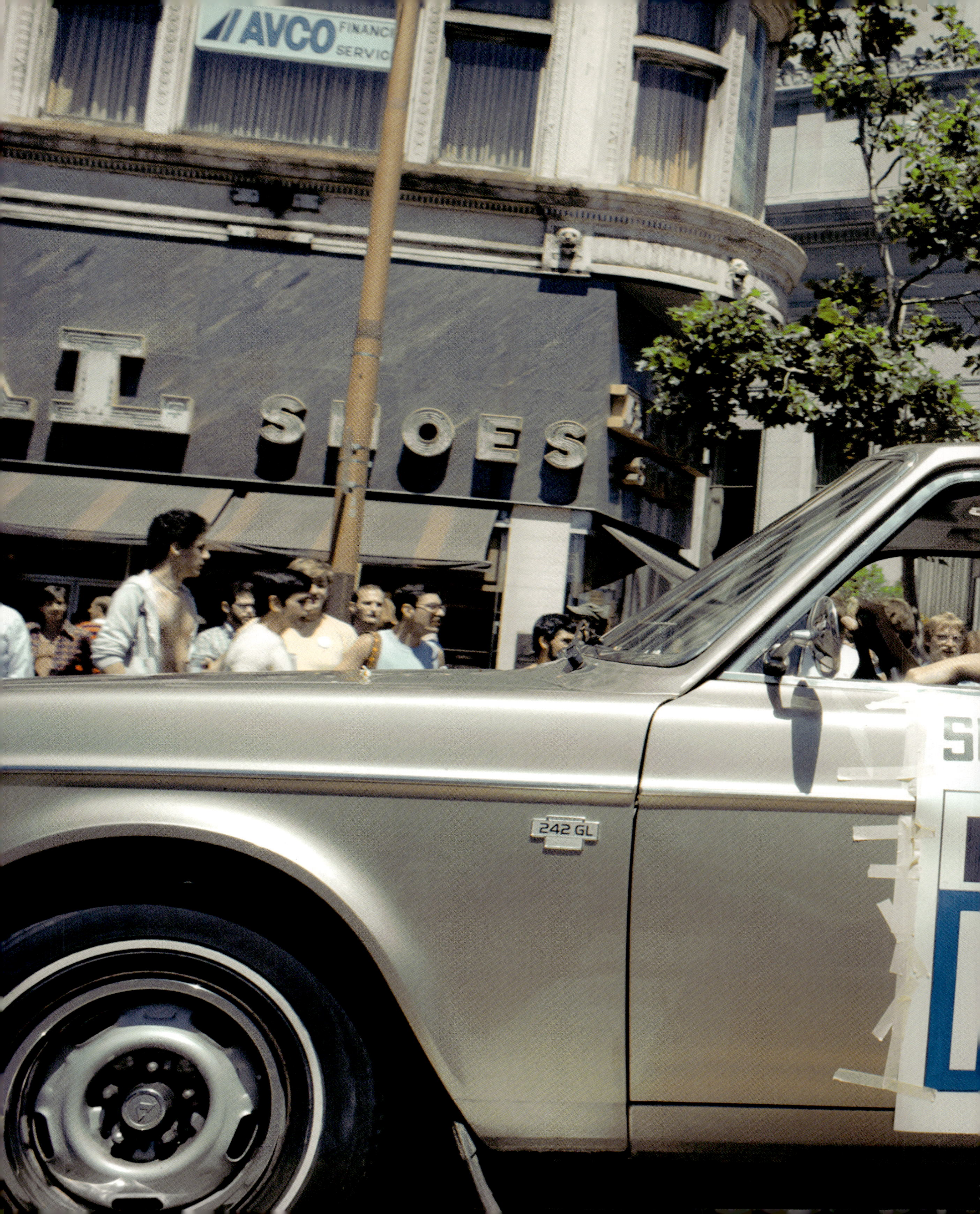
AVCO
242 GL

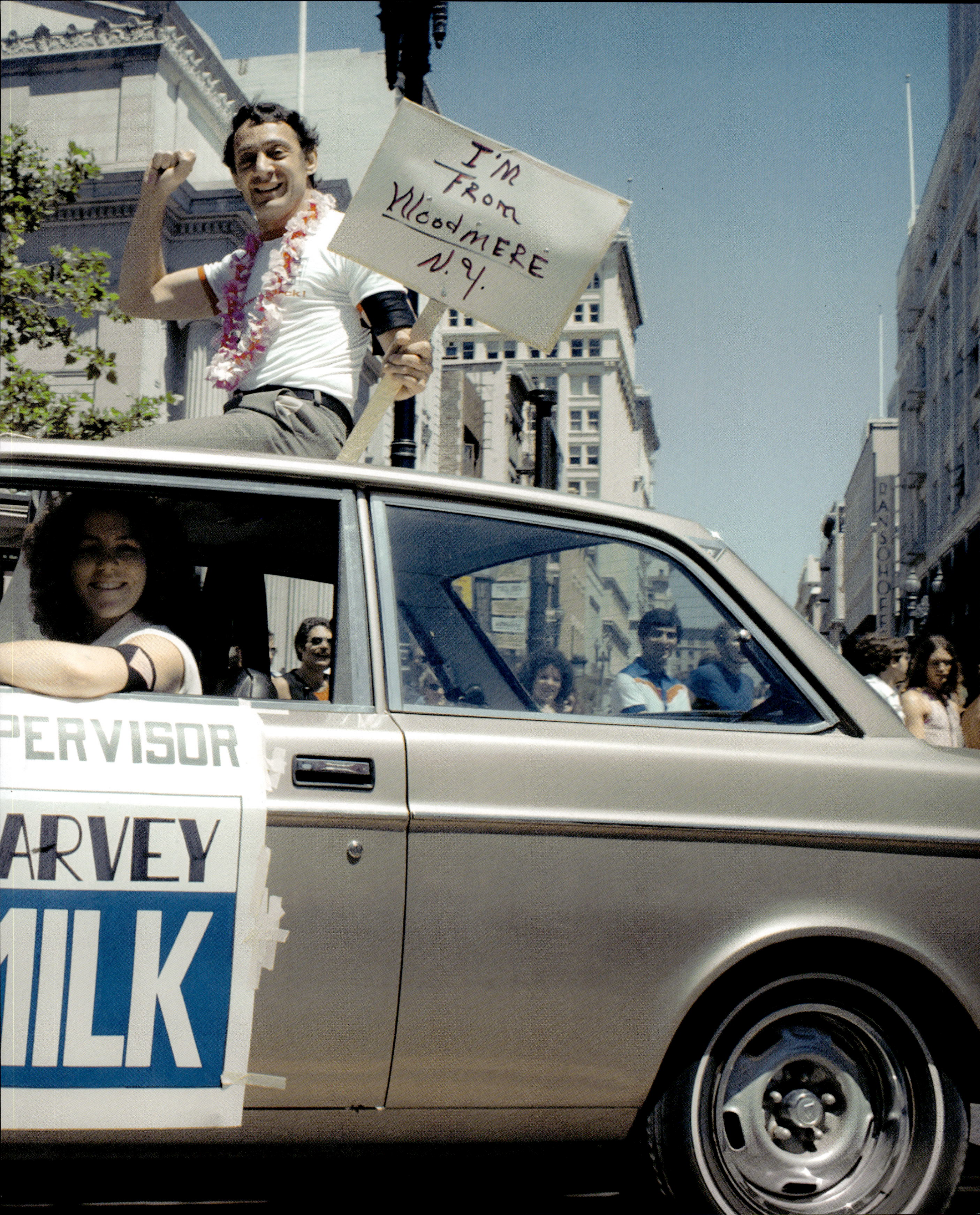
I'M FROM WOODMERE N.Y.
PERVISOR
ARVEY
MILK

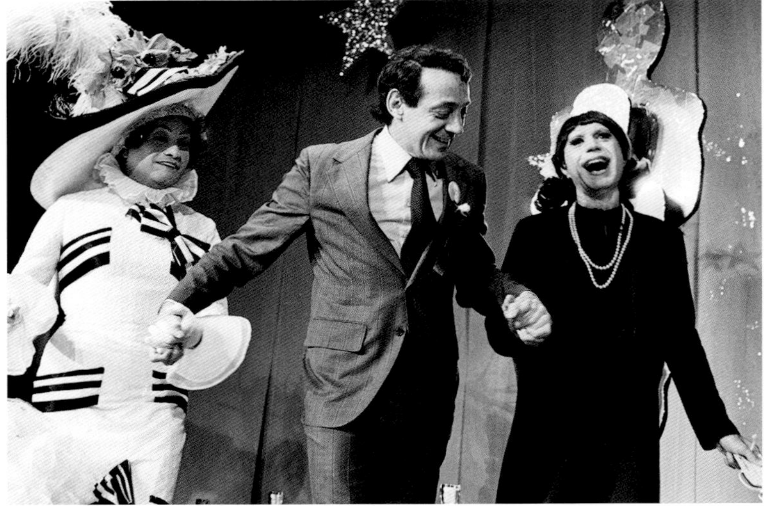

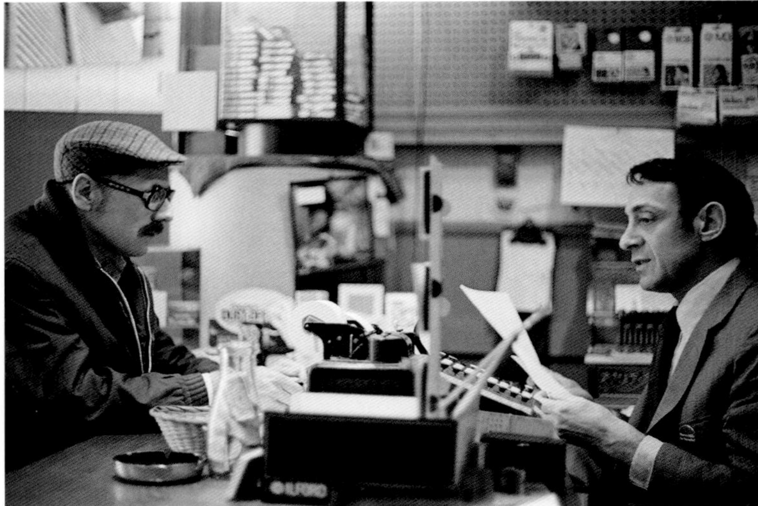

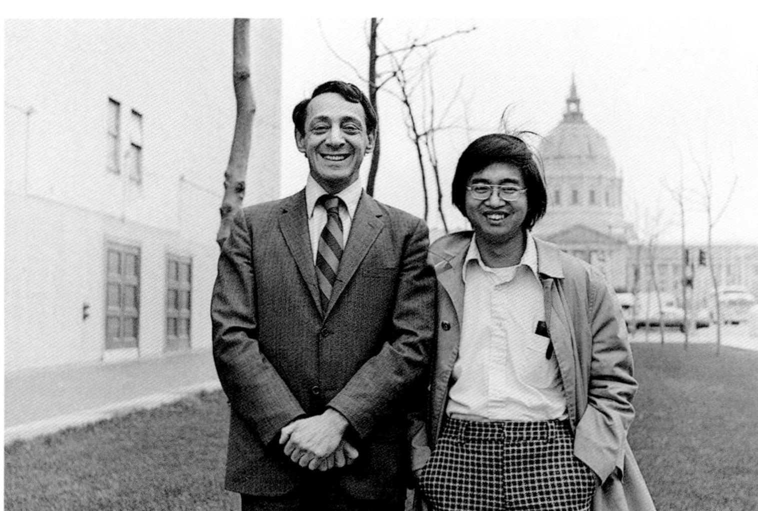

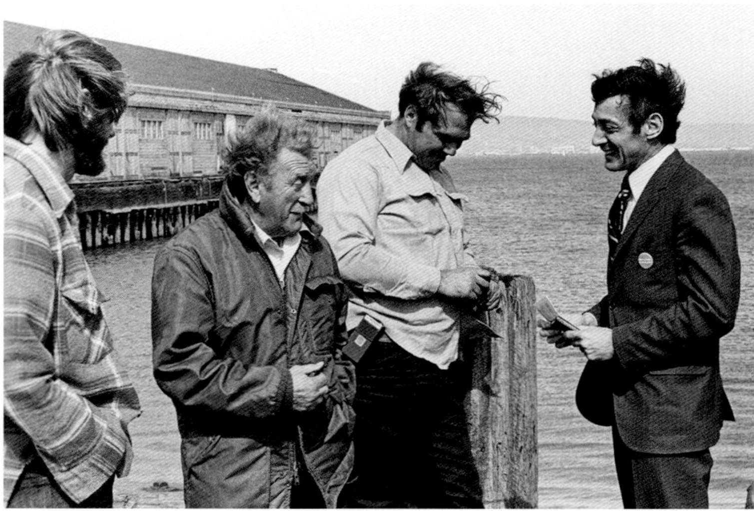

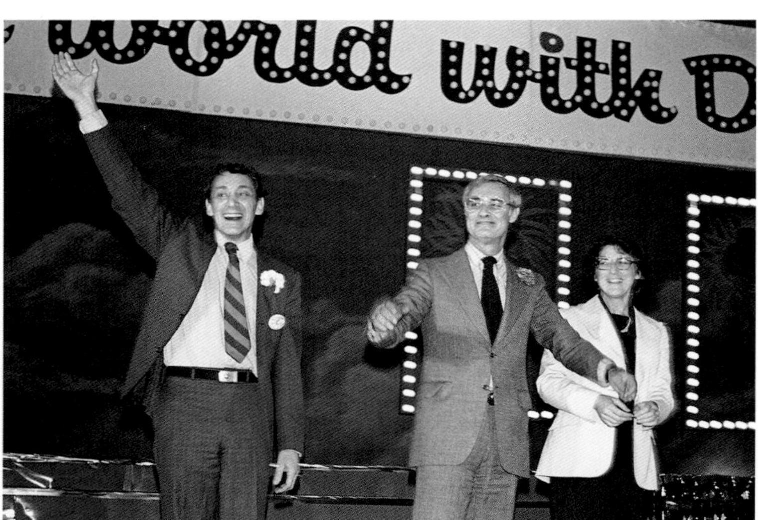

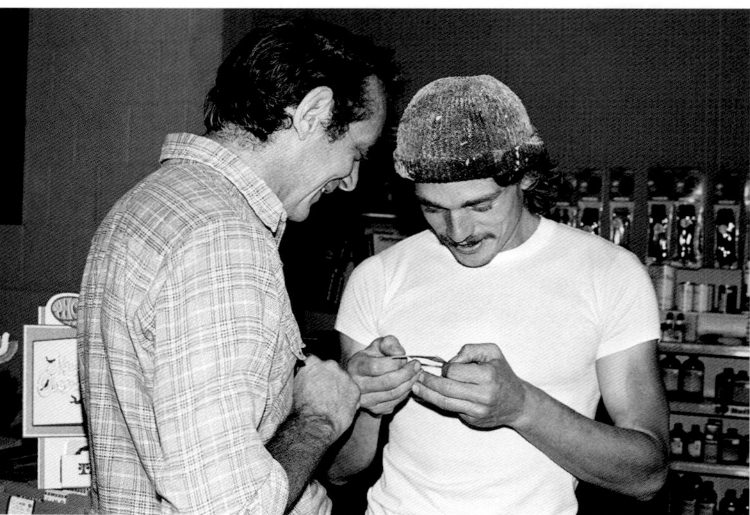

Above: *(Clockwise from top left)* José Sarria, Supervisor Harvey Milk and Mavis at The Imperial Council's Beaux Arts Ball, presenting a check from an anonymous donor to purchase uniforms for the first ever Gay and Lesbian Freedom Marching Band, October 28, 1978;
Frank Robinson proofing Harvey's writing, circa 1976; Harvey speaking to longshoremen at the Embarcadero, spring 1976; Harvey and Denton Smith share a comic strip at Castro Camera, spring 1976; Supervisor Harvey Milk, Mayor George Moscone and Supervisor Carol Ruth Silver at The Imperial Council's Coronation, January 28, 1978; Harvey and Michael Wong, March 7, 1978.
Opposite: Harvey as Deputy Mayor for a day at the dedication of a cafe at One United Nations Plaza, 1978.

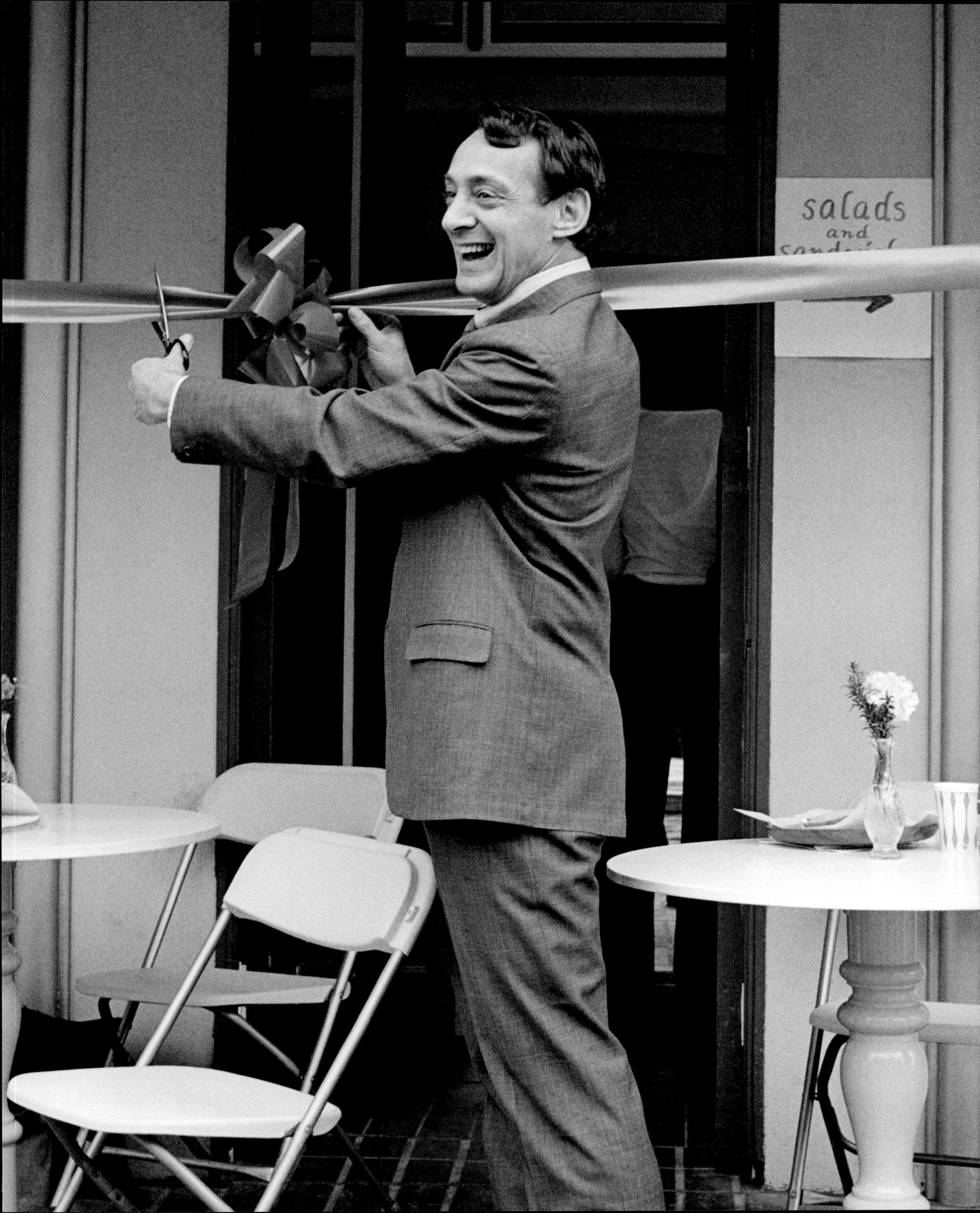
salads
and

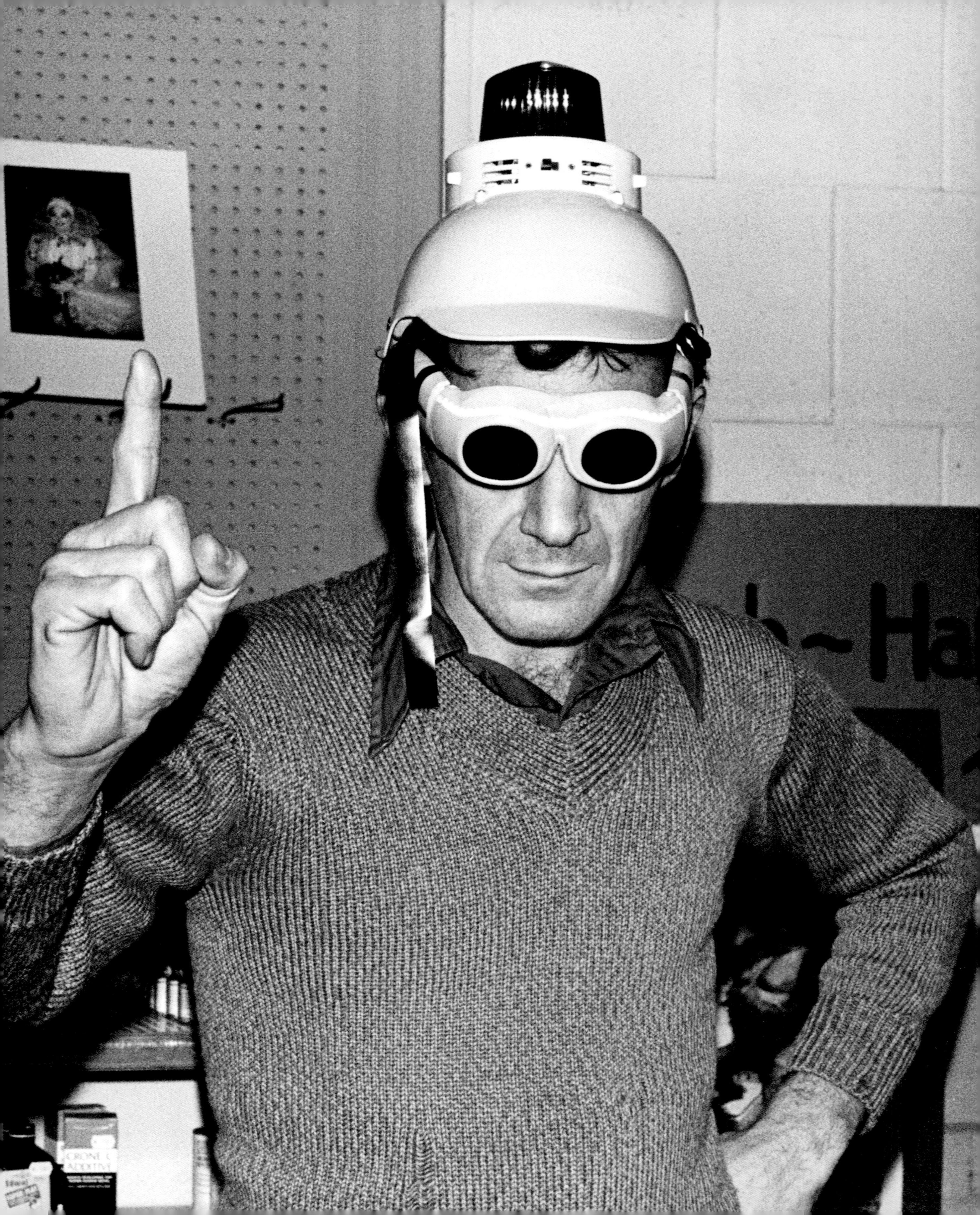

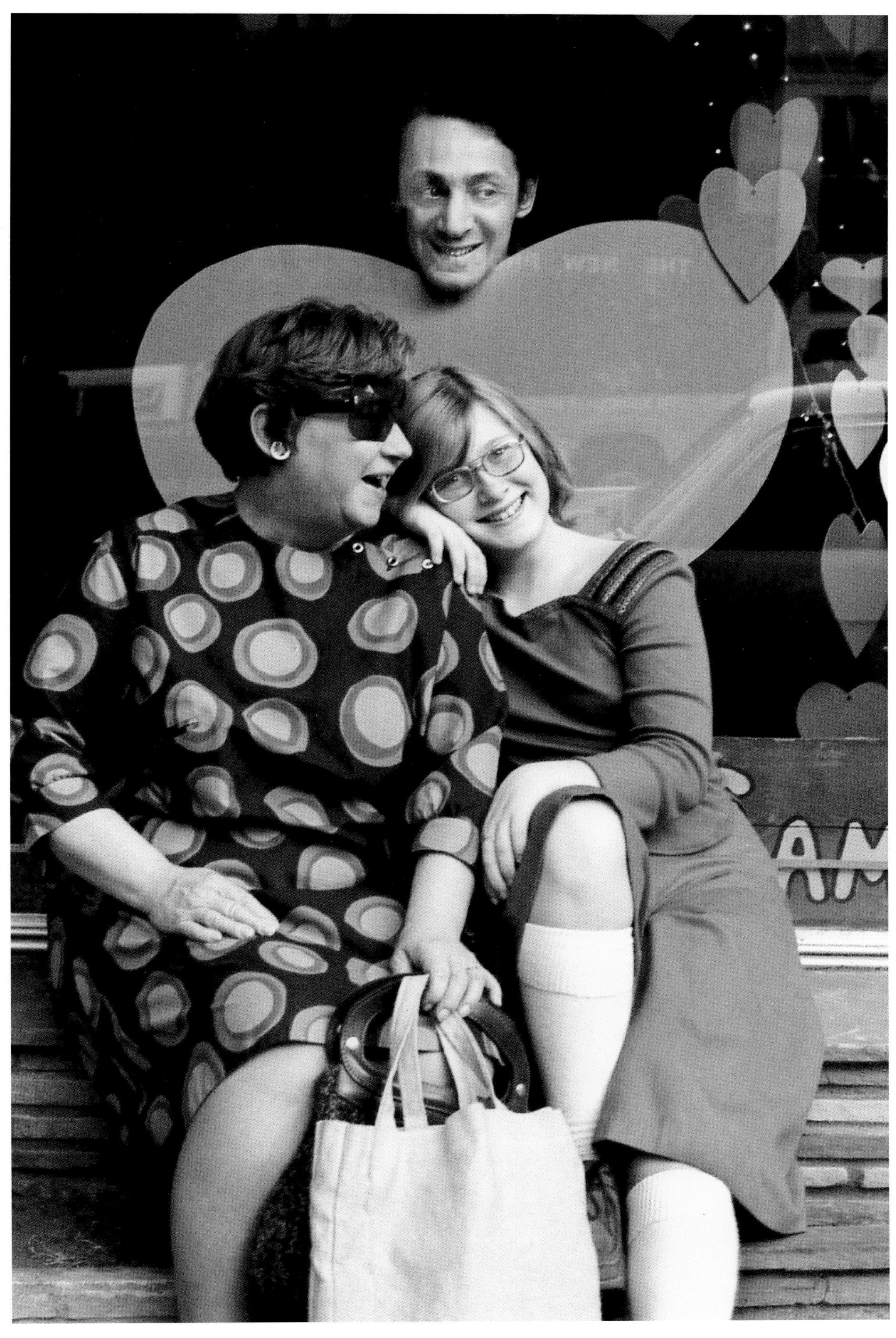

Above: Harvey at Castro Camera with campaign worker Medora Payne and her mother Gretchen, 1977.
Opposite: Harvey clowning around at Castro Camera, 1977.

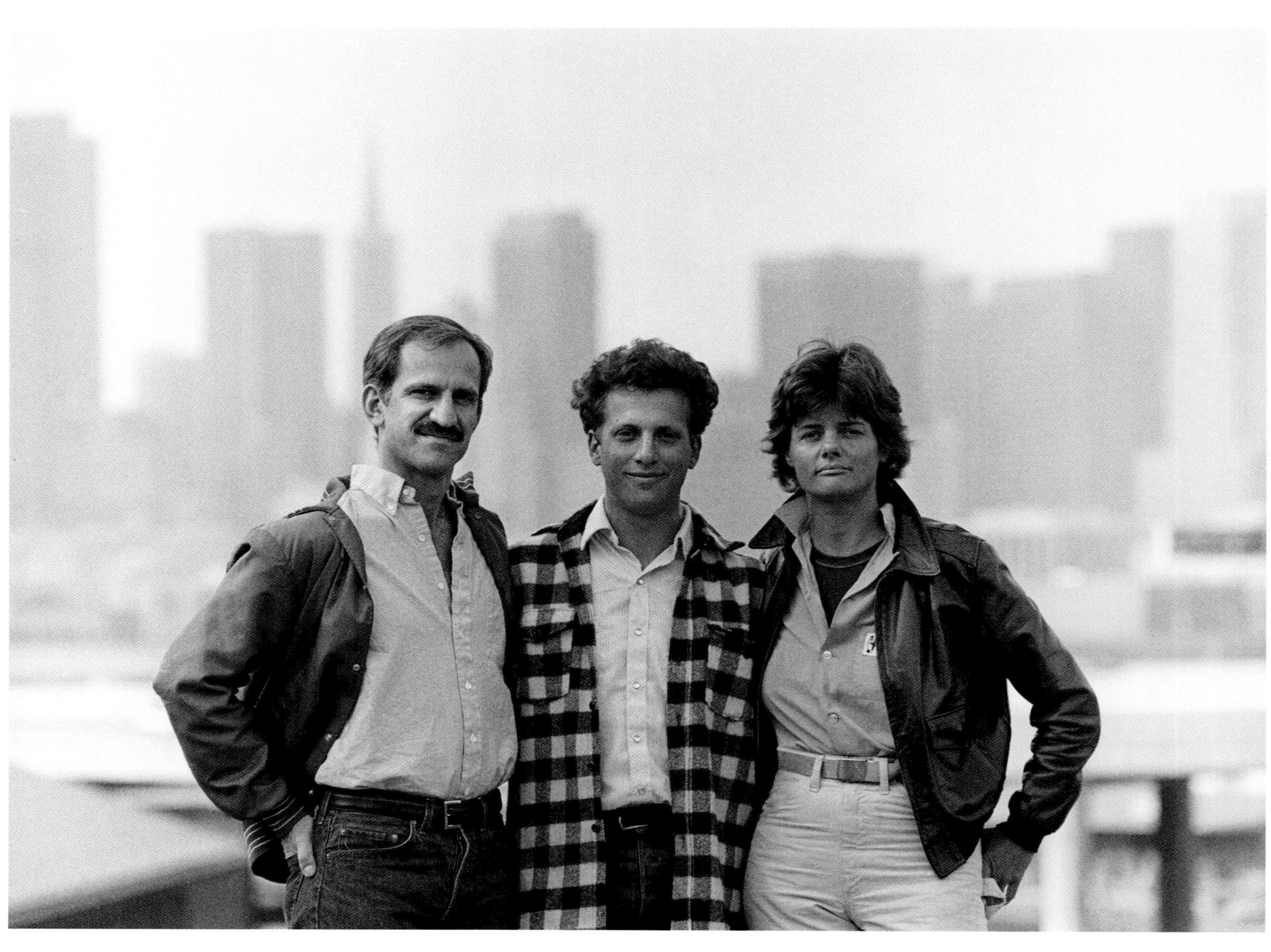

The Life and Times of Harvey Milk documentary film crew, Richard Schmiechen, Robert Epstein and Francis Reid, April 8, 1983.

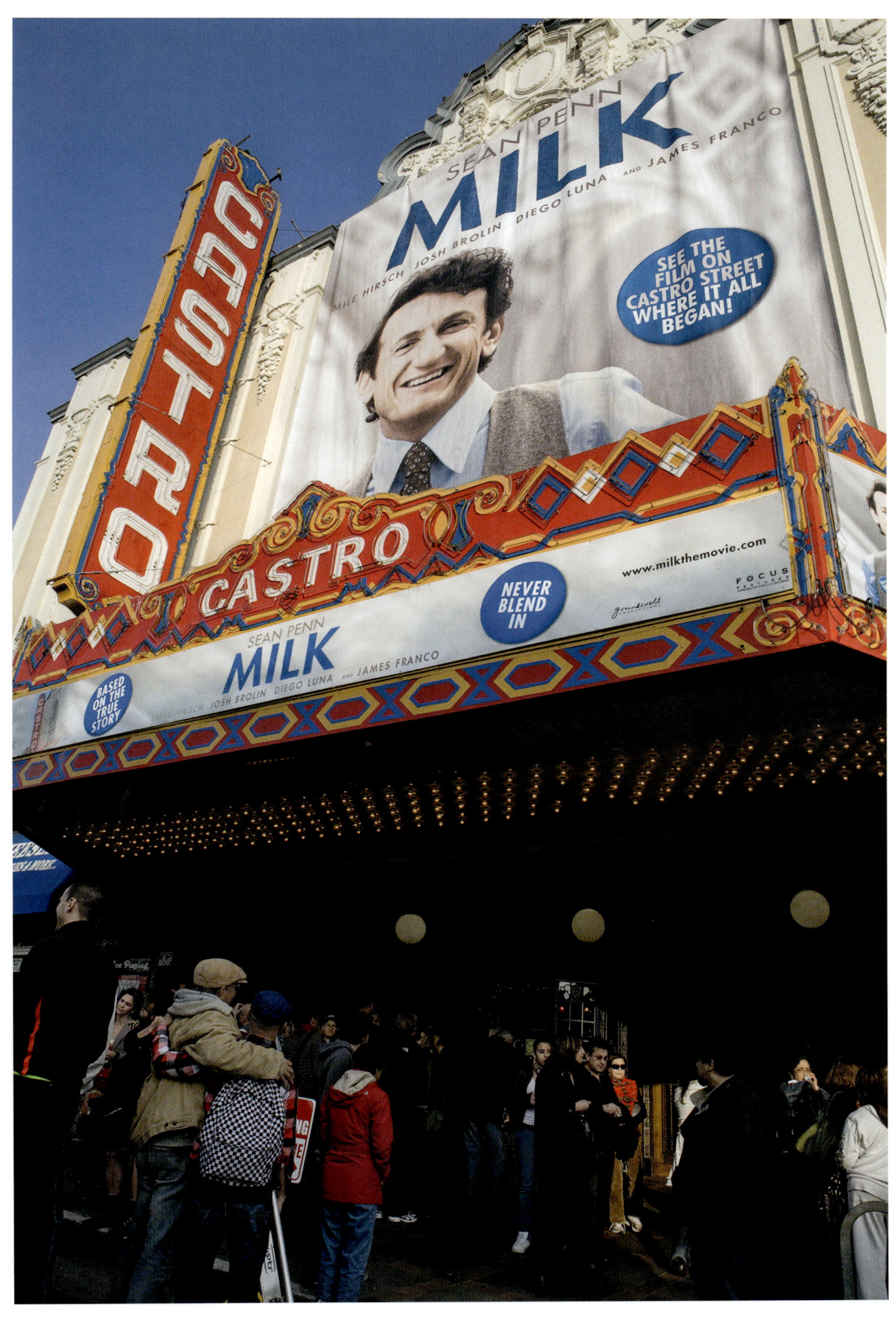

Post-matinee crowd spilling onto the street at the Castro Theatre during the first theatrical run of *Milk*, November 28, 2008.

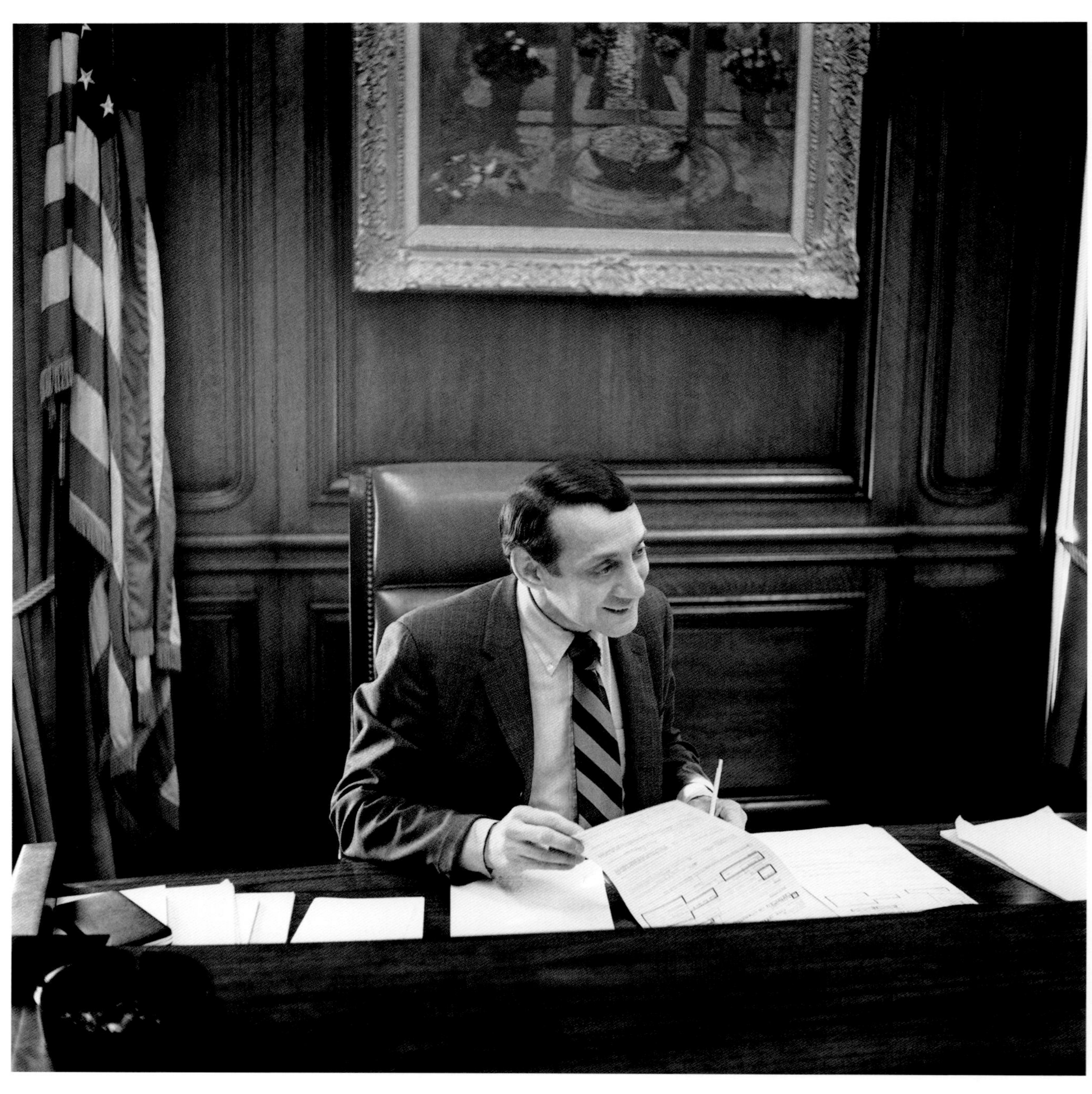

Above: Supervisor Harvey Milk as Deputy Mayor for a day, Mayor's Office, March 7, 1978.
Opposite: *Milk*; Sean Penn as Harvey Milk, March 16, 2008.

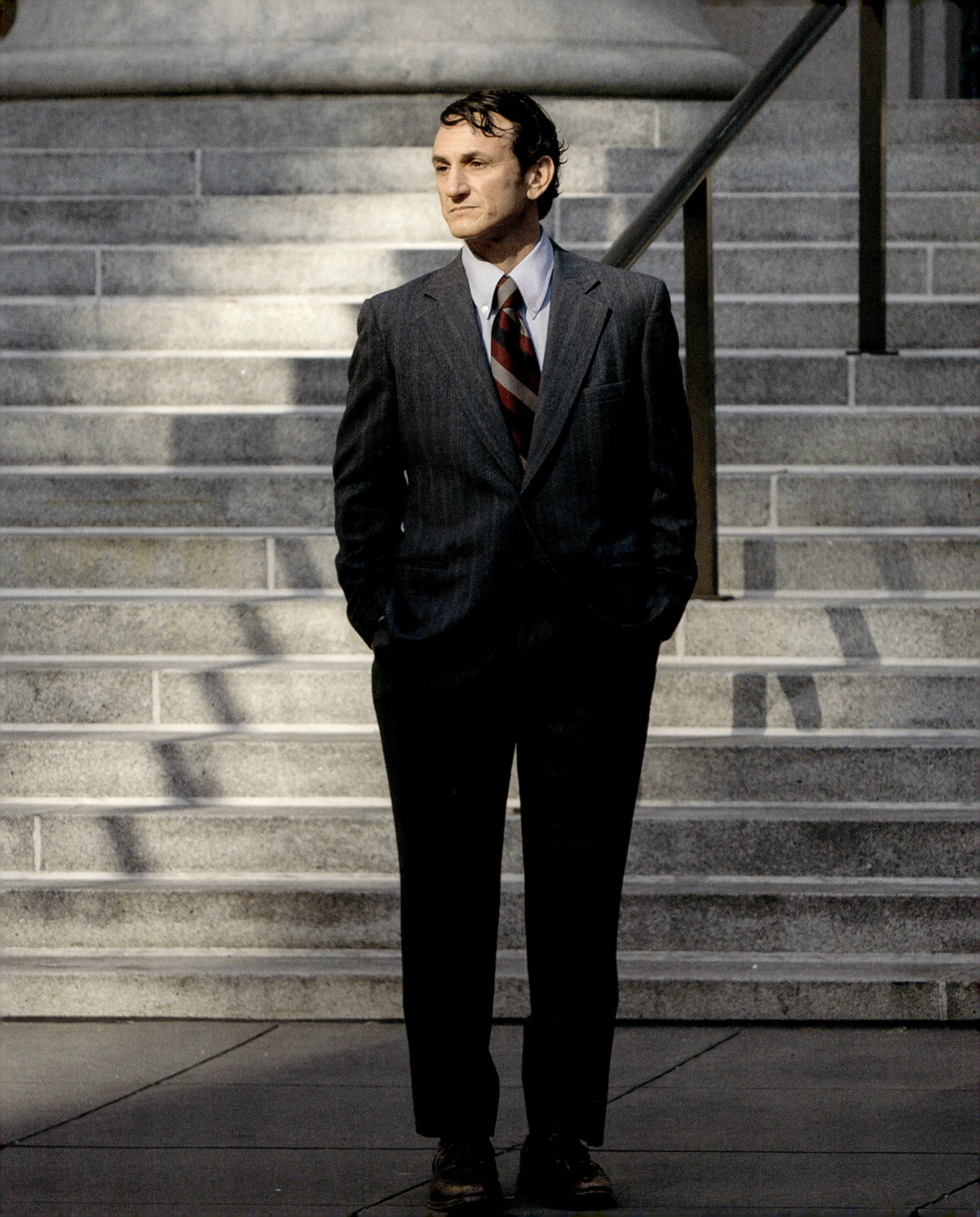

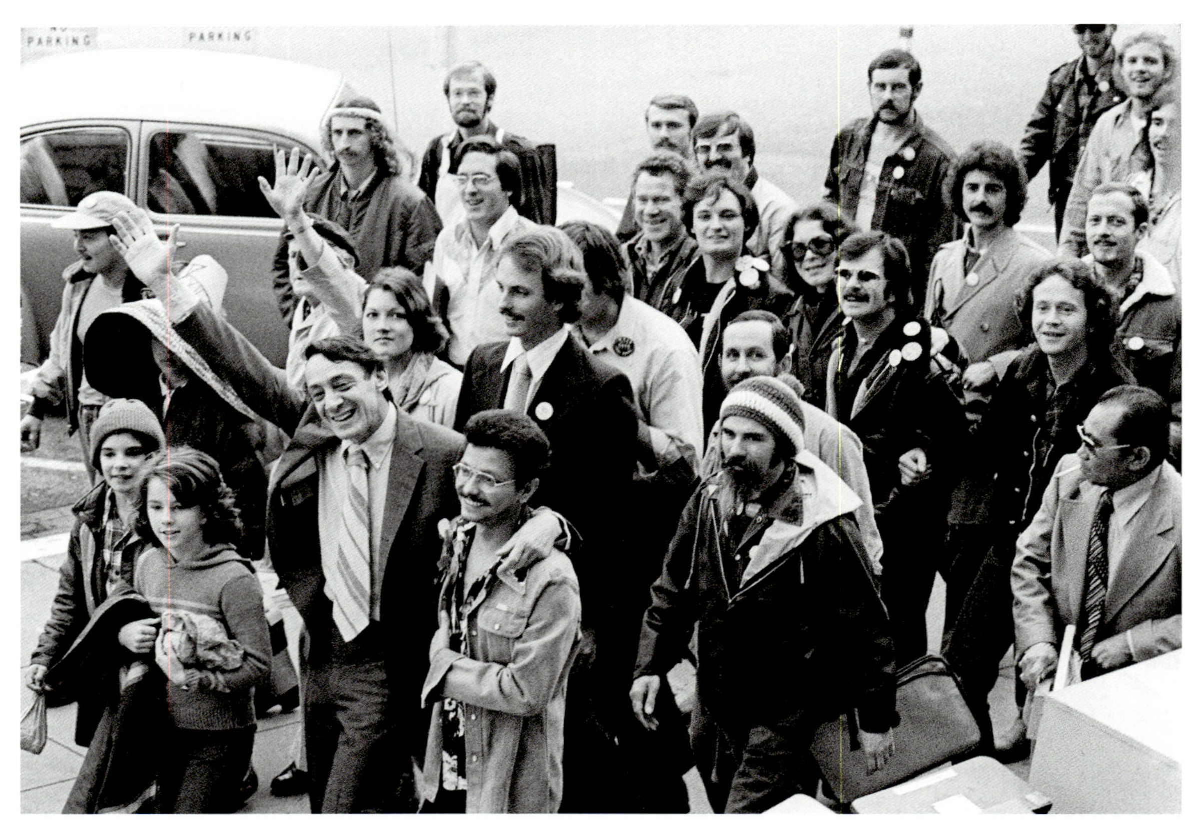
PARKING
PARKING

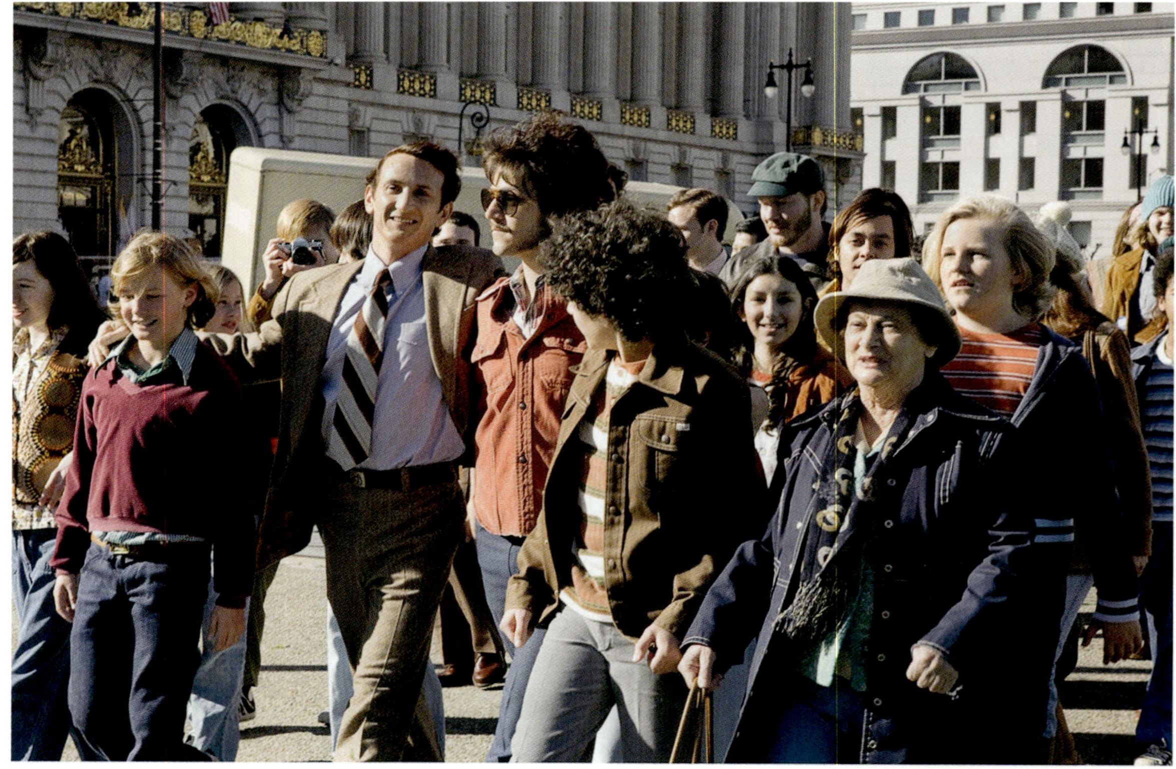

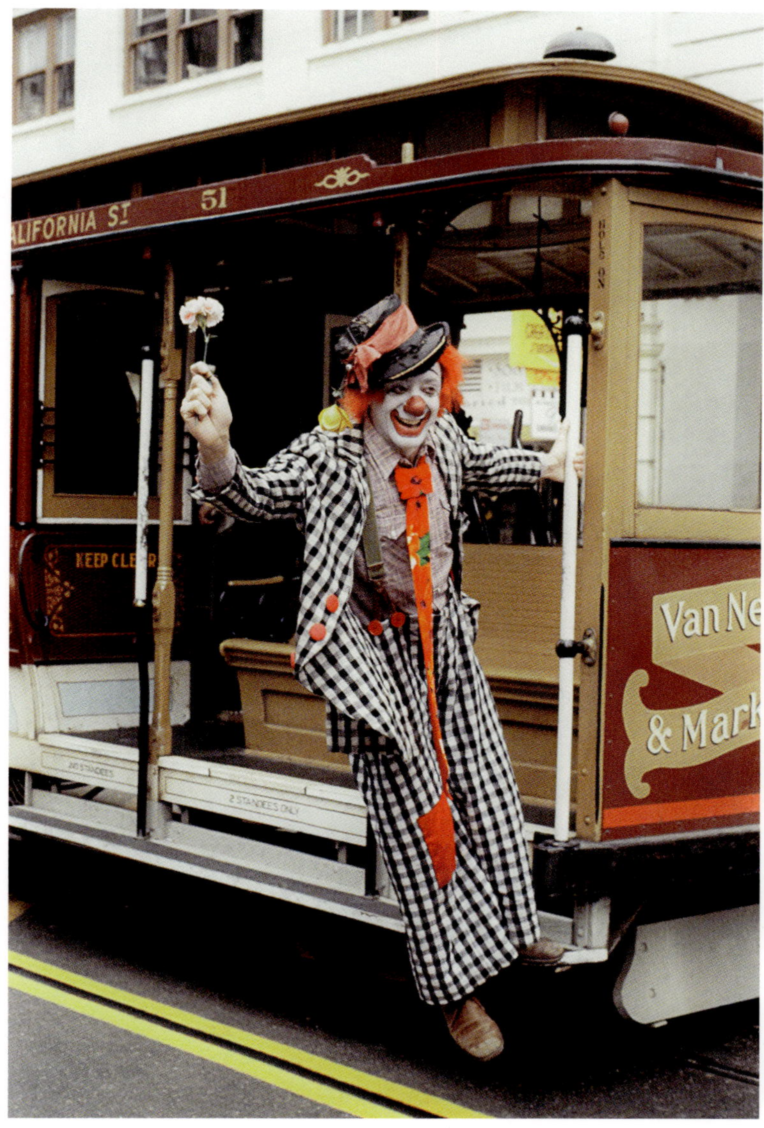

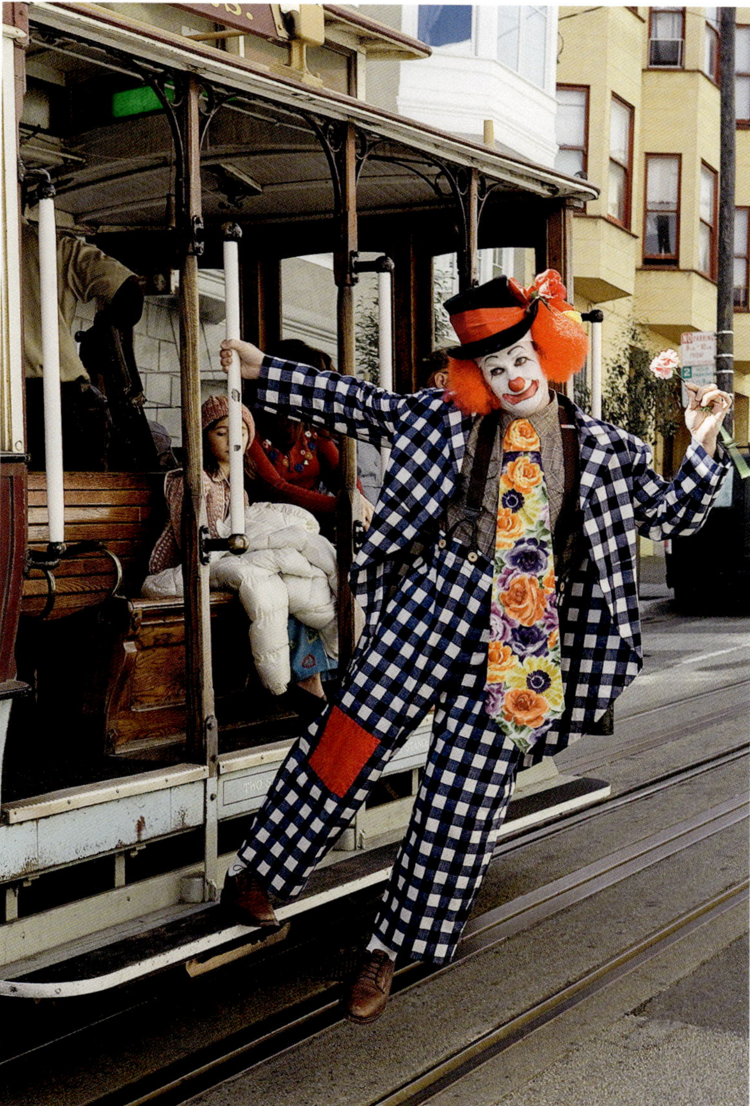

Above: *(left)* Harvey as a Ringling Bros, Barnum & Bailey "clown for a day," May 21, 1978; *(right) Milk*; Sean Penn as Harvey, March 14, 2008.
Opposite: *(top)* Supervisor Harvey Milk's Inaugural Walk from Castro Street to City Hall, with his lover Jack Lira and supporters, January 9, 1978; *(bottom) Milk*; the Inaugural Walk re-enactment, March 22, 2008.

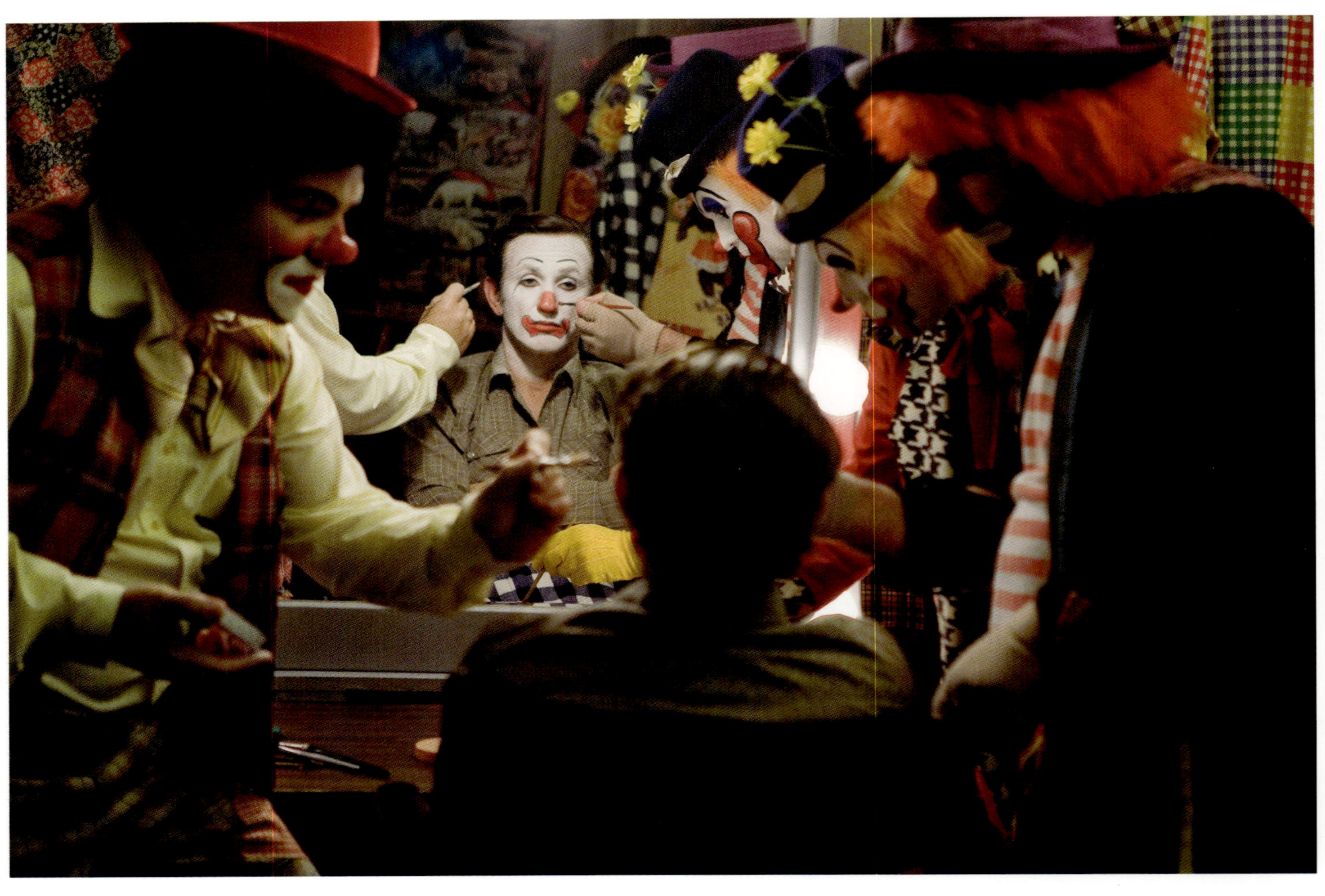

Above: *Milk*; Sean Penn as Harvey getting made up by Ringling Bros. and Barnum & Bailey clowns, March 14, 2008. David Magidson as Boswick the clown, Sean Penn, John Flanagan and Pat the Hat.
Opposite: Ron and Sandy Severini from Ringling Bros. and Barnum & Bailey clown school prepare Harvey (one of six SF celebrities chosen) for an editorial in *California Living* magazine about the circus.

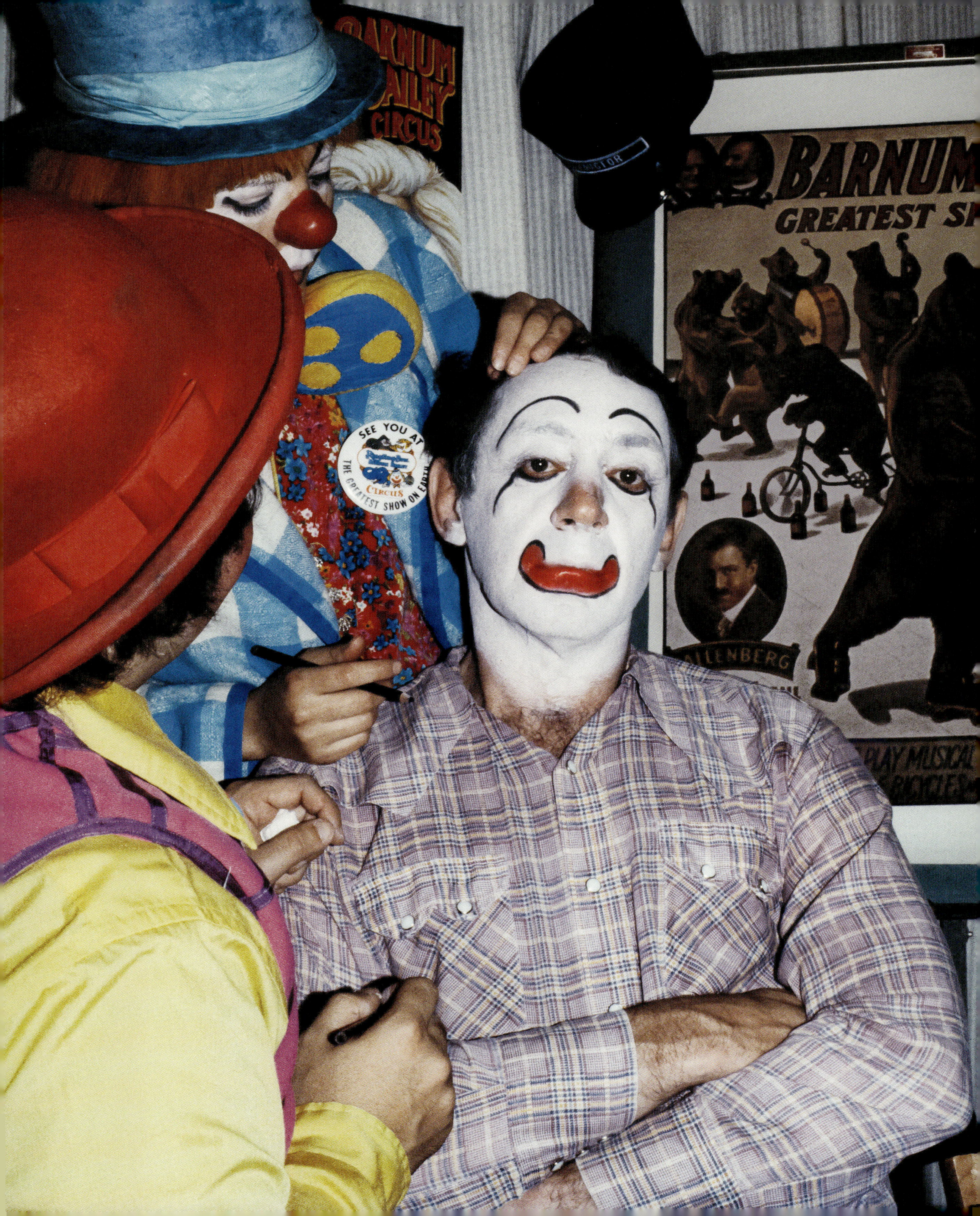
BARNUM
BAILEY
CIRCUS
SEE YOU AT
CIRCUS
THE GREATEST SHOW ON EARTH
BARNUM
PLAY MUSICAL
BICYCLES

Harvey at the seaside, May 21, 1978.

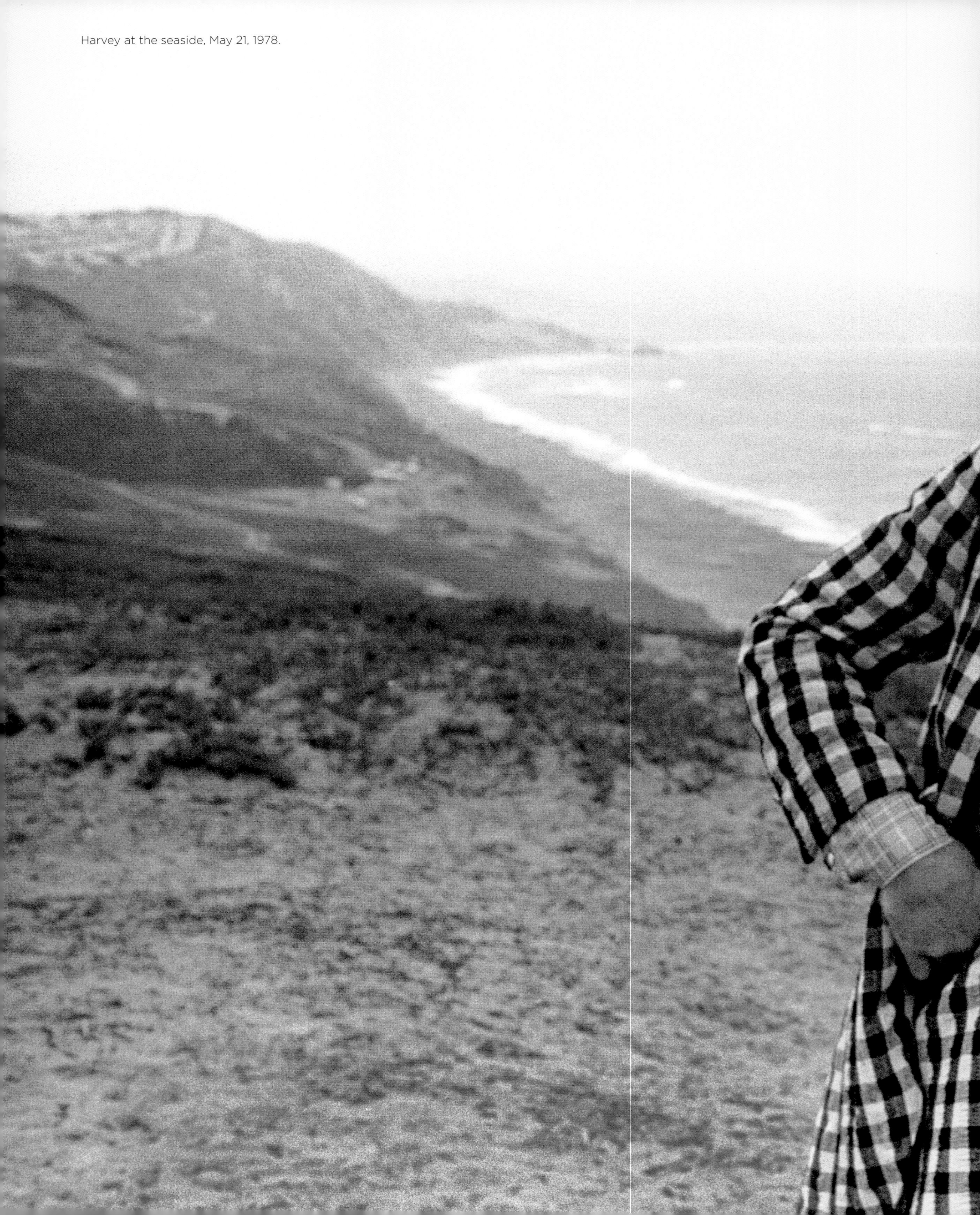

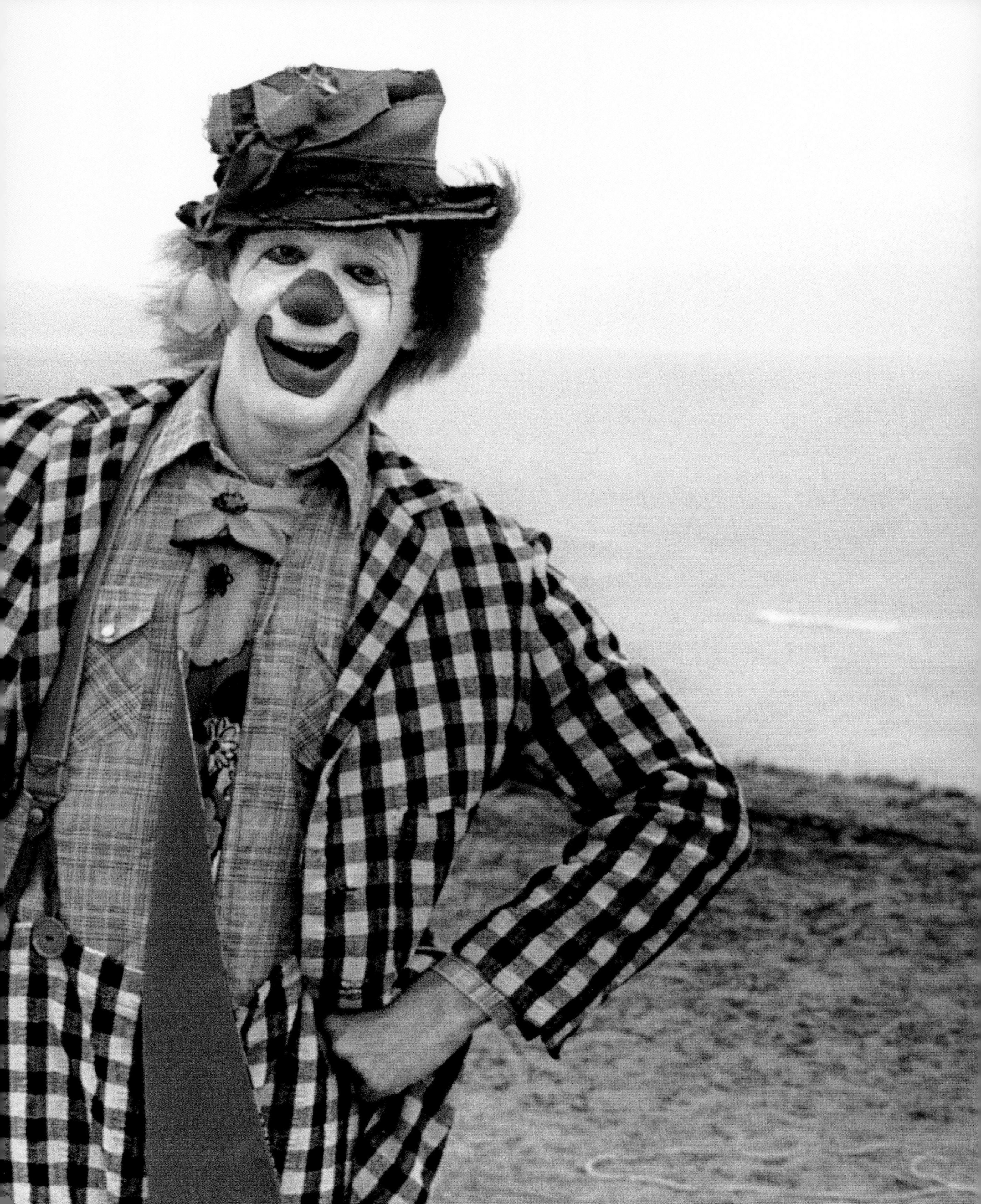

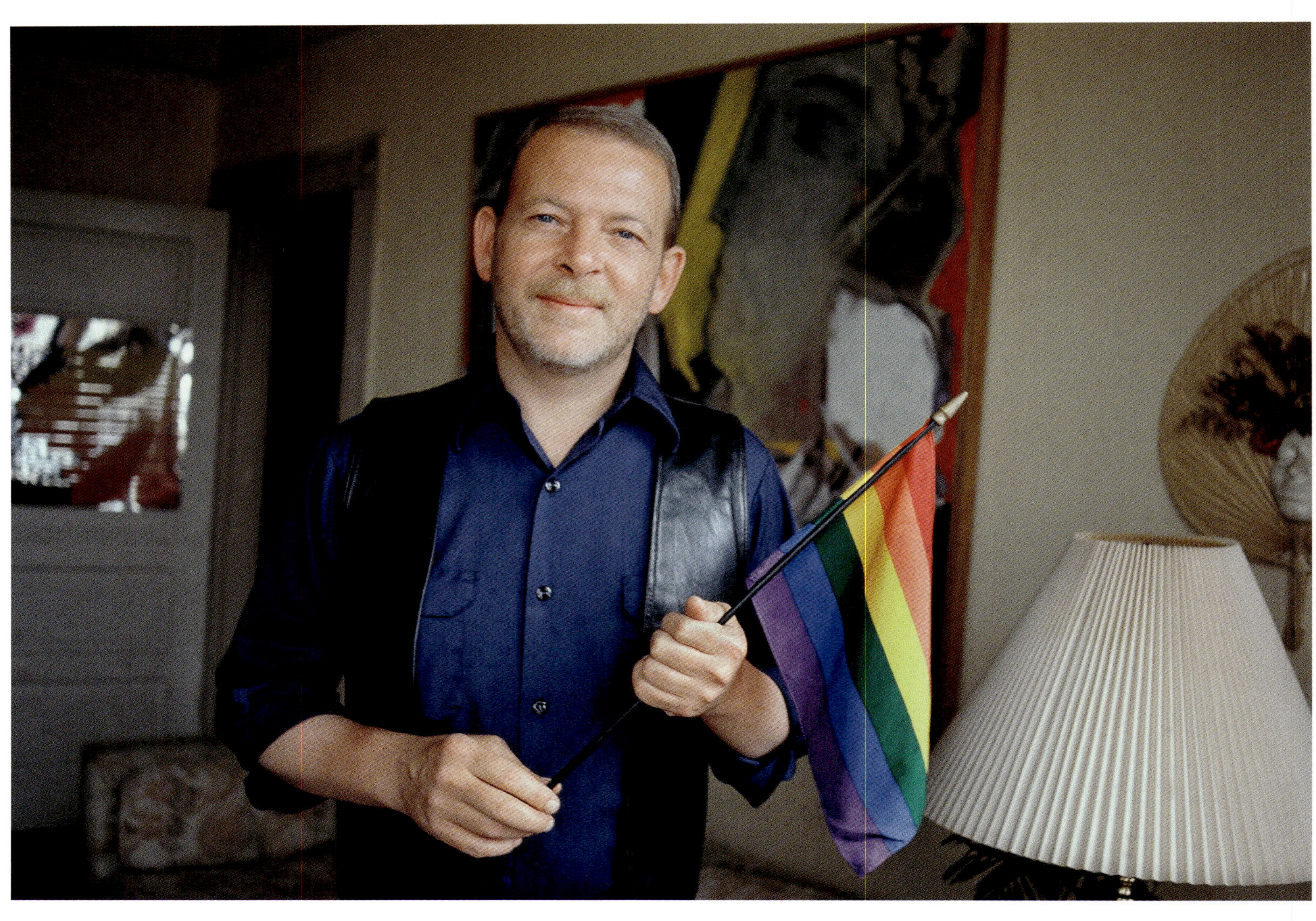

Above: Scott Smith, June 25, 1989.
Opposite: *Milk;* James Franco as Scott Smith, March 16, 2008.

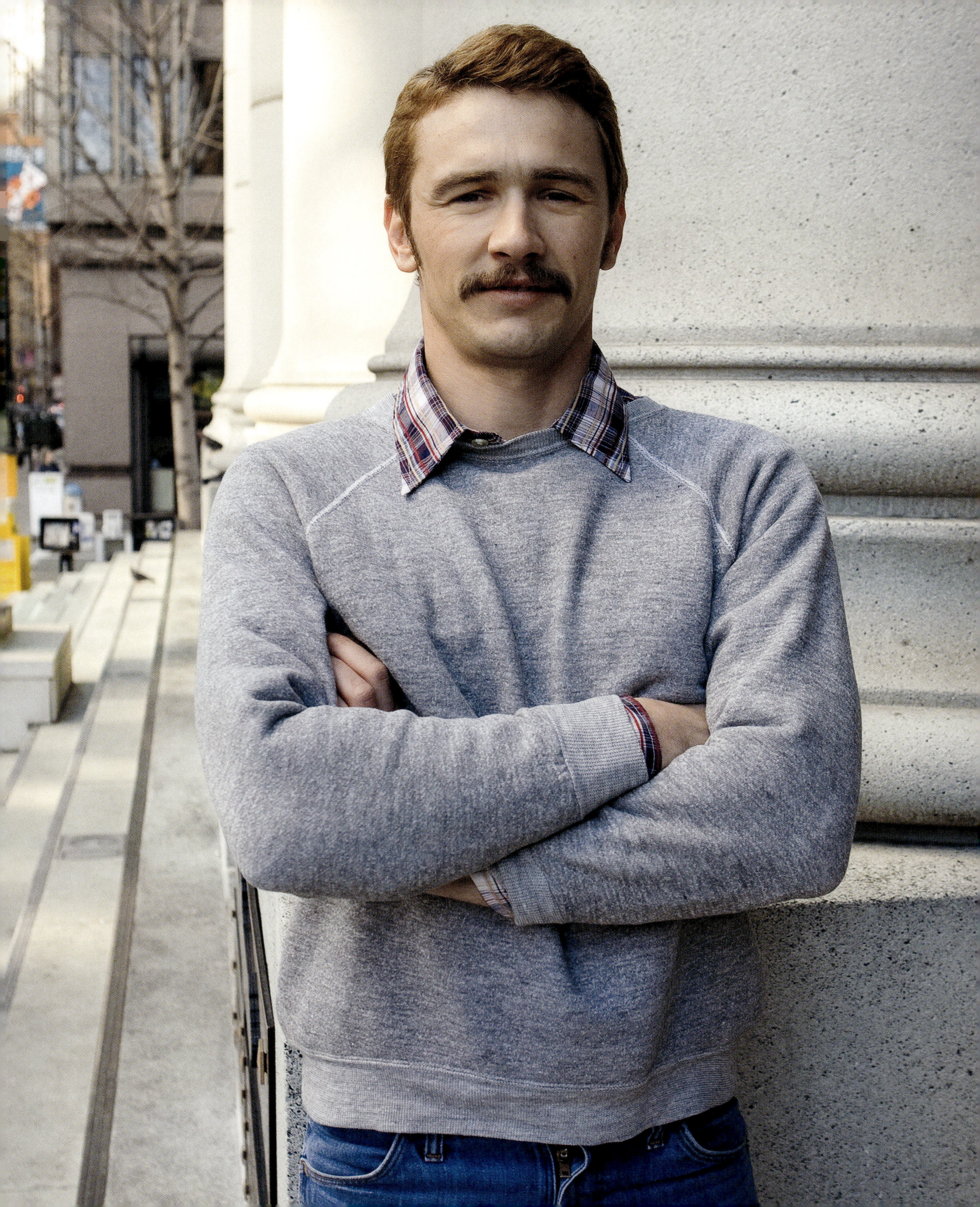

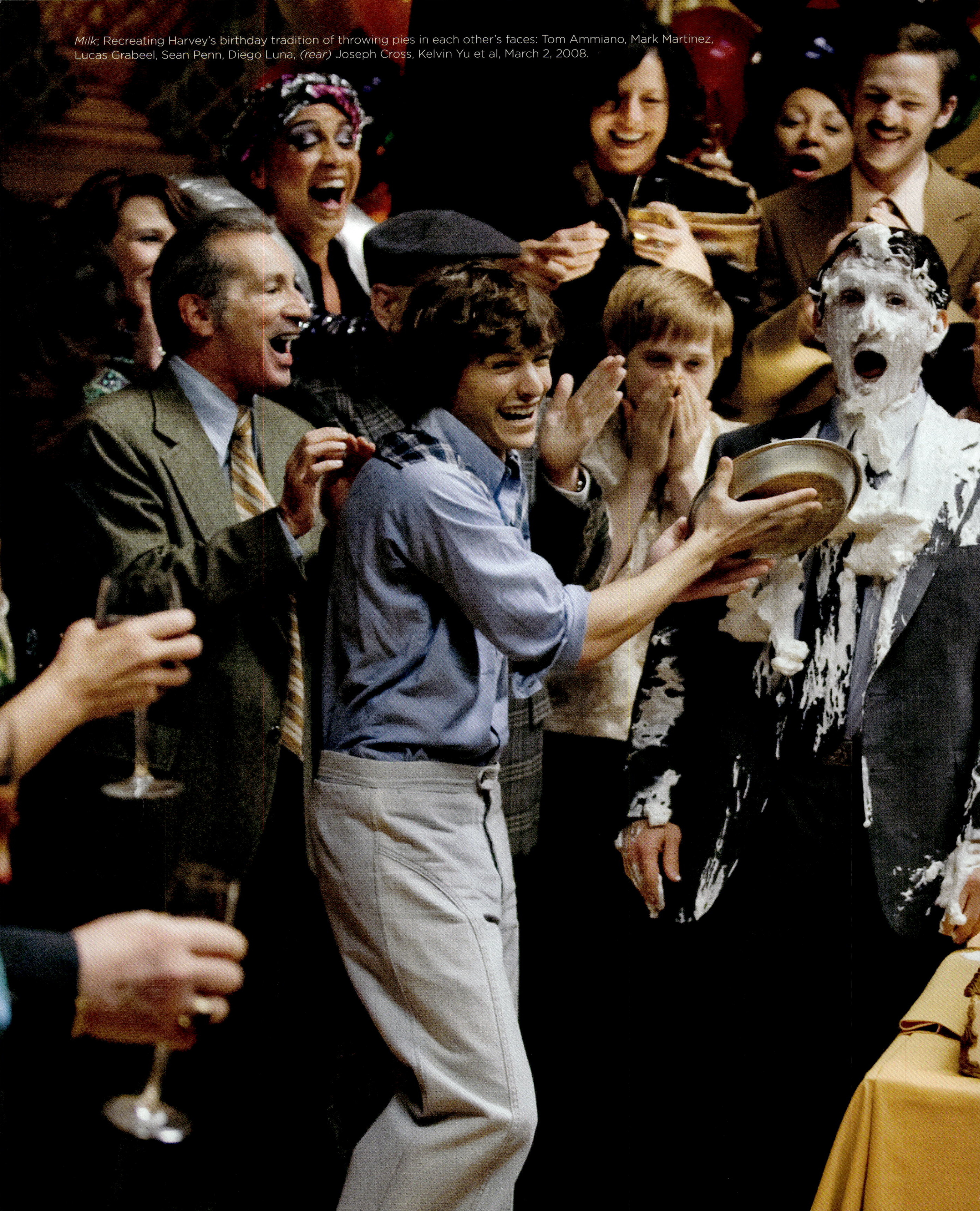

Milk; Recreating Harvey's birthday tradition of throwing pies in each other's faces: Tom Ammiano, Mark Martinez, Lucas Grabeel, Sean Penn, Diego Luna, *(rear)* Joseph Cross, Kelvin Yu et al, March 2, 2008.

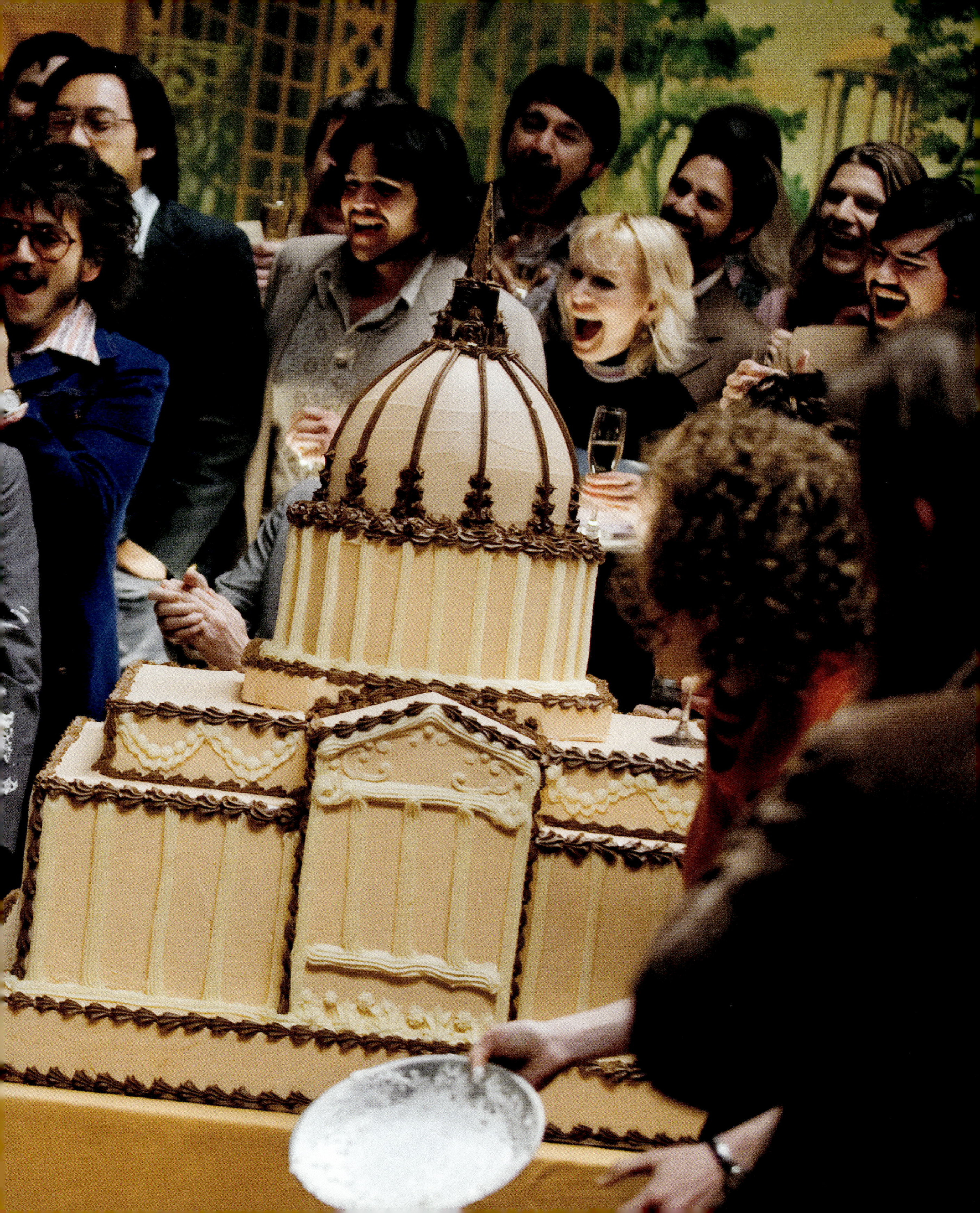

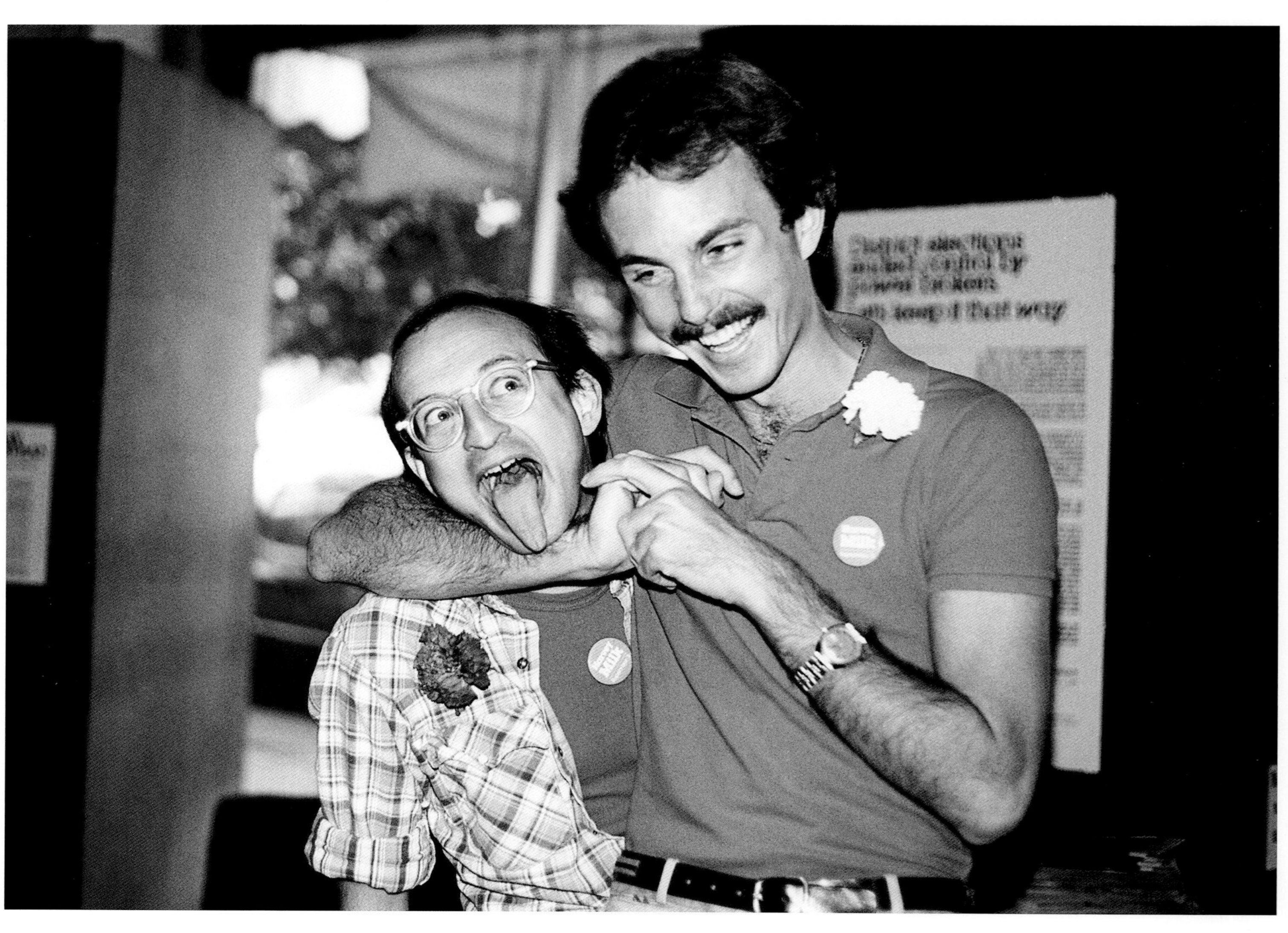

Harvey Milk's campaign strategists, Jim Rivaldo and Dick Pabich, clowning around on election day, November 8, 1977.

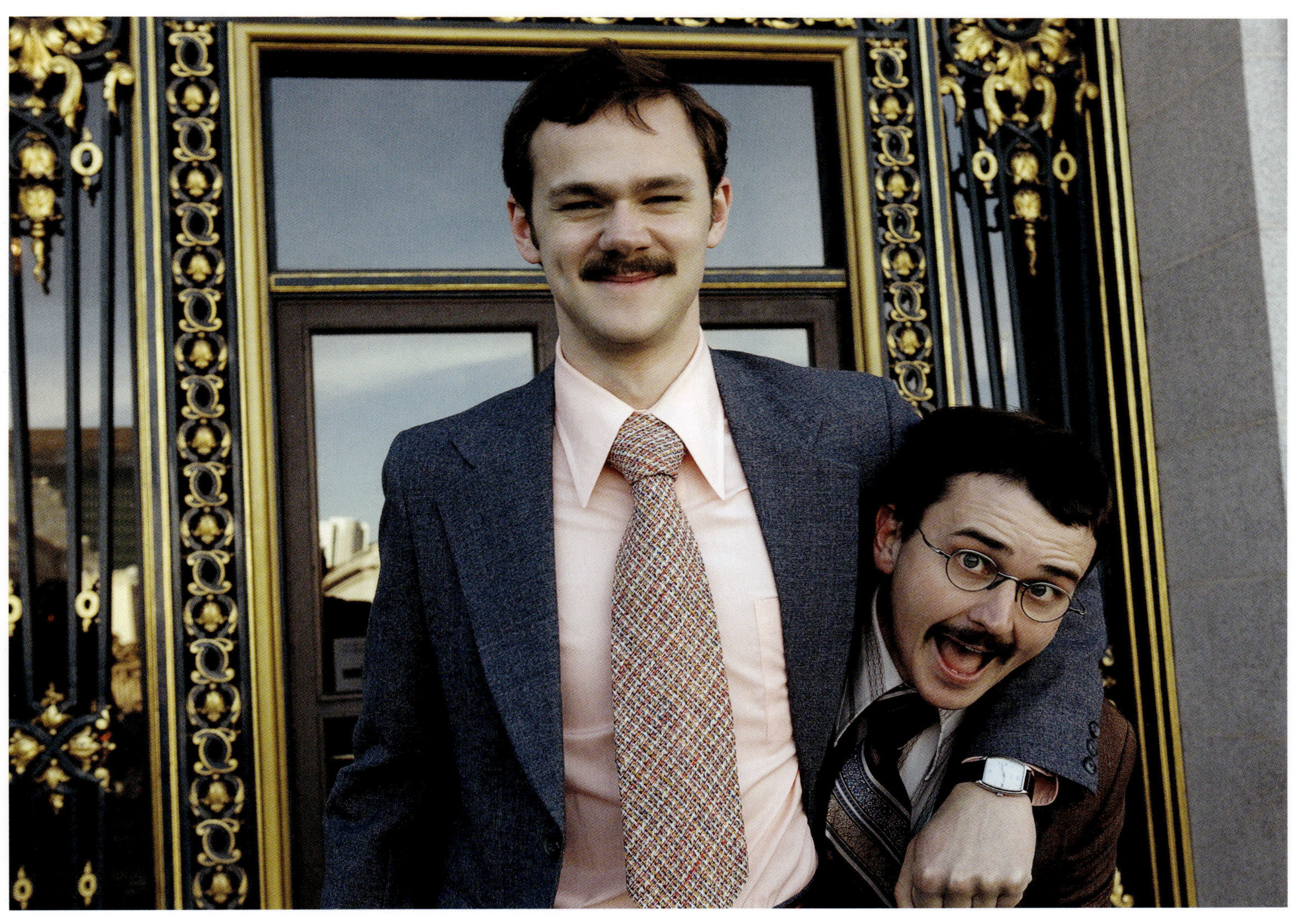

Milk; Joseph Cross as Dick Pabich and Brandon Boyce as Jim Rivaldo, March 2, 2008.

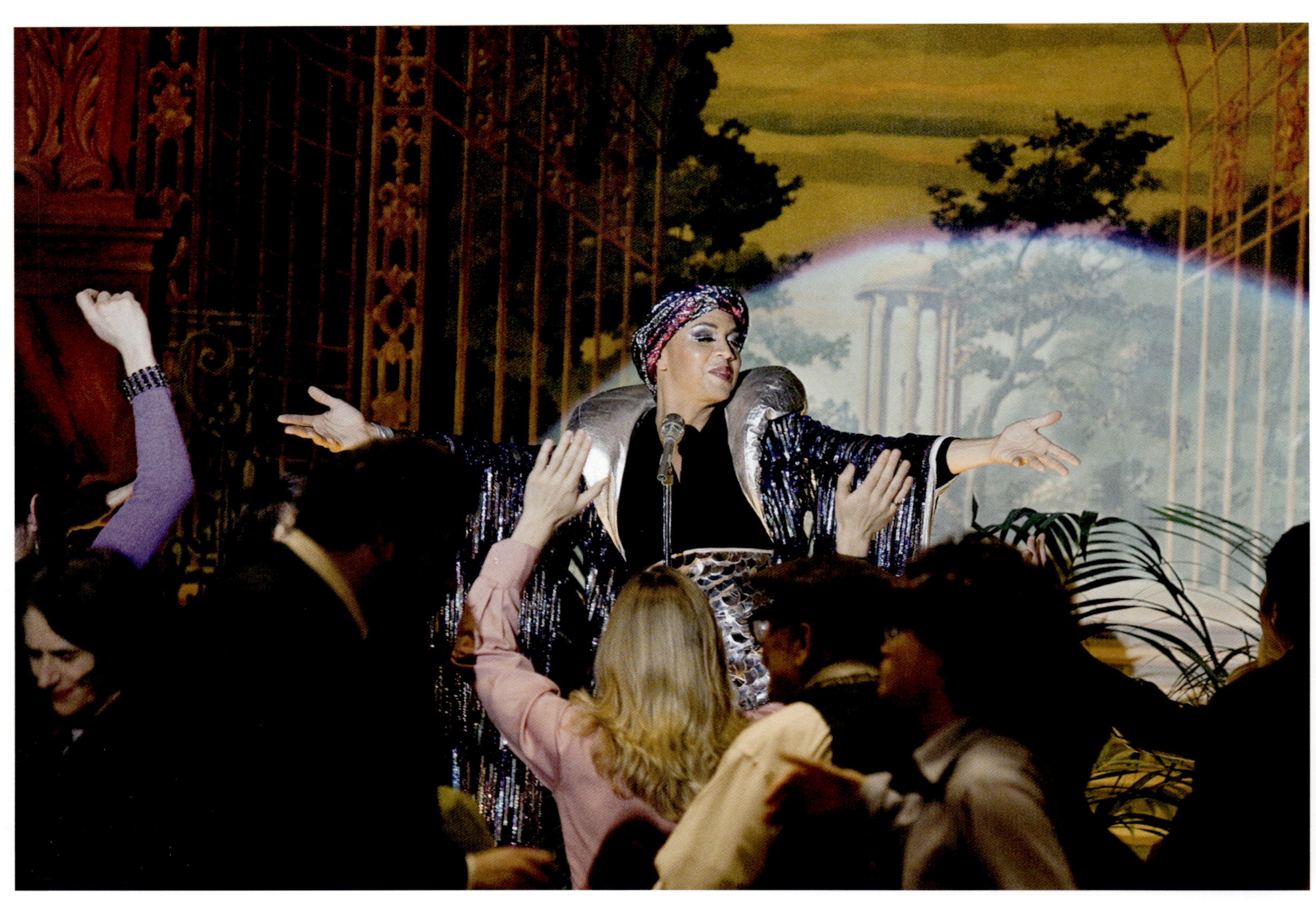

Milk; Mark Martinez as Sylvester, February 22, 2008.

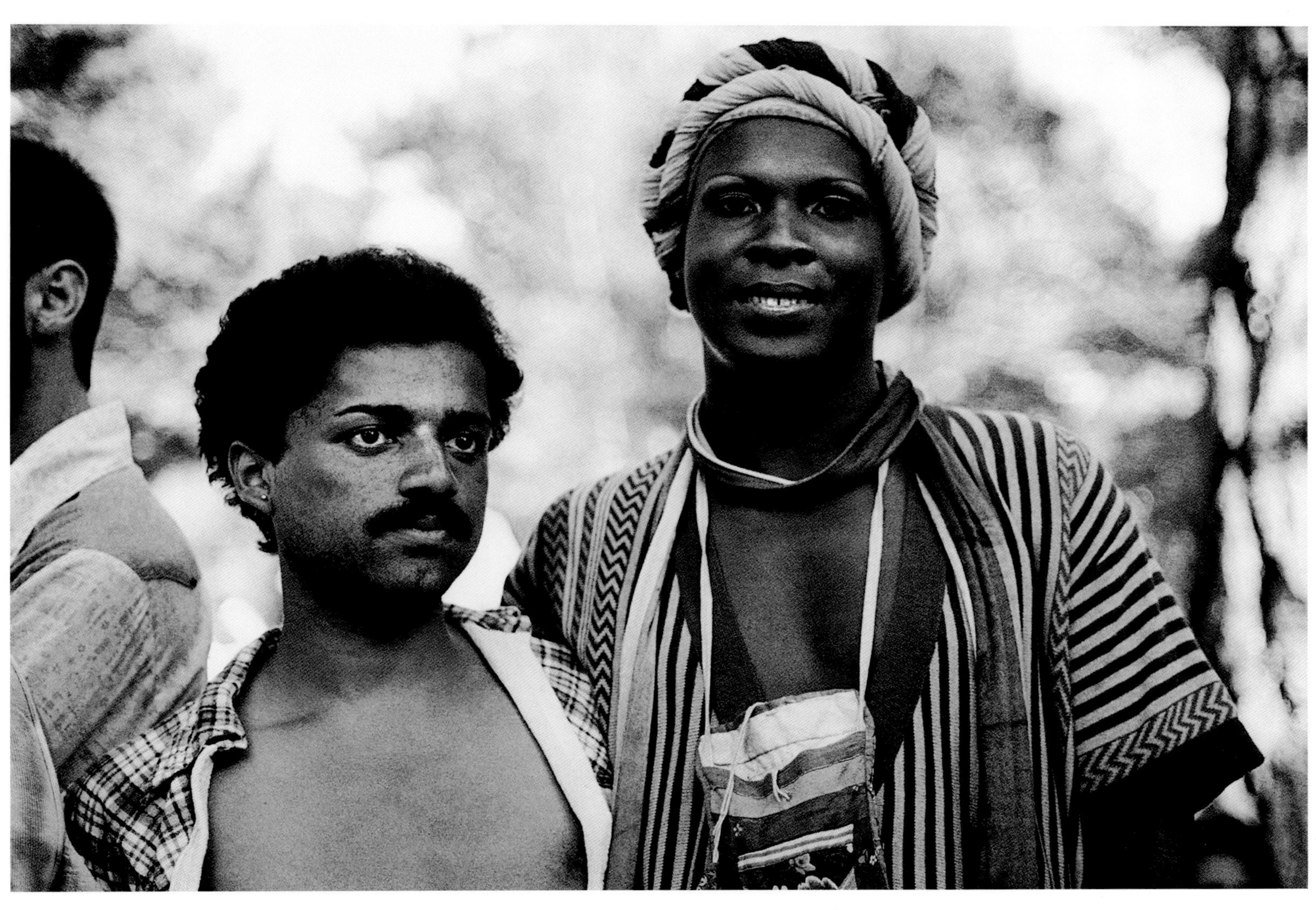

Willie and Sylvester, Gay Freedom Day celebration, Golden Gate Park, June 1976.

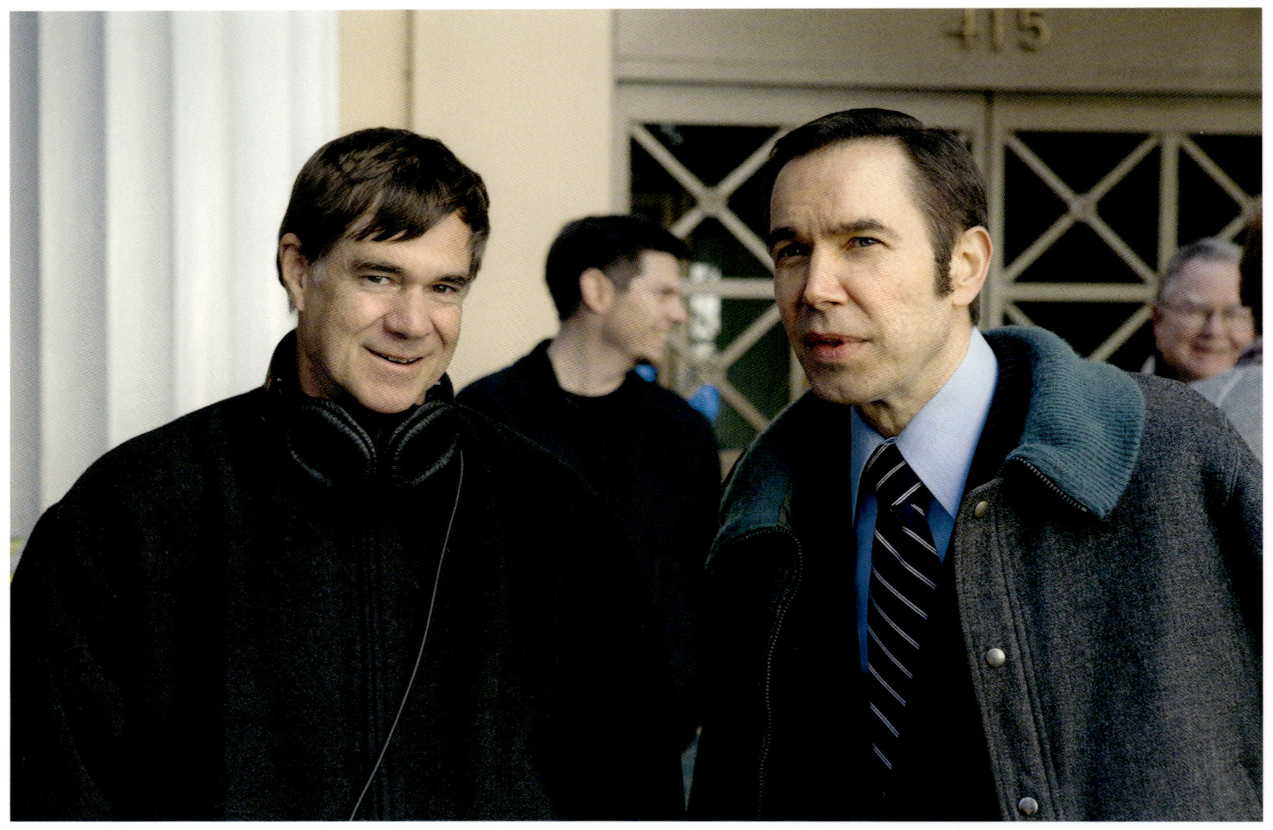

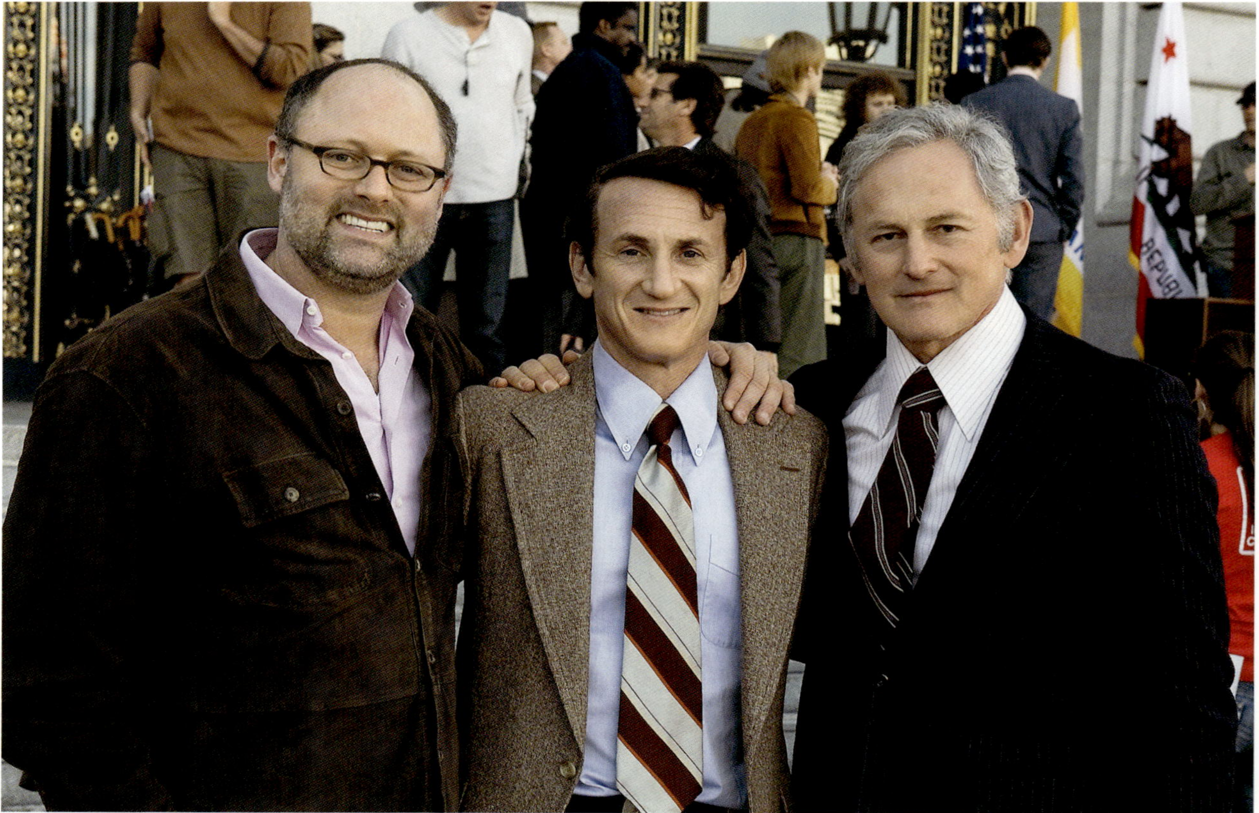

Above: *(top) Milk*; Director Gus Van Sant with Jeff Koons (playing Harvey's Assembly-race challenger, Art Agnos), March 16, 2008; *(bottom) Milk;* Jon Moscone, Sean Penn and Victor Garber (playing Mayor Moscone), March 2, 2008.
Opposite: *Milk*; Dustin Lance Black (*Milk* screenwriter) in a cameo, cuddling with Cleve Jones right before the scene, February 11, 2008.

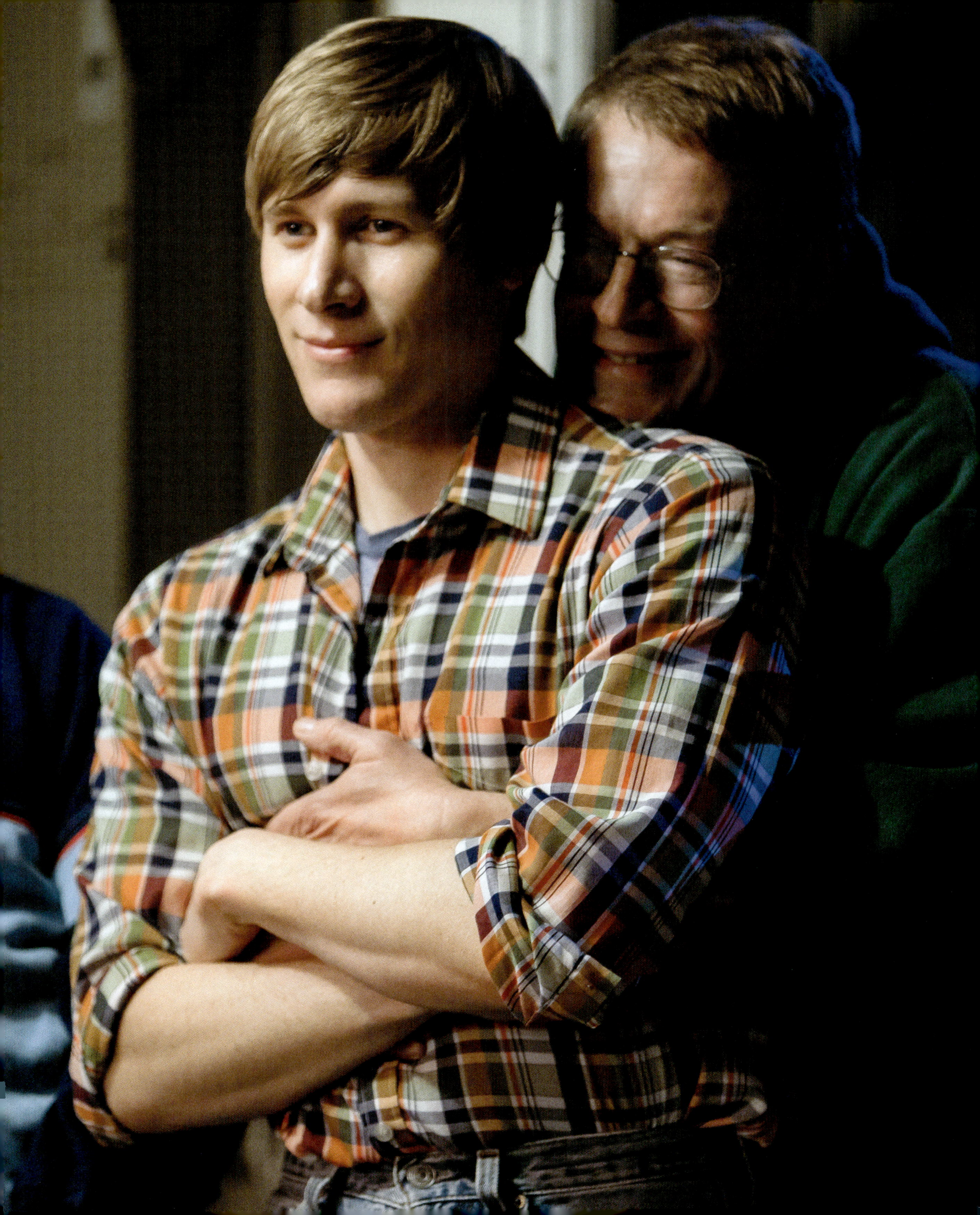

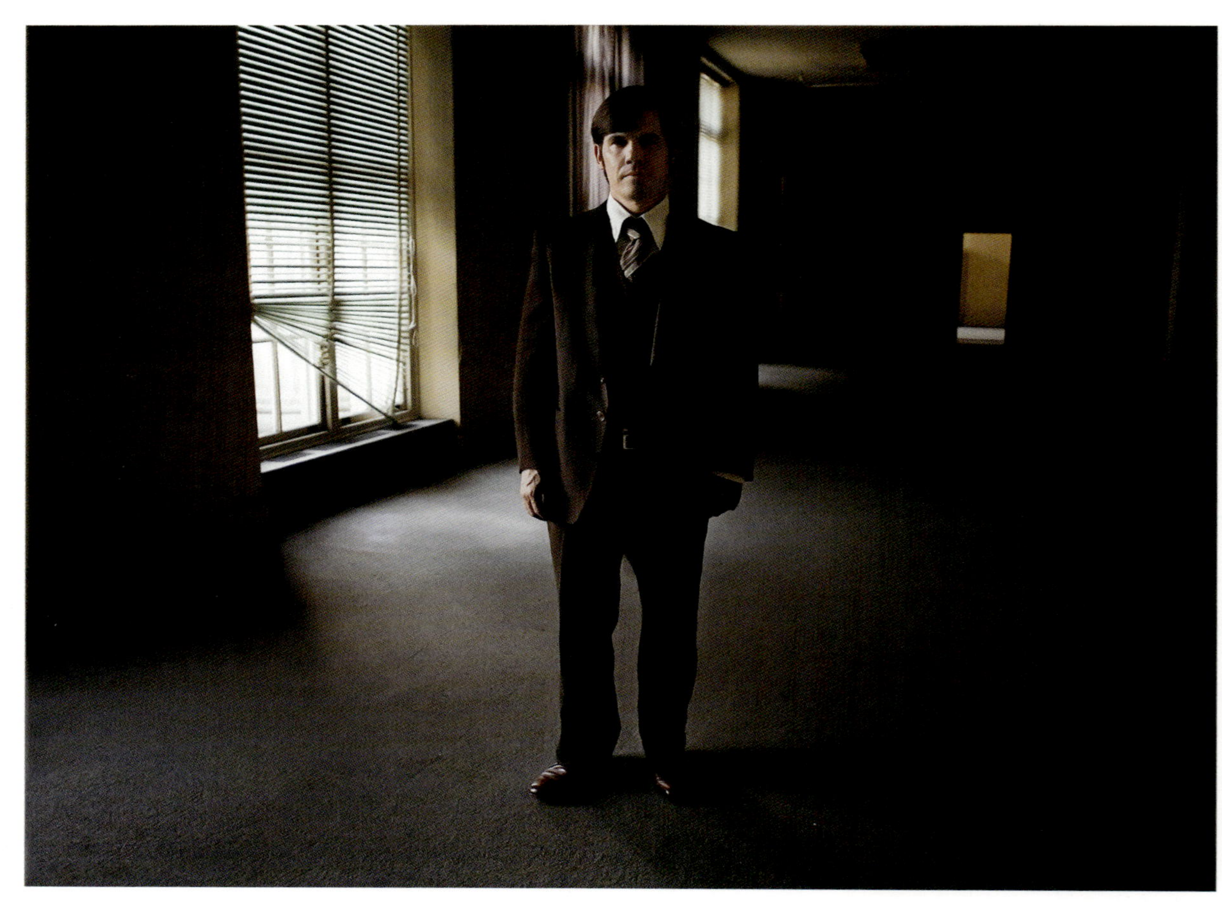

Above: *Milk*; Josh Brolin as Dan White, March 1, 2008.
Opposite: Supervisor Harvey Milk and Mayor George Moscone lying in state in SF City Hall Rotunda, December 1978.

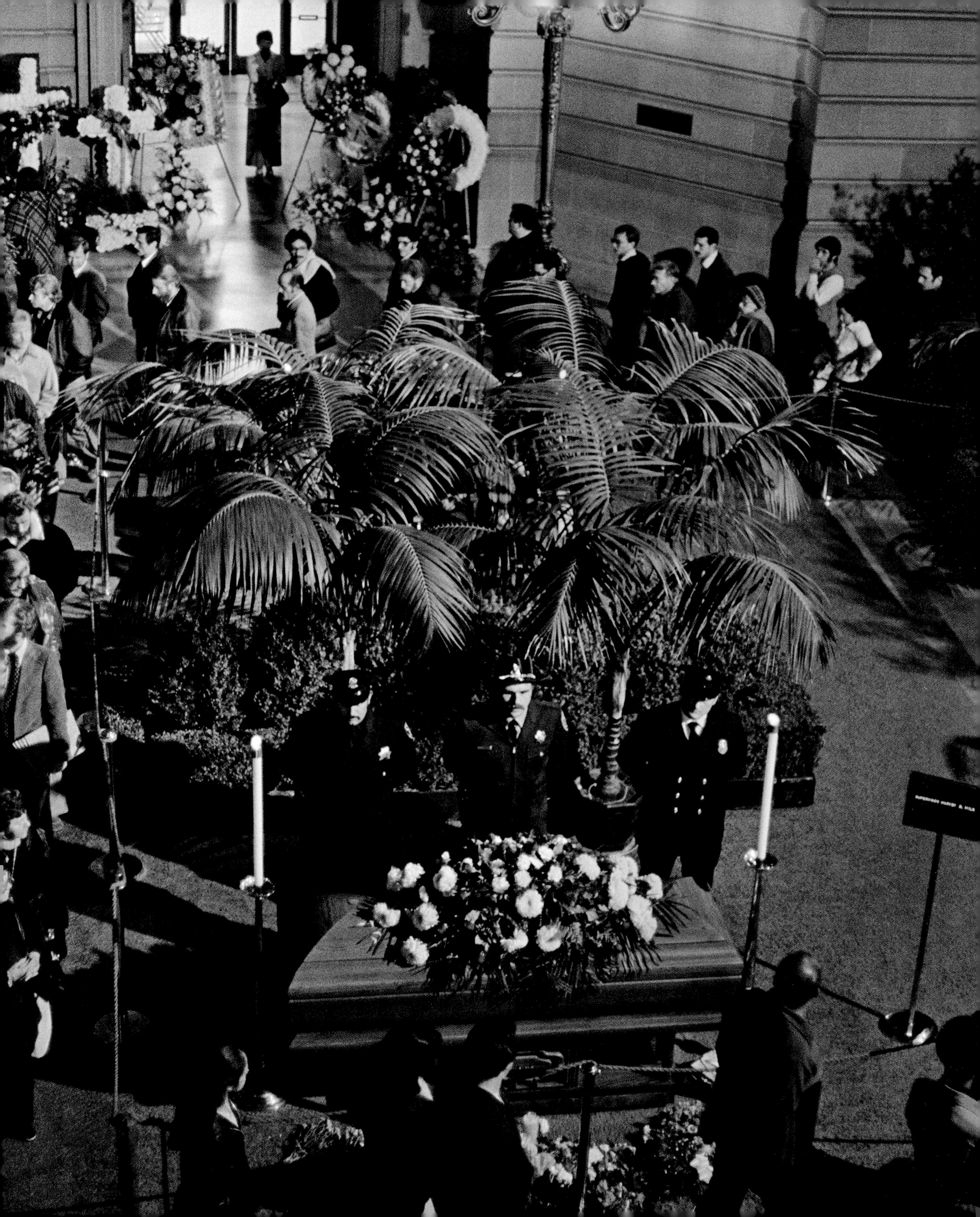

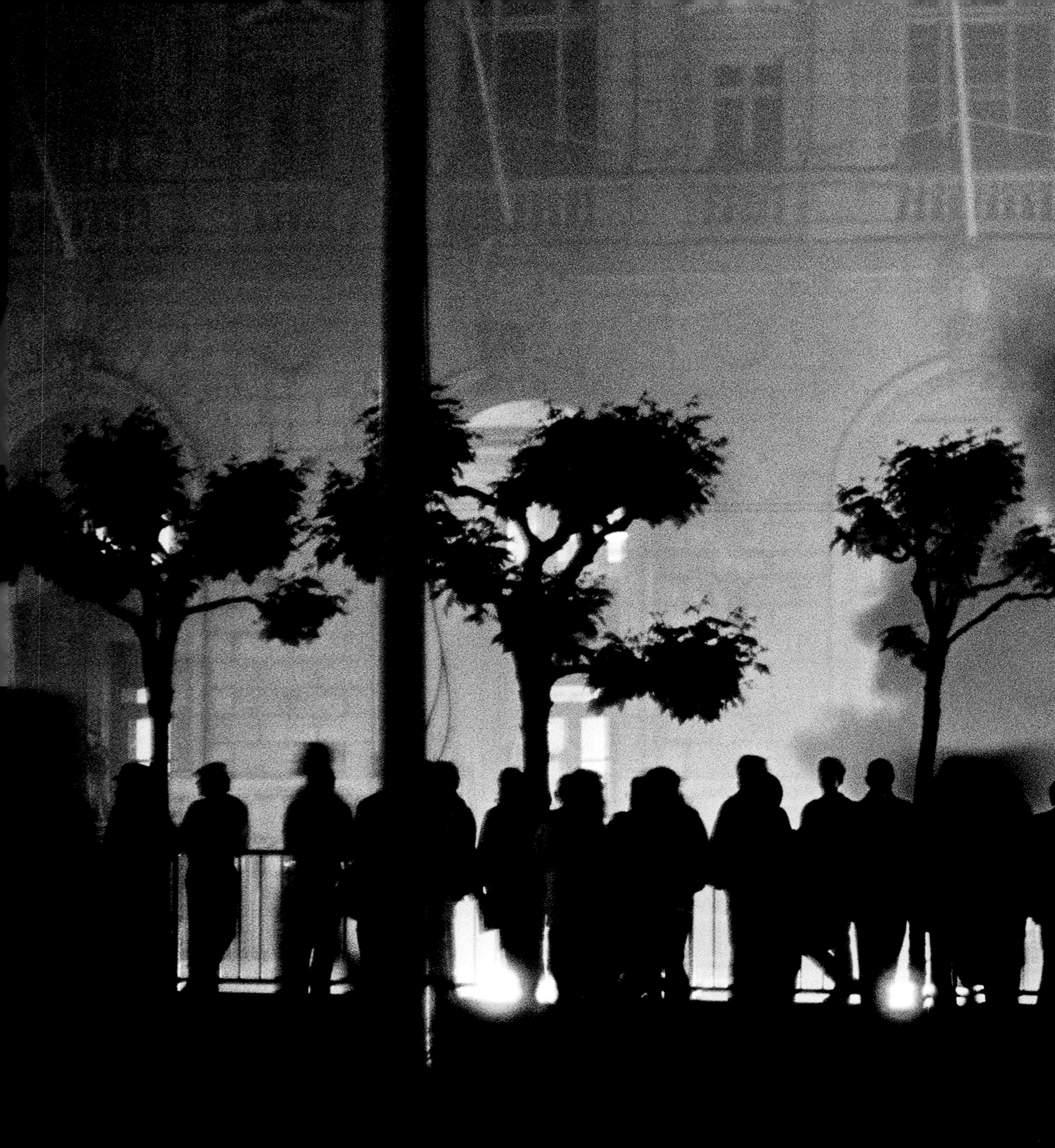

White Night riots: demonstration against the lenient “Twinkie Defense” manslaughter verdict for Dan White, the convicted assassin of Supervisor Harvey Milk and Mayor George Moscone, SF City Hall, May 21, 1979

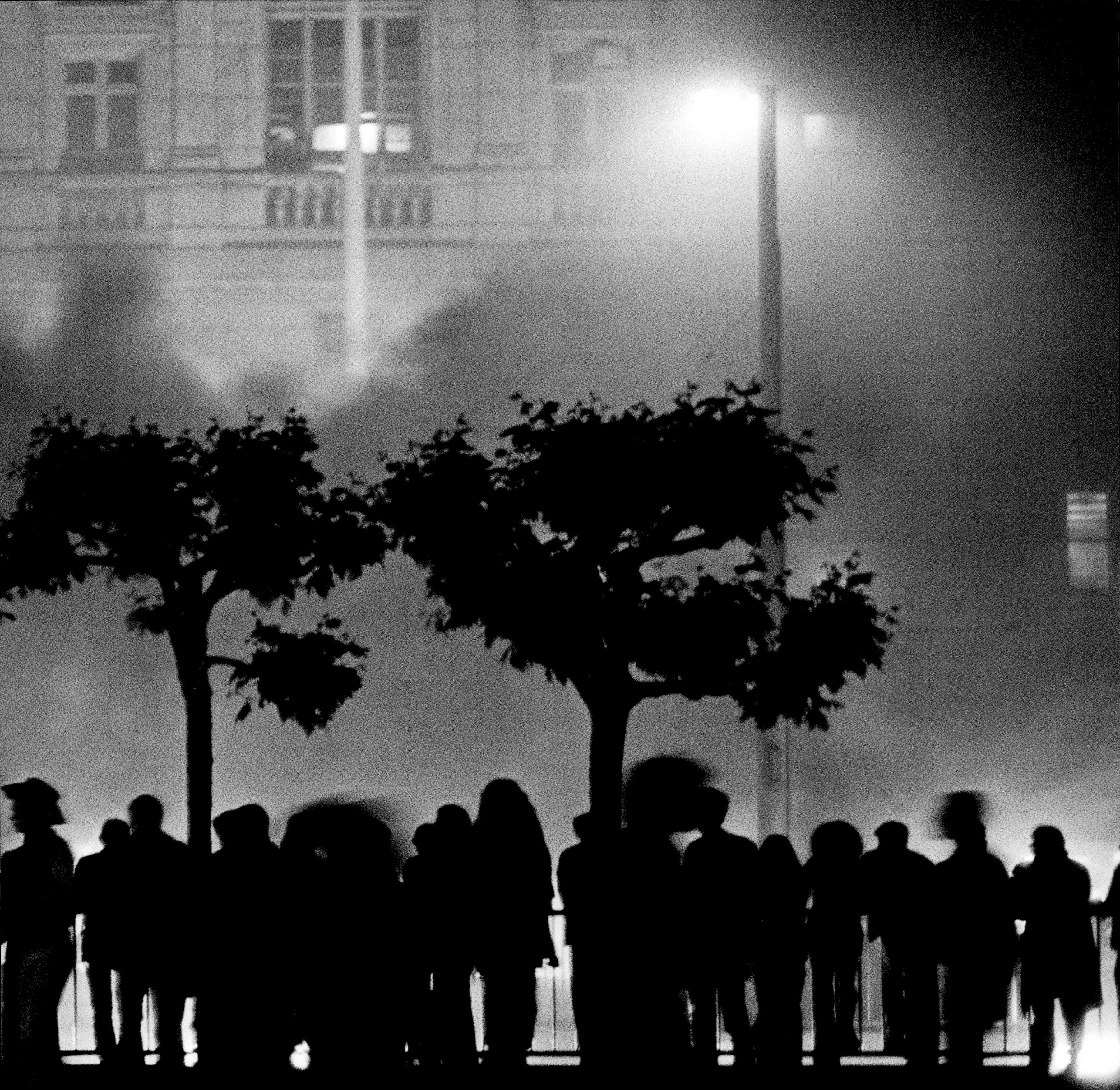

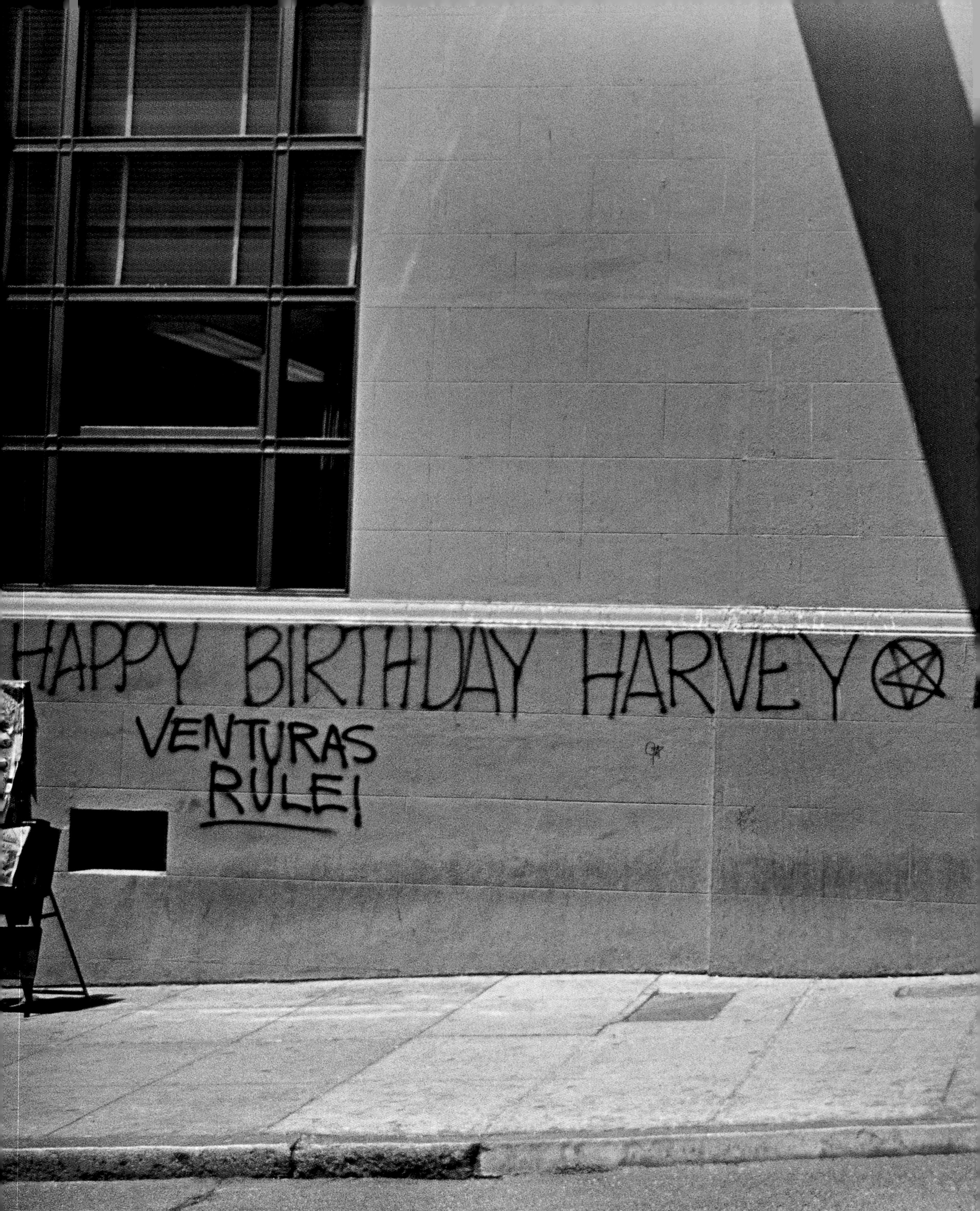
HAPPY BIRTHDAY HARVEY
VENTURAS
RULE!

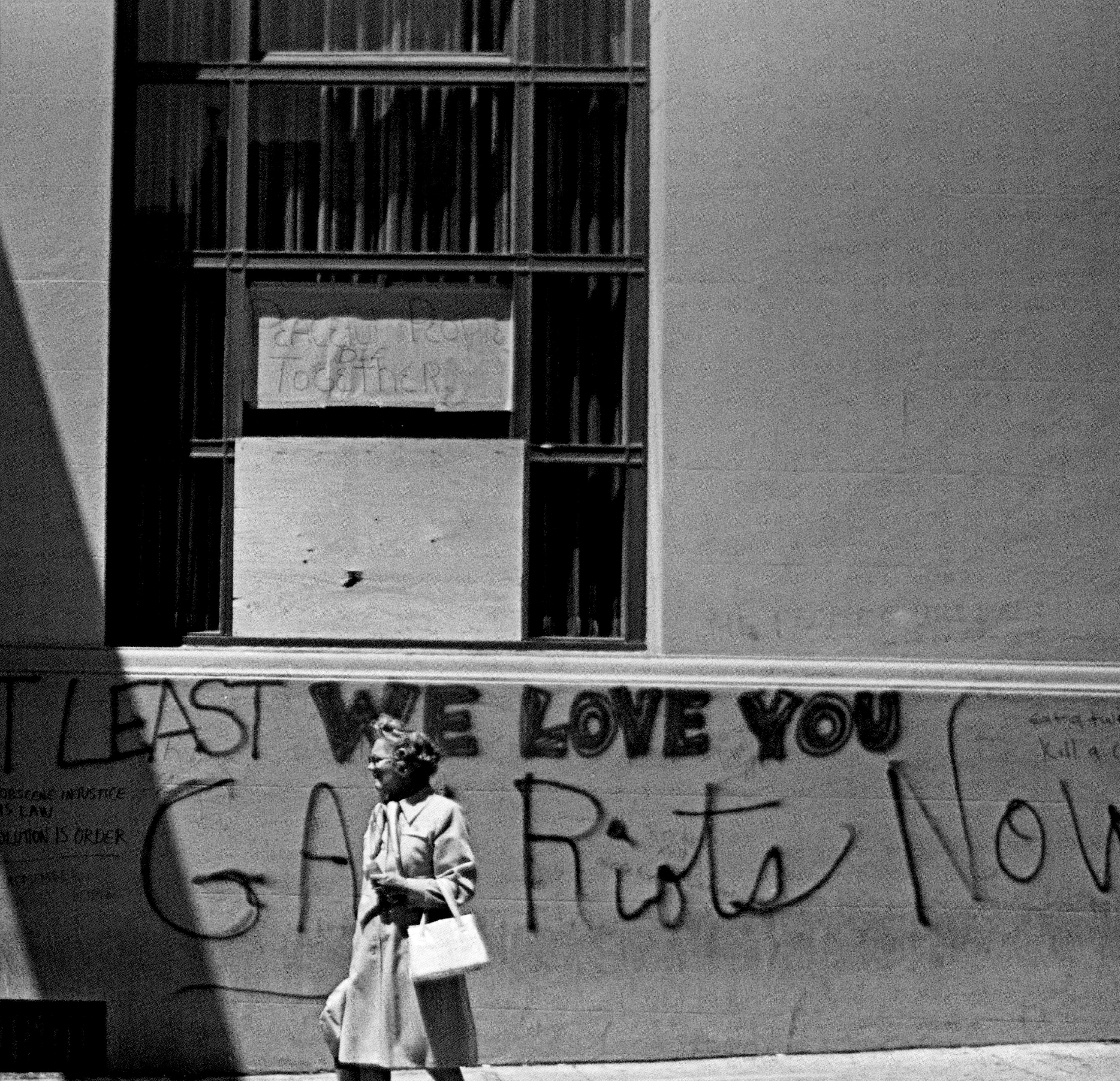

Graffiti in the Castro the day following the White Night riots, May 22, 1979 (Harvey's birthday).

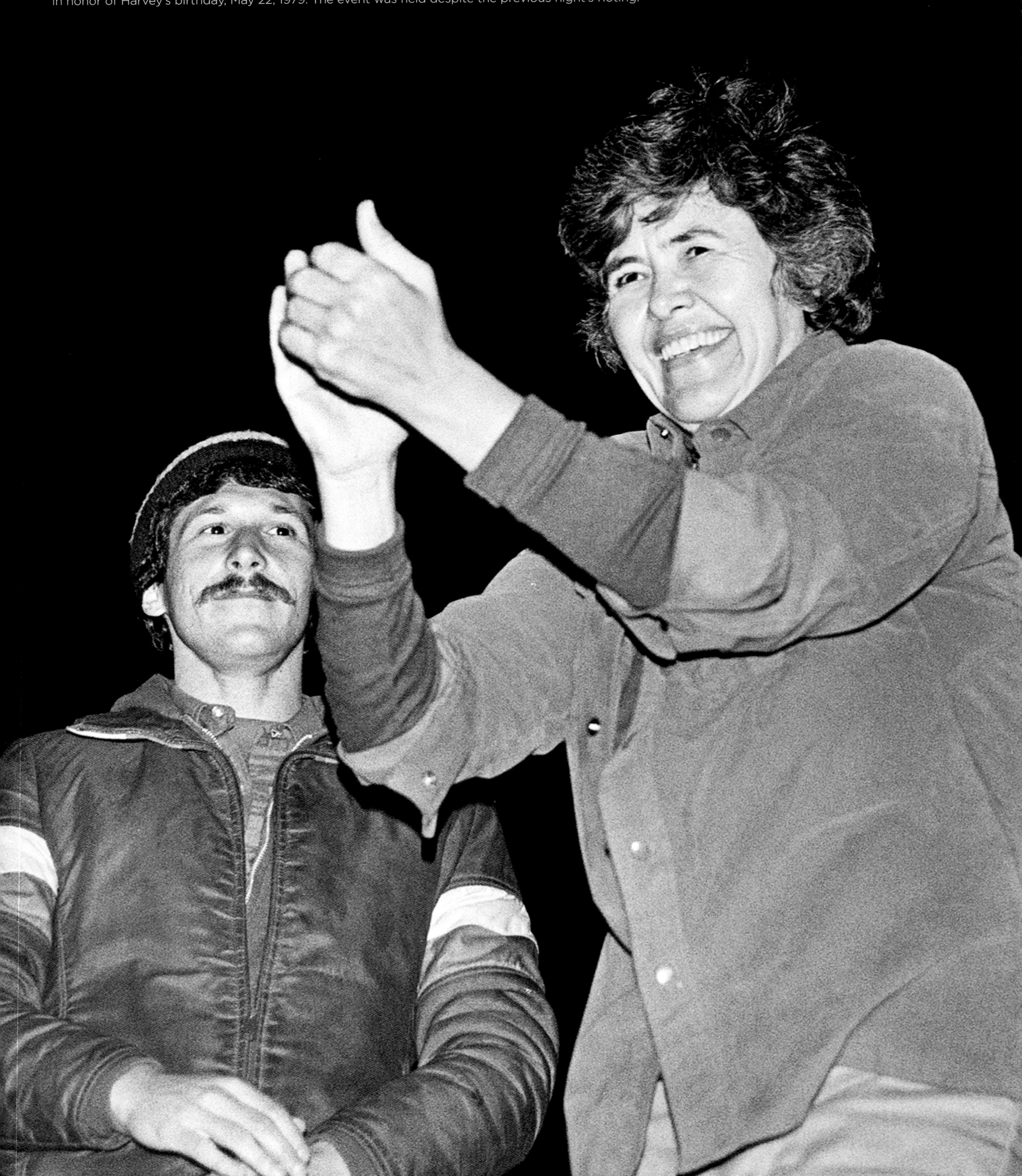

Sally Gearhart, Cleve Jones, and a sign language interpreter (left) speak at the Castro street party that was scheduled in honor of Harvey's birthday, May 22, 1979. The event was held despite the previous night's rioting.

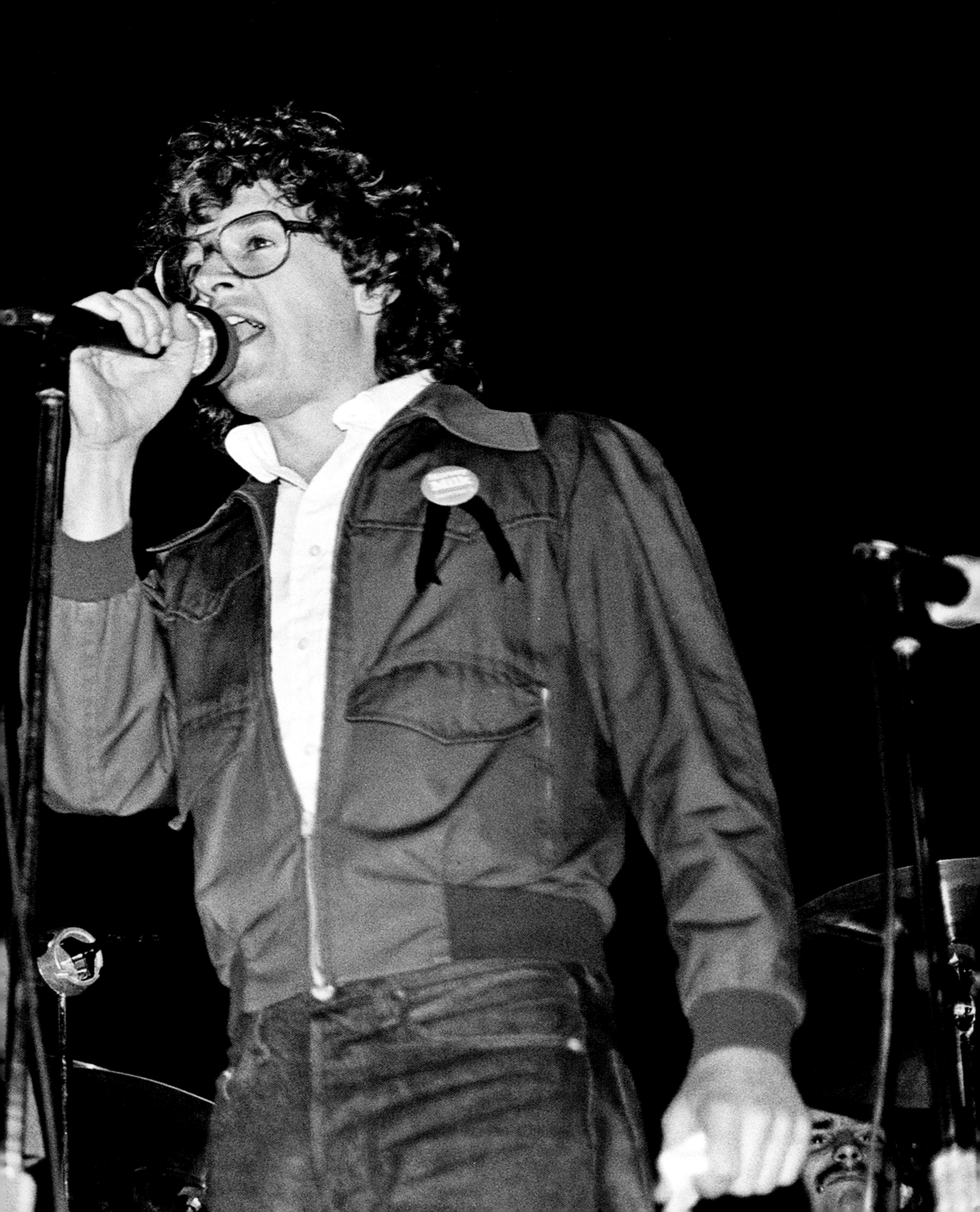

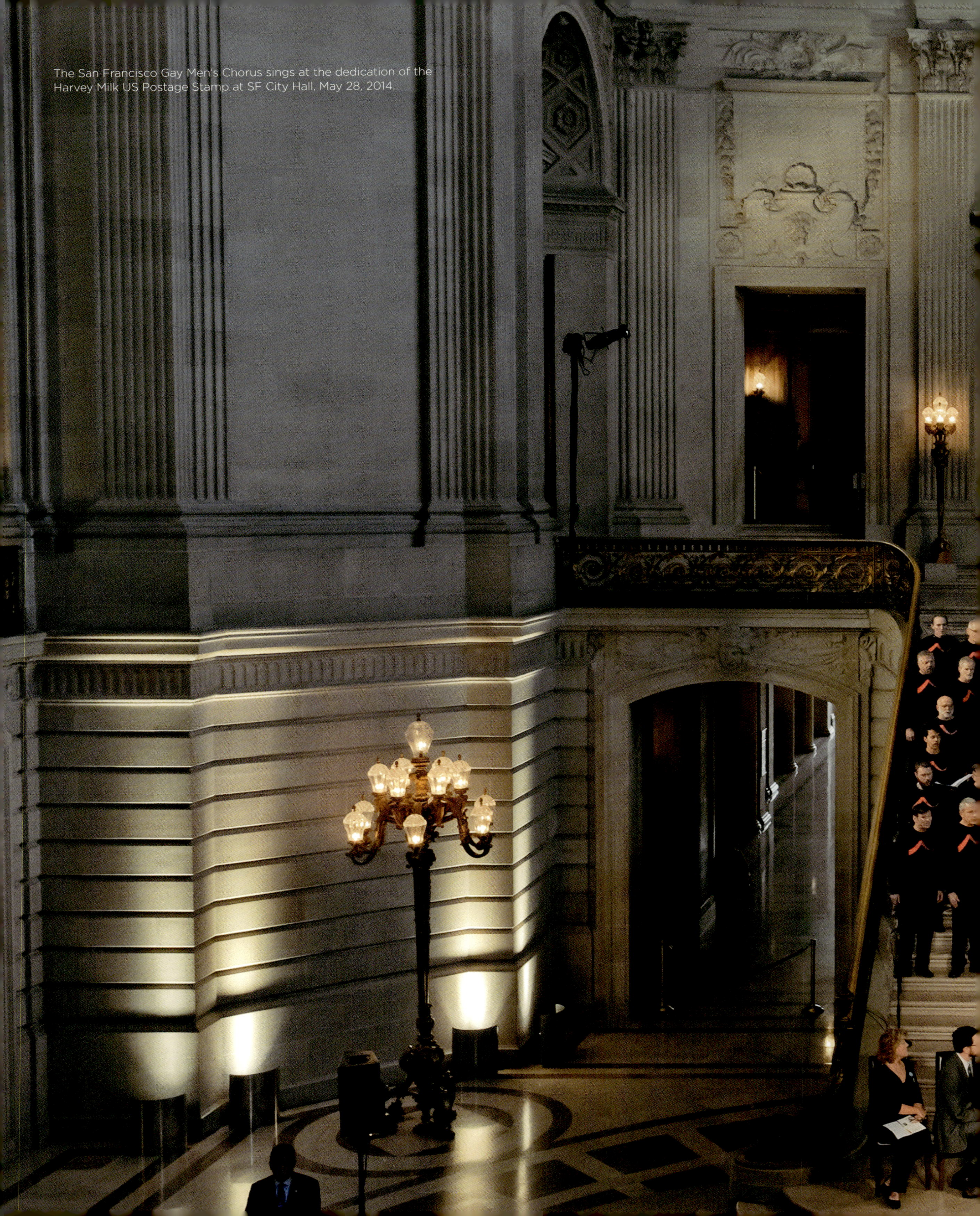

The San Francisco Gay Men's Chorus sings at the dedication of the Harvey Milk US Postage Stamp at SF City Hall, May 28, 2014.

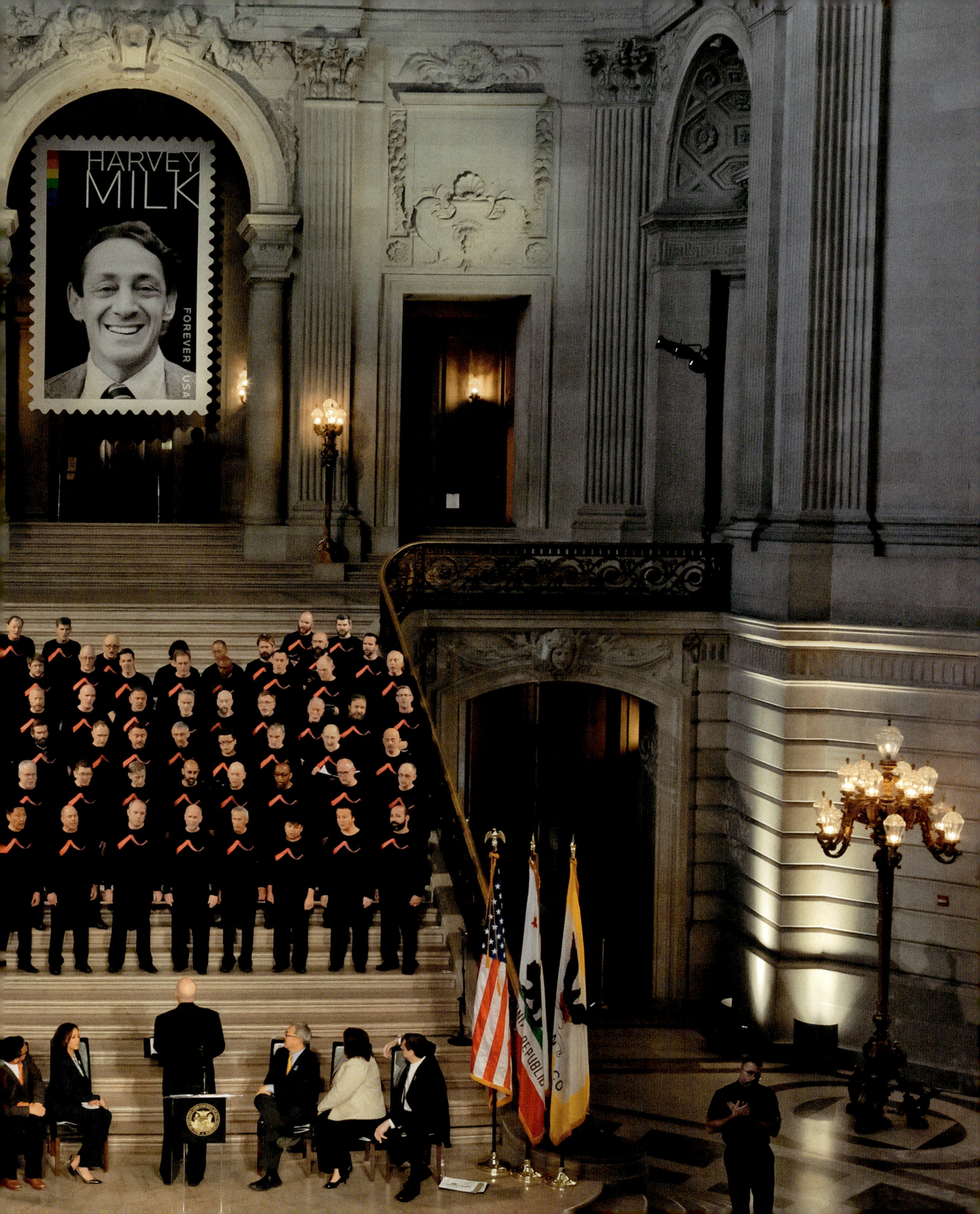
HARVEY
MILK
FOREVER
USA

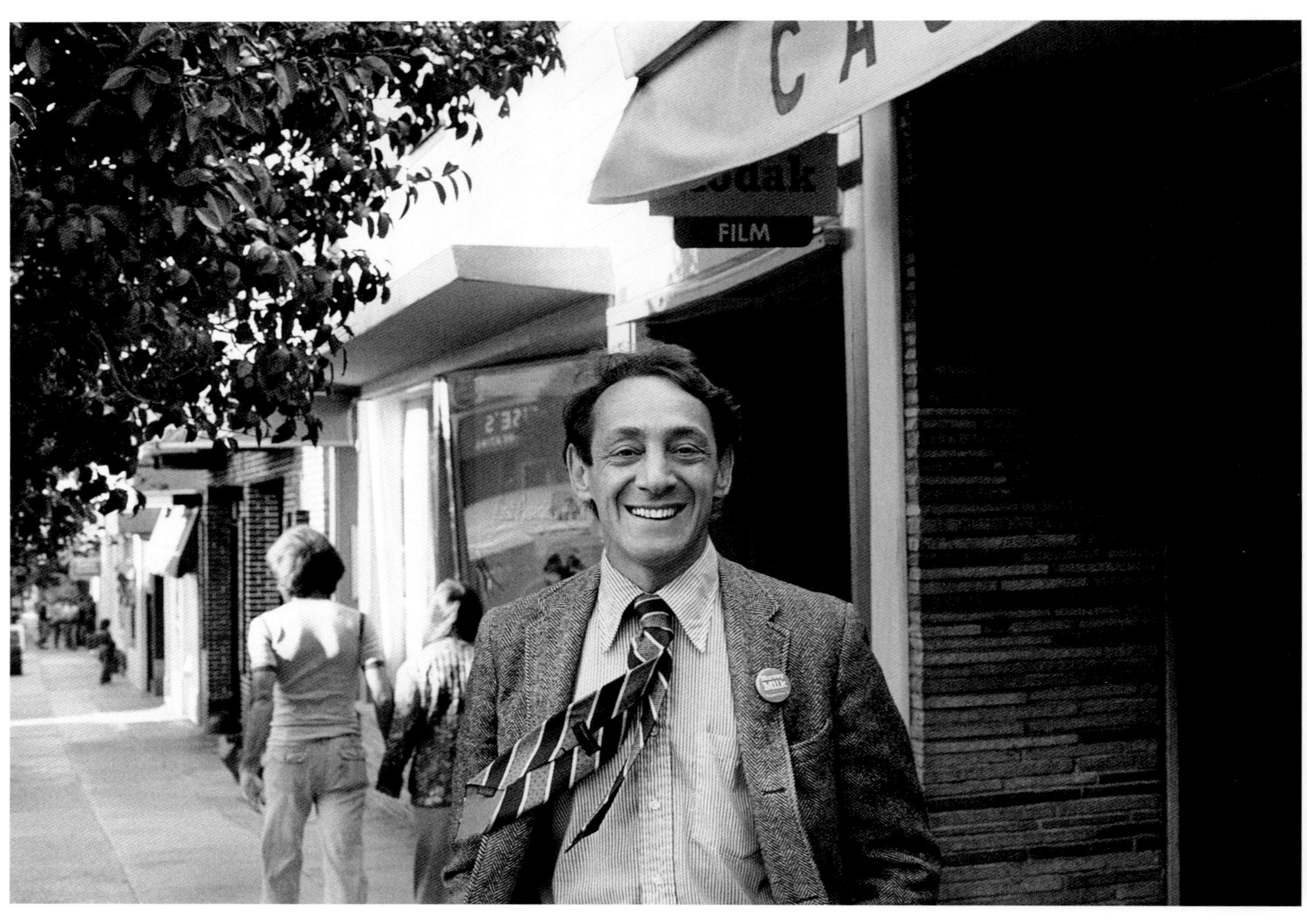

Above: Harvey in front of his Castro Street Camera Store, circa 1977.
Opposite: The US postage stamp honoring Harvey. The stamp was released on Harvey's birthday, May 22, 2014.

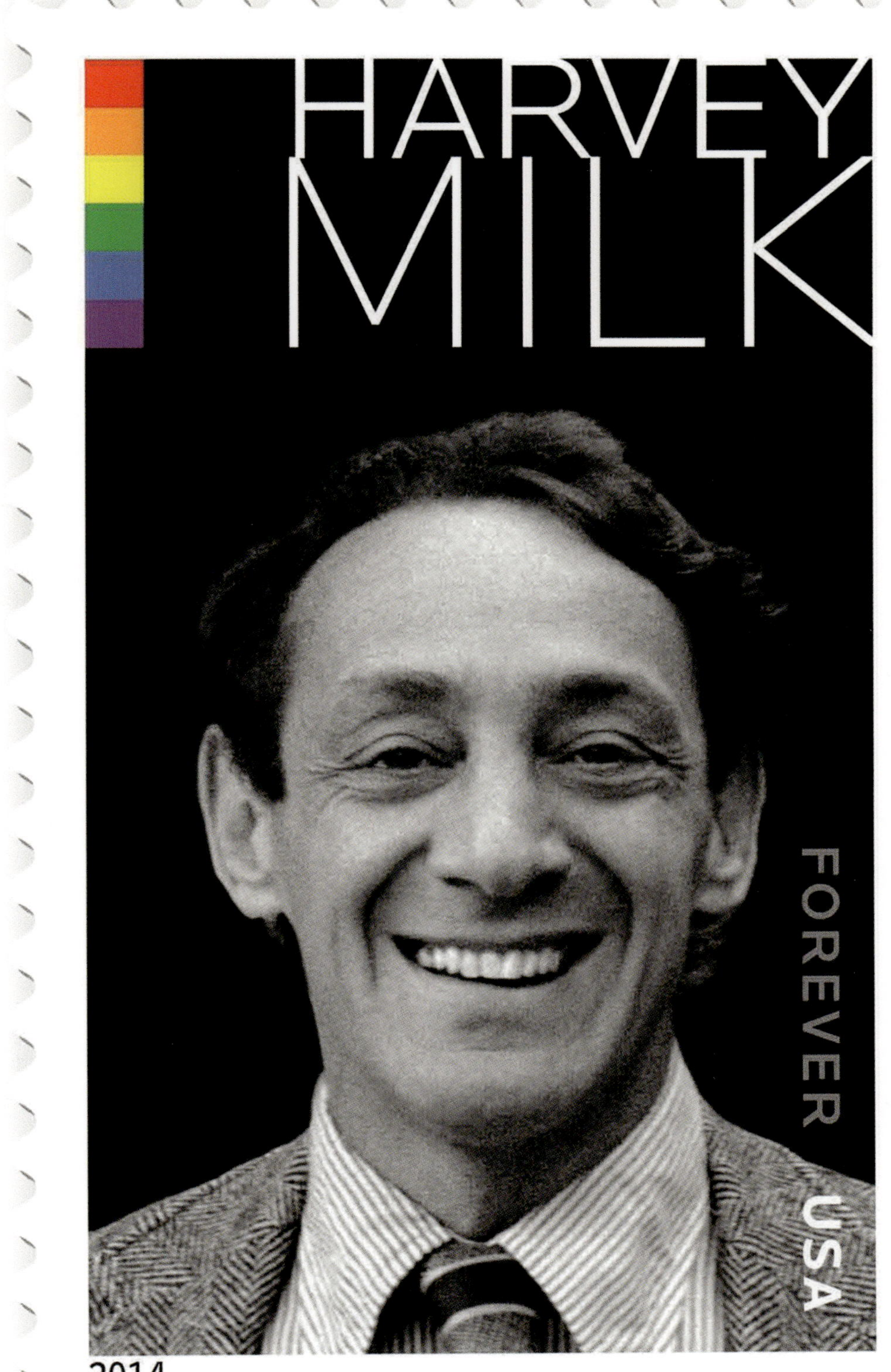
HARVEY
MILK
FOREVER
USA
2014

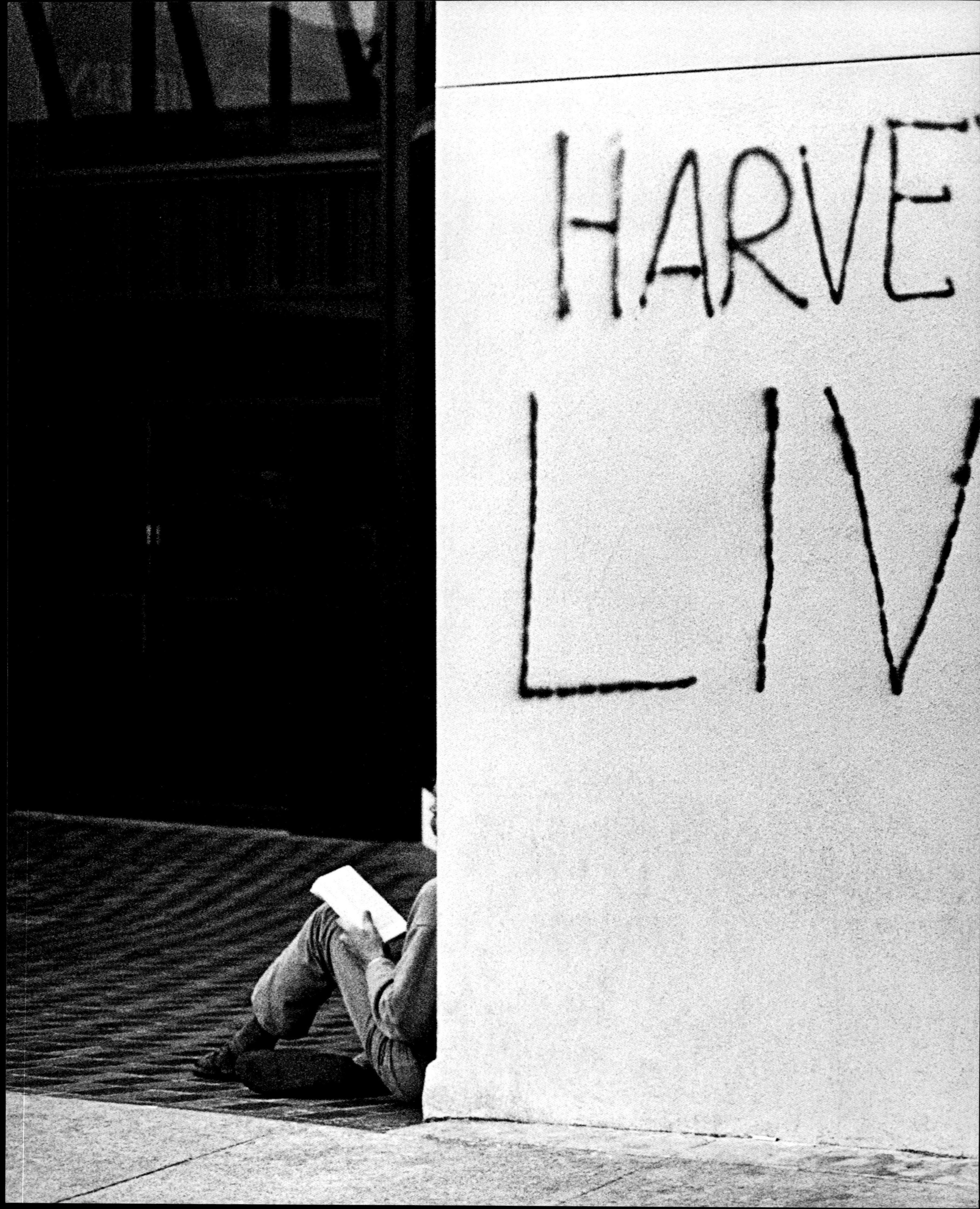

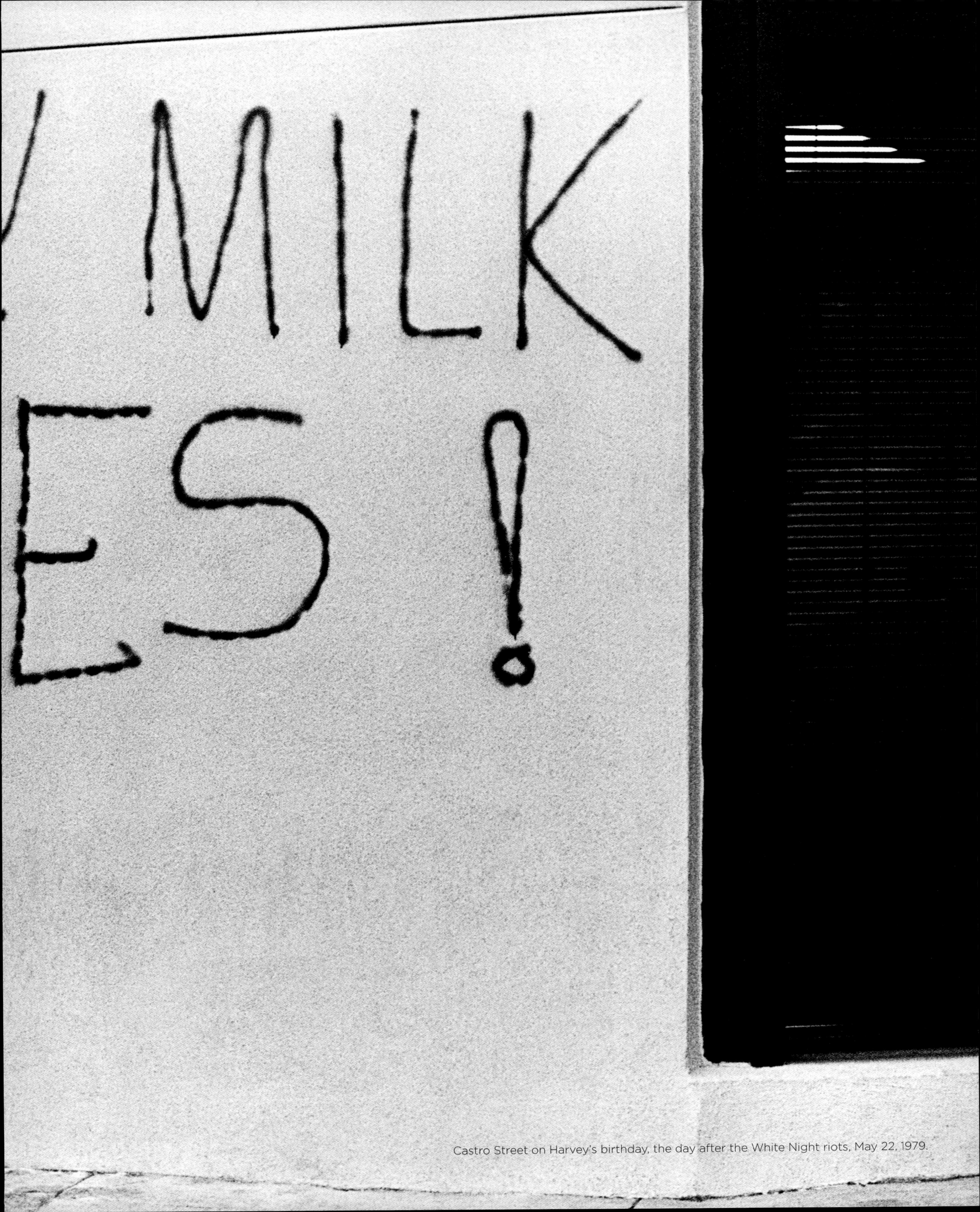

Castro Street on Harvey's birthday, the day after the White Night riots, May 22, 1979.

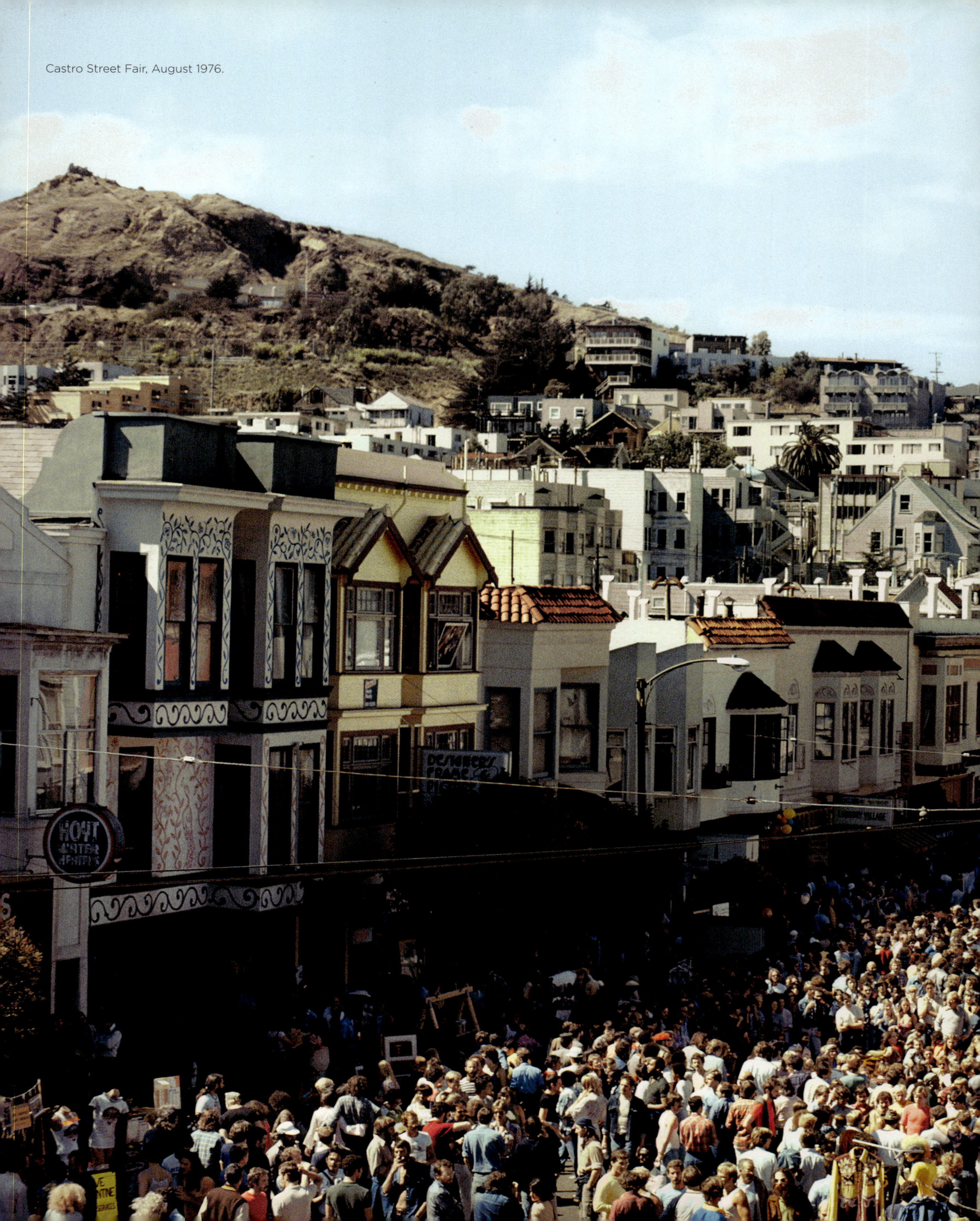

Castro Street Fair, August 1976.

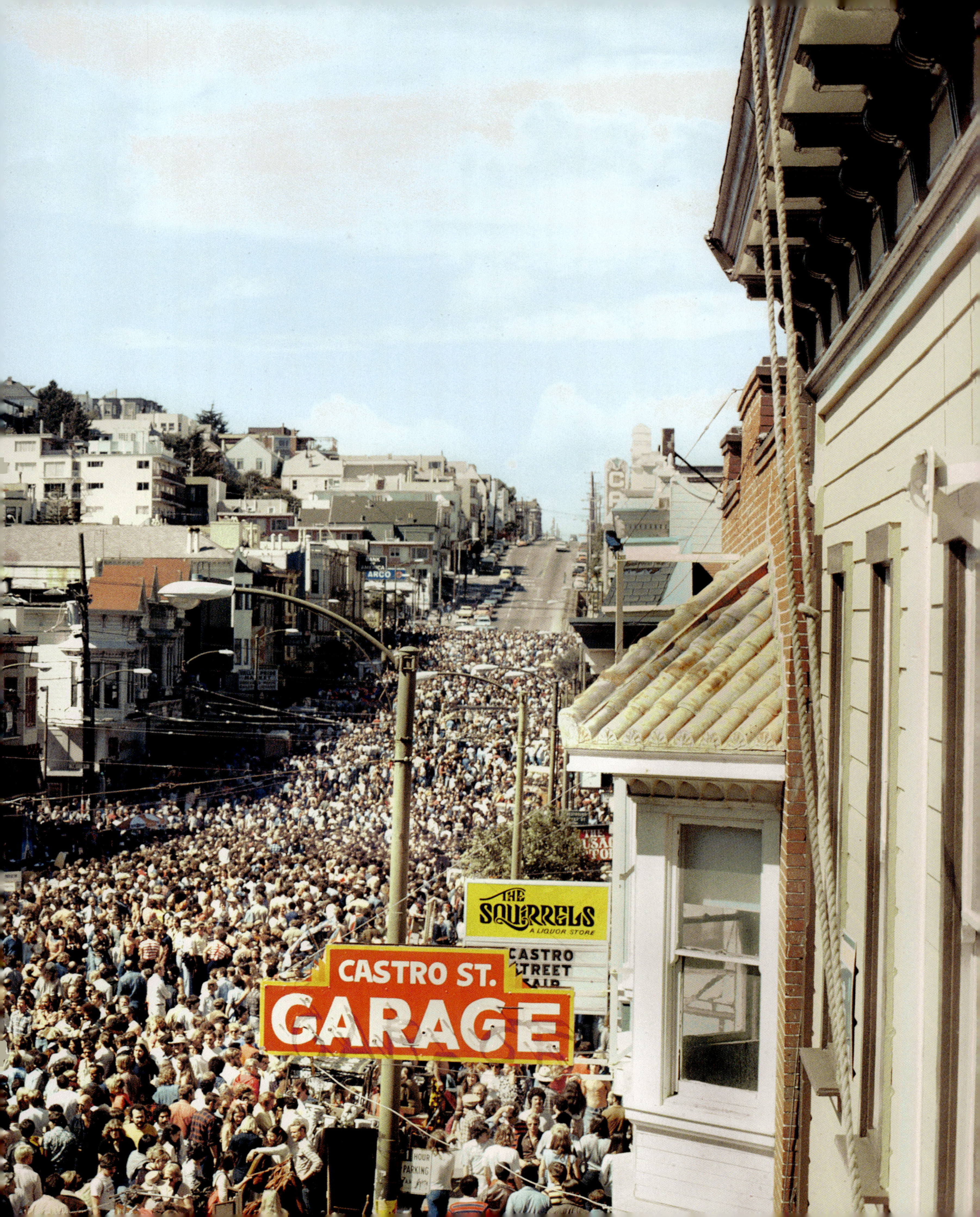
THE SQUIRRELS
A LIQUOR STORE
CASTRO
CASTRO ST.
GARAGE
ARCO

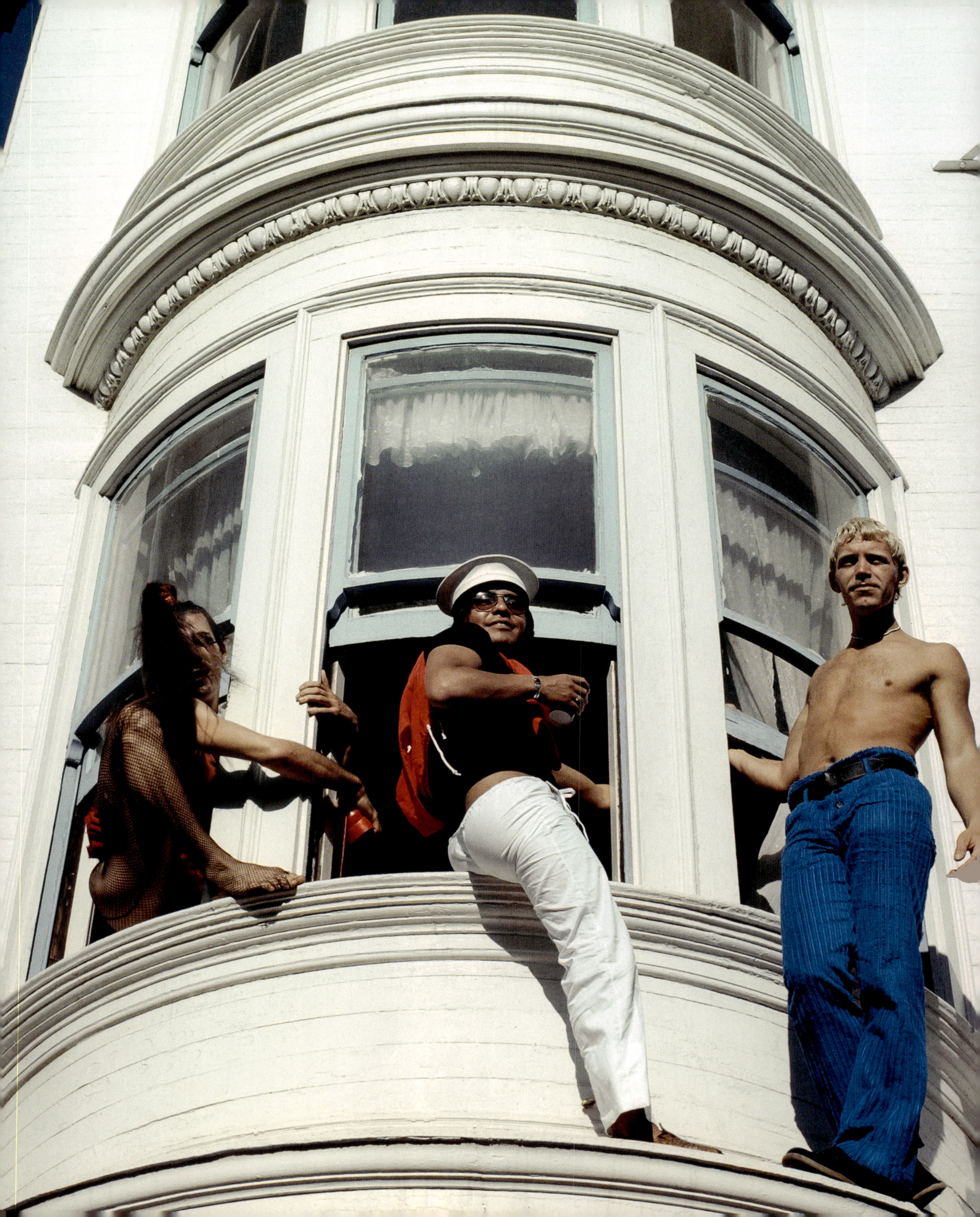

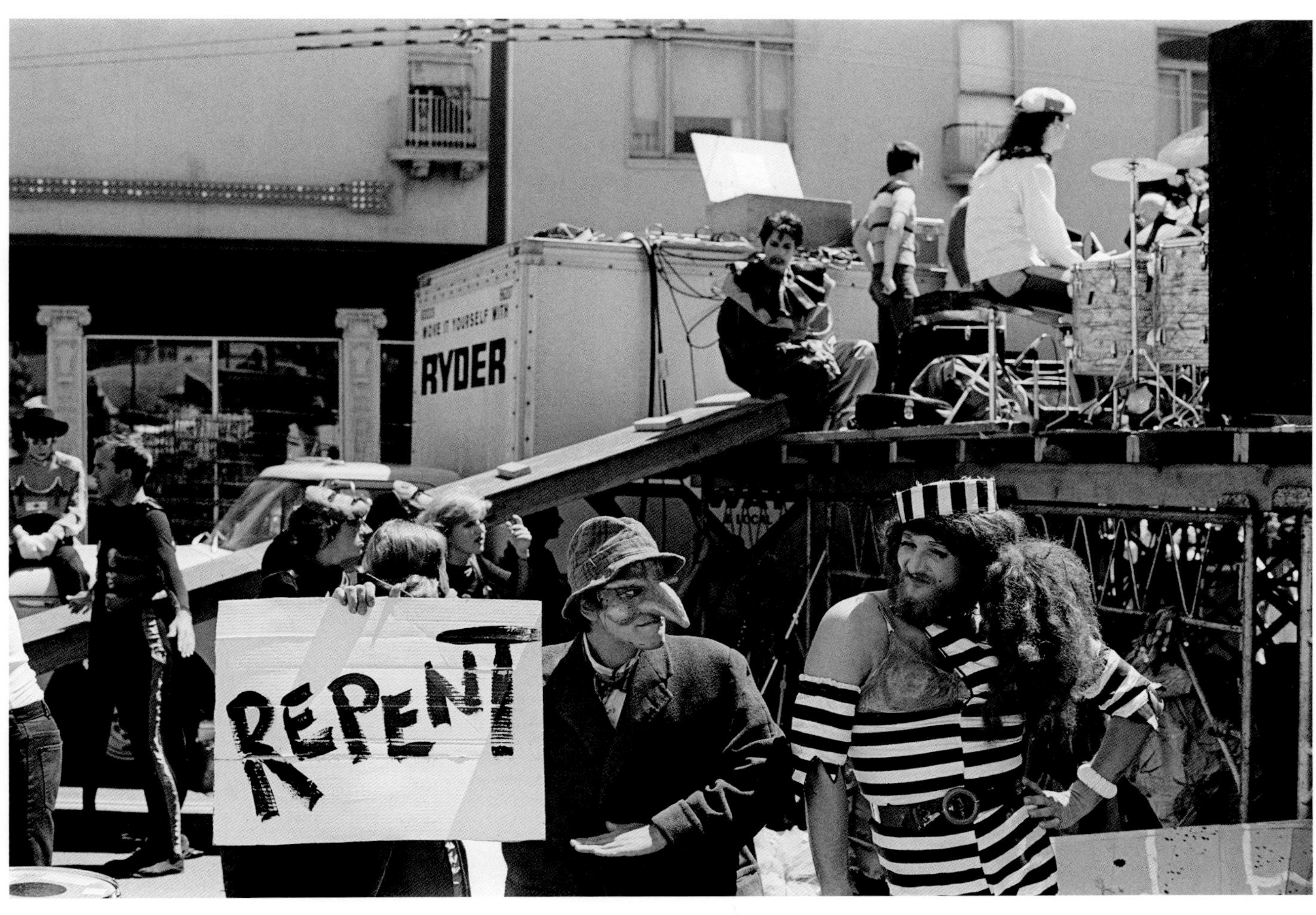

Above: Castro Street Fair, August 1978. Angels of Light, Tony Johnopoulos and Ralif Sauer.
Opposite: Castro Street Fair, August 1977. Angels of Light, Rodney Price (left) and friends.

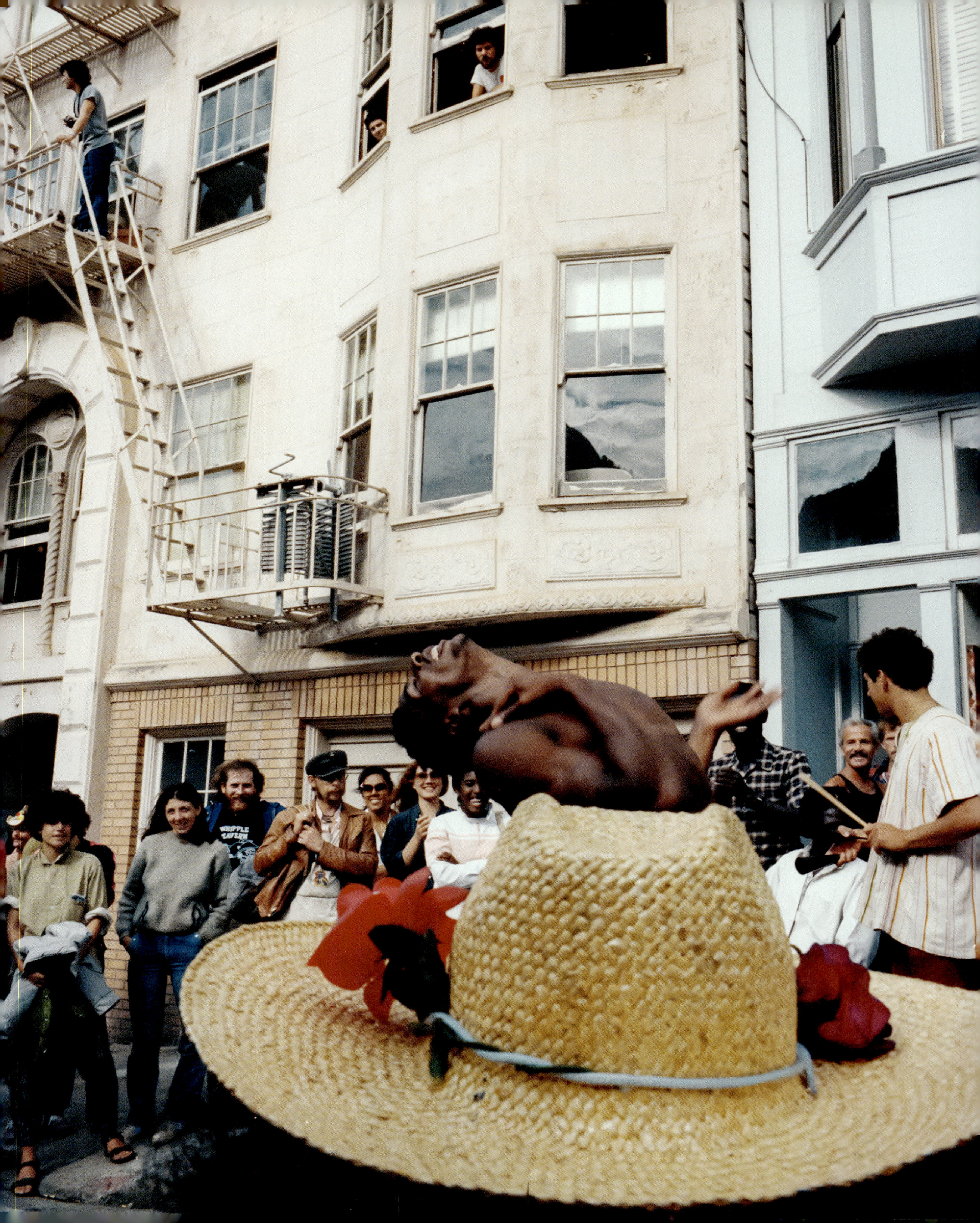
WHIPPLE

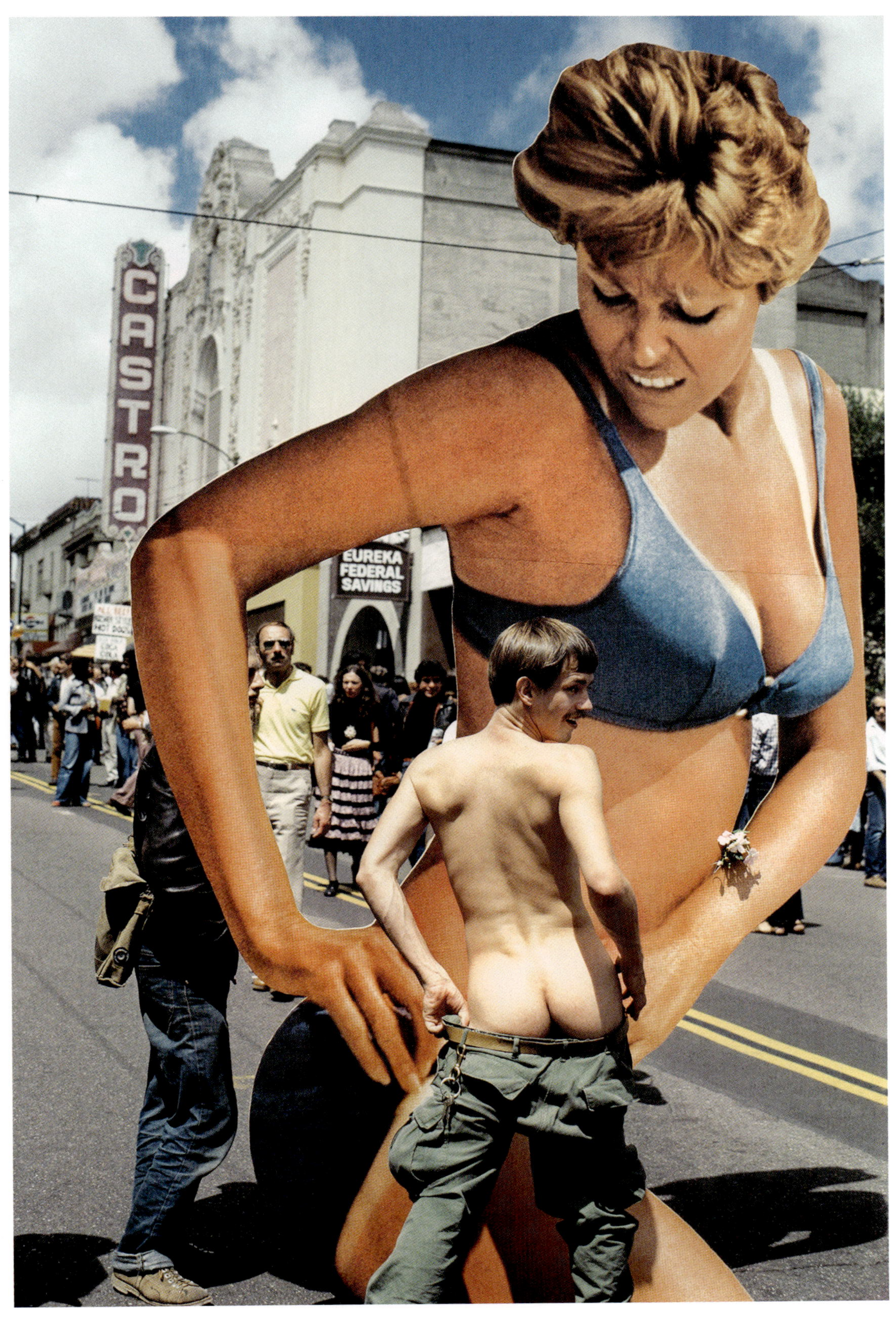

Above: Castro Street Fair, August 1976. Movable art piece by Violet Ray.
Opposite: Castro Street Fair, August 15, 1982.

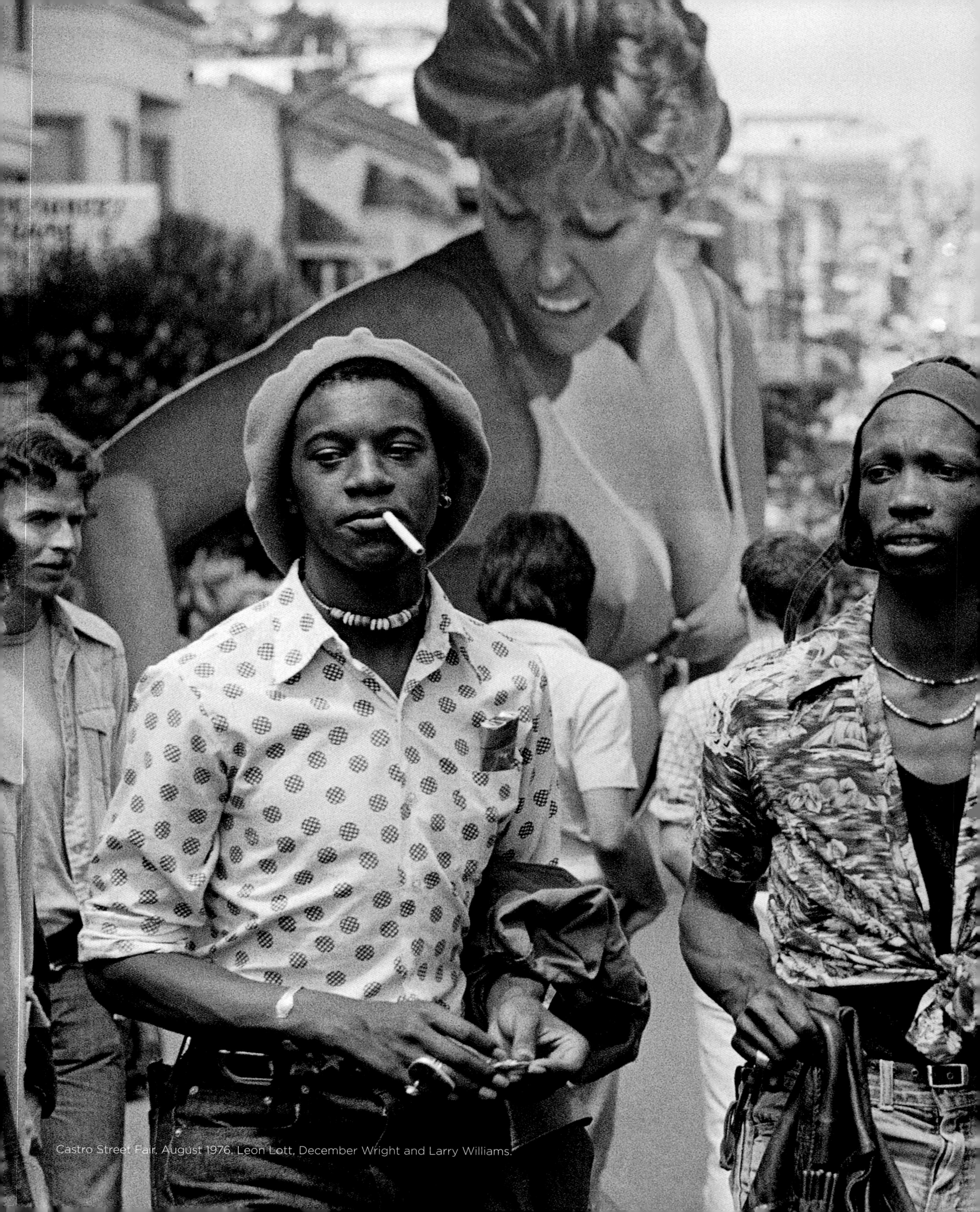

Castro Street Fair, August 1976. Leon Lott, December Wright and Larry Williams.

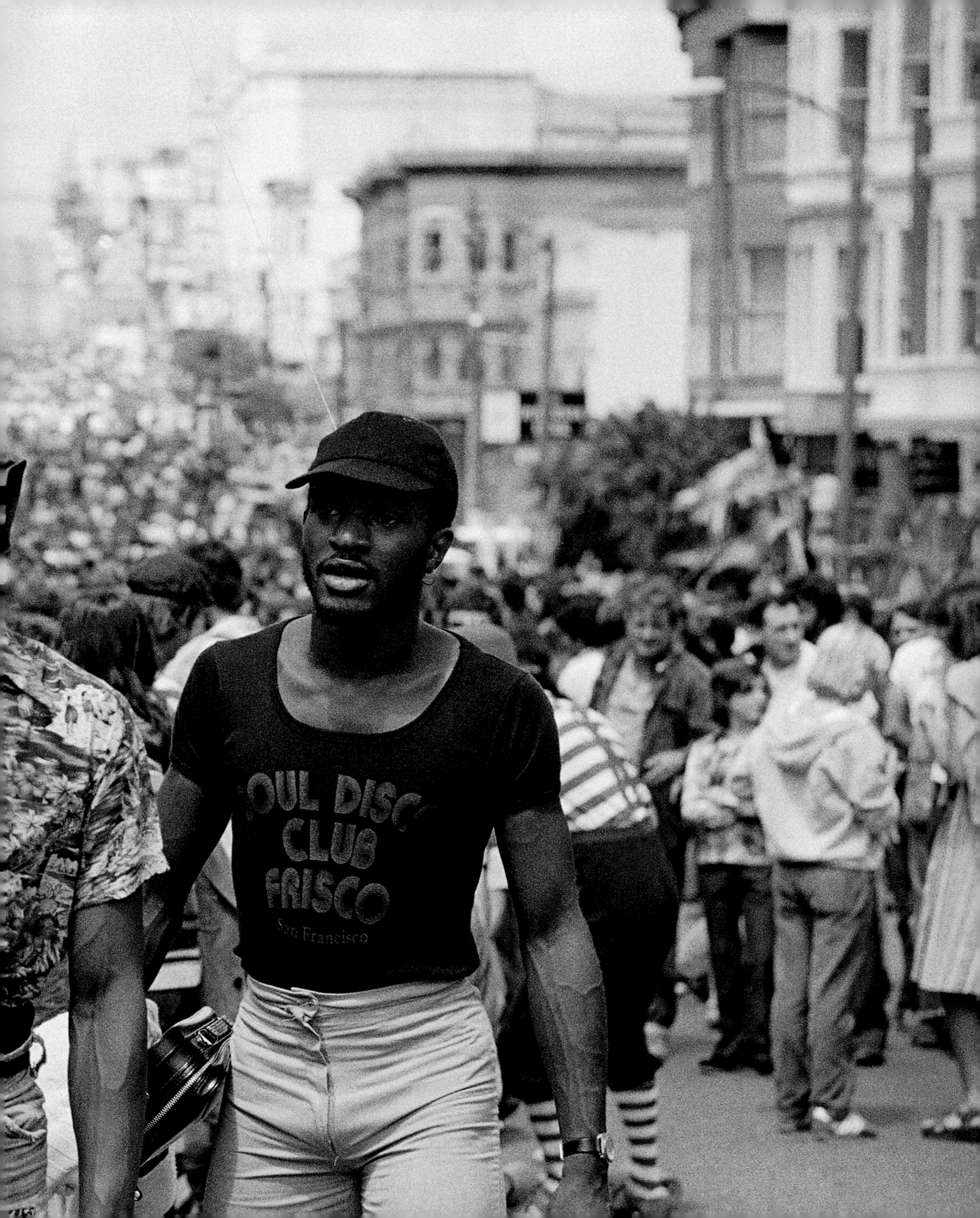
OUL DISC
CLUB
FRISCO
San Francisco

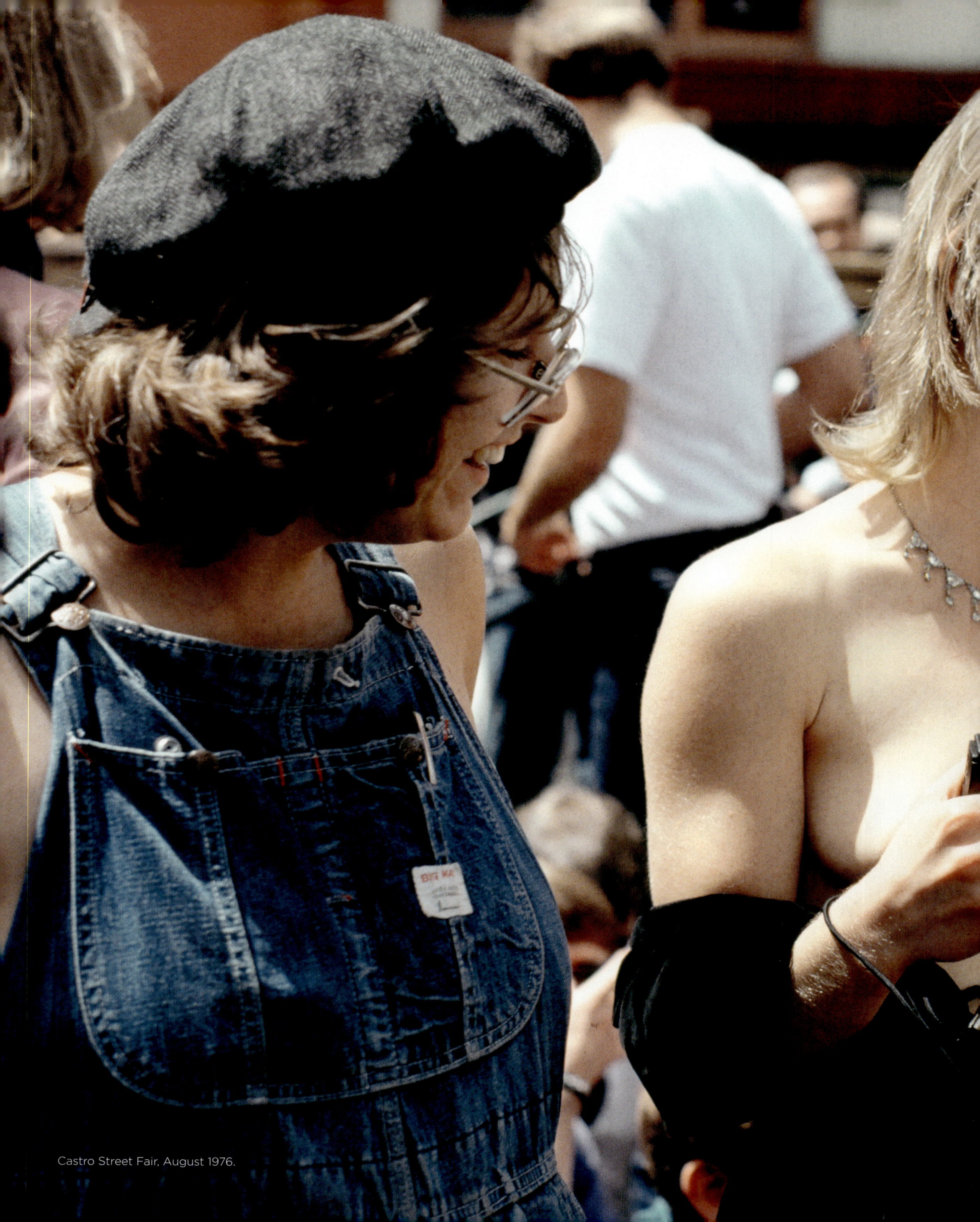

Castro Street Fair, August 1976.

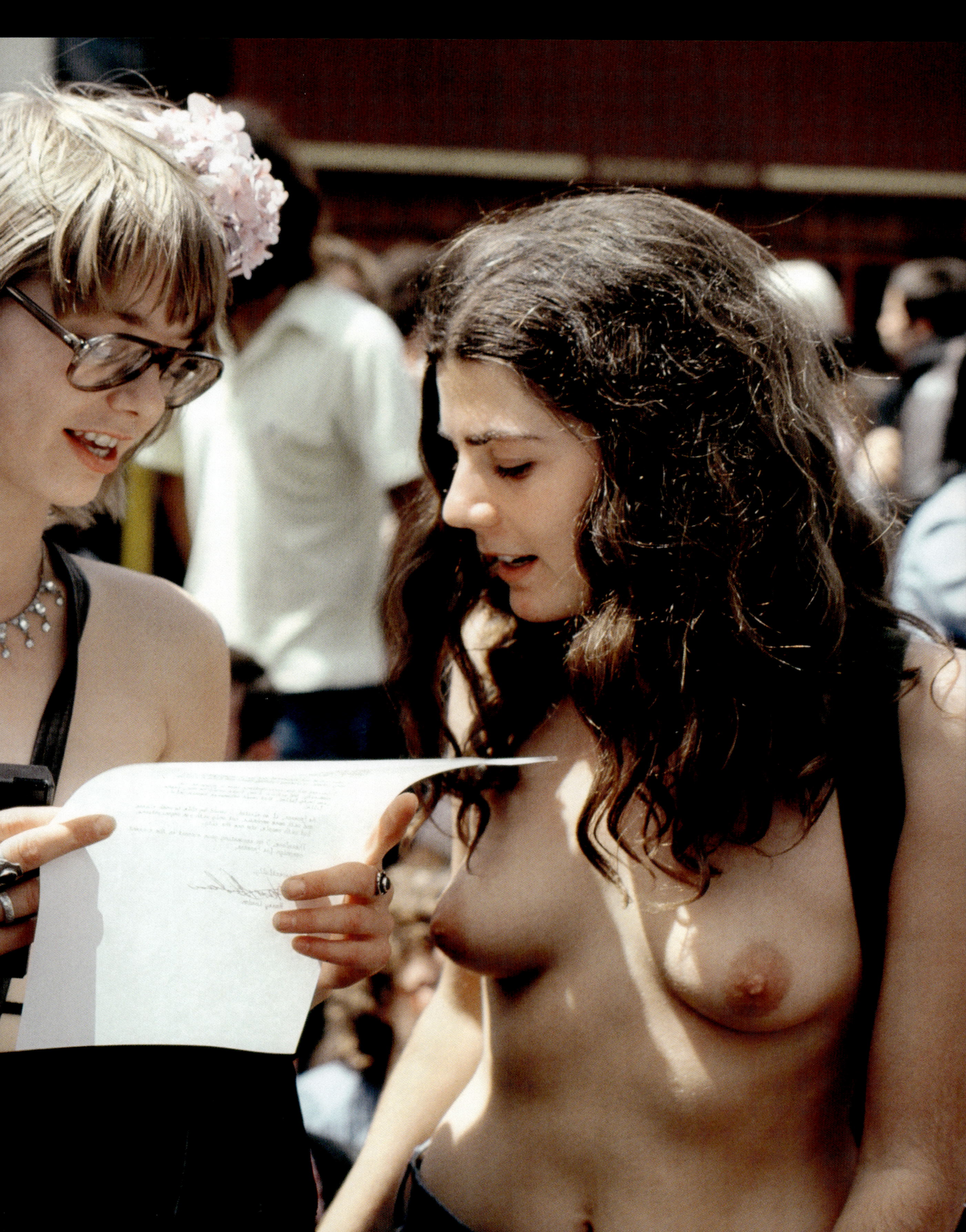

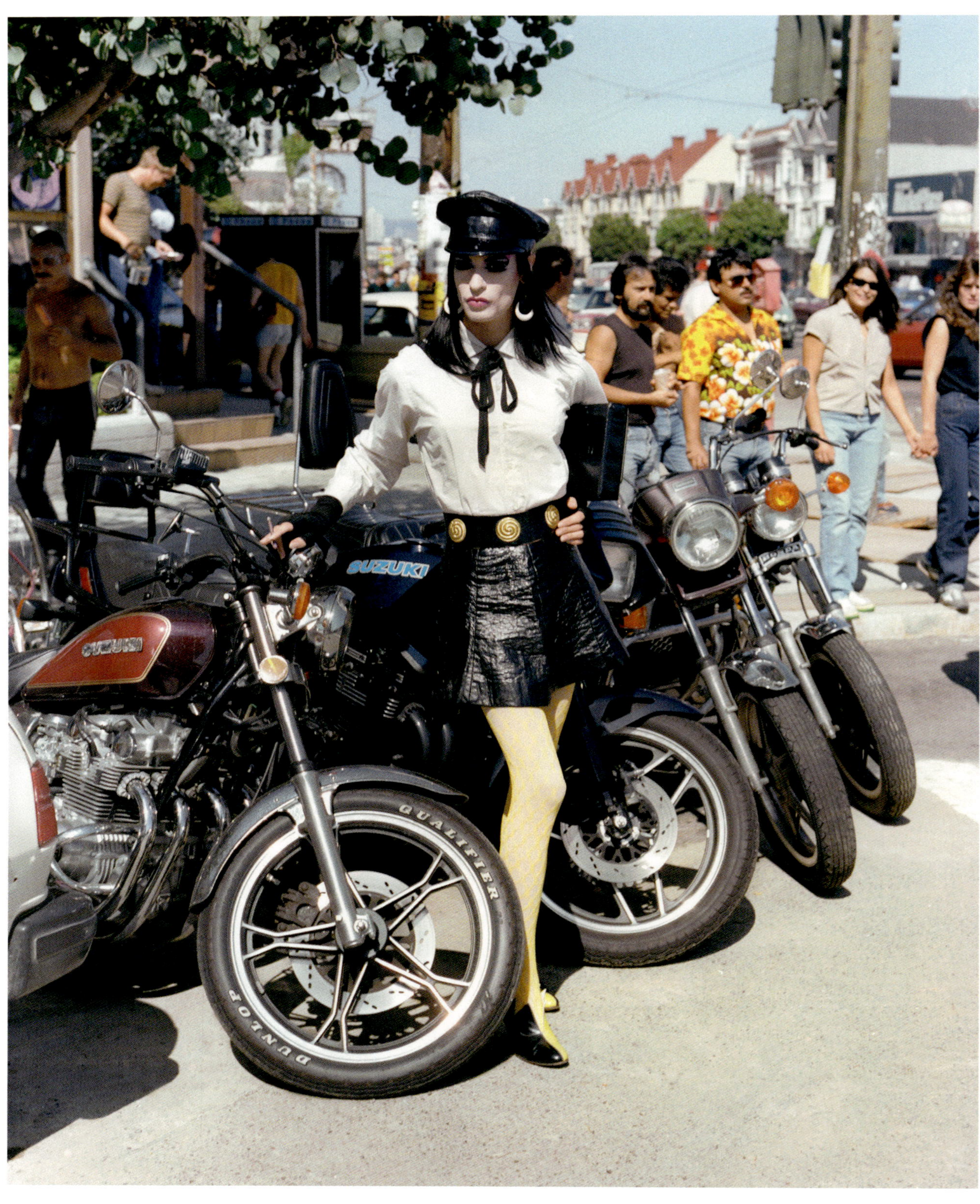

Above: Castro Street Fair, August 8, 1983. Miss X.
Opposite: Castro Street Fair, August 21, 1983. Billy Phillips and David Puckett.

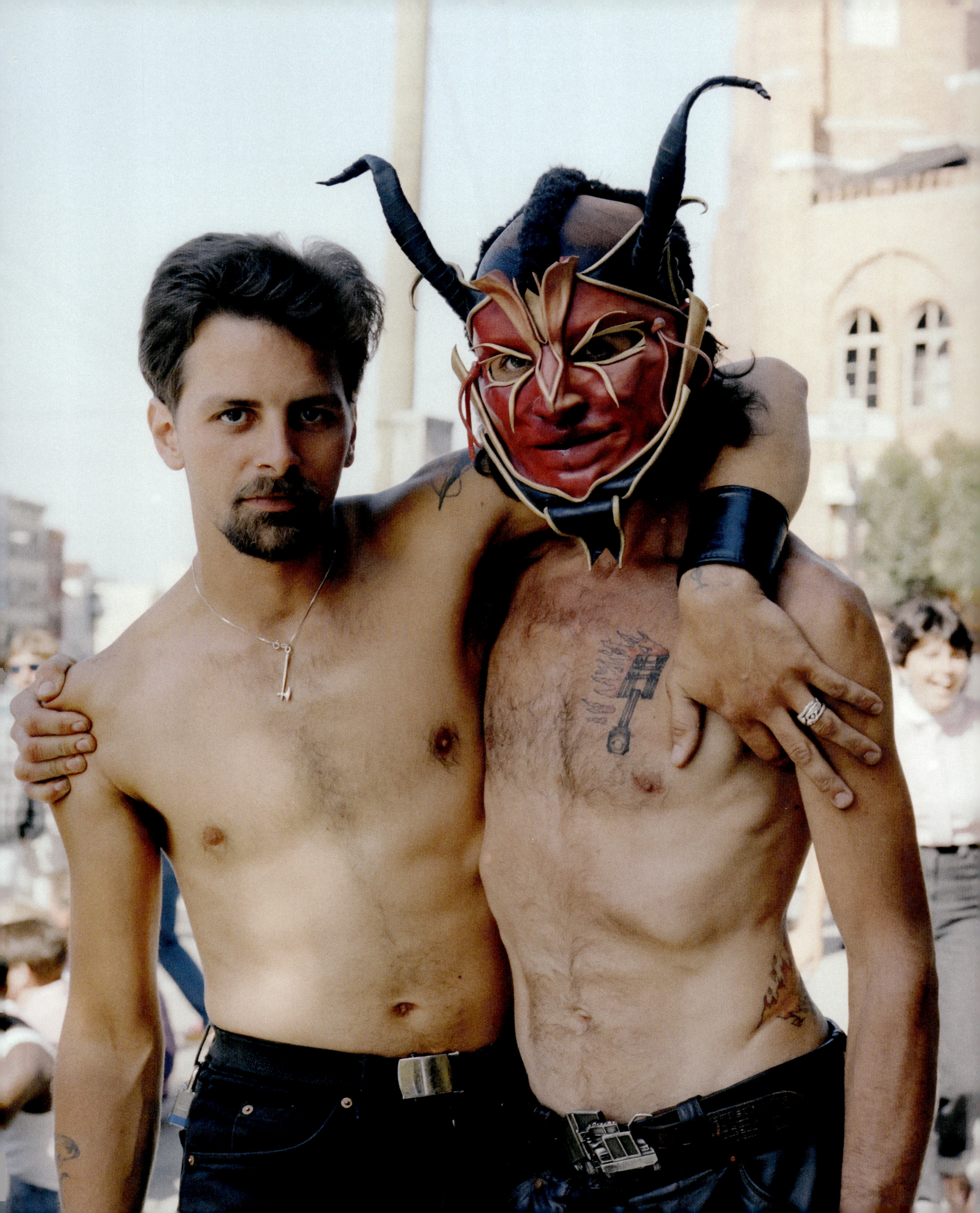

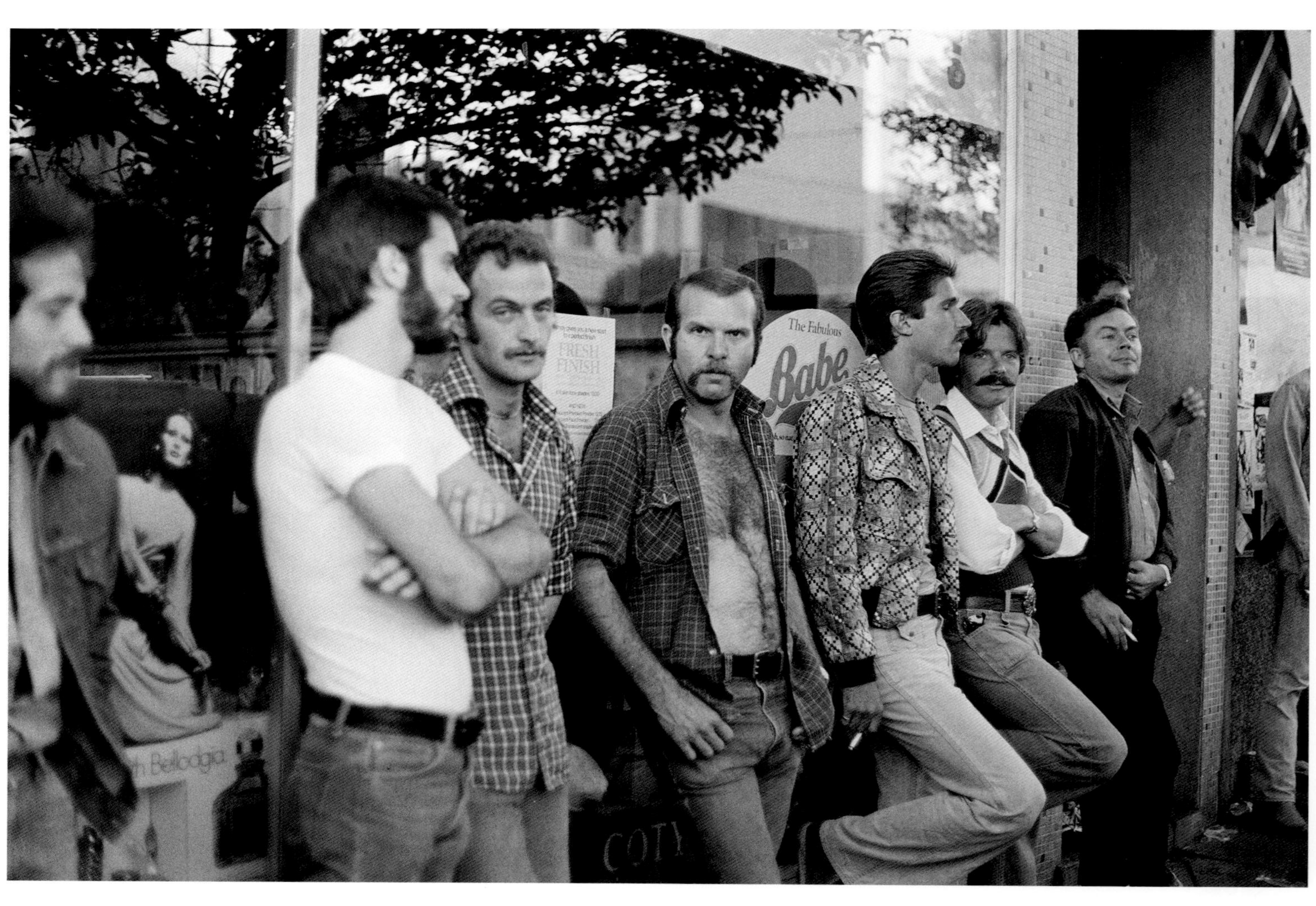

Above: Castro Street cruising, August 1976.
Opposite: Castro Street Fair, August 1977. Peppe Olvadez (far left).

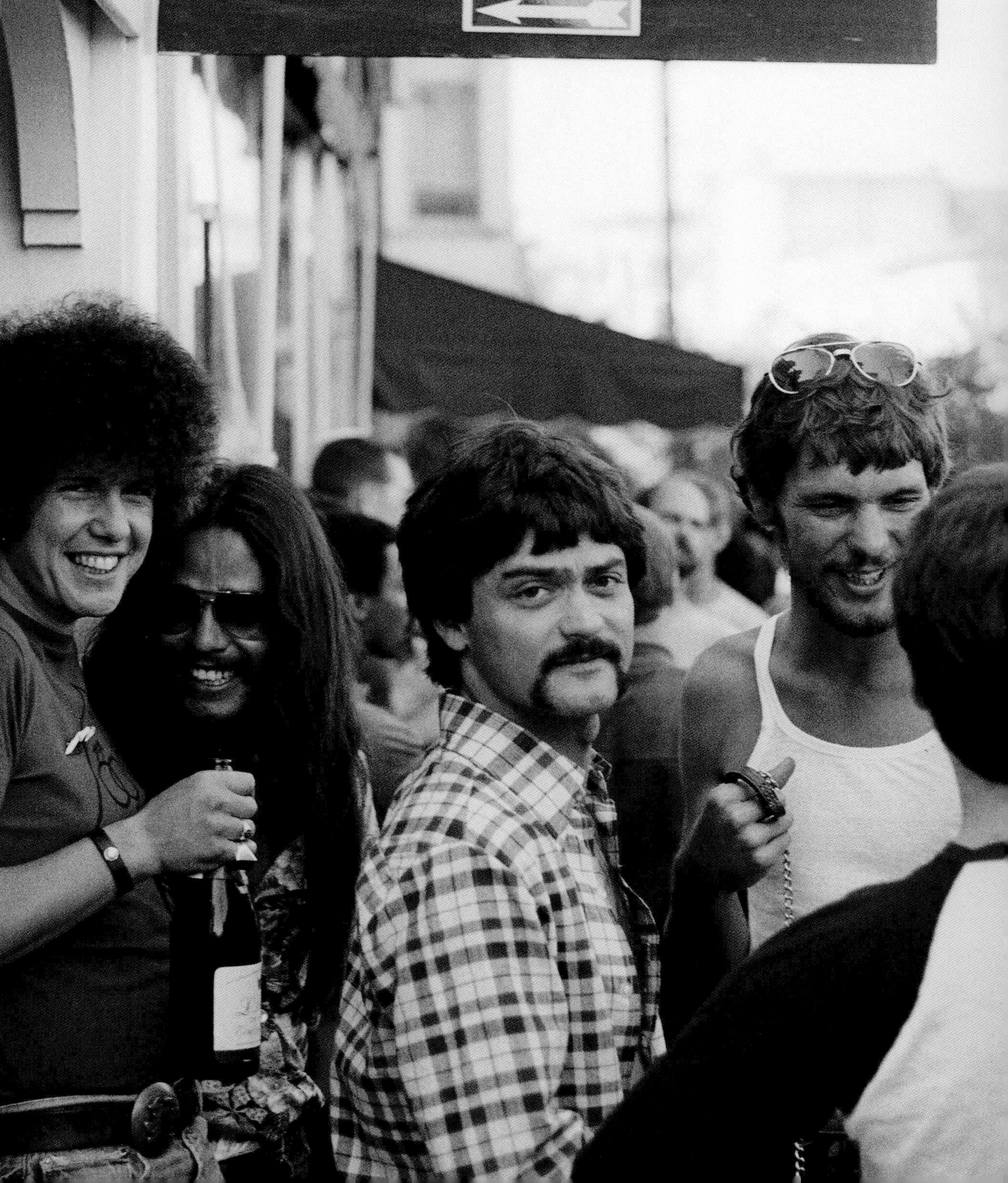
CASTRO ROCK
STEAM·BATHS

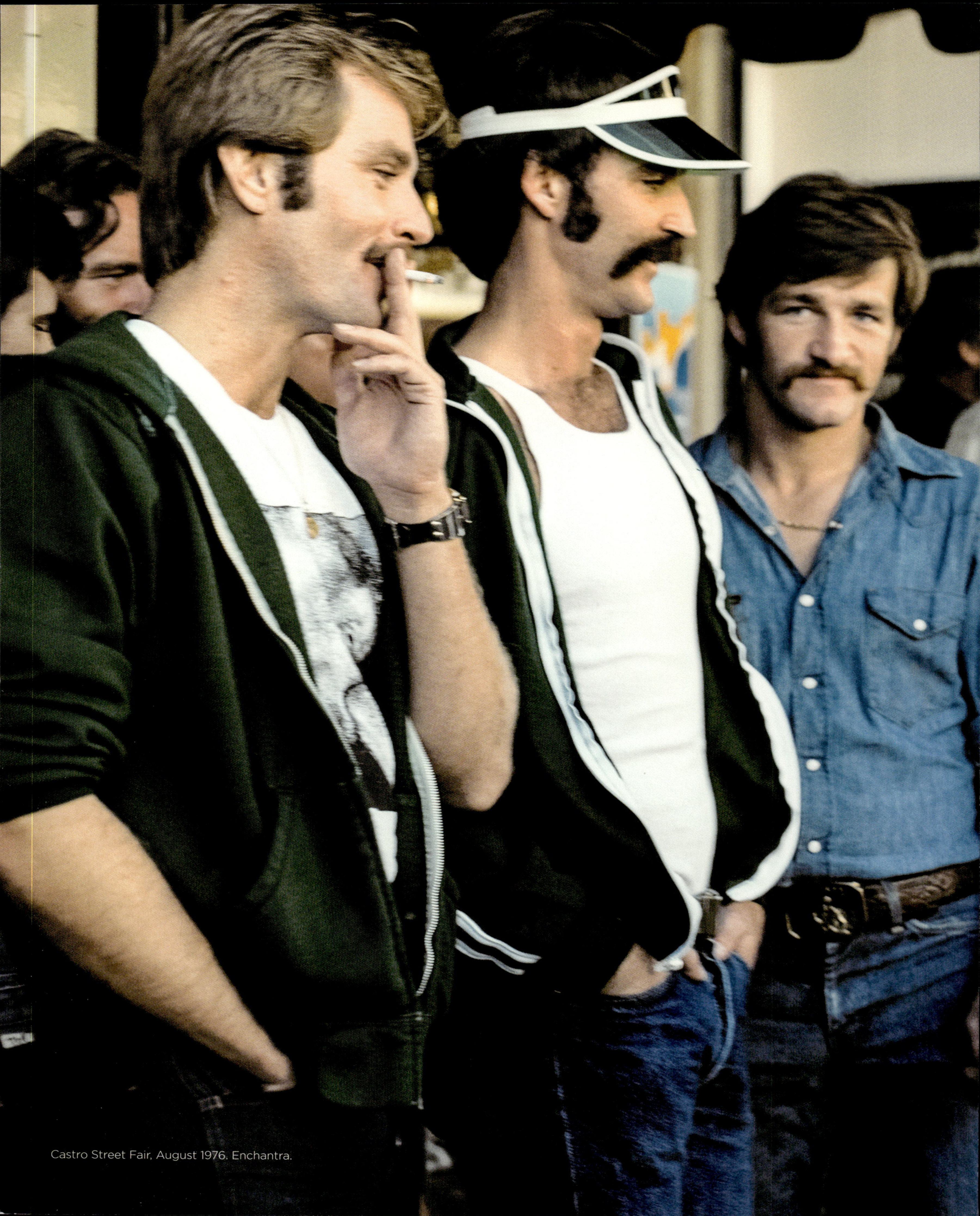

Castro Street Fair, August 1976. Enchantra.

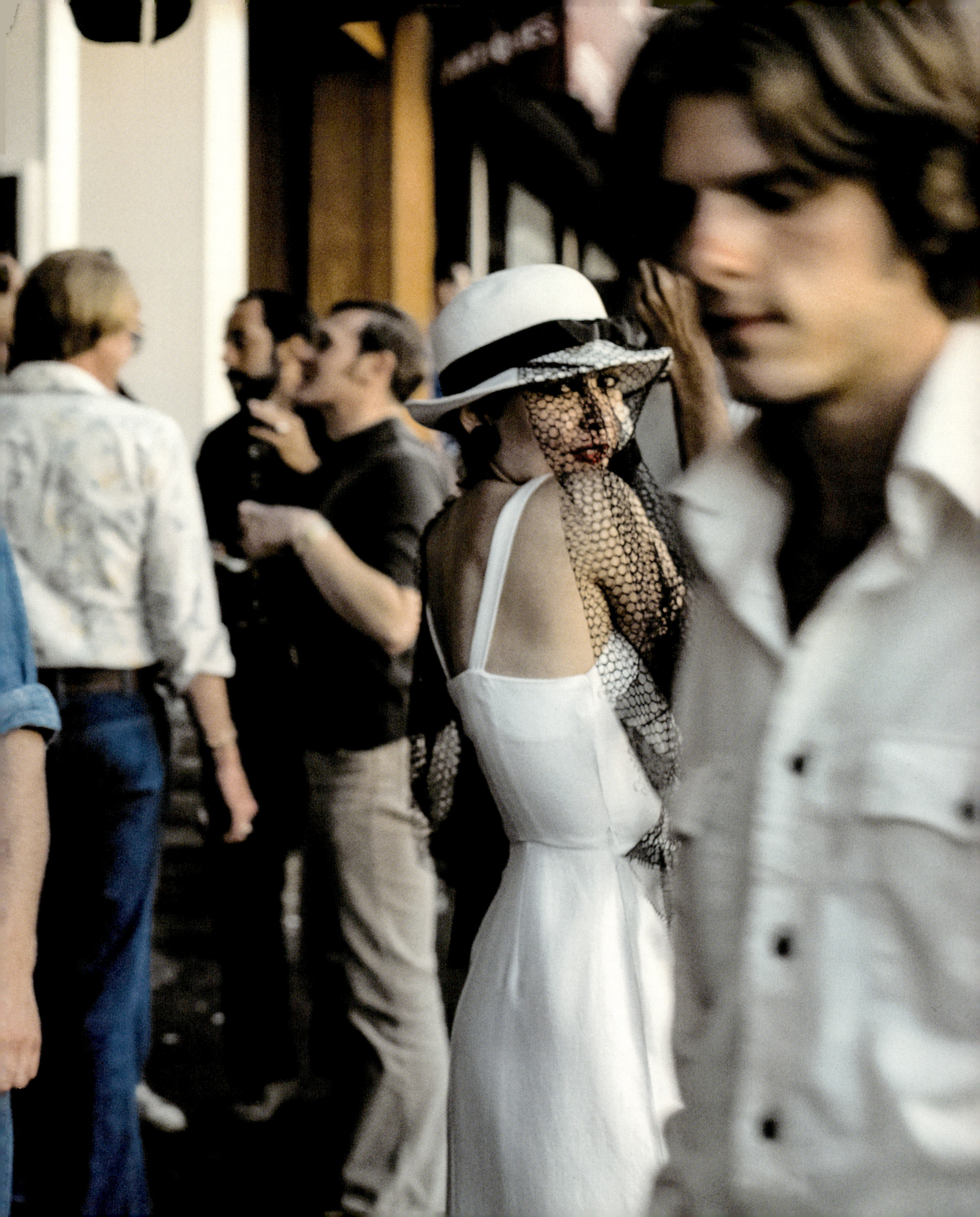

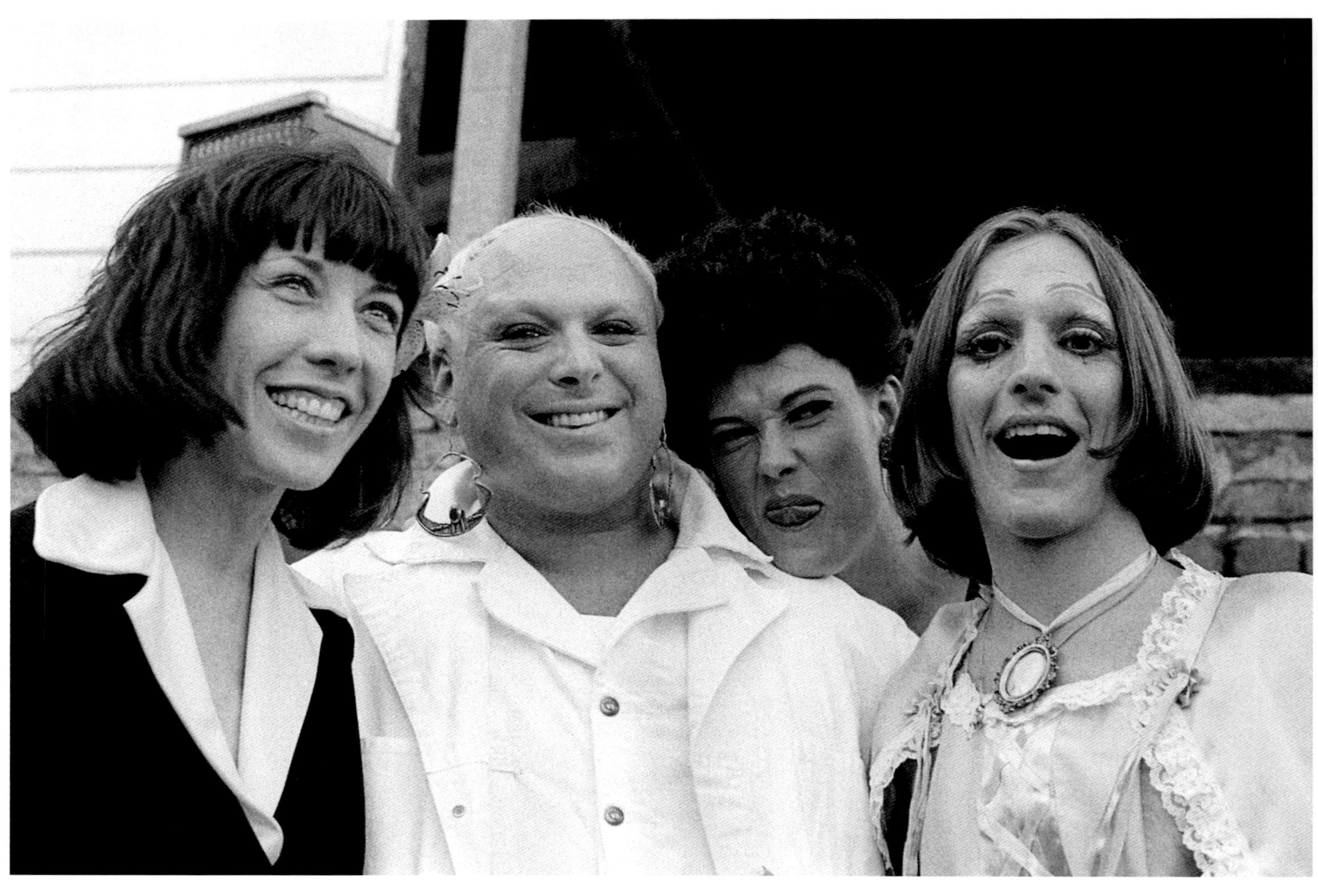

Above: Lily Tomlin, Divine, Sister Ed and Cockette Pristine Condition at an autograph party for Divine at the Bakery Cafe on Castro, 1975.
Opposite: Castro Street Fair, August 1975. Harmodius and Hoti.

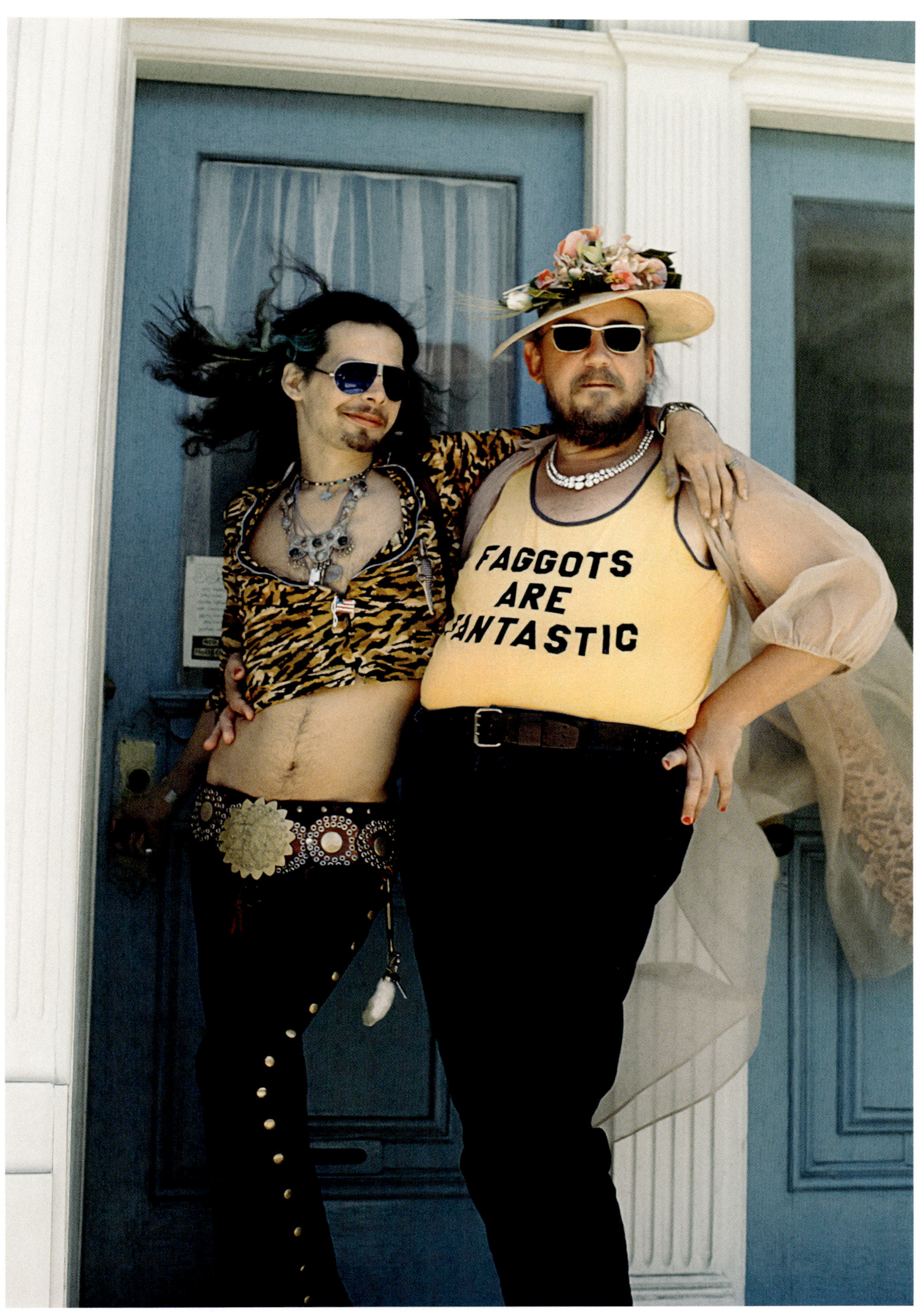
FAGGOTS
ARE
ANTASTIC

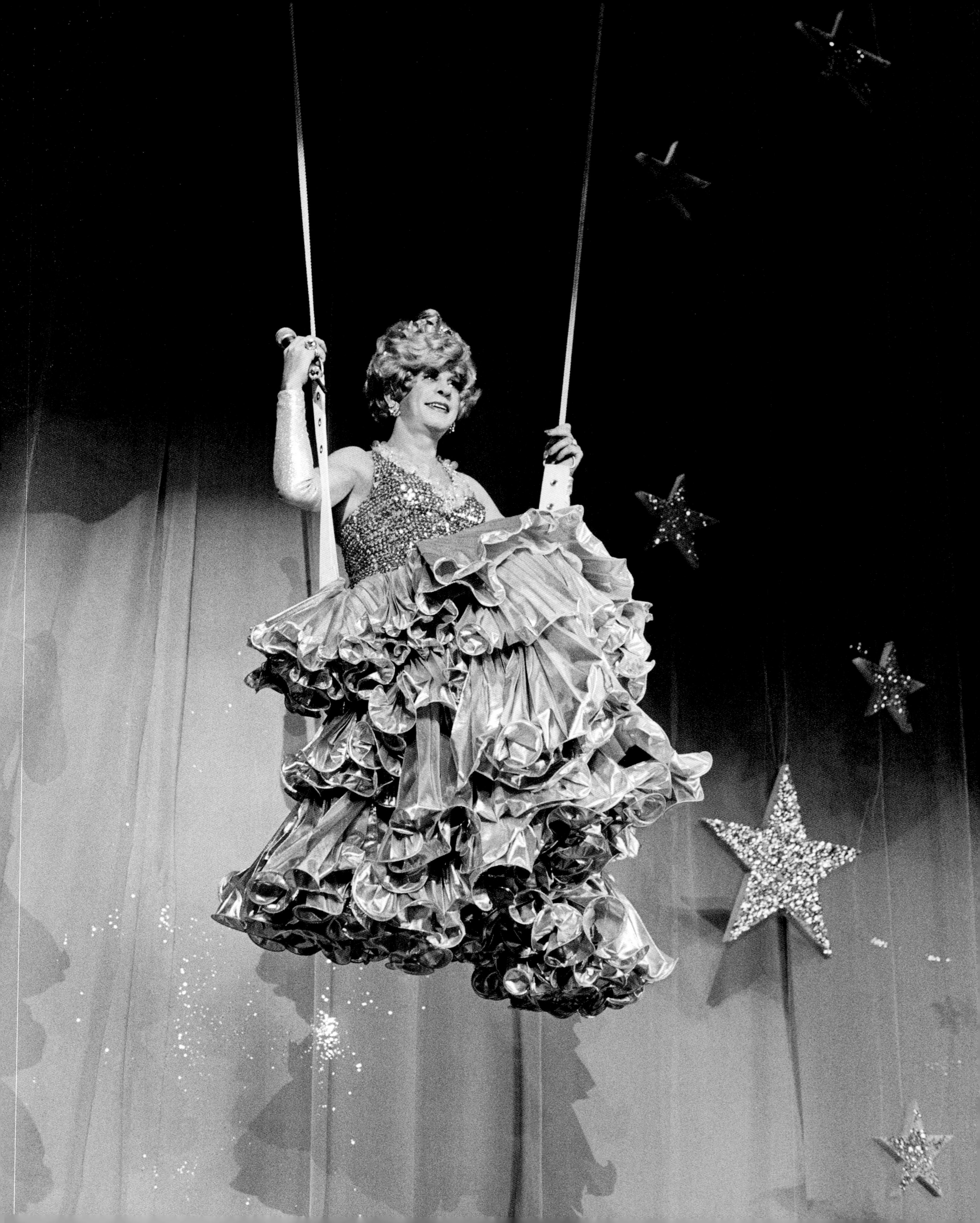

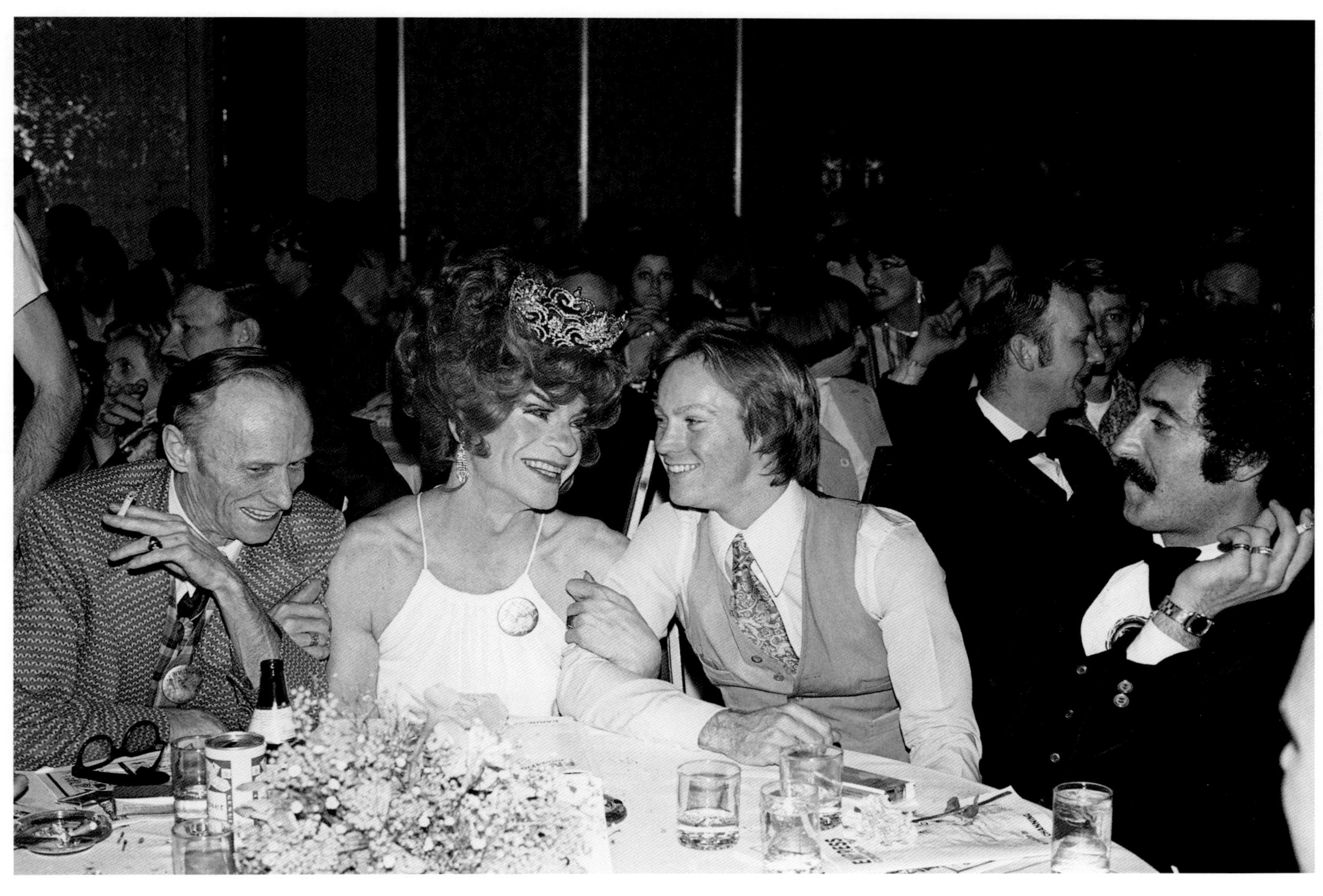

Above: The Imperial Council Annual Coronation, January 28, 1978. LaKish Hayworth and friends.
Opposite: The Imperial Council Annual Beaux Arts Ball, October 28, 1978. Michelle, aka Czarina de Castro.

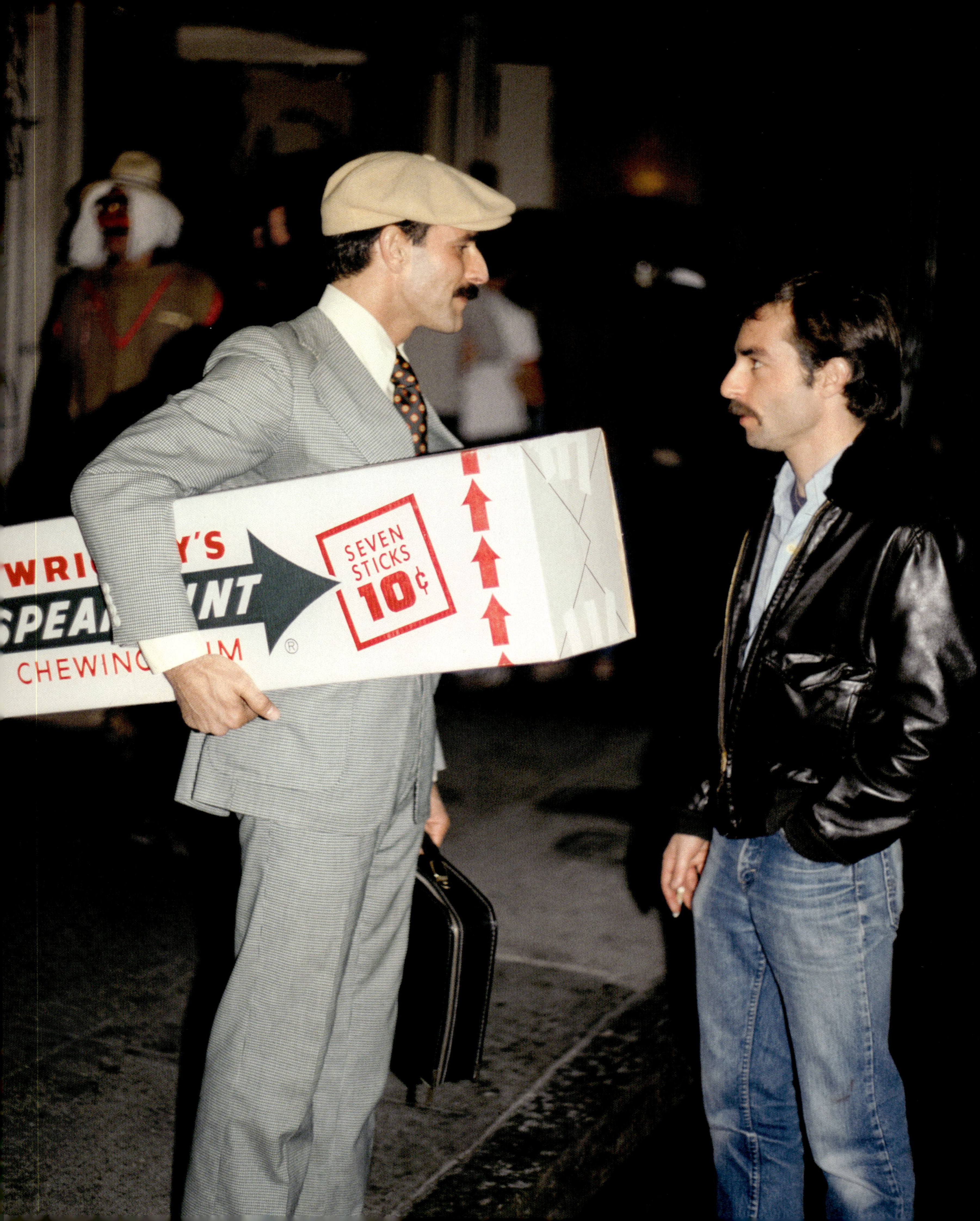
SEVEN
STICKS
10¢

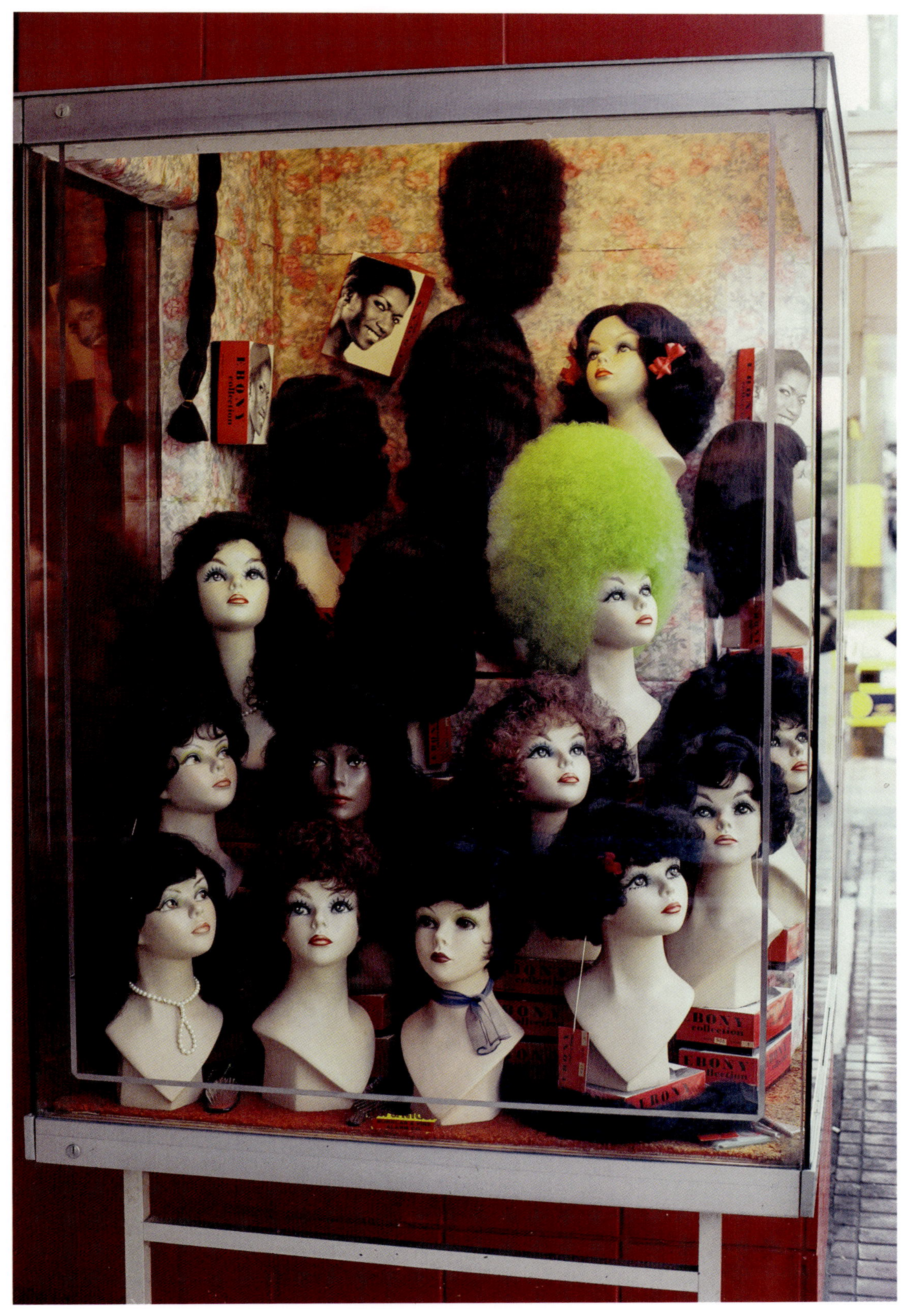

Above: Wig America, Market Street, October 1976.
Opposite: Halloween on Polk Street, October 31, 1976.

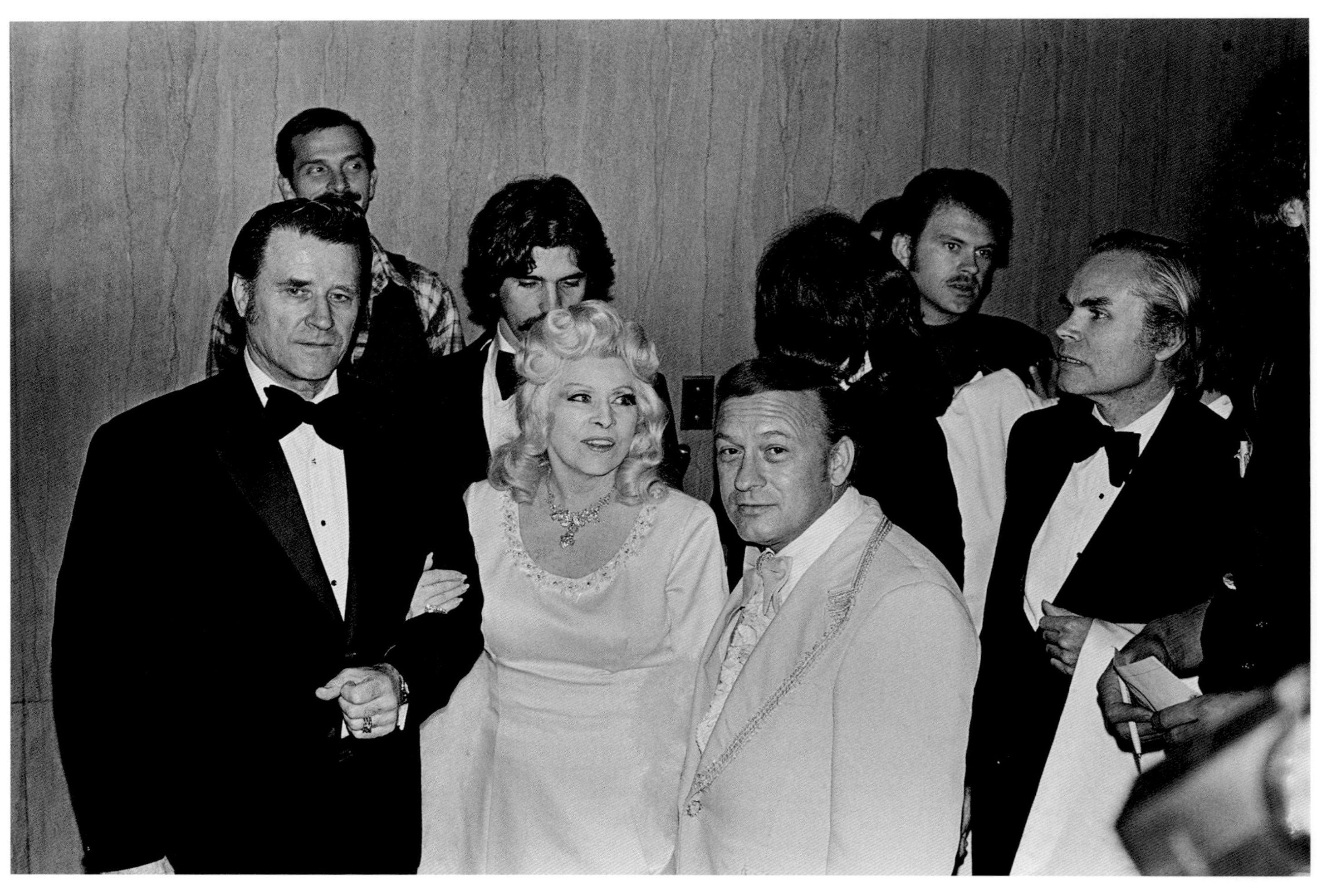

Premiere of *Sextette* at The Warfield theatre, November 16, 1978.
(Above) Mae West and entourage backstage; *(opposite)* Mae West fan.

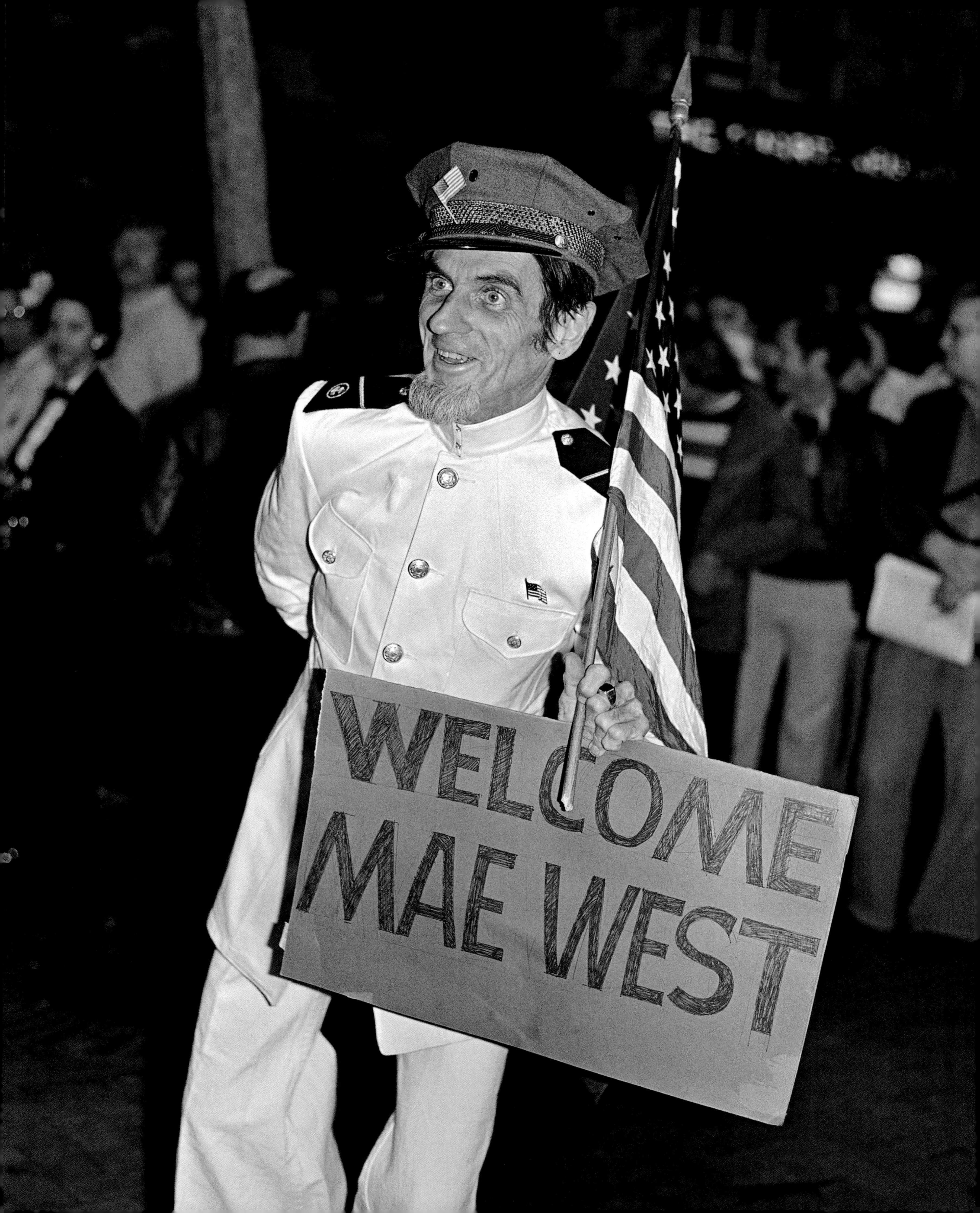
WELCOME
MAE WEST

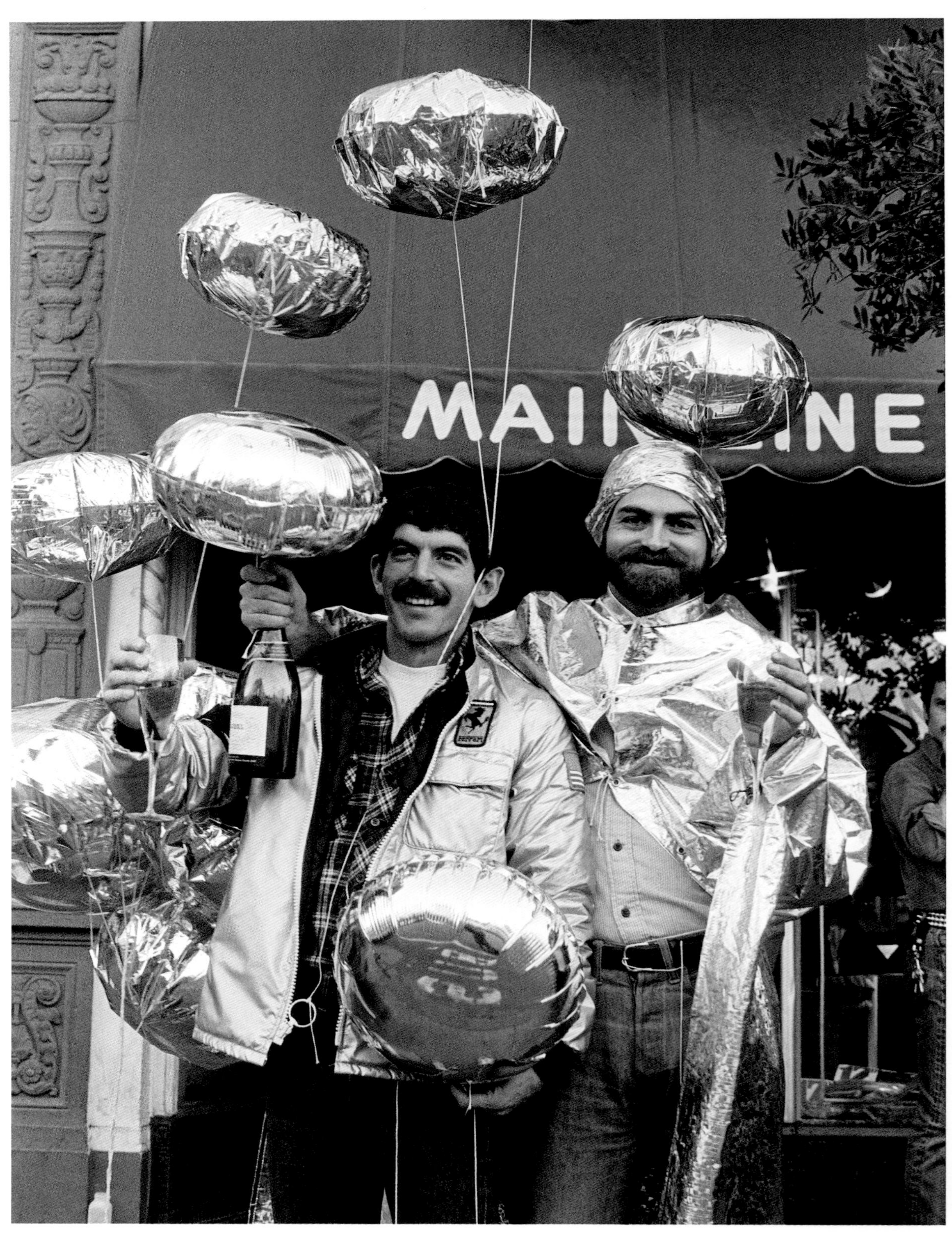

New Year's Eve Day on Castro Street, December 31, 1977. Jim Beale and Michael Jordan.

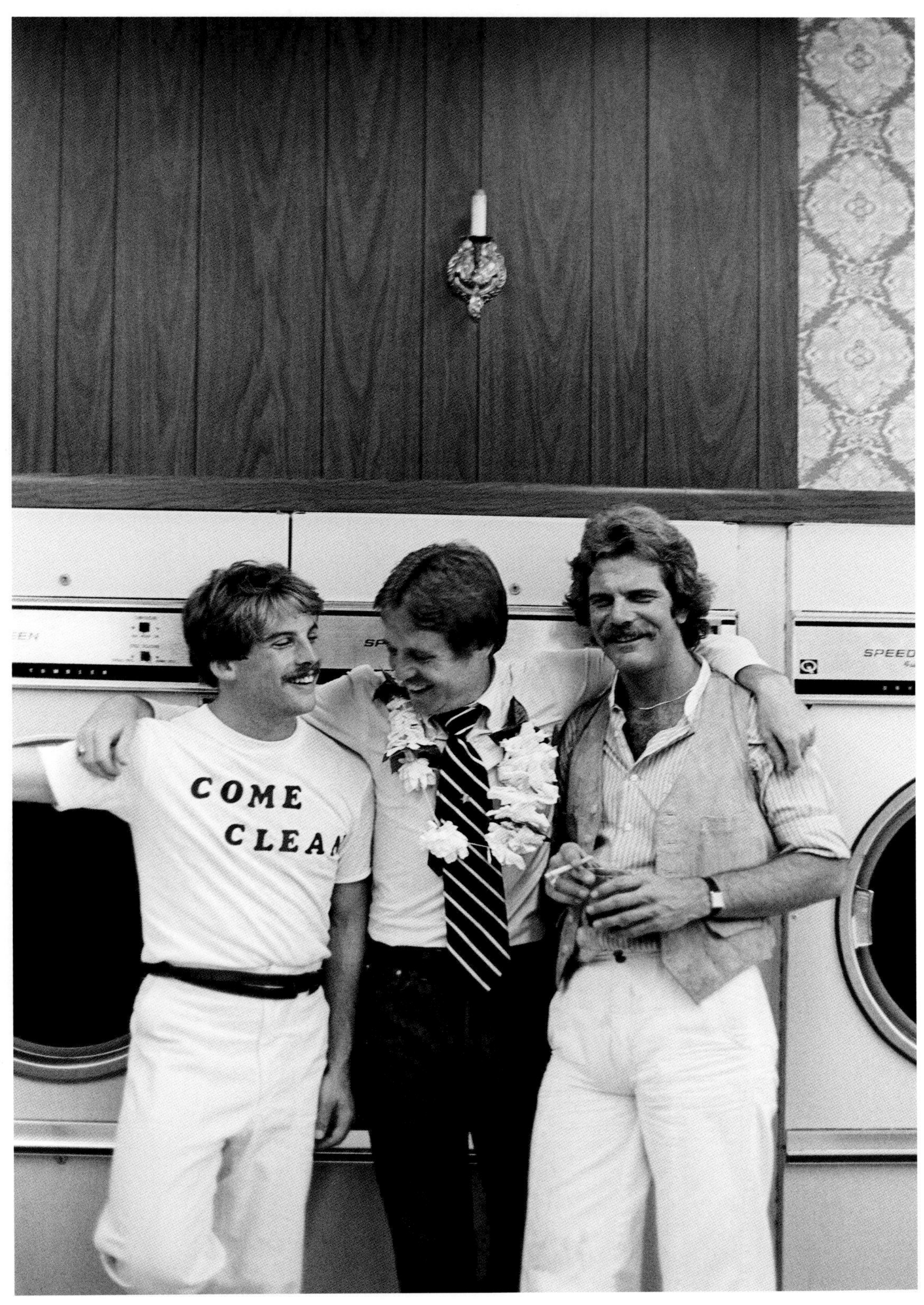

Tales of the City book launch party at the Marina Laundromat, August 23, 1978.
Daniel Katz, author Armistead Maupin and Michael Poniatowsky.

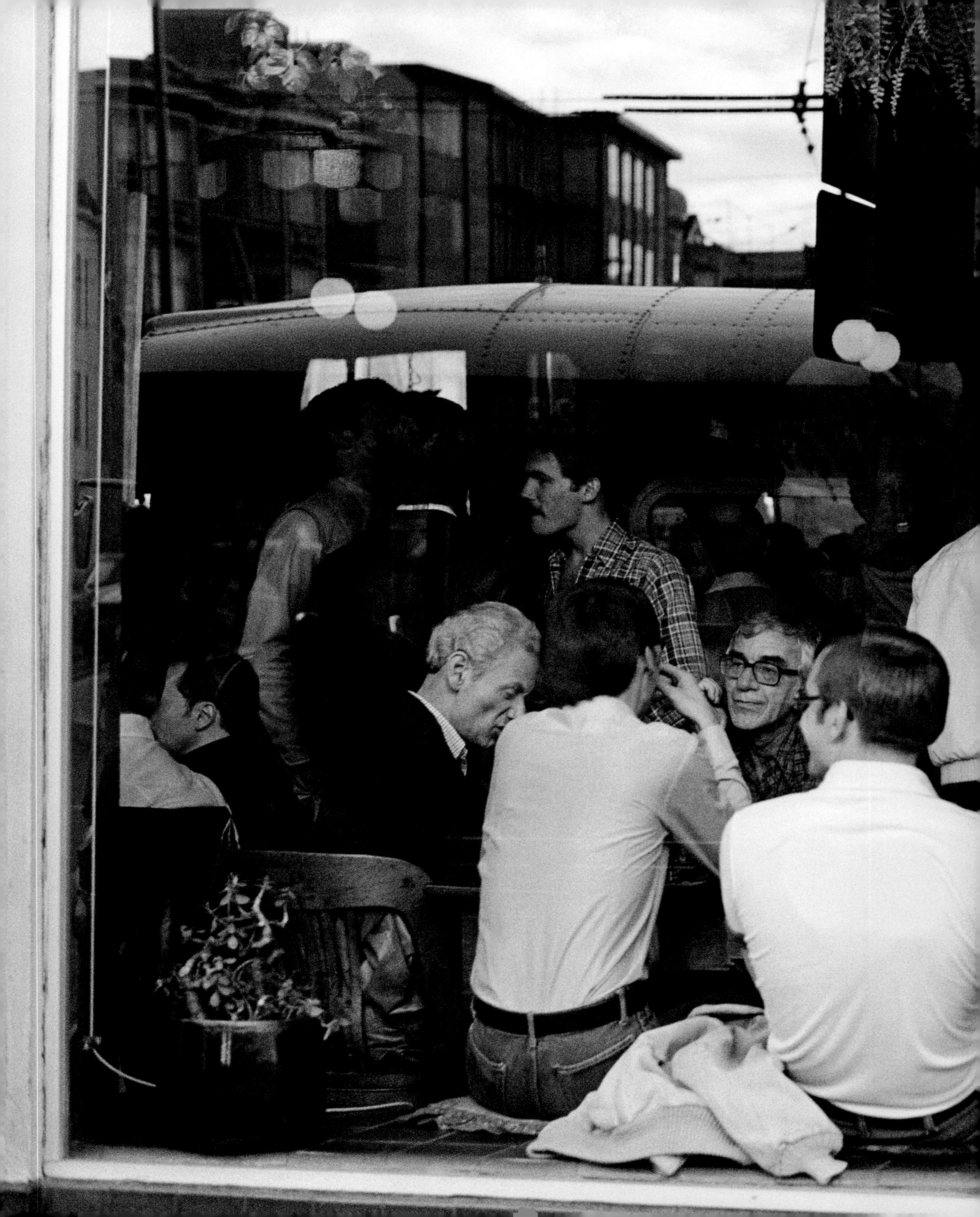

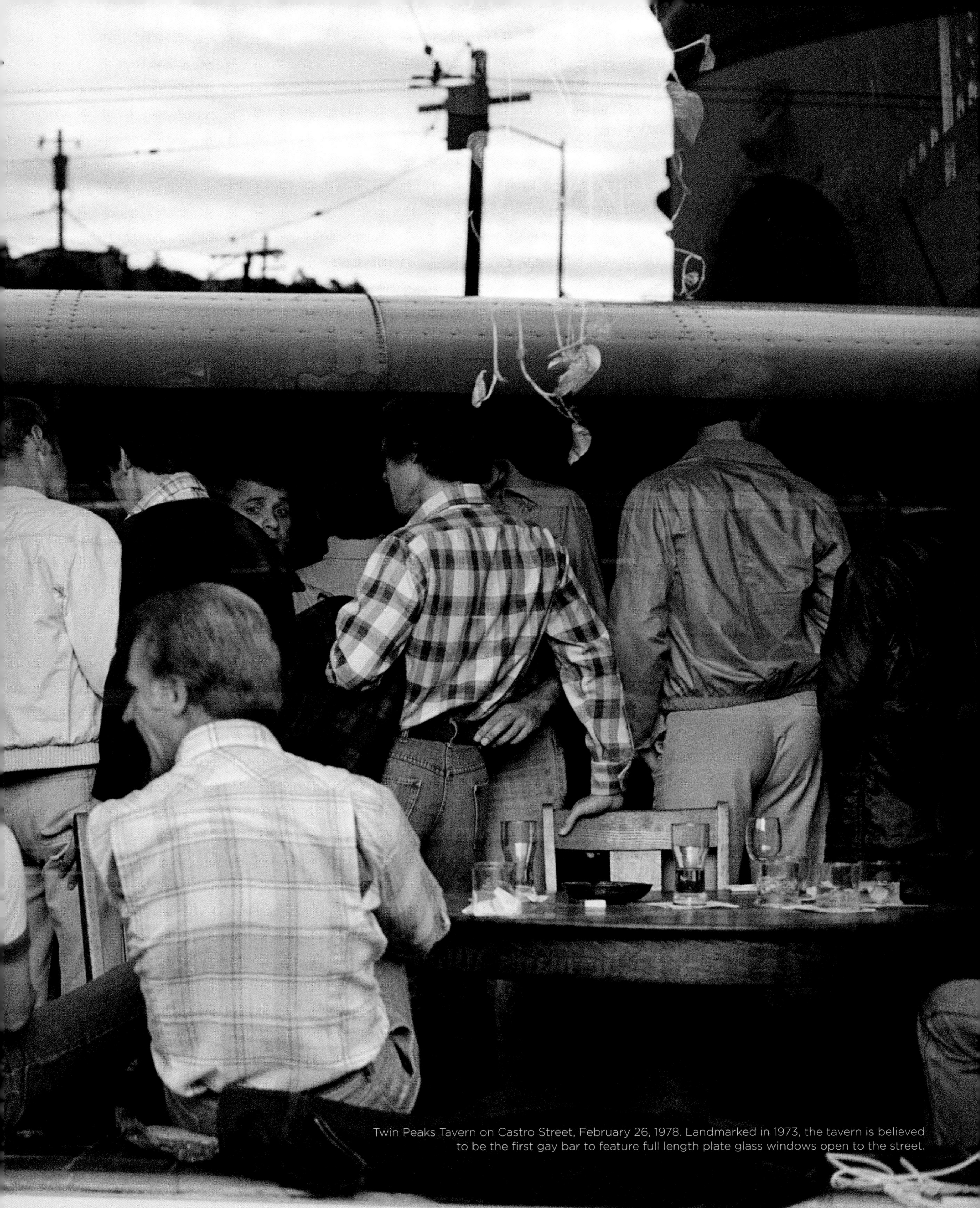

Twin Peaks Tavern on Castro Street, February 26, 1978. Landmarked in 1973, the tavern is believed to be the first gay bar to feature full length plate glass windows open to the street.

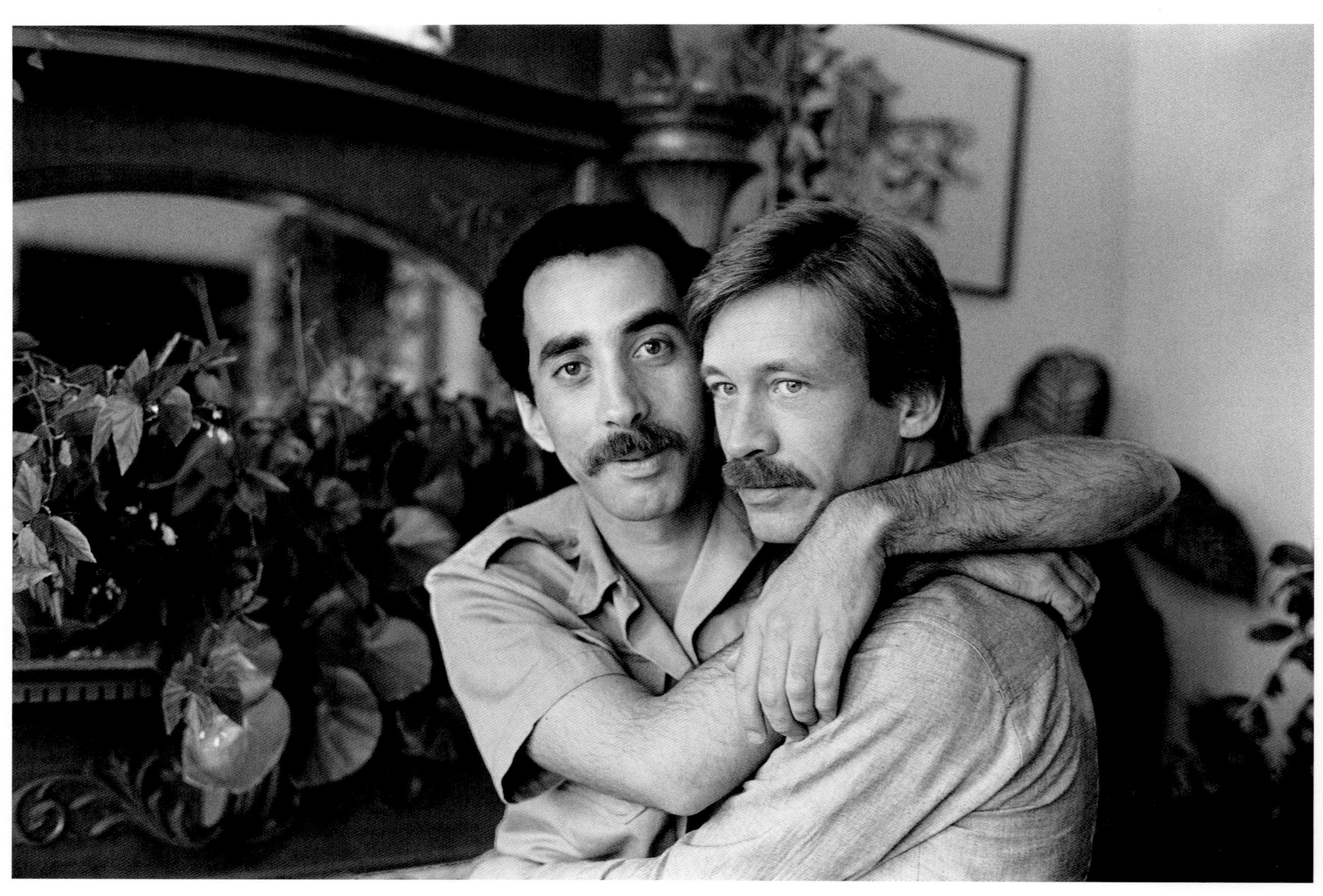

Above: Daniel Goldstein and Tom Cox, spring, 1976.
Opposite: Michael England and Roger Madison, summer, 1976.

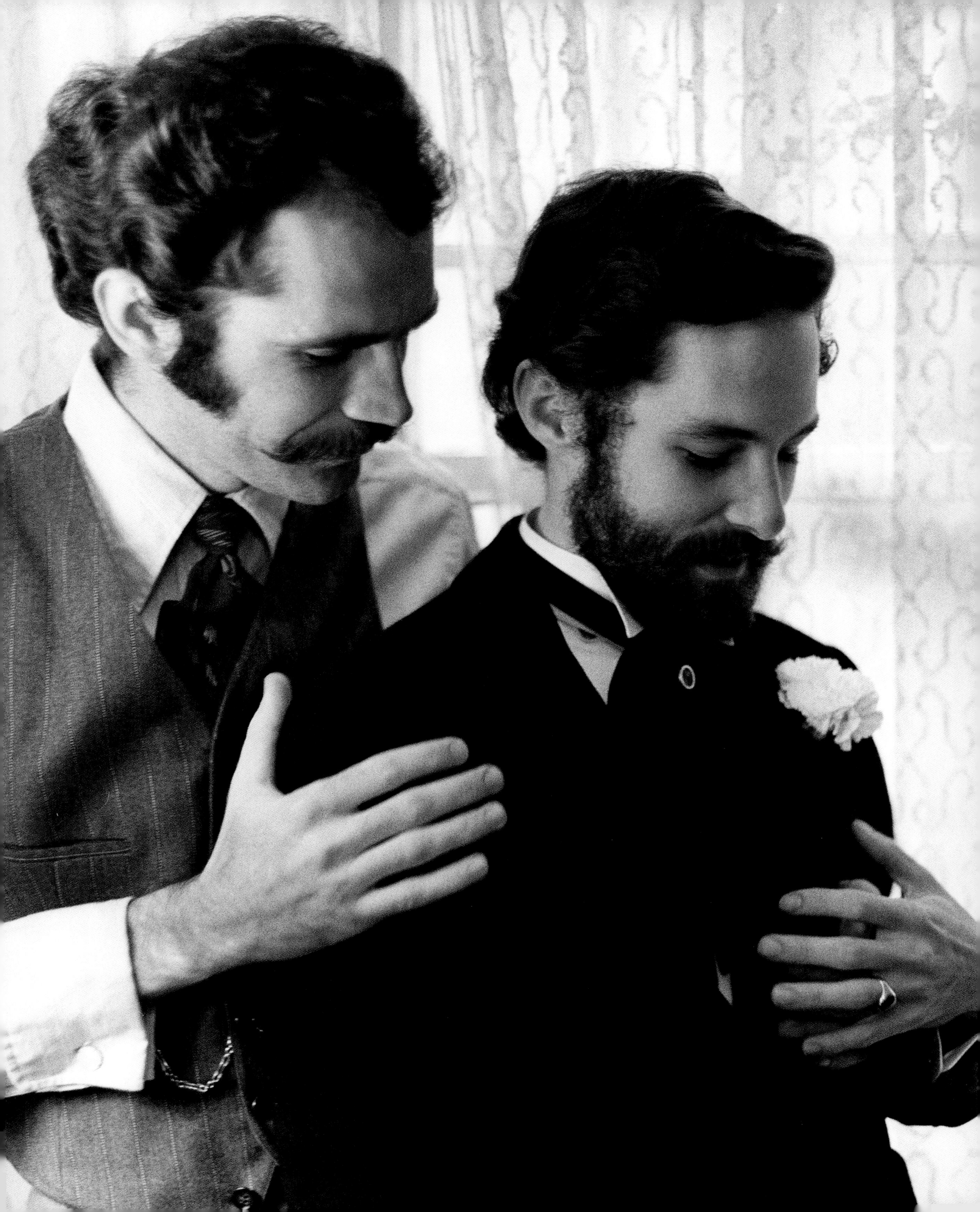

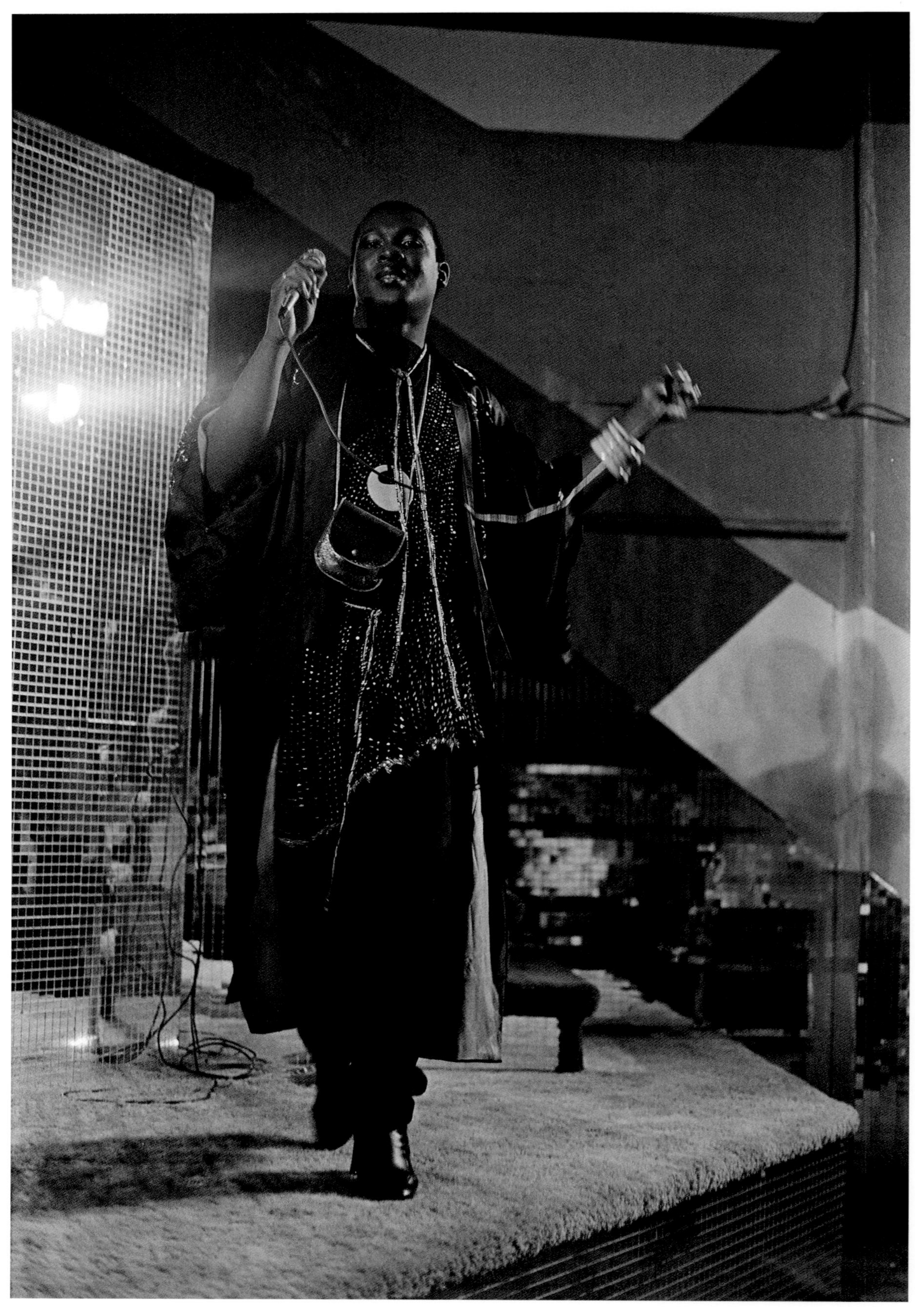

Above: Sylvester at Trocadero dance club, spring 1978.
Opposite: Divine at Trocadero dance club, October 29, 1978.

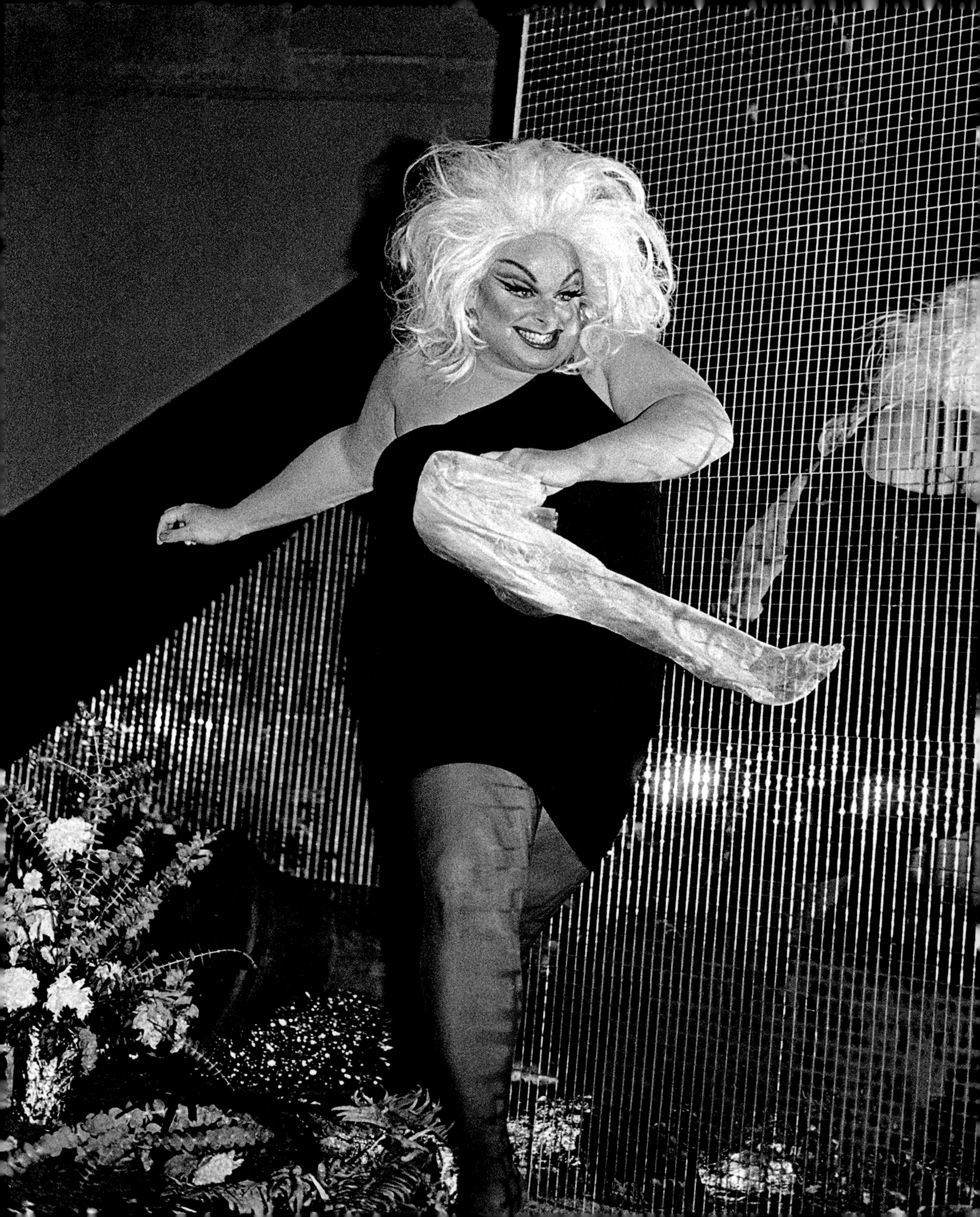

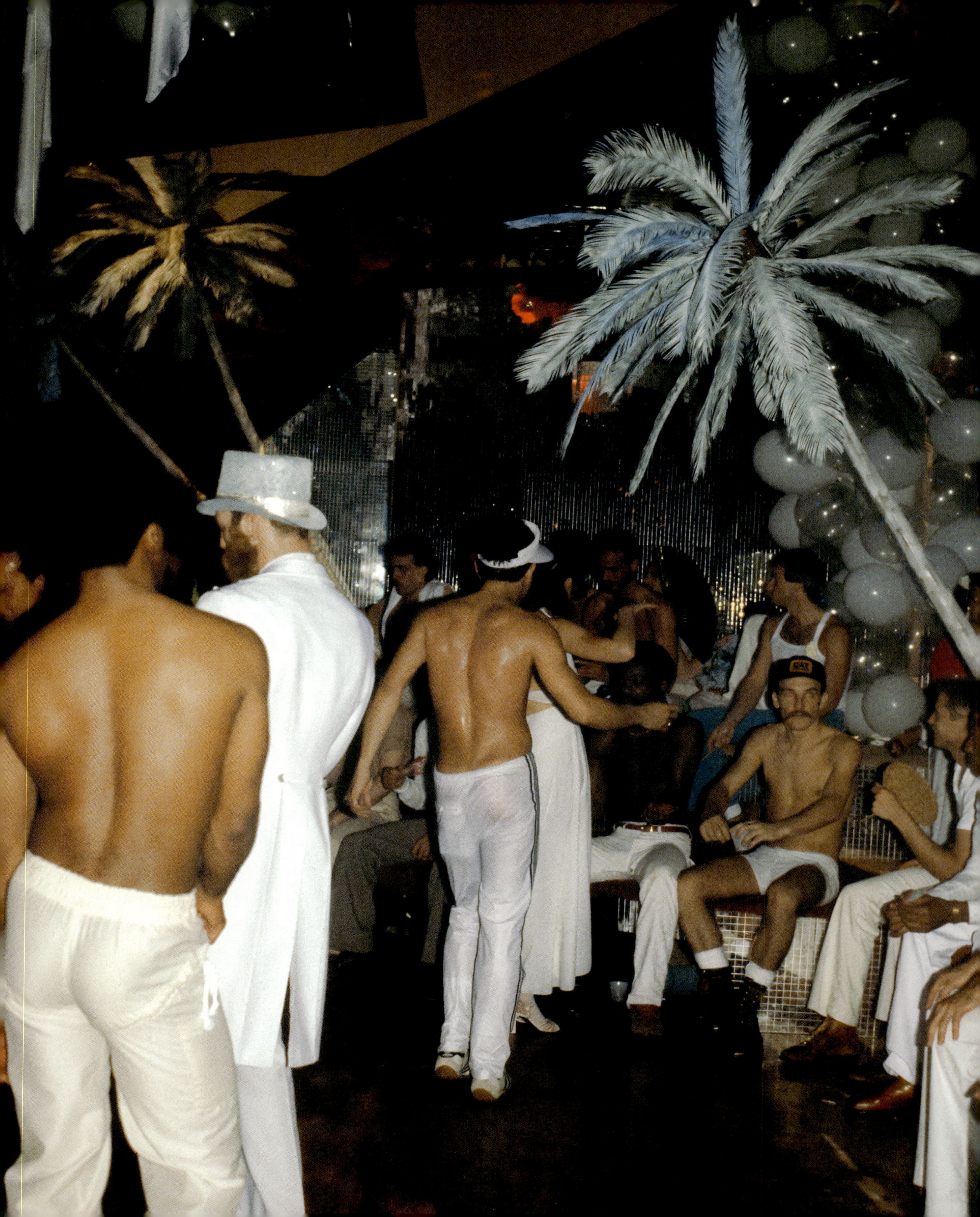

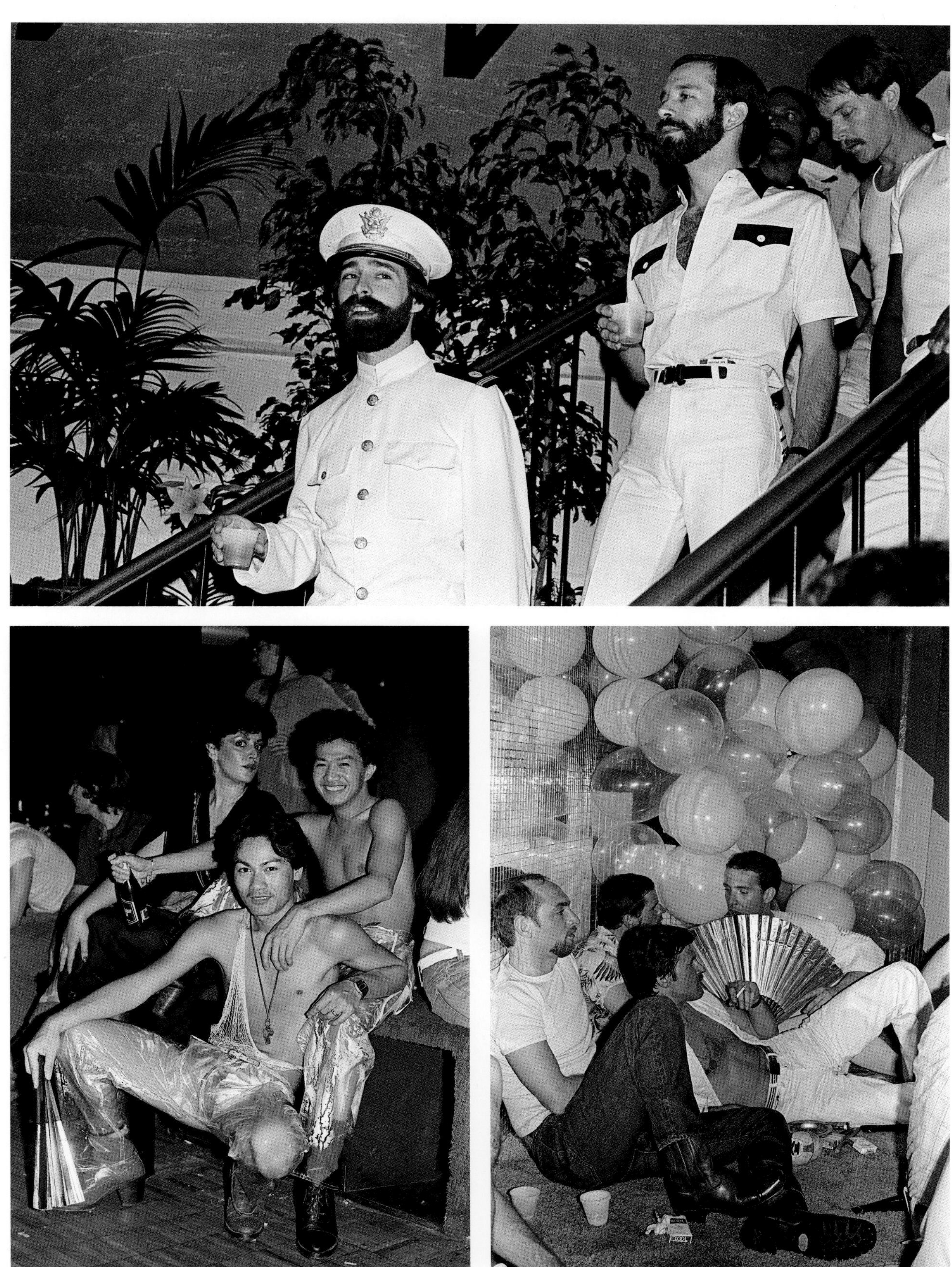

Above: Trocadero dance club. *(Clockwise from top)* White Party, spring 1978; White Party, 1978; I Love A Parade party, May 2, 1978;
Opposite: Trocadero dance club, White Party, spring 1978.

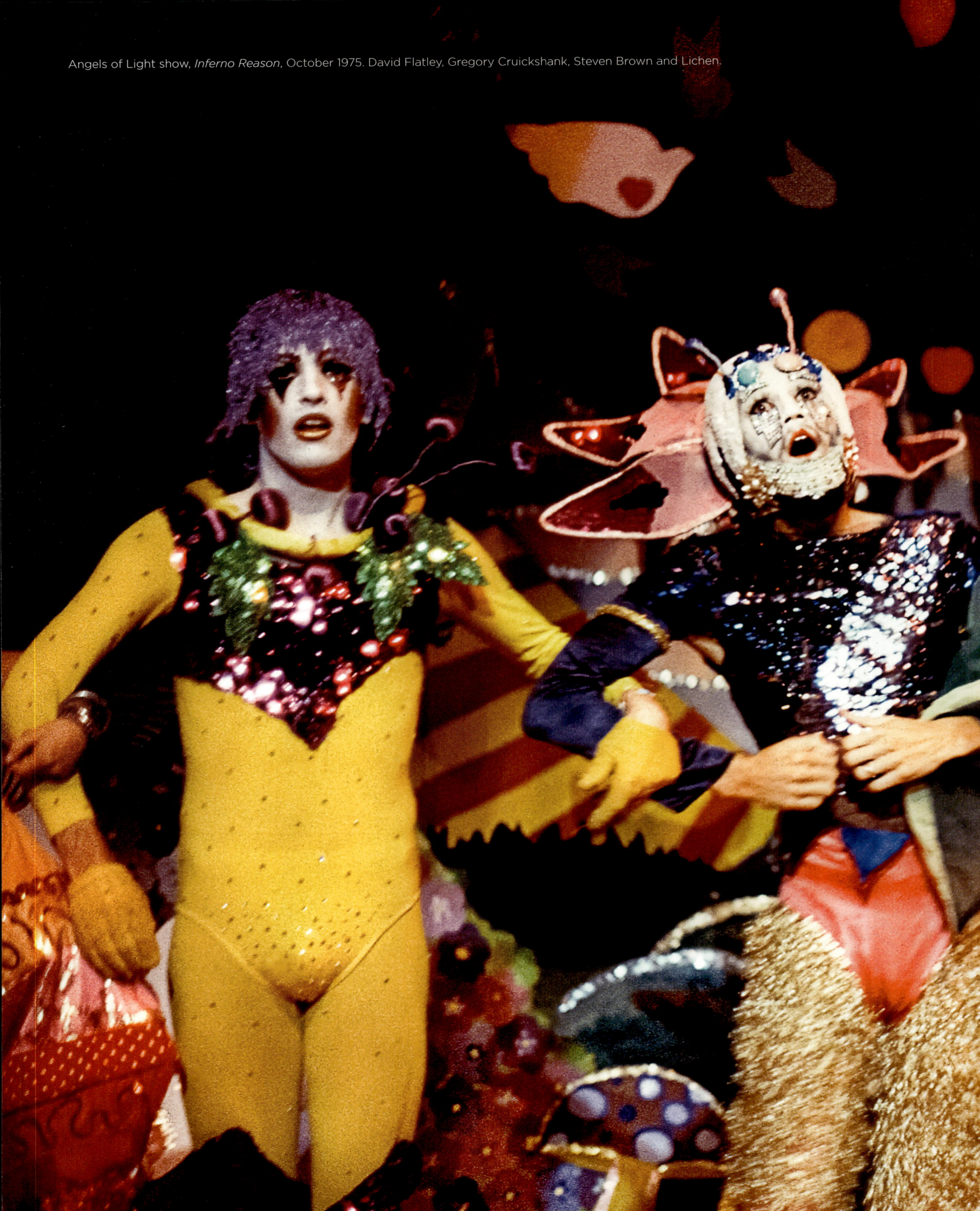

Angels of Light show, *Inferno Reason*, October 1975. David Flatley, Gregory Cruickshank, Steven Brown and Lichen.

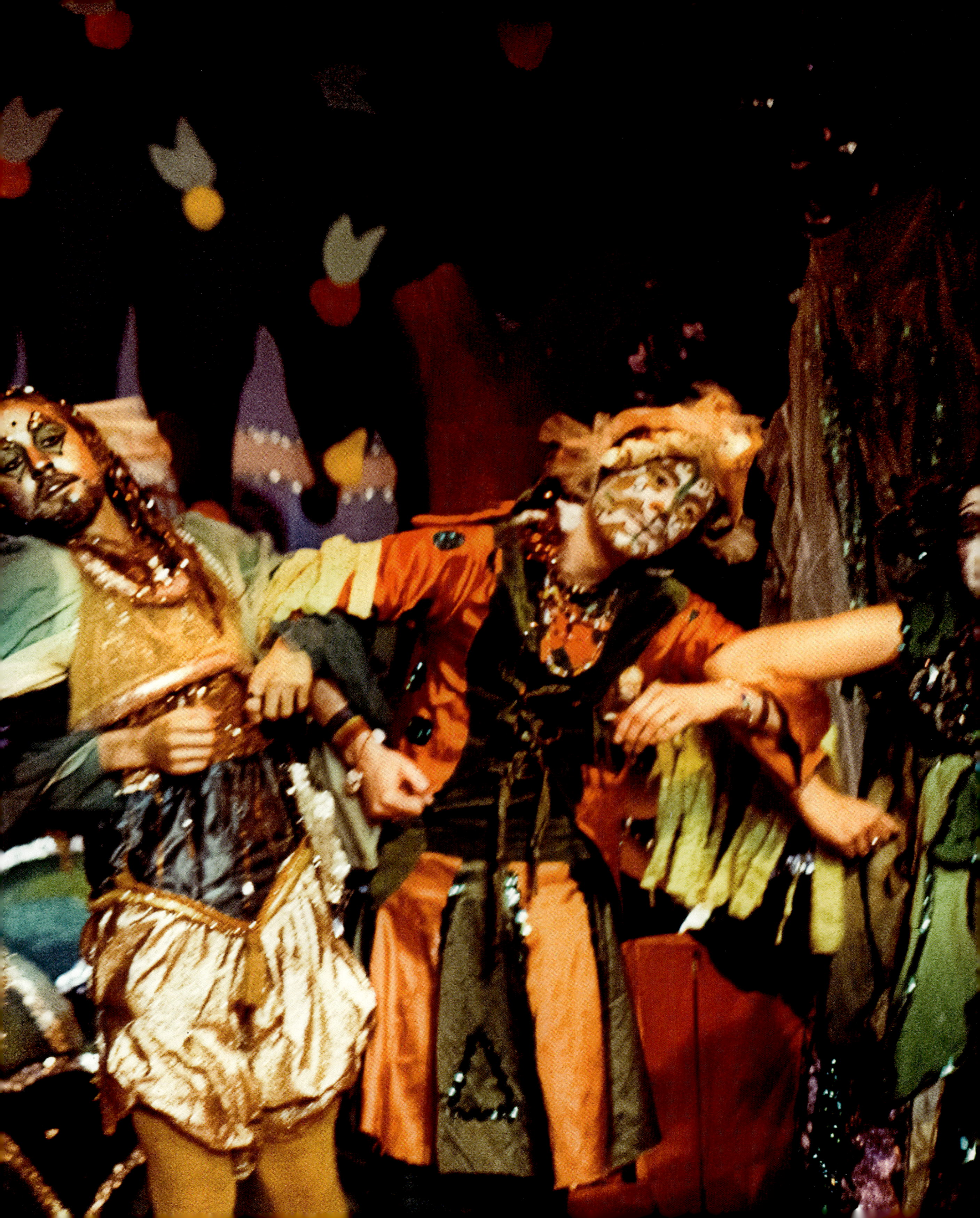

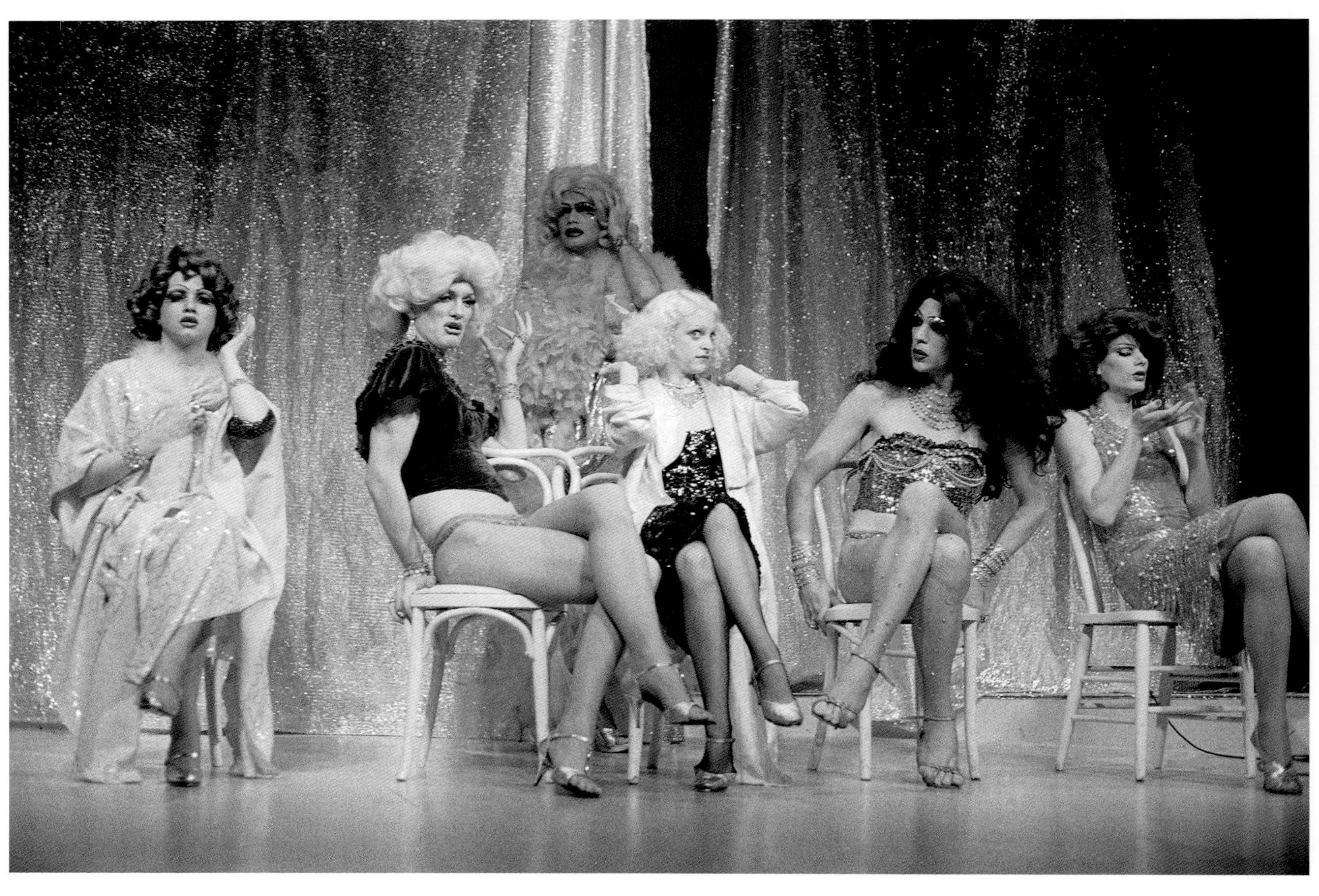

Angels of Light in *Femme Fatale*, September 1976.
(Above) Louise Harris, Ginger, Hibiscus, Chi Chi Wilson, Angel Jack and Java Jet, aka Bambi Lake;
(opposite) Hibiscus and Sandy, aka Eboni St. Gerard.

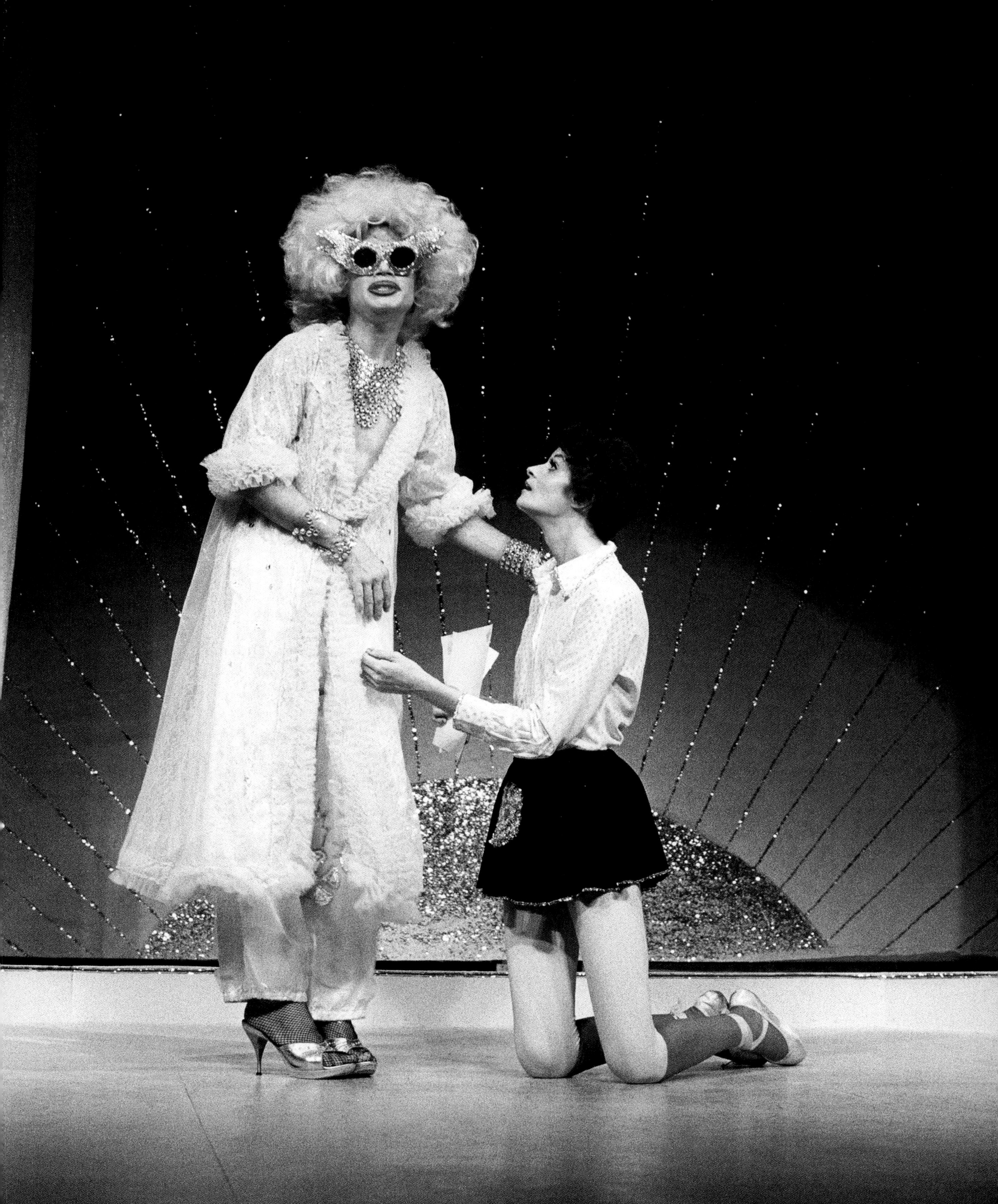

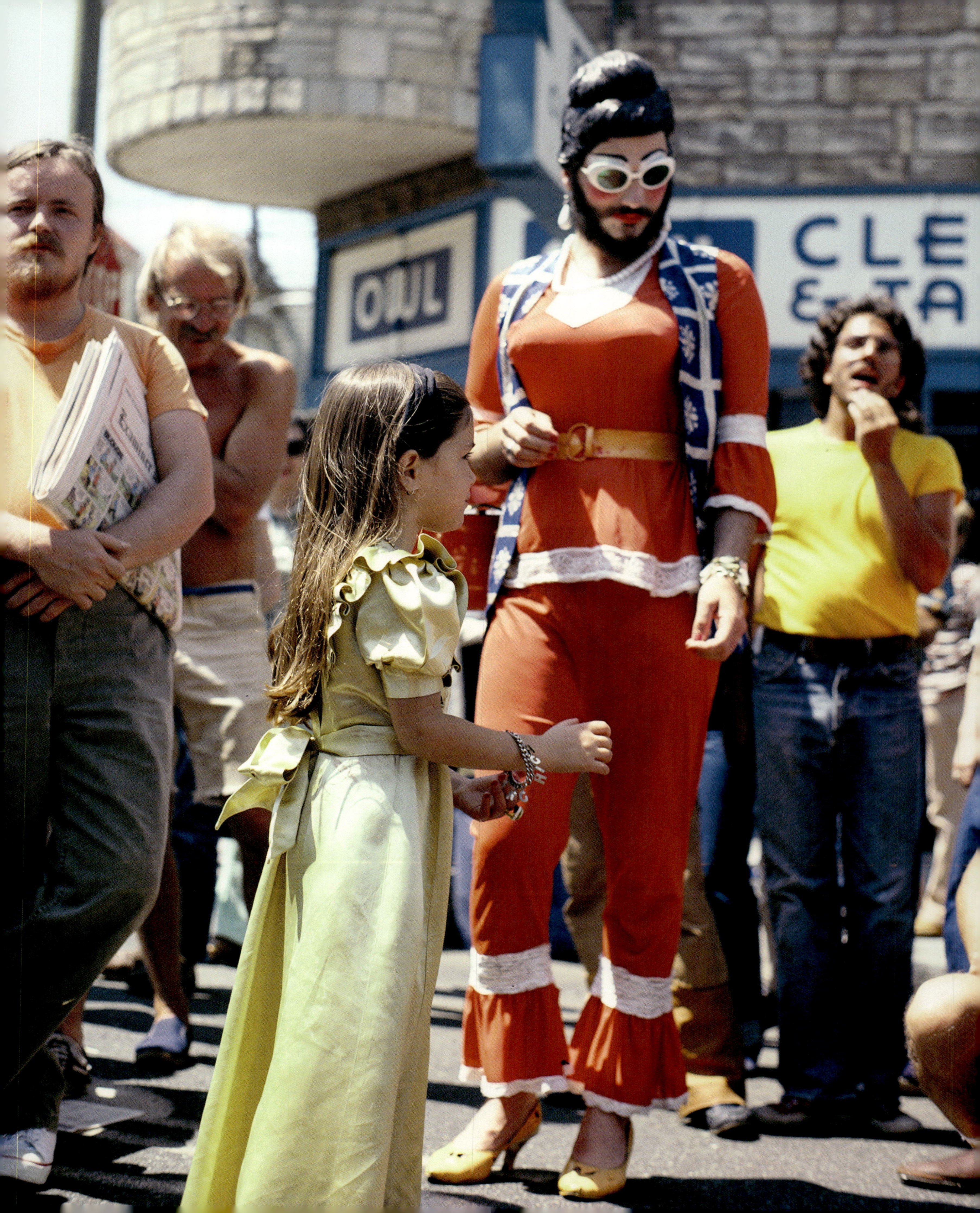
OWL
CLE
& TA

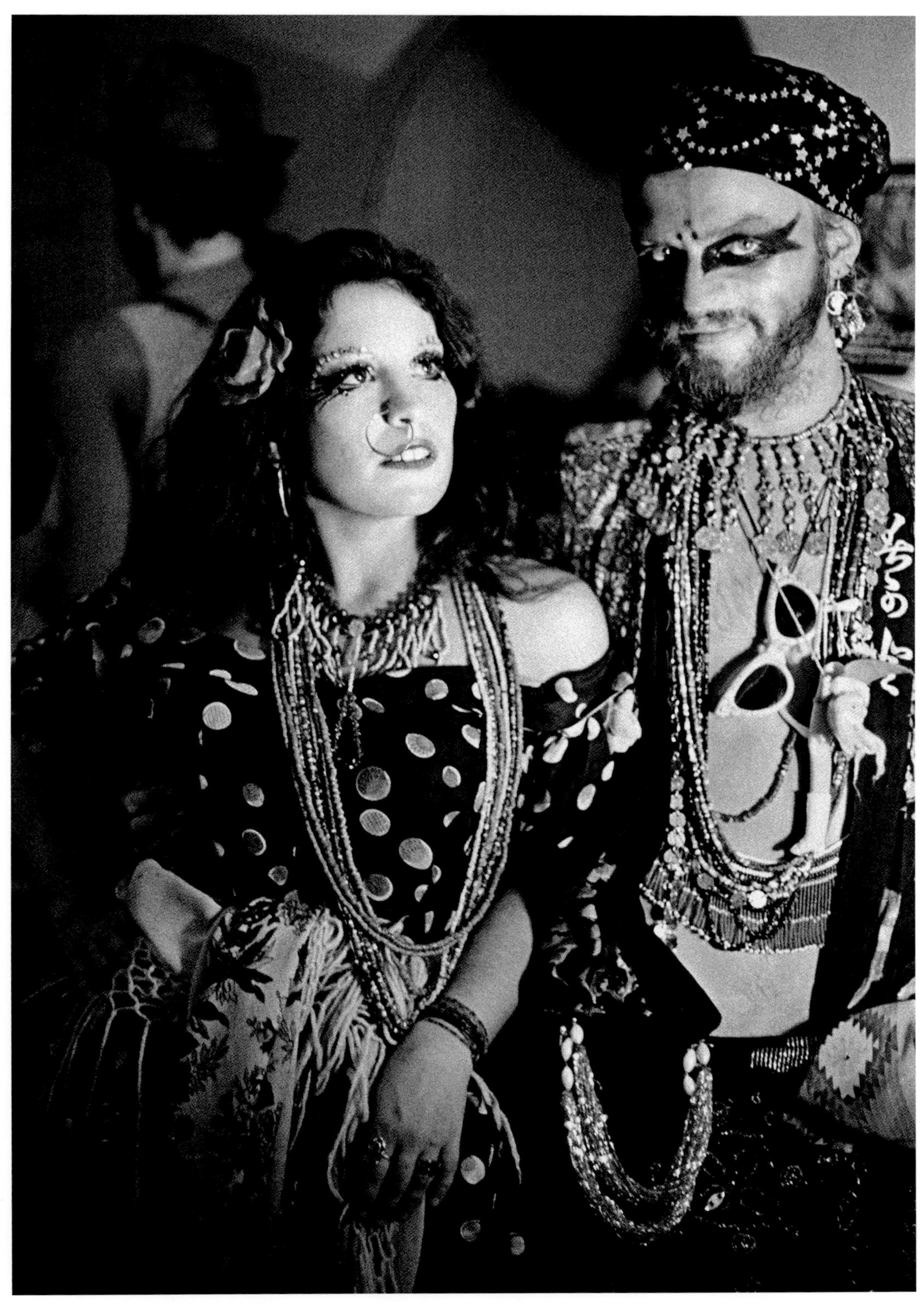

Above: Angels of Light, backstage *Mind Kamp Kabaret*, August 1976. Esmerelda and Lulu.
Opposite: Castro Street Fair, August 1977. Angels of Light, Ananda Johnopoulos and Tahara.

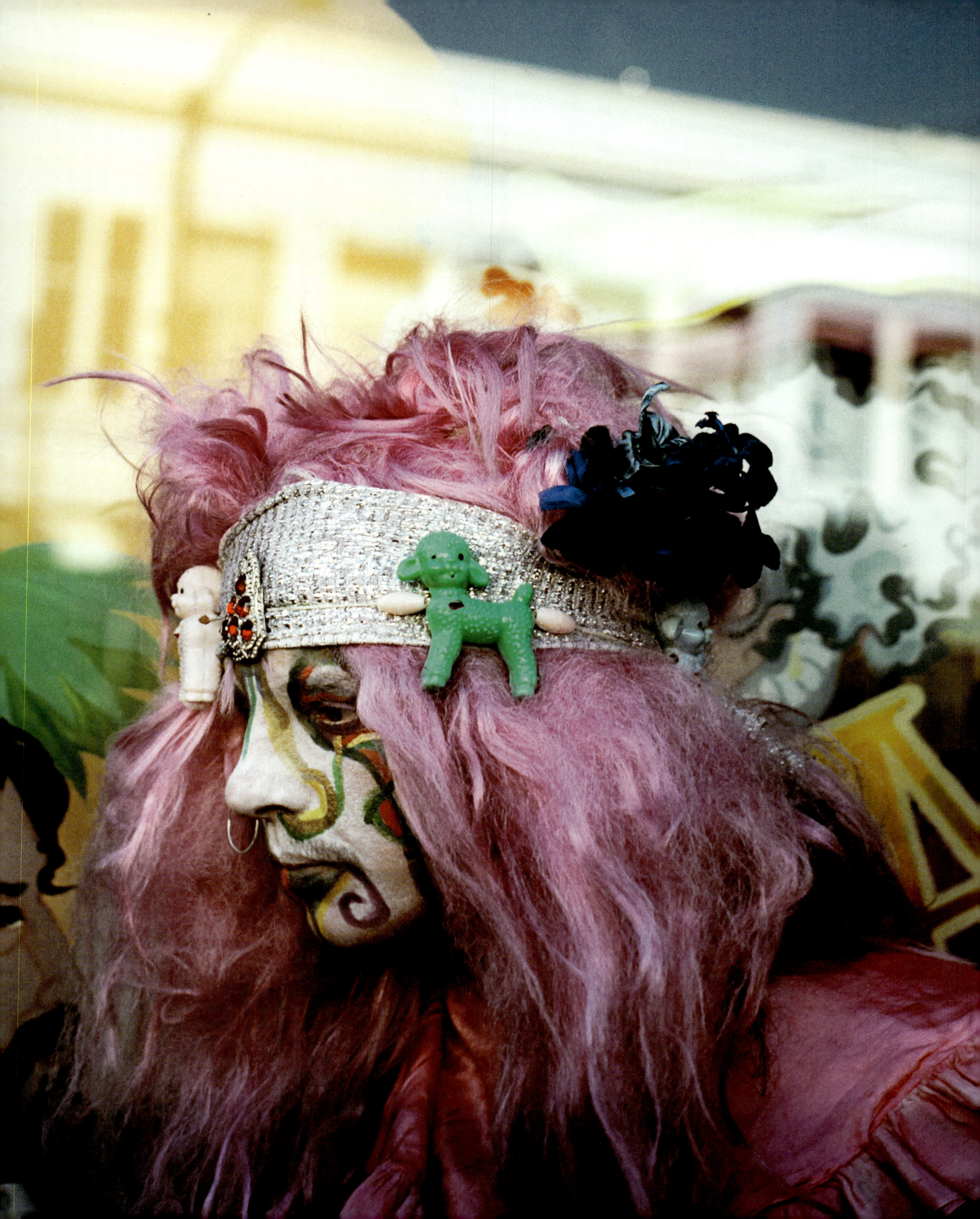

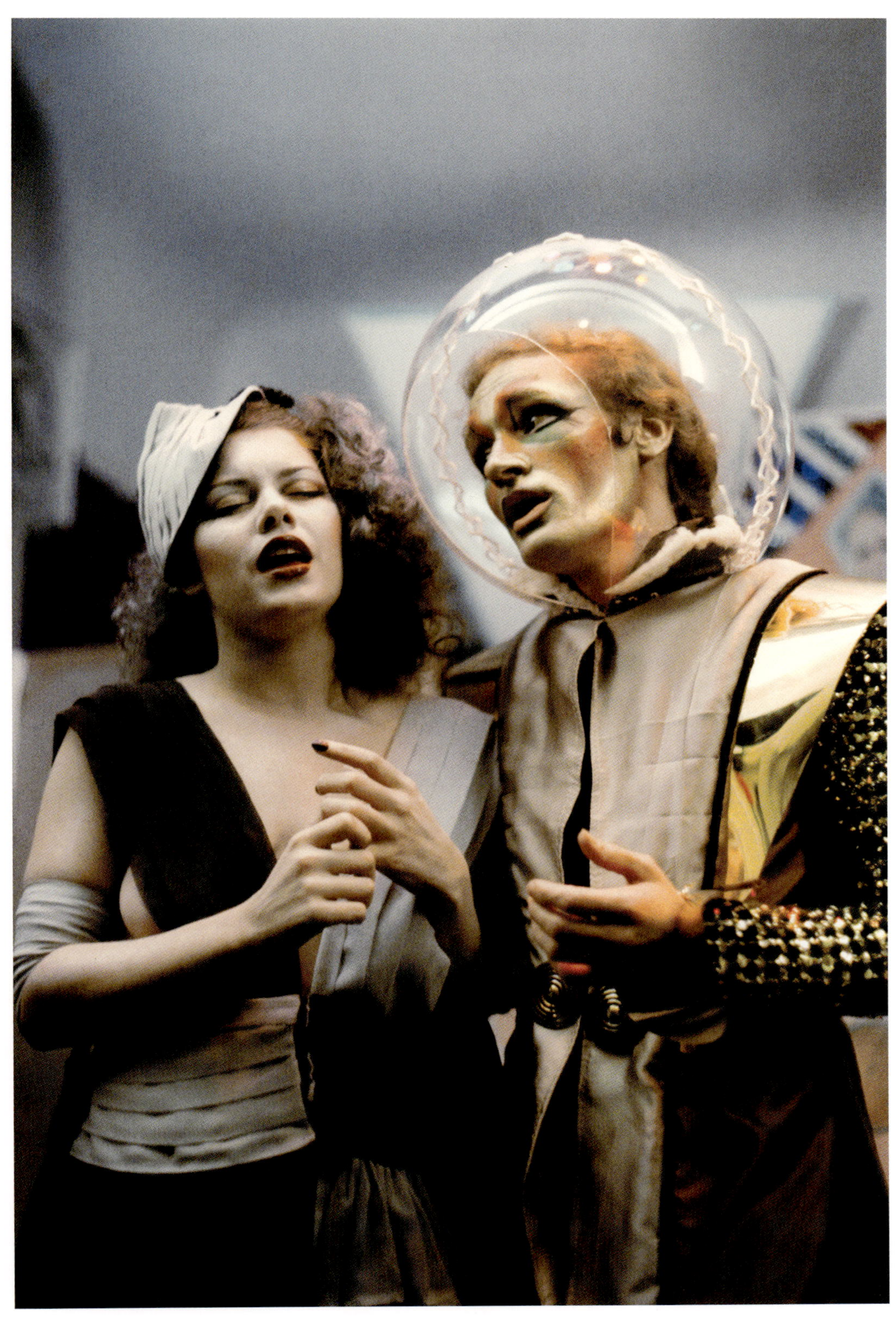

Above: Hulah Palace Salon, winter 1975. Candice Vadala and Cockette Michael Shain. (Performance and fashion show for Lourdan Kimbrell's costuming.)
Opposite: Castro Street Fair, August 1975. Angels of Light, Lichen.

Angels of Light show, *Paris Sights Under The Bourgeois Sea*, June 1975. Steven Brown.

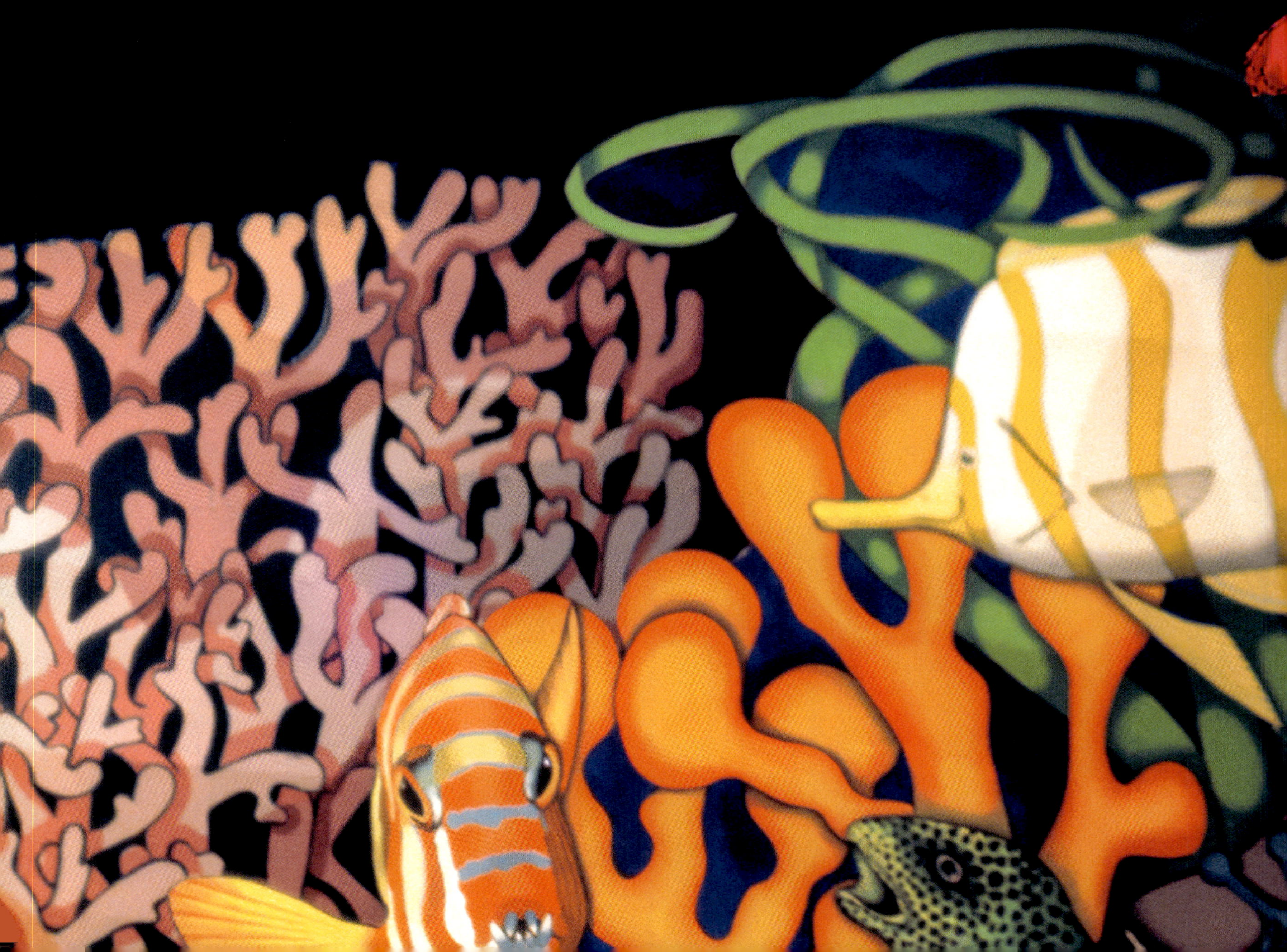

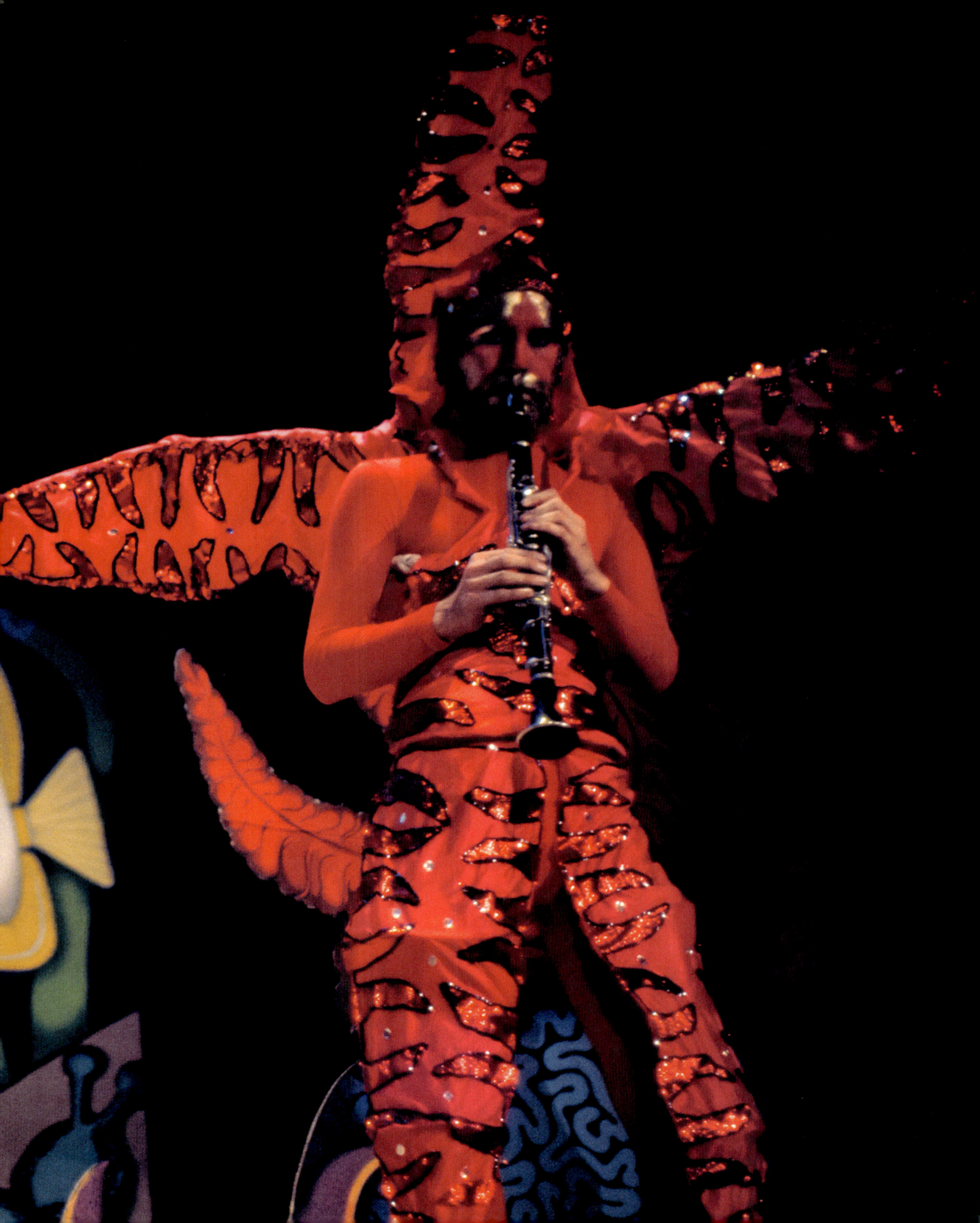

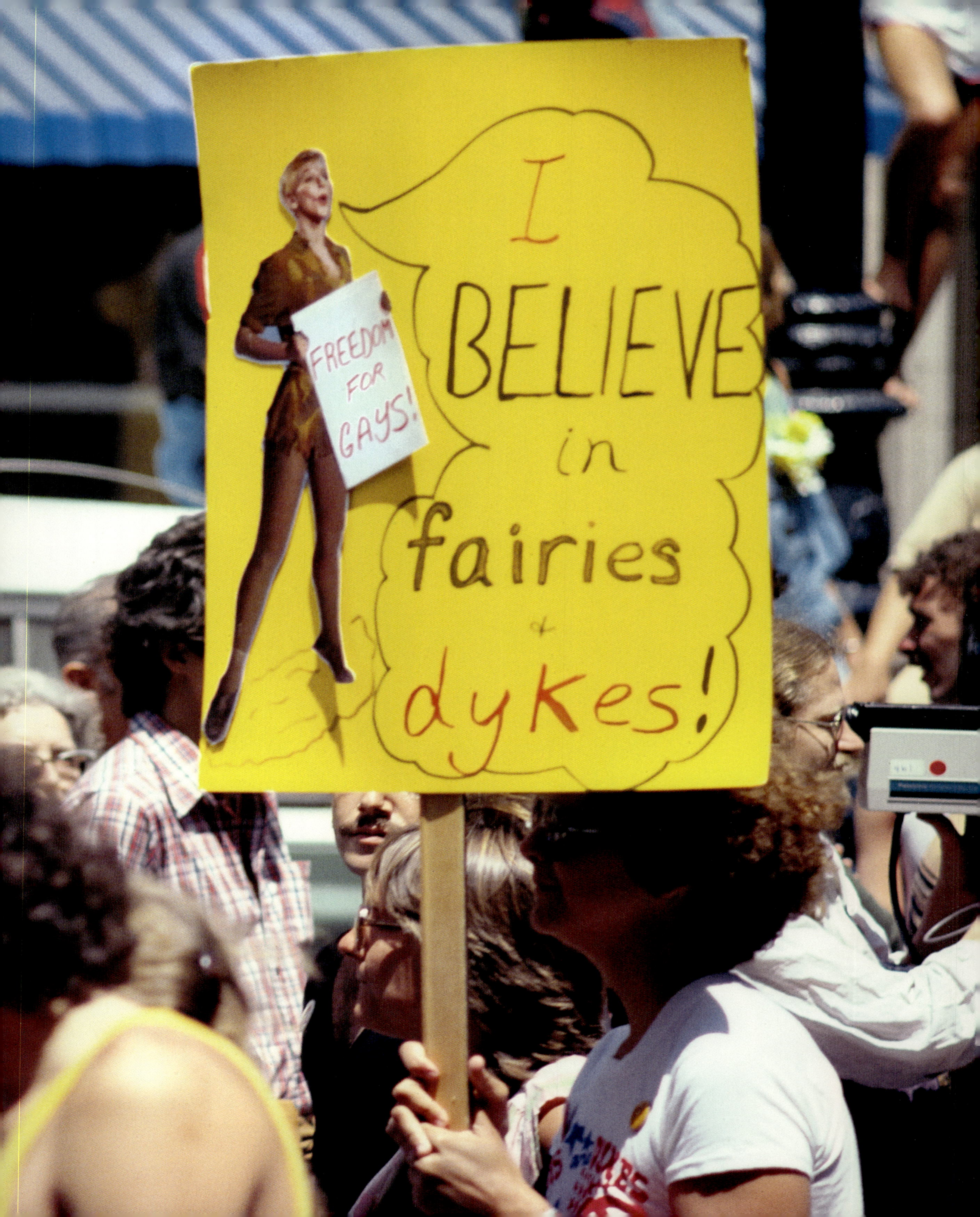
I BELIEVE in fairies & dykes!
FREEDOM FOR GAYS!

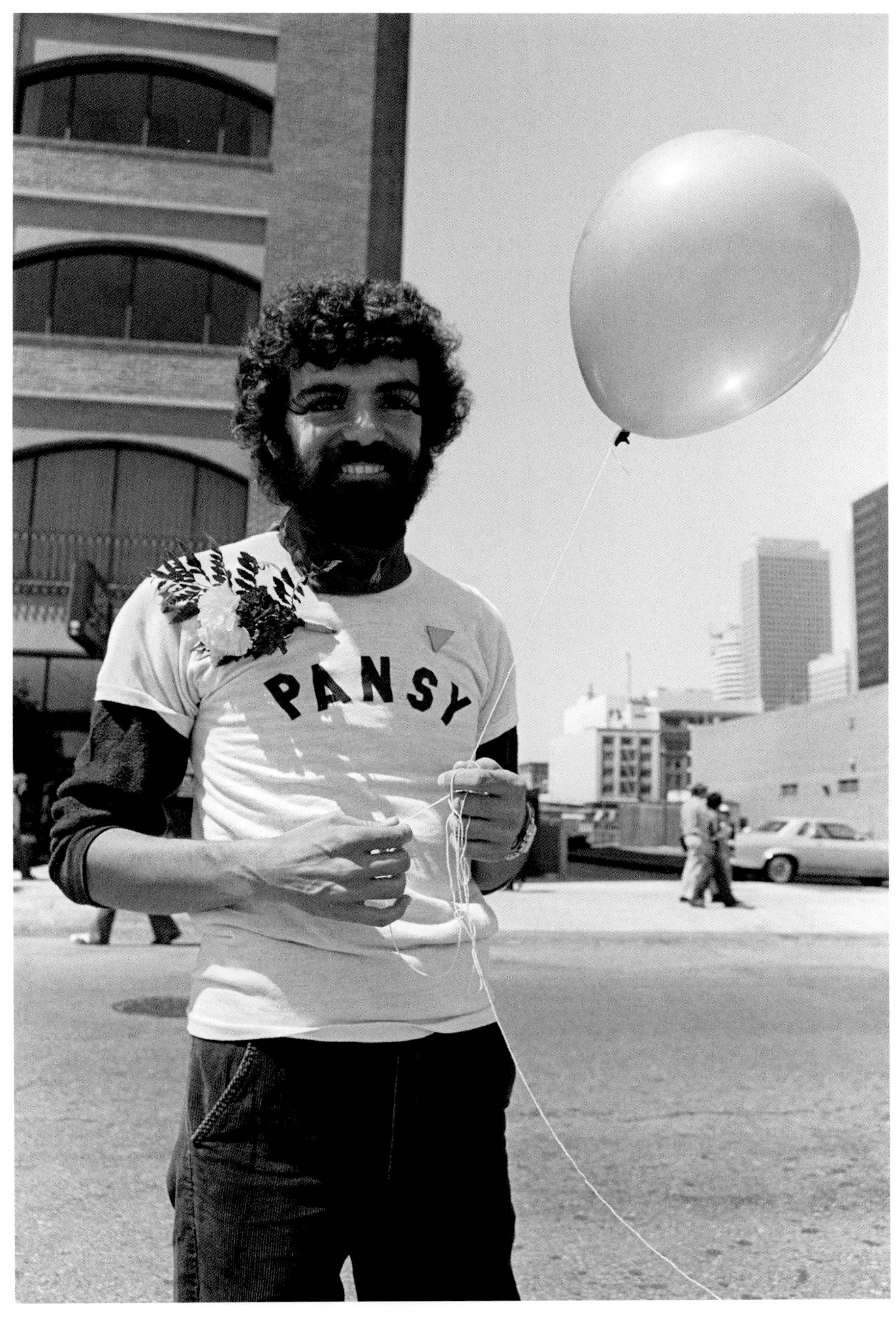

Above: SF LGBT Pride, June 25, 1978. Allan Bérubé.
Opposite: SF LGBT Pride, June 1977.

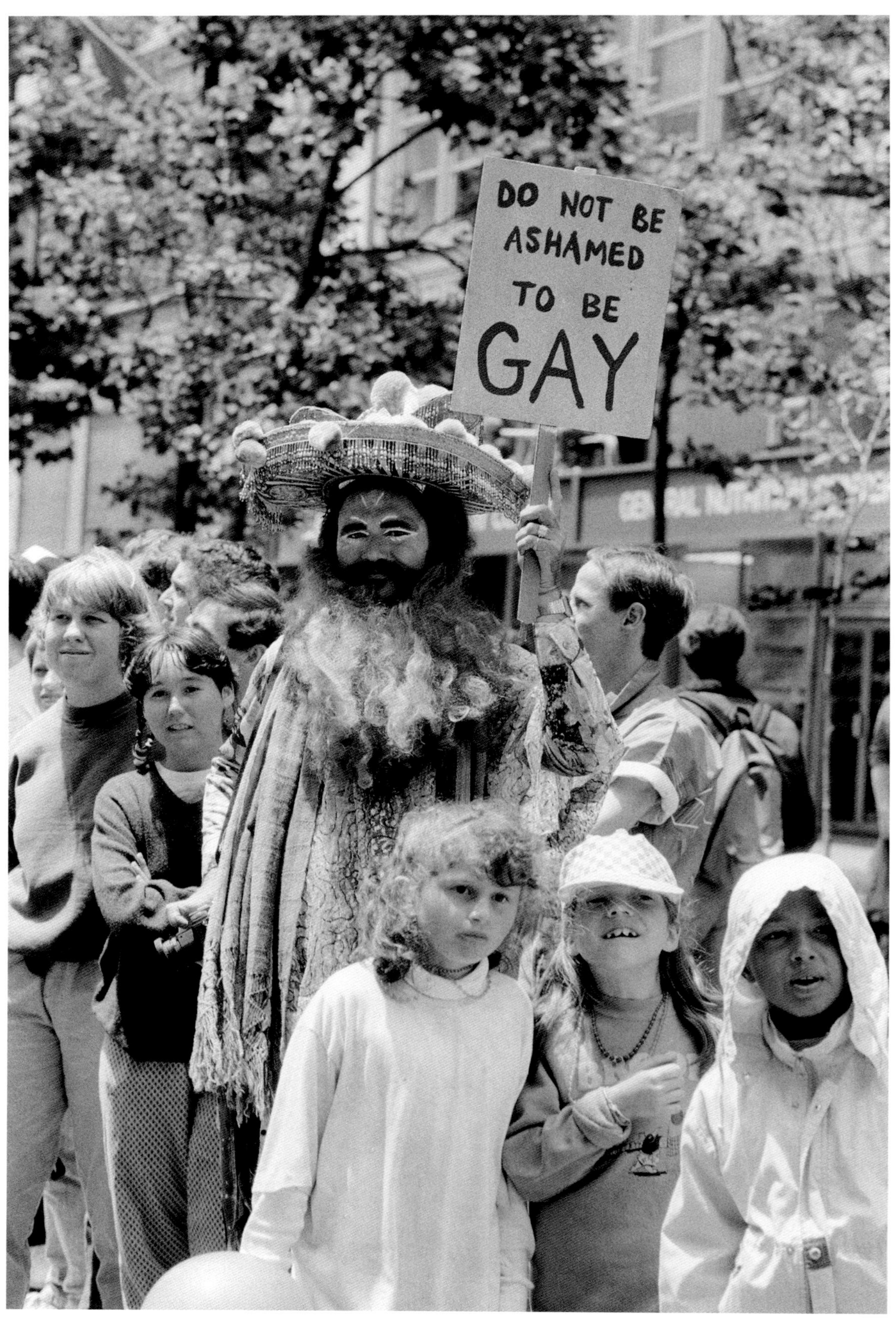

SF LGBT Pride, June 1988. Angels of Light, Tahara.

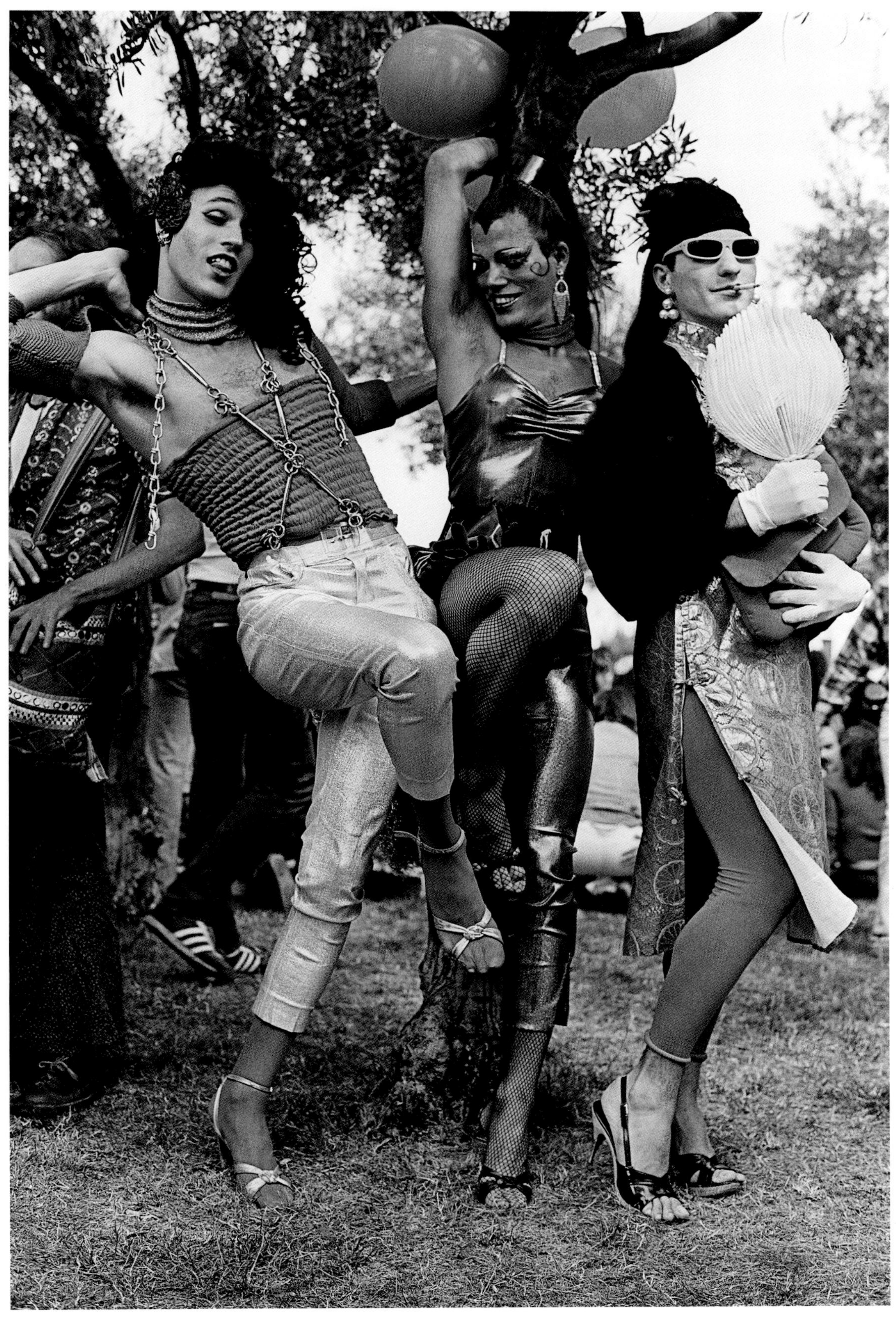

SF LGBT Pride, June 1977. Angels of Light, Gregory Cruickshank, Rodney Price and Joe Morocco.

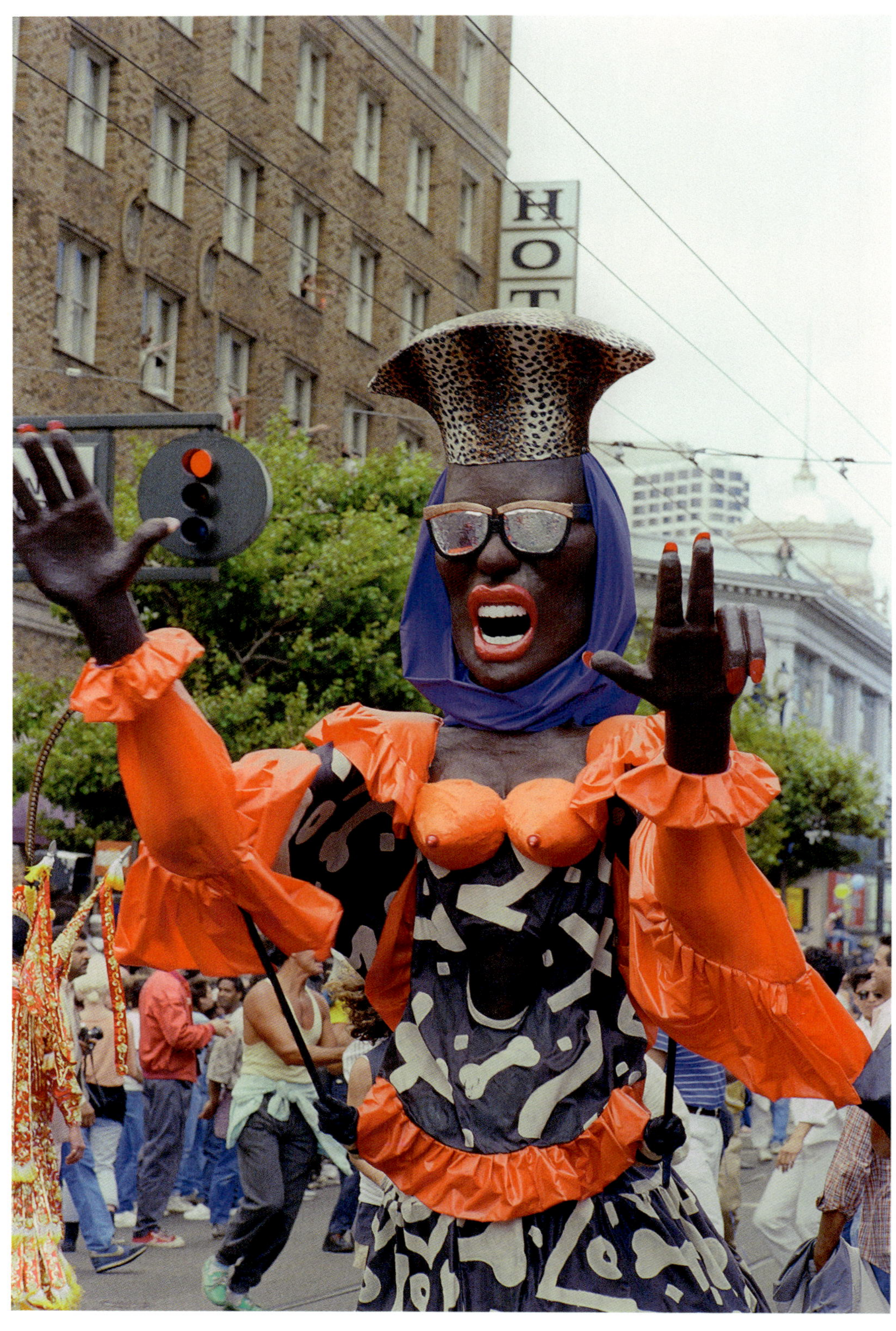

Above: SF LGBT Pride, June 28, 1987. Grace Jones puppet by Philippe Ruiz.
Opposite: SF LGBT Pride, June 1977. Grace Jones (dance club Oil Can Harry's parade float).

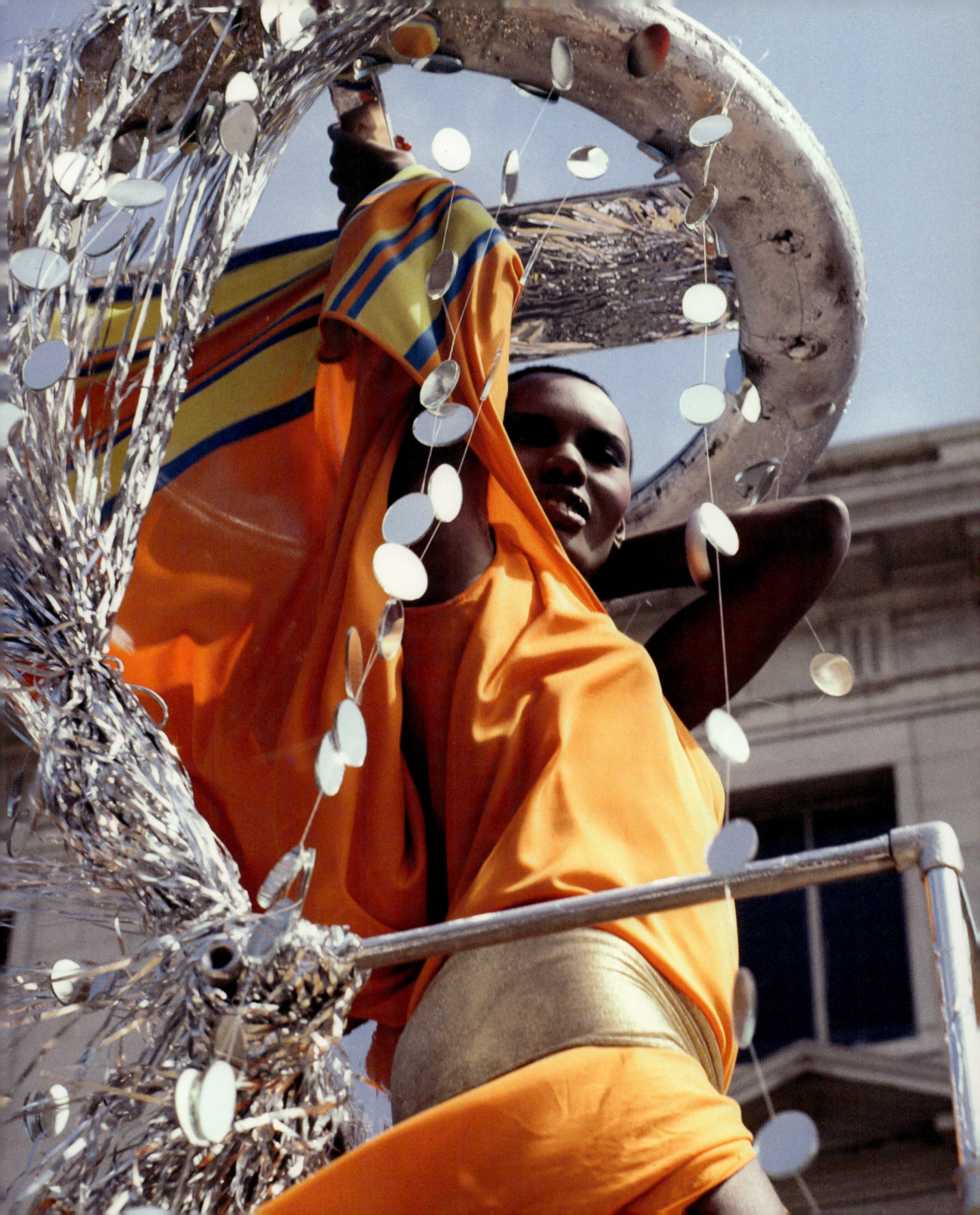

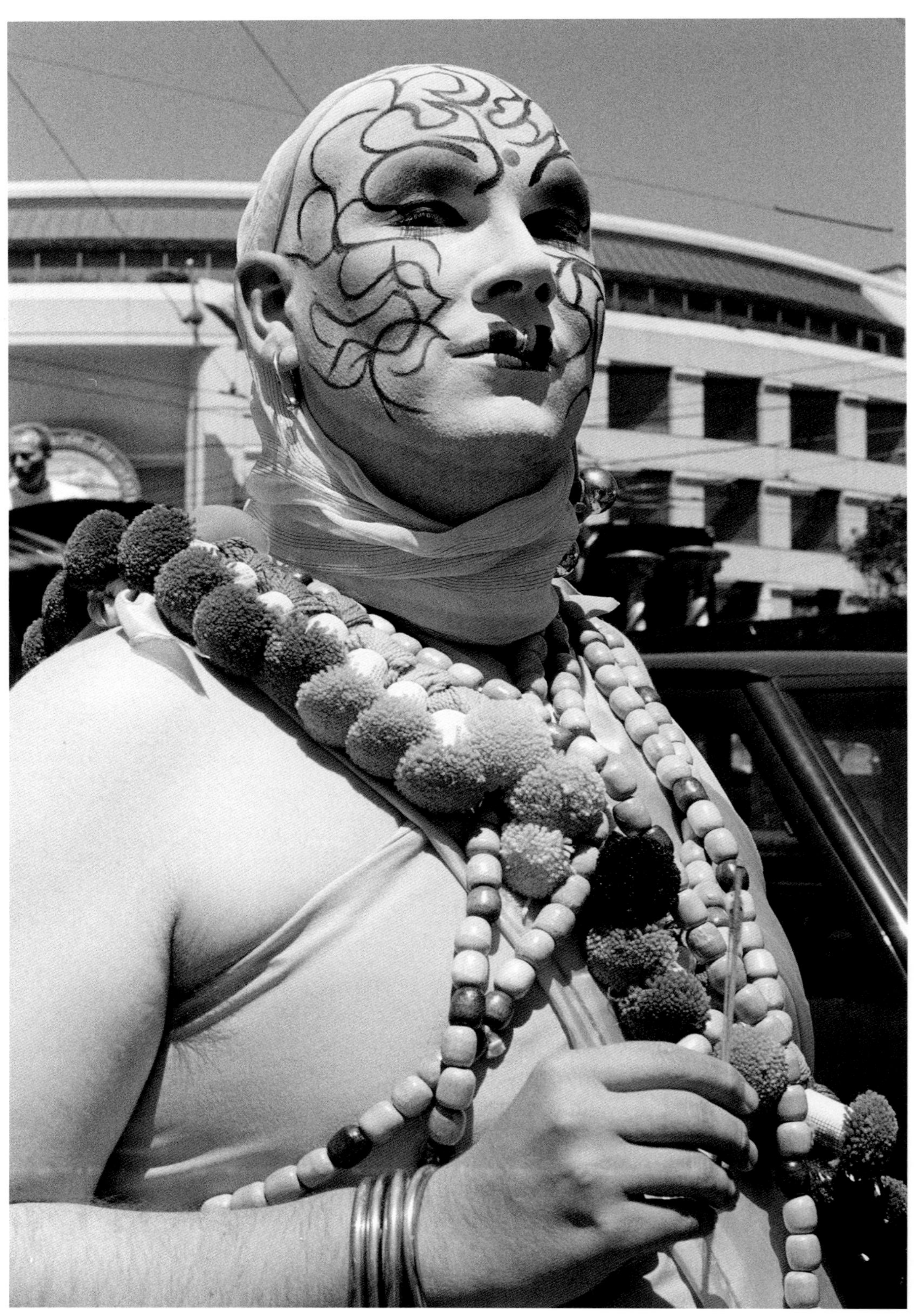

SF LGBT Pride, June 27, 1993. Phatima.

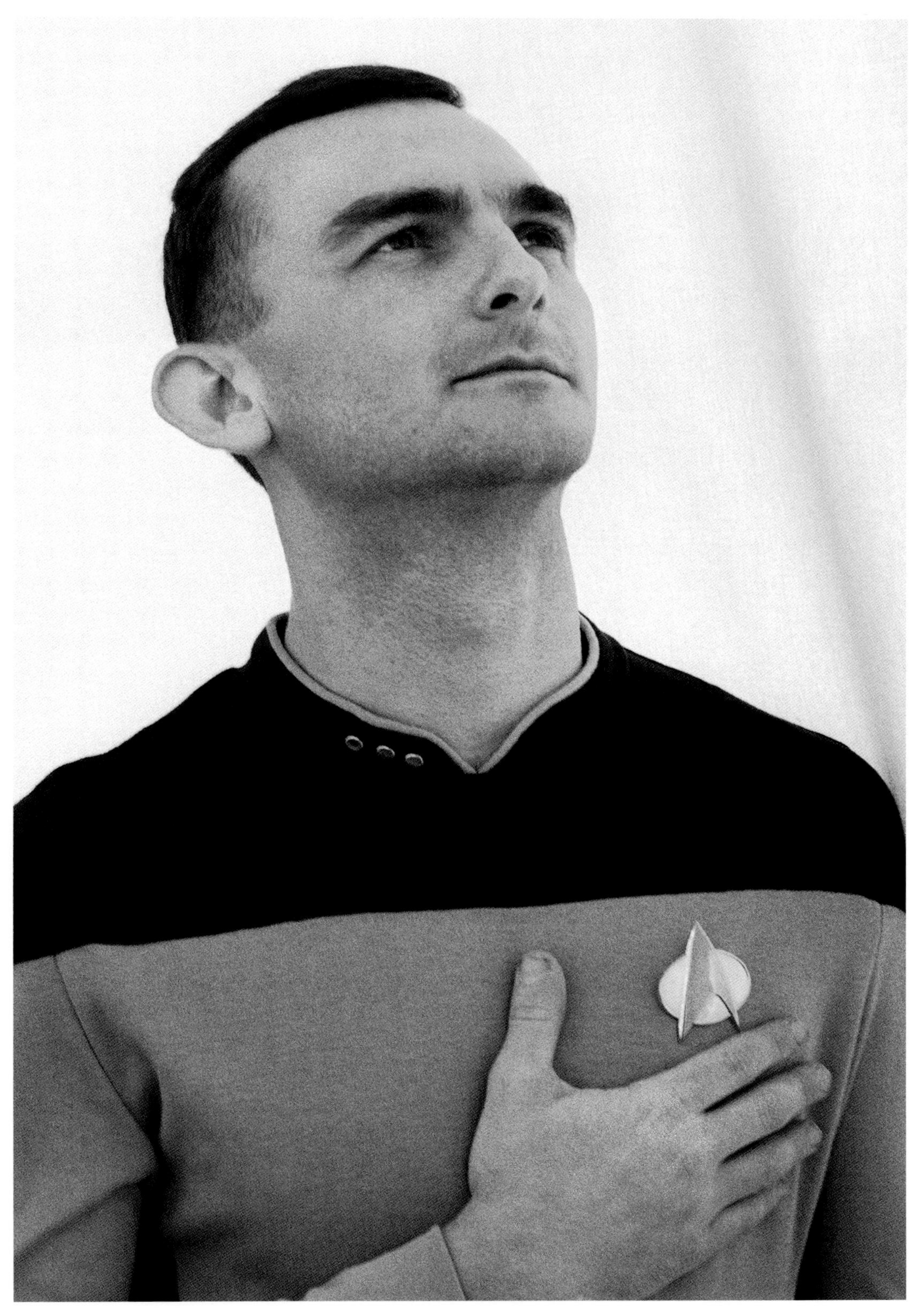

SF LGBT Pride, June 27, 1993. Randy Webb (from the band Gravity).

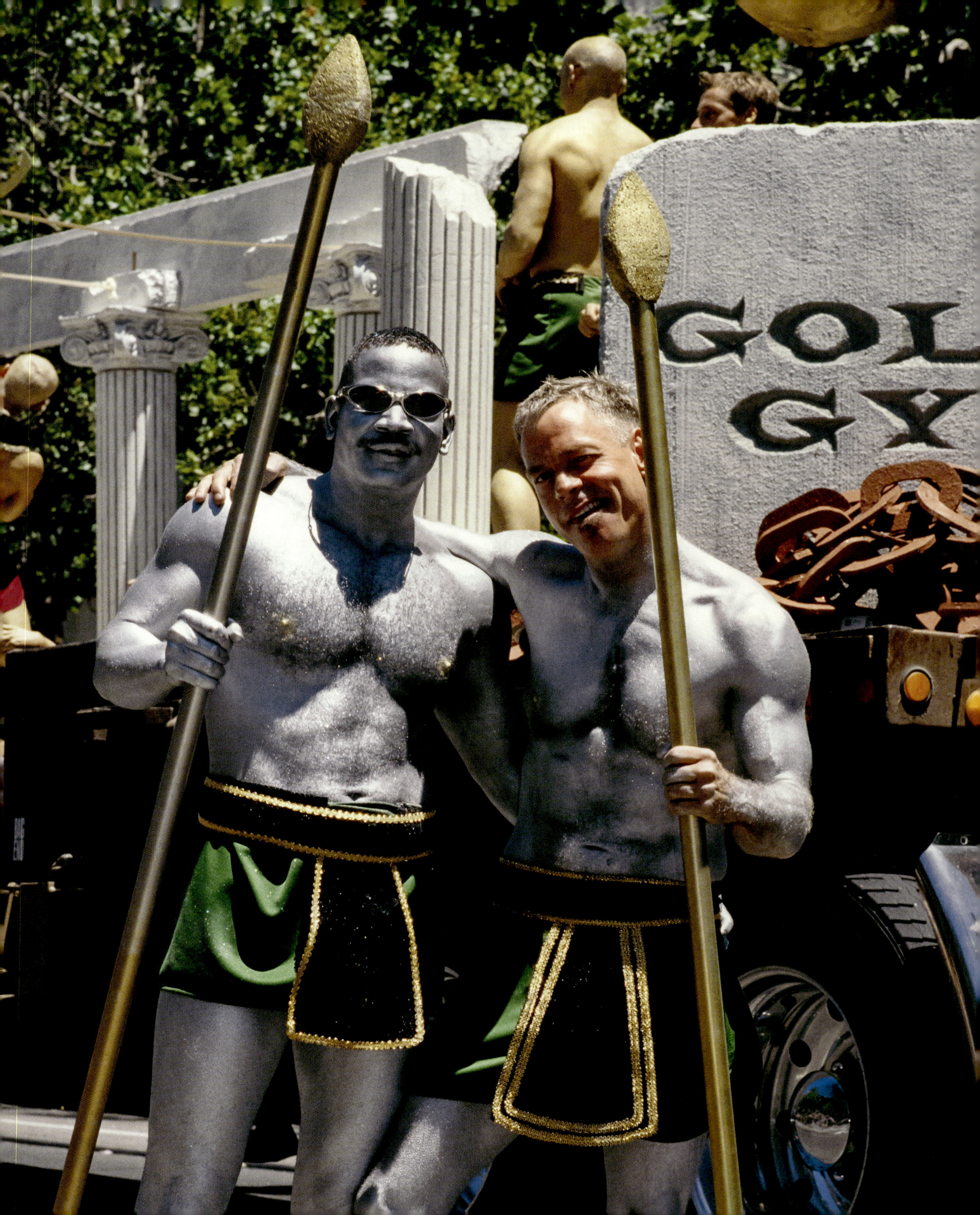

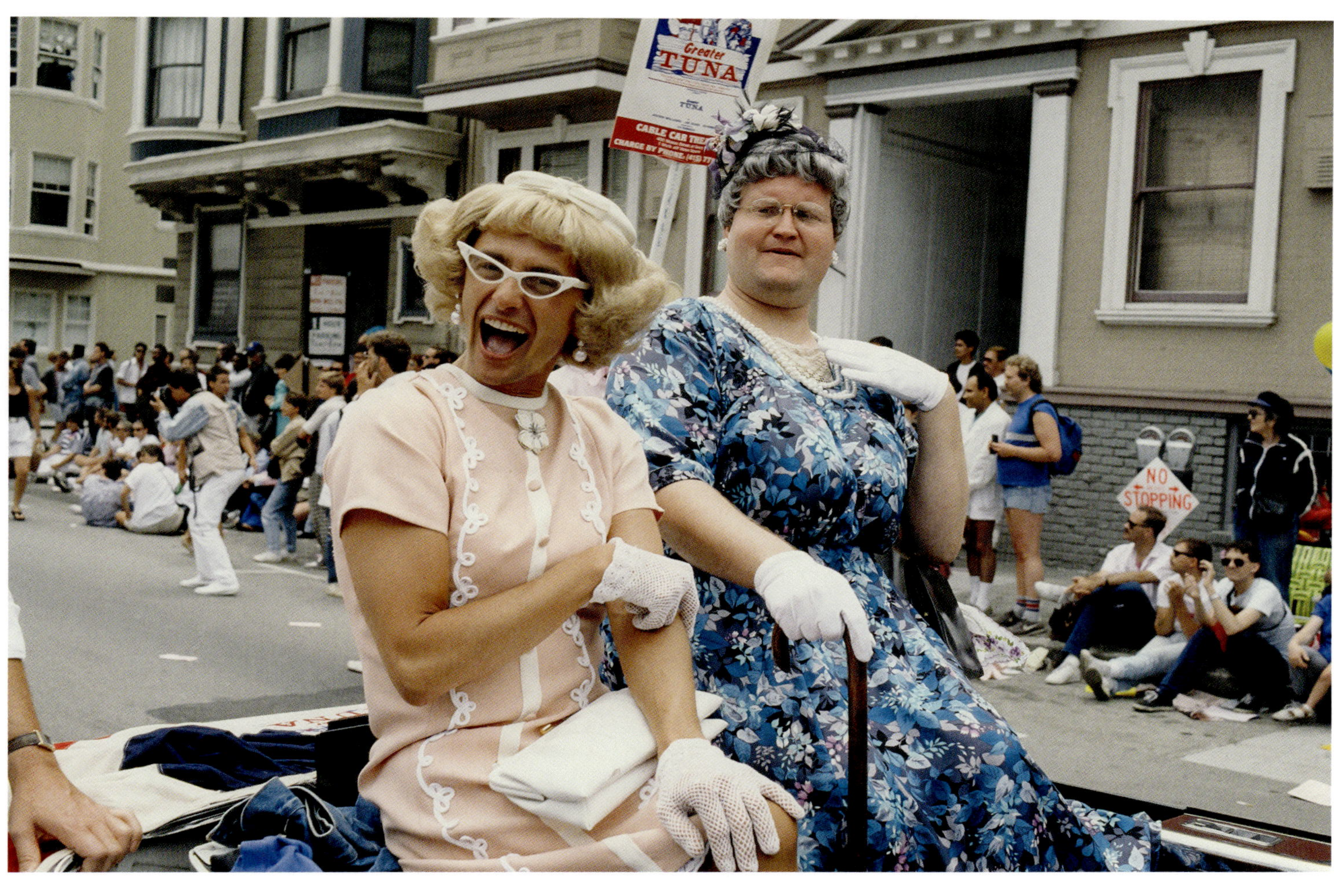

Above: SF LGBT Pride, June 25, 1989. Greater Tuna show, Greg Currie and Chip Steltz.
Opposite: SF LGBT Pride, June 27, 1999. Steve Britt (right) and friend.

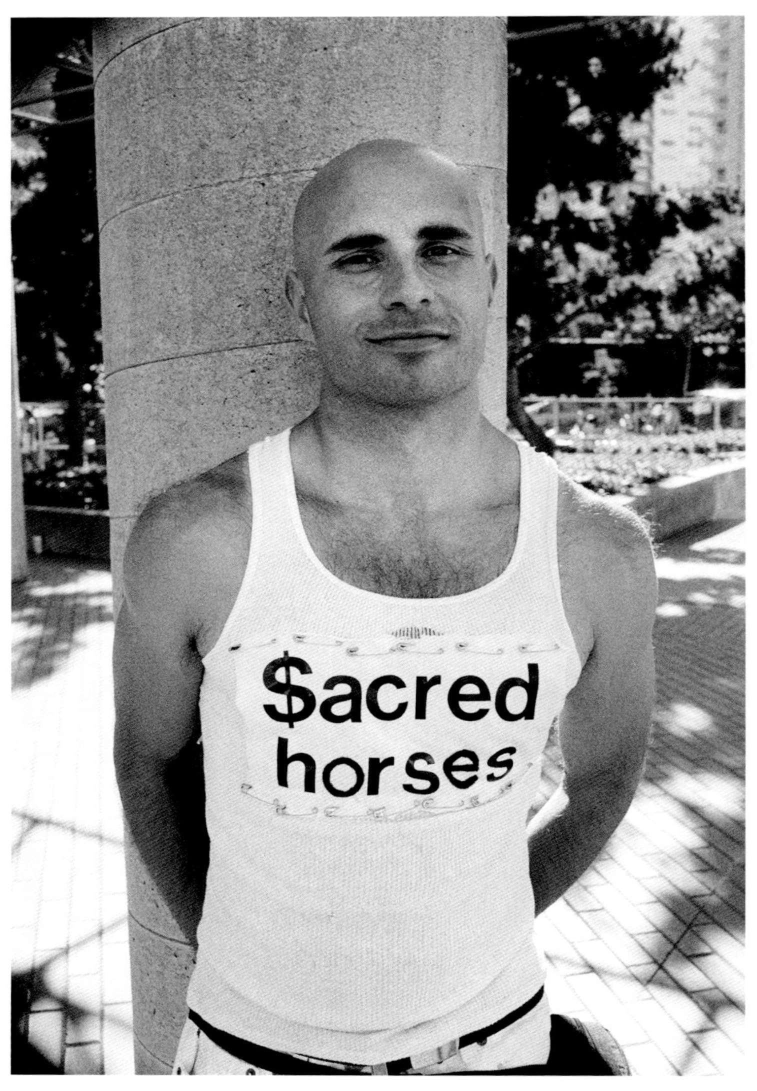

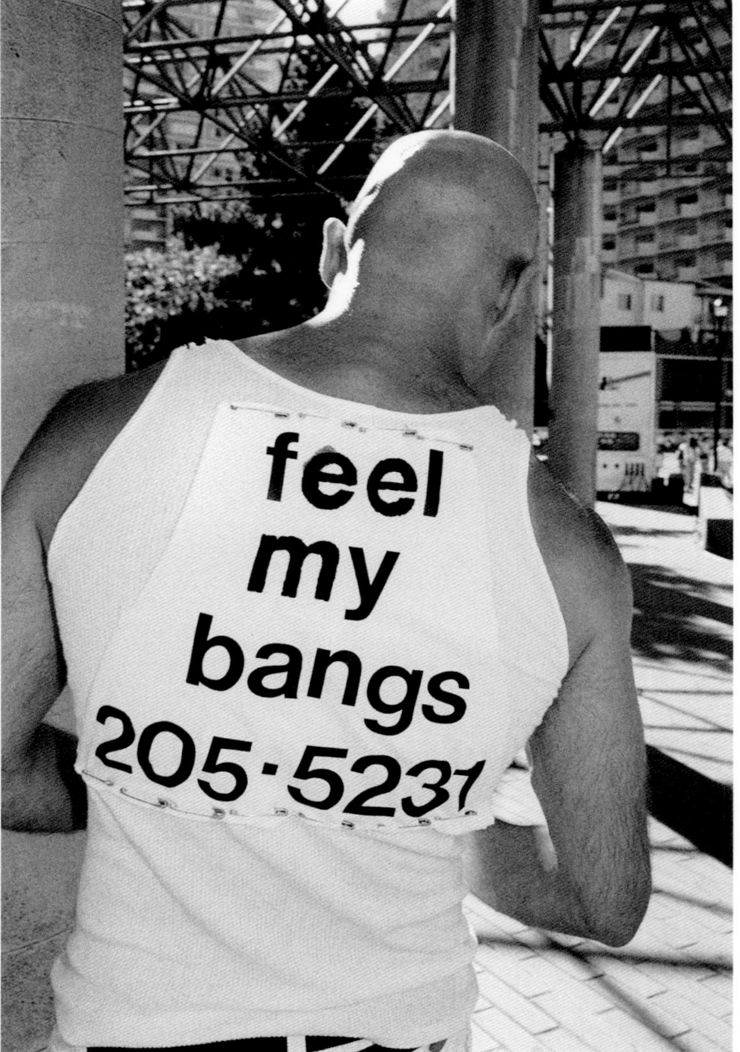

SF LGBT Pride, June 30, 1996. Vic St. Blaise.

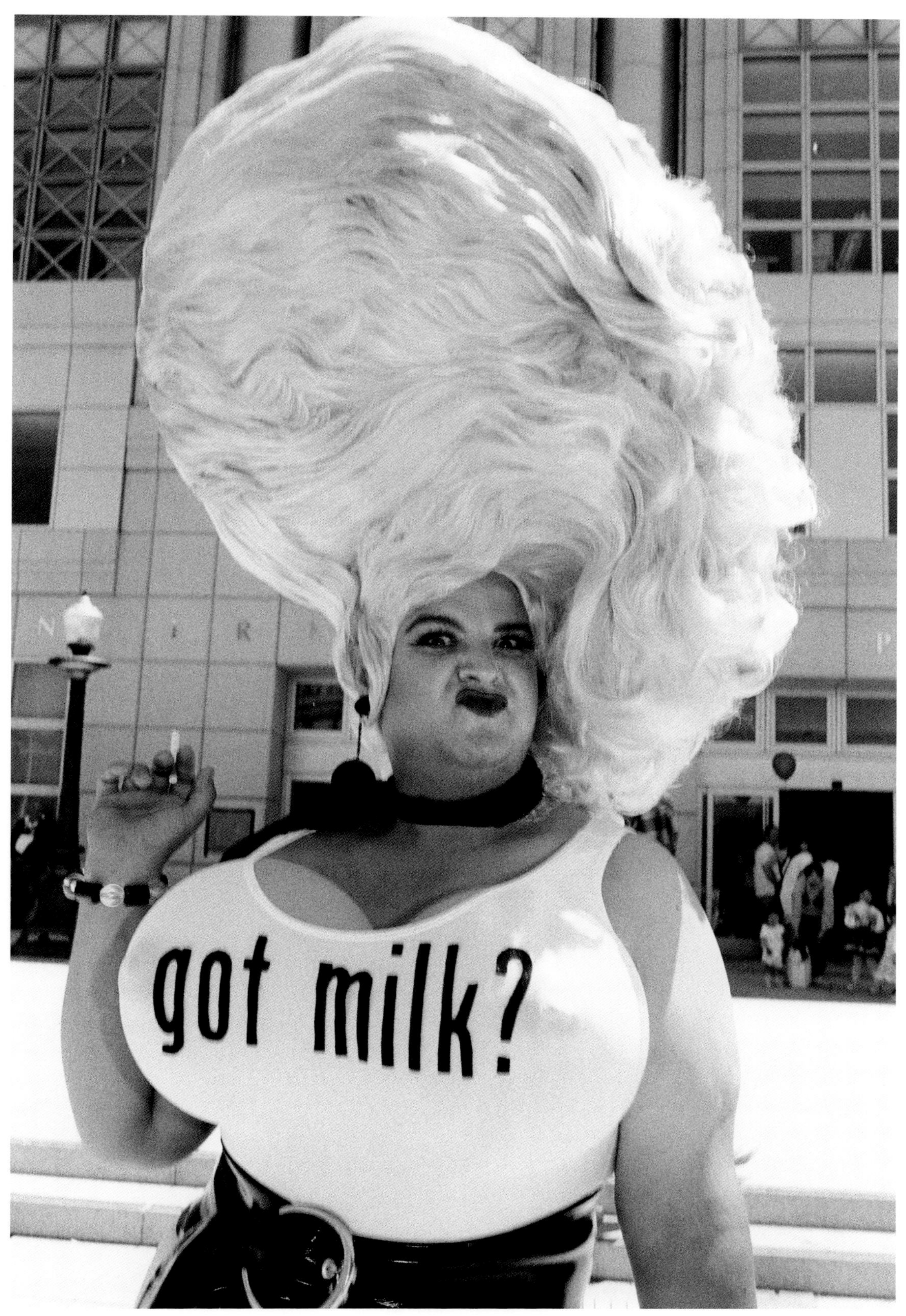

SF LGBT Pride, June 30, 1996. Chris March.

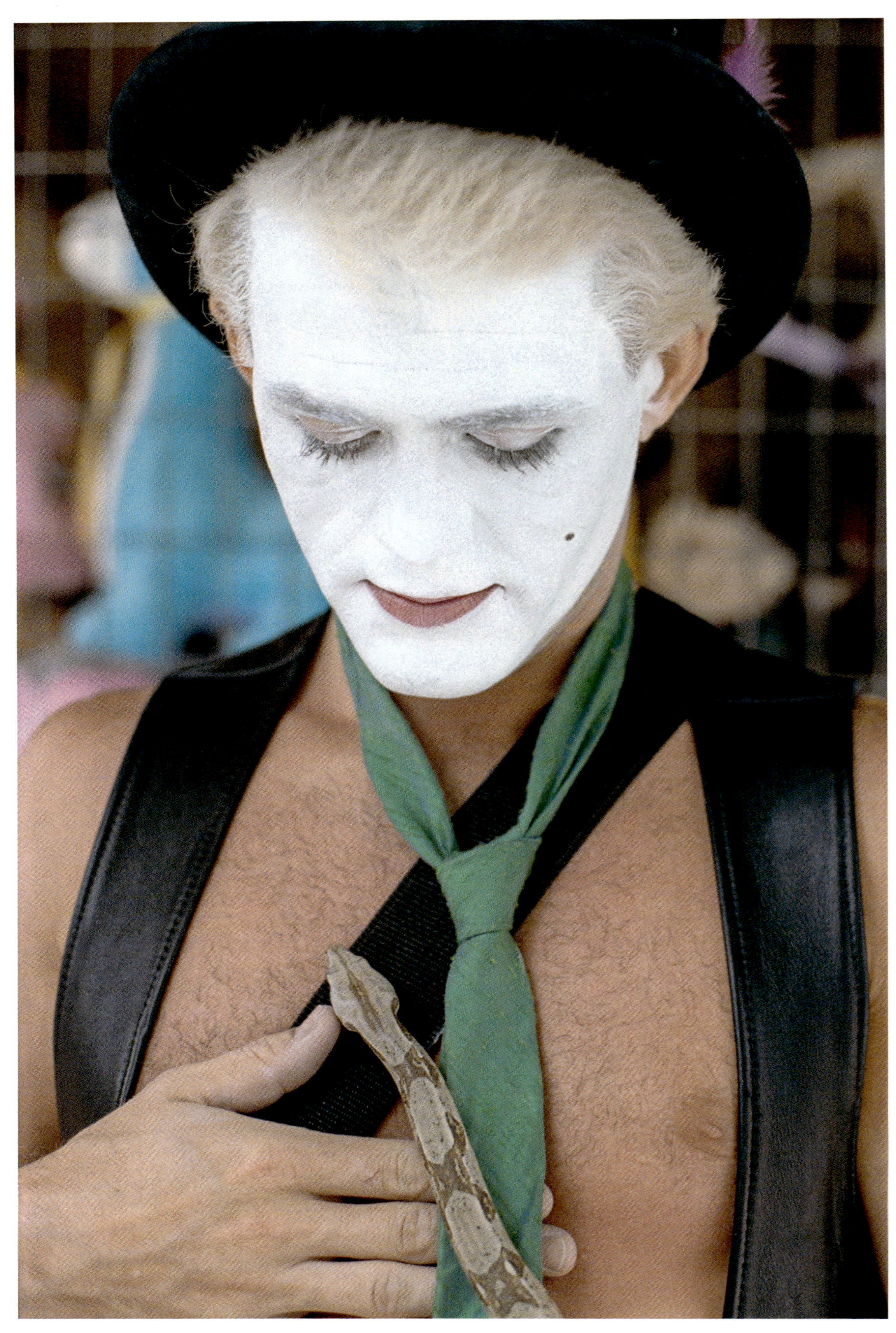

SF LGBT Pride, June 29, 1980.

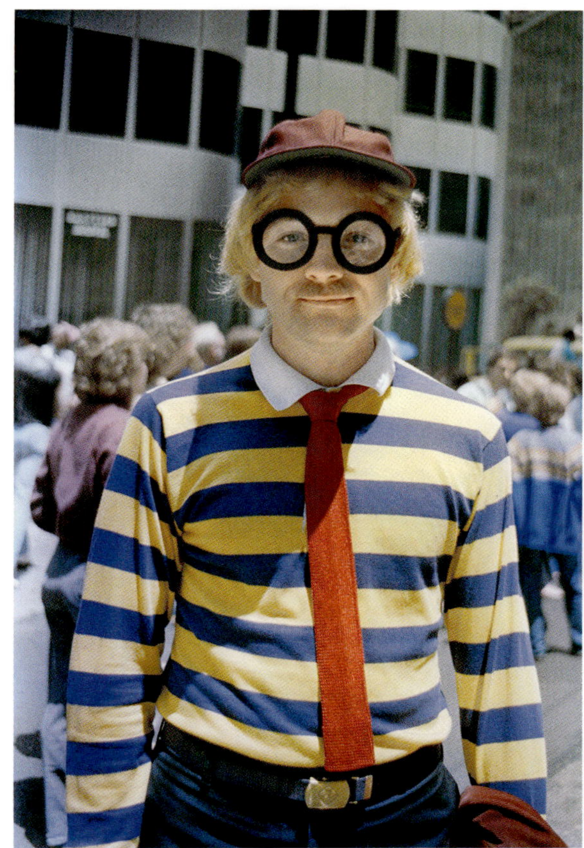

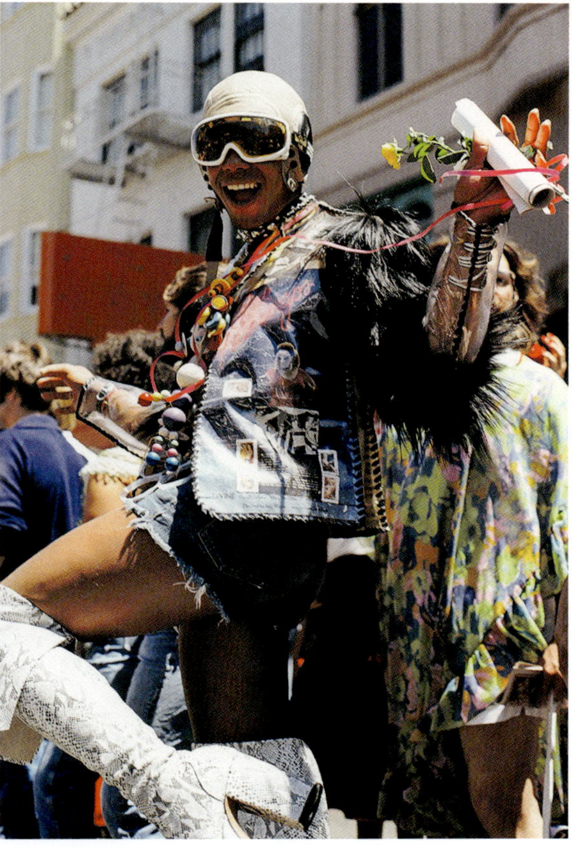

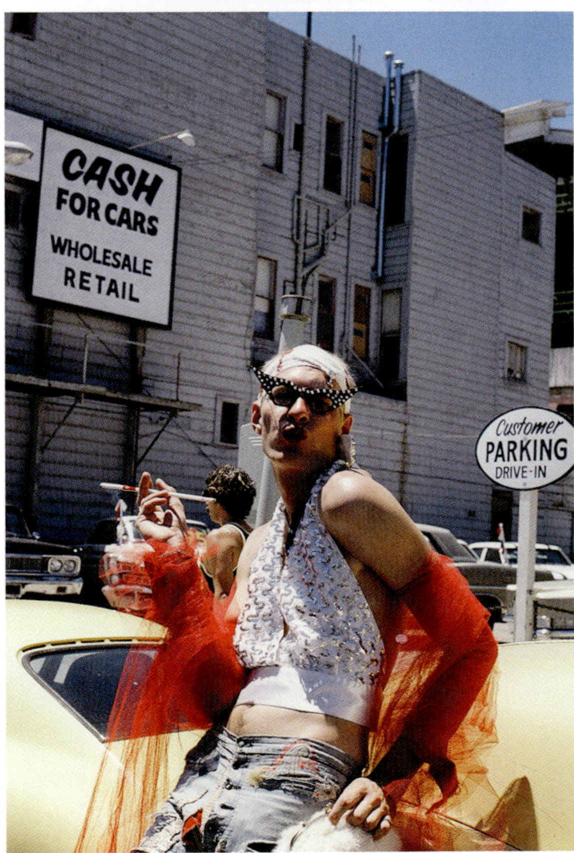

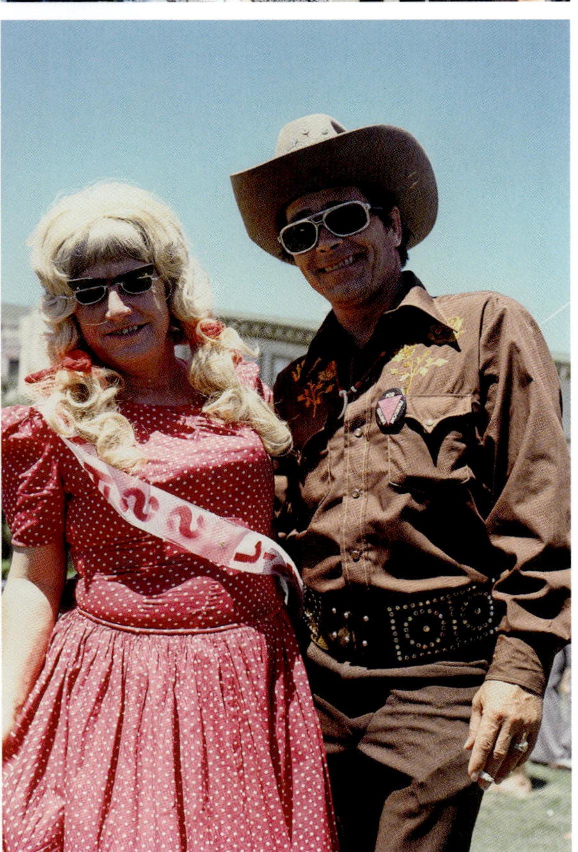

SF LGBT Pride. *(Clockwise from top left)* Robert Morgan as David Hockney, June 27, 1982; Cockette Reggie, aka Anton Dunnigan, June 1975; June 1976 (both).

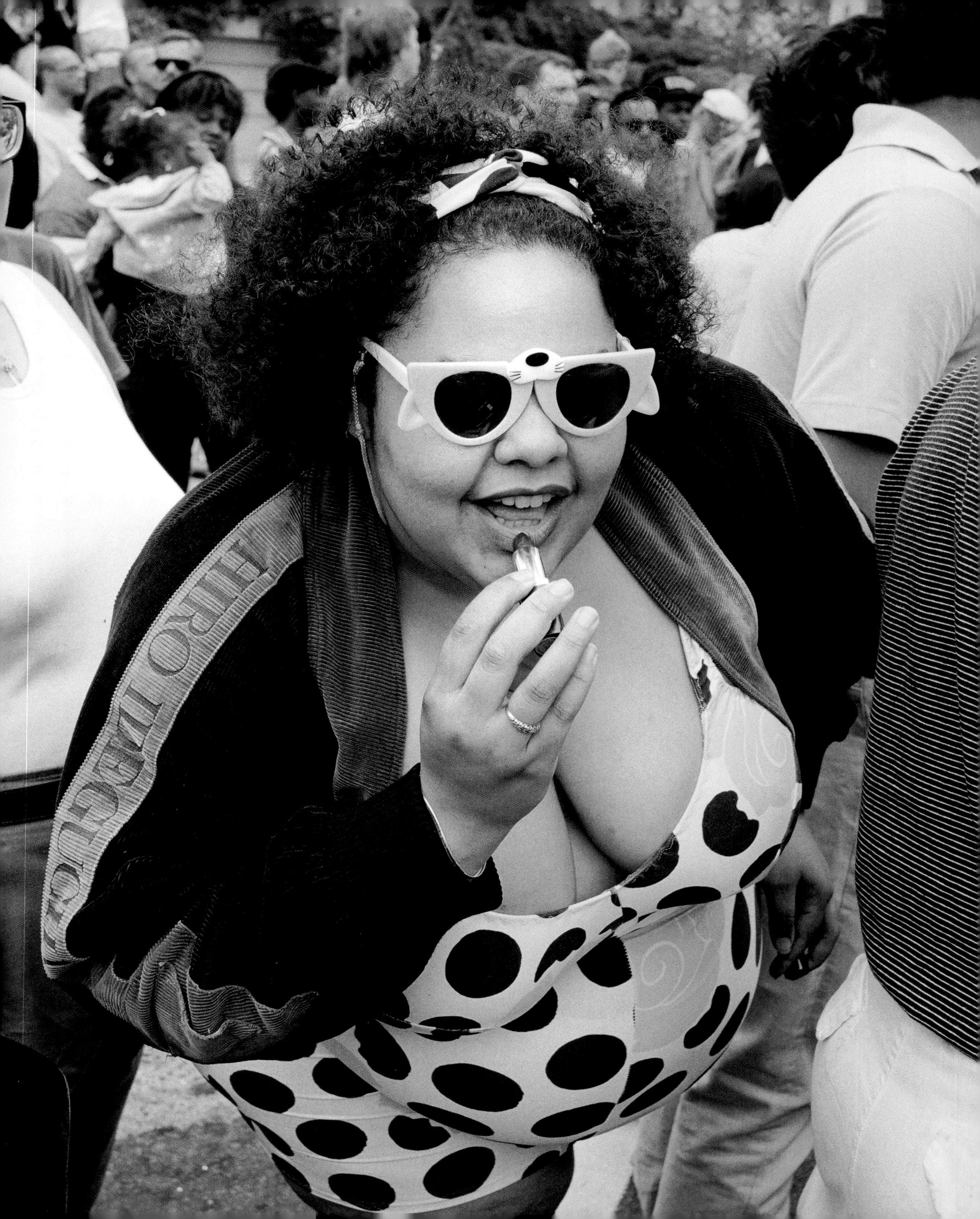

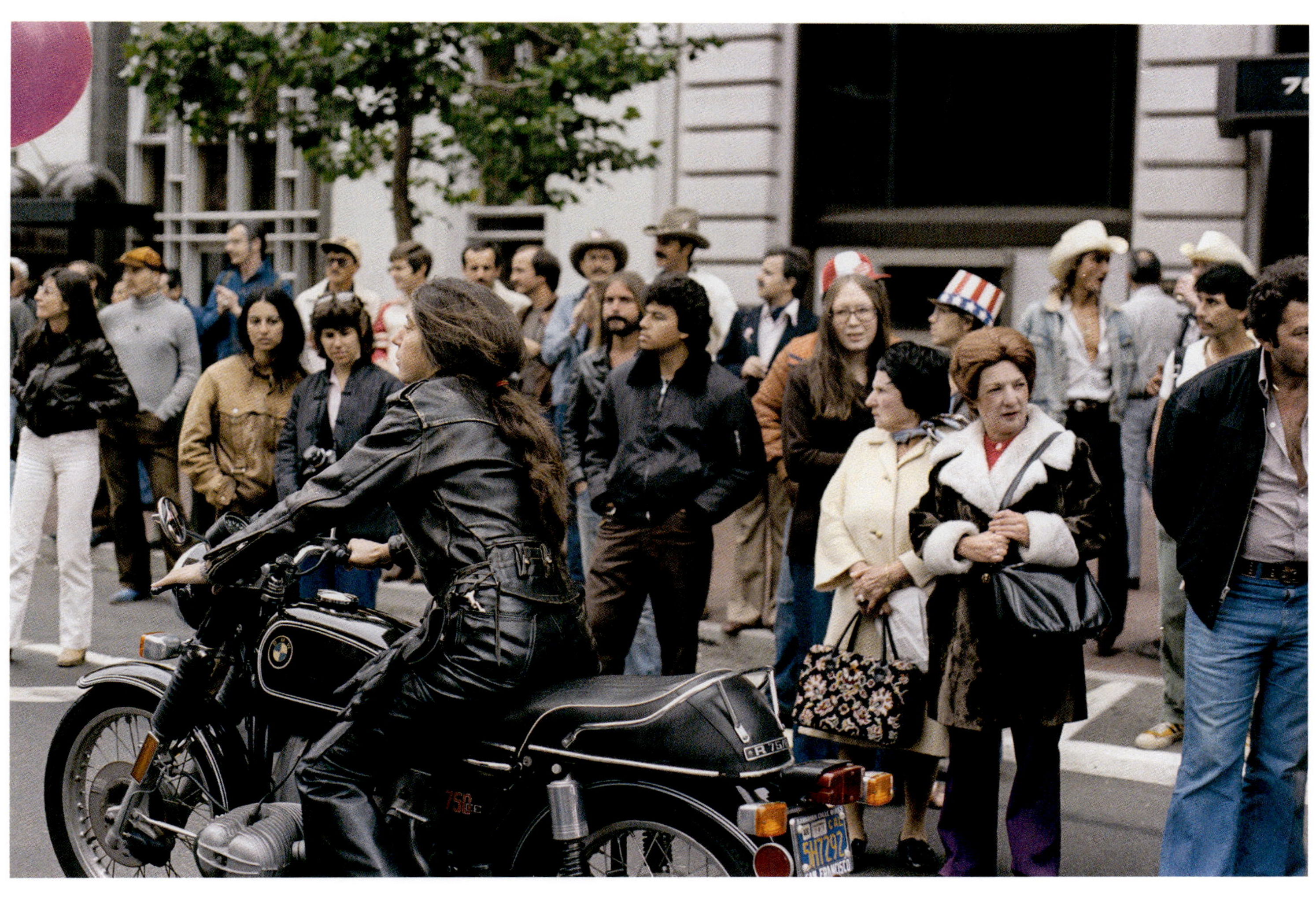

Above: SF LGBT Pride, June 24, 1979. Joyce Garay.
Opposite: SF LGBT Pride, June 25, 1986.

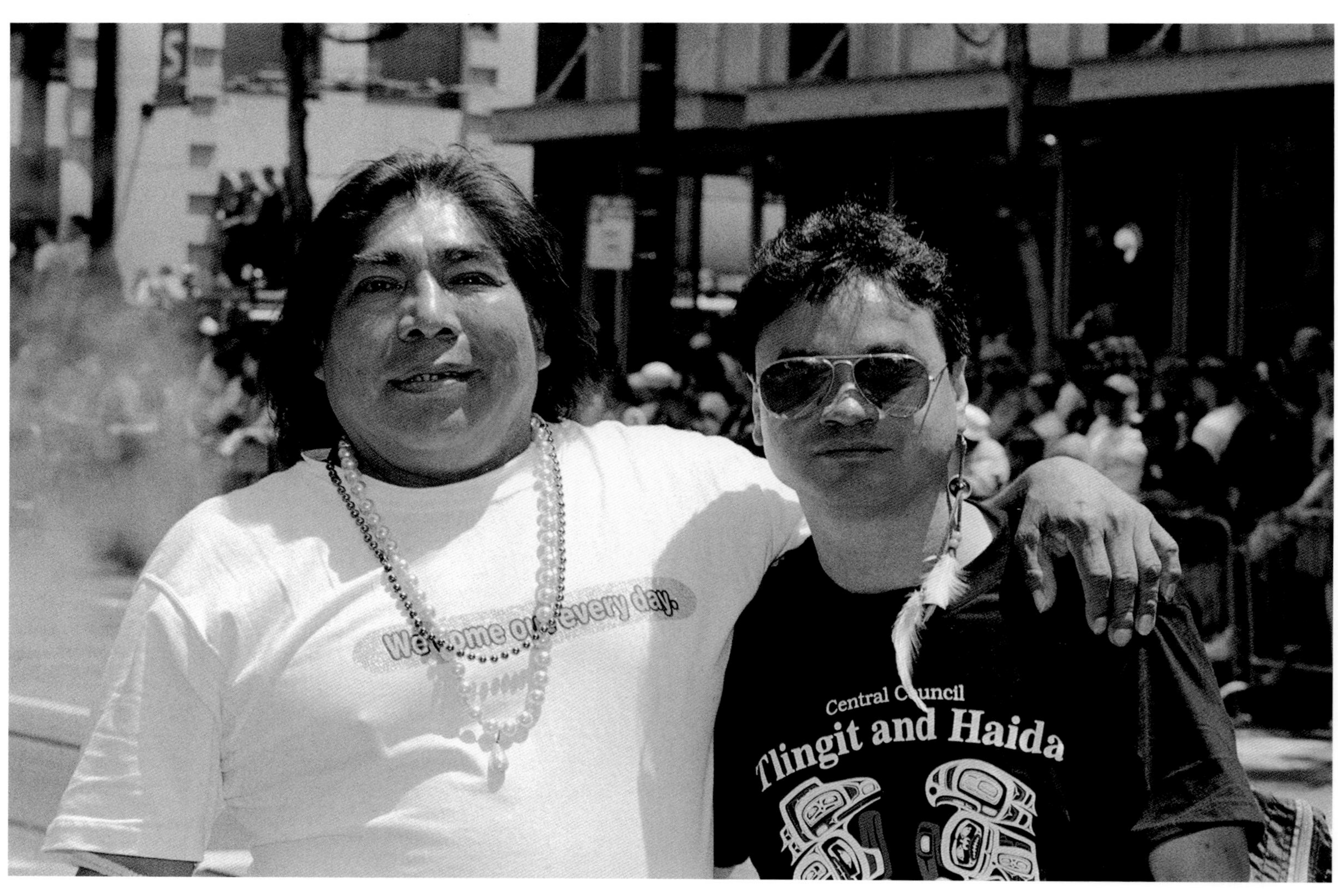

Above: SF LGBT Pride, June 25, 2000. Randy P. Burns (Pyramid Lake Paiute Tribe and co-founder of Gay American Indians in 1975) and Bambi Raven Littlefeather (Tlingit Nation, Takdeintaan Raven Clan).
Opposite: SF Dyke March, June 24, 2000. Ruth Villasenor (Chiricahua Apache and Mexican Tribes and Bay Area American Indian Two Spirit member).

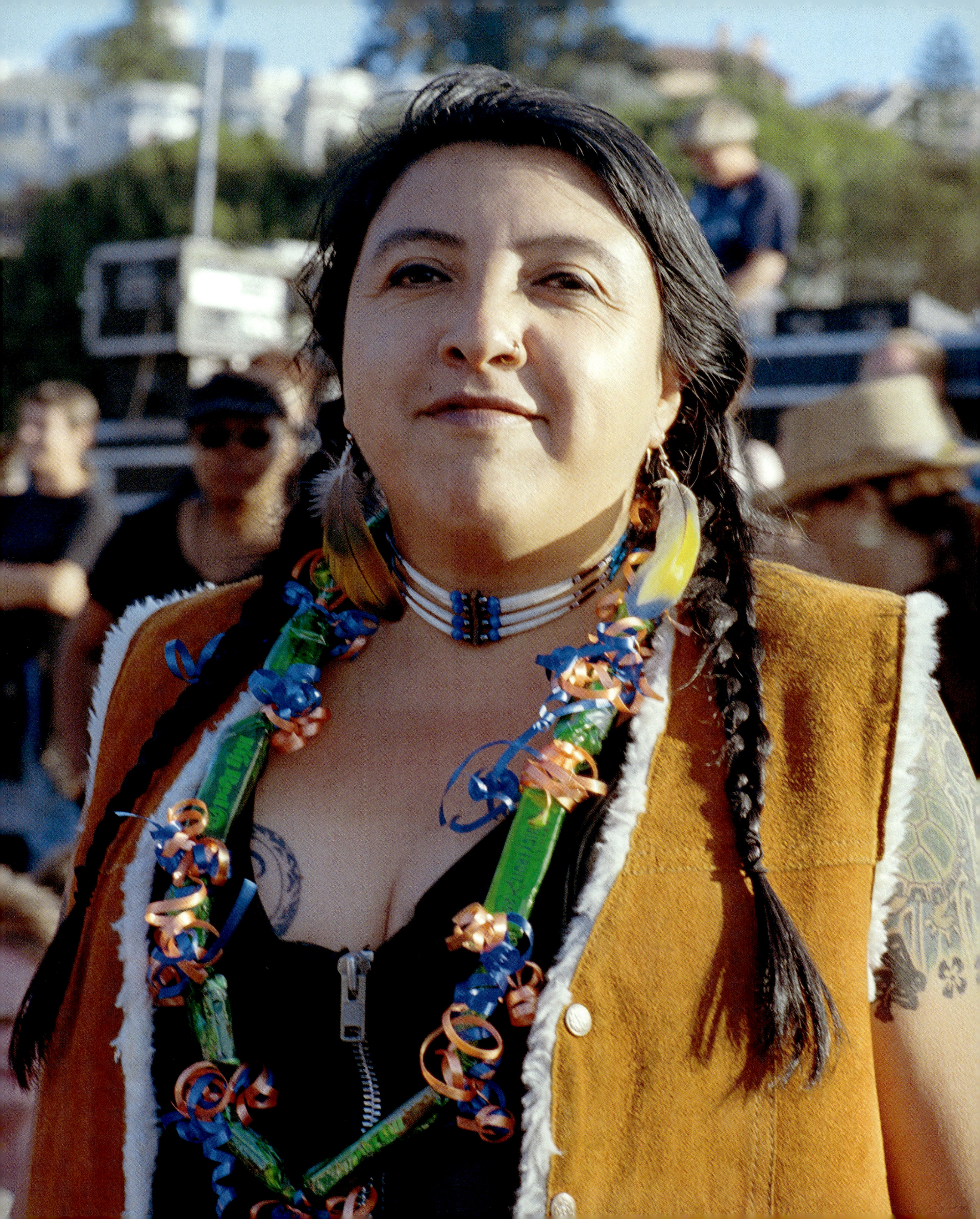

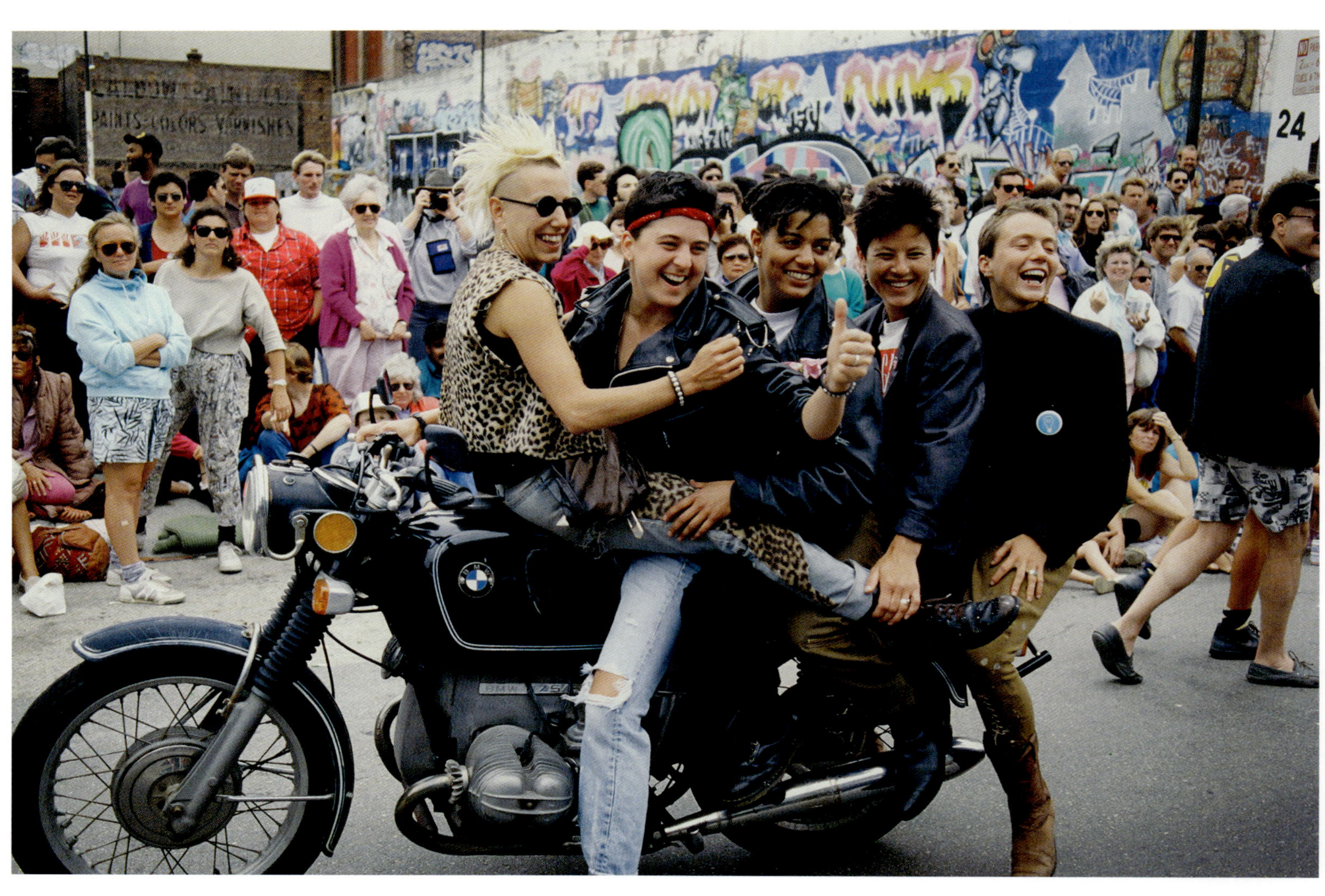

Above: SF LGBT Pride, June 25, 1989.
Opposite: SF LGBT Pride, June 24, 2001. The Stud bar float, Portia Peeples.

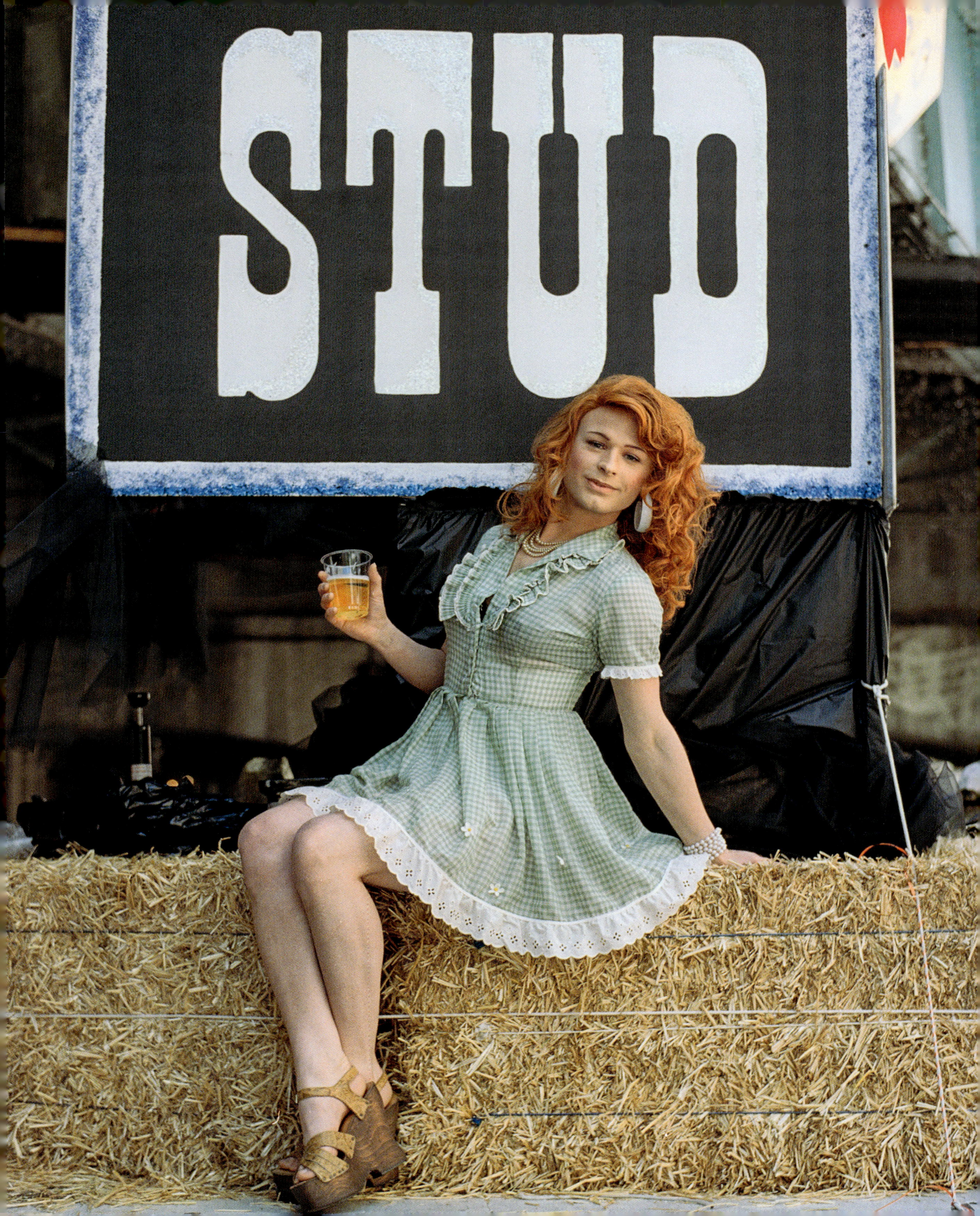
STUD

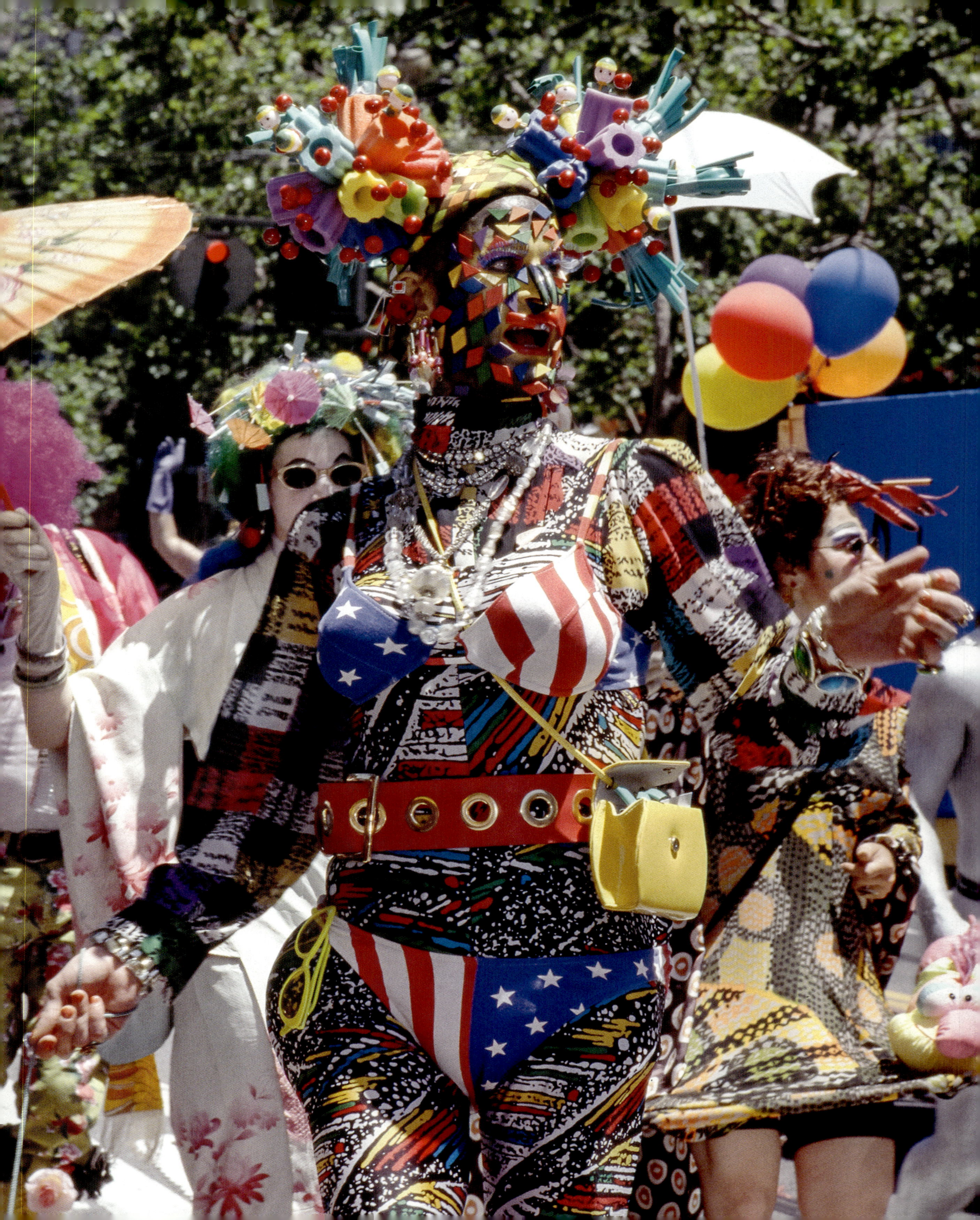

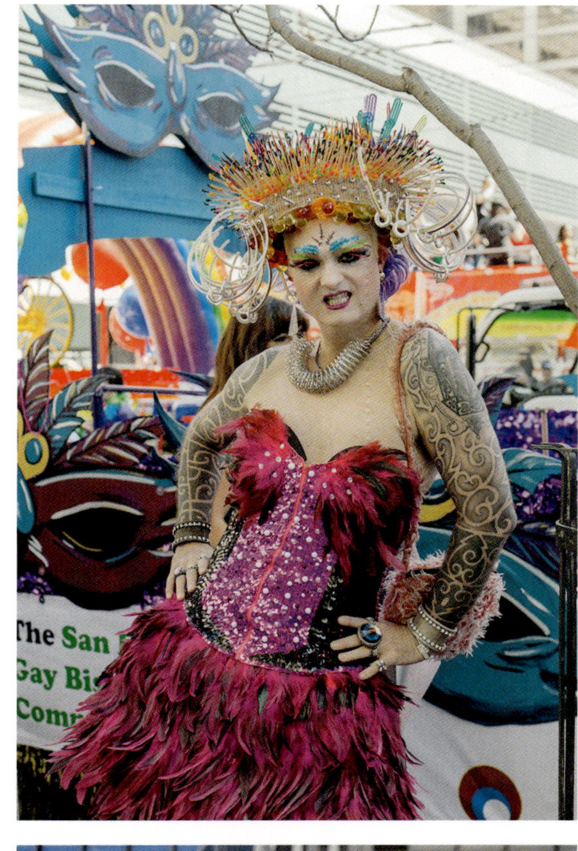

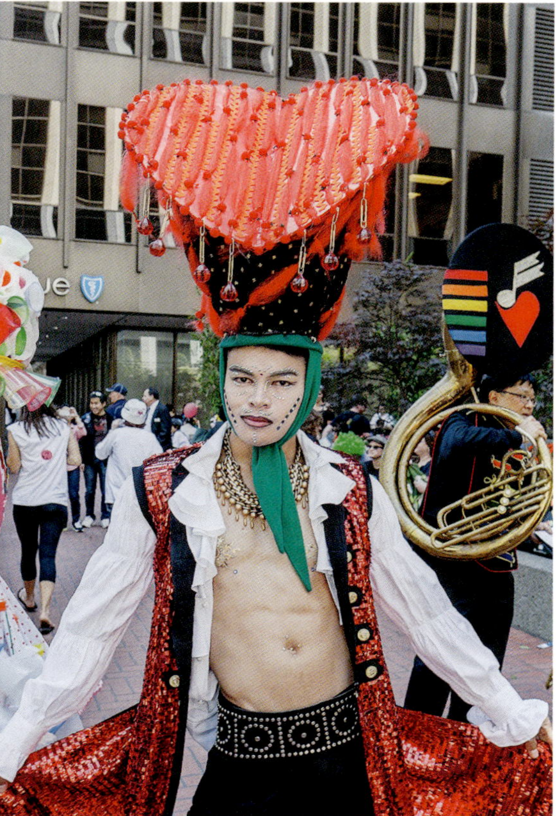

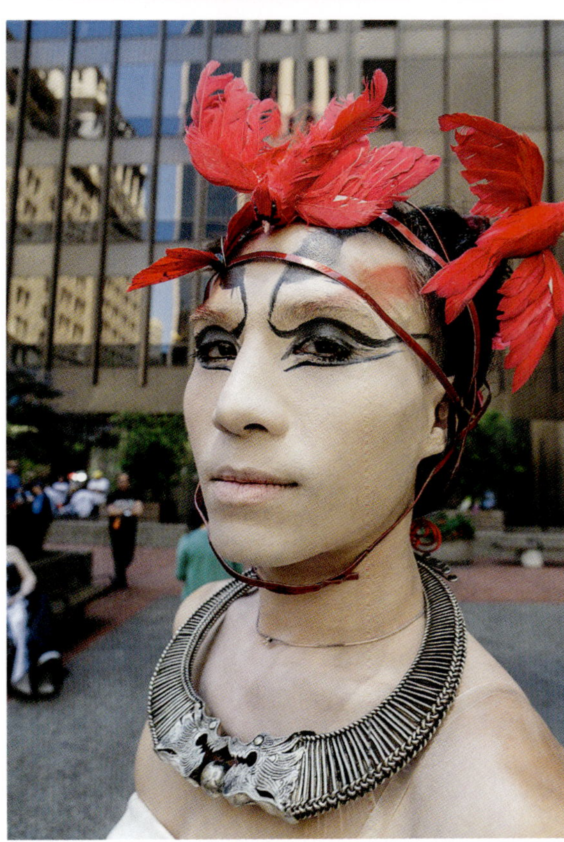

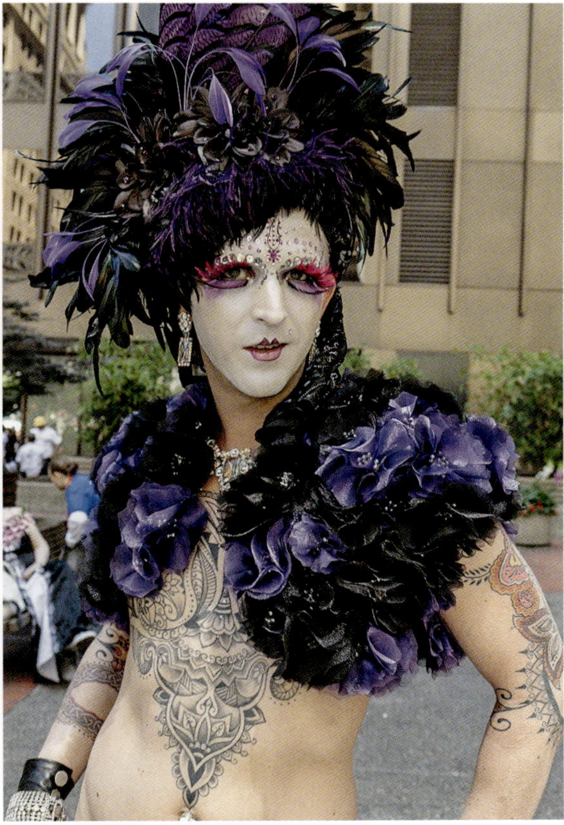

Above: SF LGBT Pride, June 2011 and 2012. Verasphere
(Clockwise from top left): Cameron, Roger Madayung, Sean Lord, Ethan Raysvag.
Opposite: SF LGBT Pride, June 27, 1999. Verasphere; Mrs. Vera (aka David Faulk, co-founder of Verasphere).

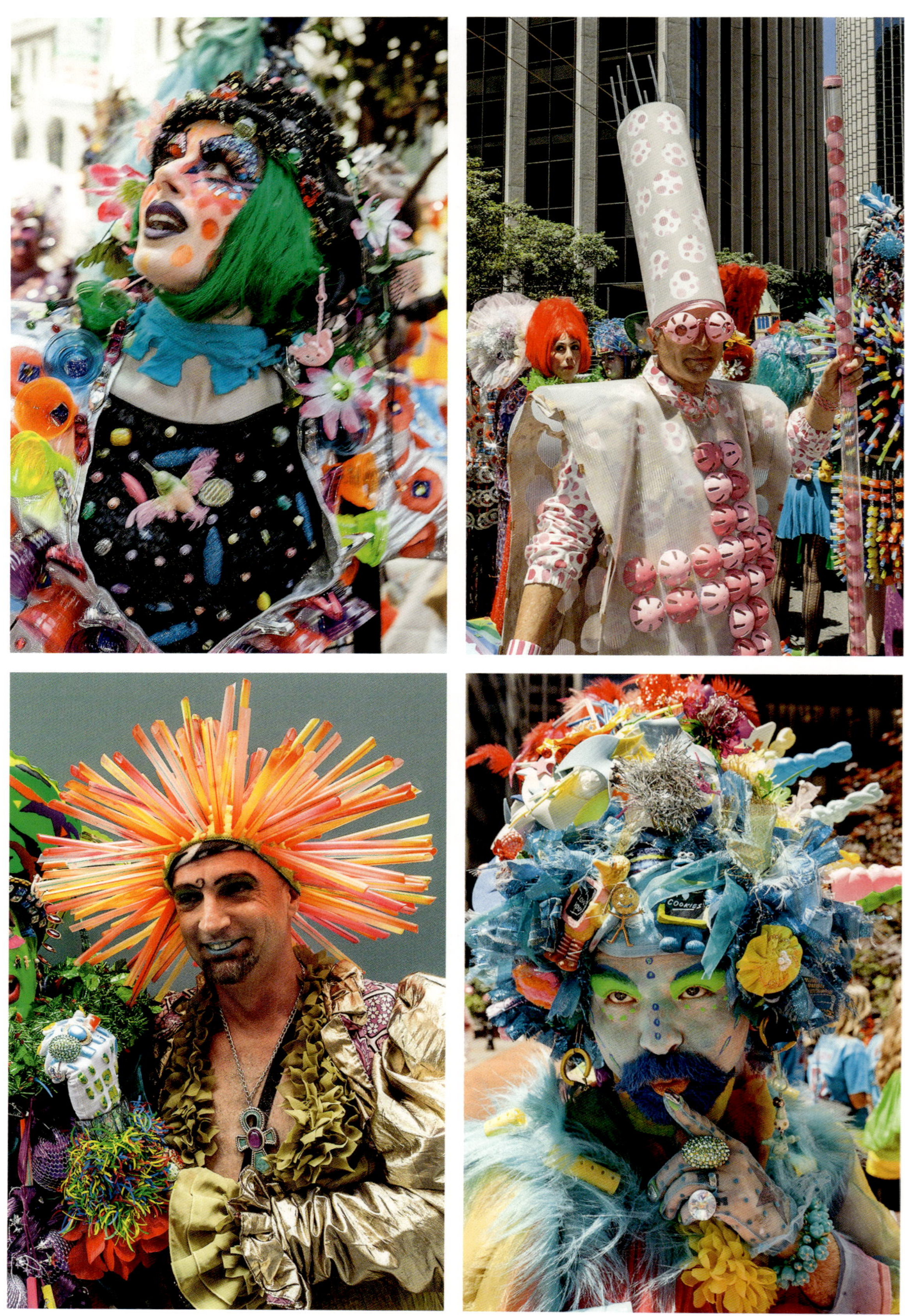

Above: SF LGBT Pride, June 2008 to 2012. Verasphere *(Clockwise from top left)*: Elron Hubby, Bruce Beaudette, Ginger Snap, Teena (aka Michael Johnstone, co-founder of Verasphere).
Opposite: SF LGBT Pride, June 28, 1998. Verasphere; Dale Van Dusen.

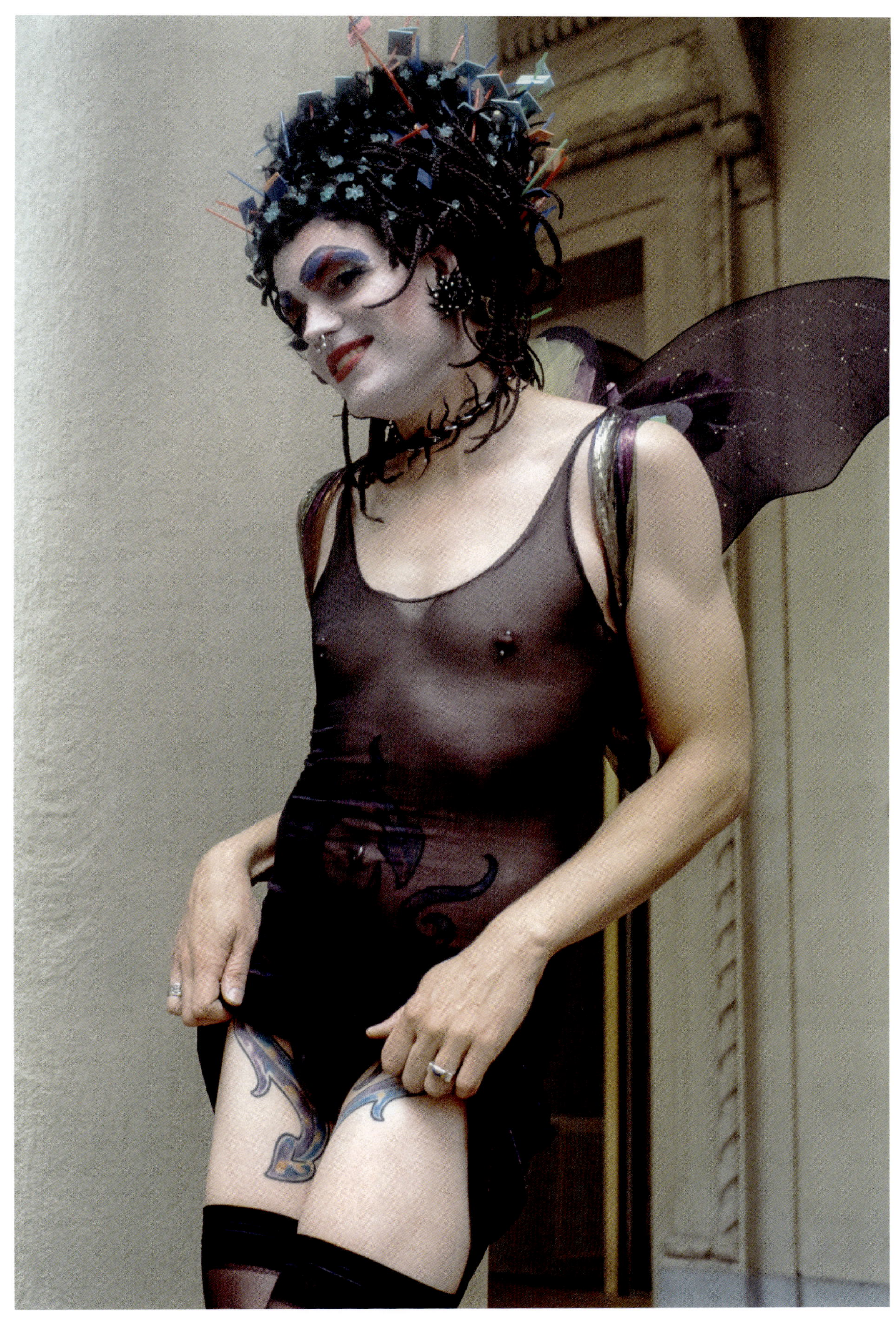

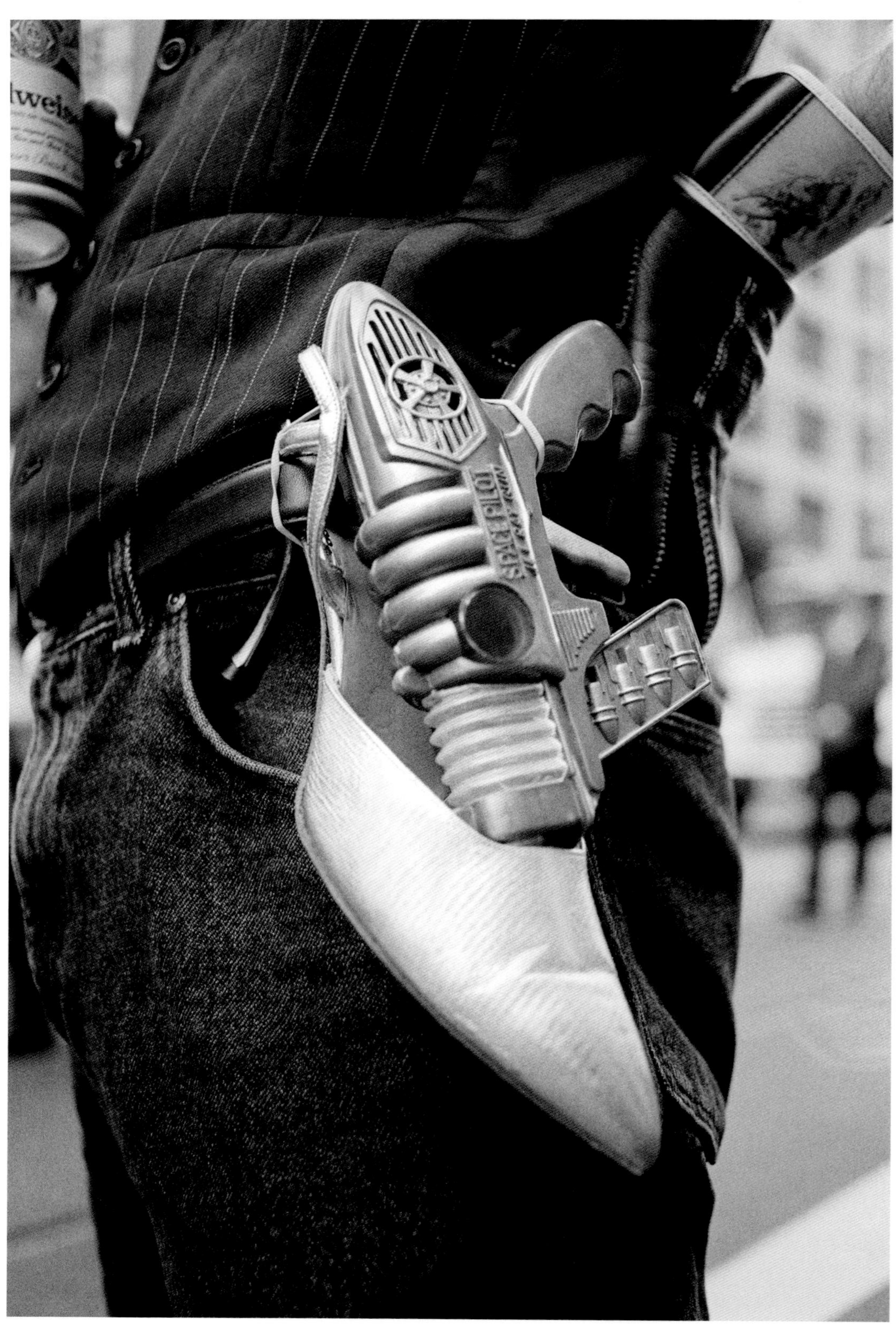

SF LGBT Pride, June 28, 1992. Scorchy's holster.

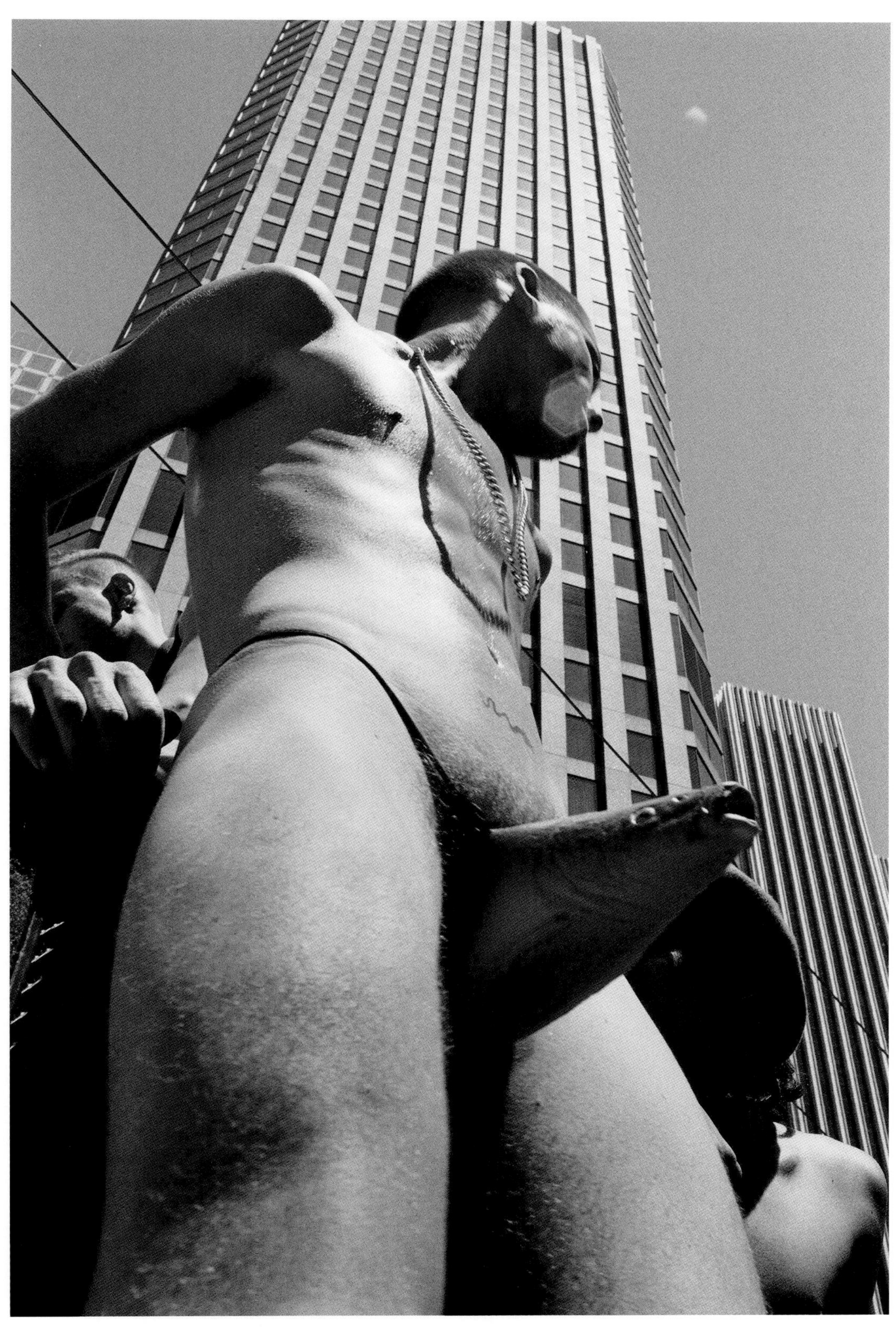

SF LGBT Pride, June 30, 1991. The EndUp bar float (Klubstitute and Club Uranus), Drew Macaroni n Cheese.

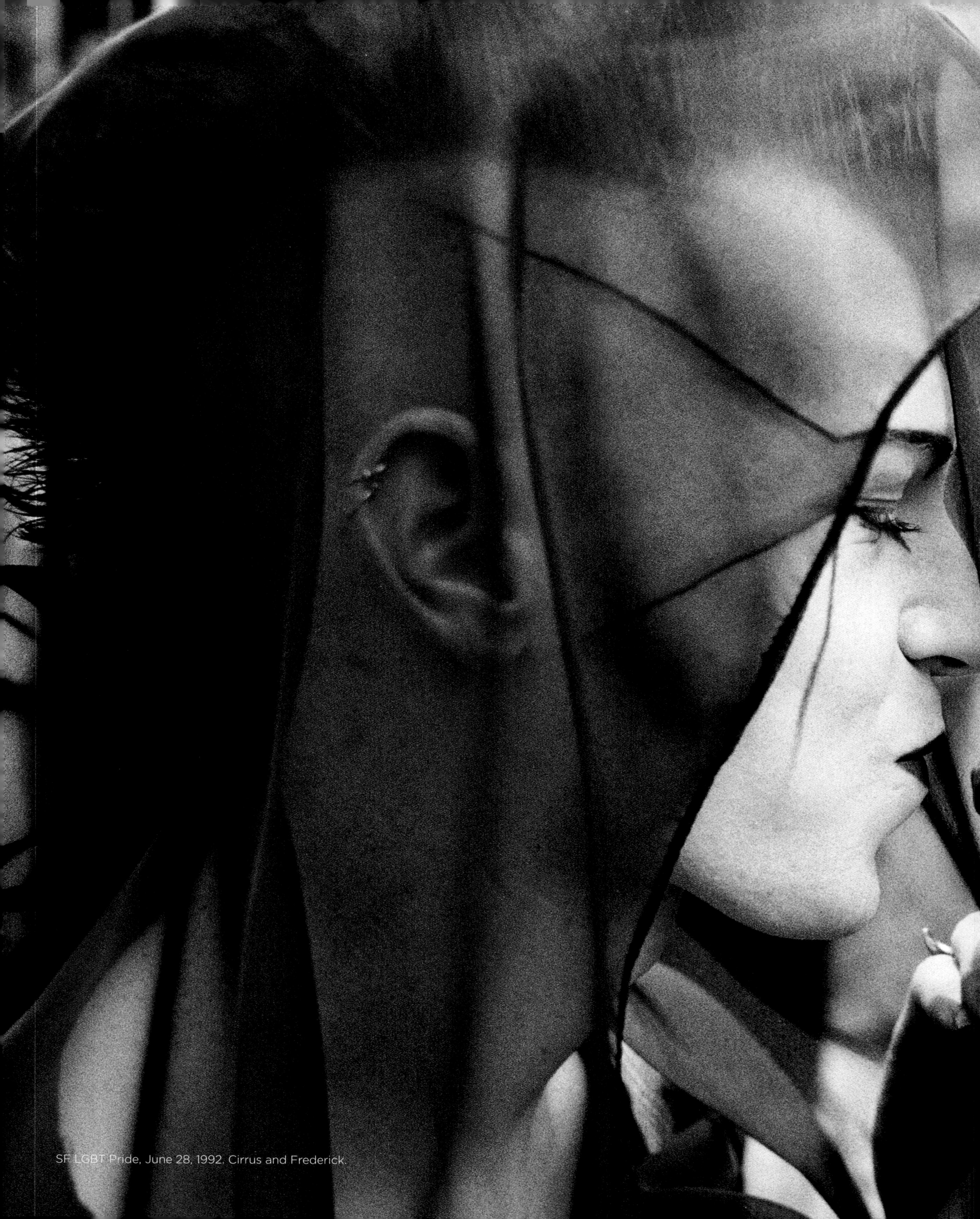

SF LGBT Pride, June 28, 1992. Cirrus and Frederick.

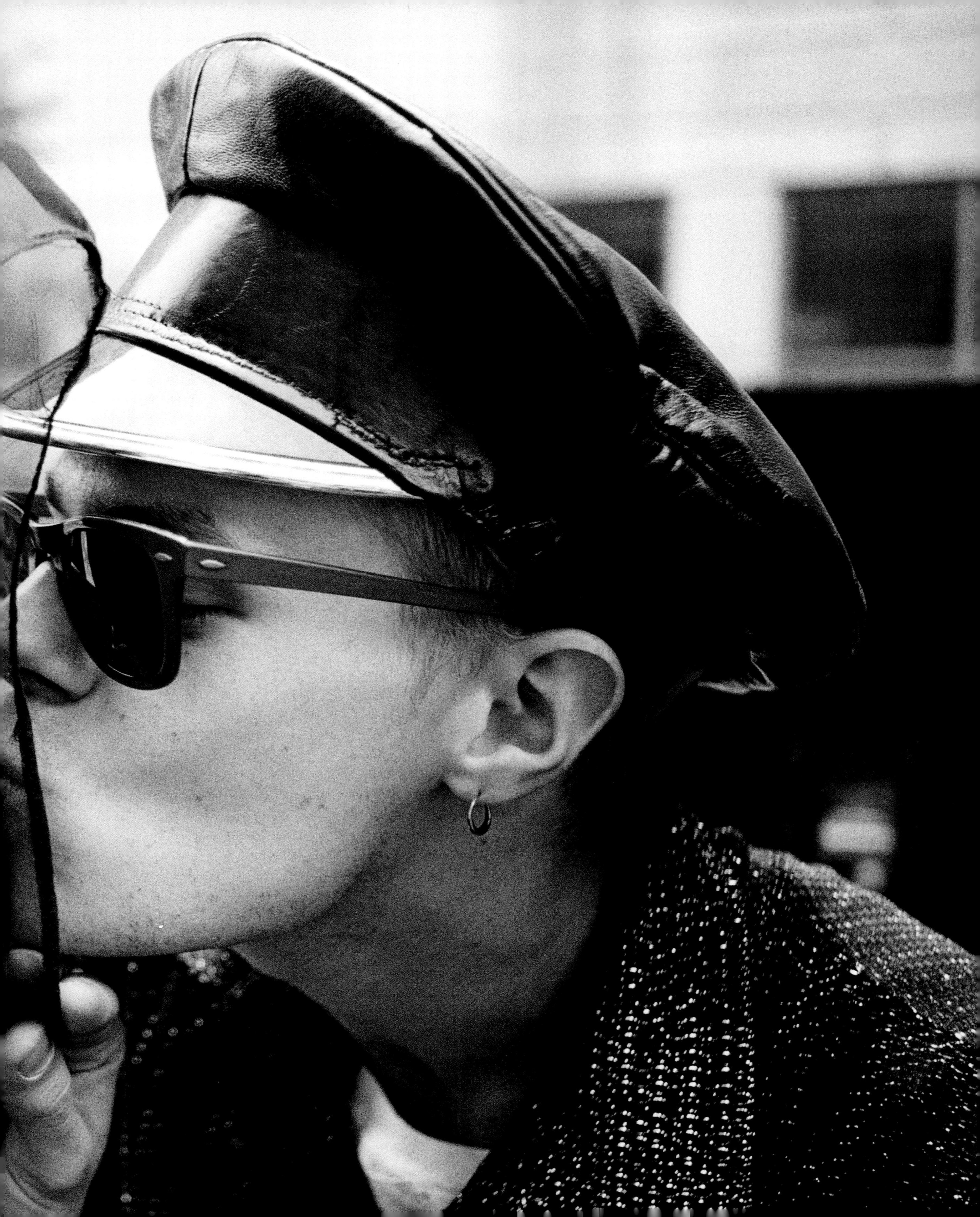

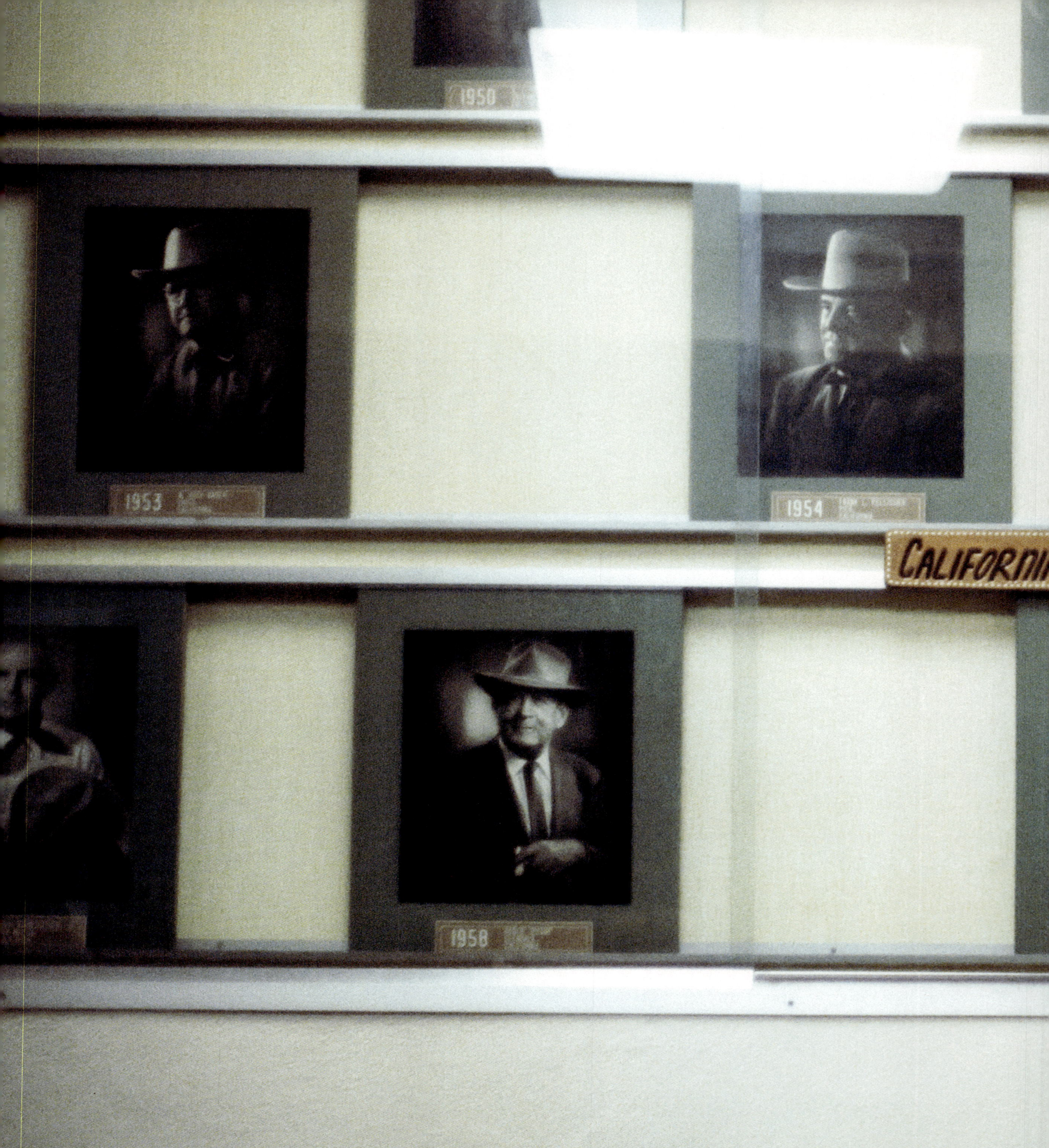

David Bowie concert at the Cow Palace auditorium, 1976. Kent Denning.

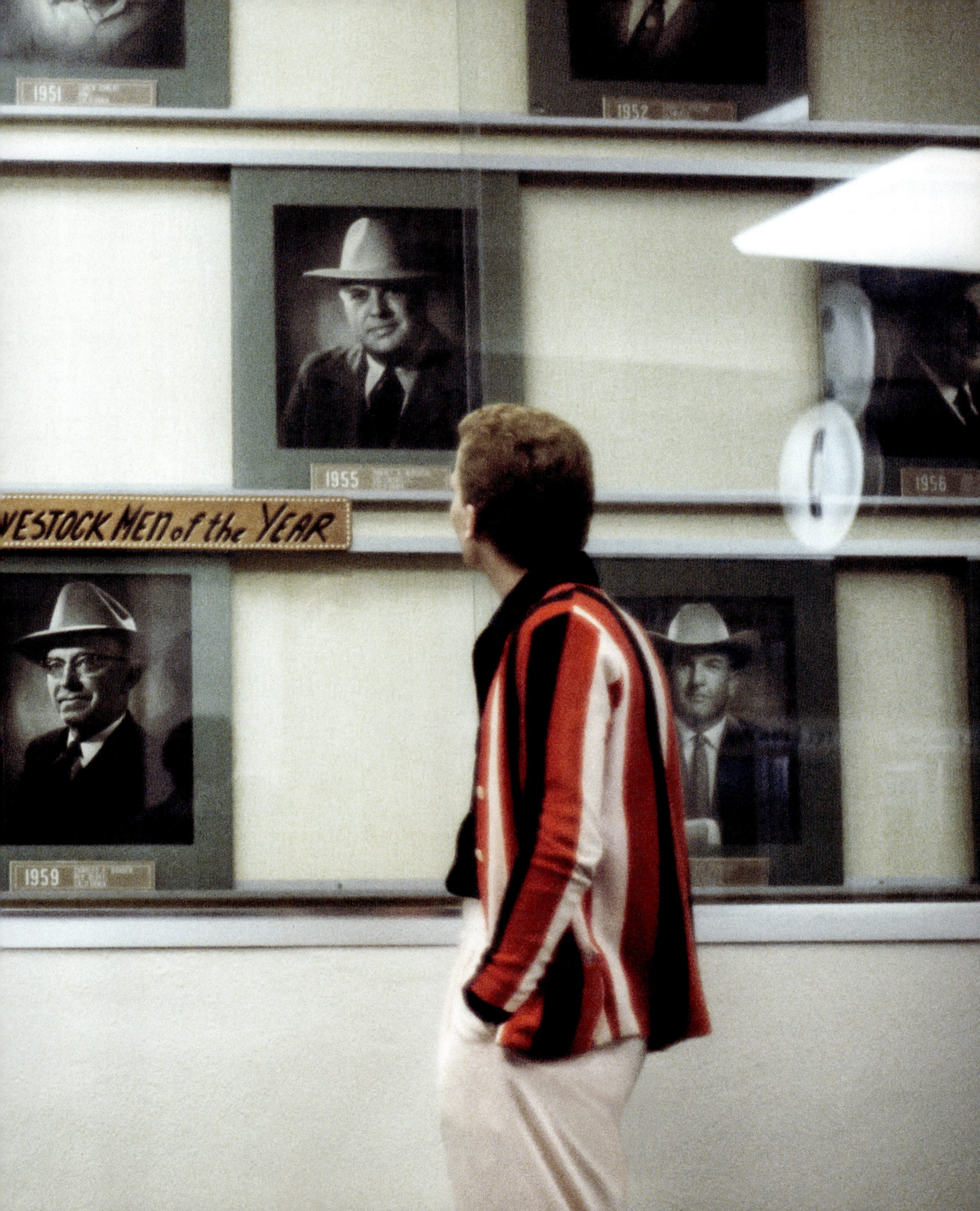
1951
1952
1955
1956
VESTOCK MEN of the YEAR
1959

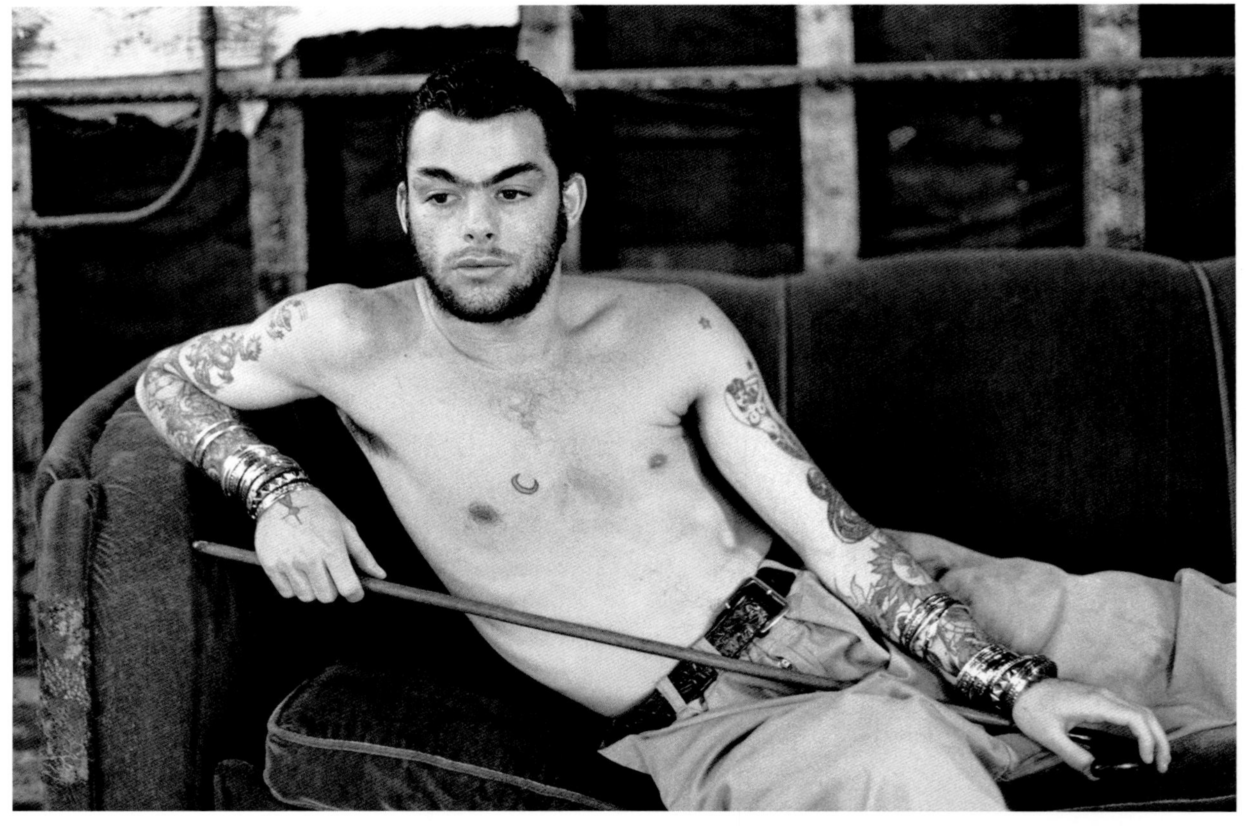

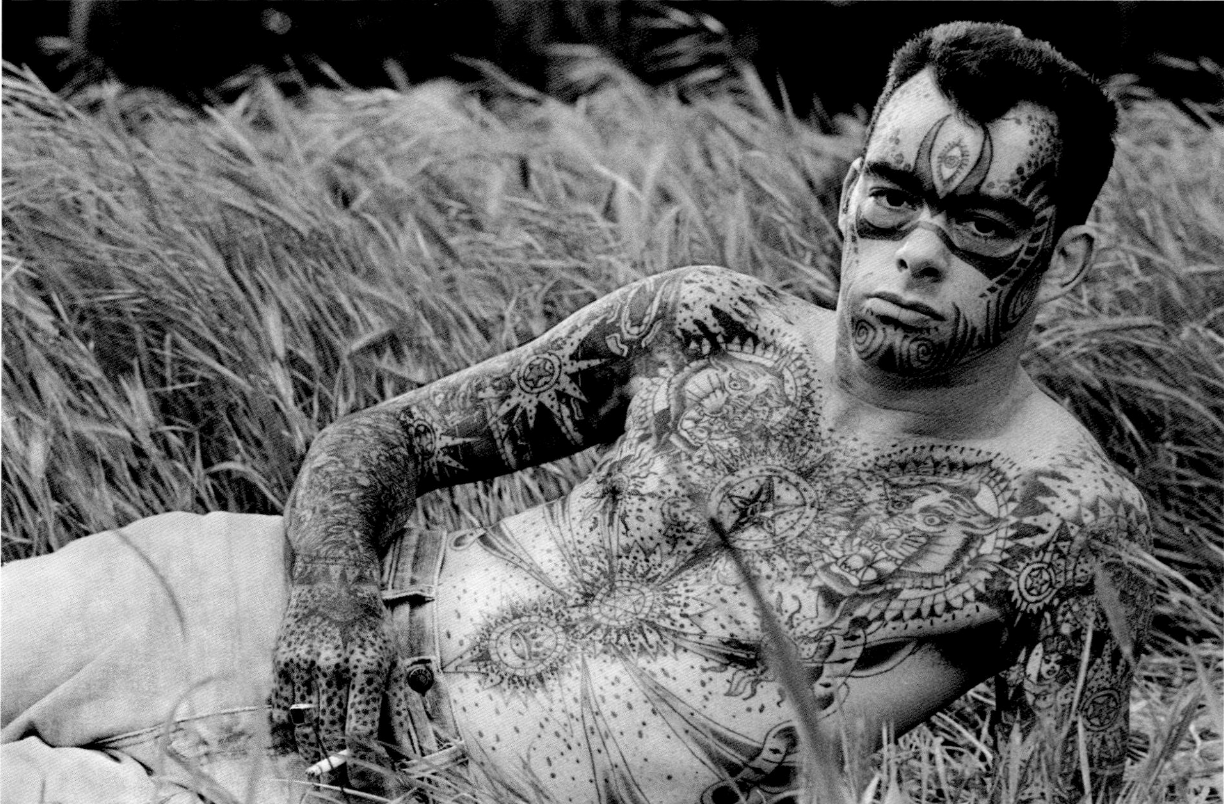

Above: *(top)* Tattoo Mike Wilson, spring 1976; *(bottom)* Tattoo Mike Wilson, March 19, 1987. Homage to Diane Arbus' portrait of Jack Dracula.
Opposite: Carmel Strelein at her Pink Tarantula hair salon, October 22, 1989.

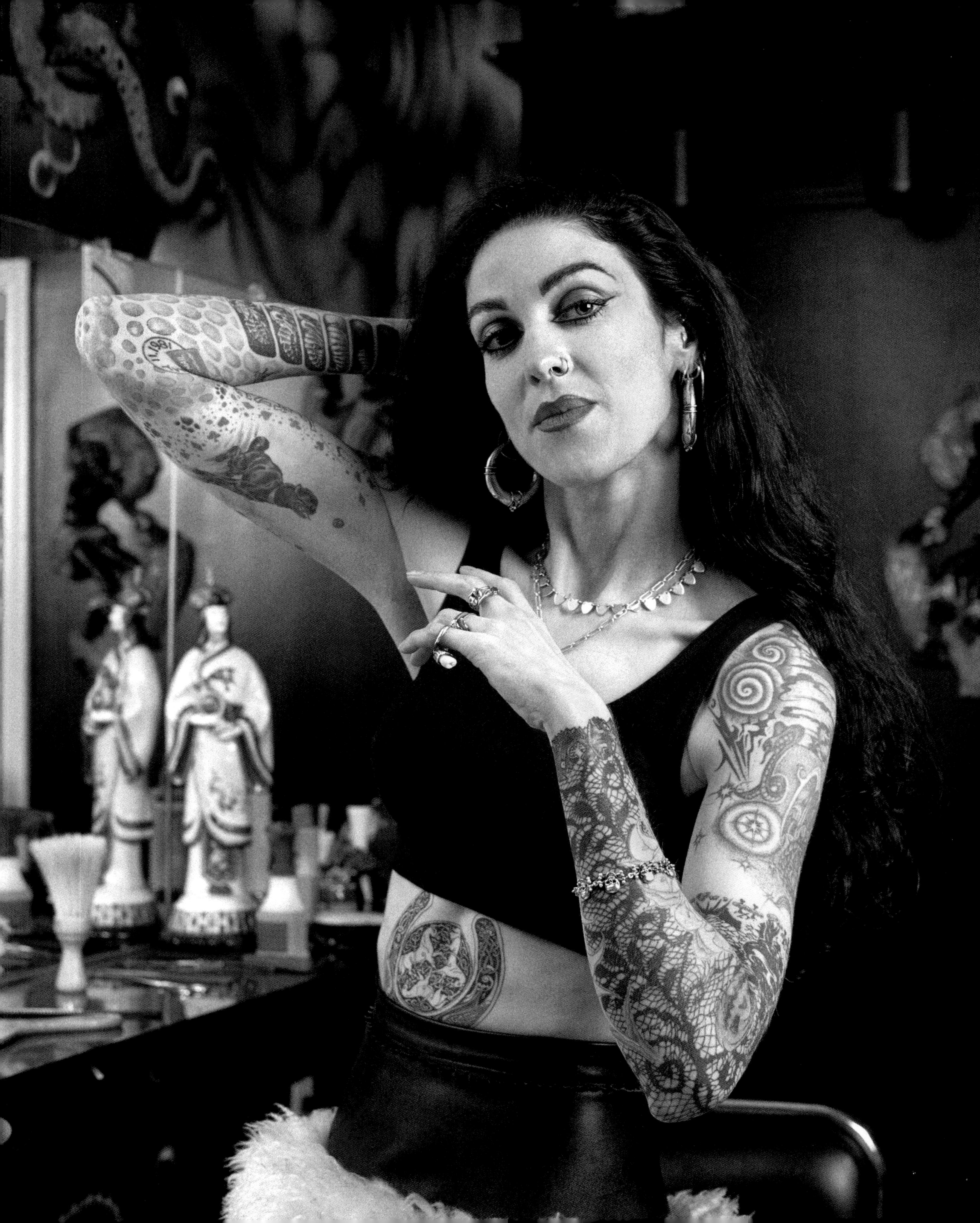

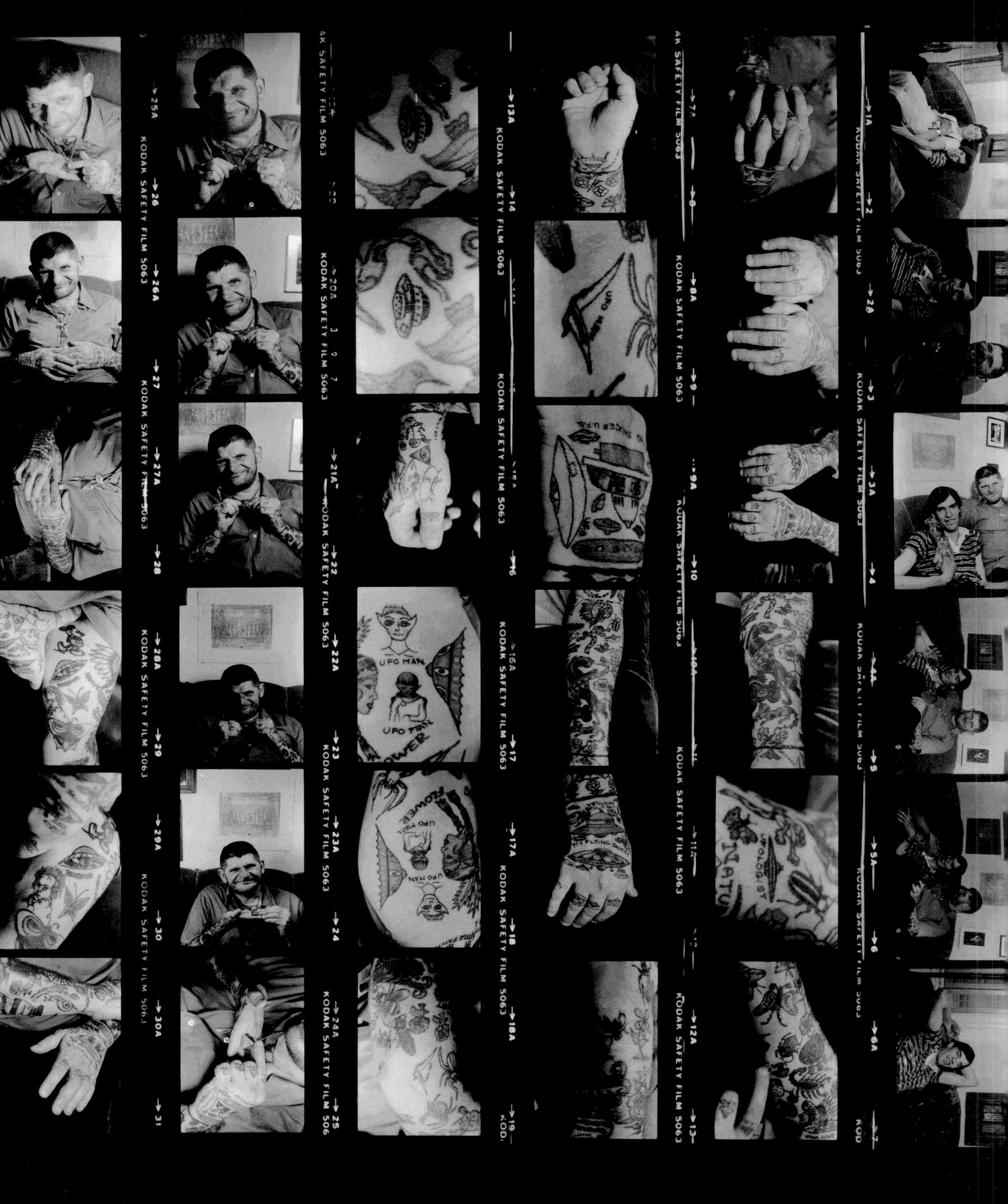
KODAK SAFETY FILM 5063
UFO MAN
UFO MAN

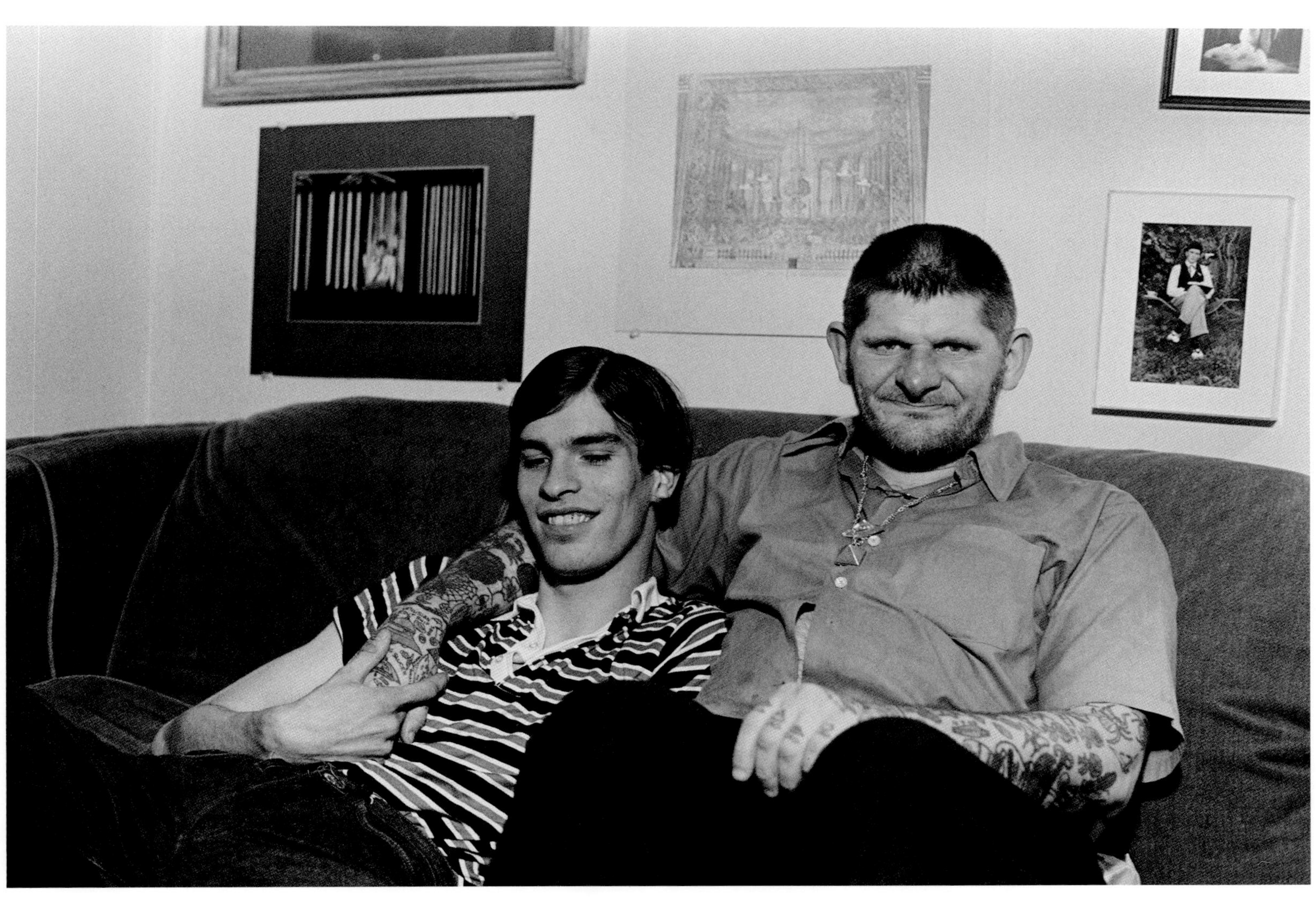

Paul and Zorthon visit Dan at his Ashbury Street apartment, March 18, 1979.

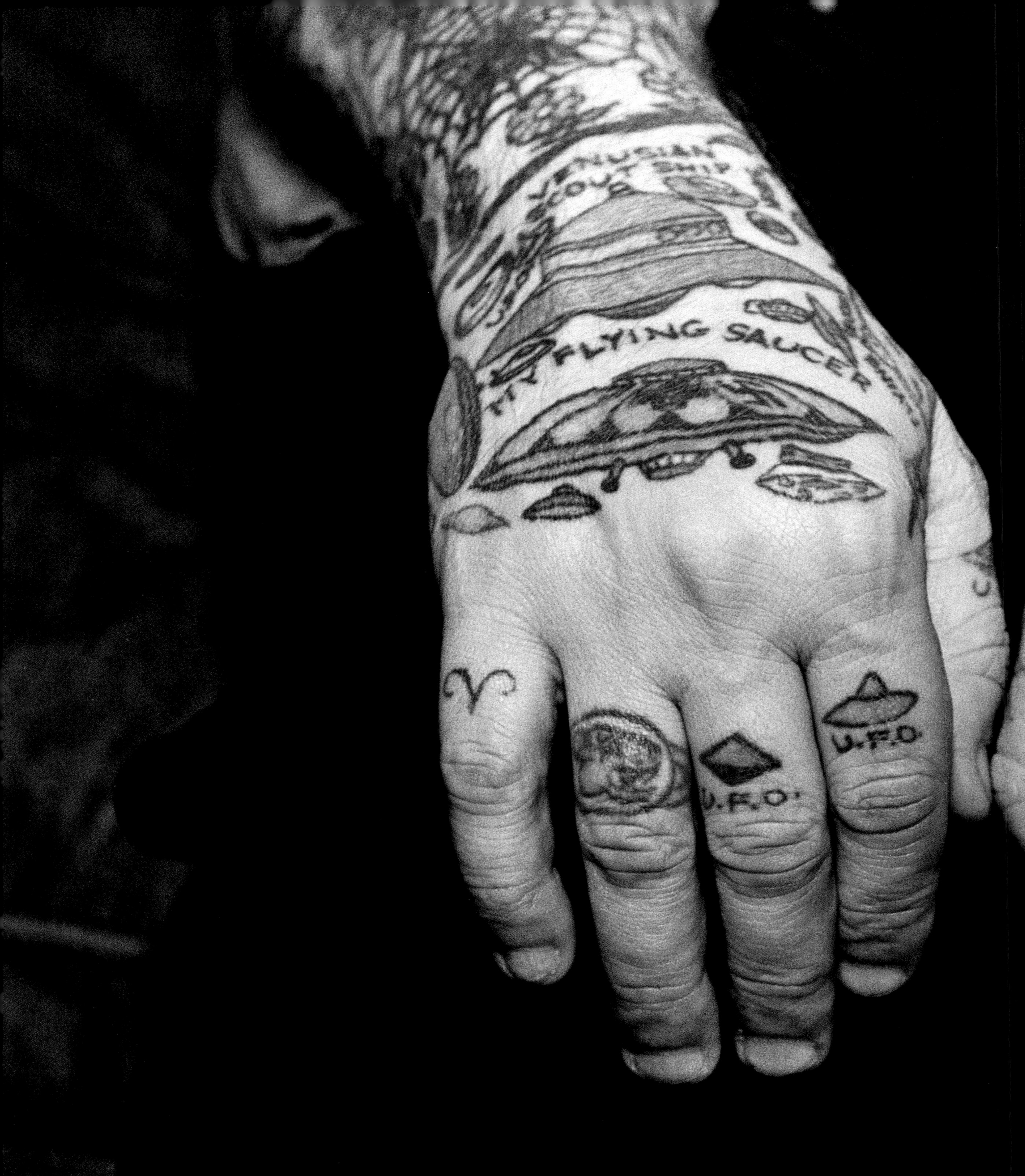

Zorthon's hands, March 18, 1979.

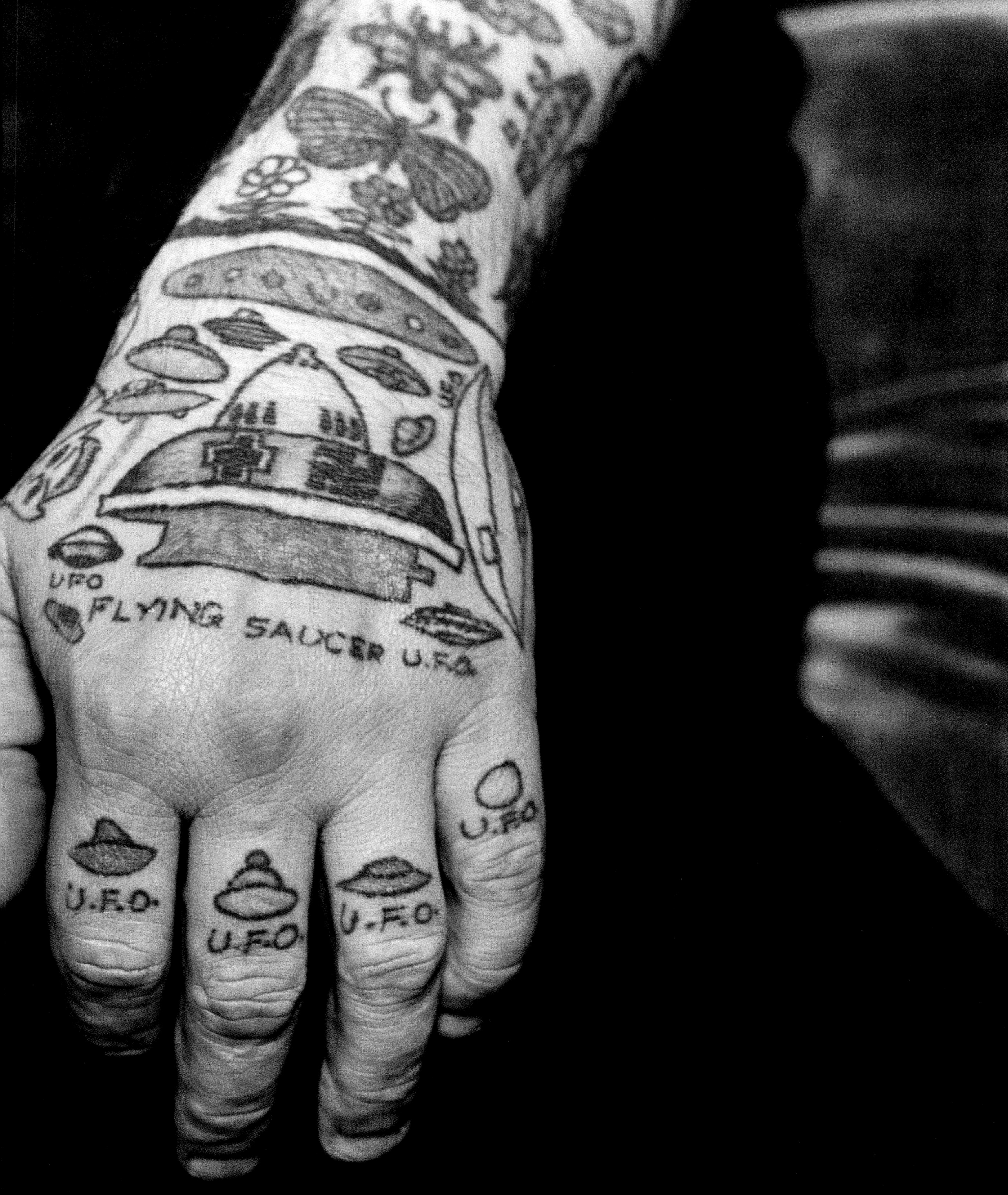
UFO
FLYING SAUCER U.F.O.
U.F.O.
U.F.O.
U.F.O.
U.F.O.

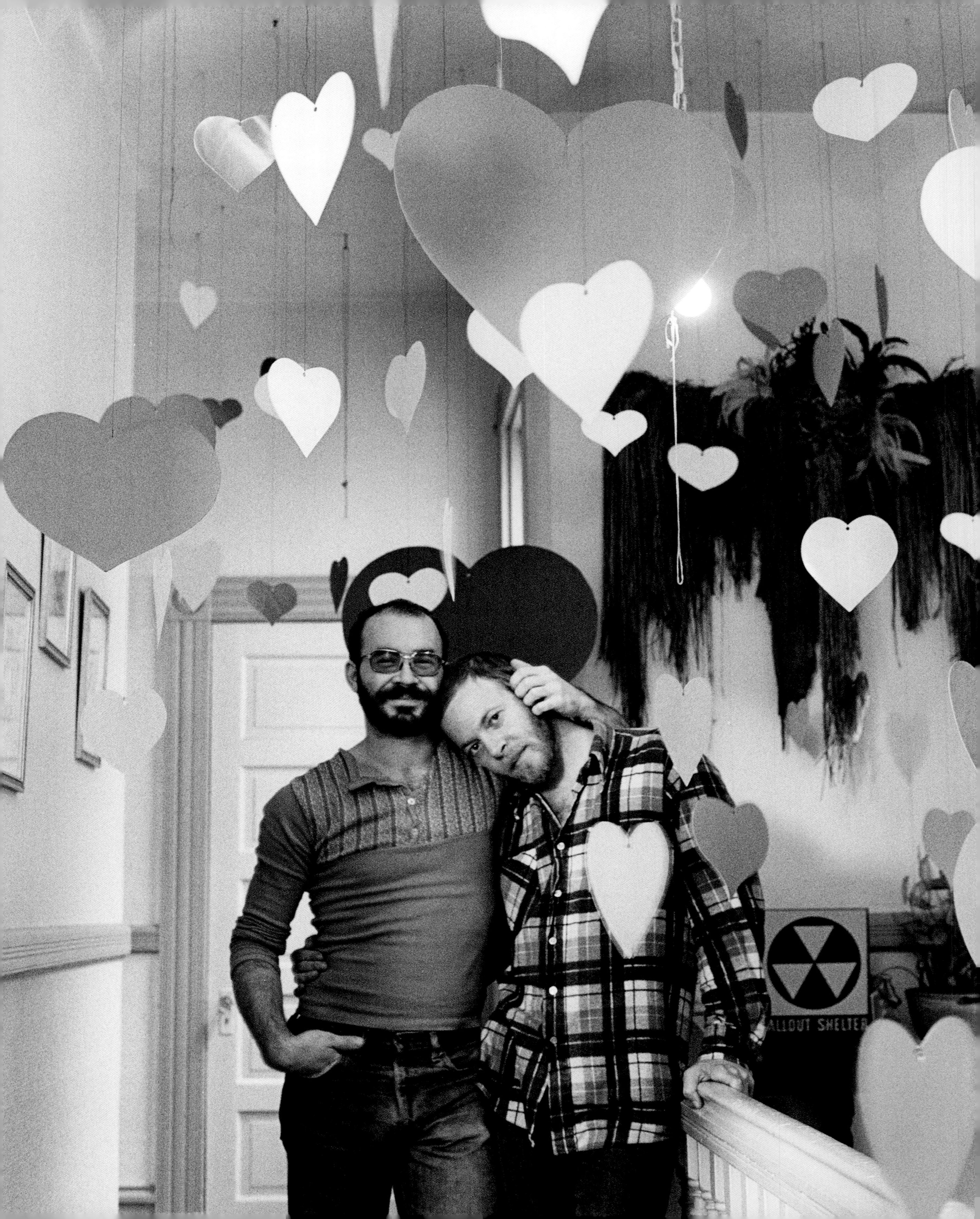
ALLOUT SHELTER

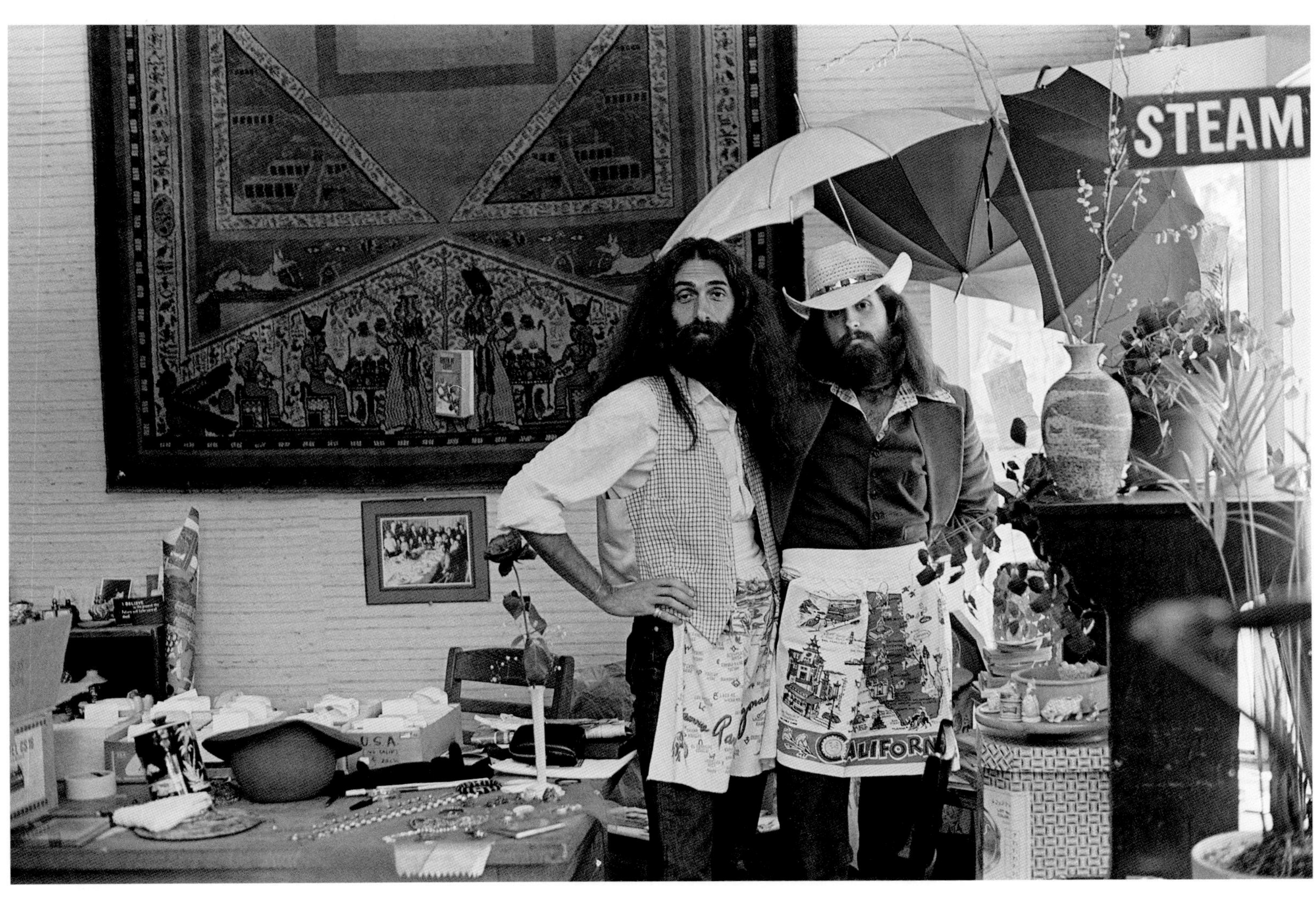

Above: Haight Street thrift store, May 15, 1979. Lawanda Rose and Chaudoin.
Opposite: Chuck Frutchey and Scott Smith, February 15, 1981.

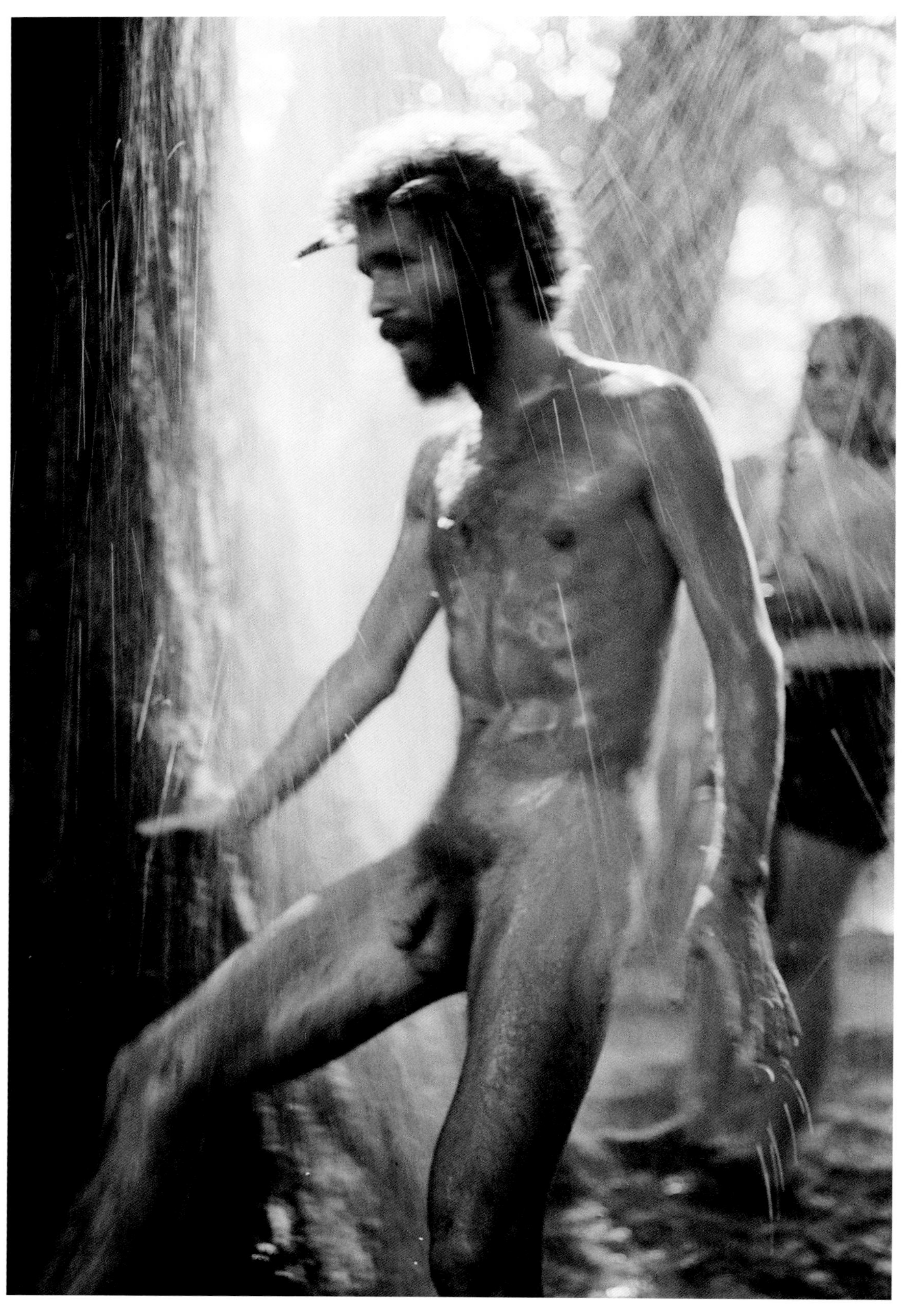

Above: SF LGBT Pride, Golden Gate Park, June 1976.
Opposite: Castro Street Fair, August 17, 1980. Fuschia, aka Najib (rear: Strawberry, Swale and Takim).

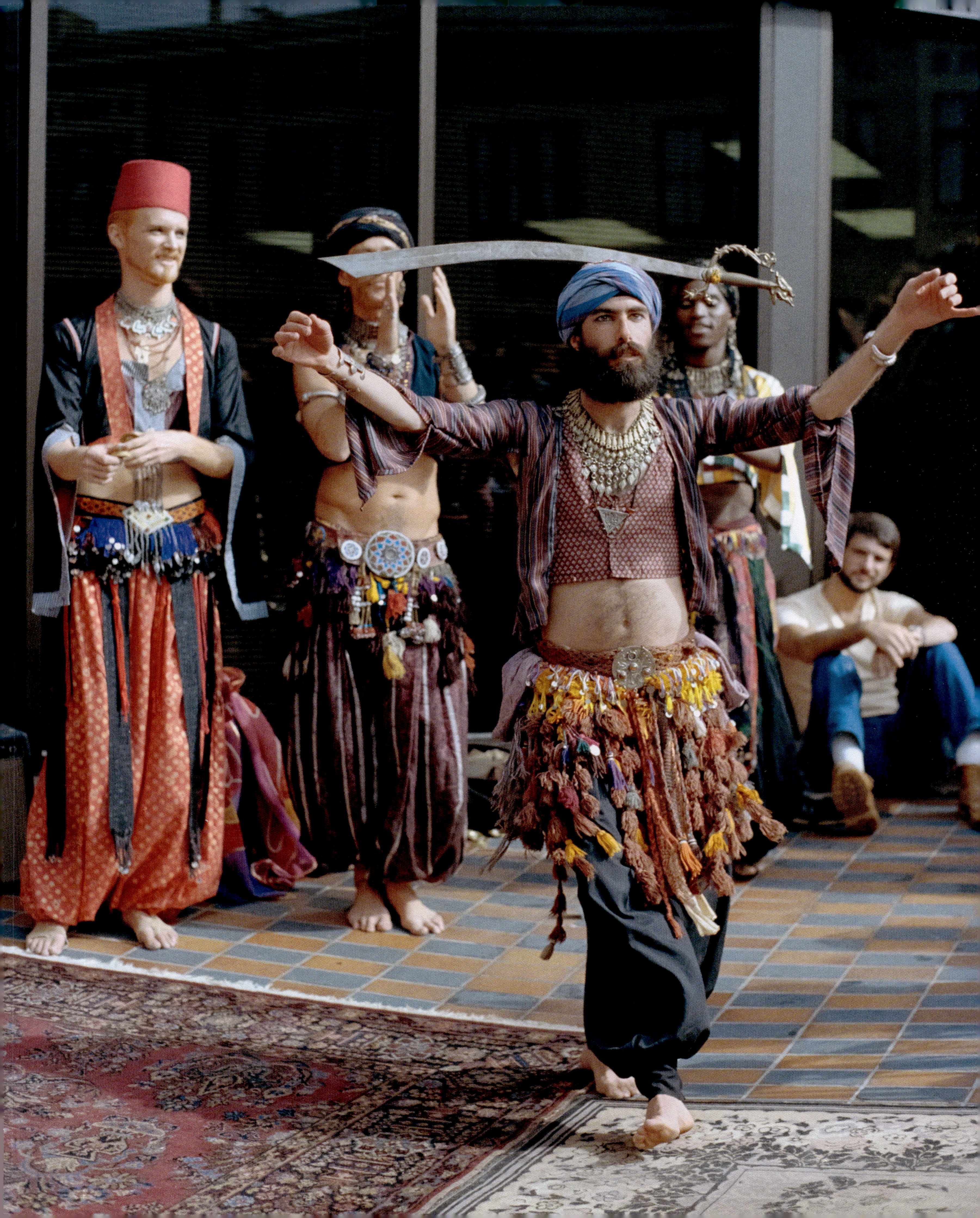

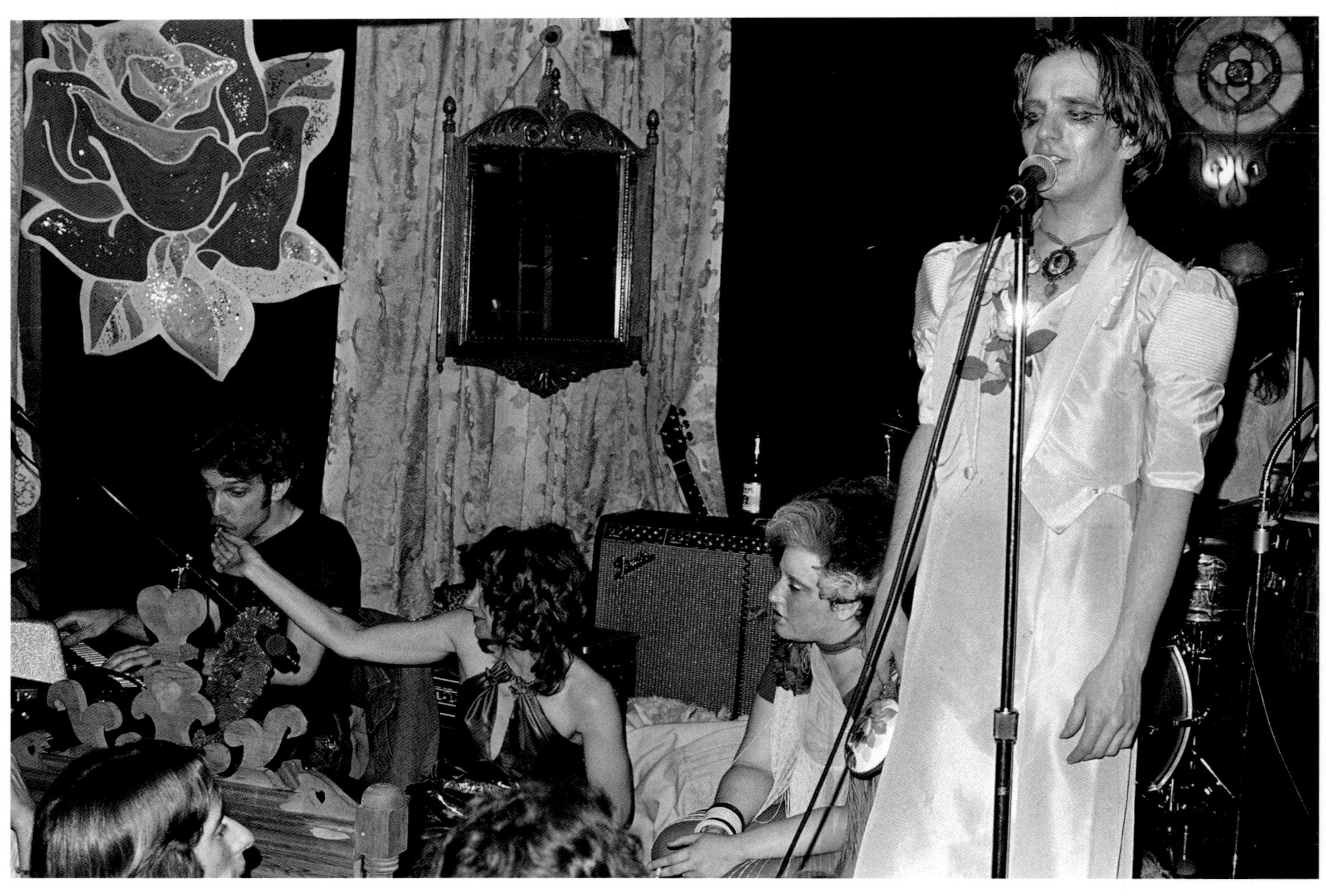

Above: Pristine Condition's Valentine's Day show, The Stud bar, February 1977.
Billy Philadelphia, Naomi Ruth Eisenberg, Patty Rodriguez and Pristine Condition.
Opposite: SF LGBT Pride, June 26, 1977.

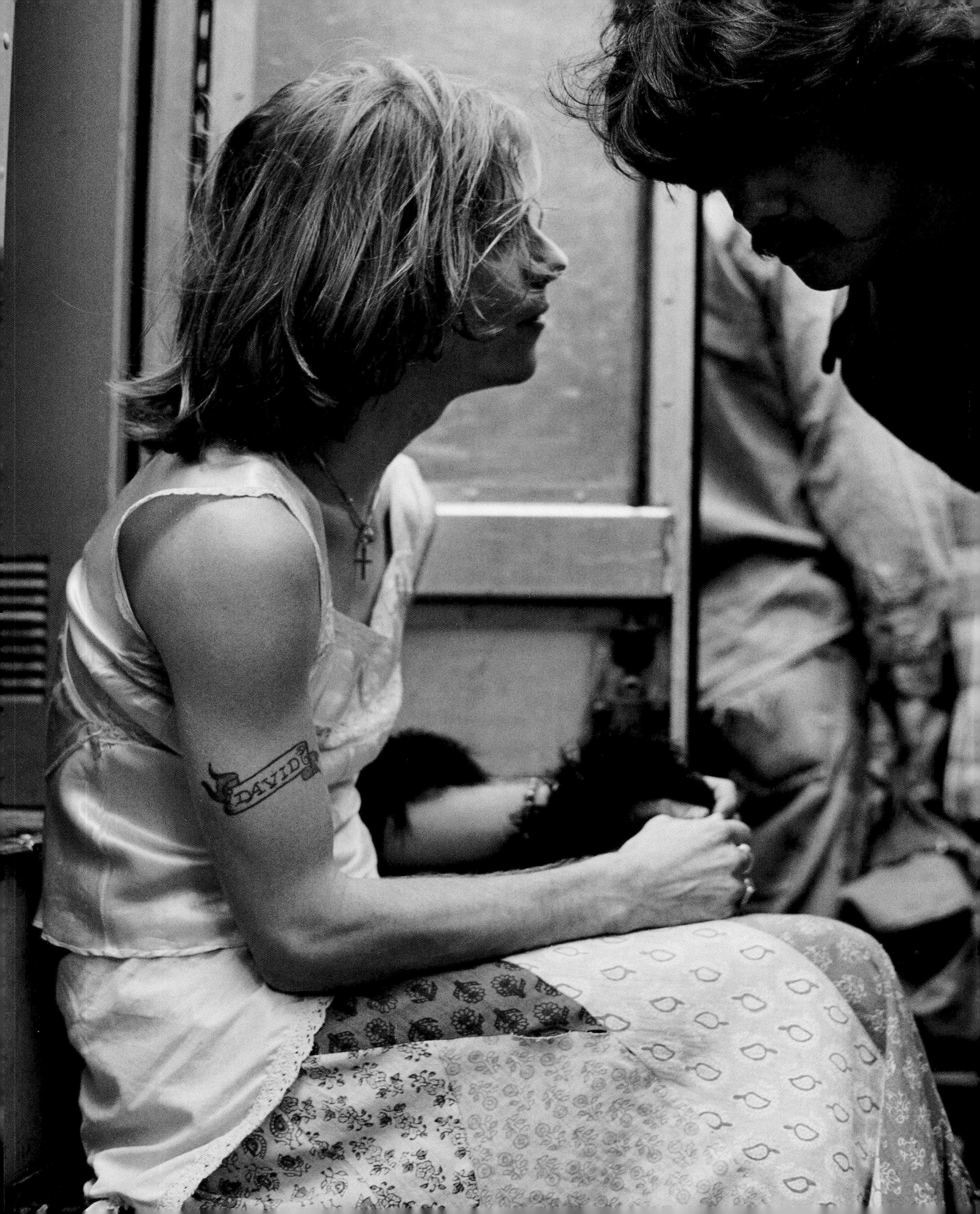
DAVID

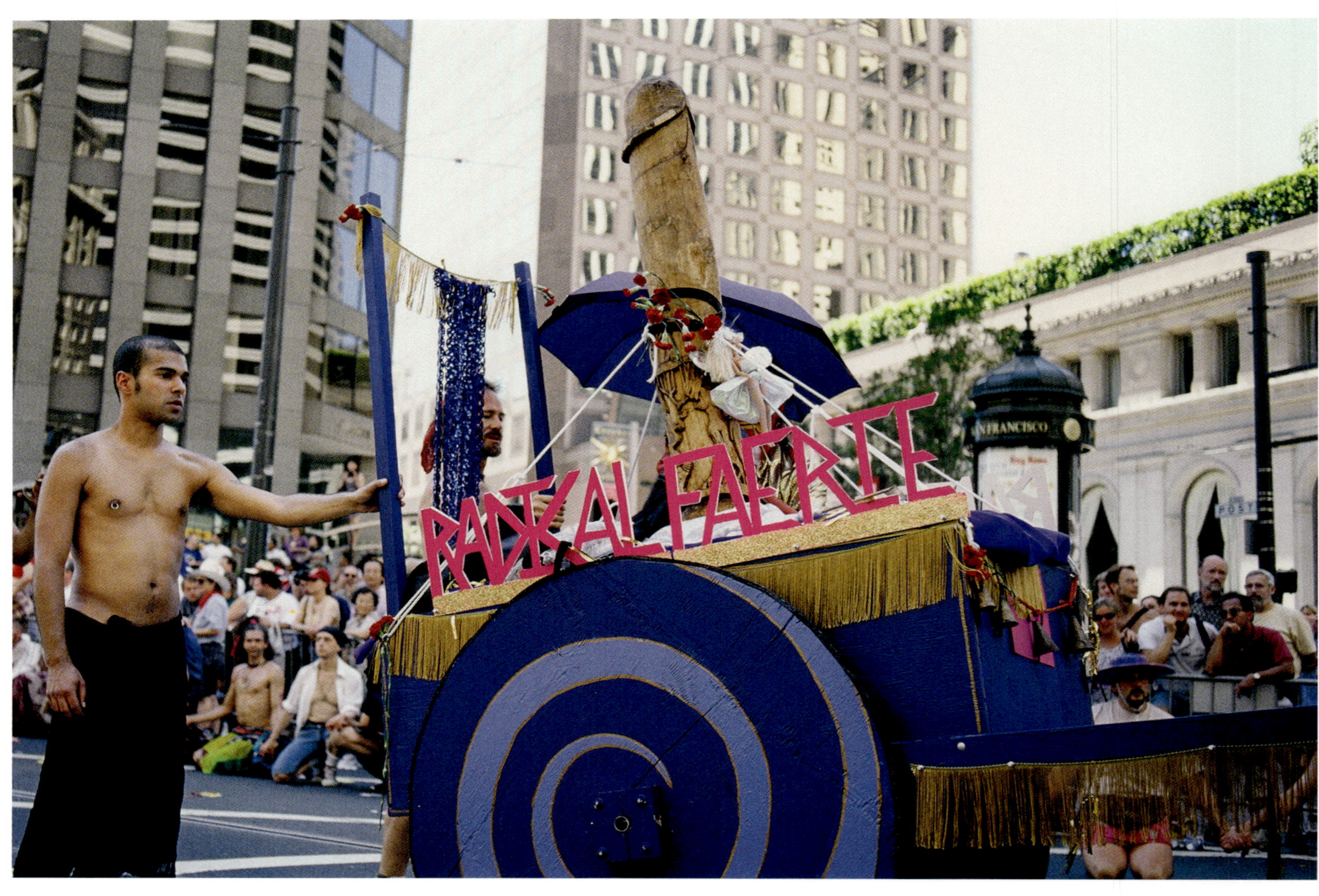

SF LGBT Pride, June 30, 1996. Radical Faerie contingent, Yvain Reed.

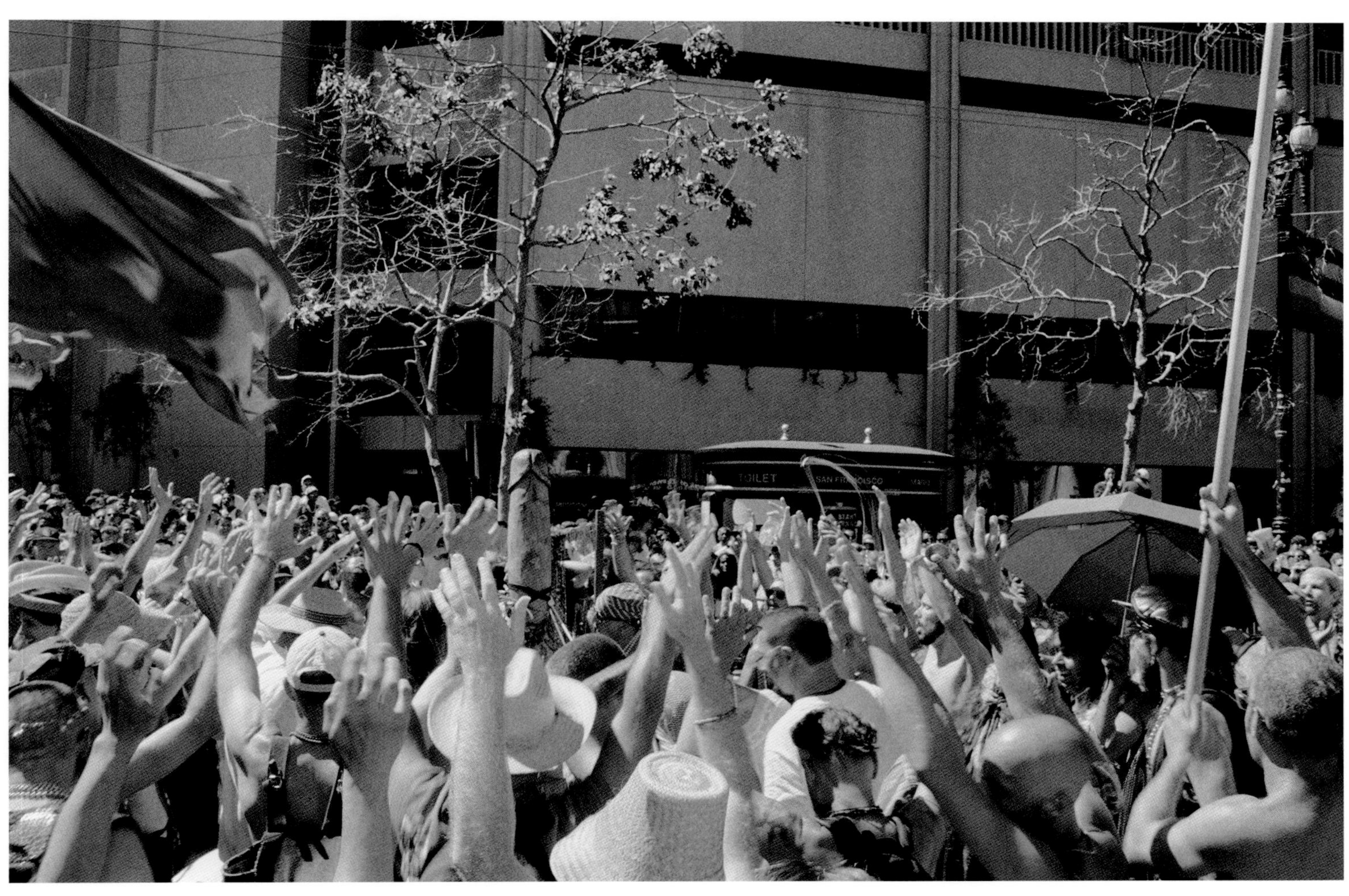

SF LGBT Pride, June 30, 1996. Pause in parade route for a moment of phallus worship.

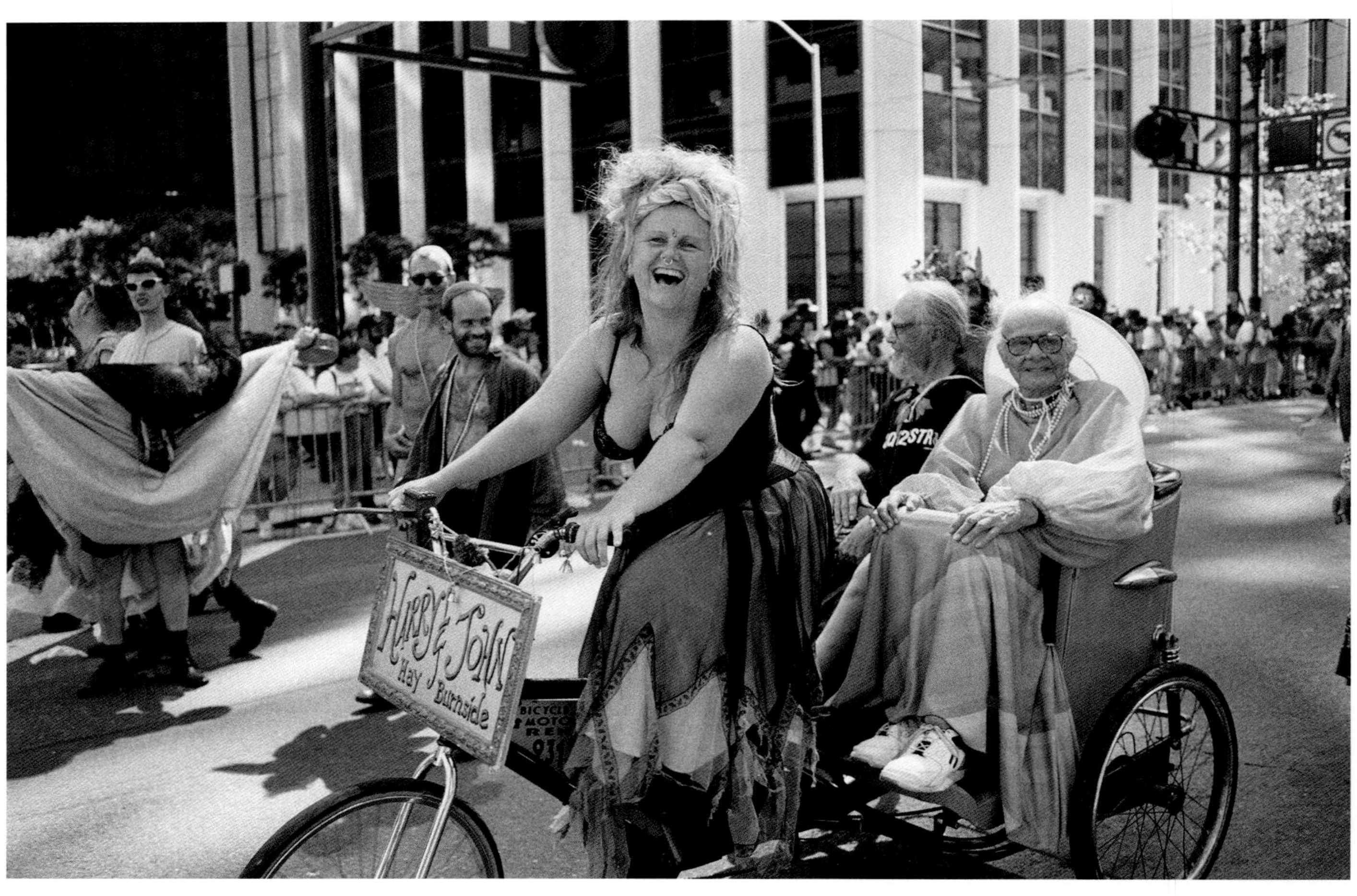

SF LGBT Pride, June 30, 1996. Madrone Jack, John Burnside and Harry Hay, with Buckwheat (rear left).

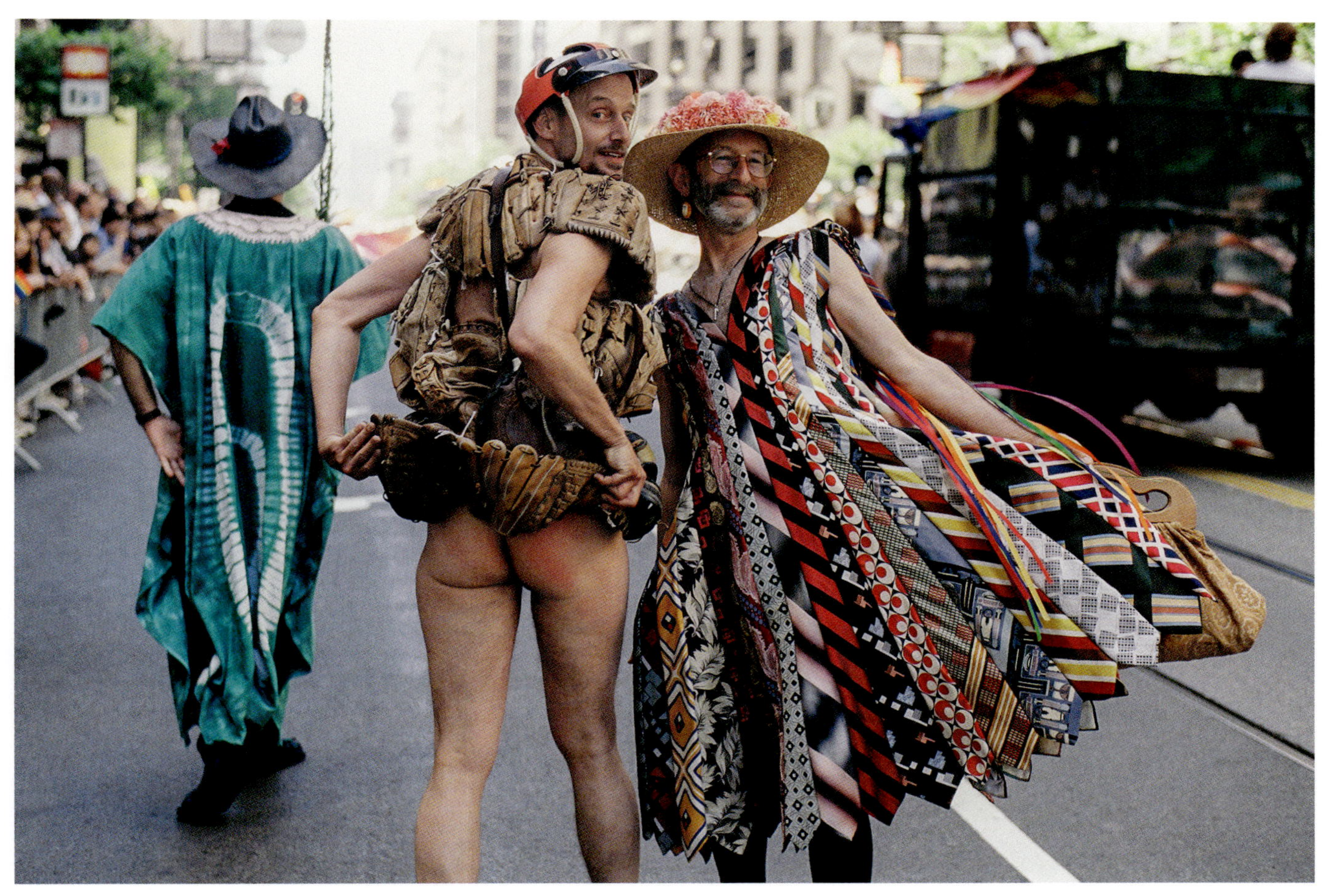

SF LGBT Pride, June 30, 1996. Jim Bernard, Bur McAllester and Karr (clothes by Bur McAllester).

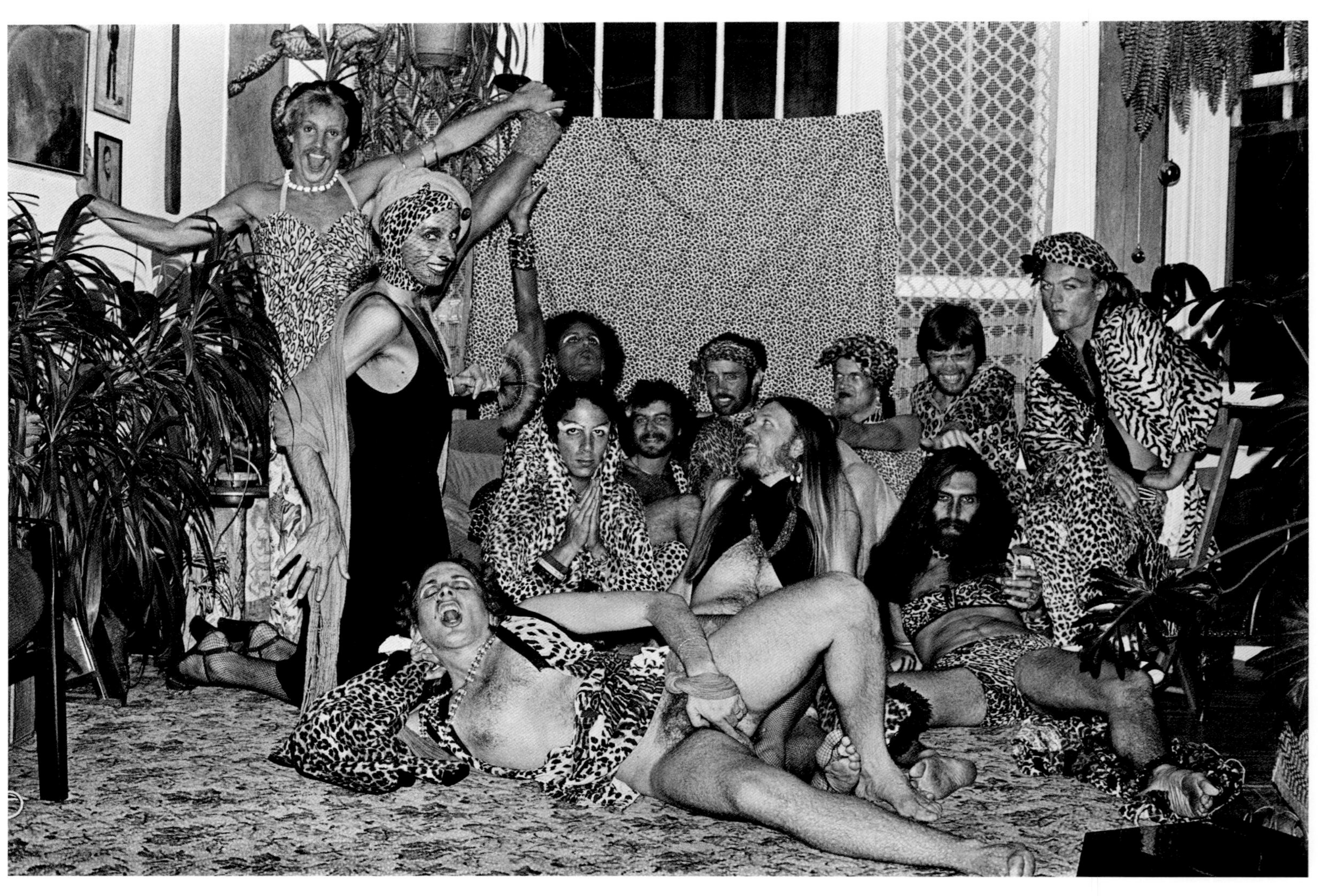

Puss print pajama party, May 1978. *(Back)* Doug Caldwell, Silvana Nova, Zelik Mintz, Jon Gould, Jamal, Bobby, Morningstar and Lulu; *(middle)* Ruven, Larry Hermsen and Lawanda Rose; *(front)* Tede Matthews.

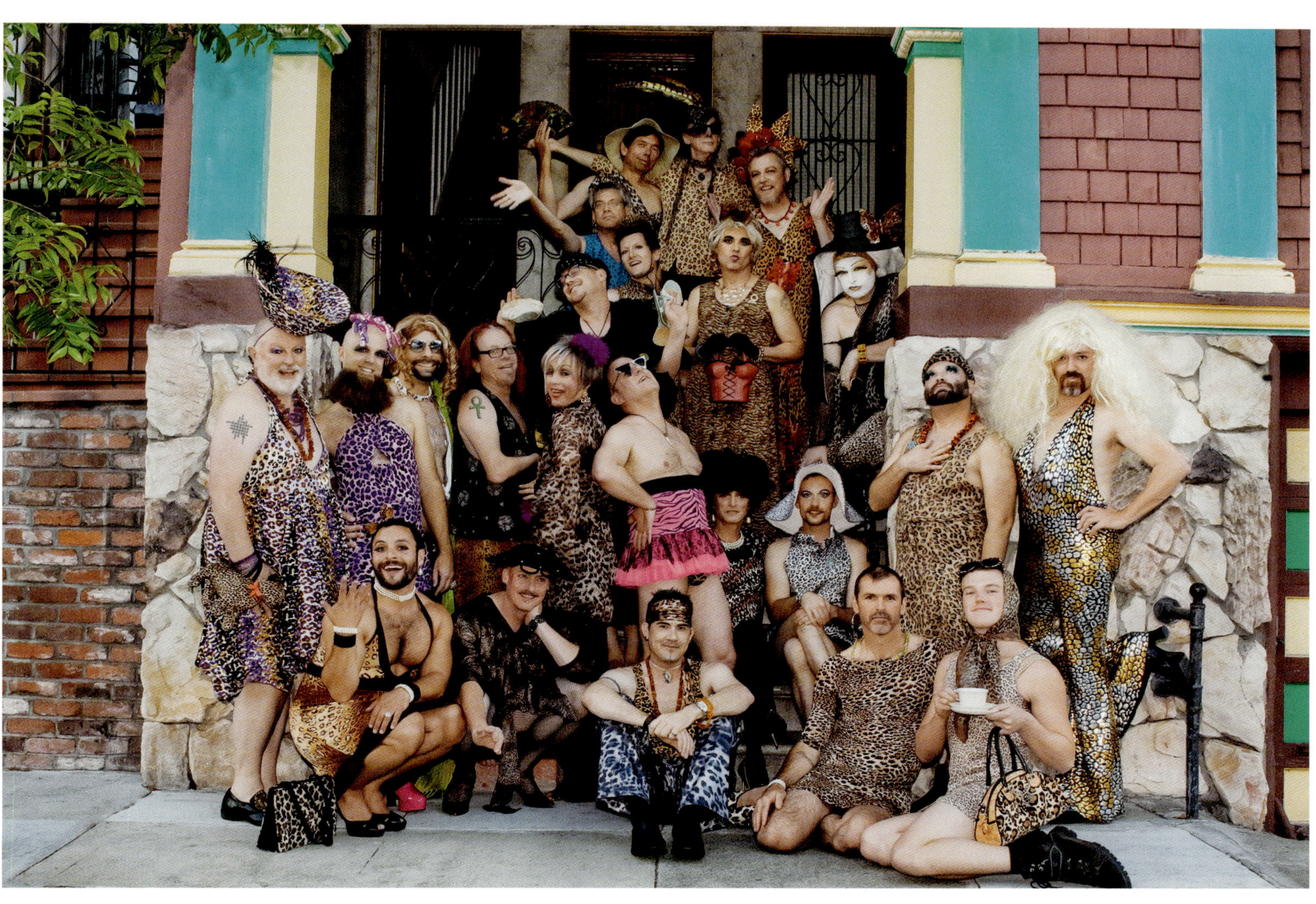

Radical Faerie puss print themed party for Jack Davis' 60th birthday at the home of Cayenne and Jack, September 25, 2010. *(Back row)* Jerry the Faerie, Dean Dalton, Terry Trout and Patrick Dorman; *(third row)* Pachez, Meesha Petty, Scott Madden, Sister Selma Soul; *(second row)* Jack Davis, Tim Lubic, Johnny Thunder, Double Snake, Cayenne, Tiger Lily, Benjamin Patterson, Clayton Robbins, Jason Dimick, Carl Crossgrove; *(front row)* Adam Barrett, Brian Fairbrother, Todd Herriott, Keith Hennessy and Dennis Collective.

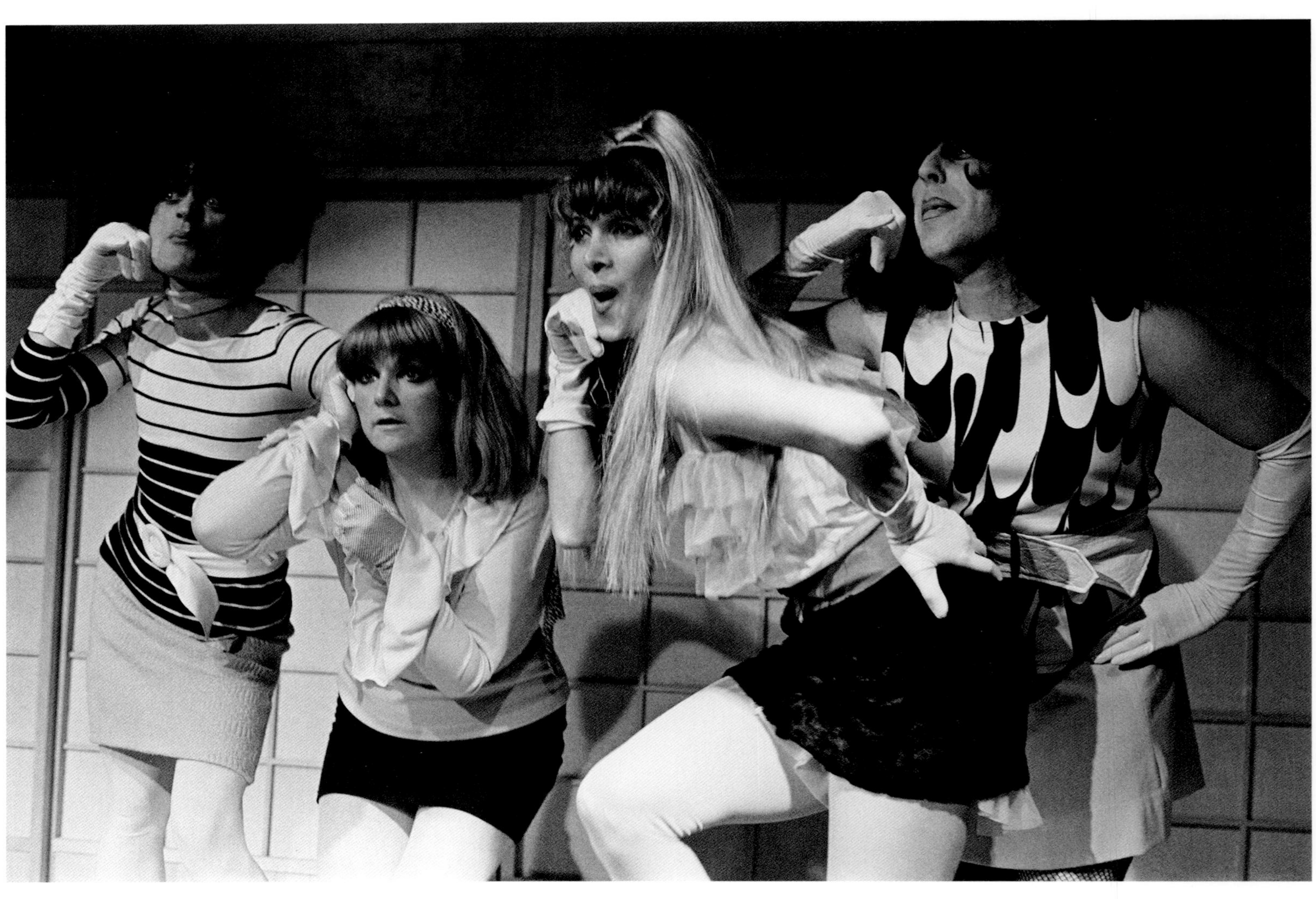

Above: The Four Beauties perform at 544 Natoma, April 11, 1981. Lulu, Maura Nolan, Teena Rosen and Tommy Pace.
Opposite: Doris Fish in *Blonde Sin*, June 26, 1980.

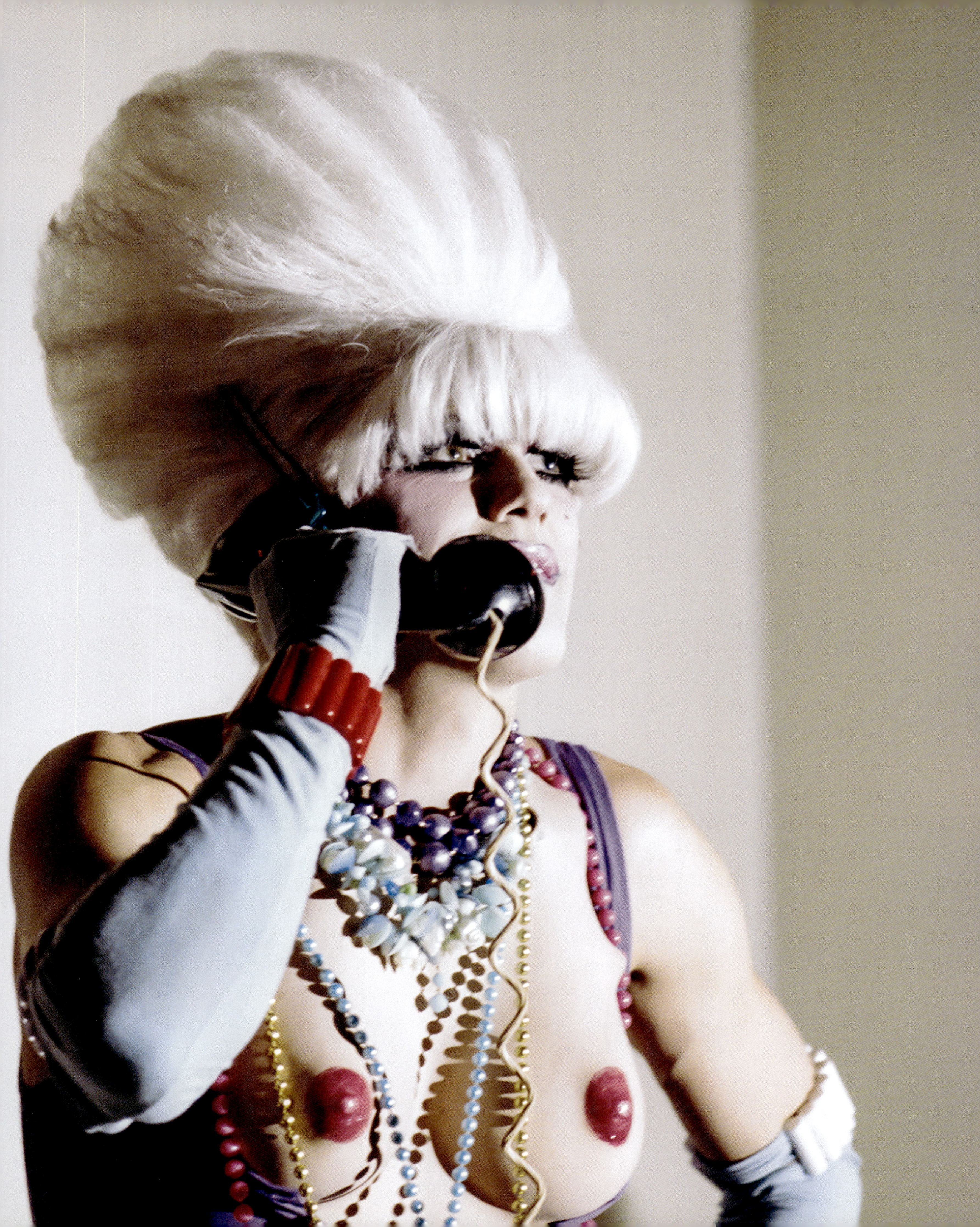

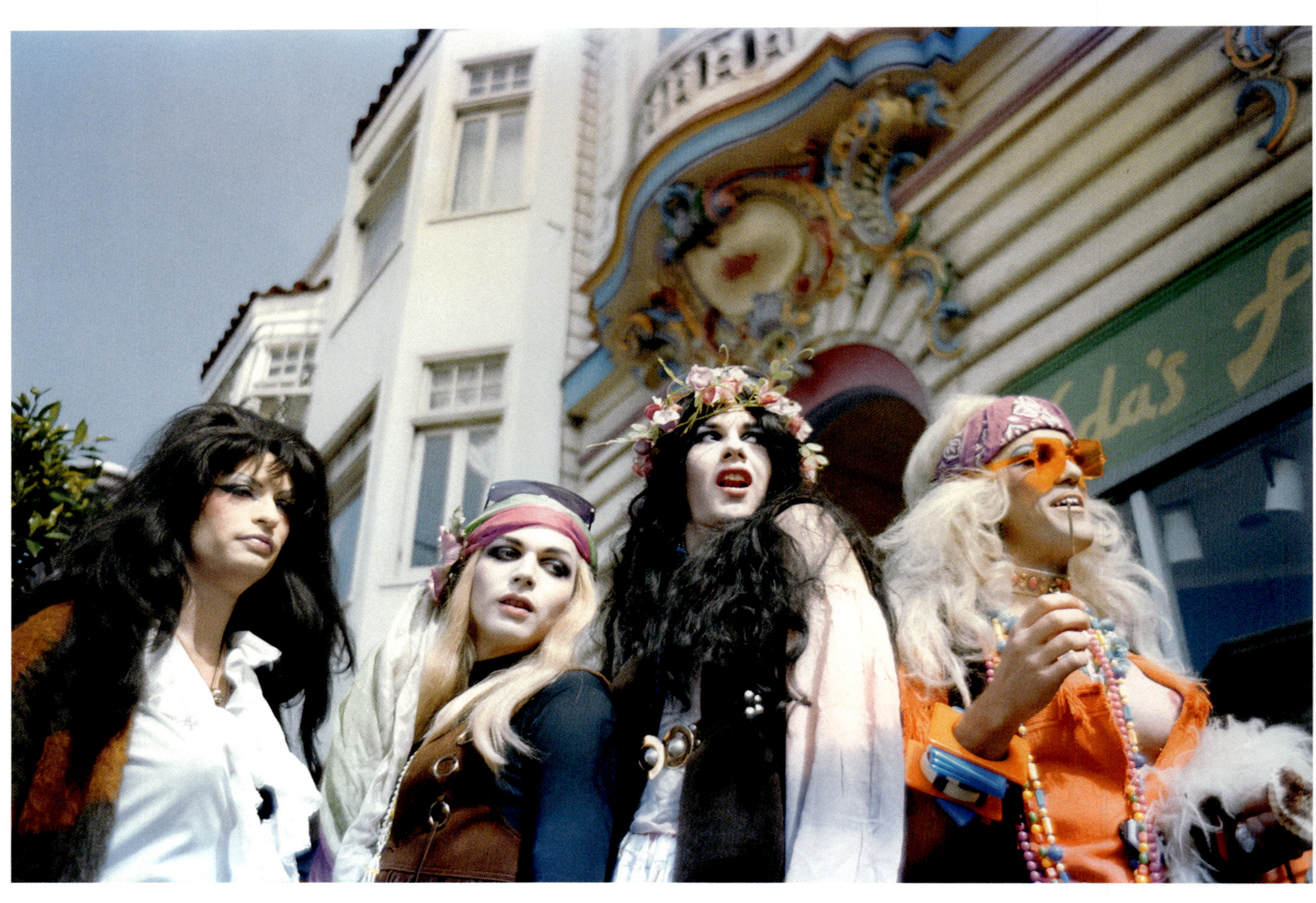

Above: Haight Street Fair, May 18, 1980. Miss X, Tippi, Freda Lay and Doris Fish.
Opposite: Haight Street Fair, May 18, 1980. Doris Fish and Tippi.

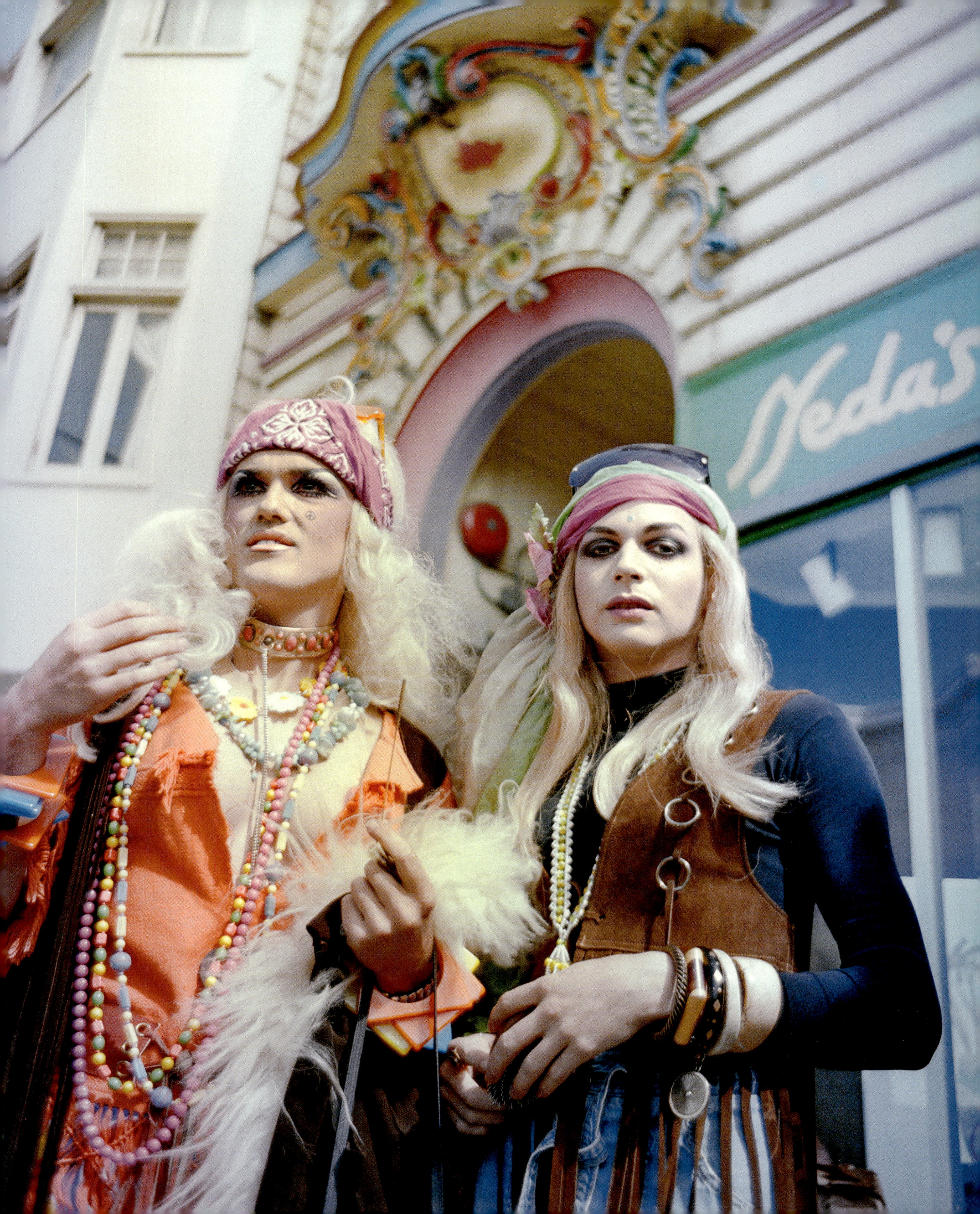
Neda's

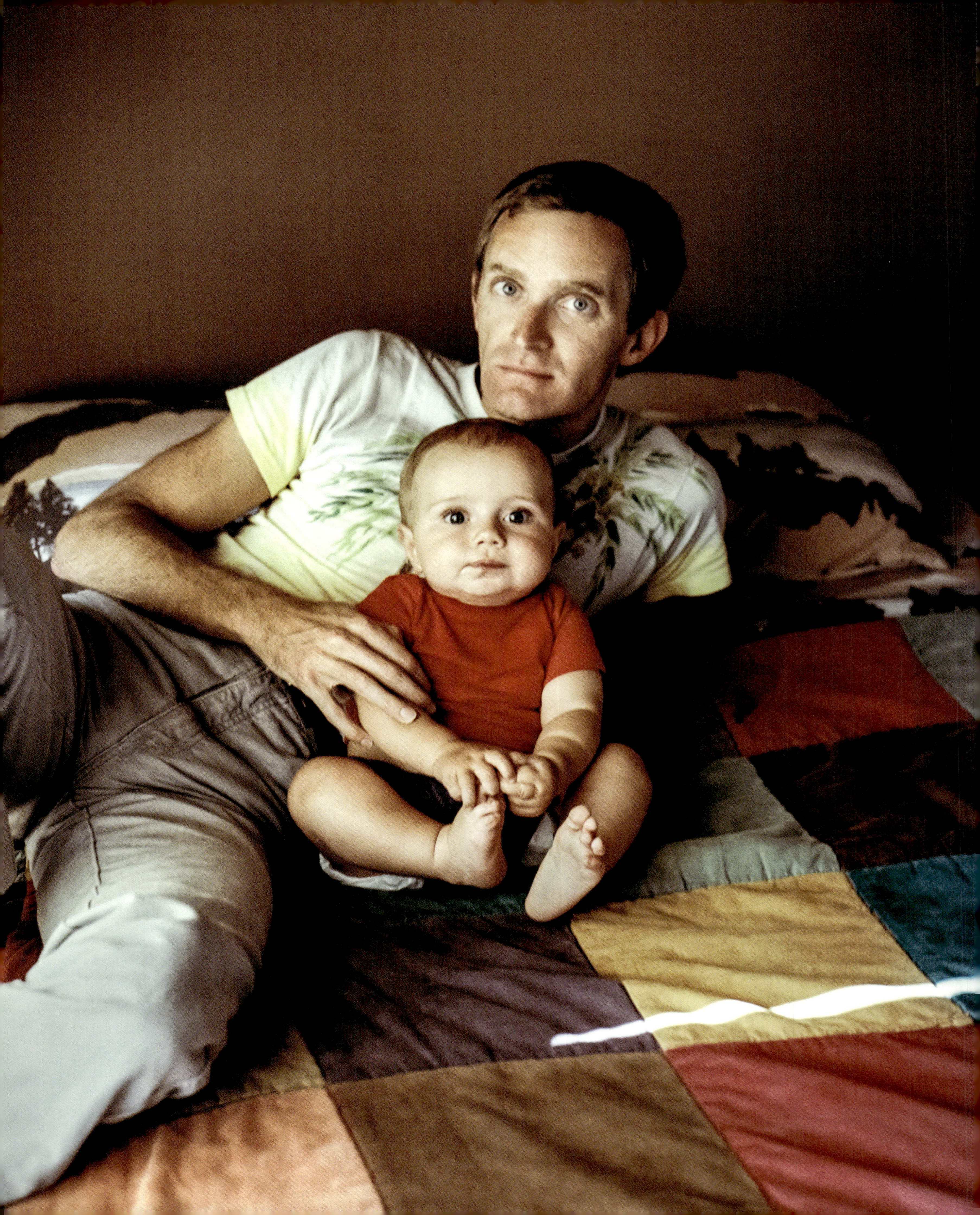

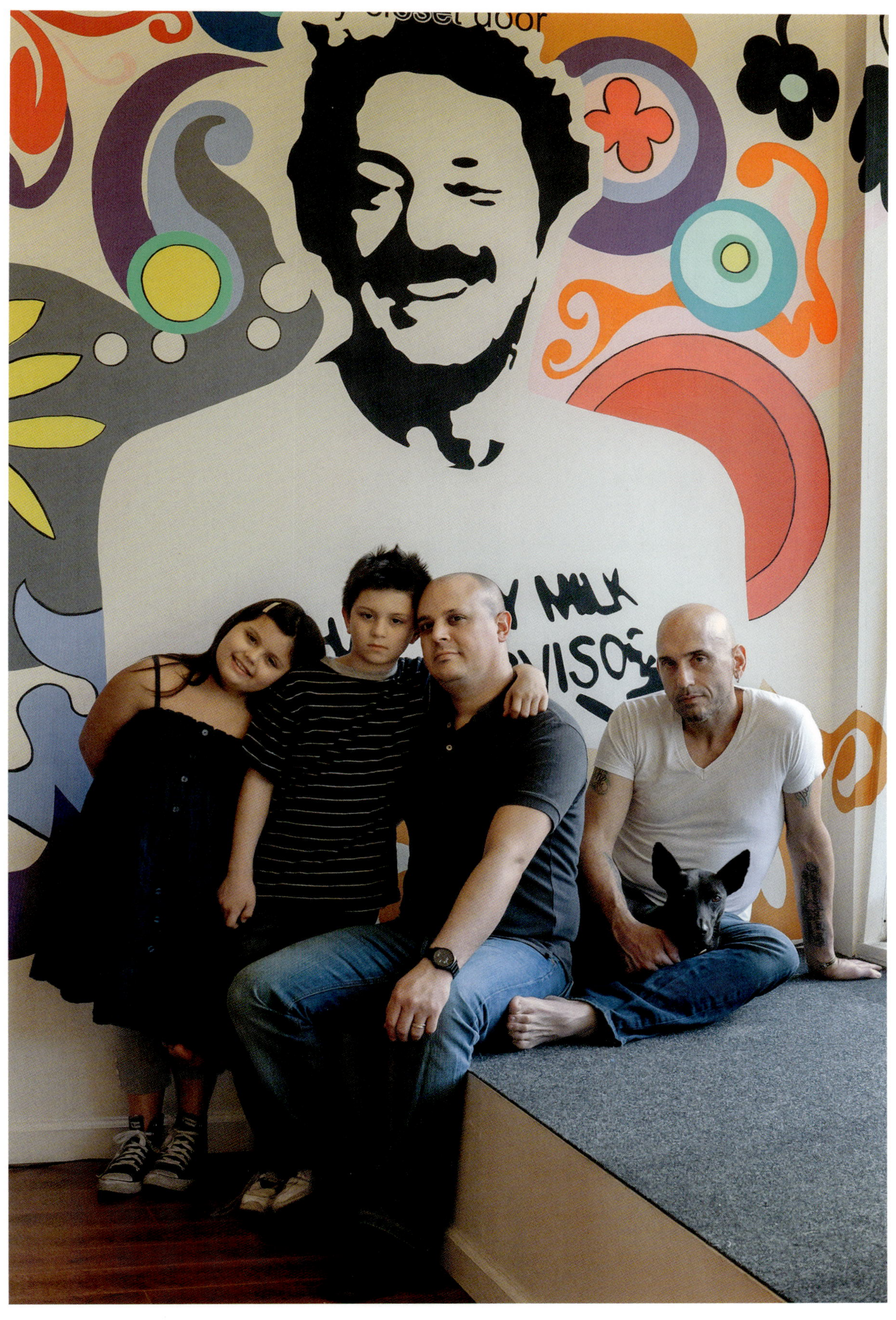

Above: Nick Romero, John Antoniades and Isabella and Elijah Romero-Antoniades at Given, their gift store at 575 Castro Street, the original location of Castro Camera Store, March 3, 2010. Harvey Milk mural by John Baden.
Opposite: Michael Pinatelli, Jr. and nephew Tony Pinatelli, August 20, 1983.

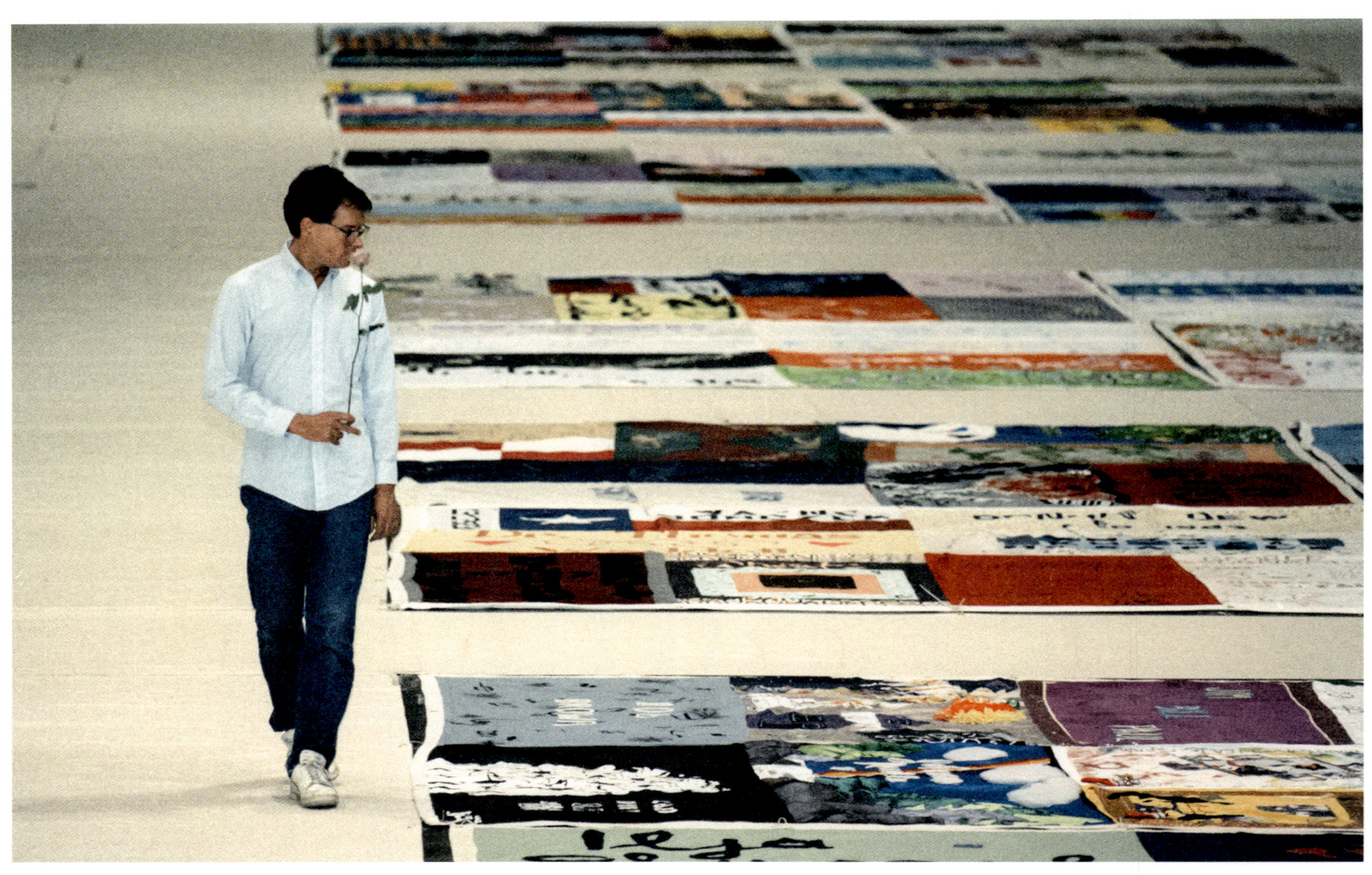

The Names Quilt AIDS memorial display at Moscone Convention Center, December 20, 1987. Cleve Jones, founder.

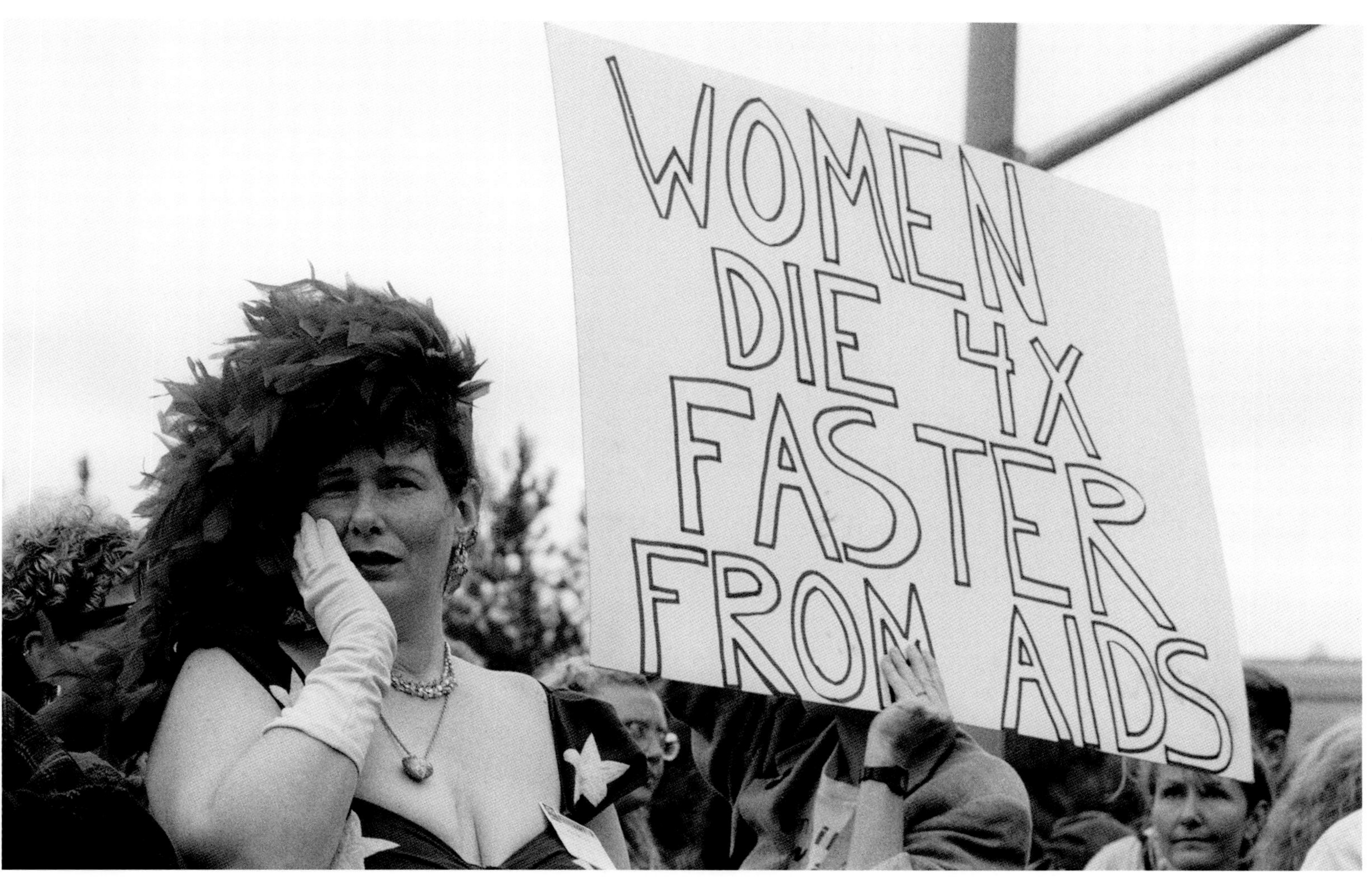

Above and overleaf: Demonstration for women's AIDS issues at the 6th International AIDS Conference, June 22, 1990. *(Above)* Scarlet Harlot; *(overleaf)* Madrid St. Angelo and Rick Jacobsen (demonstrators).

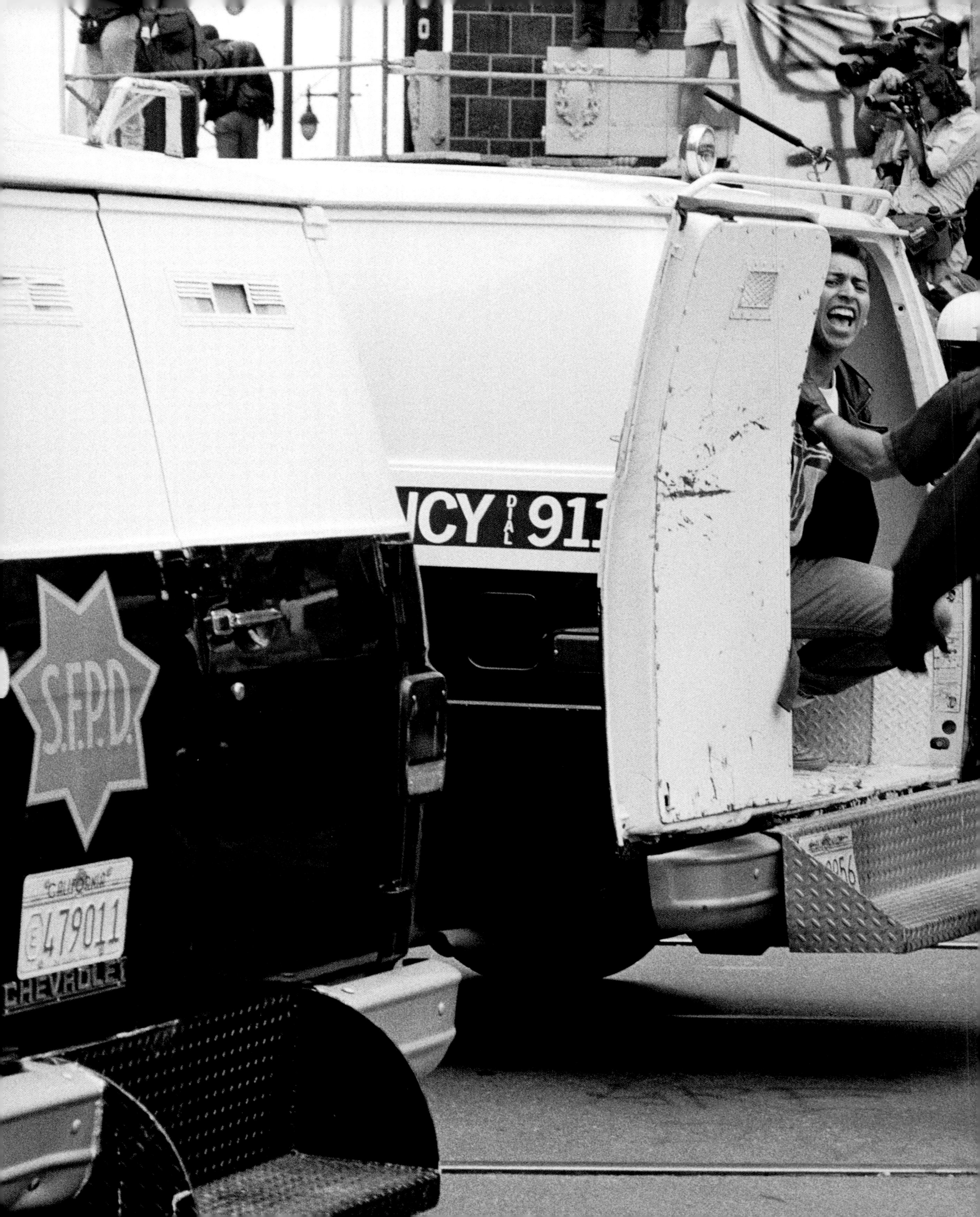

DIAL 911
S.F.P.D.
CALIFORNIA
479011
CHEVROLET

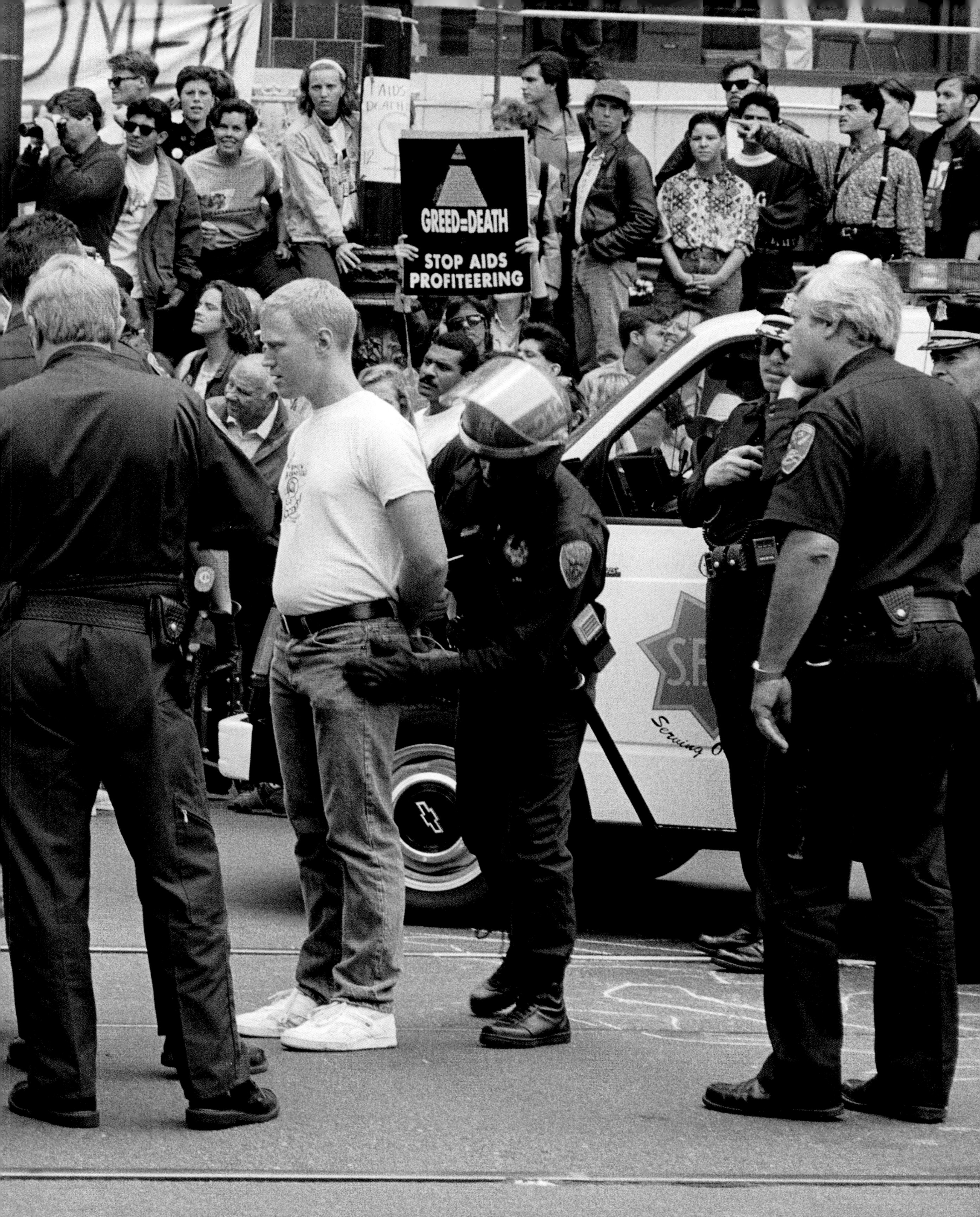
GREED=DEATH
STOP AIDS
PROFITEERING

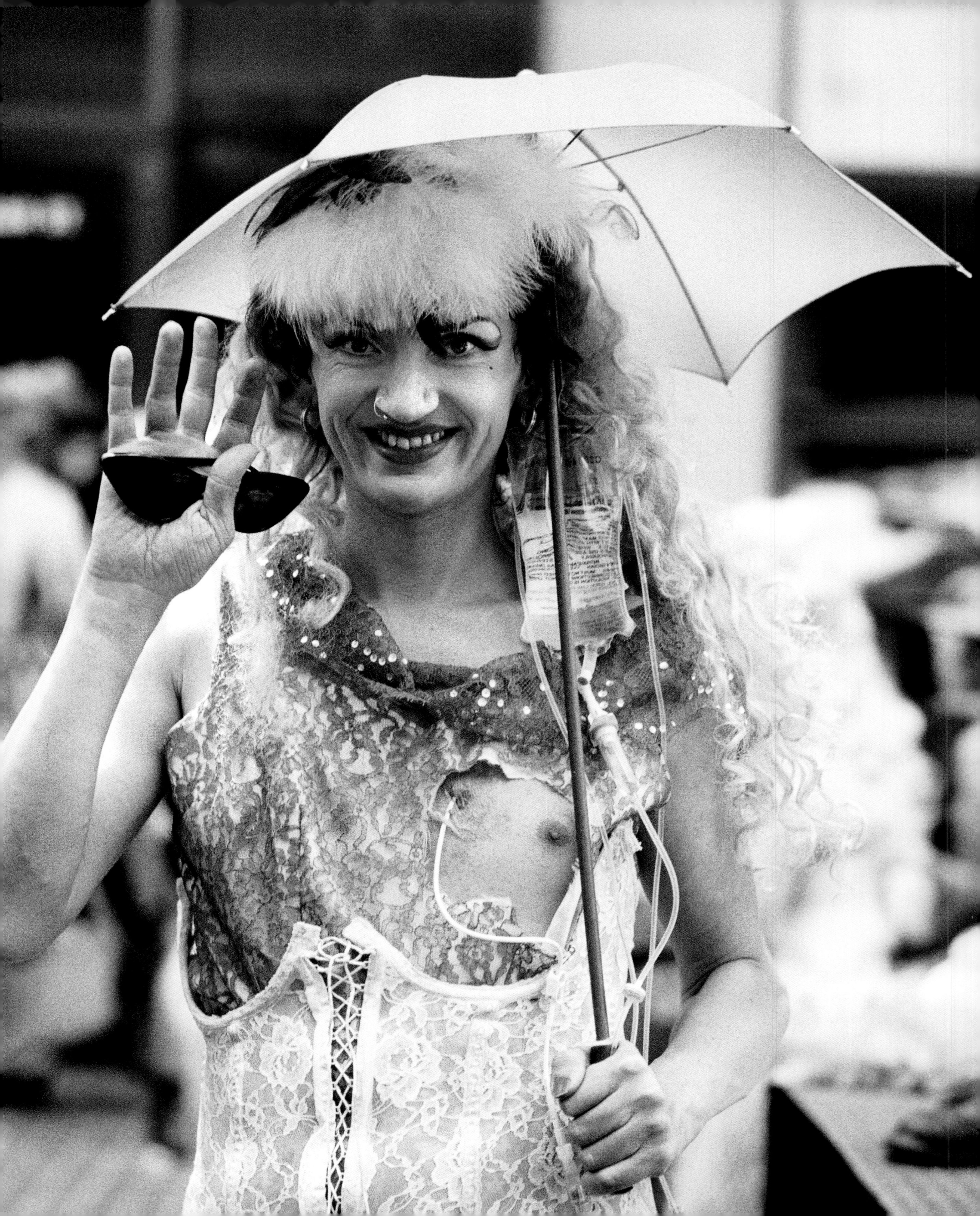

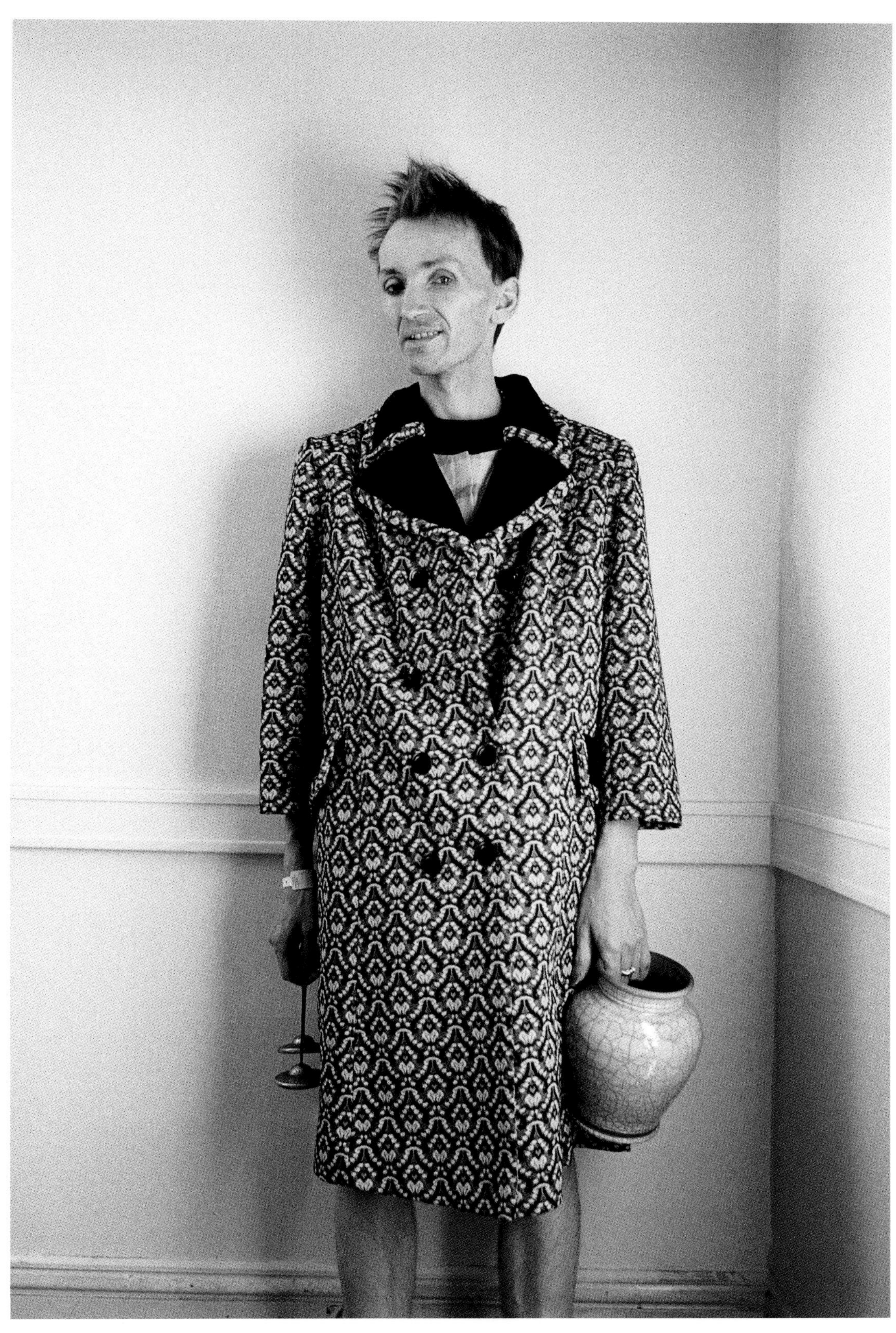

Above: Dan Jones, aka Miss Kitty, at their open studio, May 29, 1994.
Opposite: SF LGBT Pride, June 27, 1993. Dan Jones, aka Miss Kitty.

The Hospital Zone, October 28, 1997. Danny Celeri.

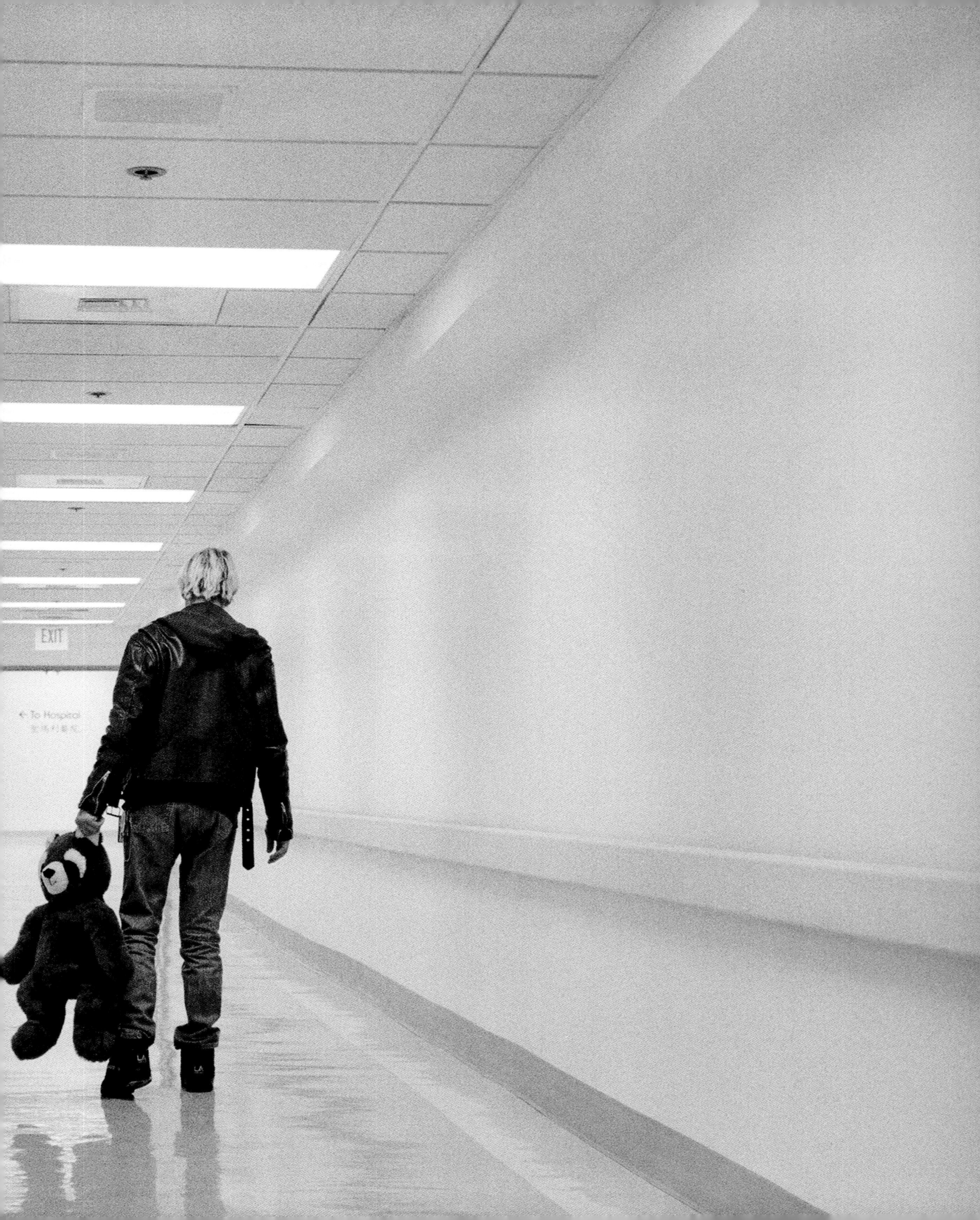
EXIT
← To Hospital

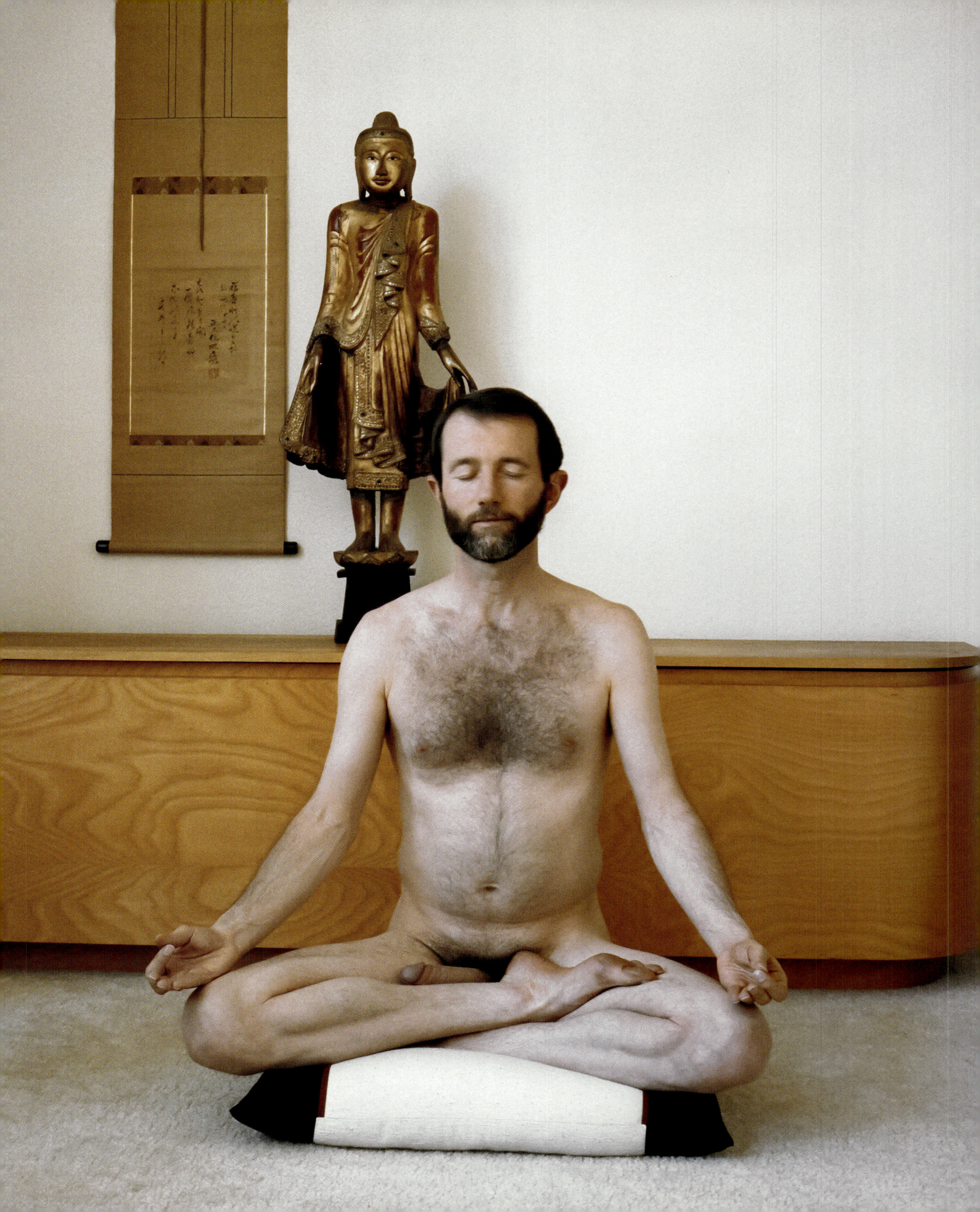

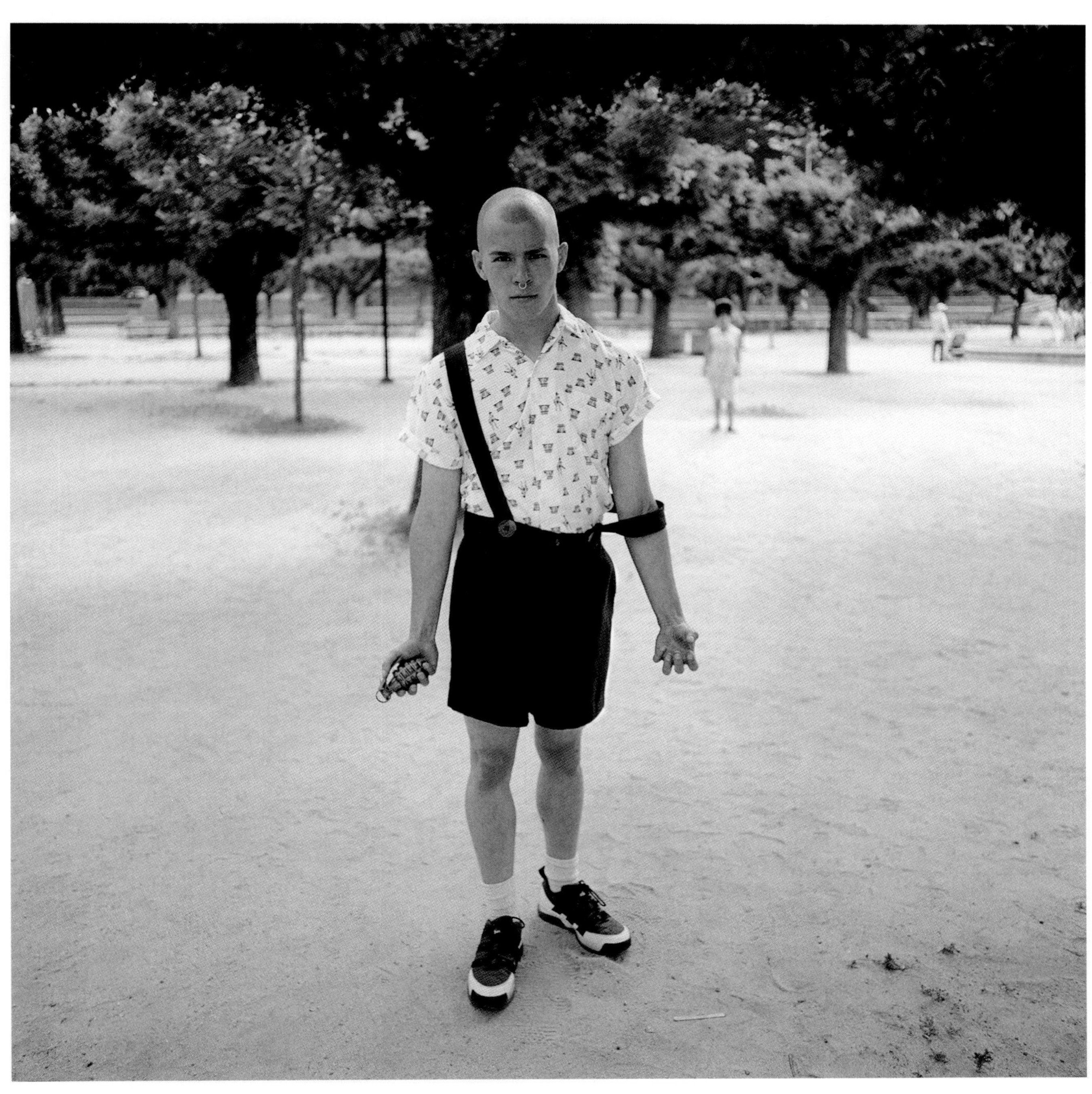

Above: Homage to Diane Arbus' *Child with Toy Hand Grenade*, May 13, 1996.
(Models: Marcus Ewert, Jillian Clark; hair: Deena Davenport; styling: Scott Pimintel.)
Opposite: Jack Love Sullivan, April 1, 1987.

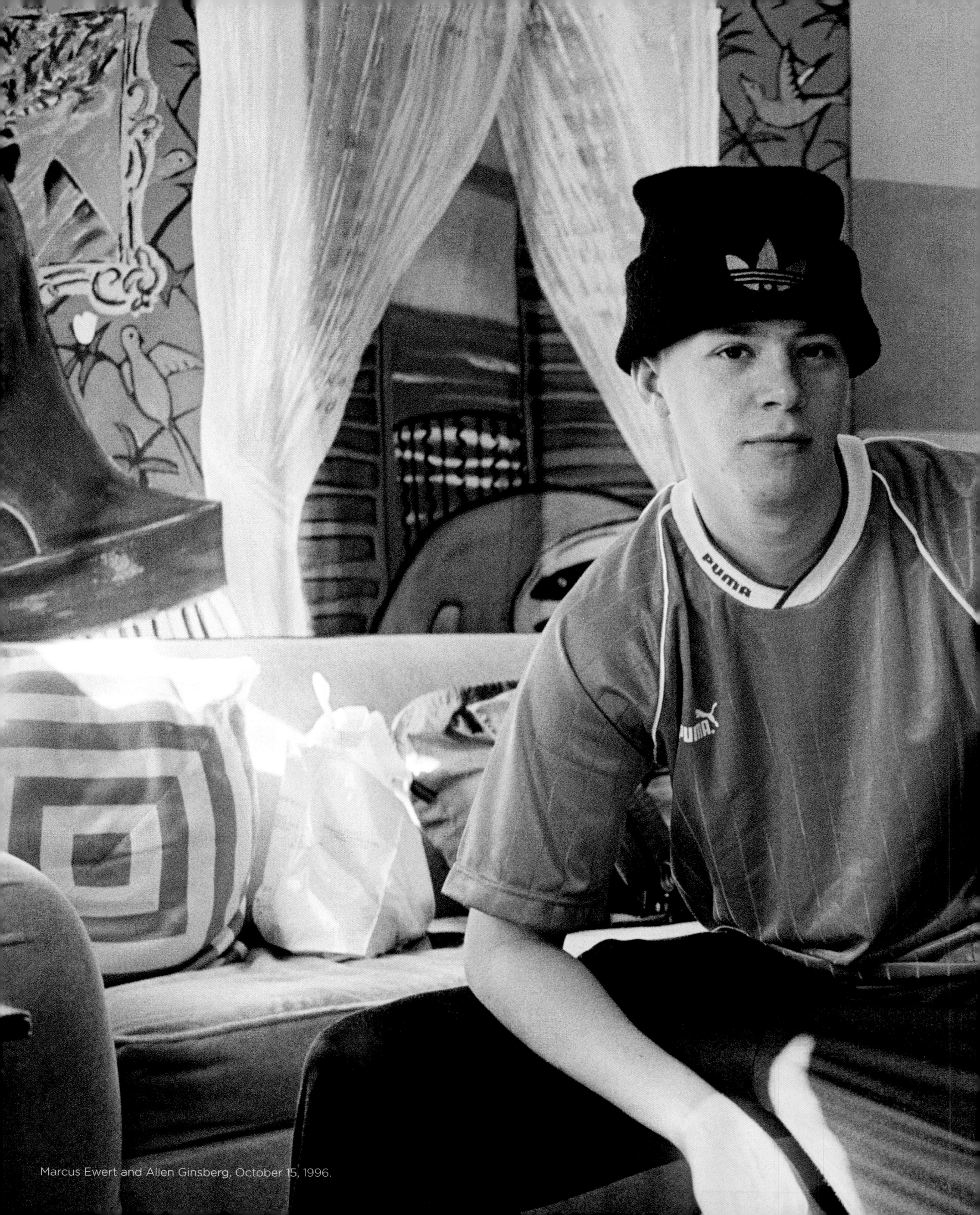

Marcus Ewert and Allen Ginsberg, October 15, 1996.

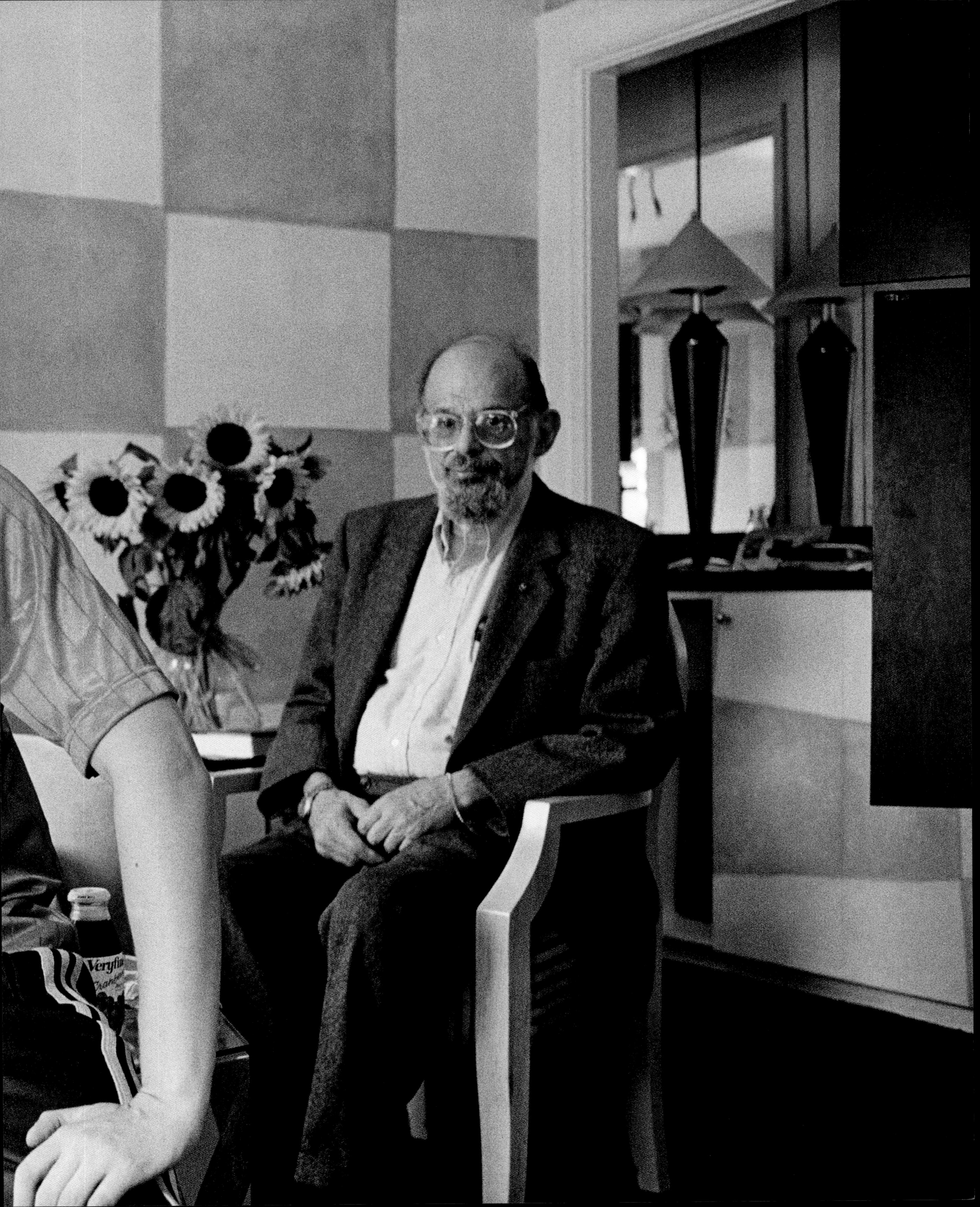

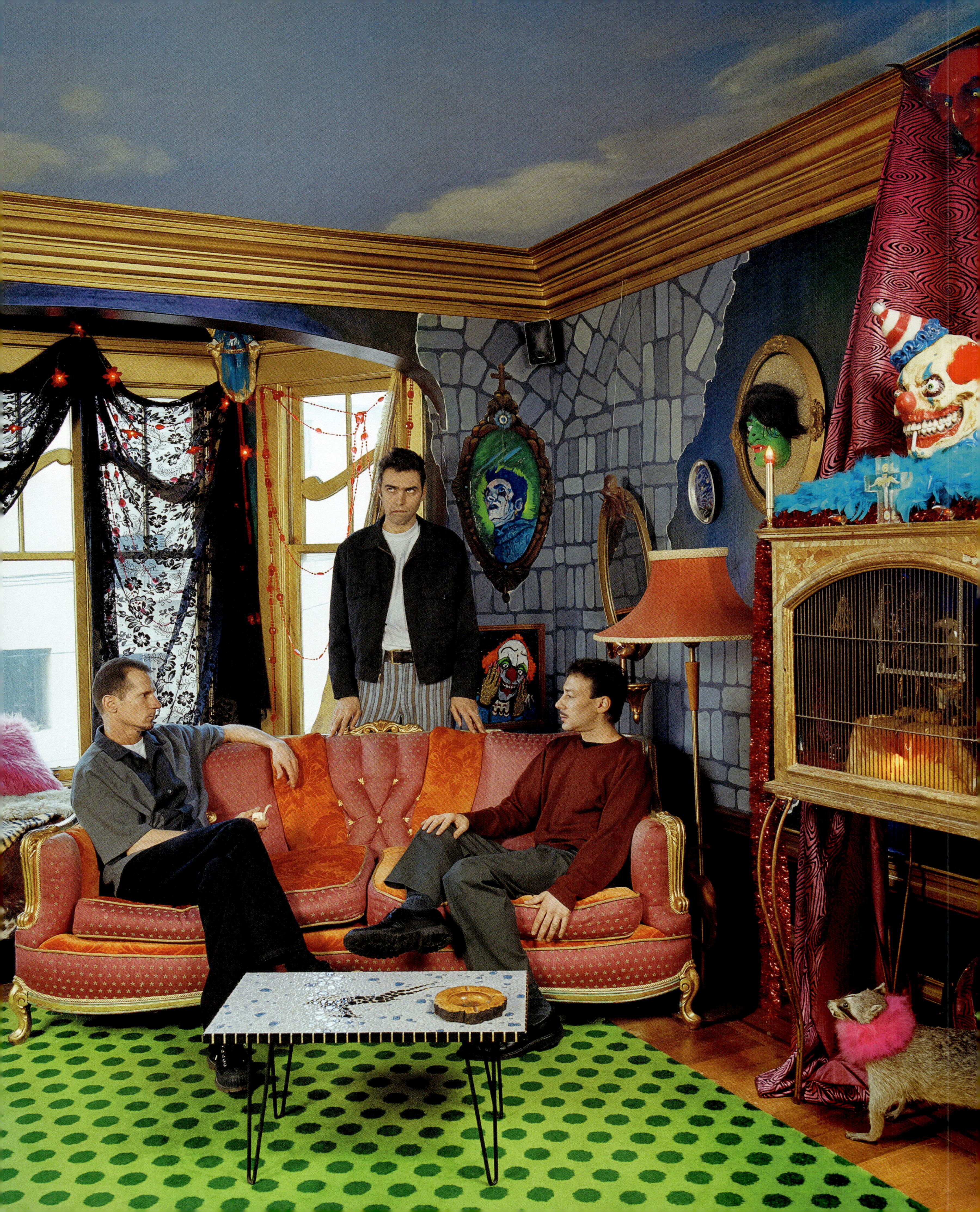

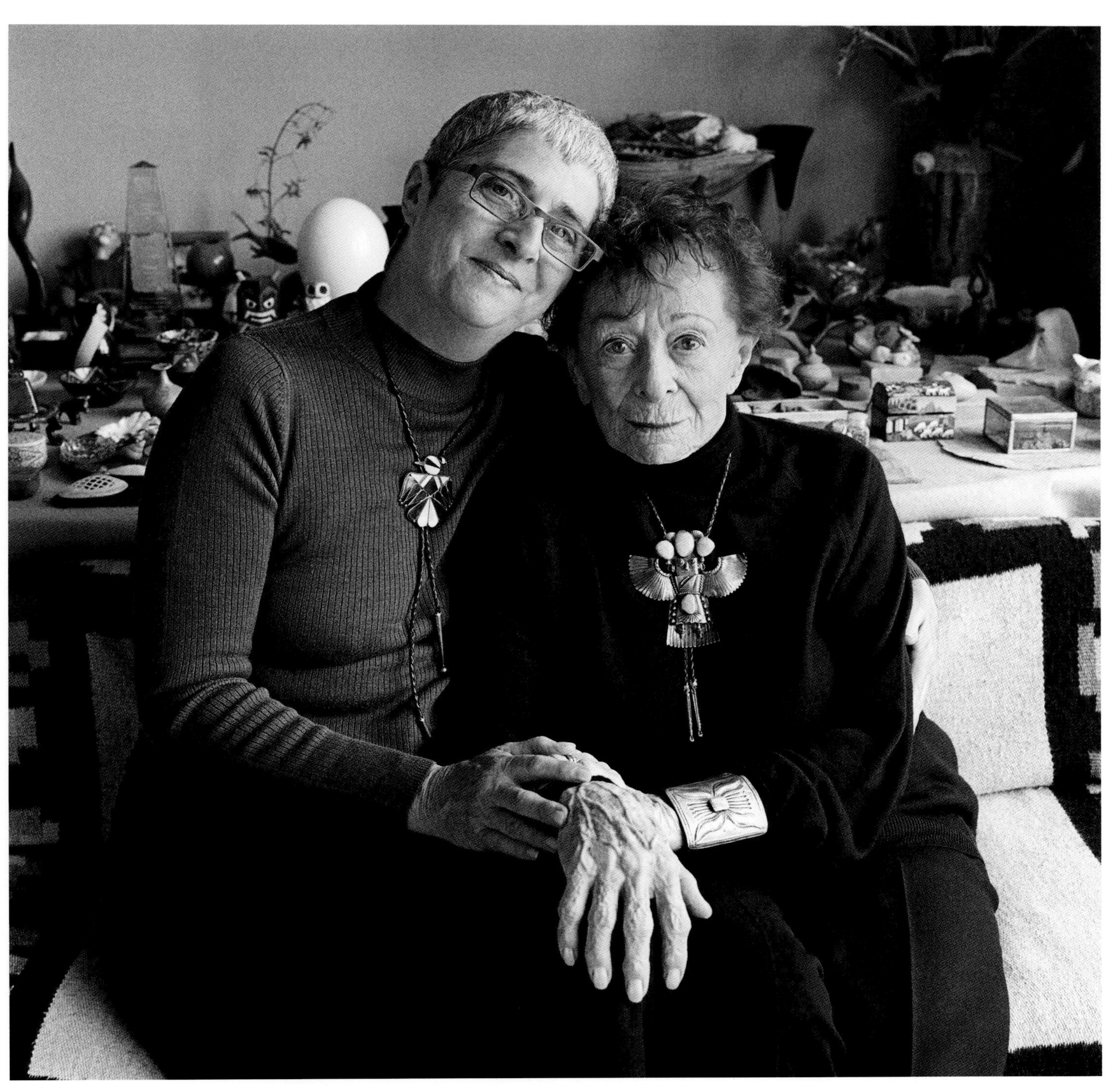

Above: Chris Mende and Ruth Bernhard, May 16, 2003.
Opposite: Scott England's home, January 3, 1998. Scott England, Gordon Henderson and Thomas Avena.
(Sofa by Granite Trudeau, murals by Charles Sexton and Jerome Caja.)

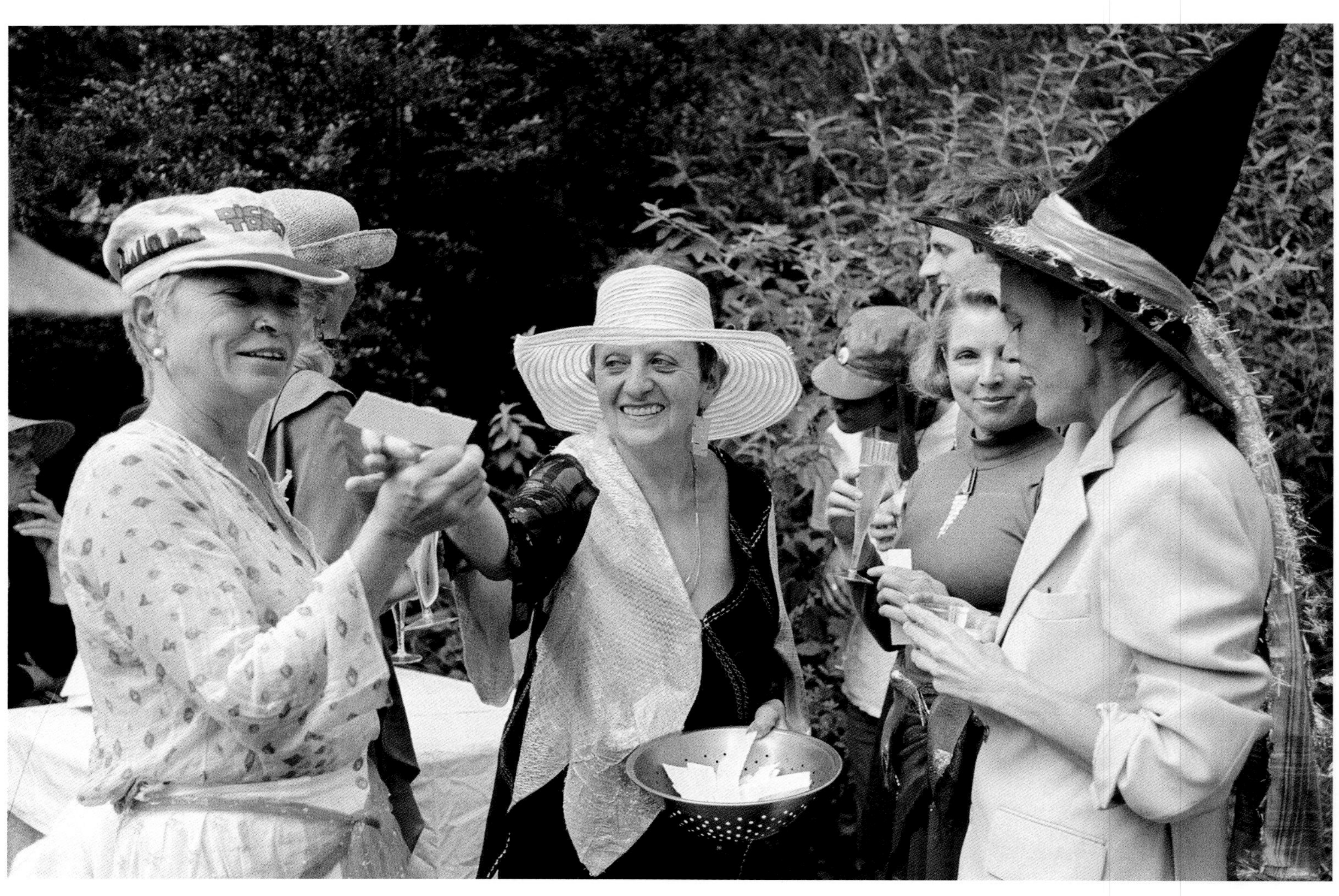

Above: Poet ruth weiss giving Wendy Dalton original haiku in ruth's garden in Albion, September 13, 1992 (far right rear: Daniel Frontino Elash and Tony Stallone).
Opposite: Dodie Bellamy and Kevin Killian, March 8, 2003.

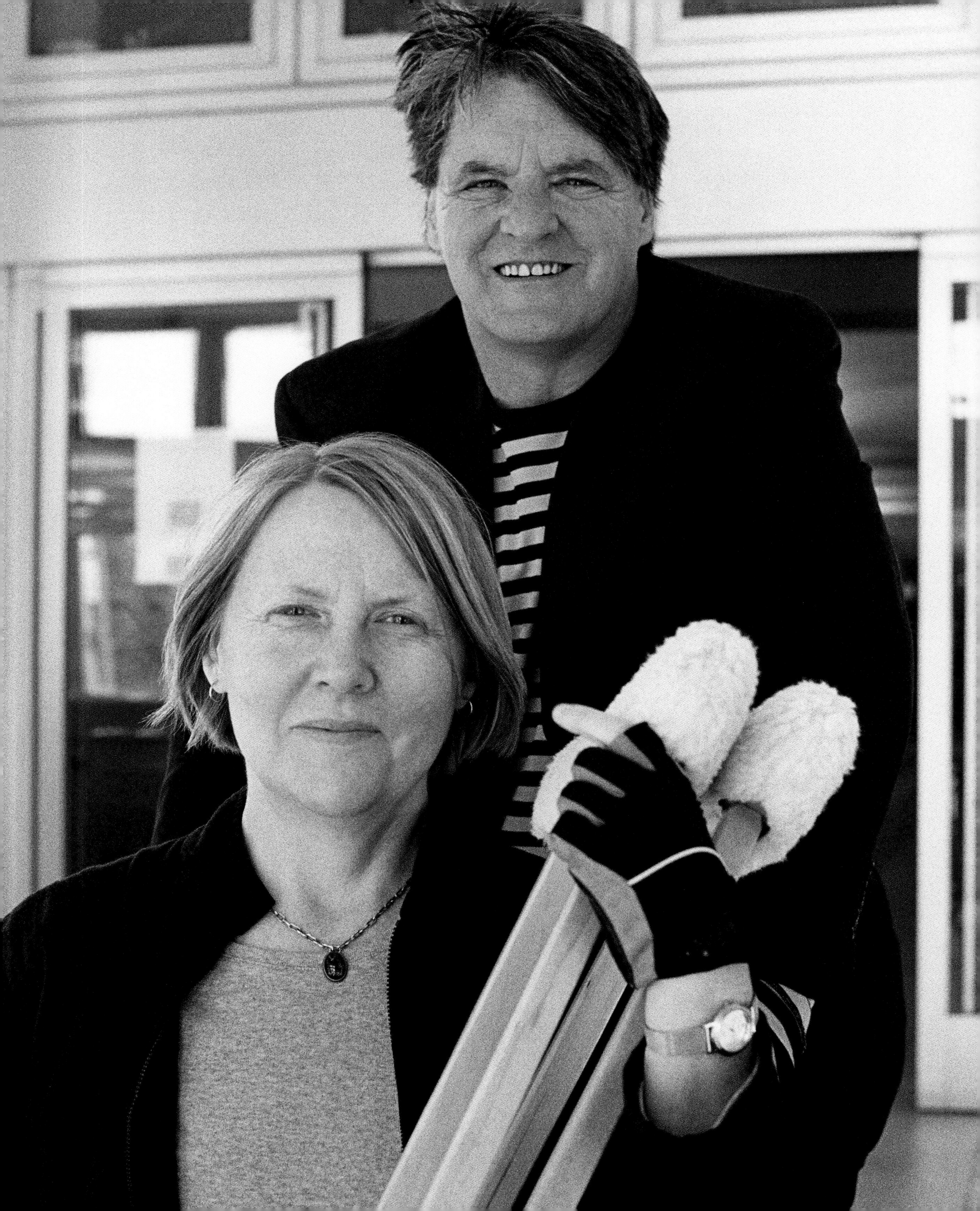

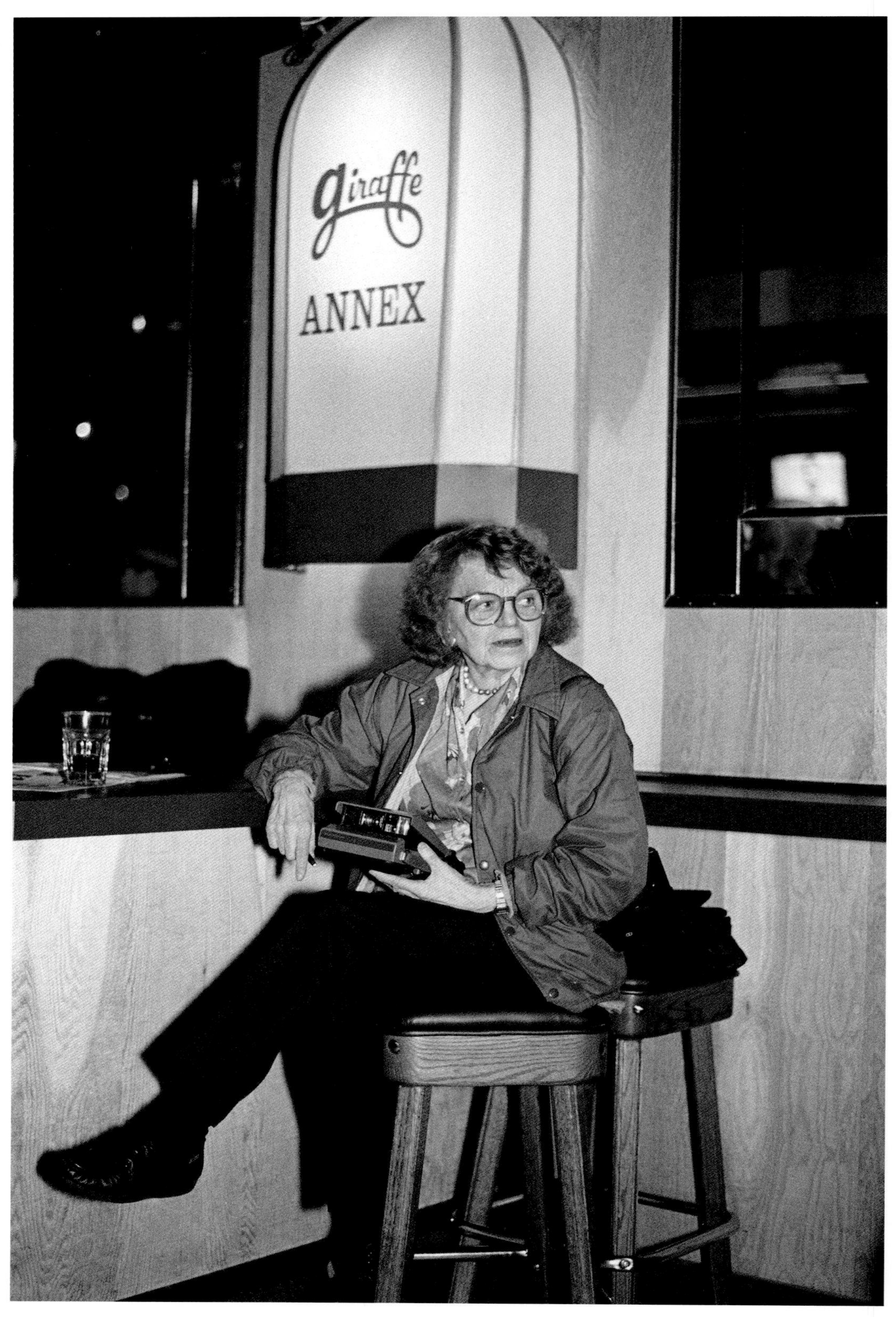

Giraffe Bar, Polk Street, February 14, 1994. Polly Polaroid.

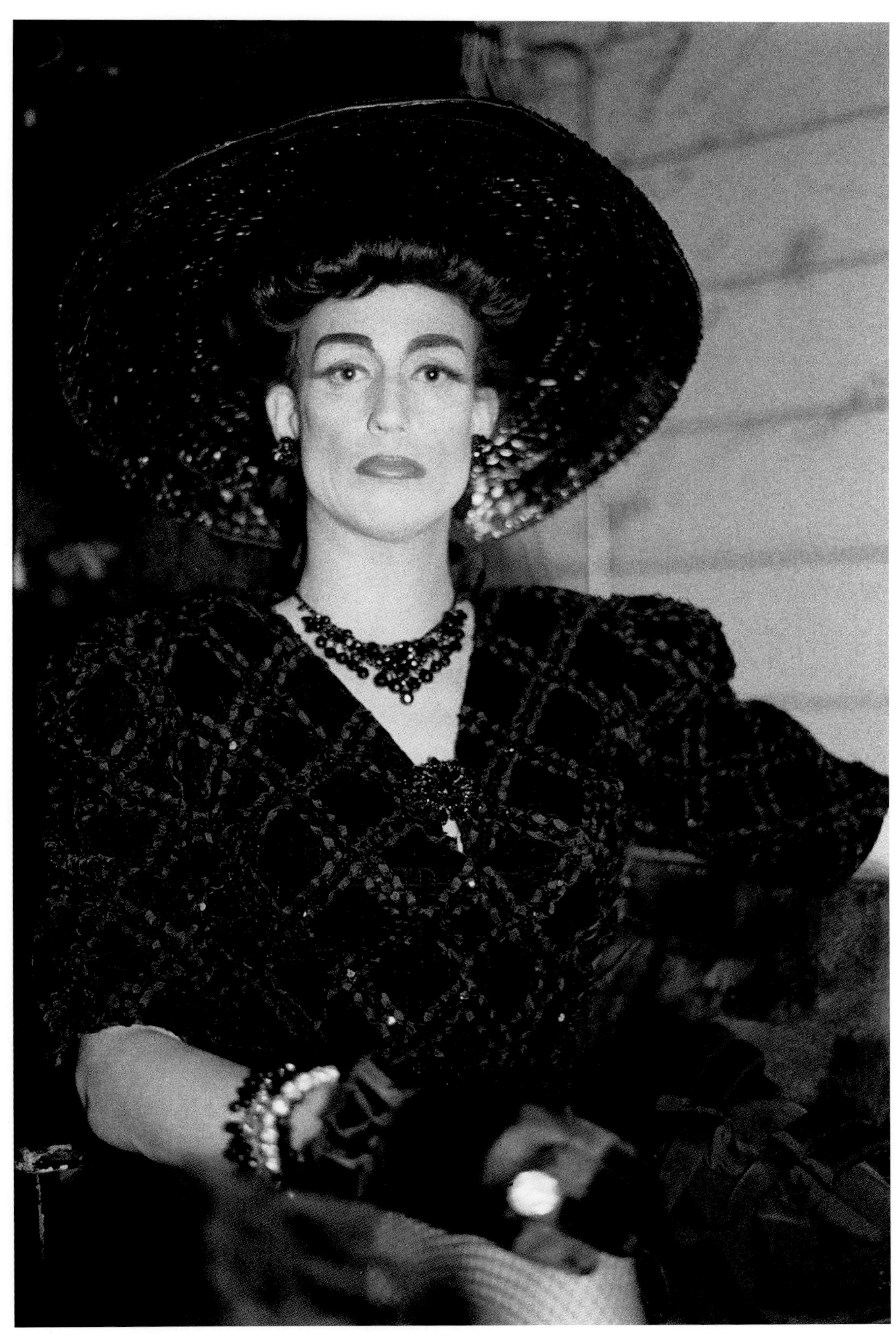

Mad Magda's Russian Tea Room, March 27, 1998. Jaymes Mark Williams.

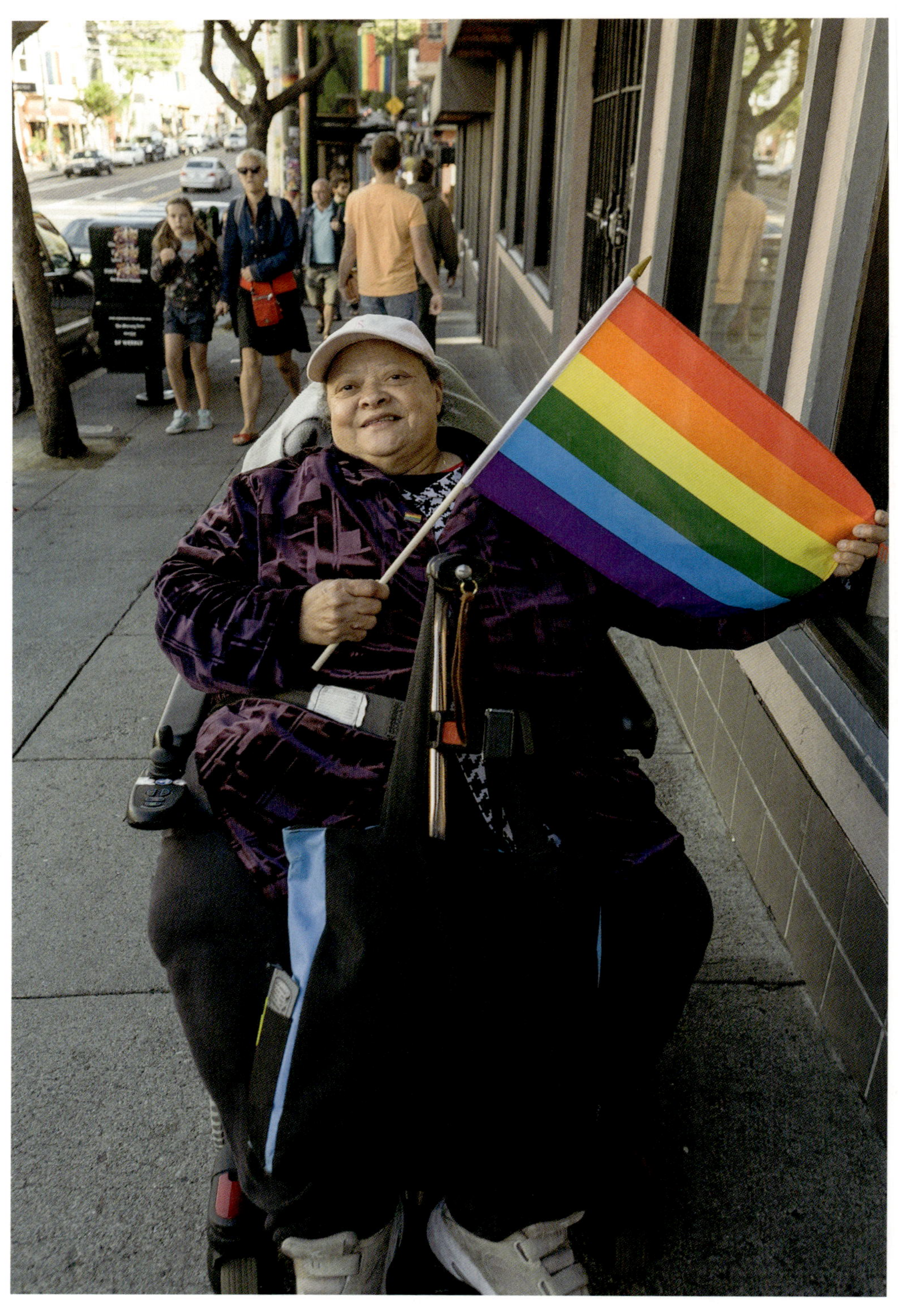

Above: Castro Street, June 2, 2009. Marion Abdullah.
Opposite: SF Police Lieutenant Stephan Thorne, June 22, 2006.

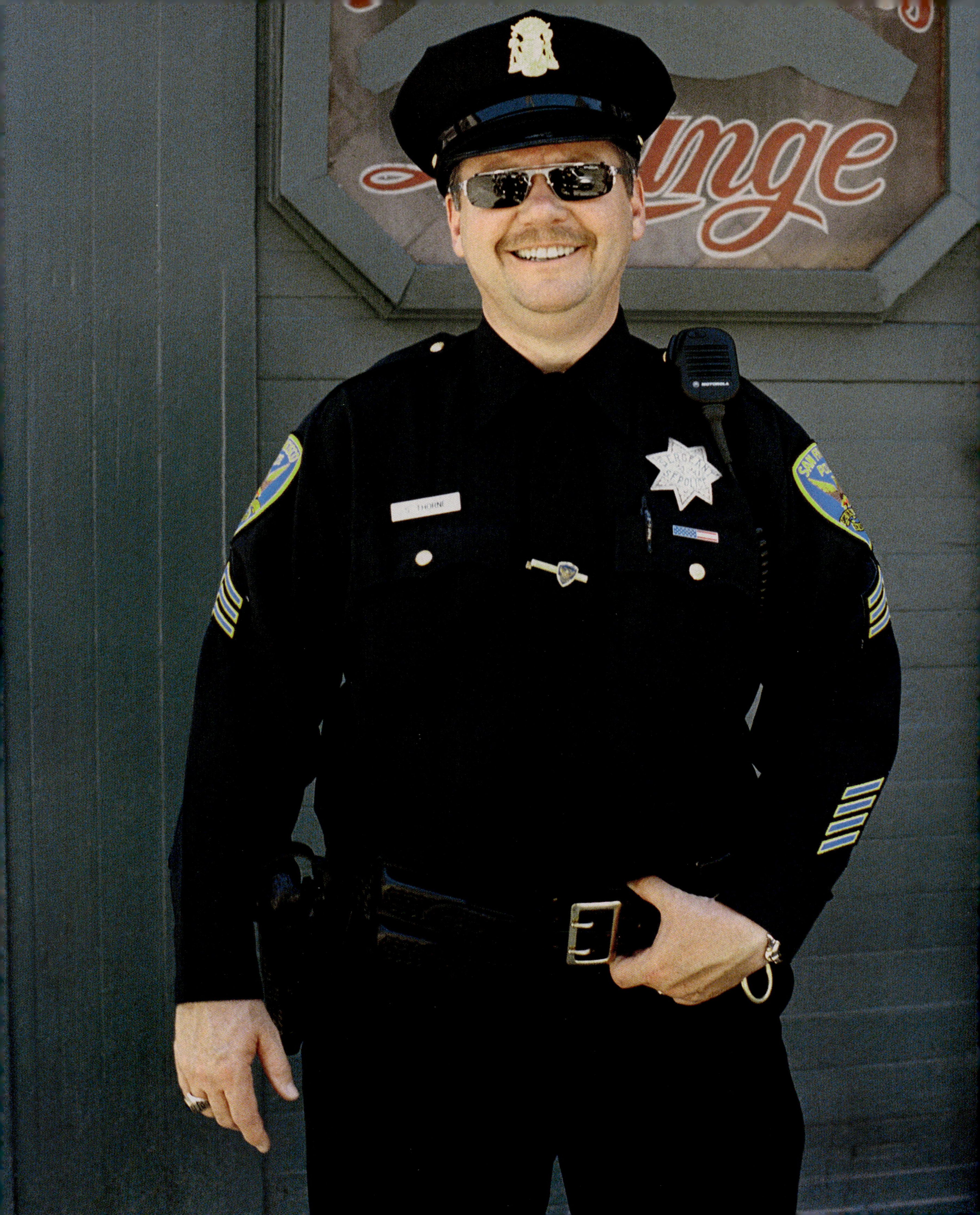
SERGEANT
S.F. POLICE
THORNE

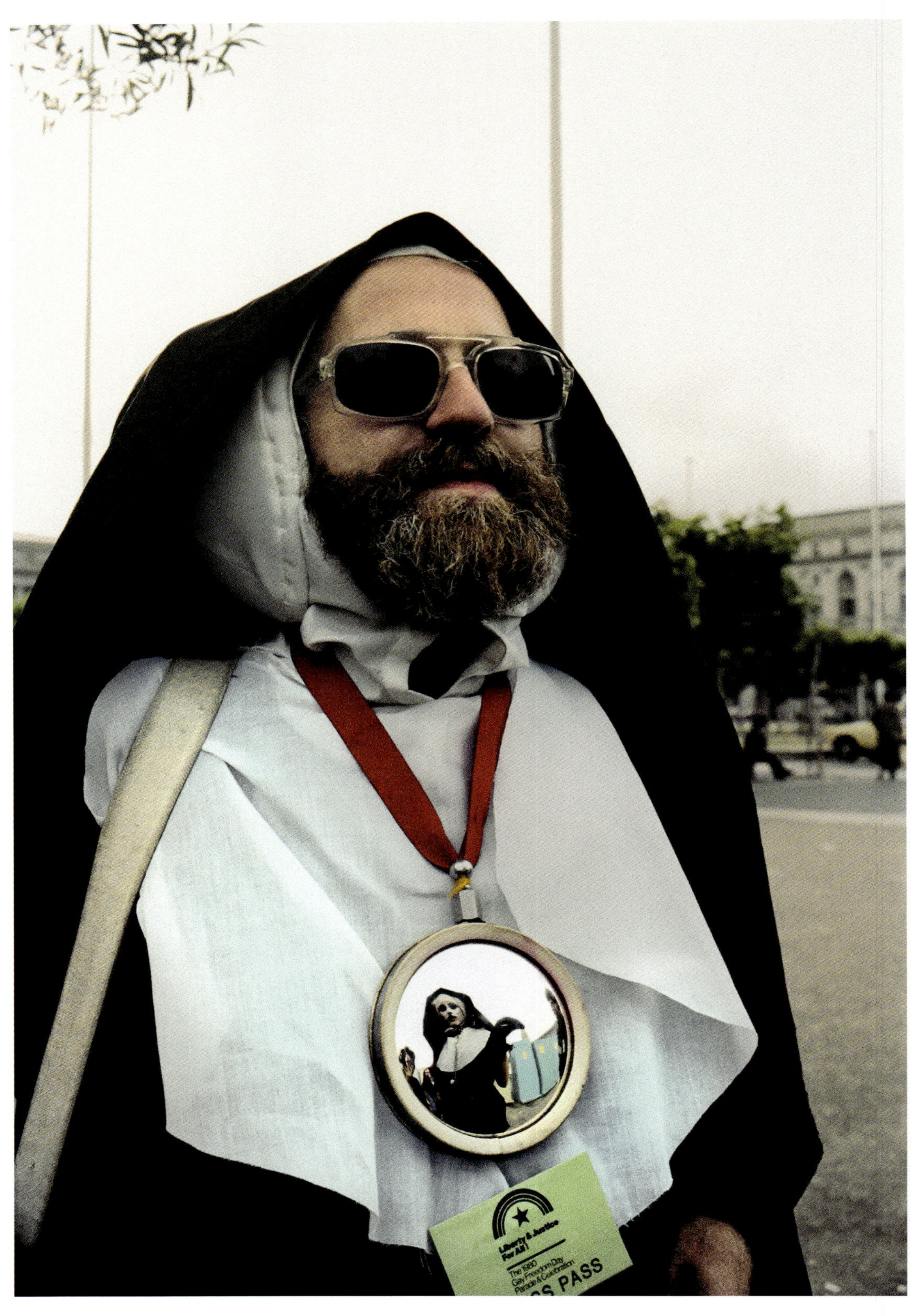

Above: SF LGBT Pride, June 29, 1980. Sister Missionary Position with mirrored Sister Vish (Adhanarisvara), co-founders of the Sisters of Perpetual Indulgence.
Opposite: Protest rally against the Pope's visit to San Francisco, September 17, 1987.

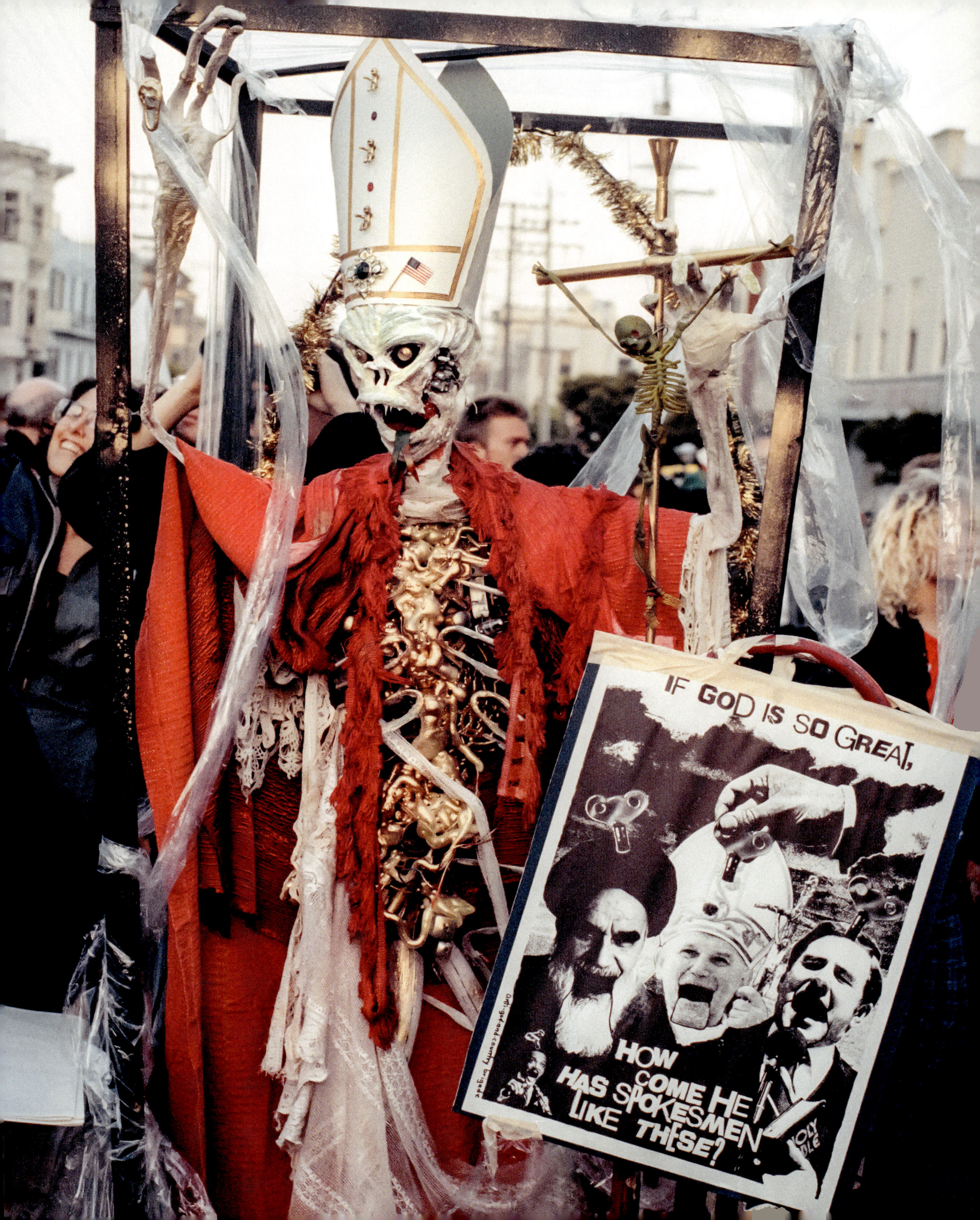
IF GOD IS SO GREAT,
HOW COME HE HAS SPOKESMEN LIKE THESE?
anti-god-and-country brigade

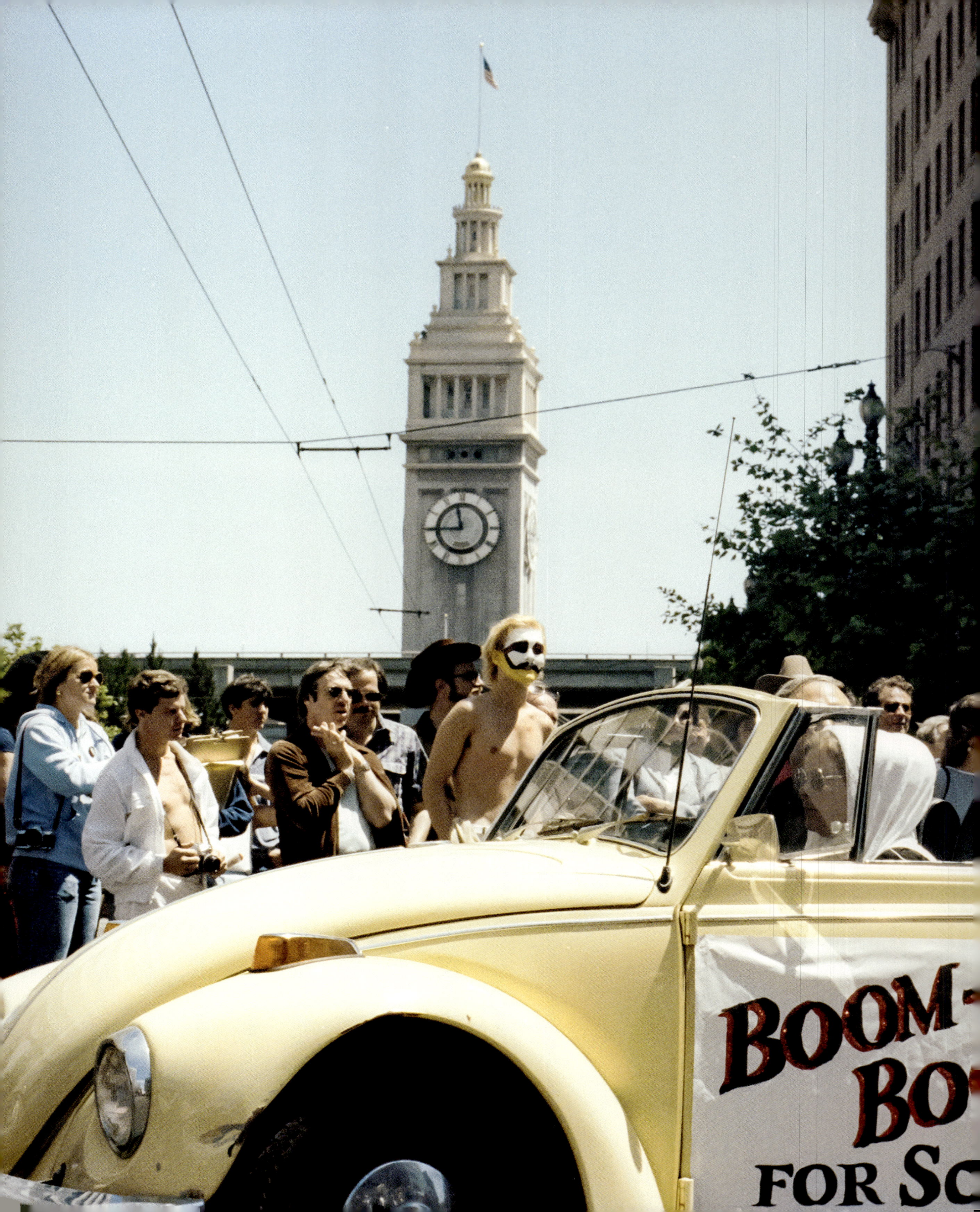
BOOM-
BO
FOR SC

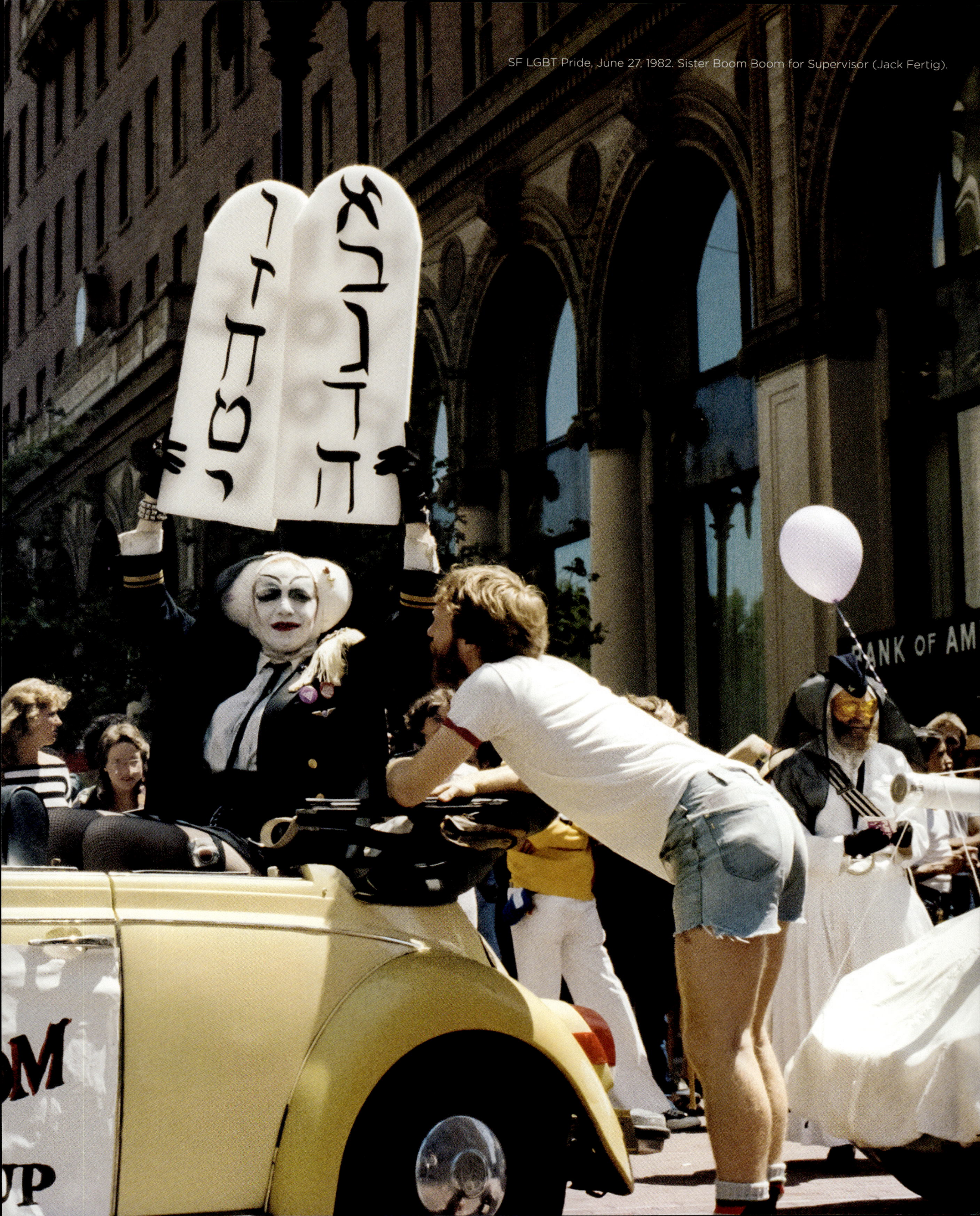

SF LGBT Pride, June 27, 1982. Sister Boom Boom for Supervisor (Jack Fertig).

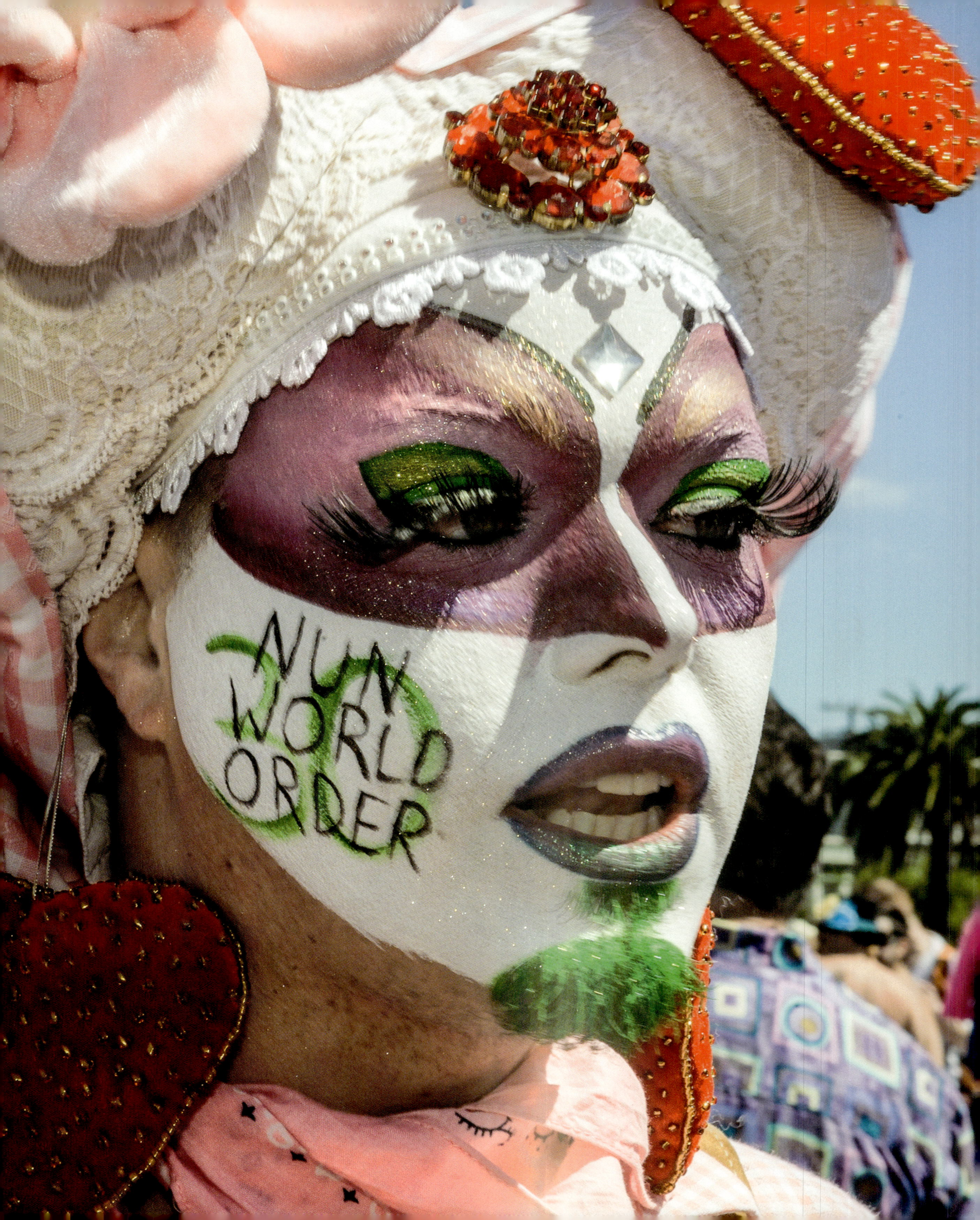
NUN
WORLD
ORDER

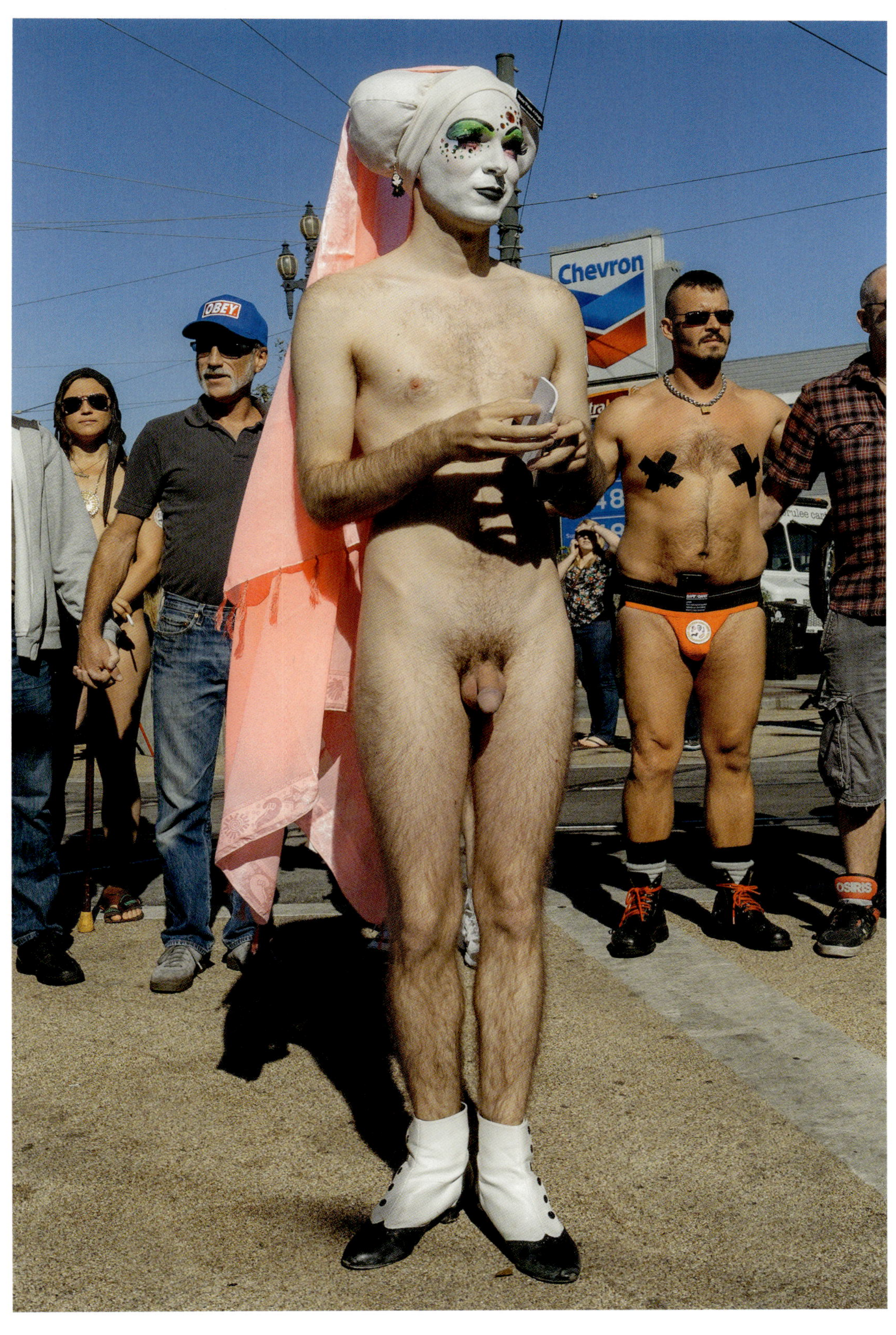

Above: Castro rally protesting local legislation prohibiting public nudity, October 10, 2012. Sister T'aint A Virgin.
Opposite: The Sisters of Perpetual Indulgence 30th Anniversary and Annual Easter Celebration in Dolores Park, April 12, 2009. Mutter Daphne.

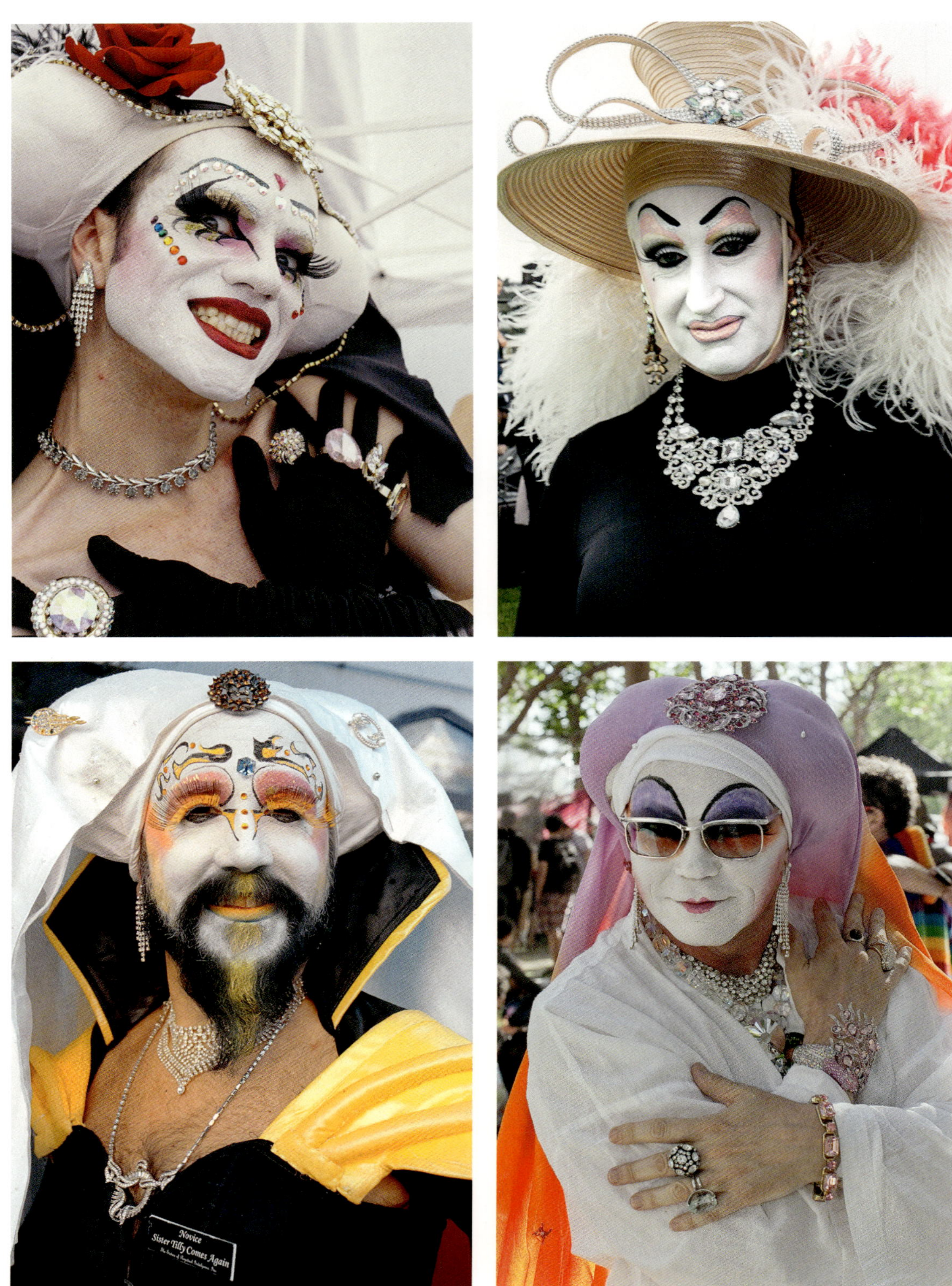

Above: The Sisters of Perpetual Indulgence. (*Clockwise from top left*) Sister VixXxen, Folsom Street Fair, September 26, 1999; Sister Roma, April 8, 2012; Sister Zsa Zsa Glamour, June 26, 2011; Sister Tilly Comes Again, Sisters Bingo, June 6, 2004.
. ***Opposite:*** The 30th Anniversary of The Sisters of Perpetual Indulgence and Annual Easter Celebration in Dolores Park, April 12, 2009. Sister Erotica Psychotica.

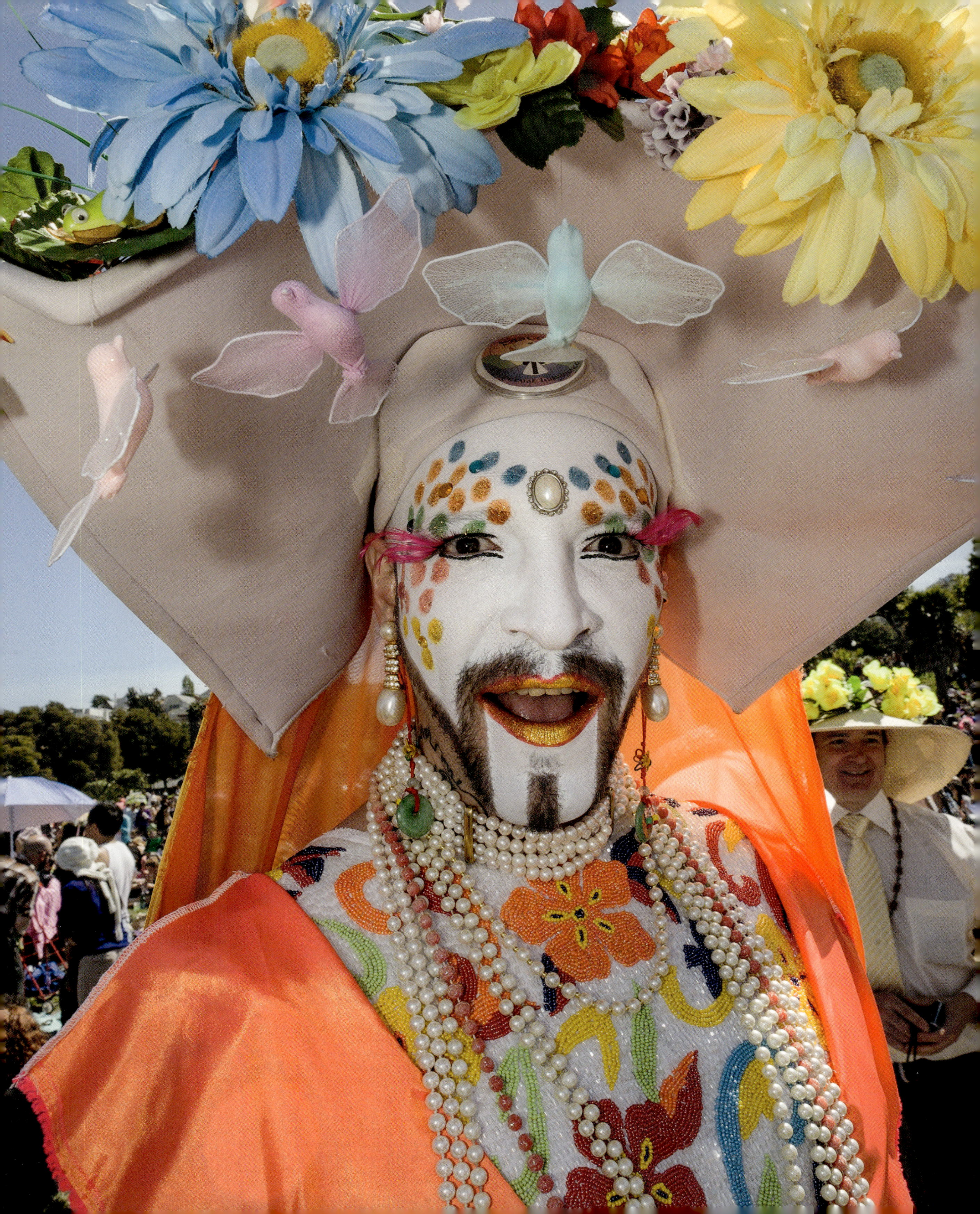

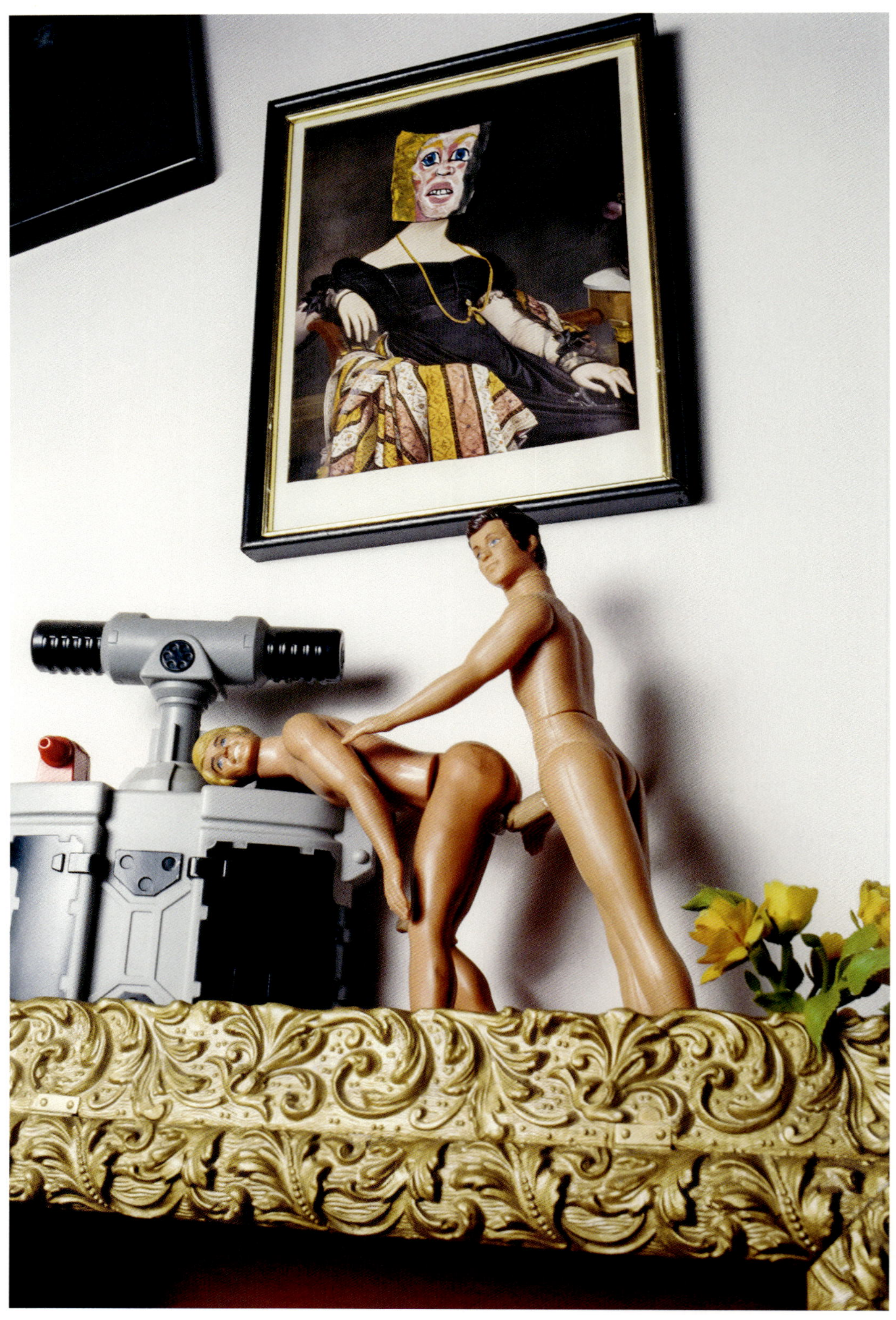

Jerome Caja's home, August 9, 1995.

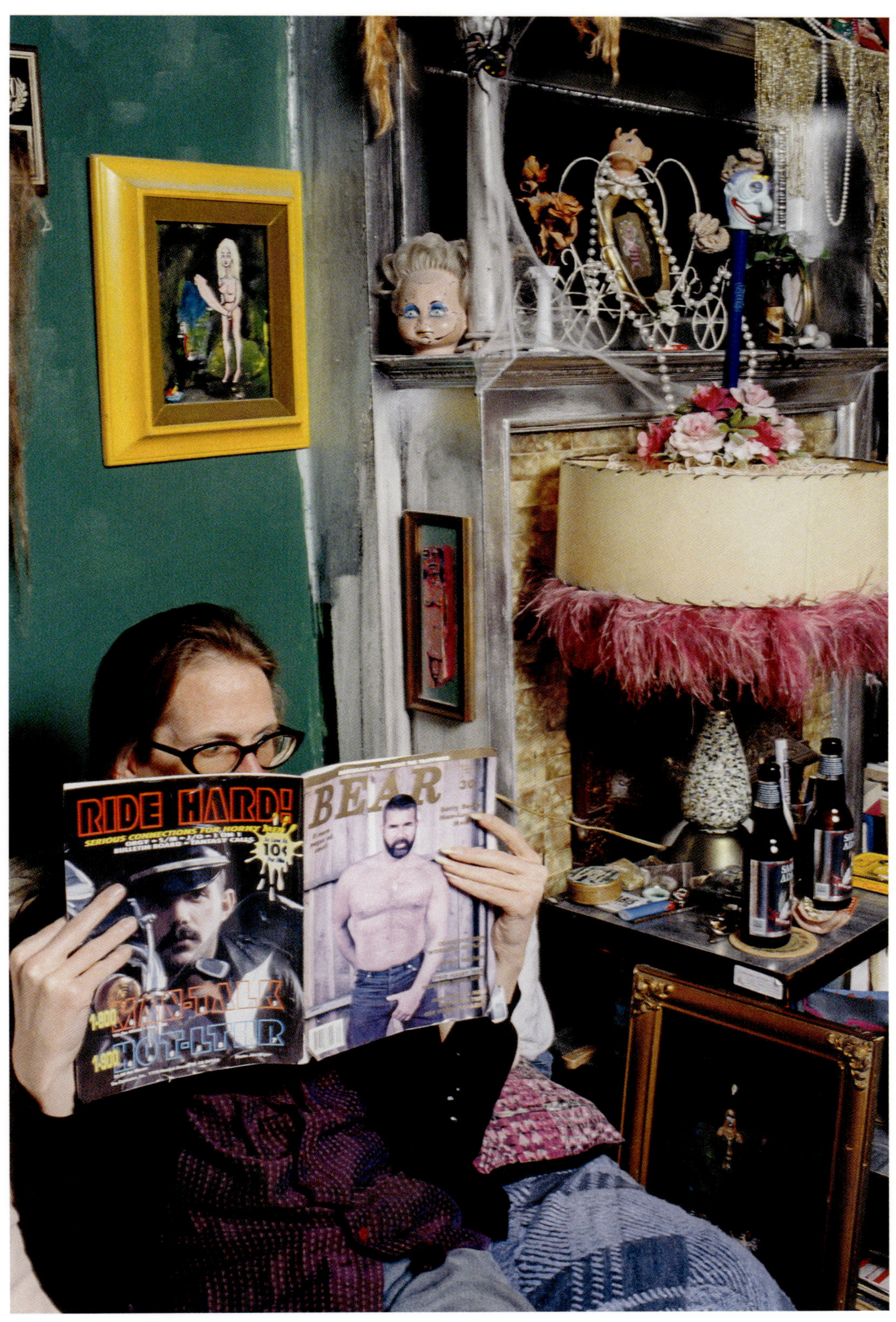

Jerome Caja at home, August 9, 1995.

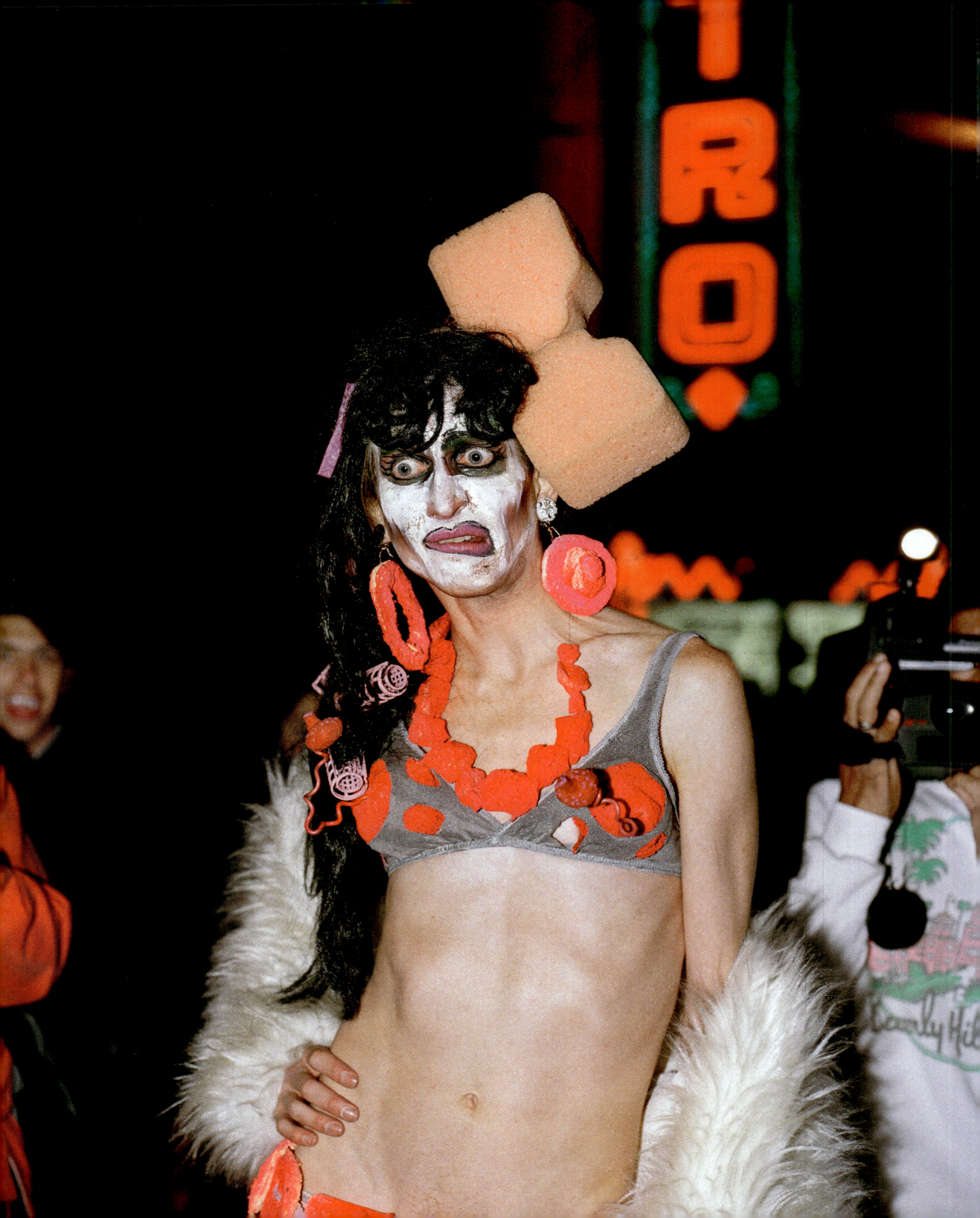

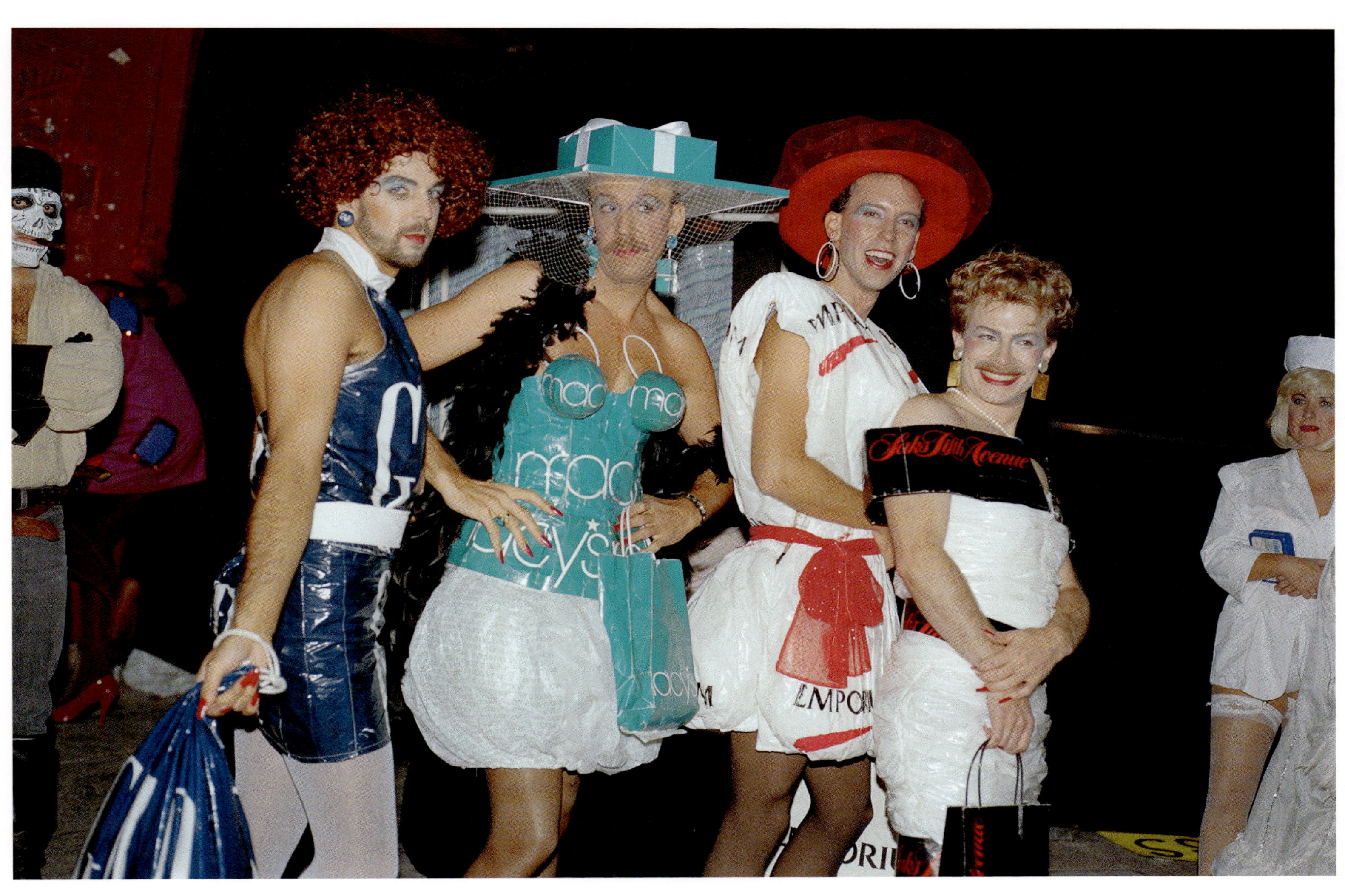

Halloween, October 31, 1990.
(Above) Retail Queens; *(opposite)* Jerome Caja on Castro Street.

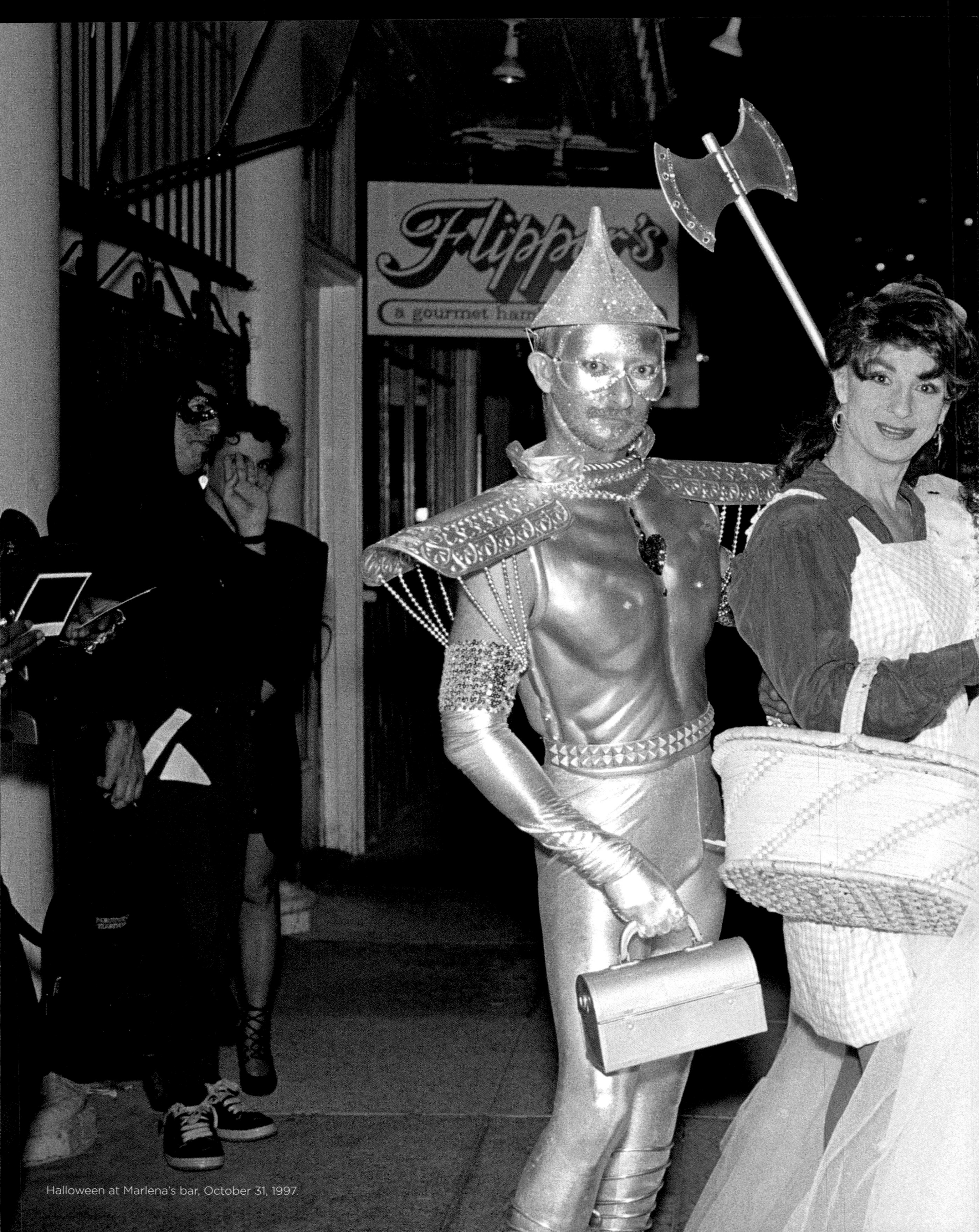

Halloween at Marlena's bar, October 31, 1997.

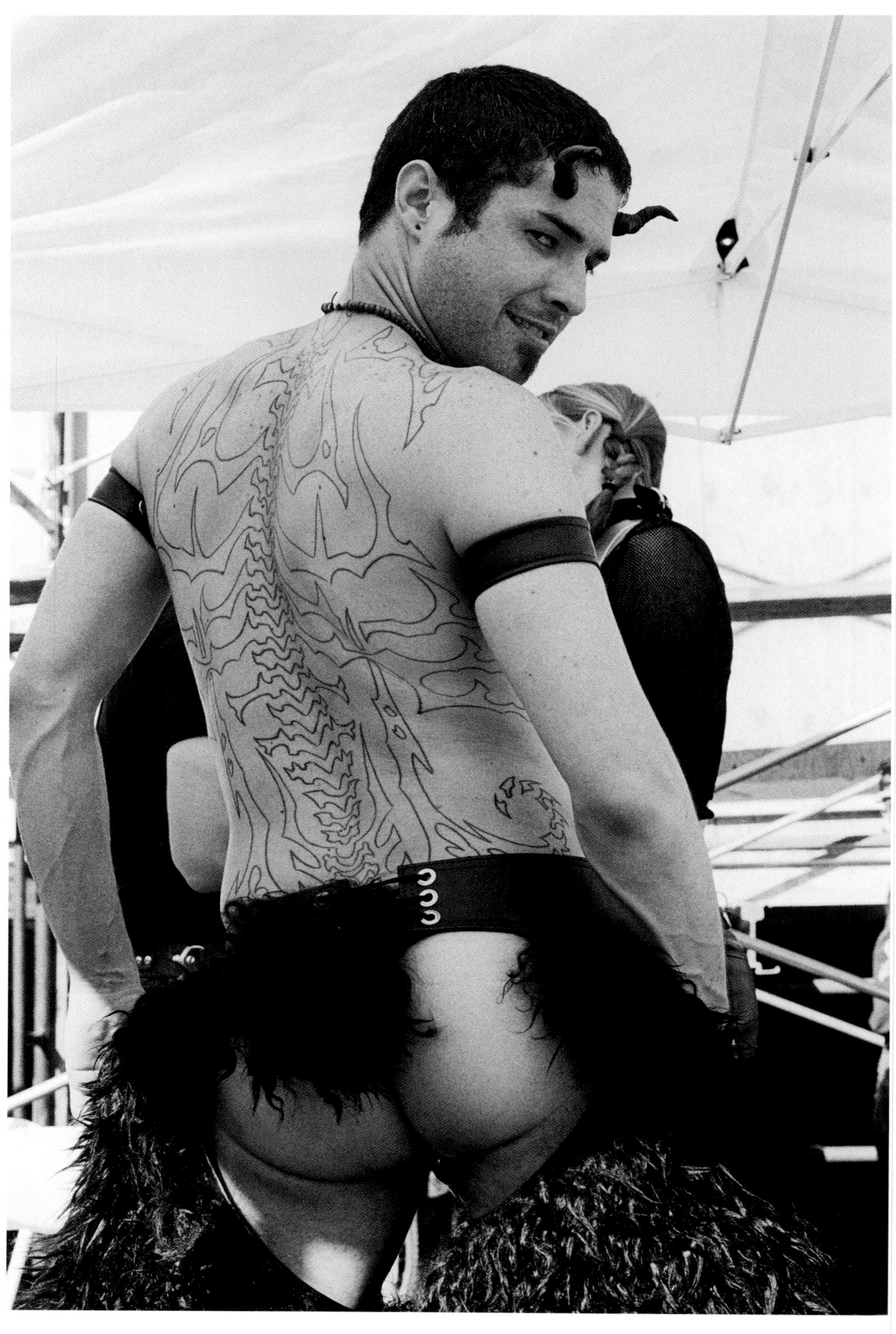

Above: Folsom Street Fair, September 26, 1999. Santiago "The Notorious Imp" Salsido.
Opposite: Folsom Street Fair, September 24, 2000.

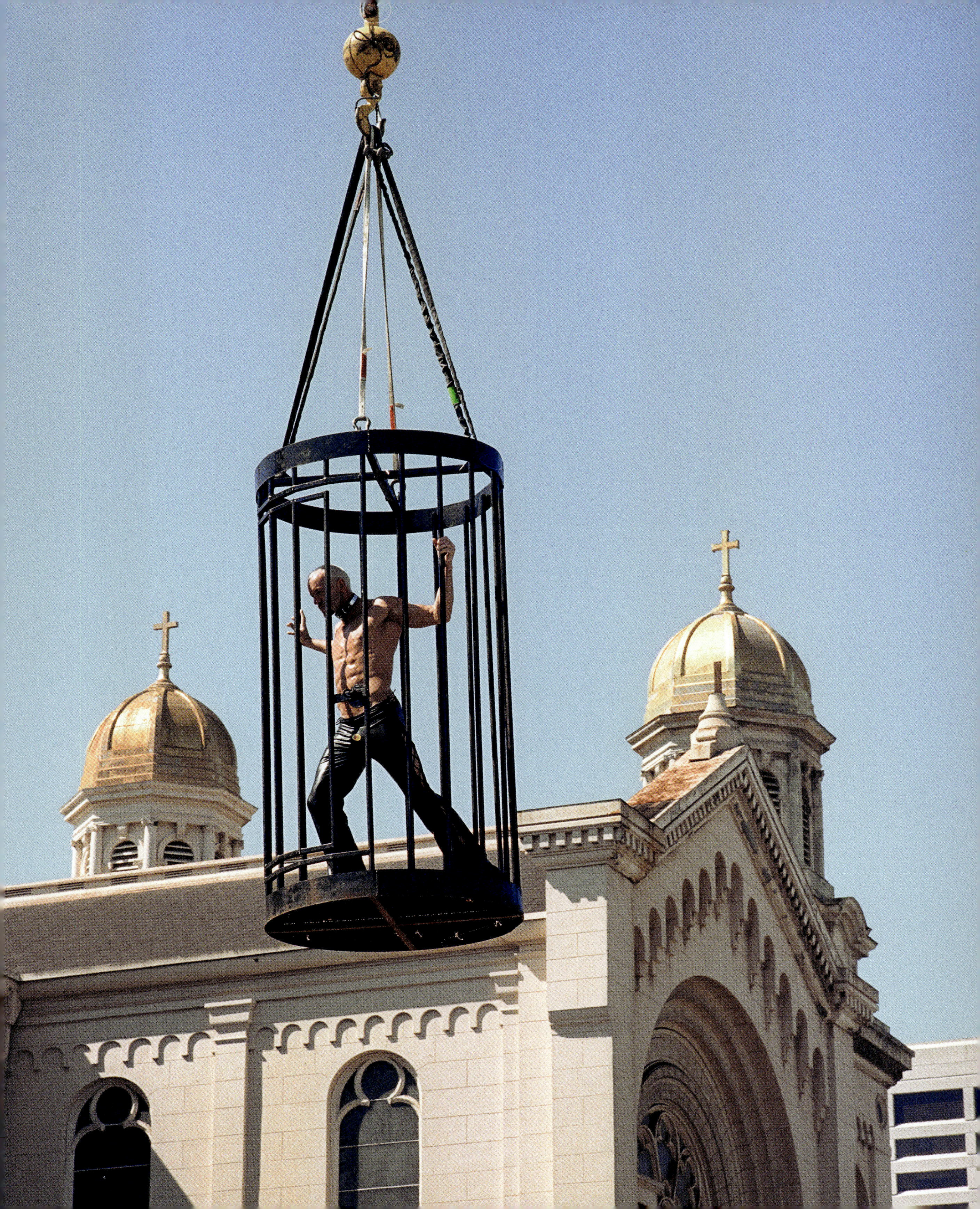

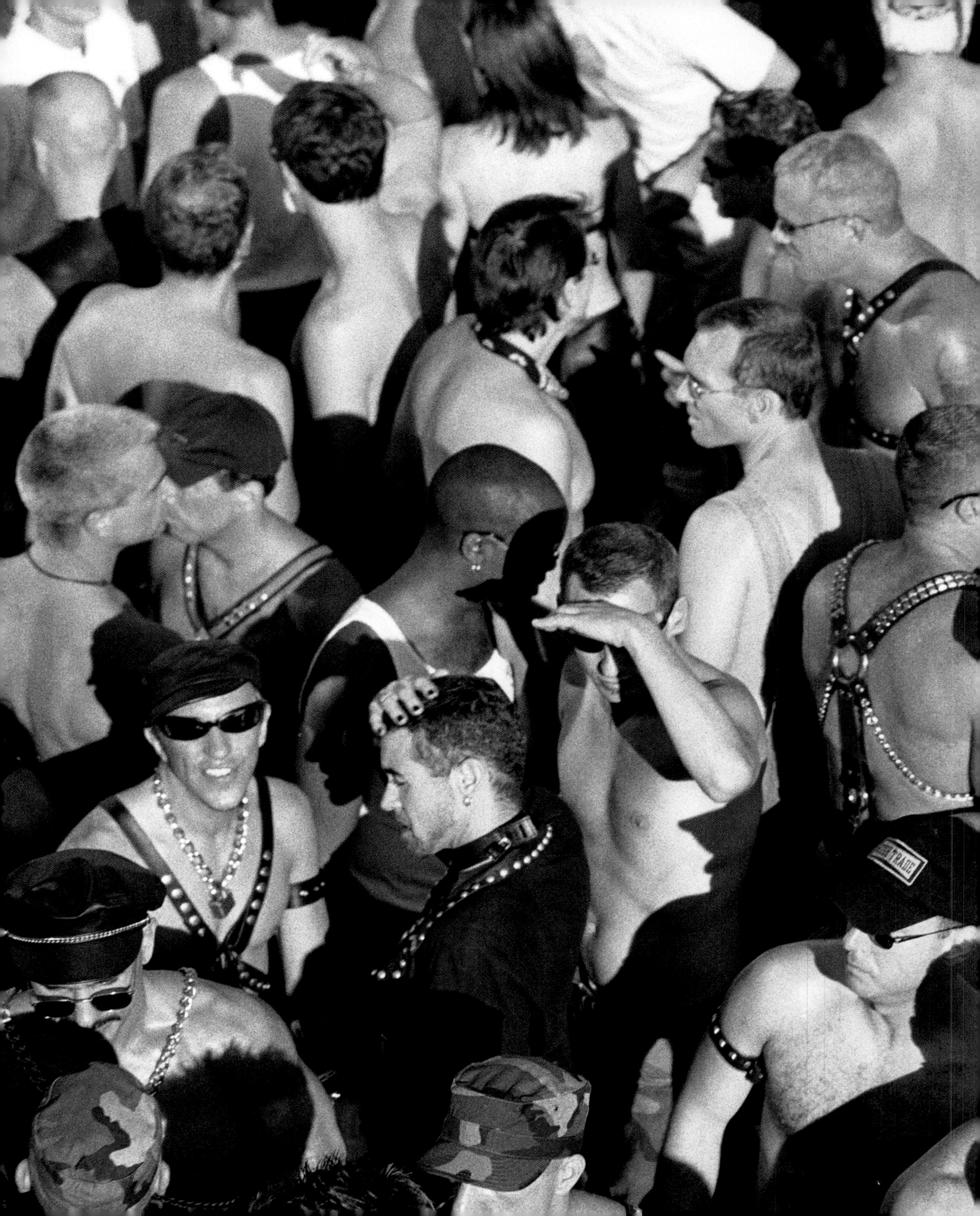
TRADE

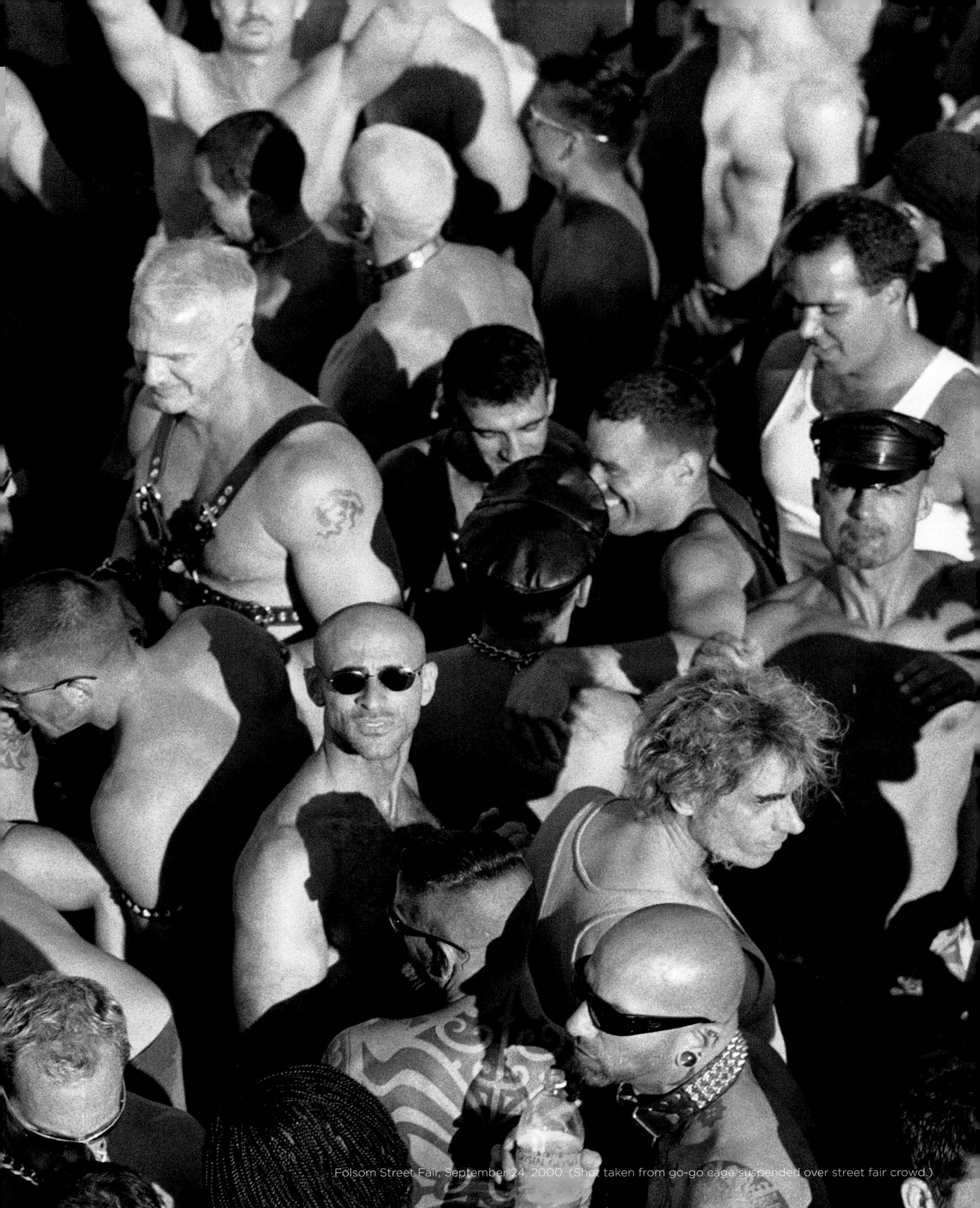

Folsom Street Fair, September 24, 2000. (Shot taken from go-go cage suspended over street fair crowd.)

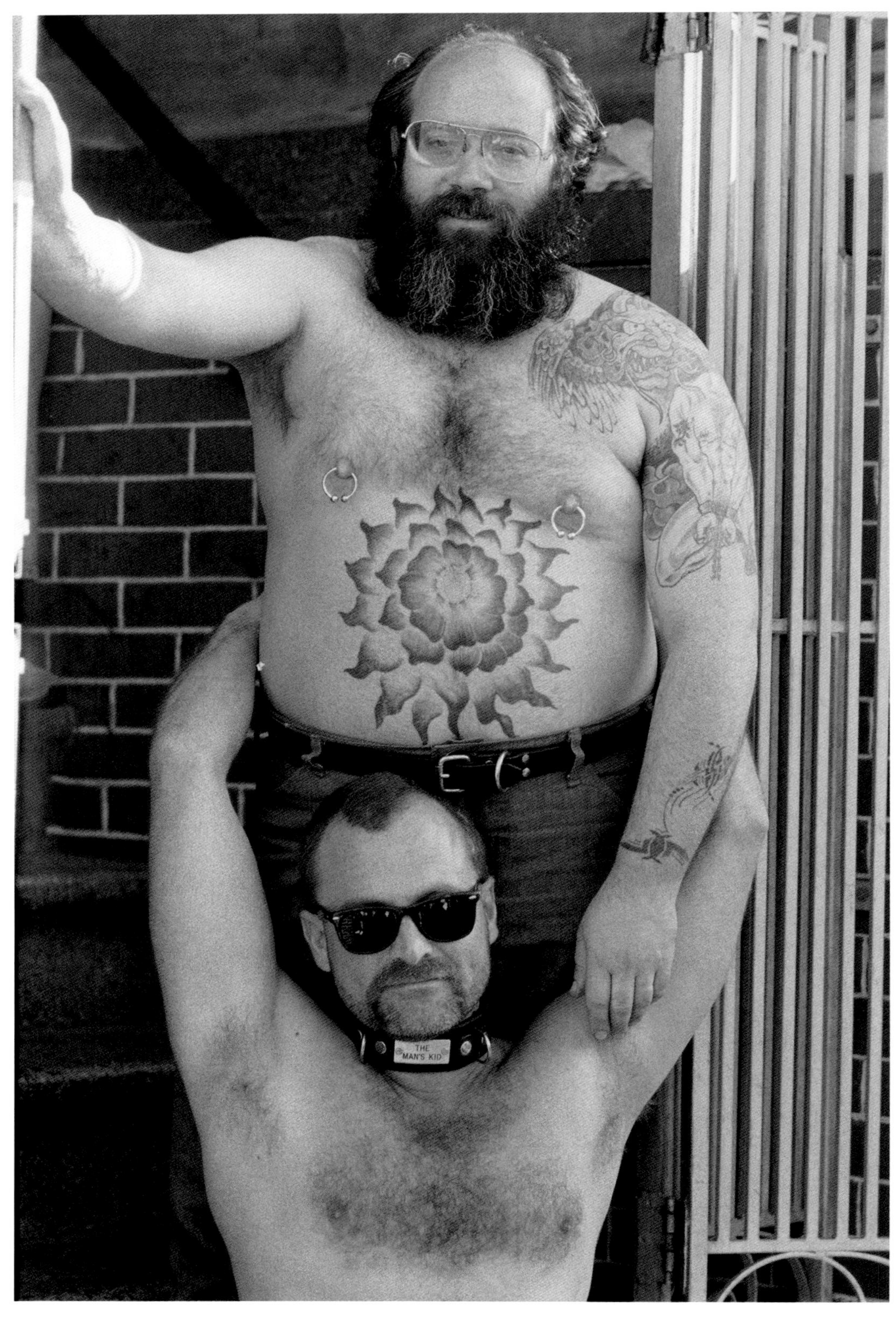

Above: Folsom Street Fair, September 20, 1987. Photographer Mark I. Chester (back) with writer Tim Barrus in front of Chester's annual Folsom St. Fair exhibit of sexual art.
Opposite: Tricycle Race, spring 1976.

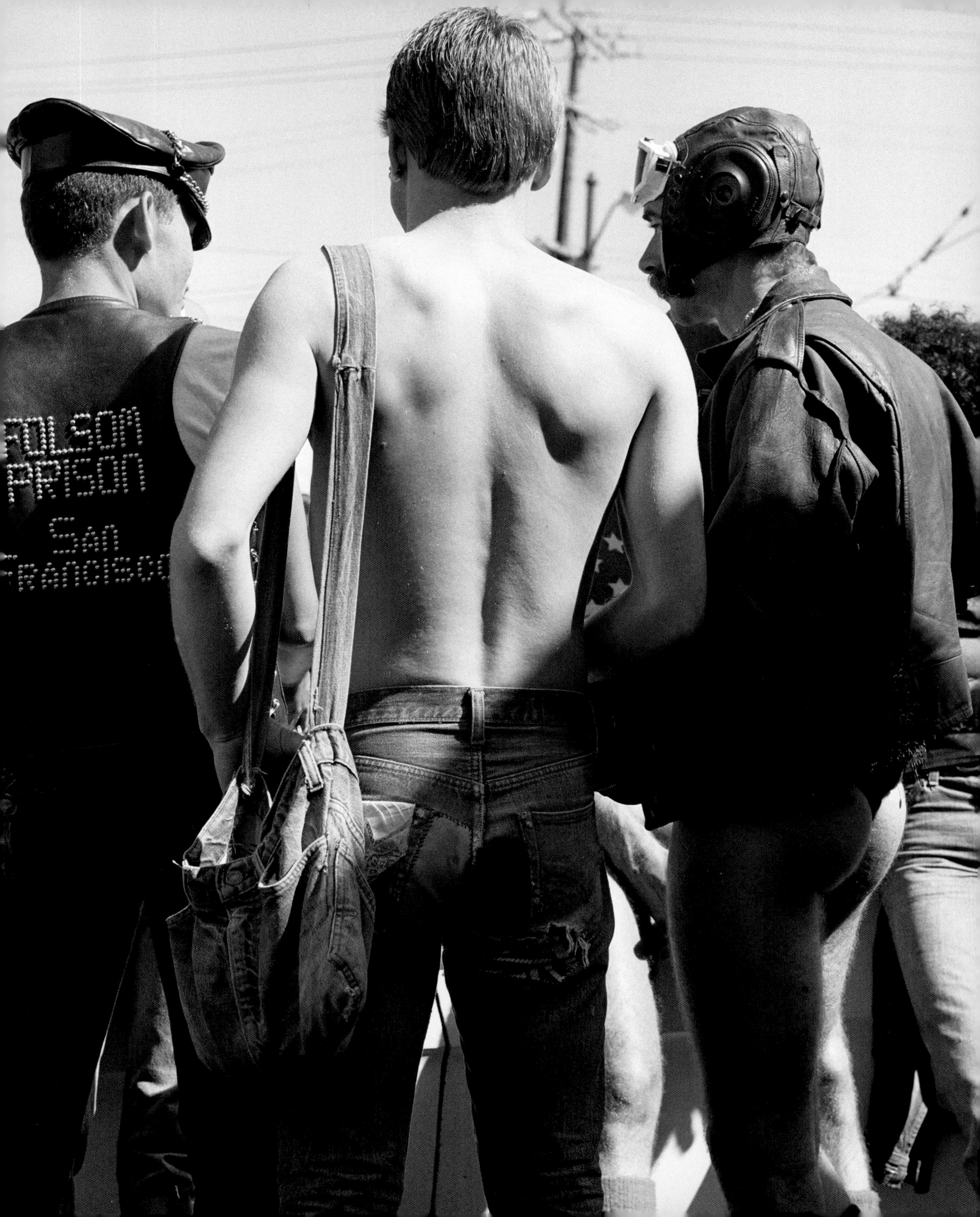
FOLSOM
PRISON
San

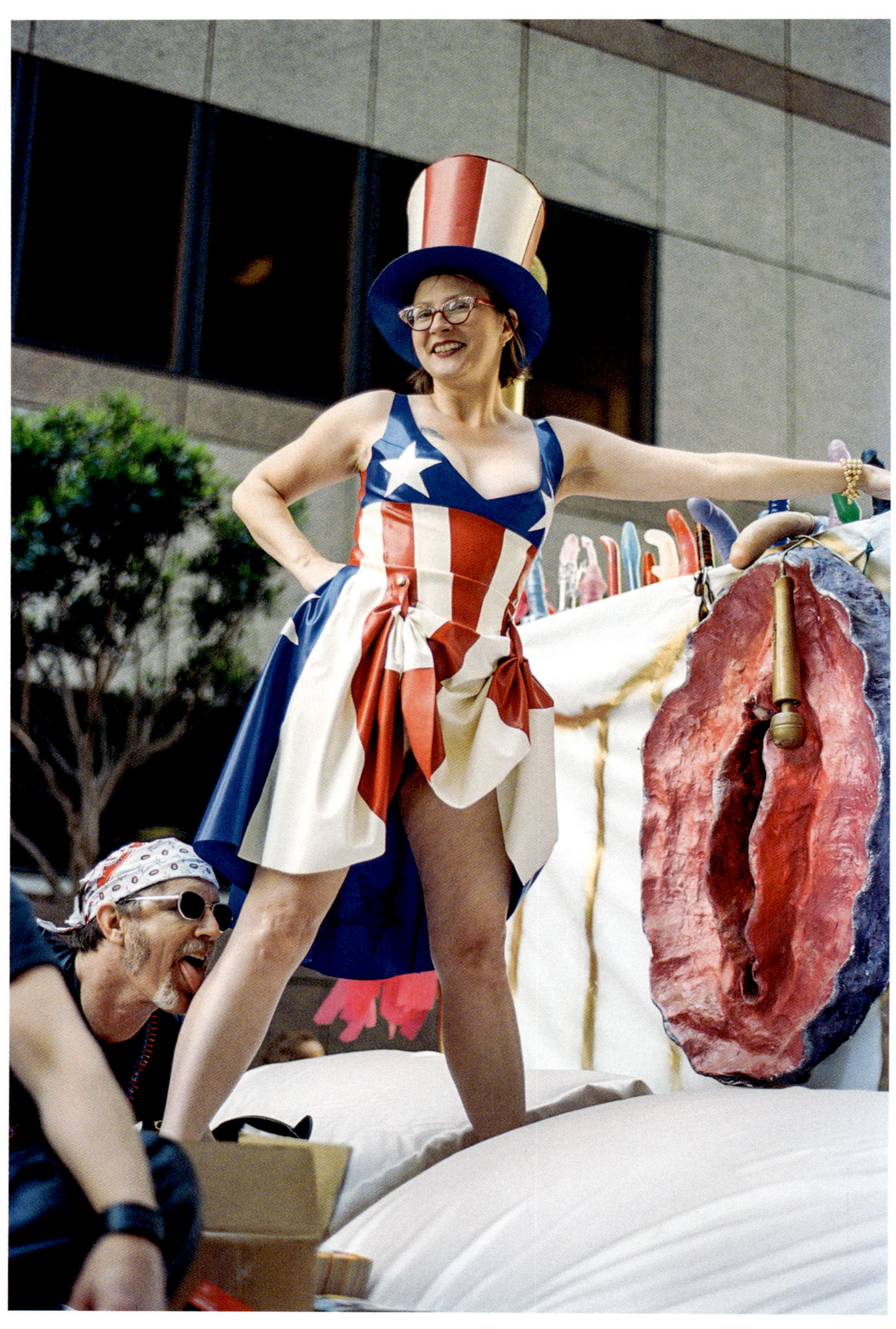

SF LGBT Pride, June 24, 2001. Robert Lawrence and Carol Queen (directors of the Center for Sex & Culture) on the Good Vibrations float.

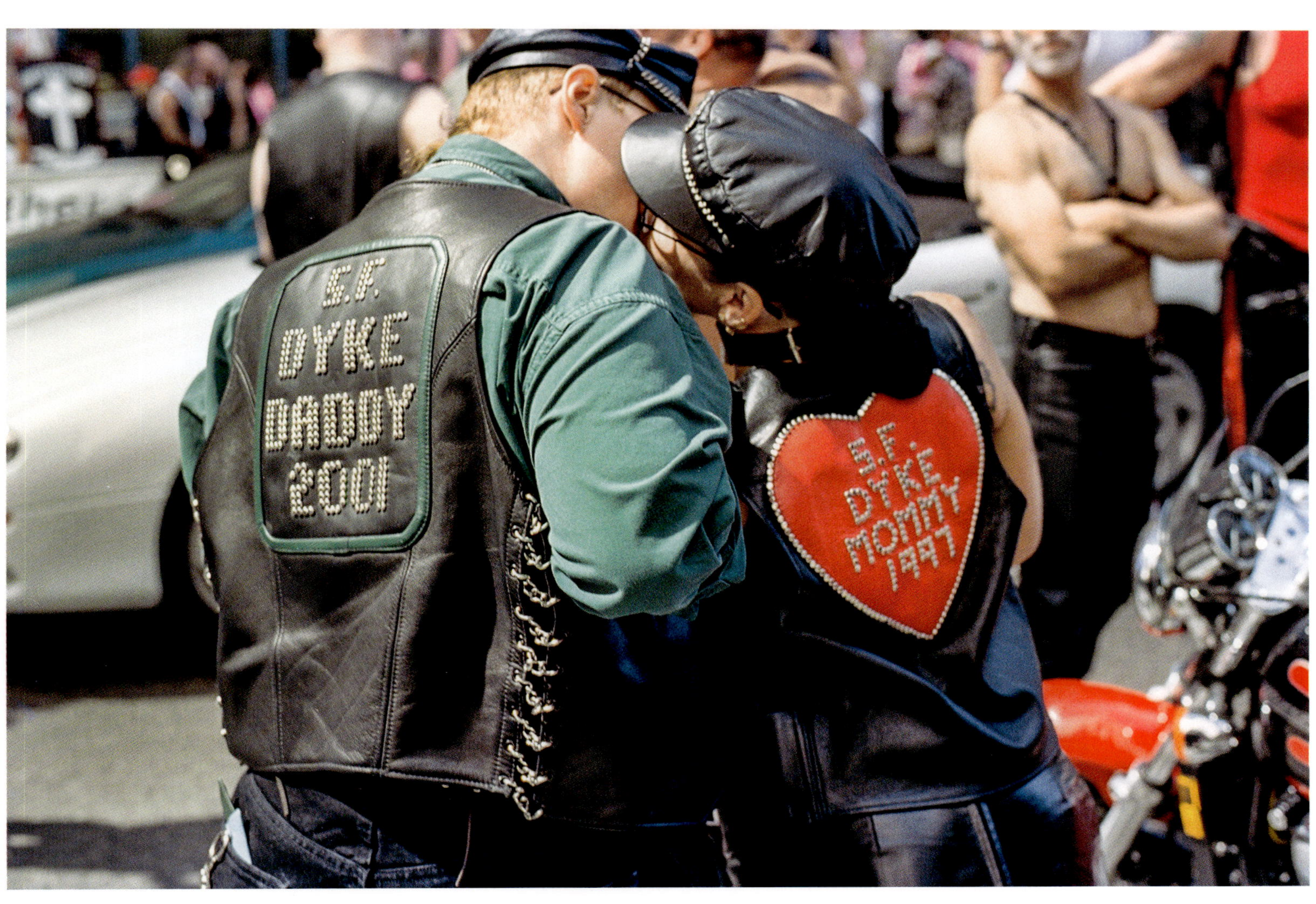

SF LGBT Pride, June 24, 2001.

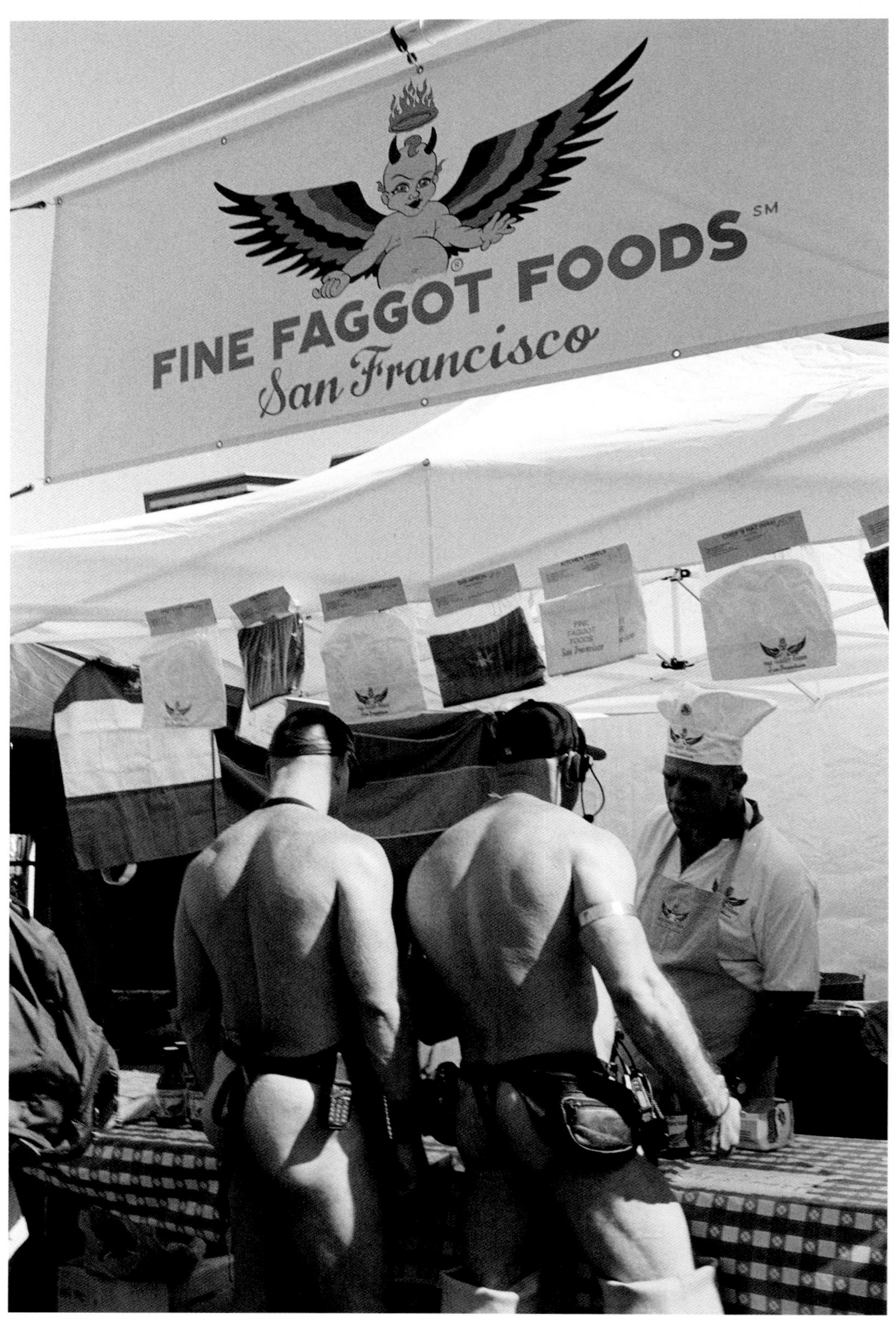

Folsom Street Fair, September 24, 2000.

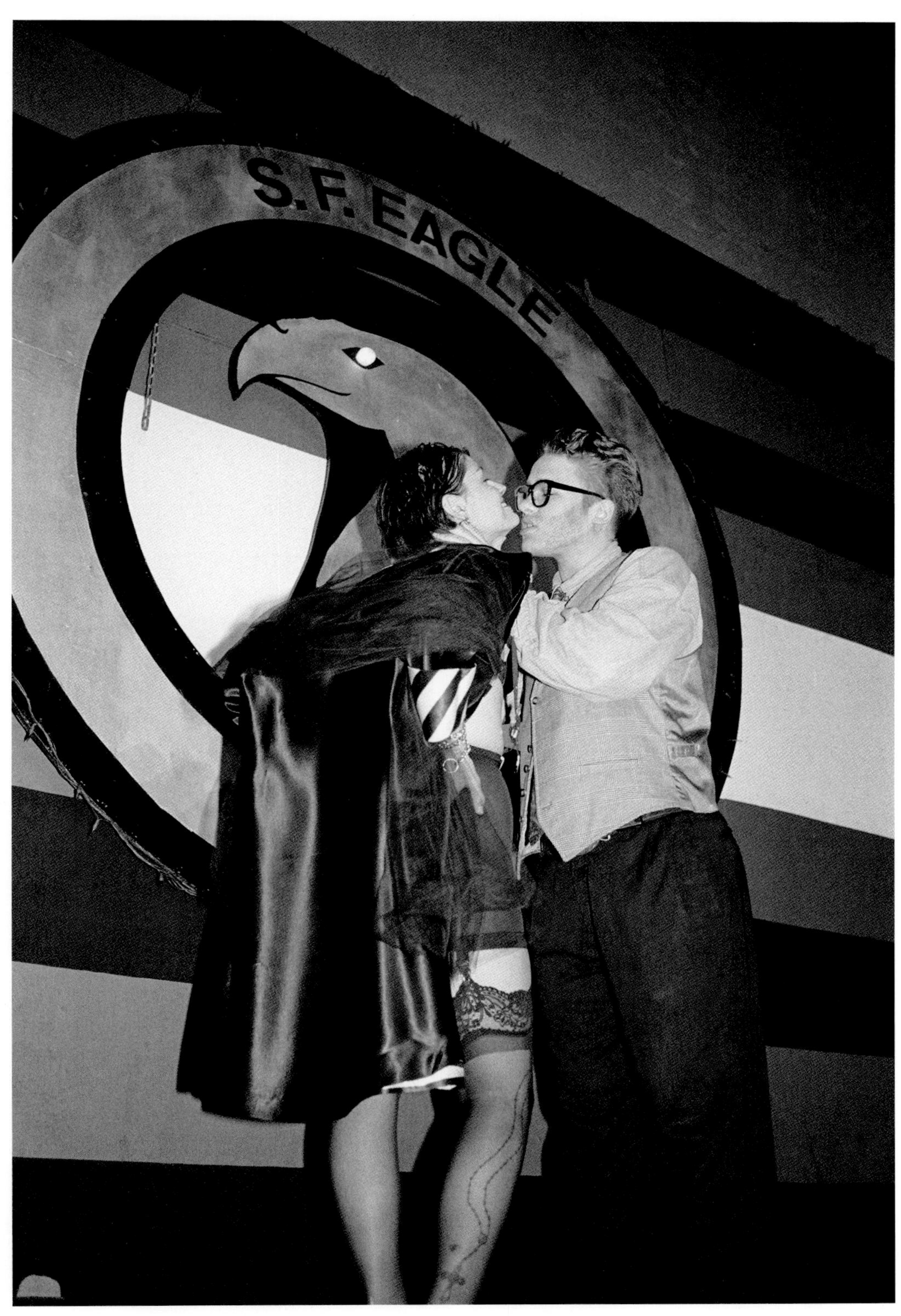

First Annual Drag King contest, SF-Eagle bar, May 15, 1994.

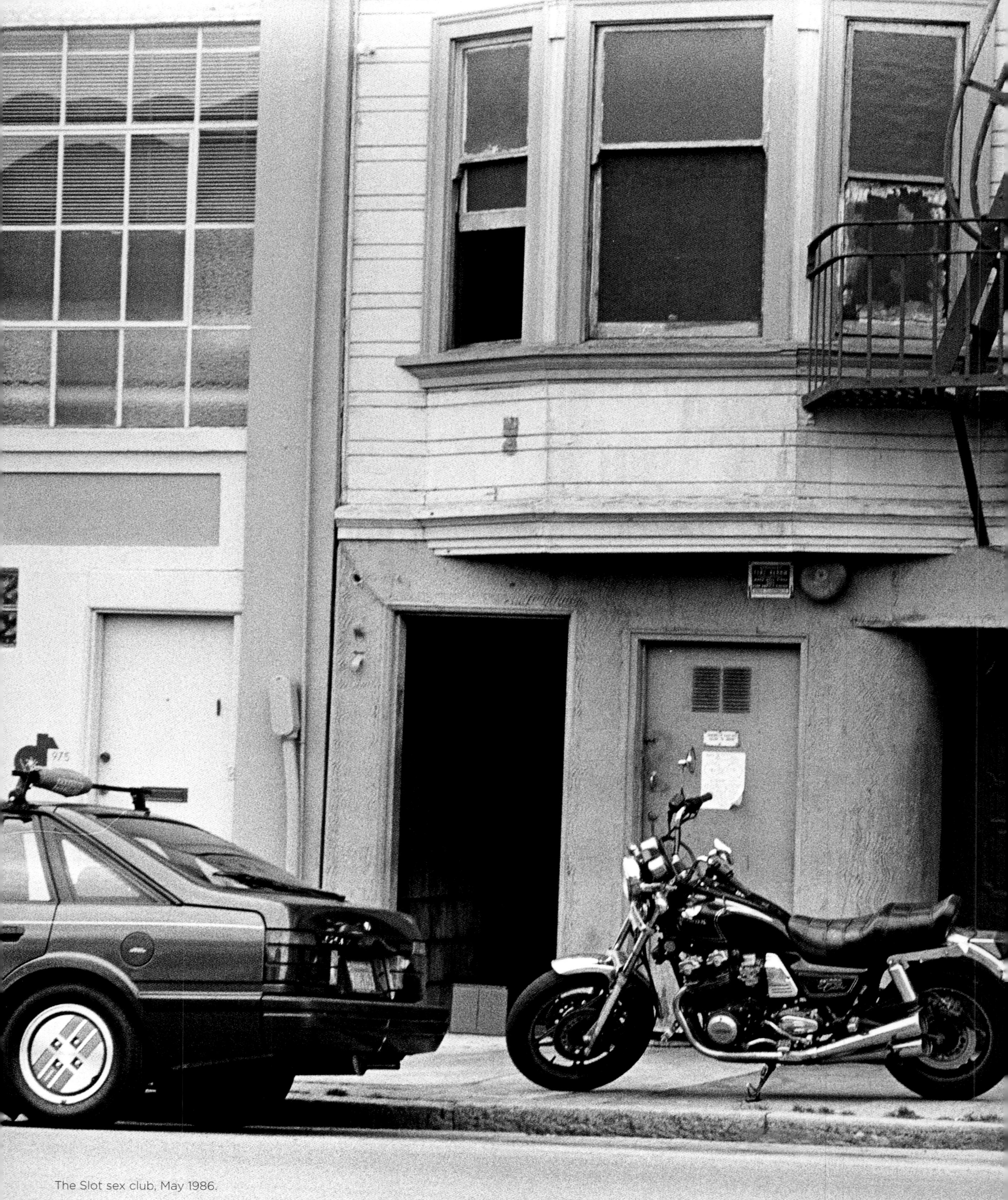

The Slot sex club, May 1986.

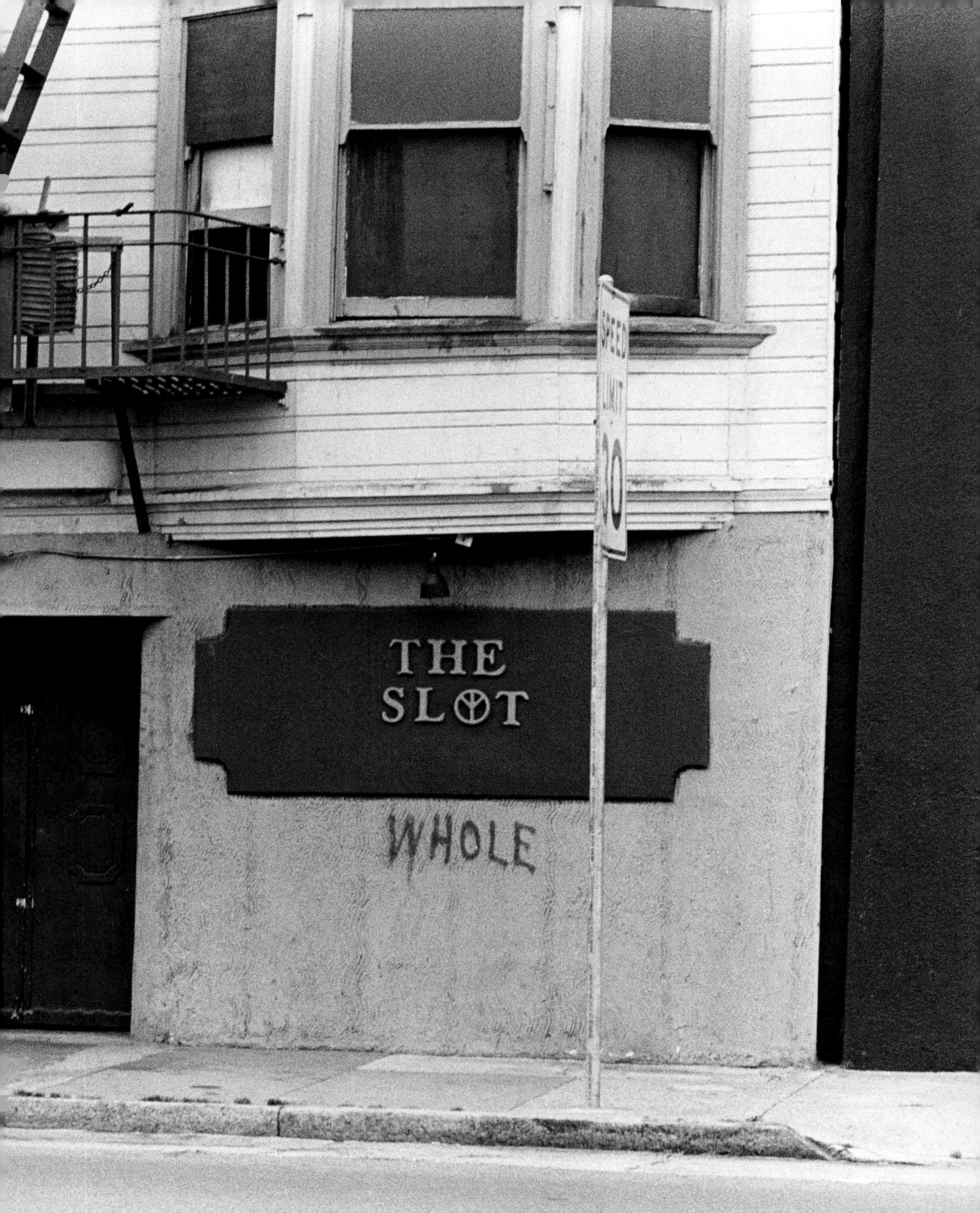
SPEED
LIMIT
30
THE
SLOT
WHOLE

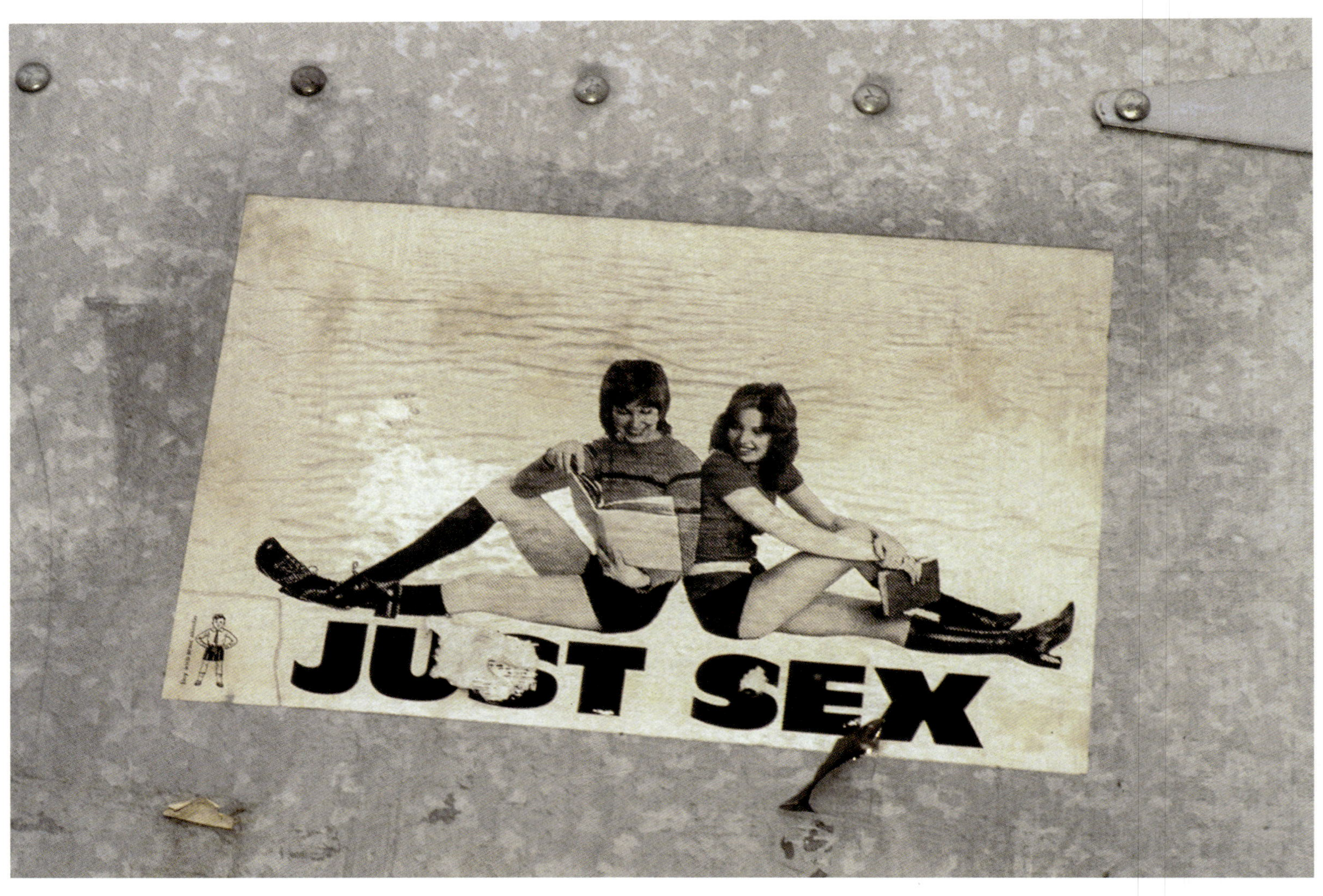

Above: *Just Sex* poster on Folsom Street, June 1991, by Boy With Arms Akimbo (an anonymous anti-censorship activist group).
Opposite: *Just Sex* poster on Castro Street, September 11, 1989, by Boy With Arms Akimbo.

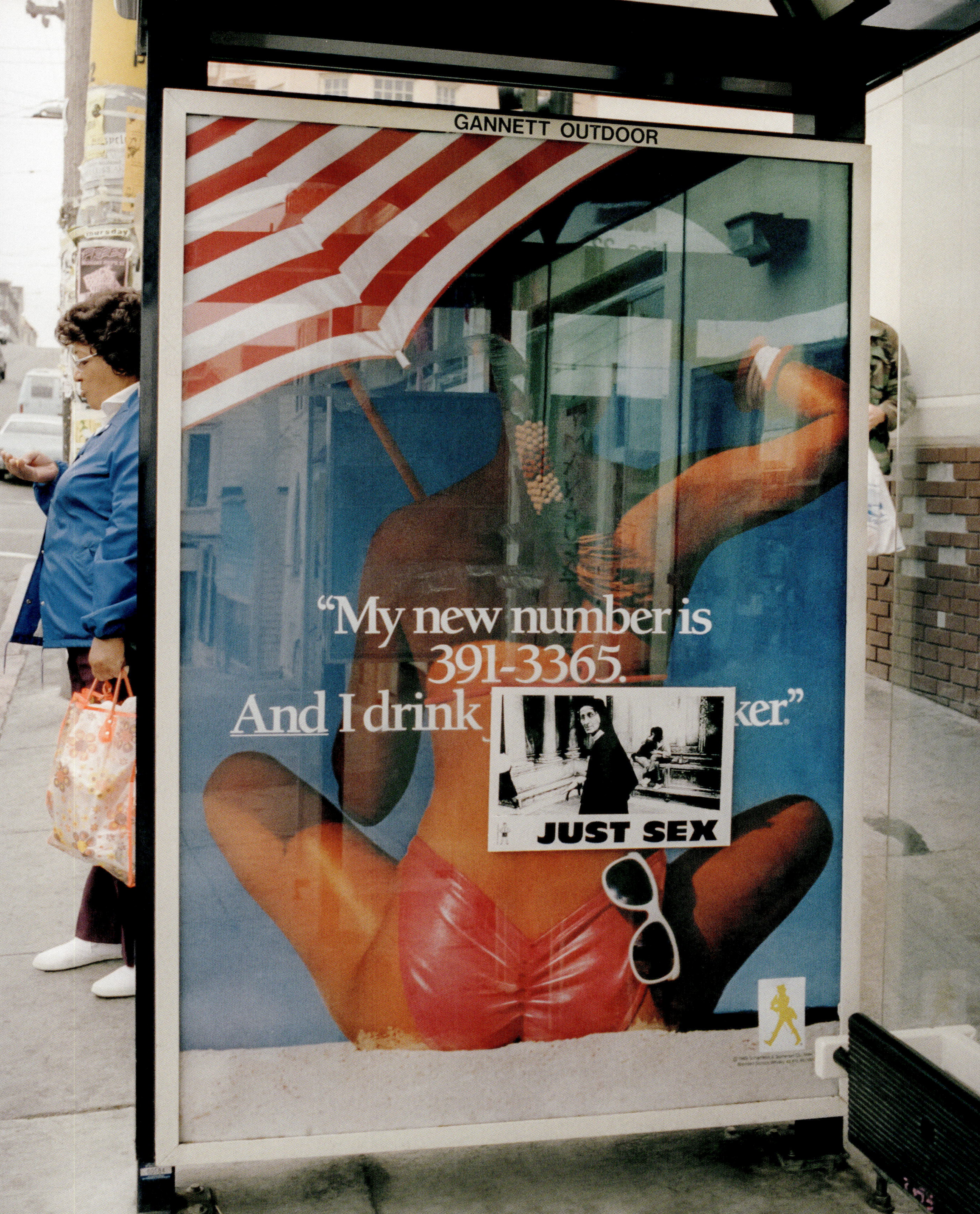
GANNETT OUTDOOR
"My new number is
391-3365.
And I drink
ker."
JUST SEX

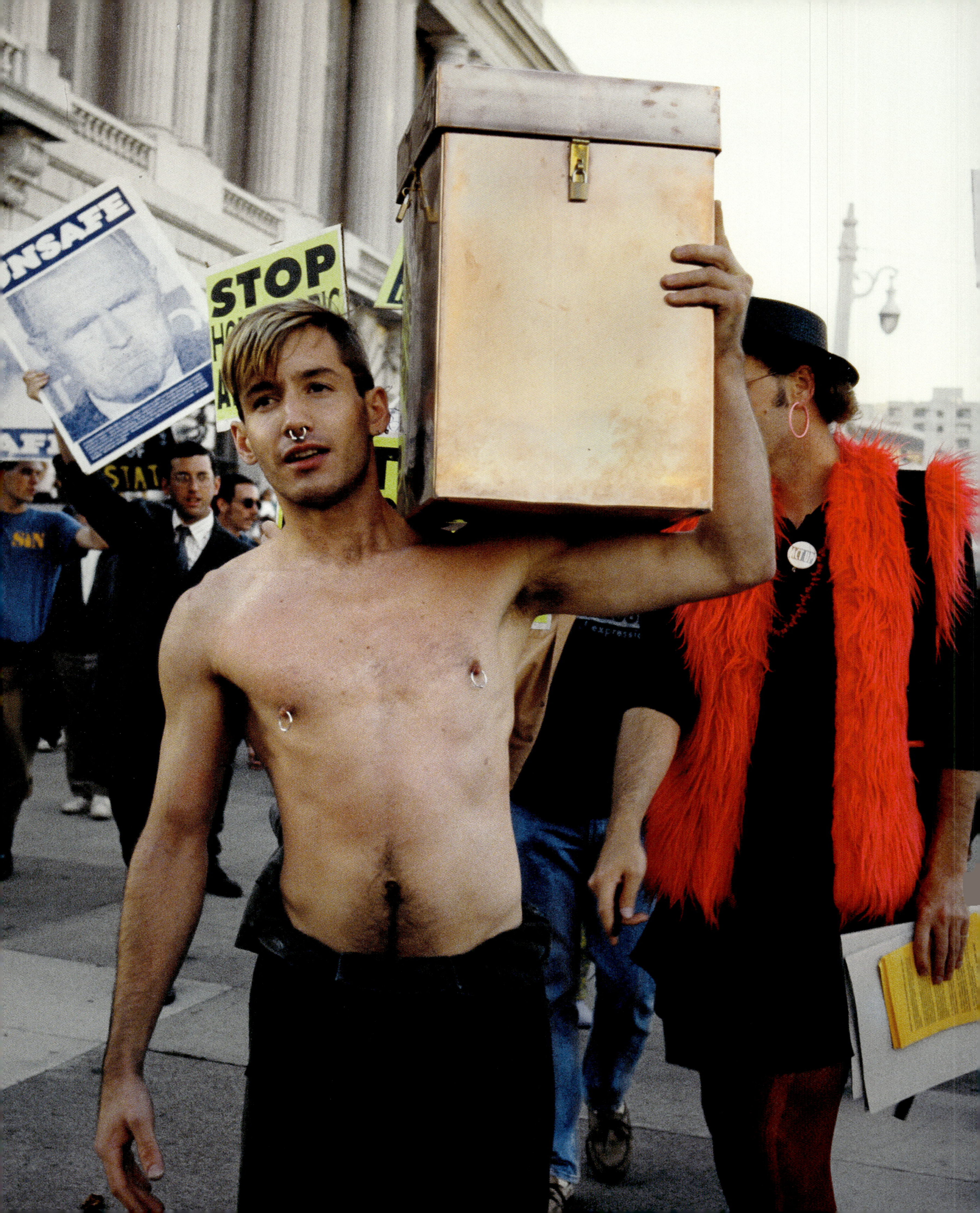
UNSAFE
STOP

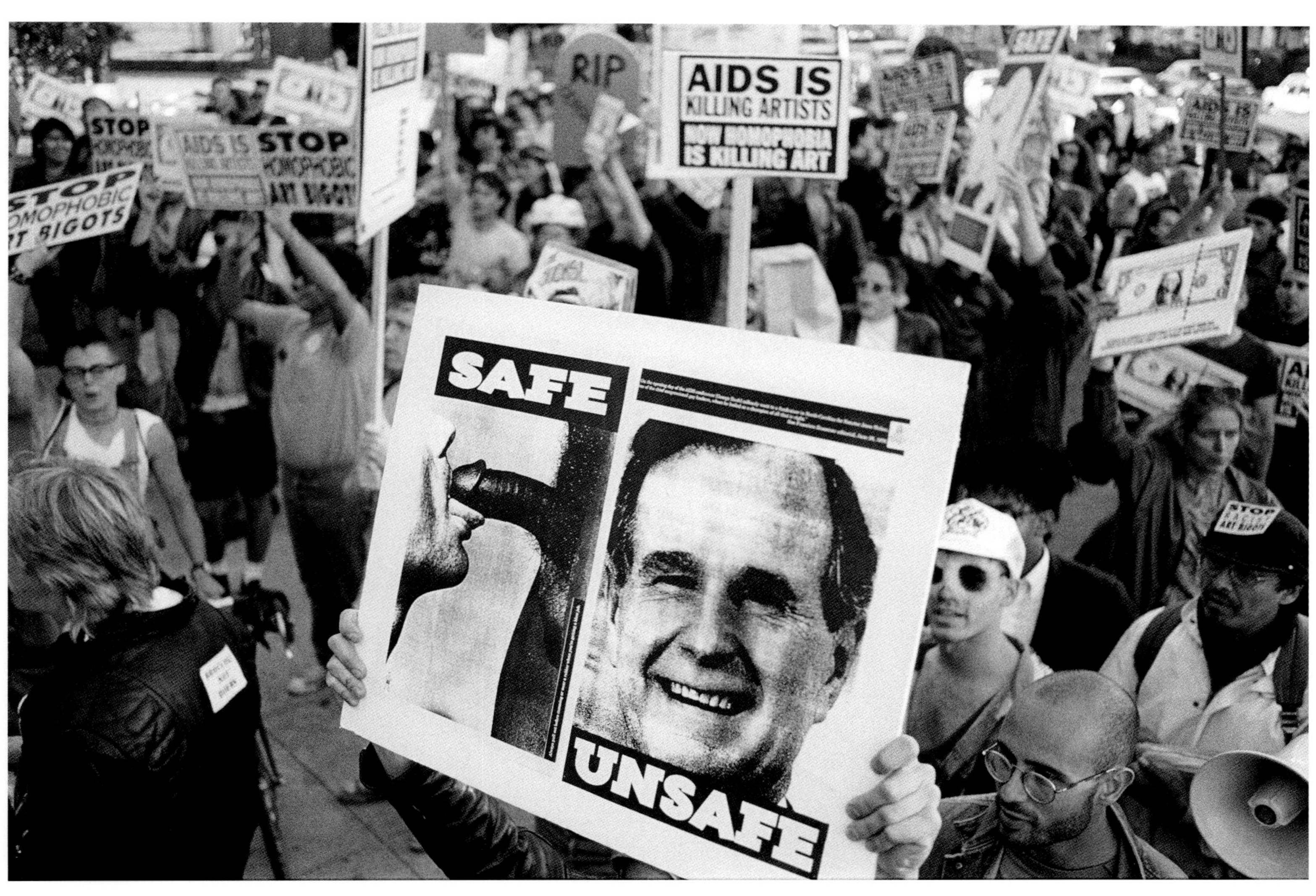

Above and opposite: Anti-censorship demonstration and time capsule burial at the San Francisco Art Commission Gallery, September 7, 1990. *(Opposite)* Nic Pereira of The High Risk Group with copper time capsule by Michael Brown.

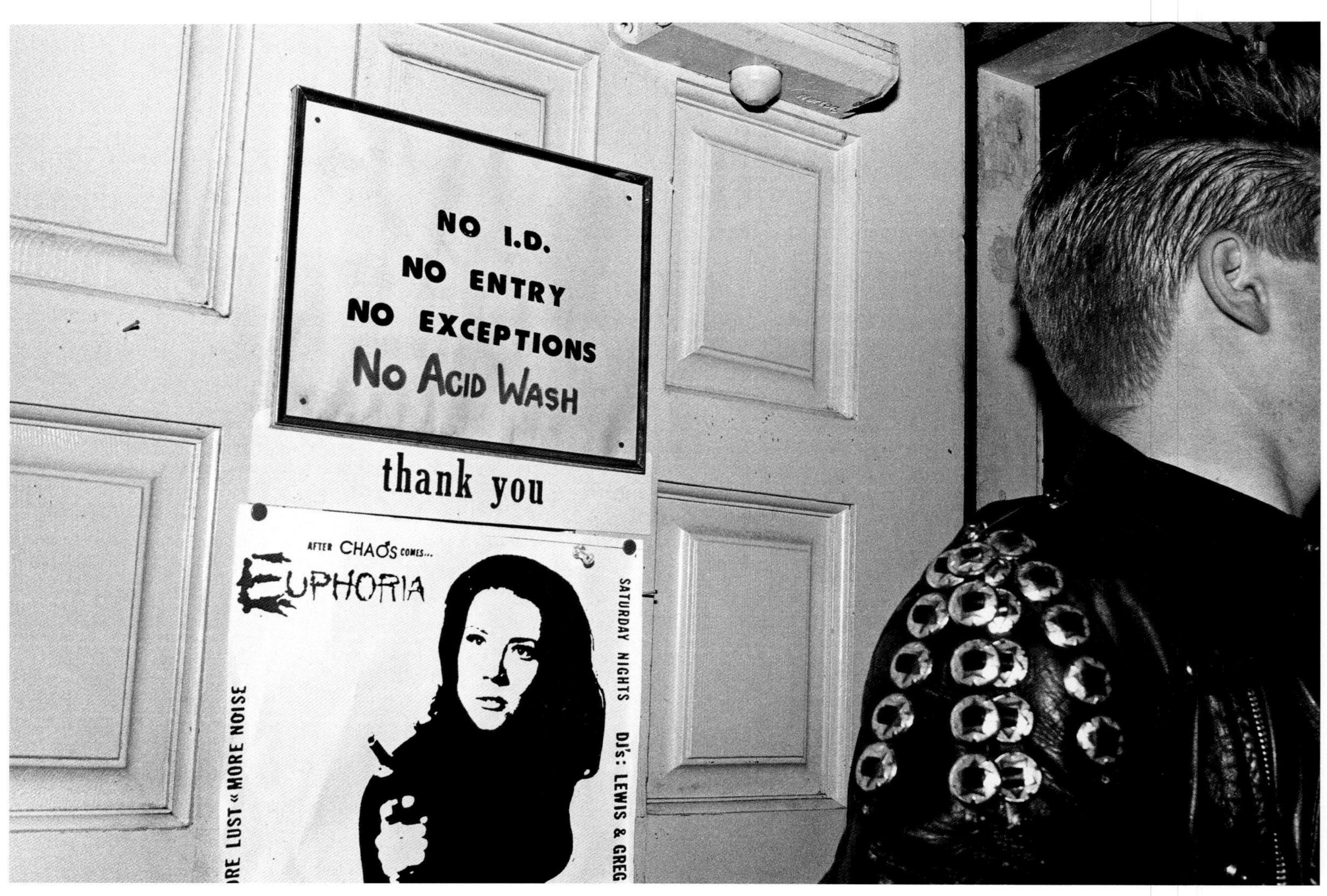

Above: Club Chaos, September 21, 1989.
Opposite: Polka Dot Party at The Stud bar, April 25, 1989. Kevin F. and Christopher Overington.

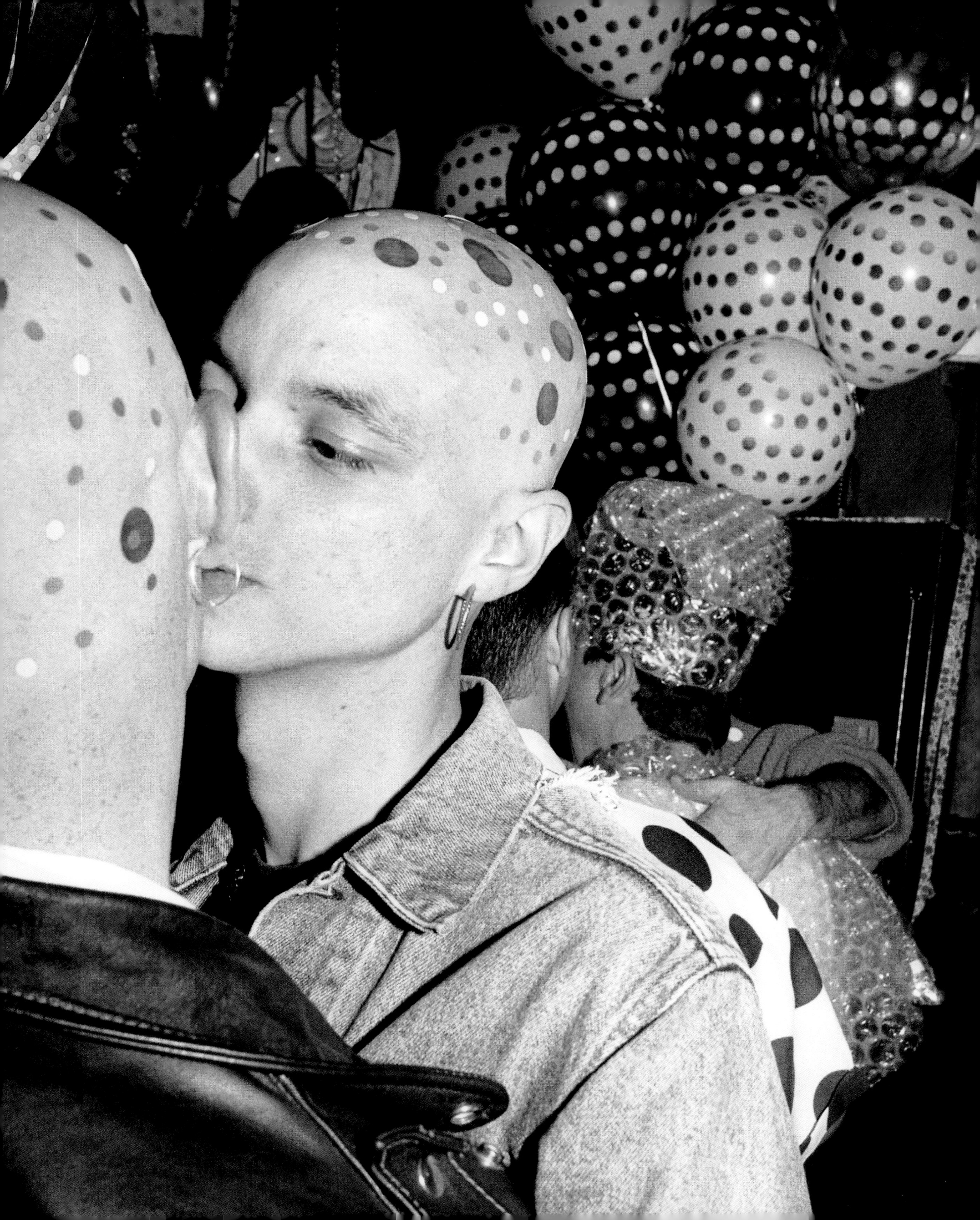

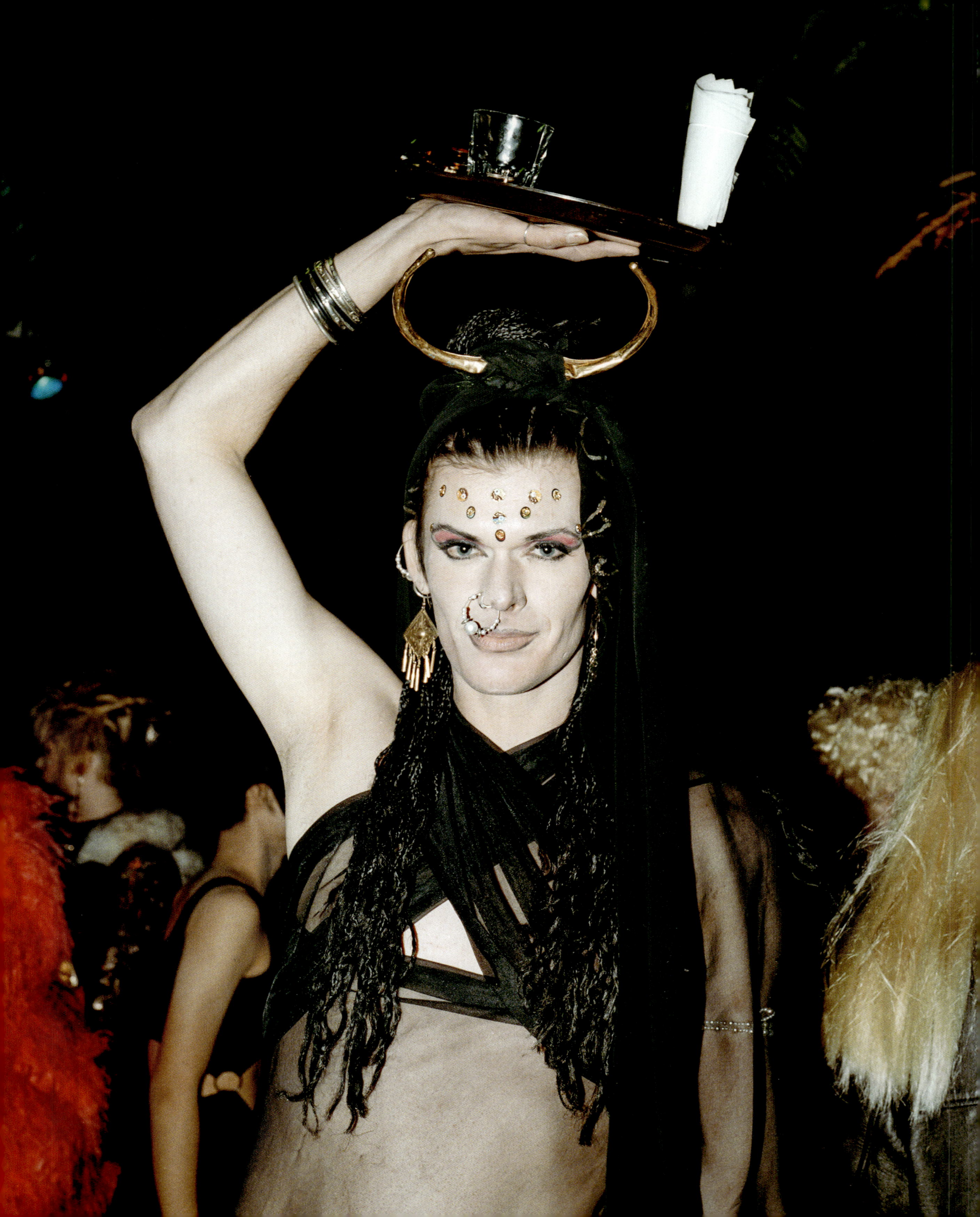

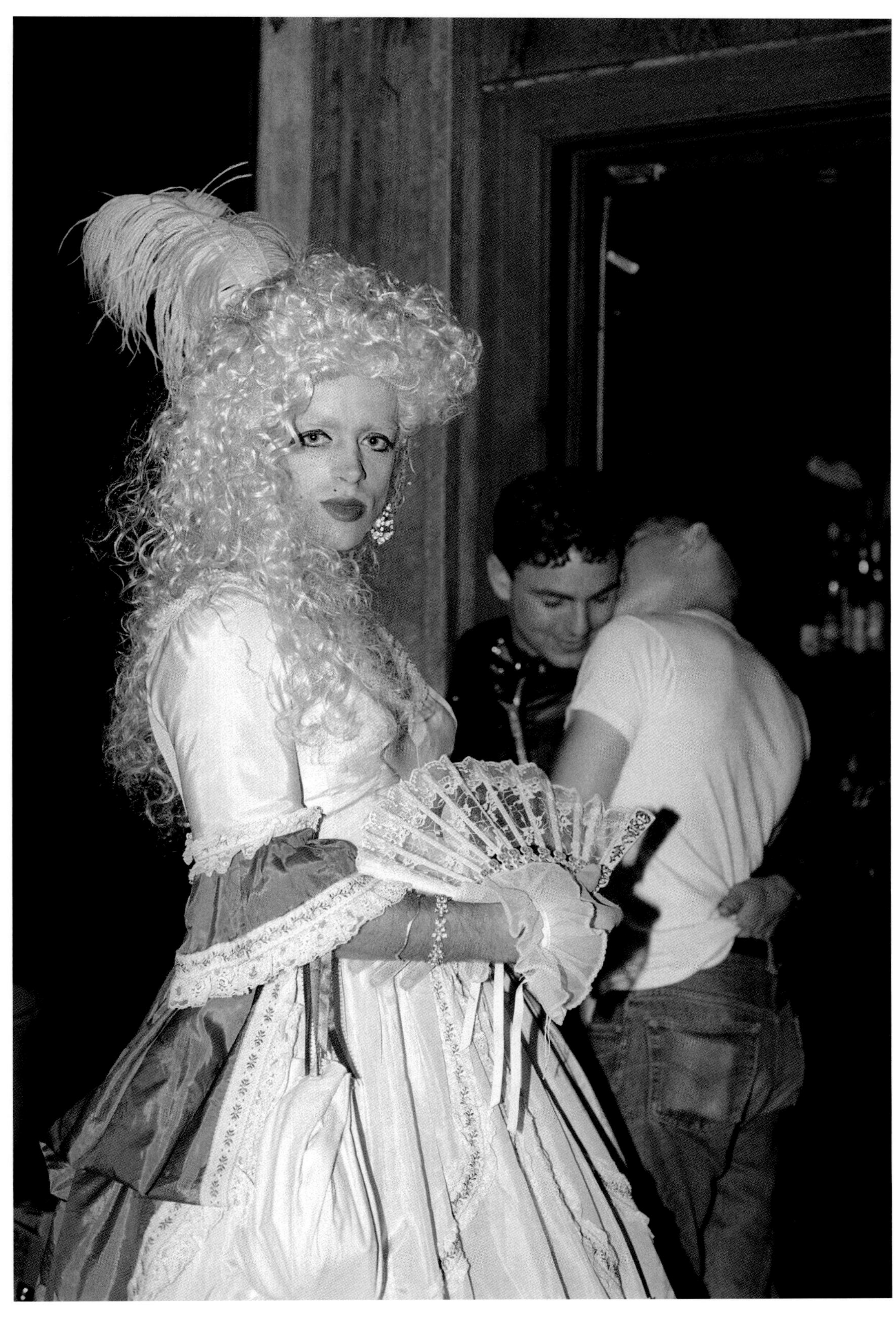

Club Uranus, October 31, 1990. *(Above)* Darren (foreground); *(opposite)* Desiree White Witch.

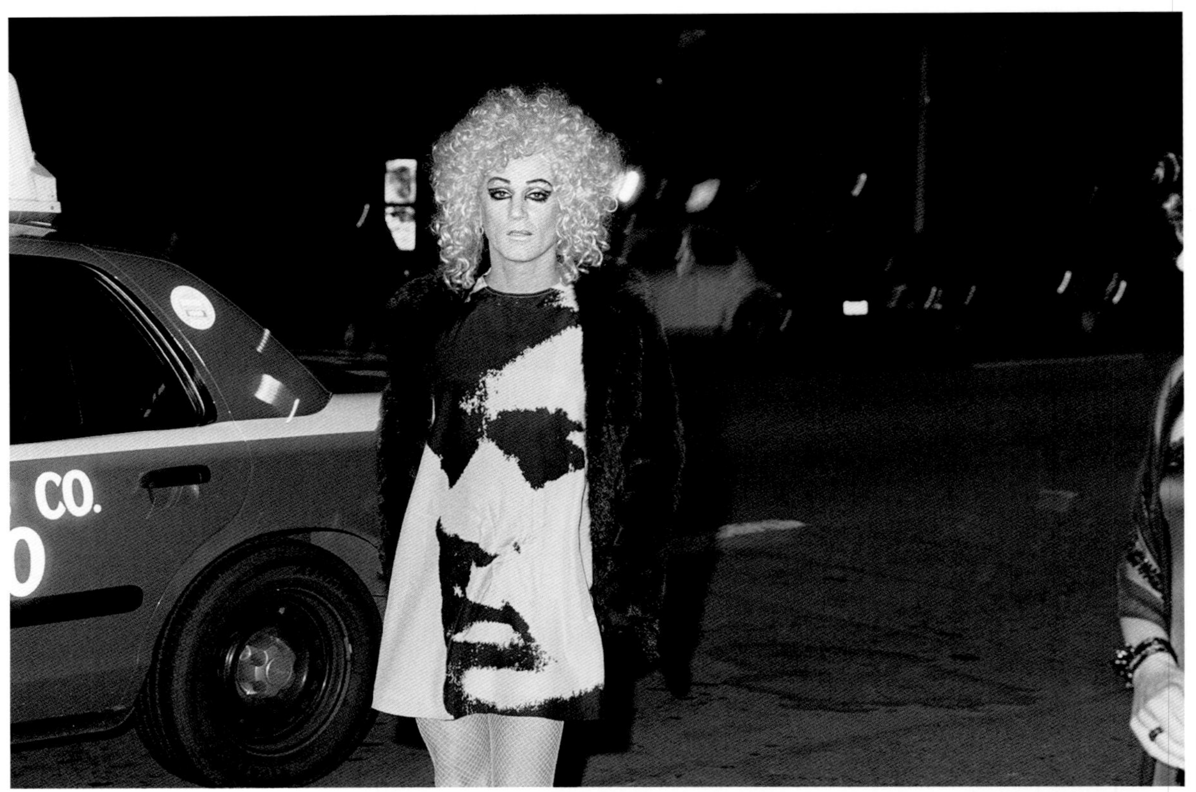

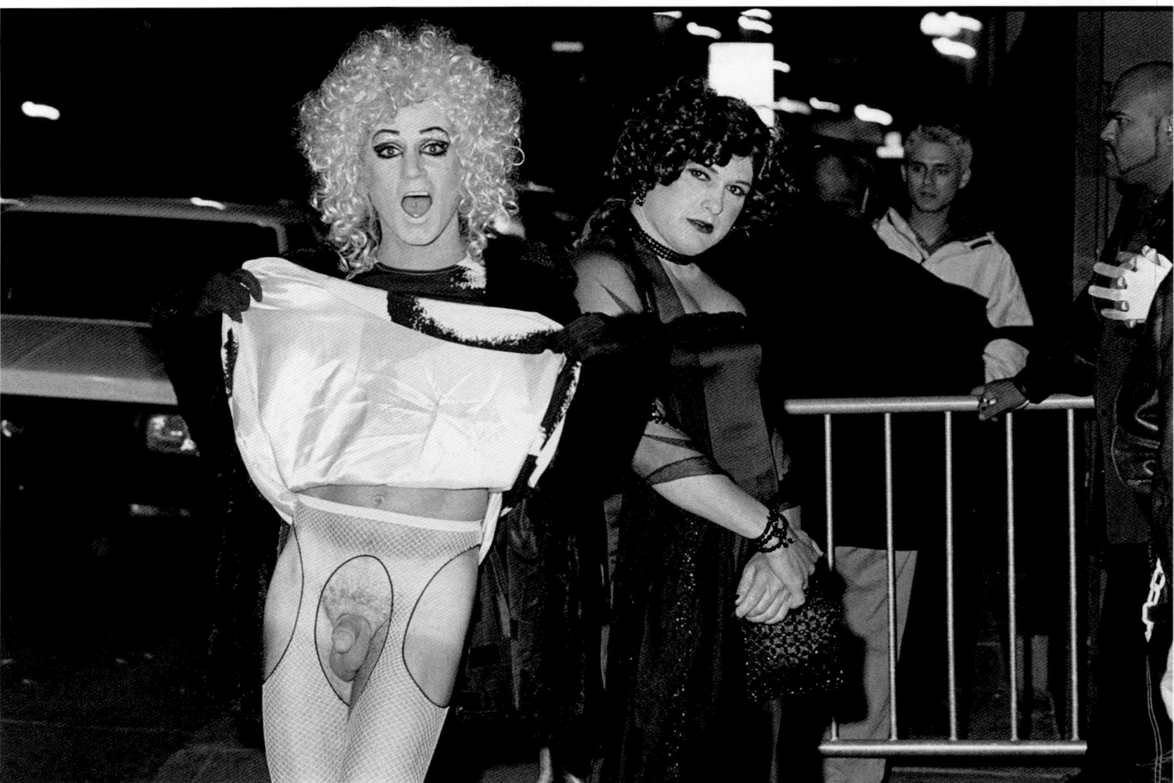

Above: The Annual Miss T-Shack Pageant, November 21, 1999. Arturo Galster and Jeff Simpson.
Opposite: DNA Lounge, June 24, 1989. Gregg Foss visiting with the Del Rubio Triplets.

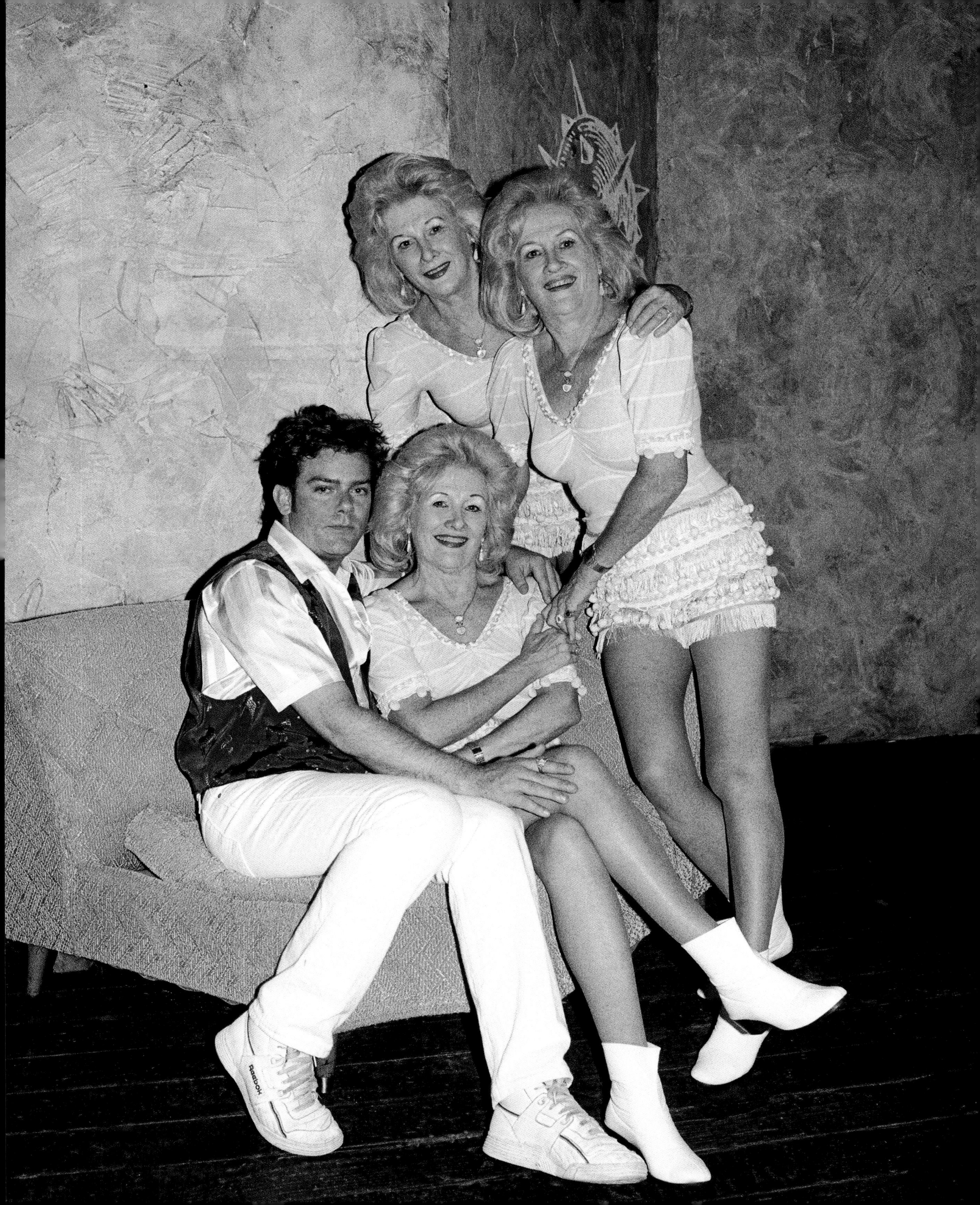
Reebok

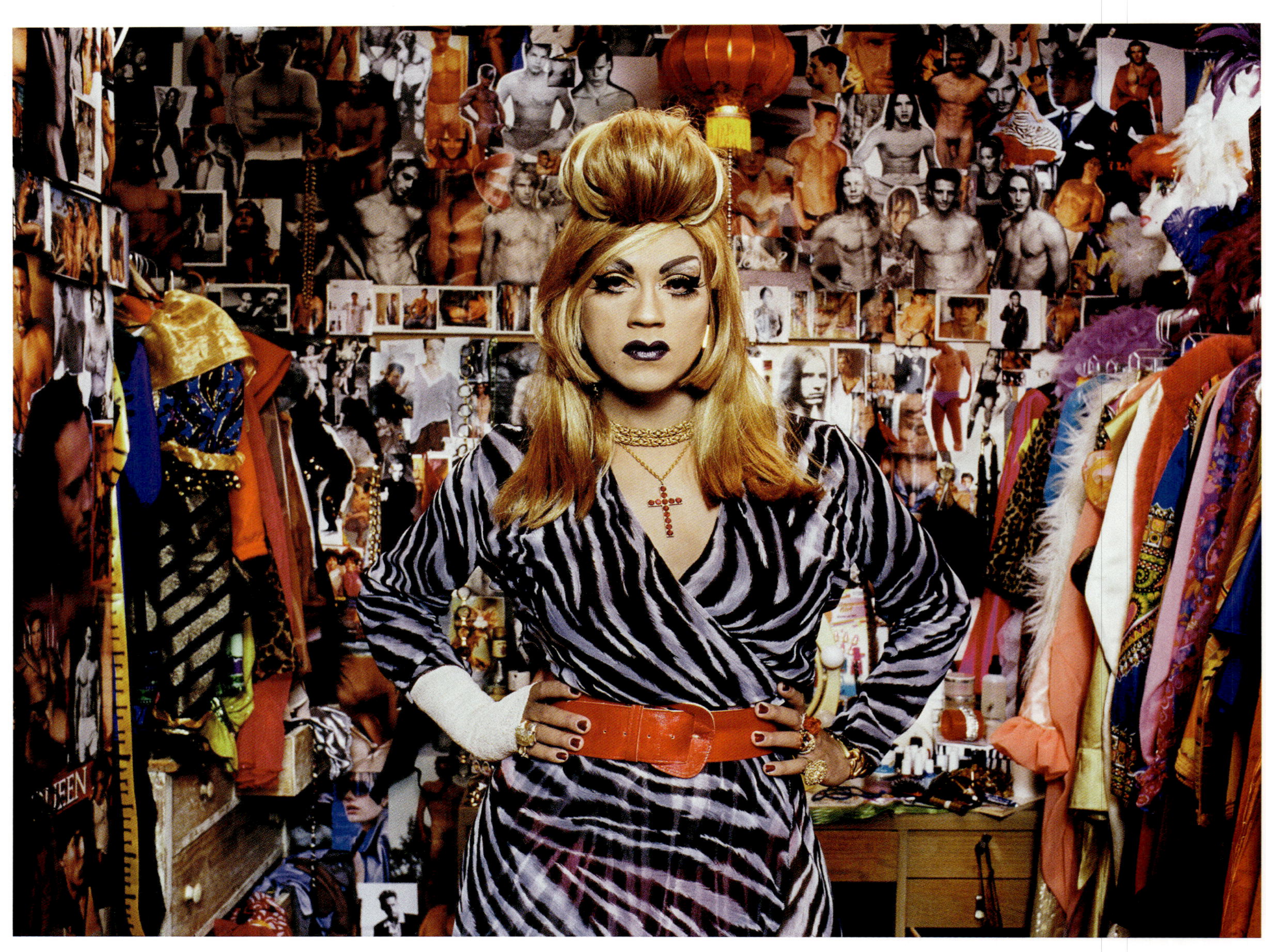

Above: Juanita More, October 8, 1996. (Hair by Brent Haas, styling by Todd Hartnett, couture by Mr. David.)
Opposite: Fauxnique, Mr. David fashion parade (Joey Arias Show at The Castro Theatre), February 15, 2013.

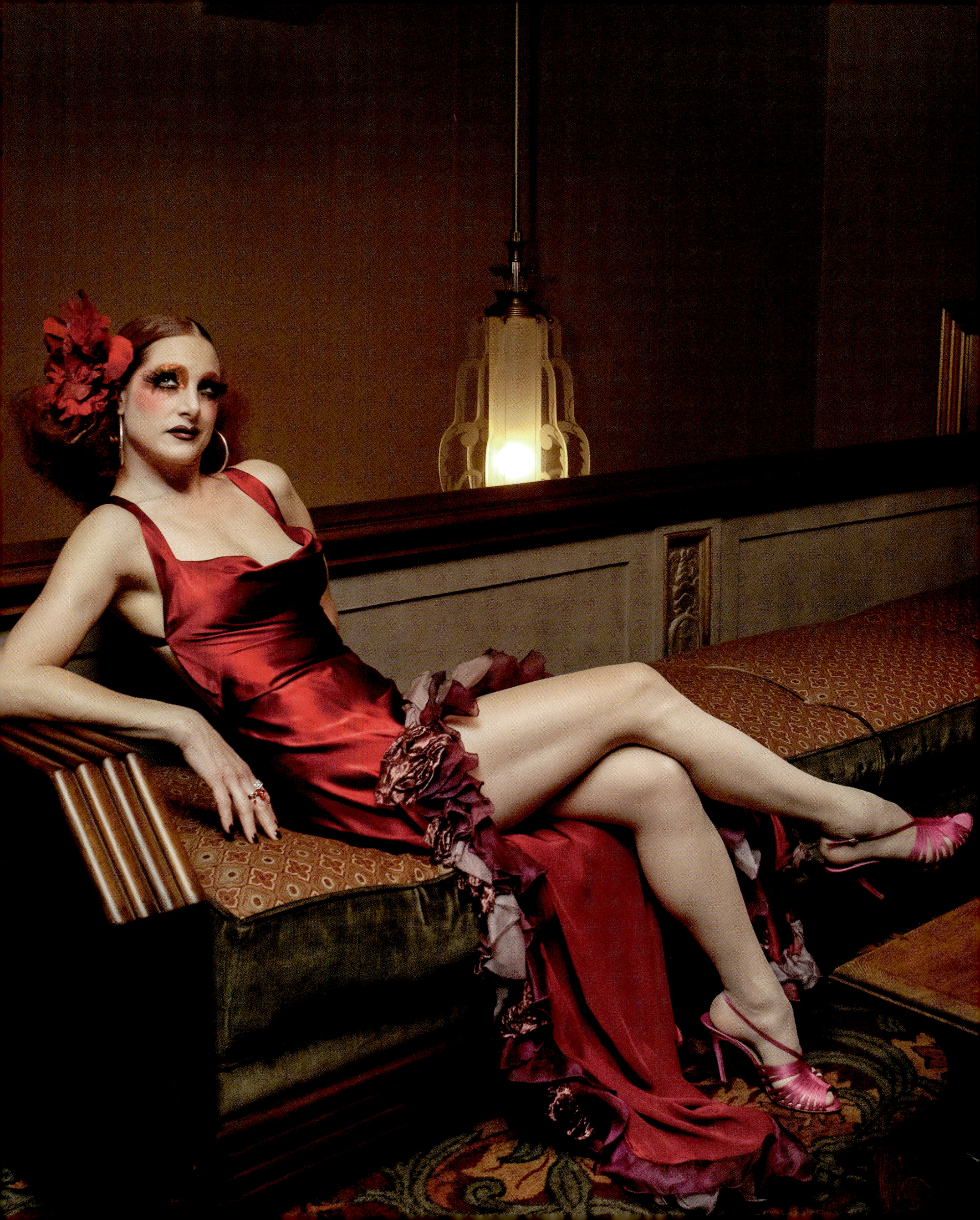

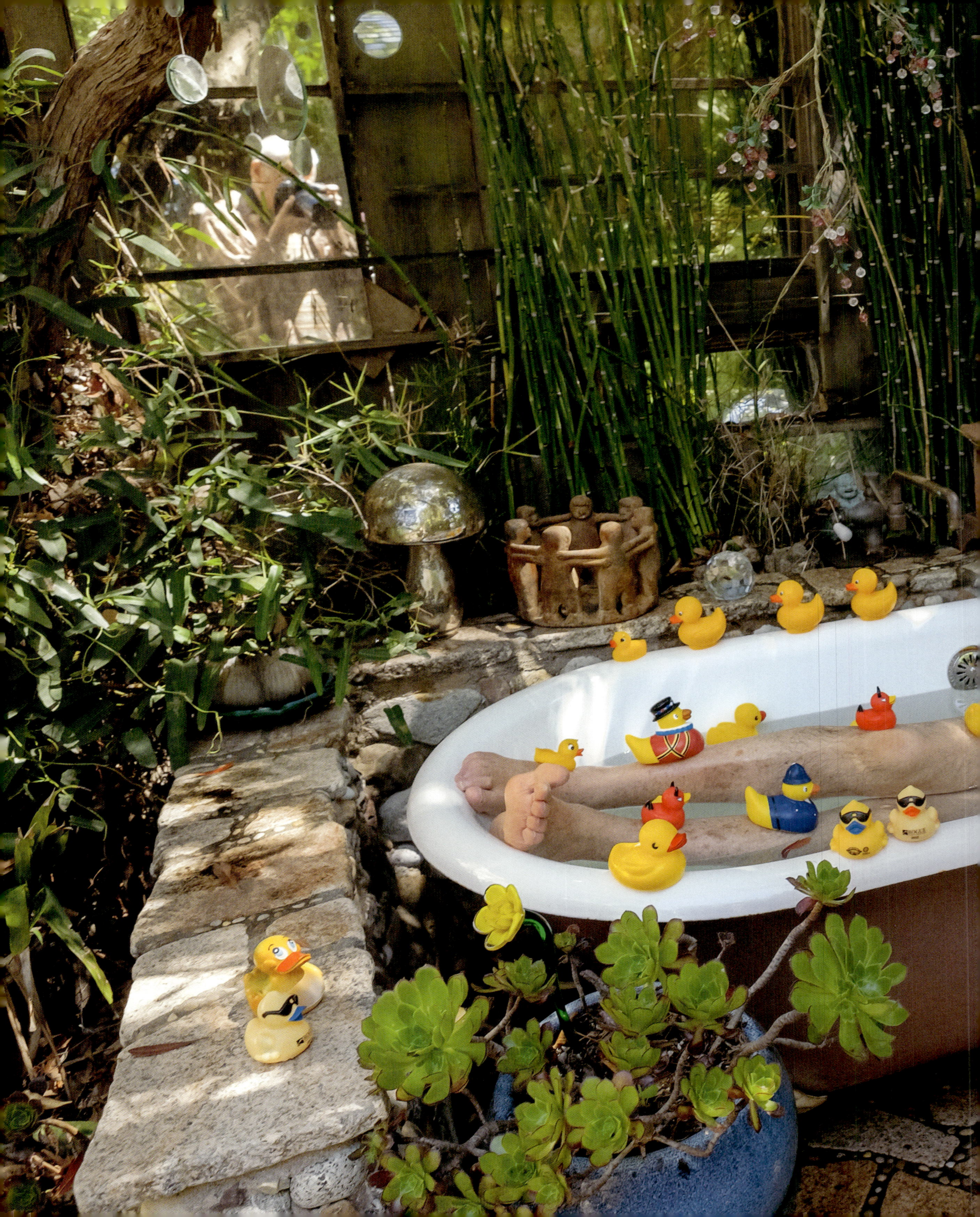

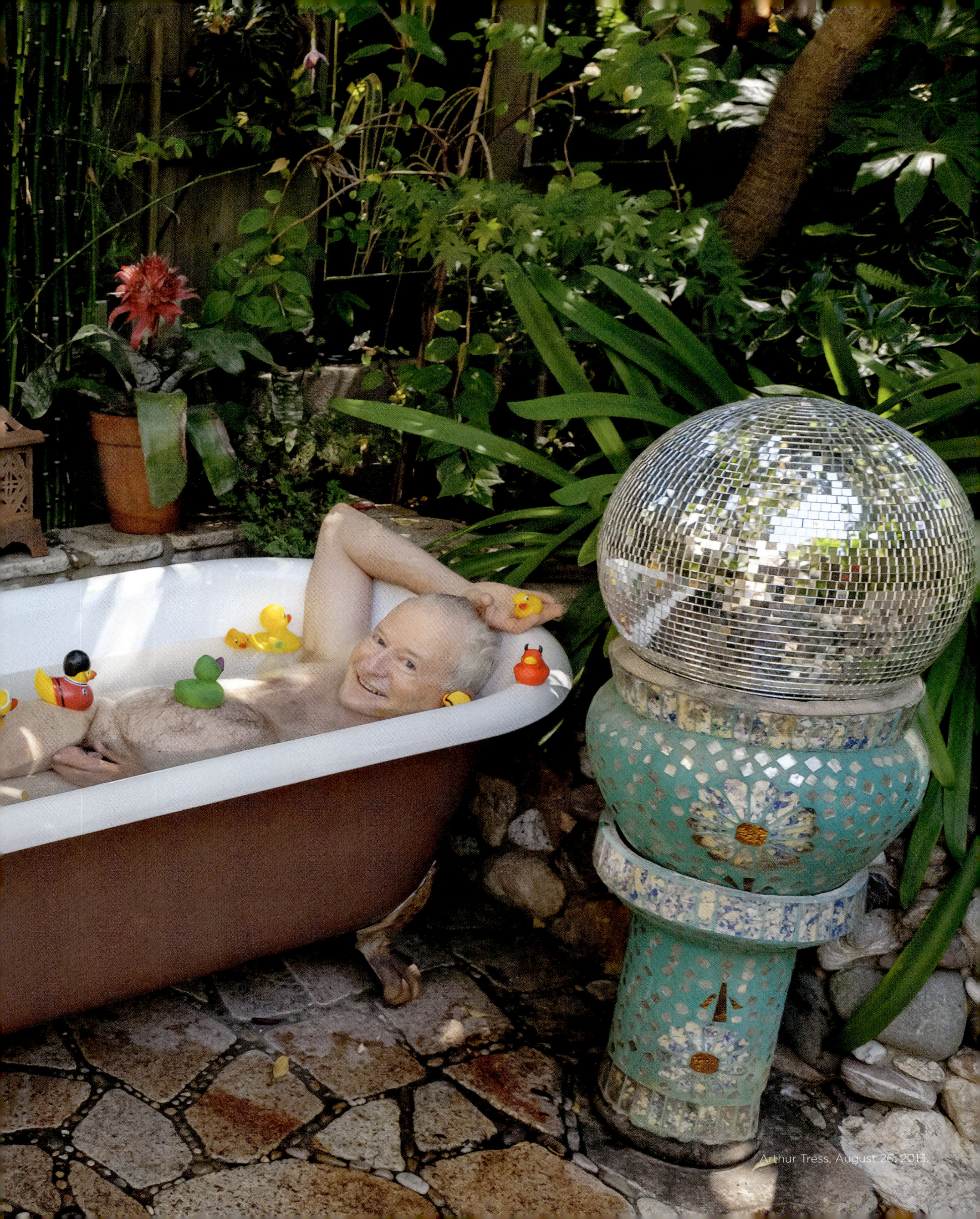

Arthur Tress, August 26, 2013

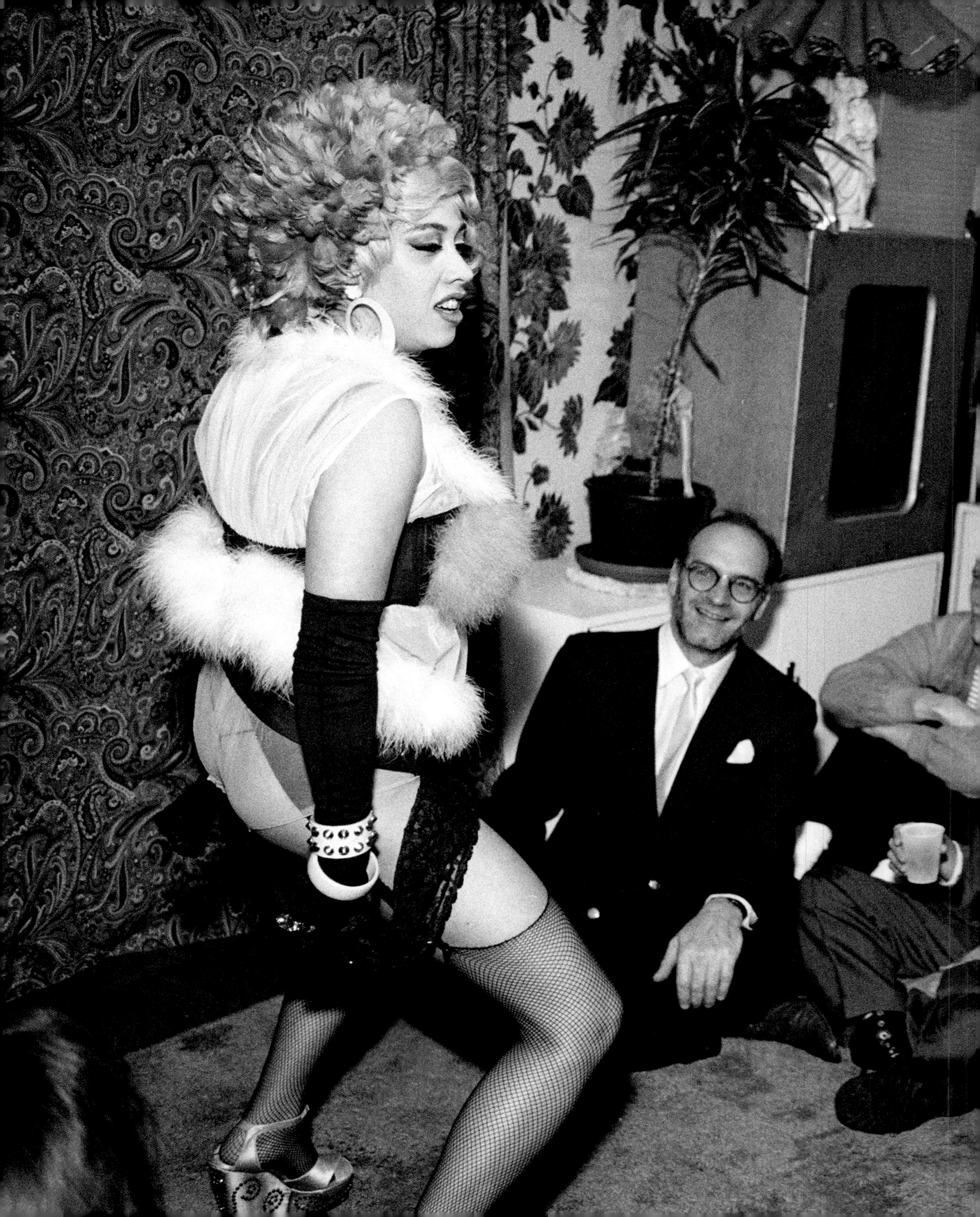

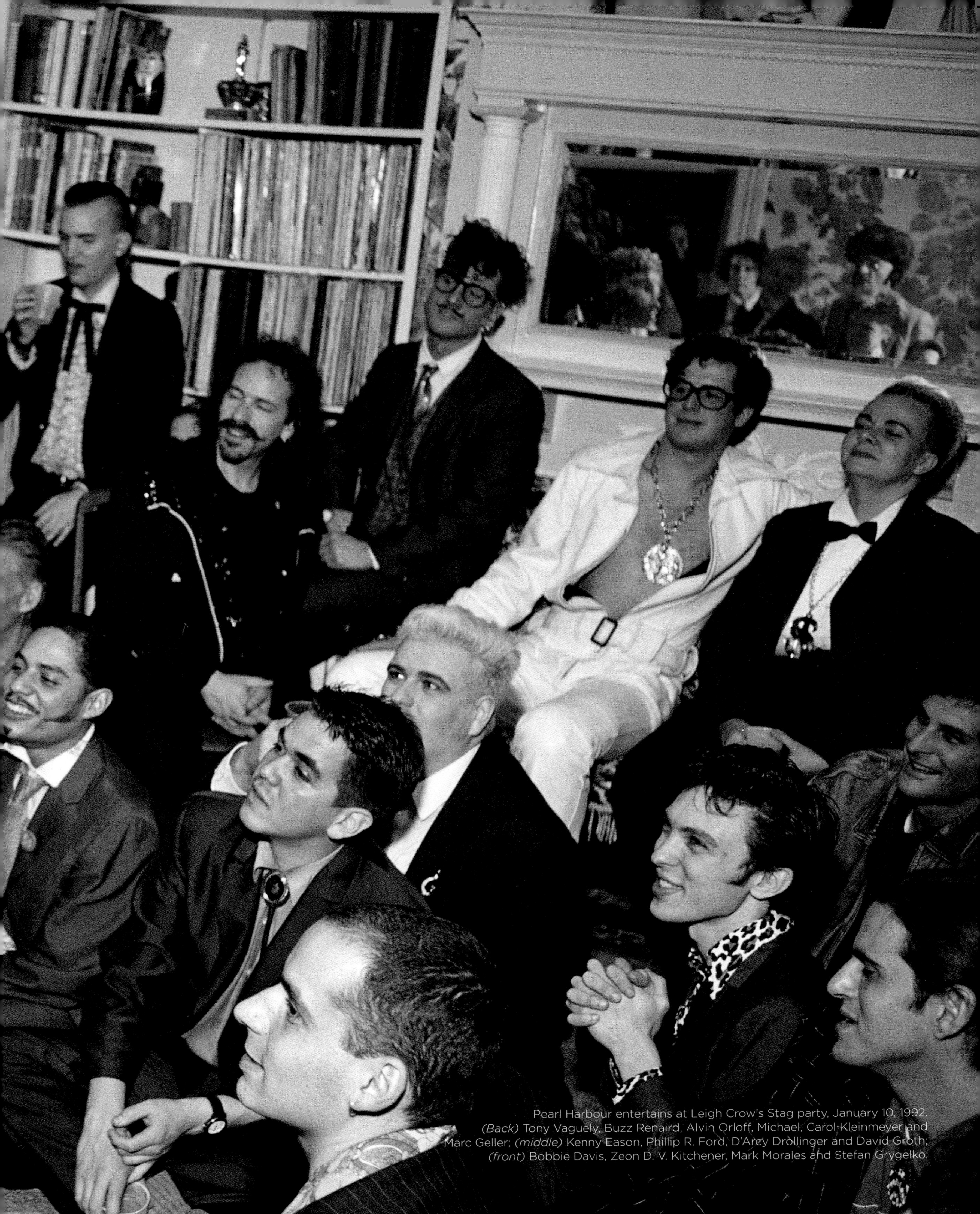

Pearl Harbour entertains at Leigh Crow's Stag party, January 10, 1992. *(Back)* Tony Vaguely, Buzz Renaird, Alvin Orloff, Michael, Carol Kleinmeyer and Marc Geller; *(middle)* Kenny Eason, Phillip R. Ford, D'Arcy Drollinger and David Groth; *(front)* Bobbie Davis, Zeon D. V. Kitchener, Mark Morales and Stefan Grygelko.

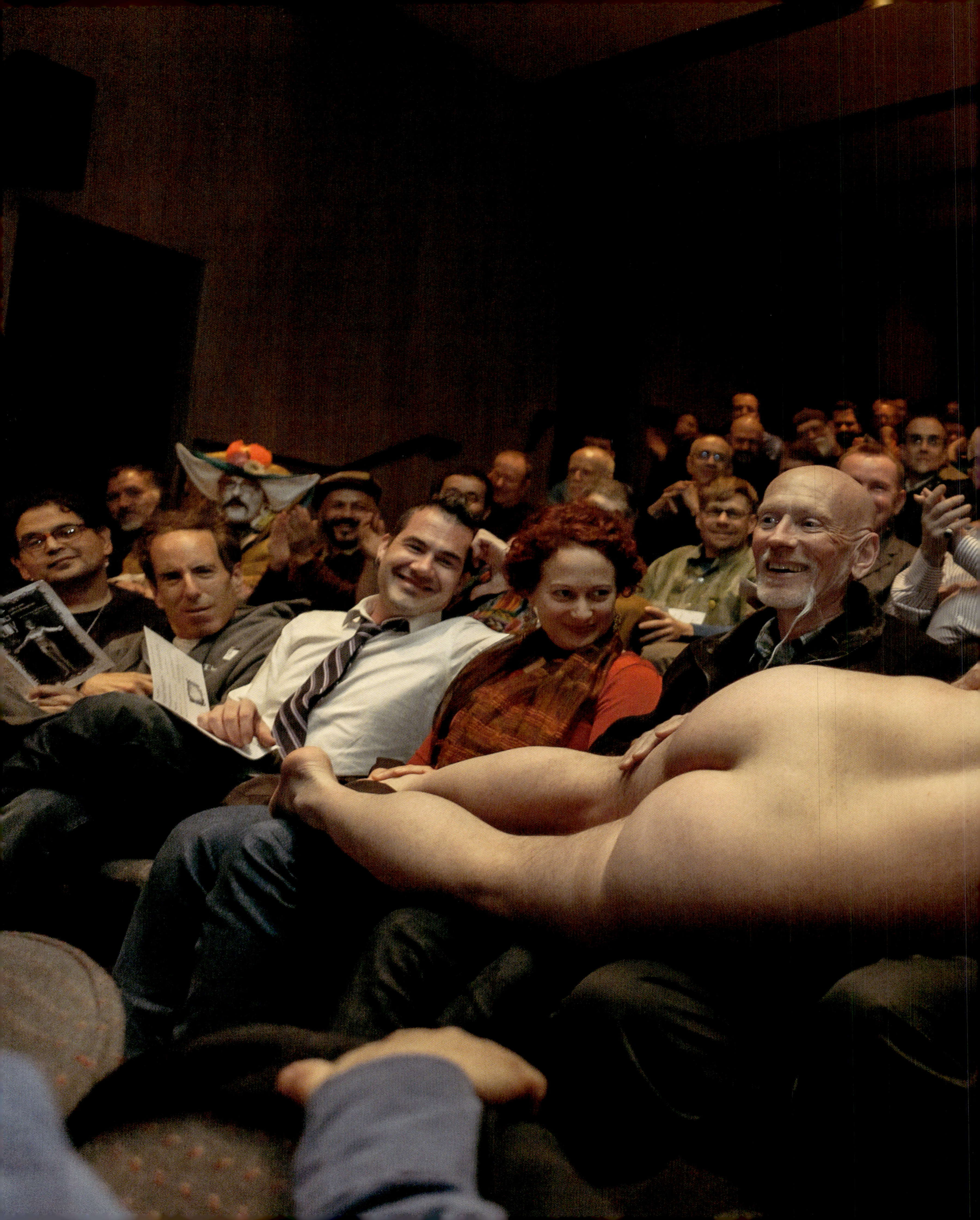

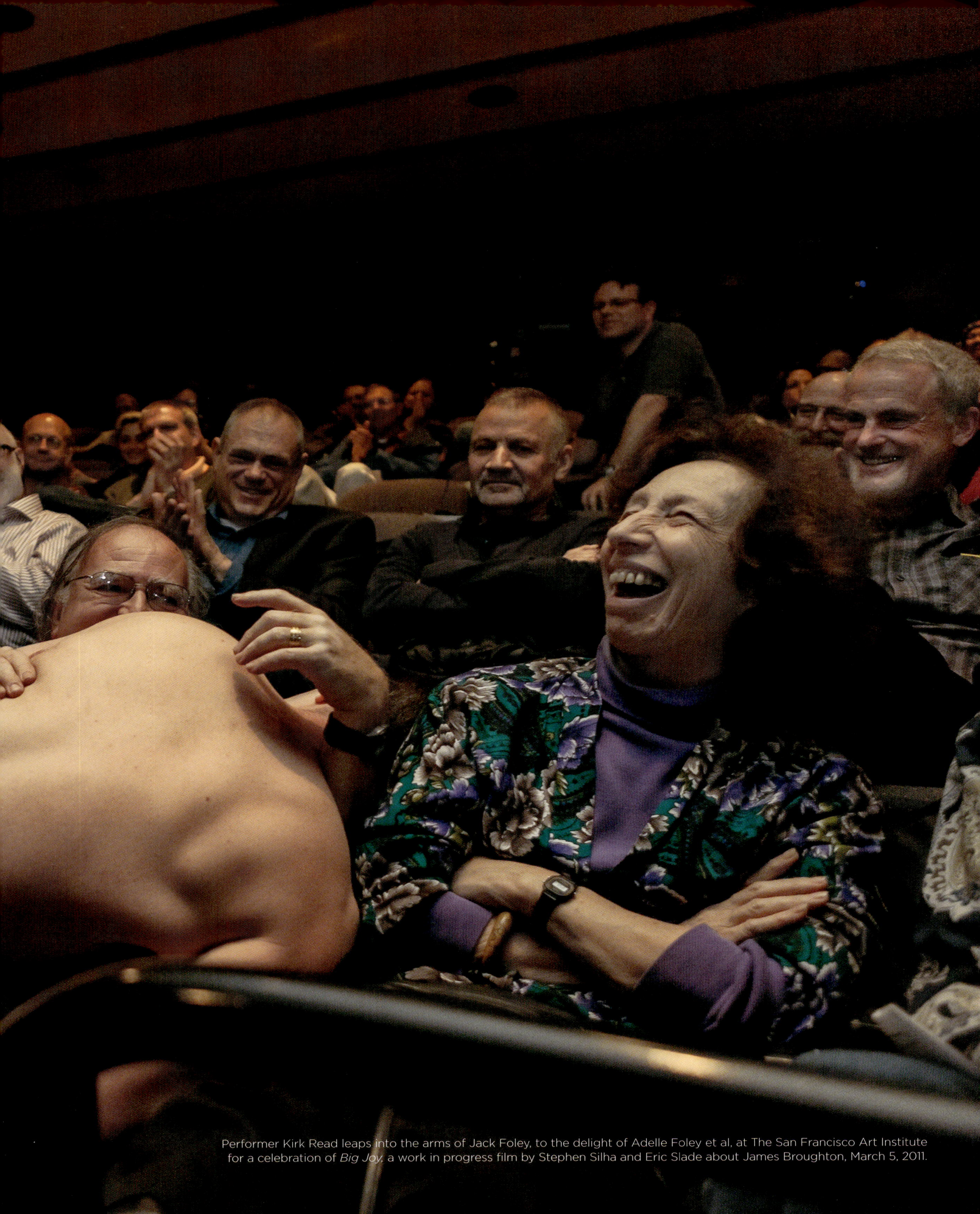

Performer Kirk Read leaps into the arms of Jack Foley, to the delight of Adelle Foley et al, at The San Francisco Art Institute for a celebration of *Big Joy*, a work in progress film by Stephen Silha and Eric Slade about James Broughton, March 5, 2011.

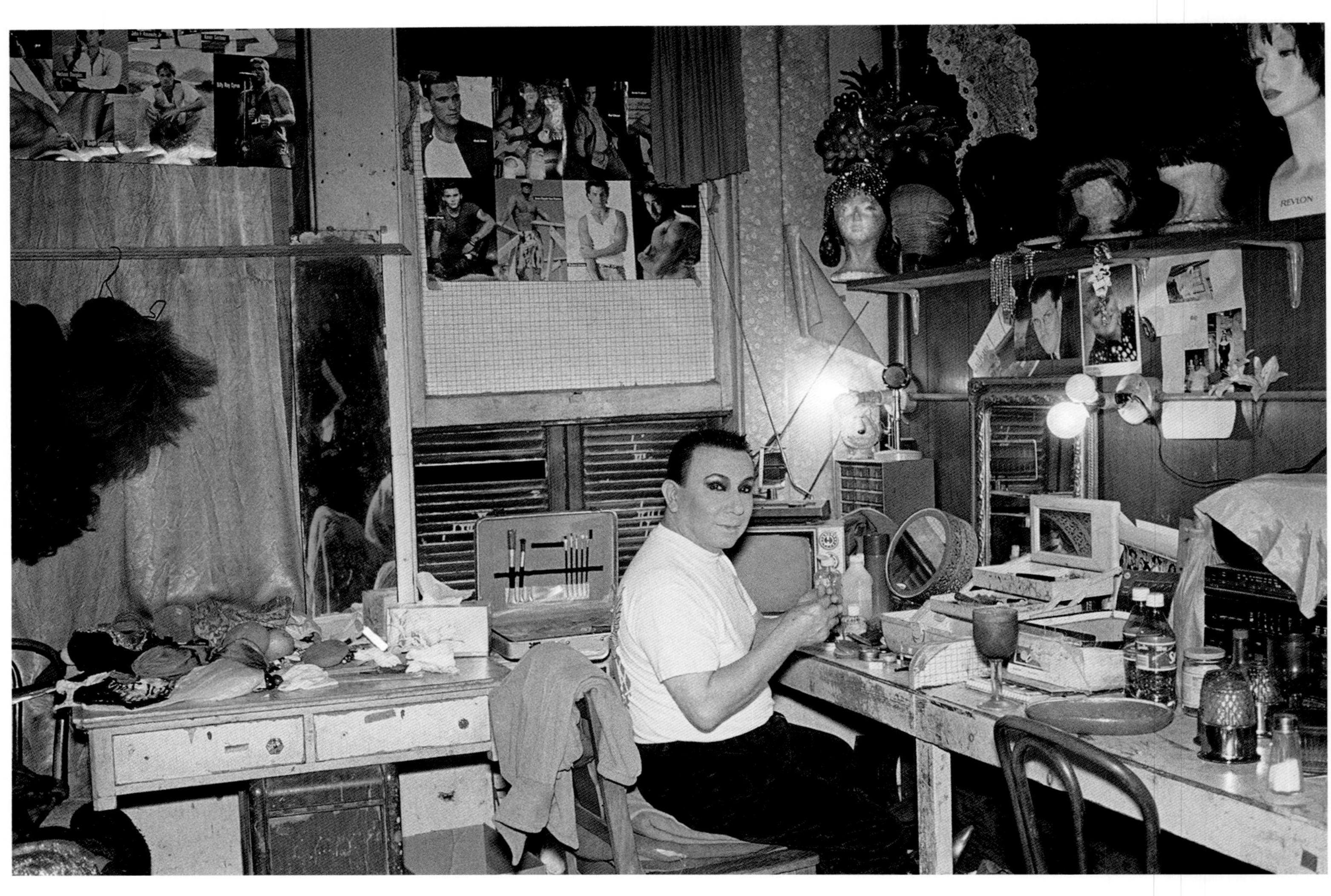

Finocchio's last week of performances, November 20, 1999.
(Above) Paco Rios, a 28-year-veteran with the review, which opened in 1933; *(opposite)* Brian Keith.

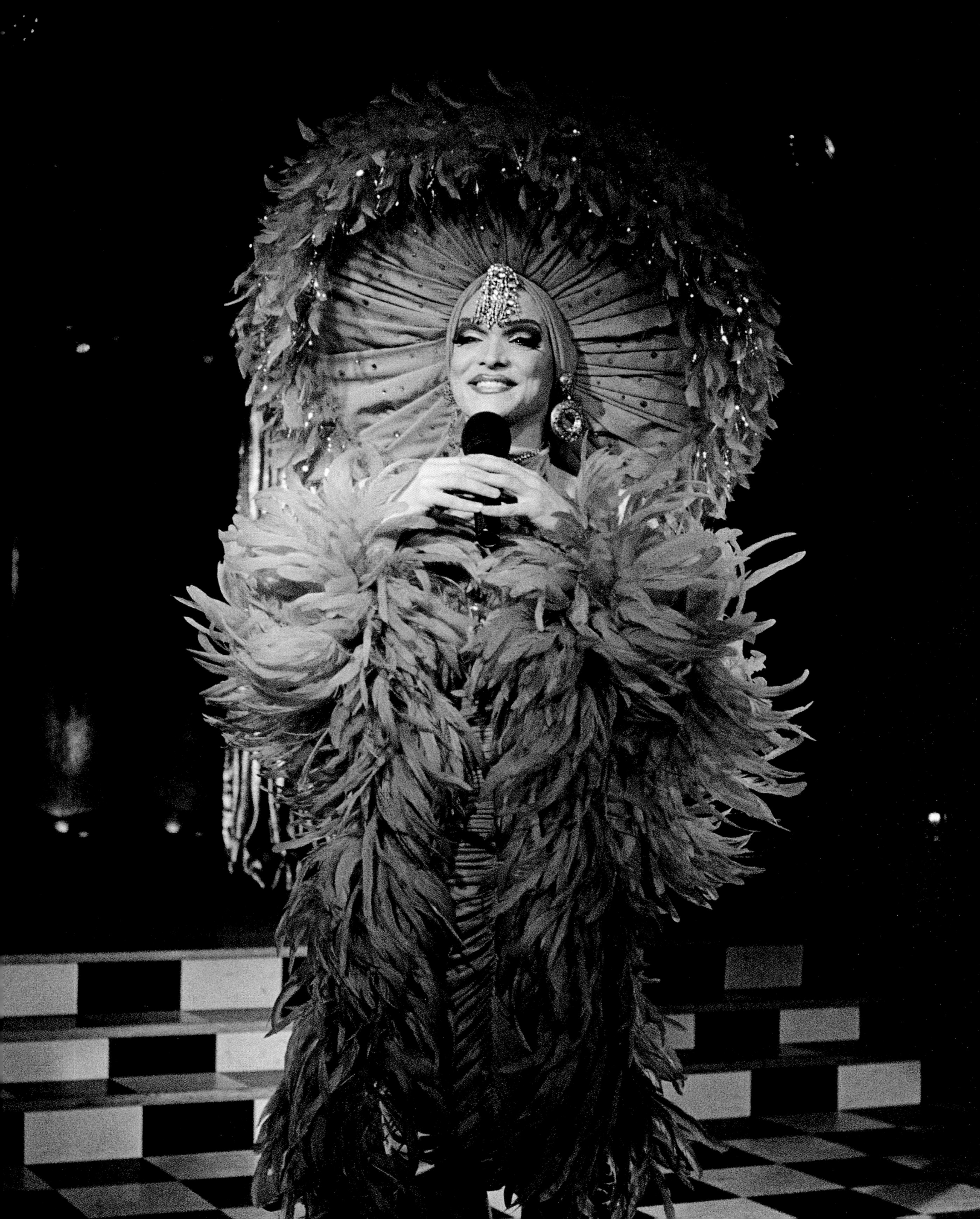

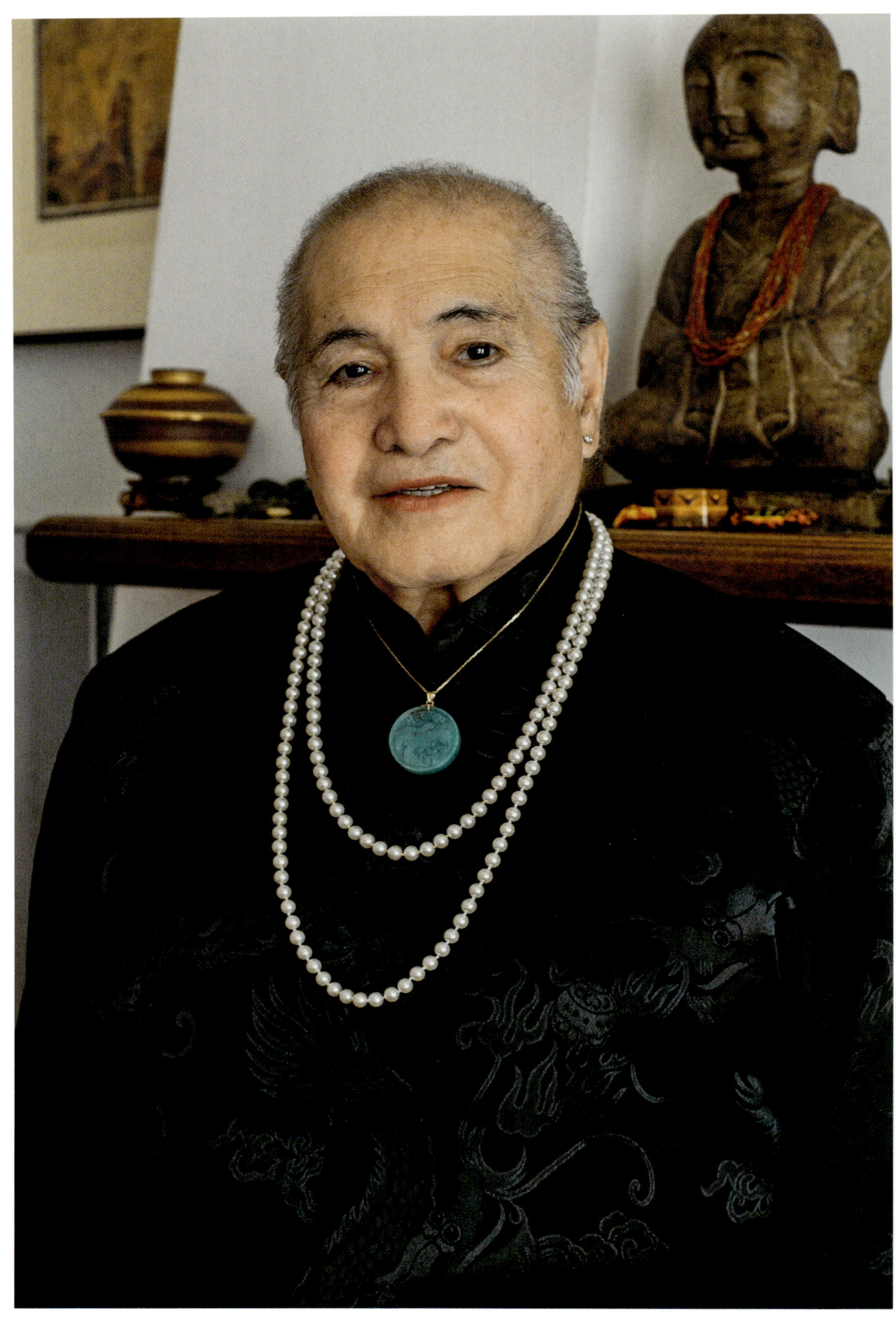

Above: José Julio Sarria, Absolute Empress I de San Francisco, aka the Widow Norton, October 27, 2011.
Opposite: Jean Franco, June 15, 2013.

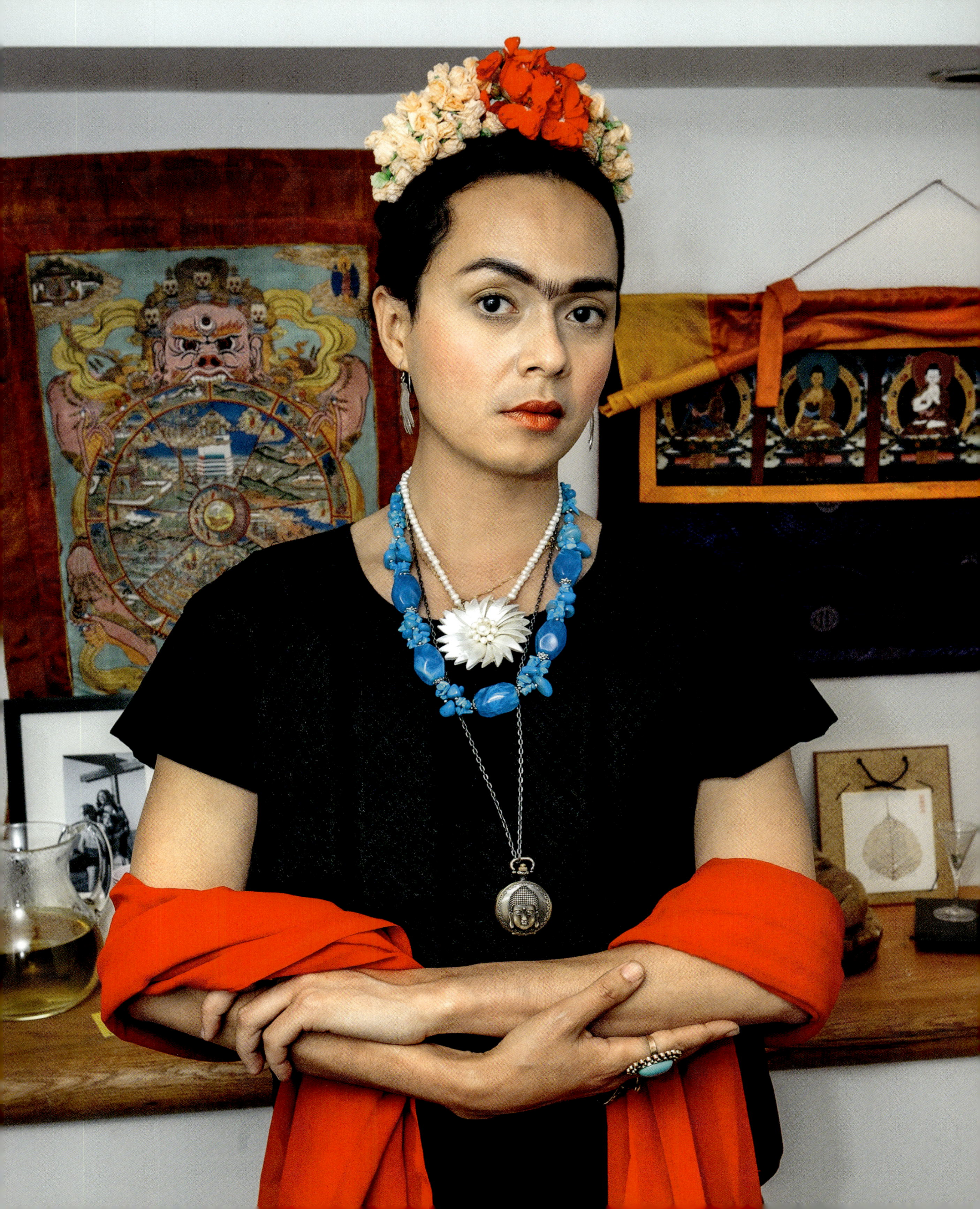

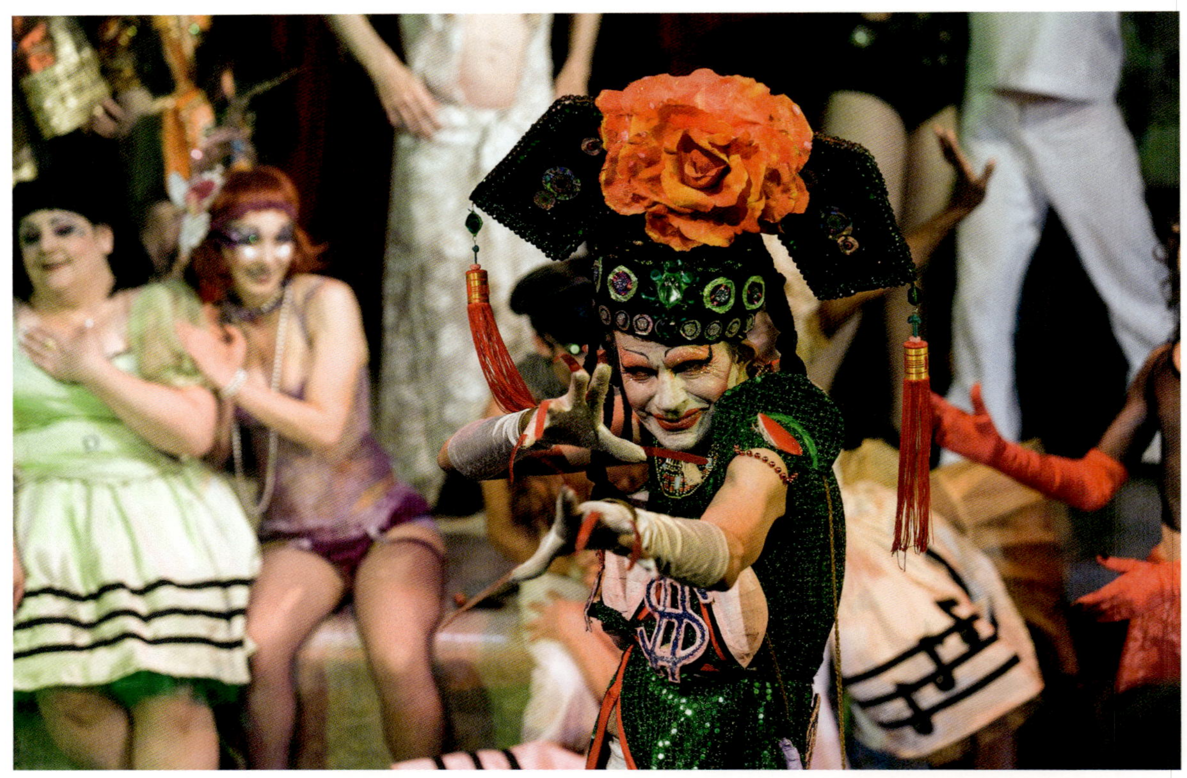

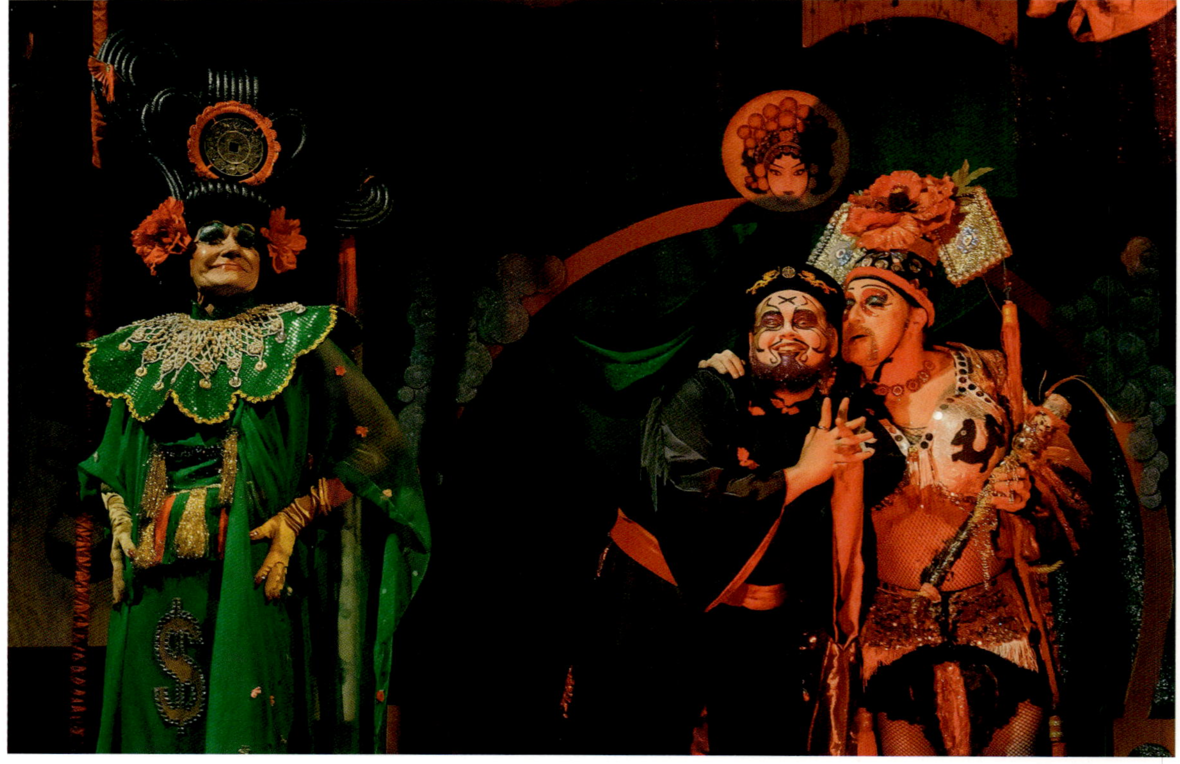

Thrillpeddlers revival of the Cockettes show, *Pearls Over Shanghai*, 2008 through 2014:
(Top) Cockette Rumi Missabu as Madame Gin Sling, June 13, 2009;
(bottom) Cockette Rumi Missabu, John Flaw and Russell Blackwood, May 31, 2014.

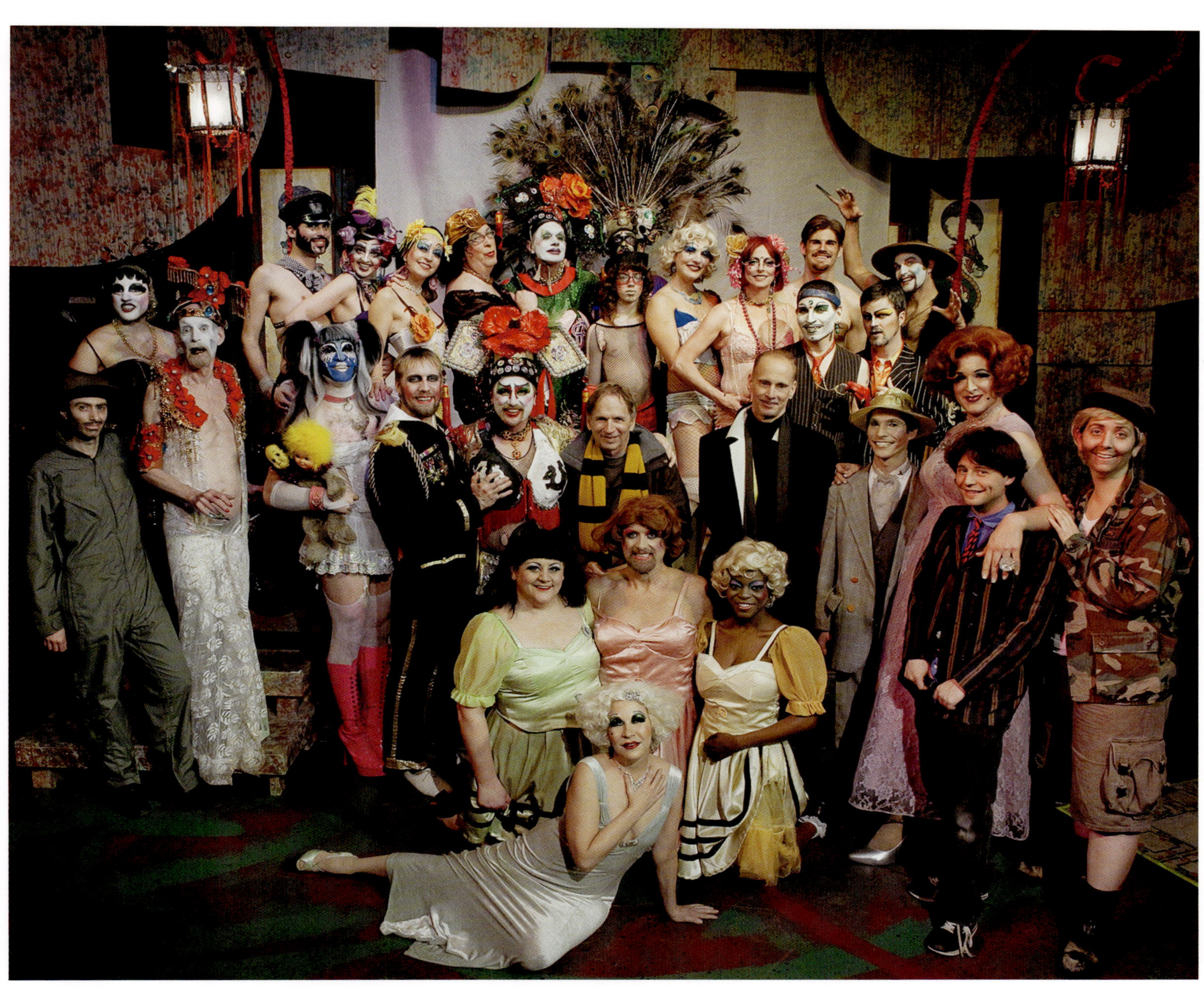

Above: The cast of *Pearls* with John Waters and Cockette Sebastian in attendance, January 8, 2010. *(Back)* Morningwood, Kegel Kater, Nancy French, Scrumbly Koldewyn, Rumi Missabu, Jimmy Toczyl, Galen Tsongas, Nahid Varjavand, Corrine Levy, Will Freitas and Tommy Buswell; *(middle)* Elron Hubby, Kara Emry, Lanny Baugniet, Eric Wertz, Steven Satryicon, Russell Blackwood, Cockette Sebastian, John Waters, Jef Valentine, Paul Ziller, Gabriel Ross, Katya Smirnoff-Skyy, Aaron Gonzo Gonzales and Laura Oz-burn; *(front)* Miss Sheldra, Eric Brizee and Adeola Role; *(center)* Connie Champagne.
Overleaf: Kegel Kater and Nancy French, Tingle Tangle Club, December 4, 2009.

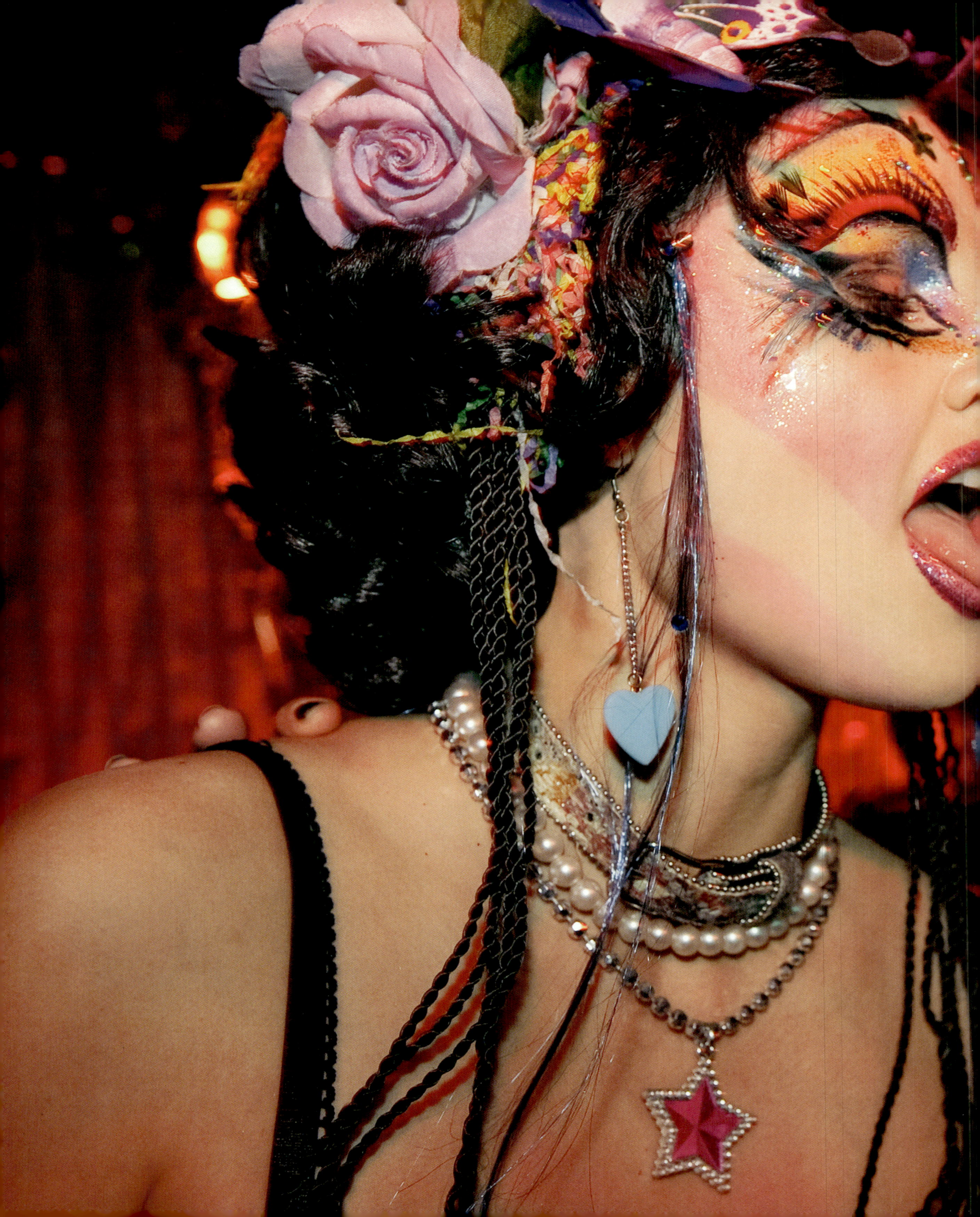

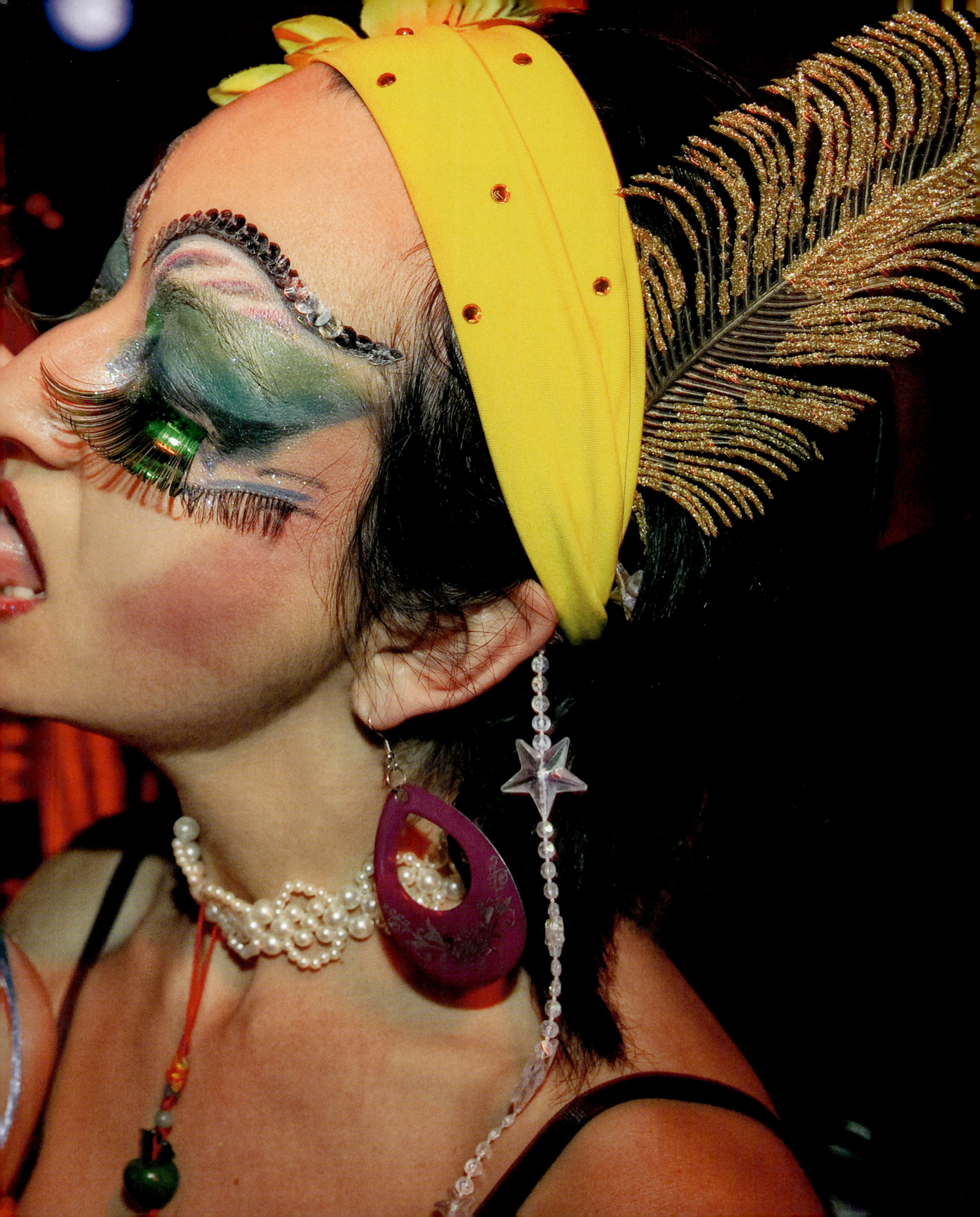

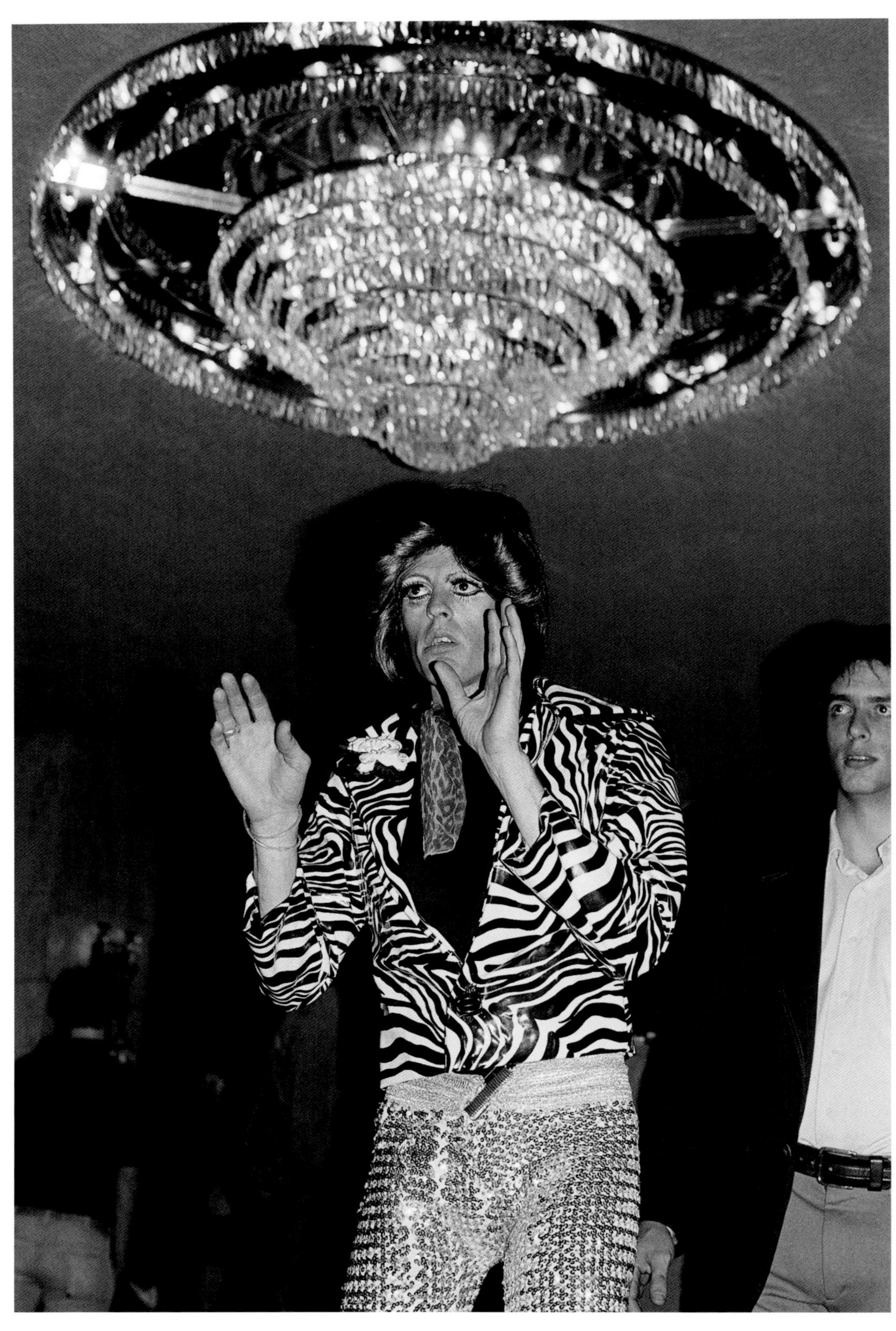

Above: Hookers Ball, October 1976. Bill Bowers.
Opposite: Peter Berlin, November 14, 2003.

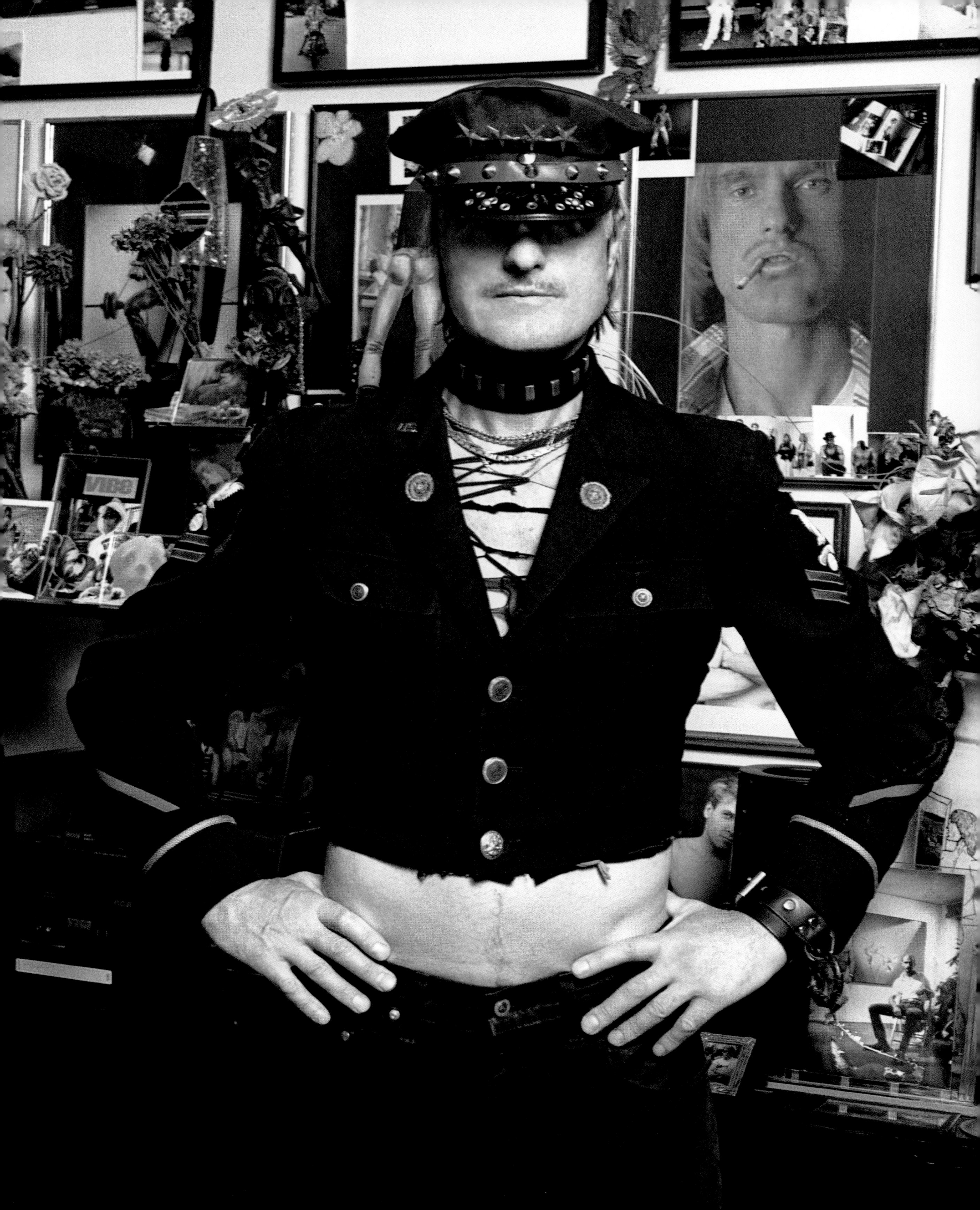
vibe

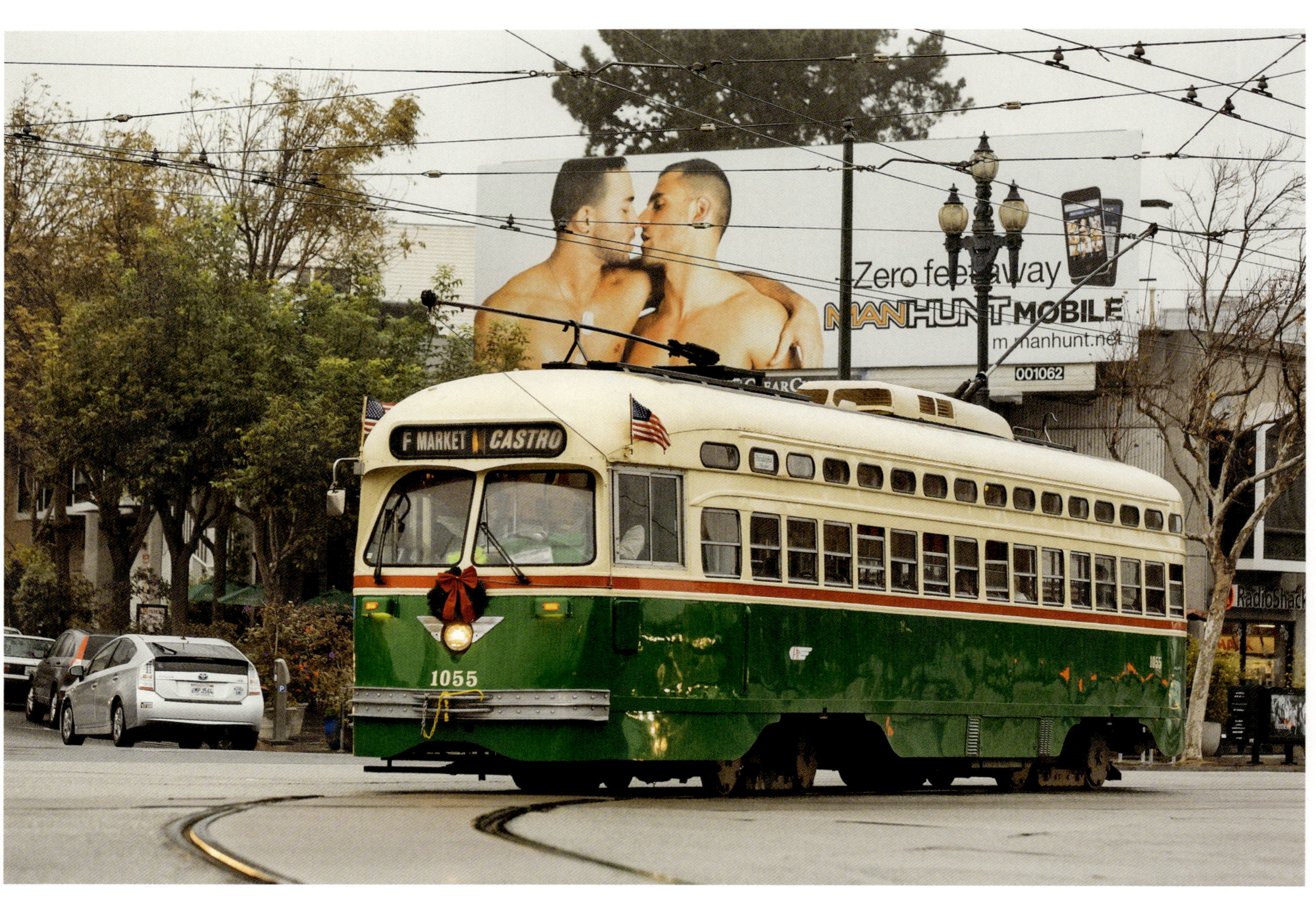

Market and Noe Streets, December 30, 2011.

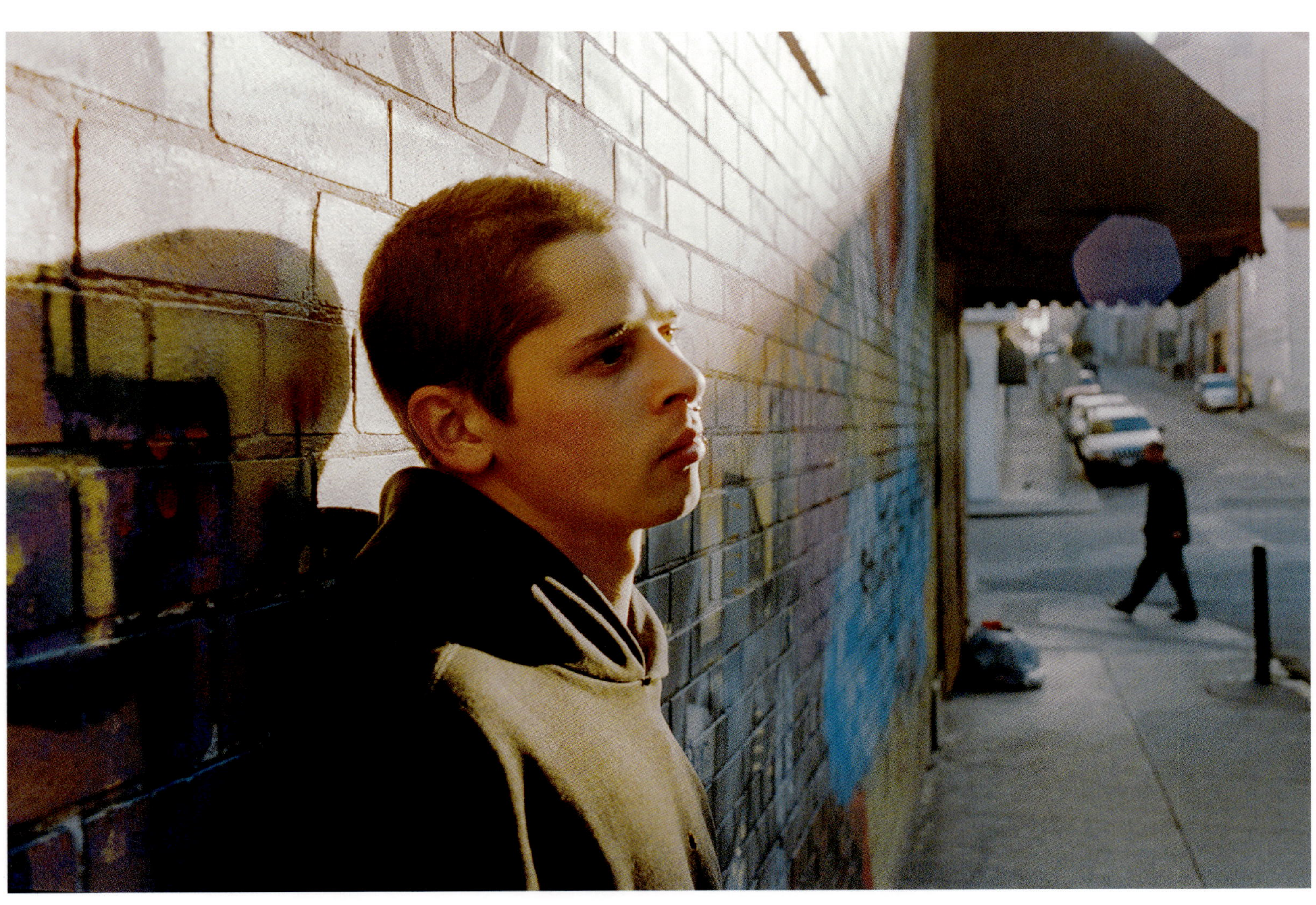

Polk Street, June 2, 2002. Simon.

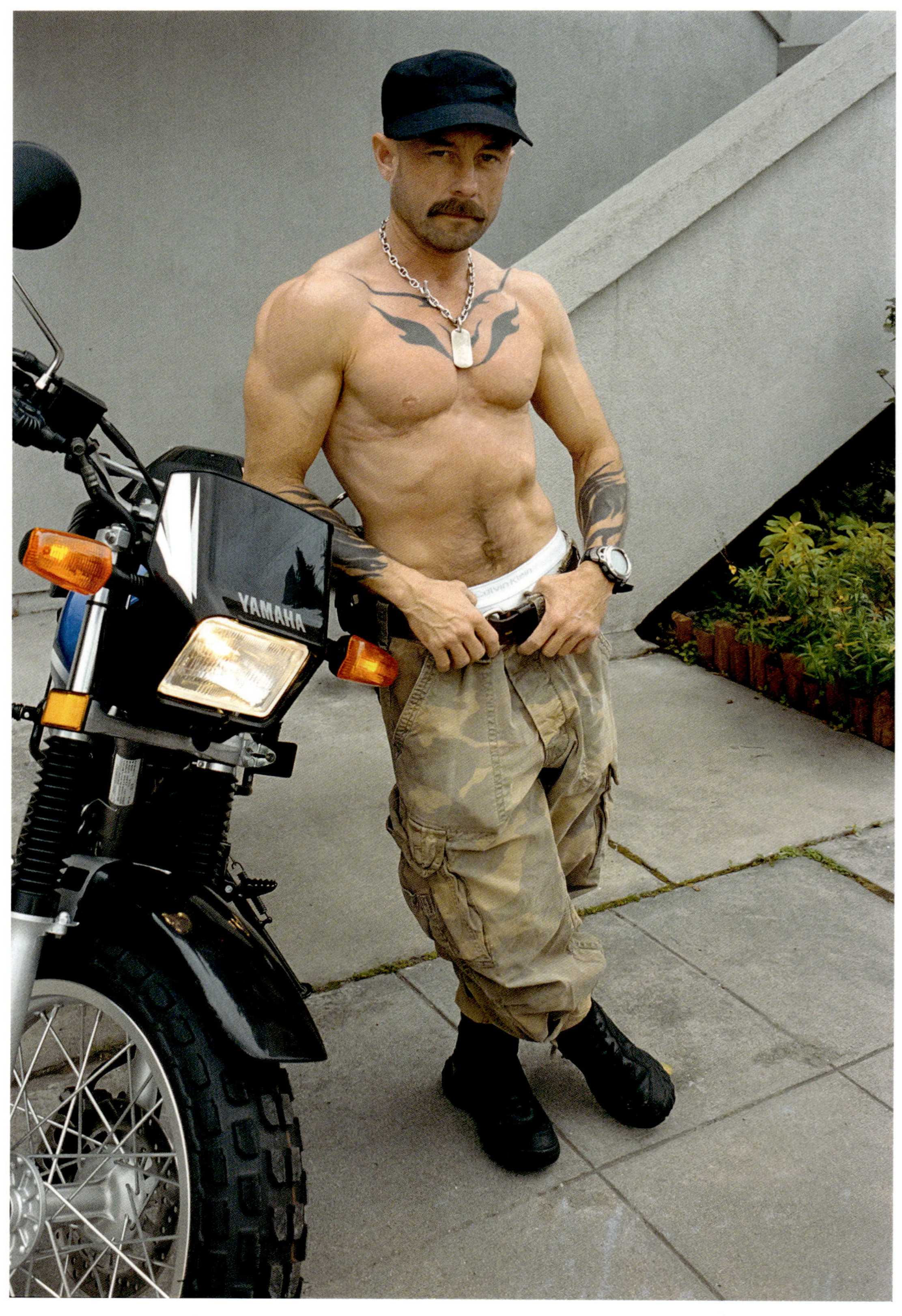

Above: Rex Cameron, April 1, 2006.
Opposite: Brad Russo, June 22, 1990.

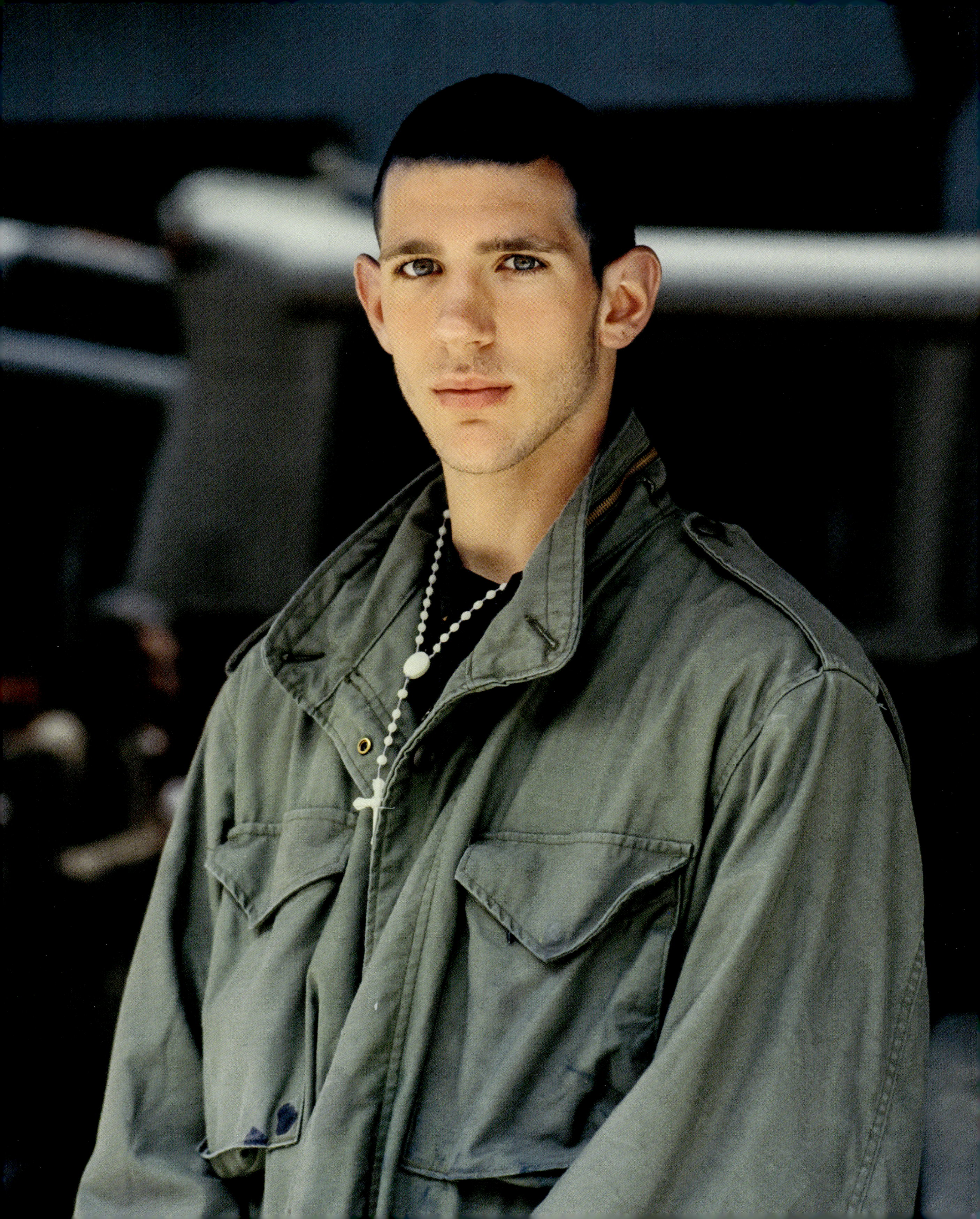

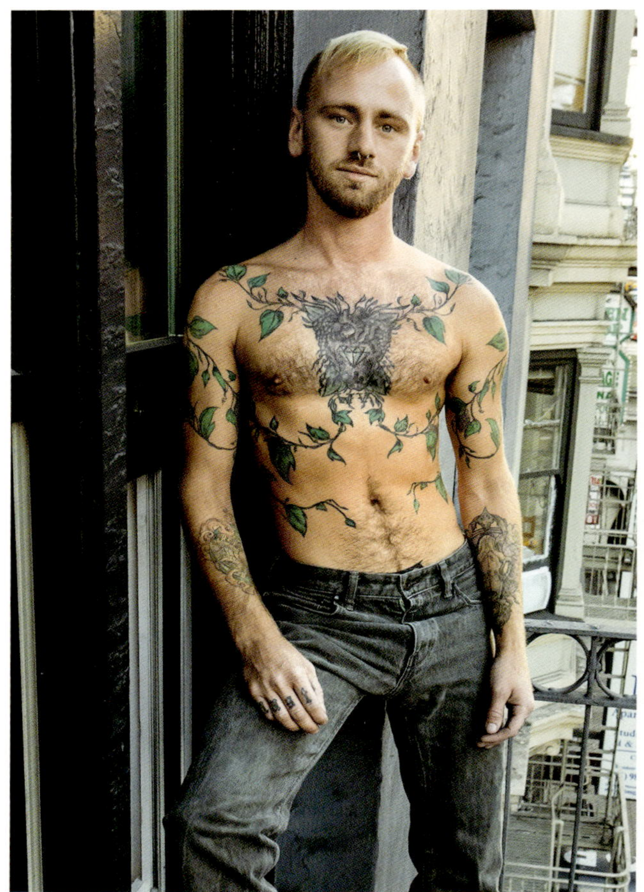

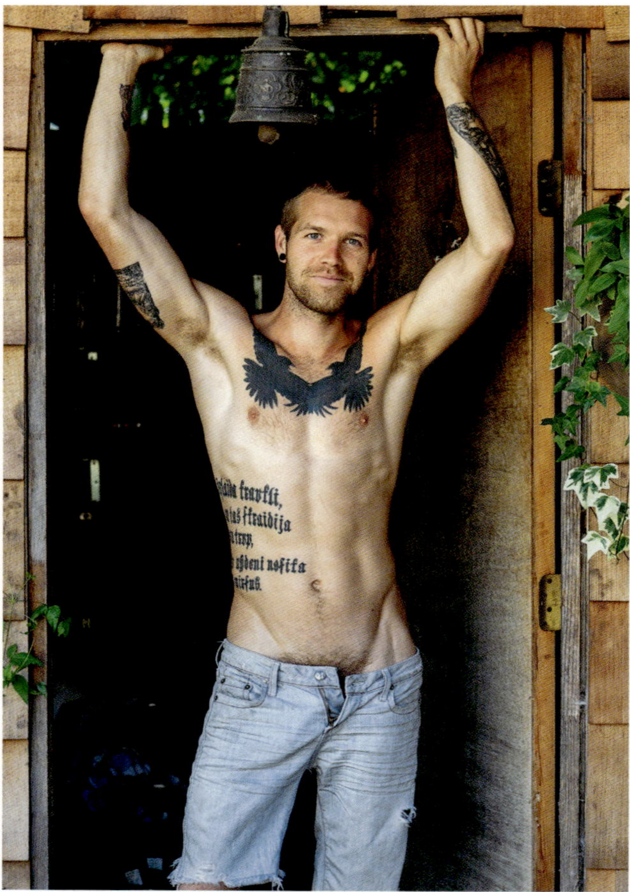

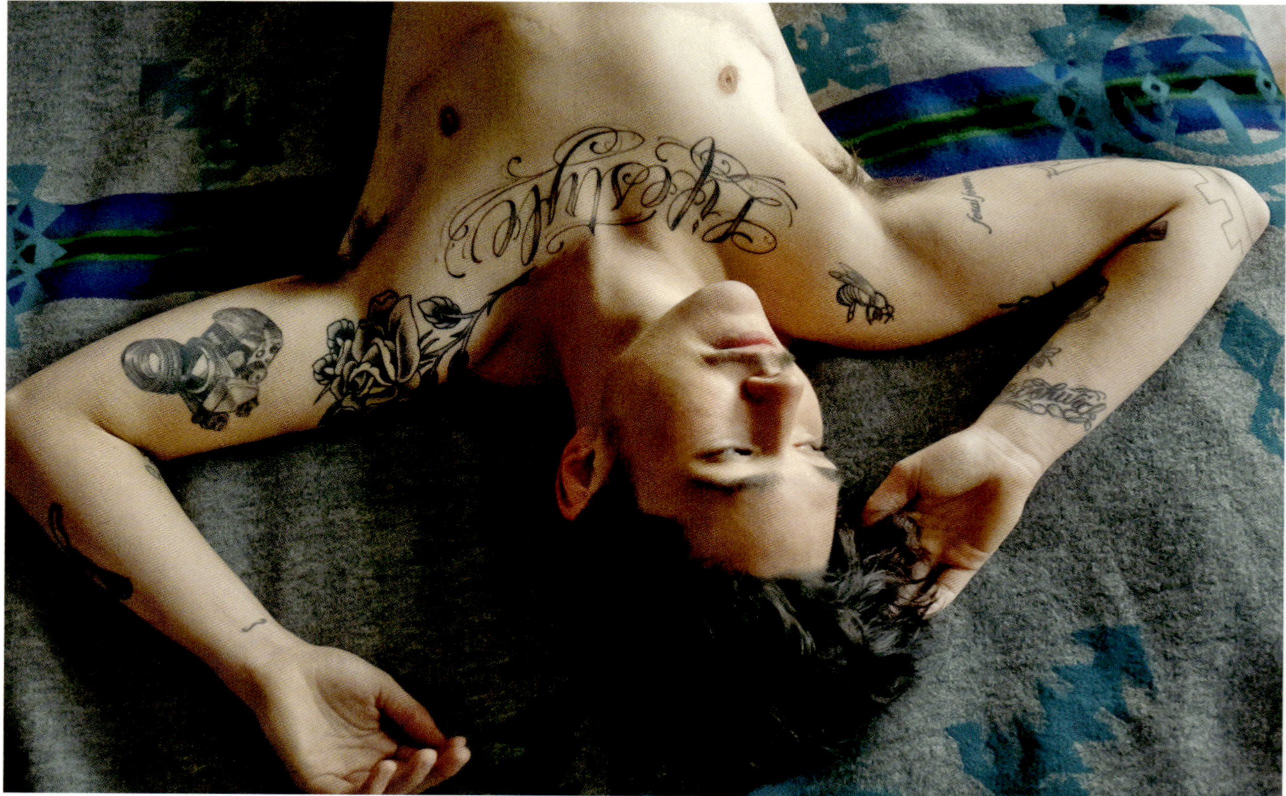

Above: *(clockwise from top left)* Ace, October 22, 2015; Leif Erickson, January 1, 2009; Amos Mac, December 9, 2009.
Opposite: Zel, May 29, 2009.

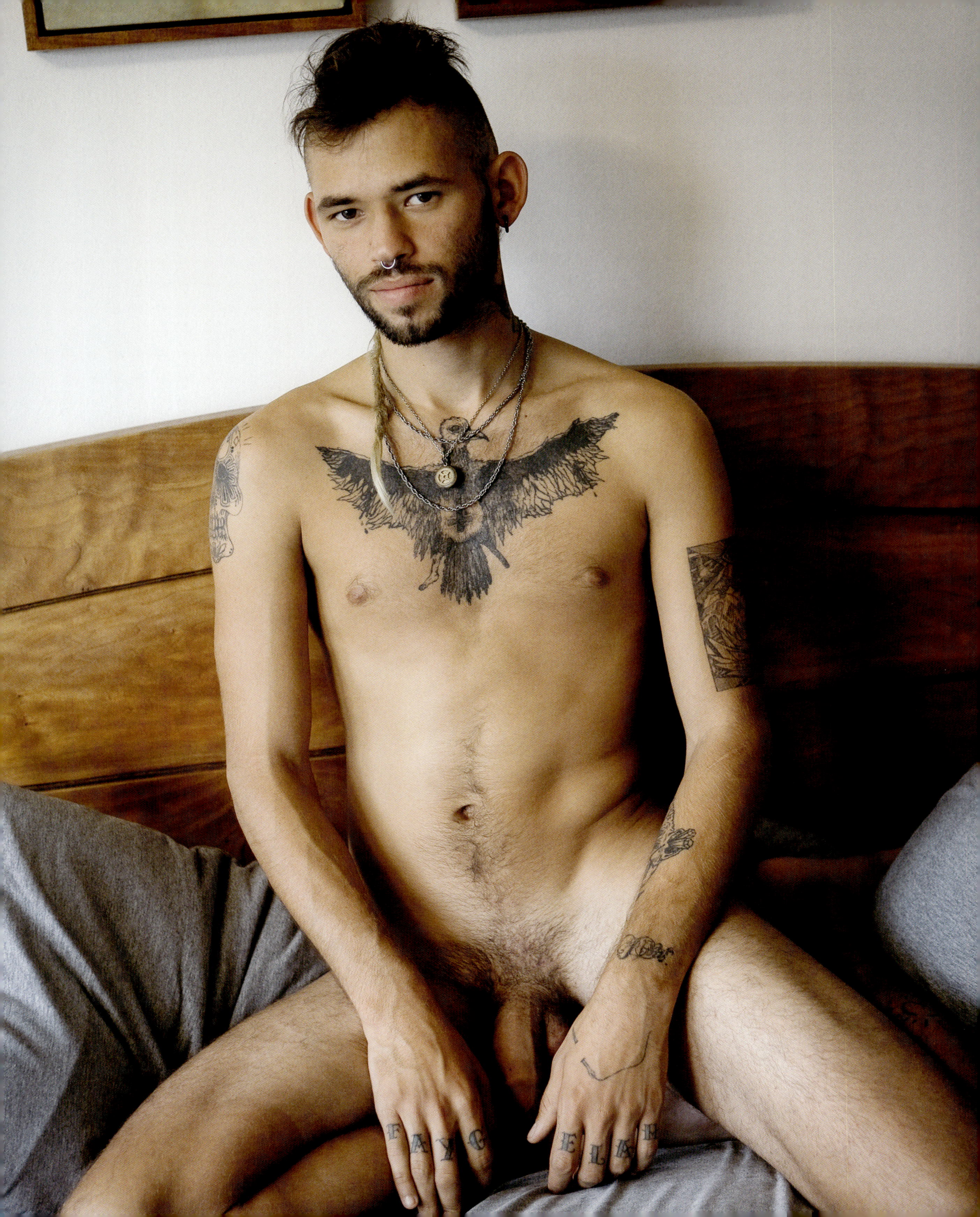
FAYG
ELAH

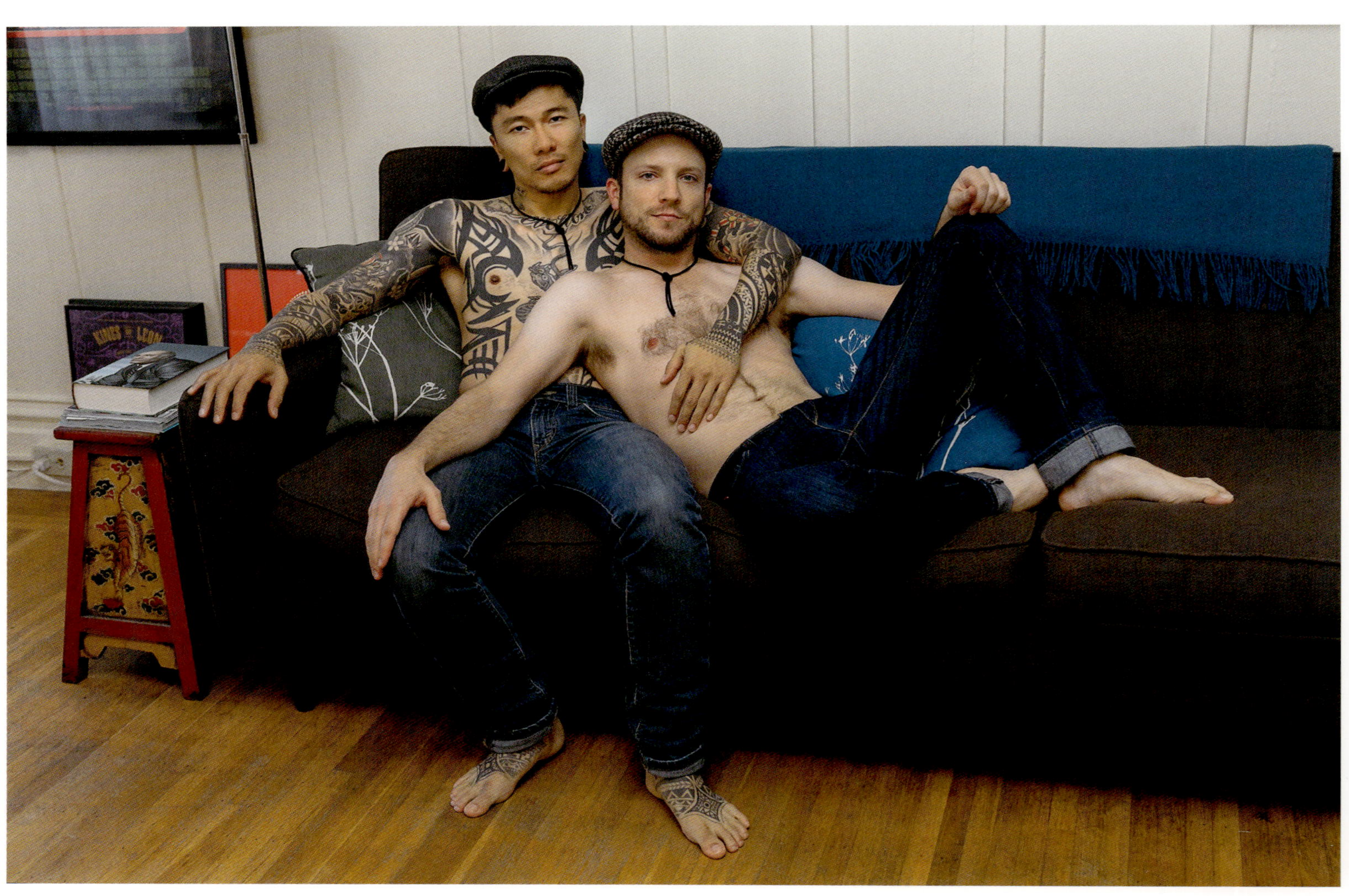

Glenn Low-A-Chee and Daniel Kayes, October 31, 2010.

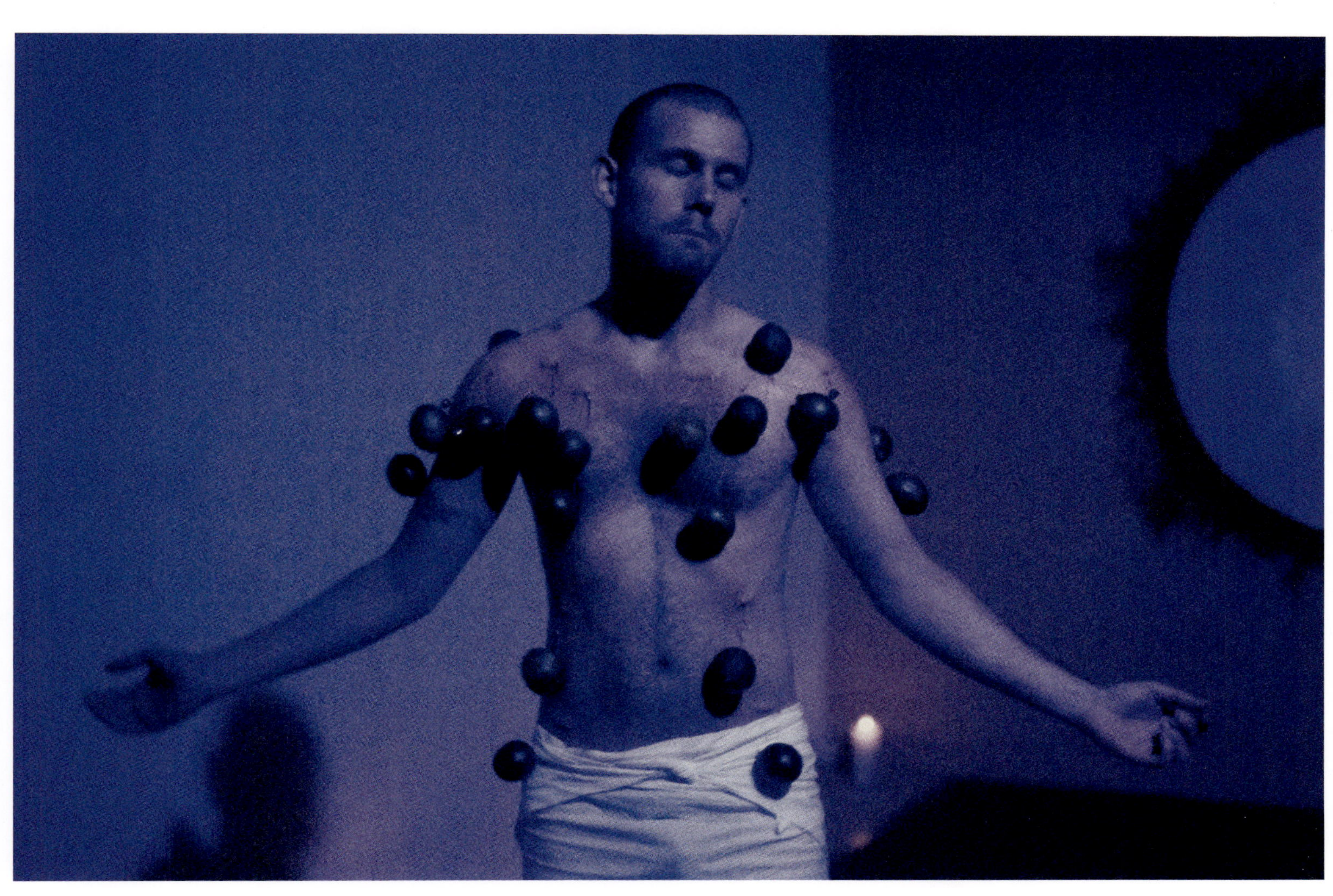

Energy pull, July 1, 1995. Beau Love.

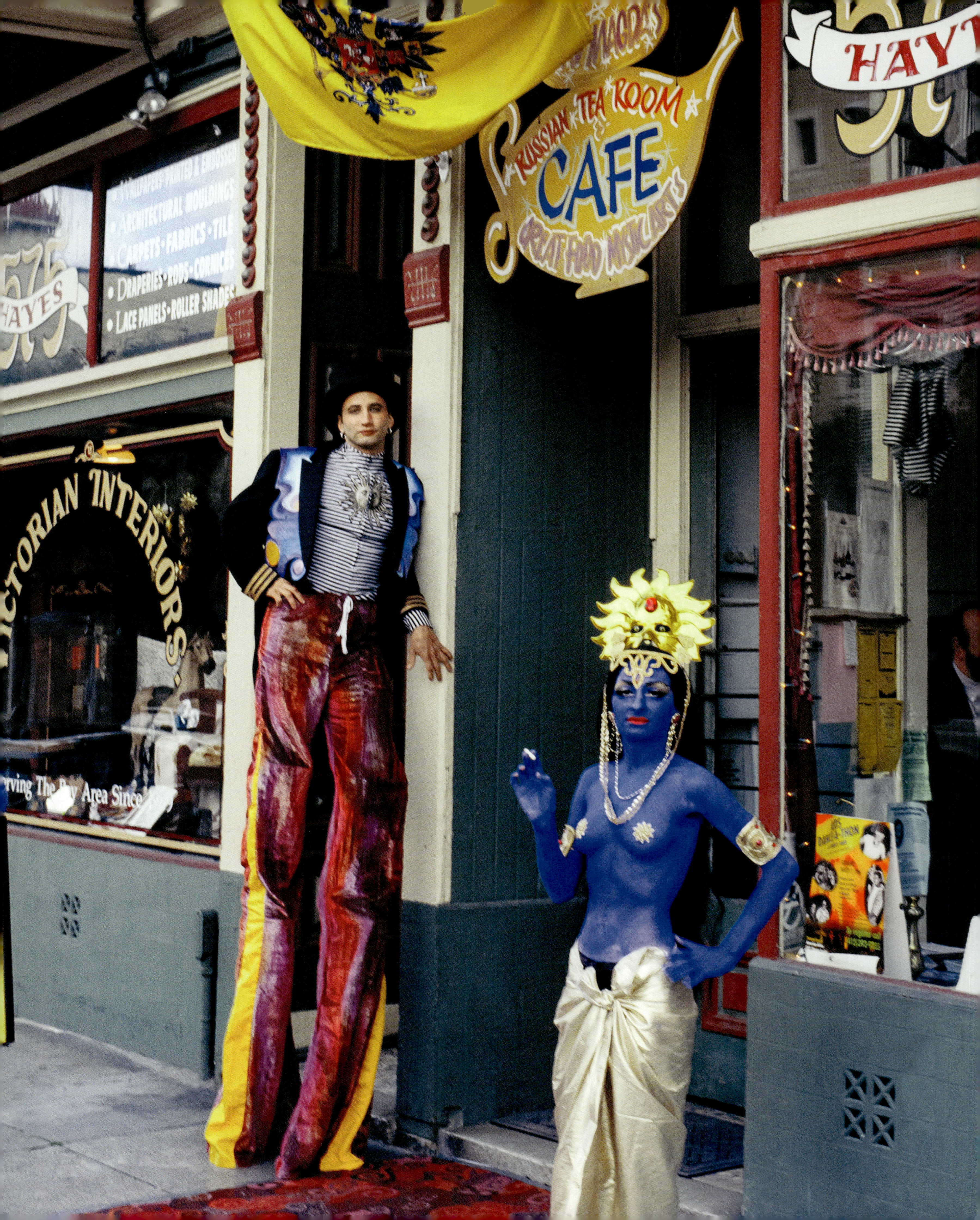

RUSSIAN TEA ROOM &
CAFE
GREAT FOOD MUSIC ARTISTS
HAYT
575 HAYES
• ARCHITECTURAL MOULDINGS
• CARPETS • FABRICS • TILE
• DRAPERIES • RODS • CORNICES
• LACE PANELS • ROLLER SHADES
ICTORIAN INTERIORS
rving The Bay Area Since

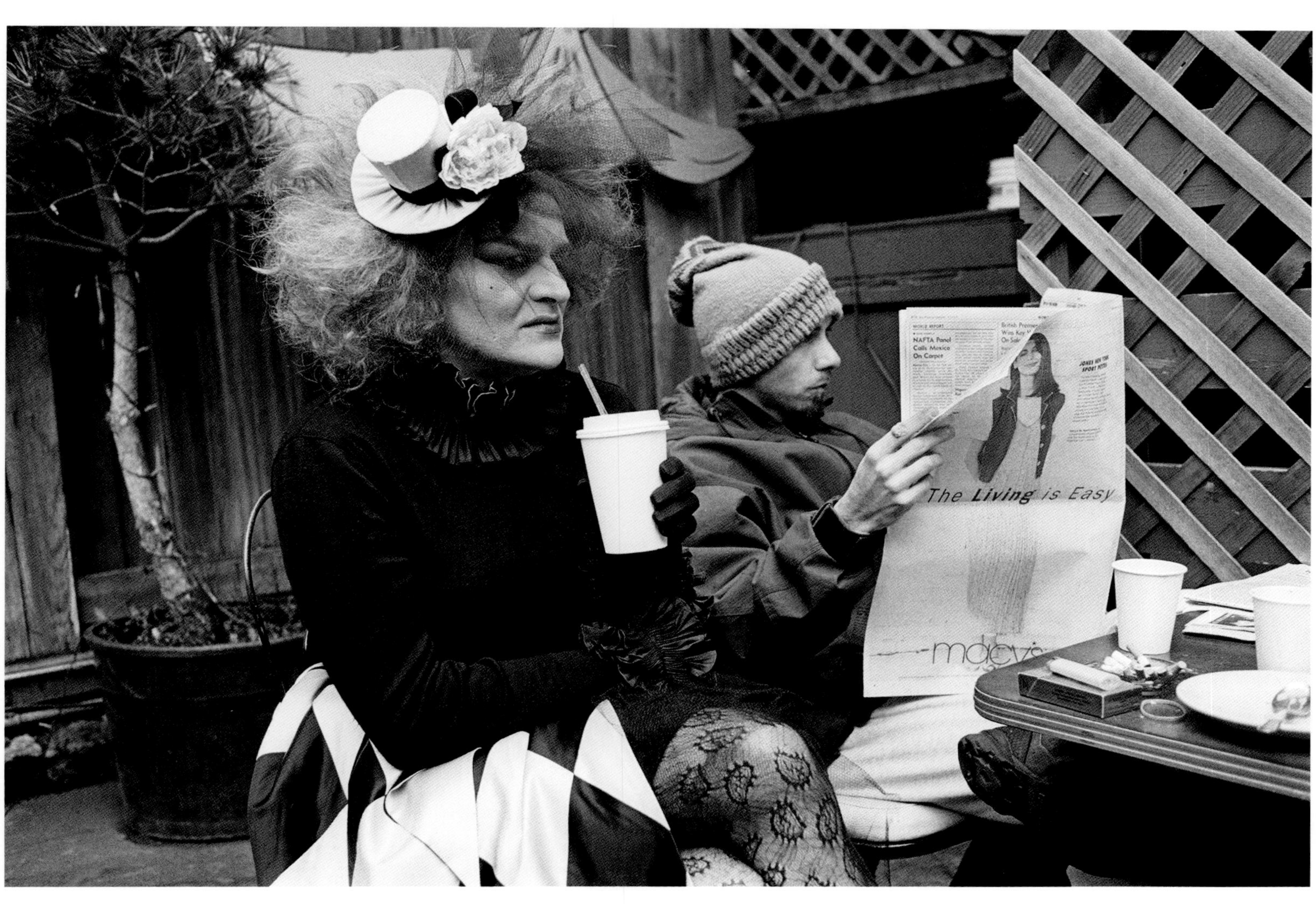

Mad Magda's Russian Tea Room and Cafe, February 27, 1996.
(Above) Glamamore and Jon Bush; *(opposite)* Fred Adler and Joanne Evangelista.

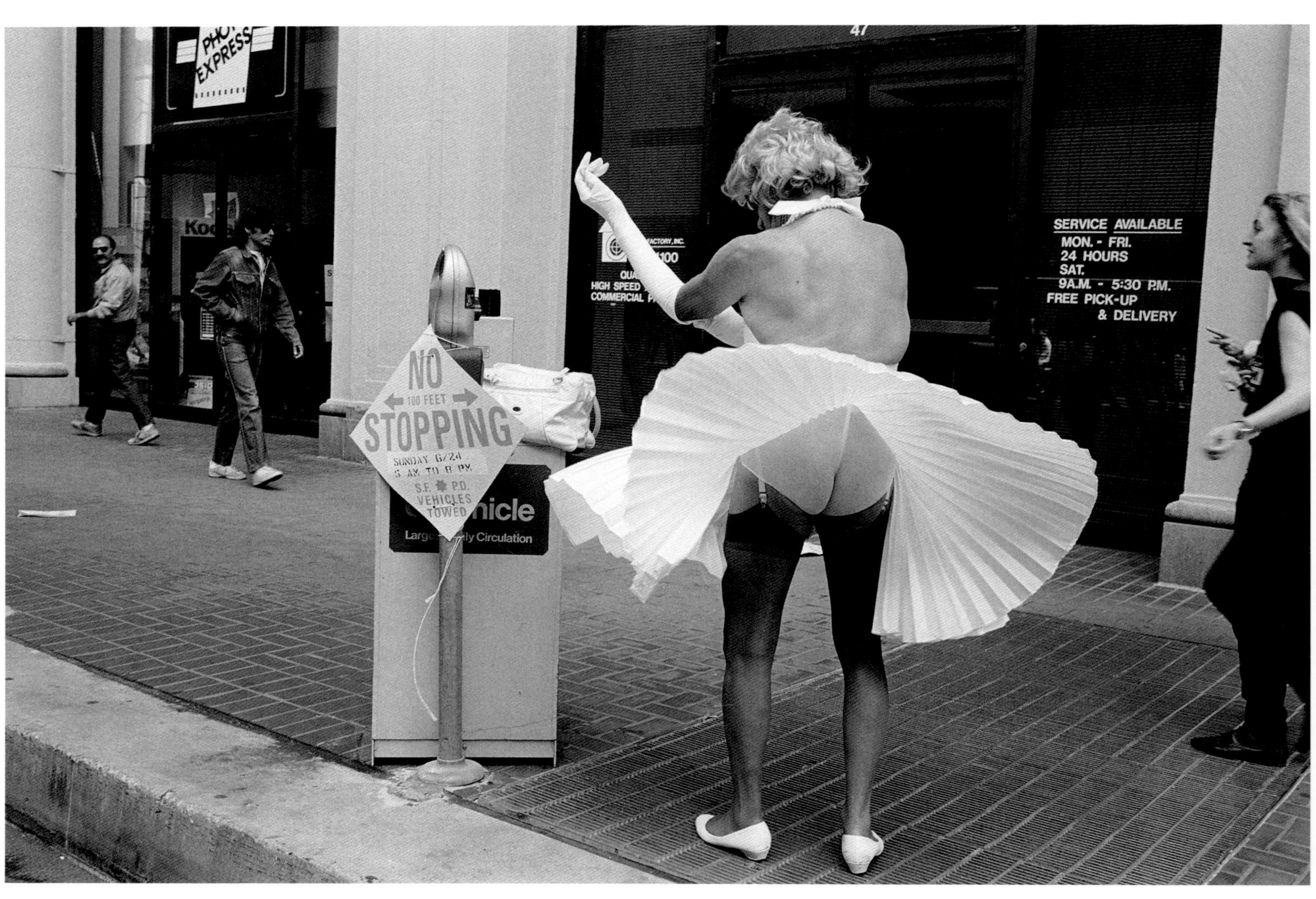

Above: SF LGBT Pride, June 24, 1990.
Opposite: Frameline SF LGBT Film Festival. Premiere of 35mm print of Gus Van Sant's film *Mala Noche*, June 13, 1993.

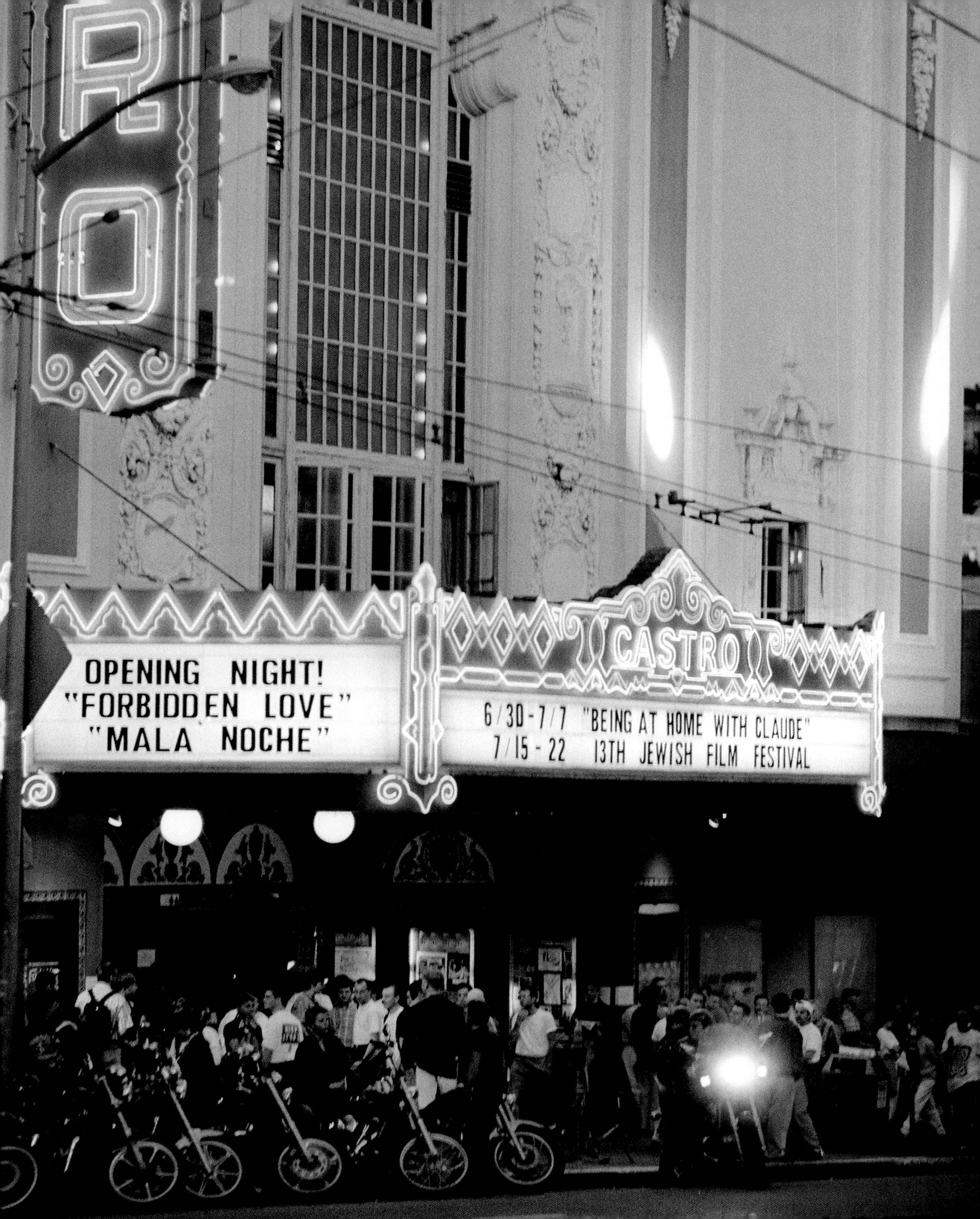
OPENING NIGHT!
"FORBIDDEN LOVE"
"MALA NOCHE"
CASTRO
6/30-7/7 "BEING AT HOME WITH CLAUDE"
7/15-22 13TH JEWISH FILM FESTIVAL

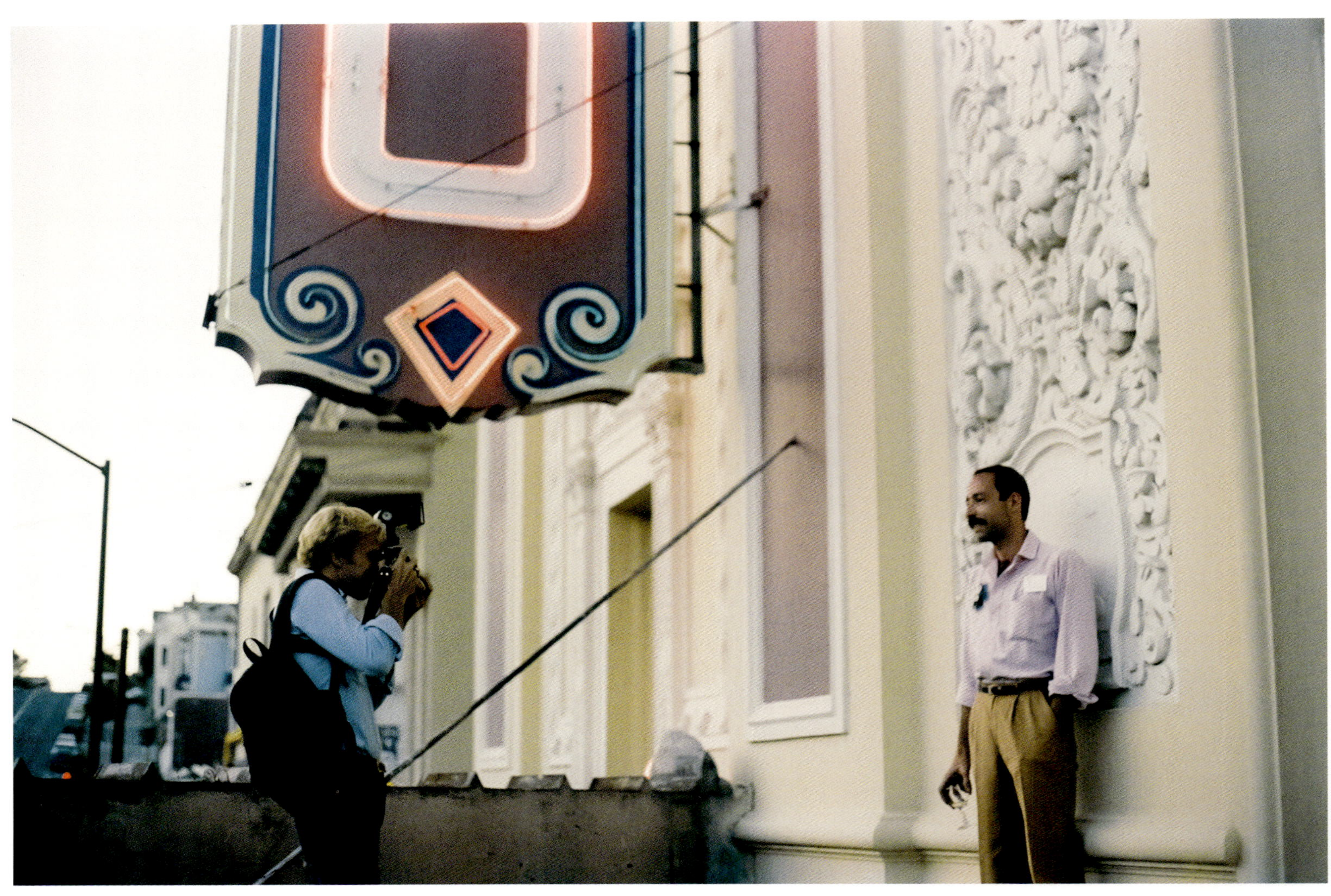

Castro Theatre premiere of Rob Epstein's film, *Greetings from Washington DC*, June 22, 1981. Mick Hicks photographing Vito Russo.

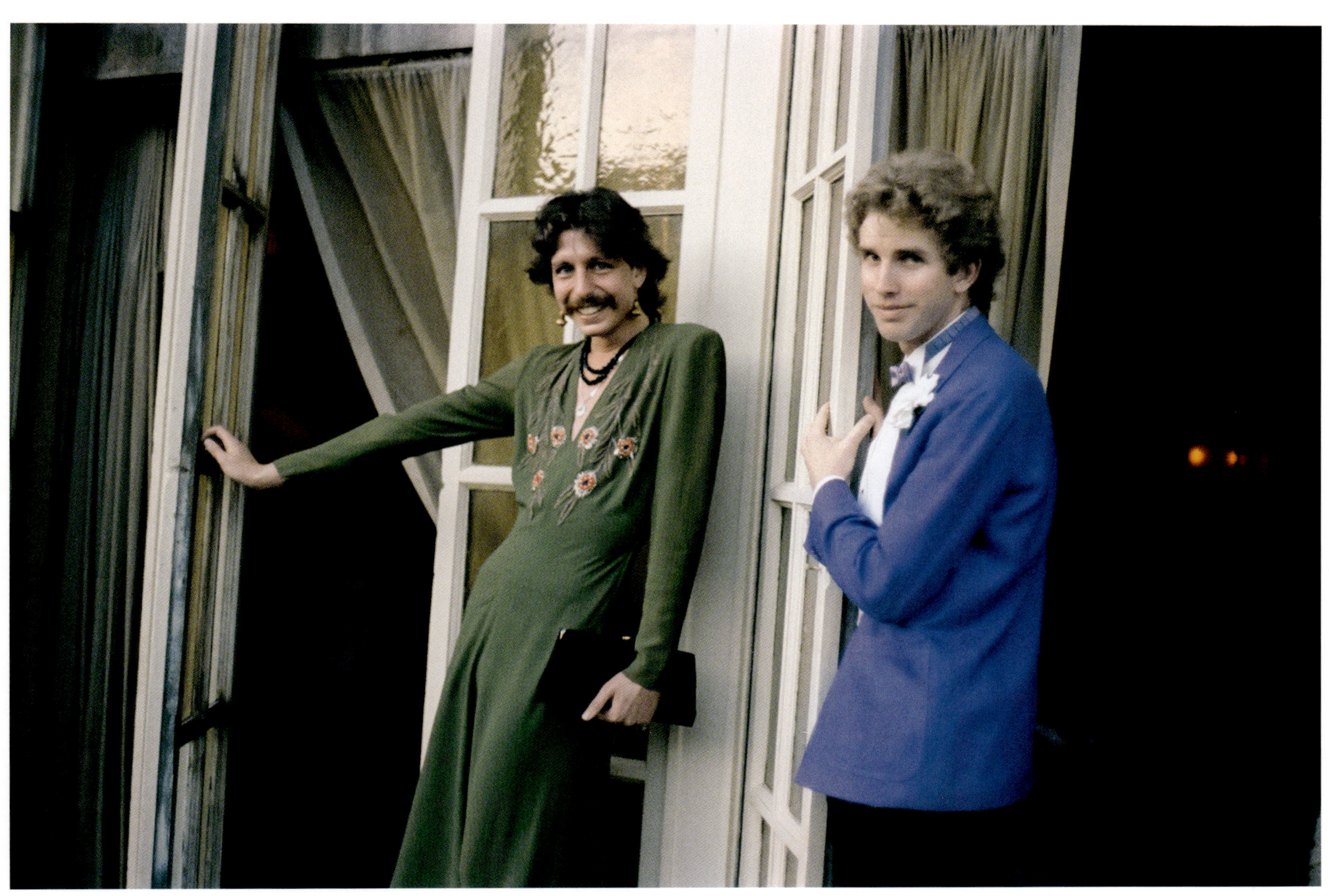

Castro Theatre premiere of Rob Epstein's film, *Greetings from Washington DC*, June 22, 1981. Michael Starkman and Alan Sawyer.

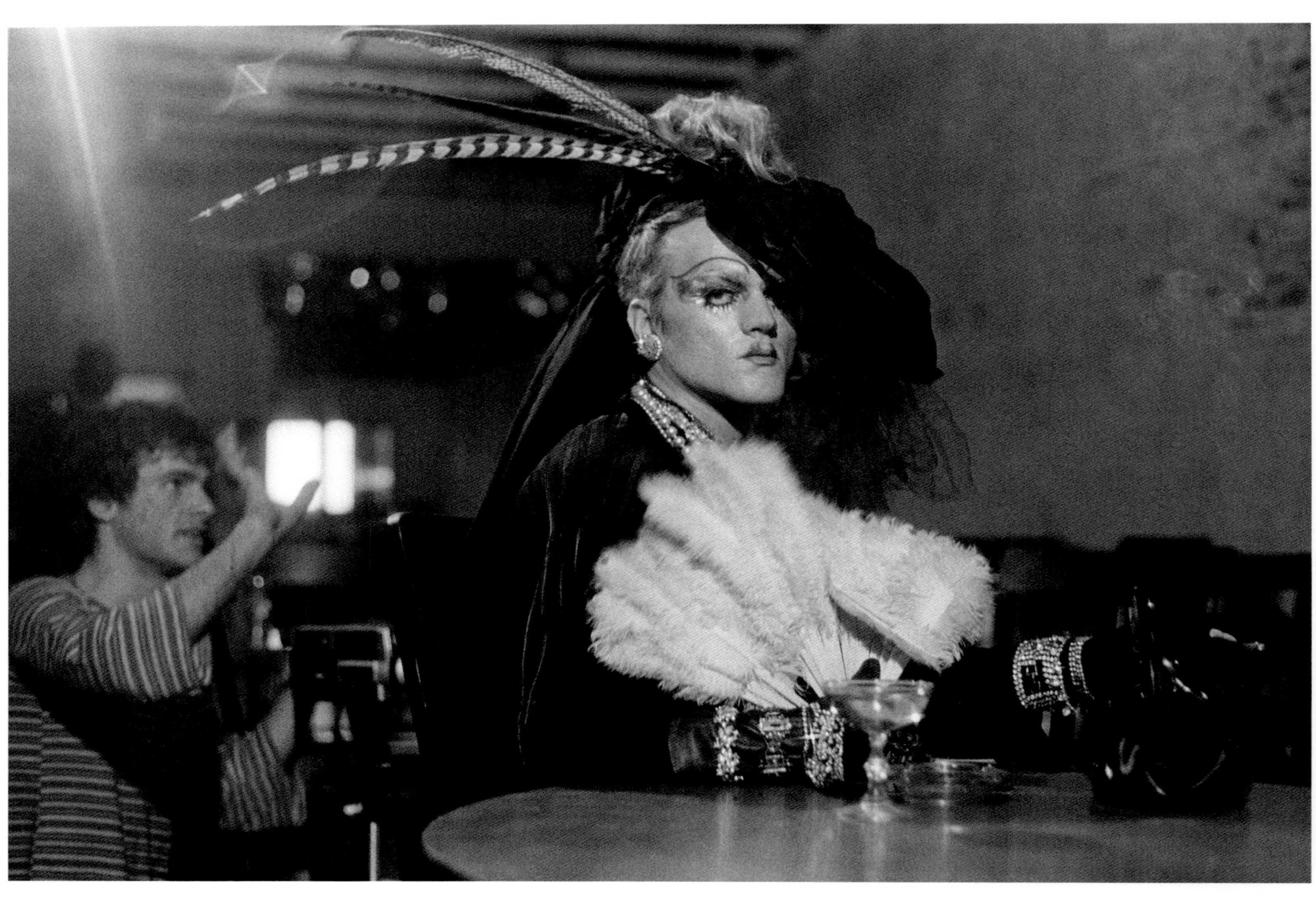

Above: *Unity*, December 4, 1977. Marc Huestis directing Lulu in his historical imagining of the end of Weimar-era cabaret life in Germany. (The motif is also a homage to Brassai's 1933 photo *La Môme Bijou*.)
Opposite: *Lulu Gets a Facelift*, a film by Marc Huestis, November 14, 2003.

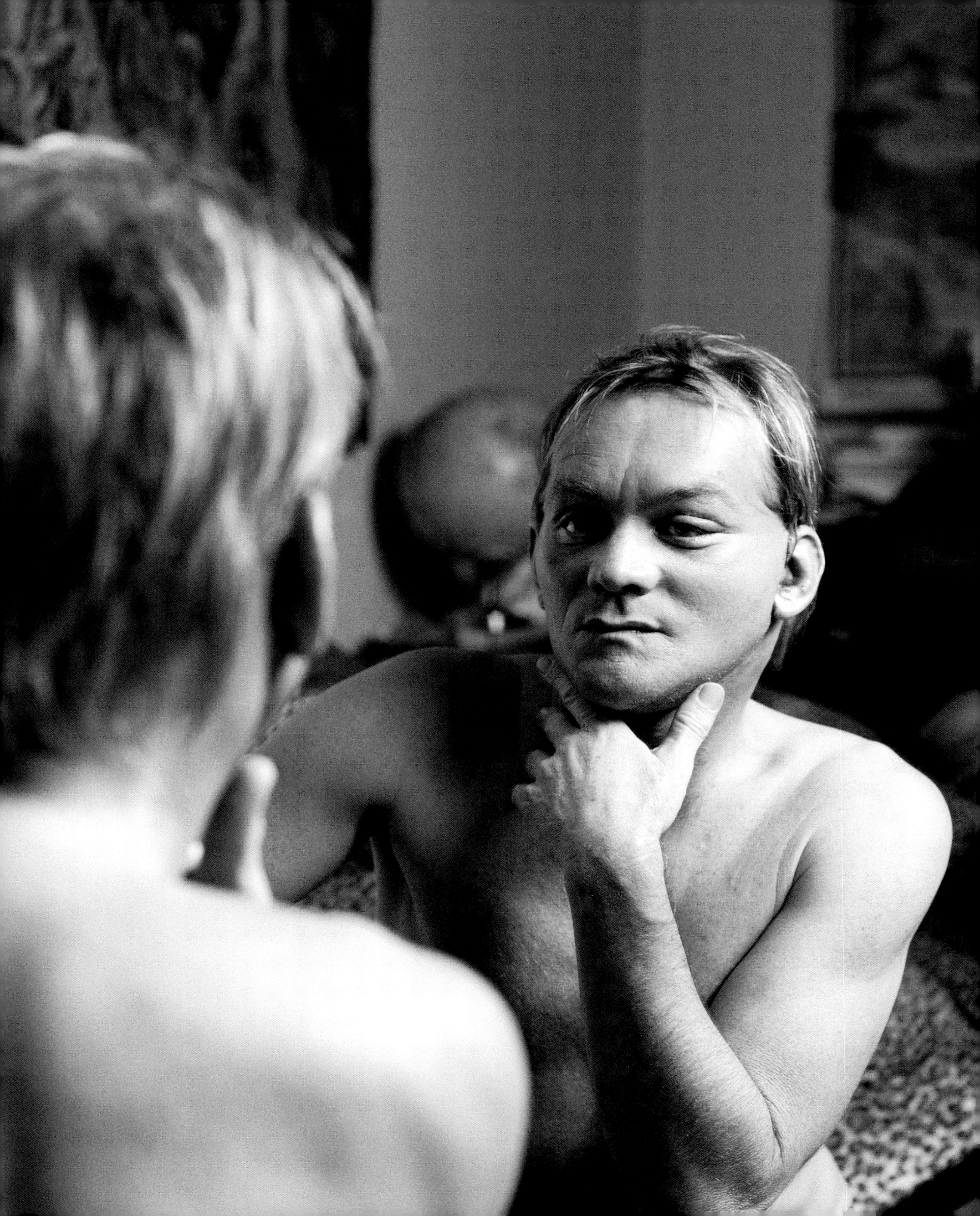

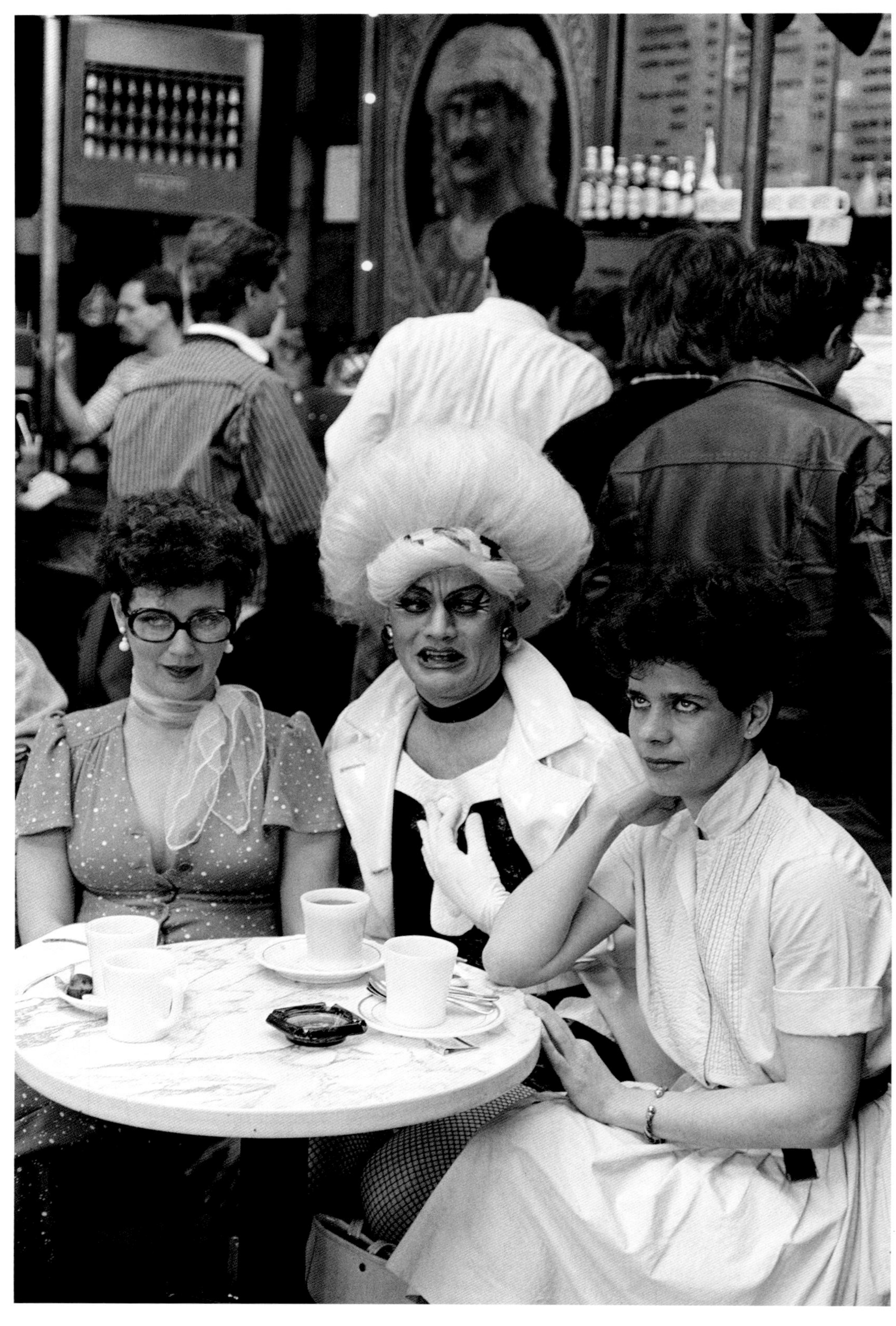

Above: *Whatever Happened To Susan Jane?*, a film by Marc Huestis, March 27, 1983. Ann Block, Lulu and Francesca Rosa.
Opposite: *Broken Dishes*, April 1977. Amber Waves and Dolores Deluxe.

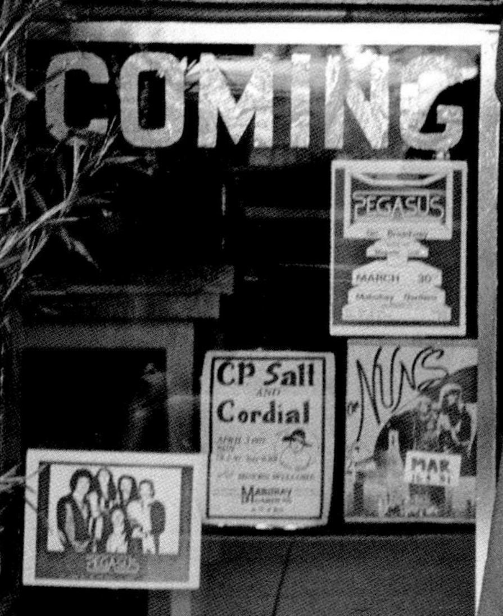
MABUHAY
Gardens Presents
BROKEN
DISHES
WITH
DOLORES DELUXE
&
AMBER WAVES
MUSIC BY
SCRUMBLY
COMING
PEGASUS
MARCH 30
CP Sall
AND
Cordial
NUNS
MAR
MEAT LOAF DINNER
FROZEN

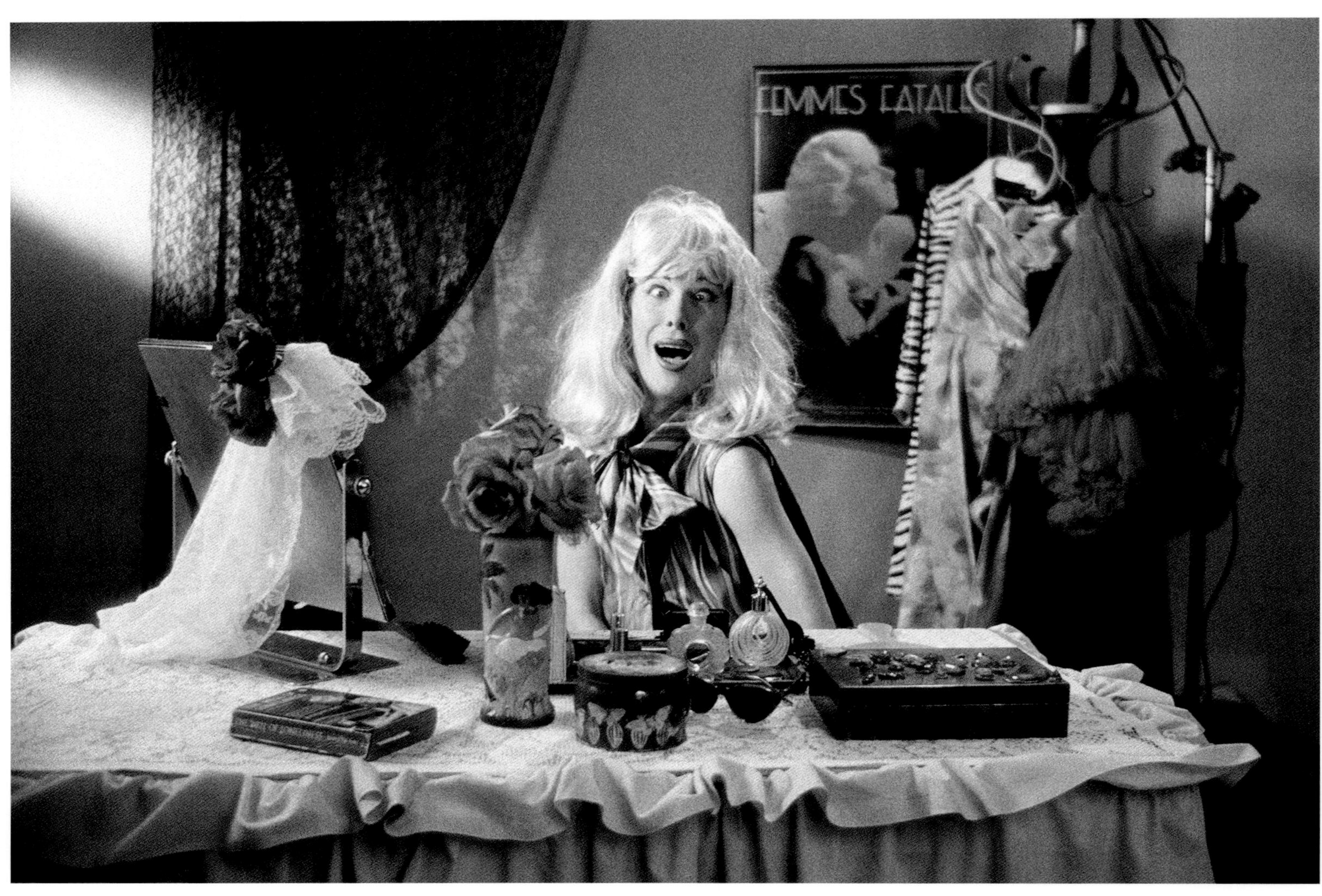

Above: *Sex Is* by Marc Huestis and Lawrence Helman, February 16, 1992. Vivian Bond in a scene for Huestis' searing re-creation of David Reuben's dim view of homosexuality in his 1960s' best seller, *Everything You Always Wanted to Know About Sex* (*But Were Afraid to Ask).*
Opposite: *Sex Is*, February 9, 1992. Madame X (set direction, Vola Ruben).

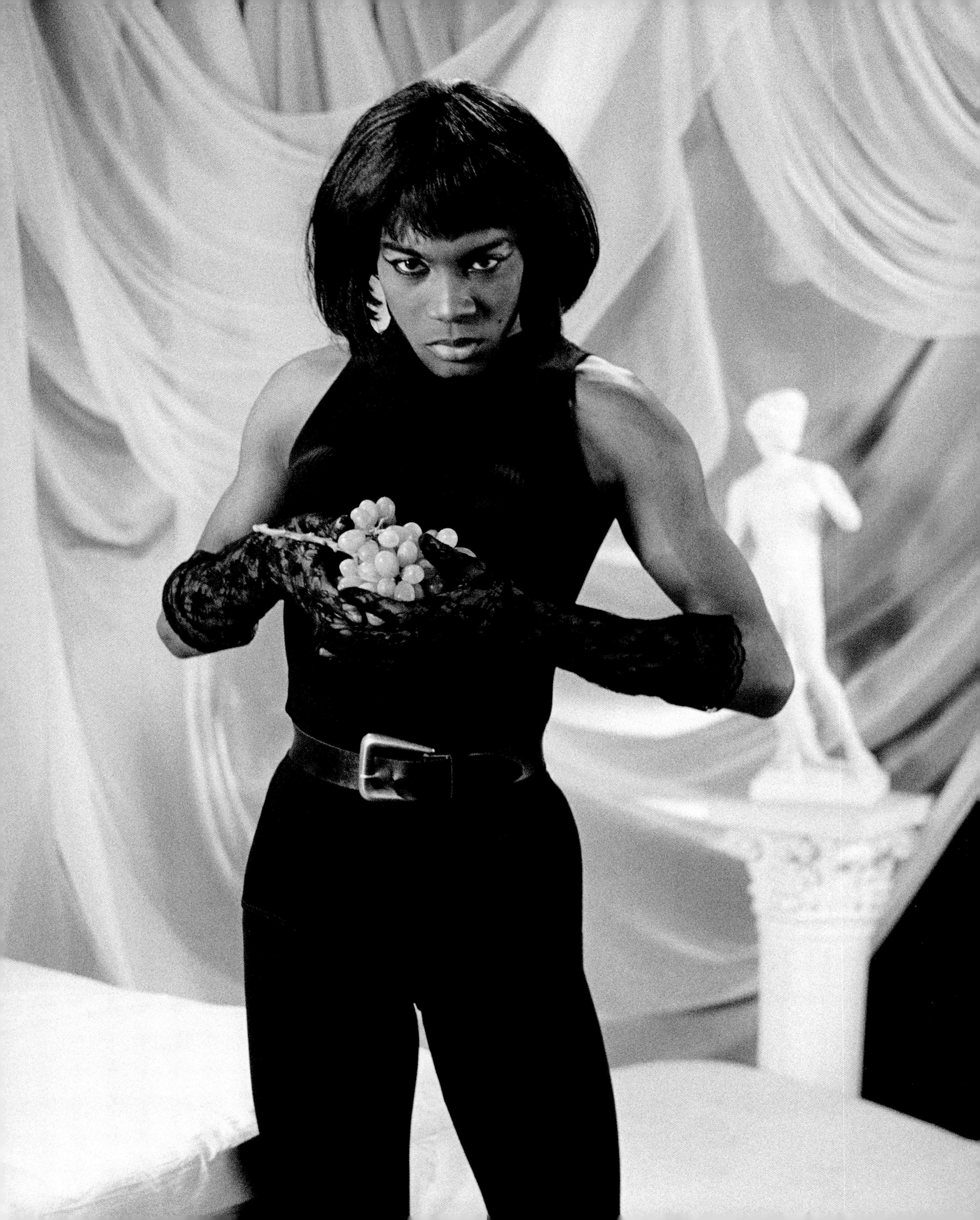

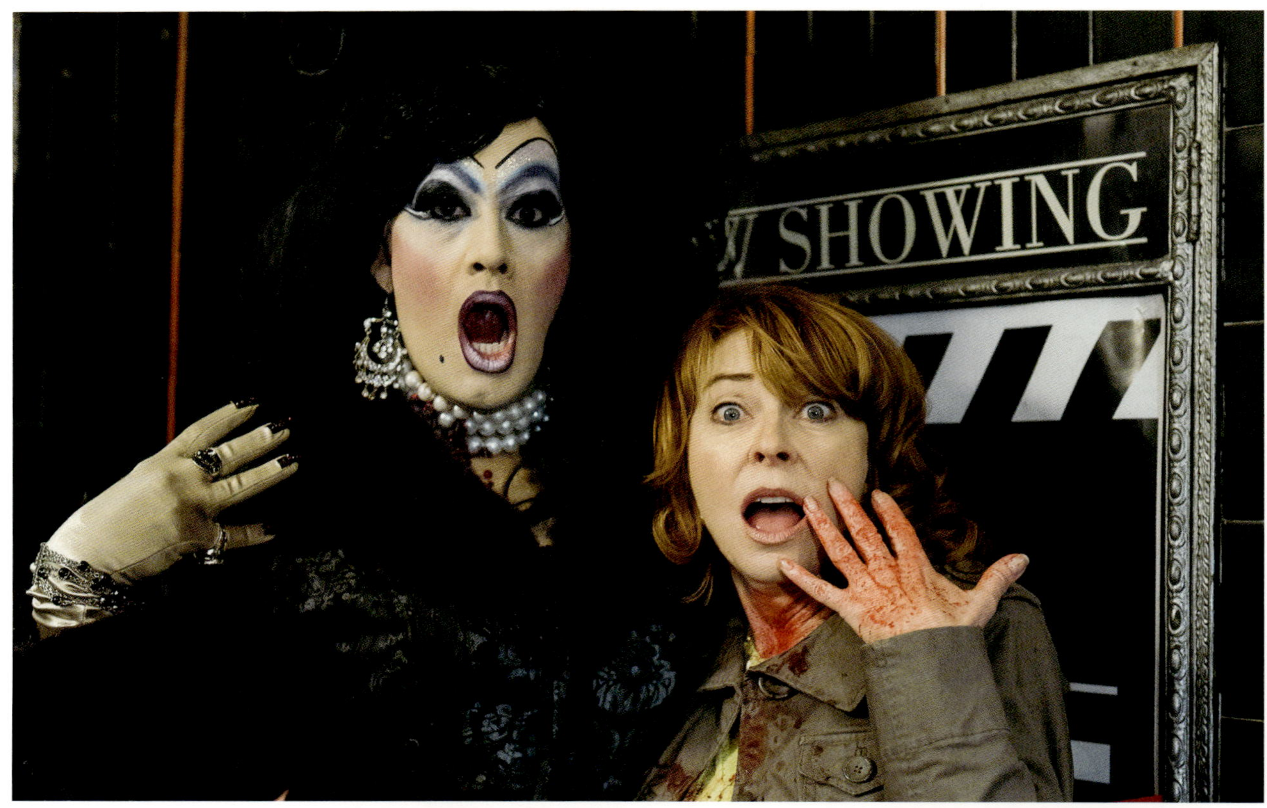

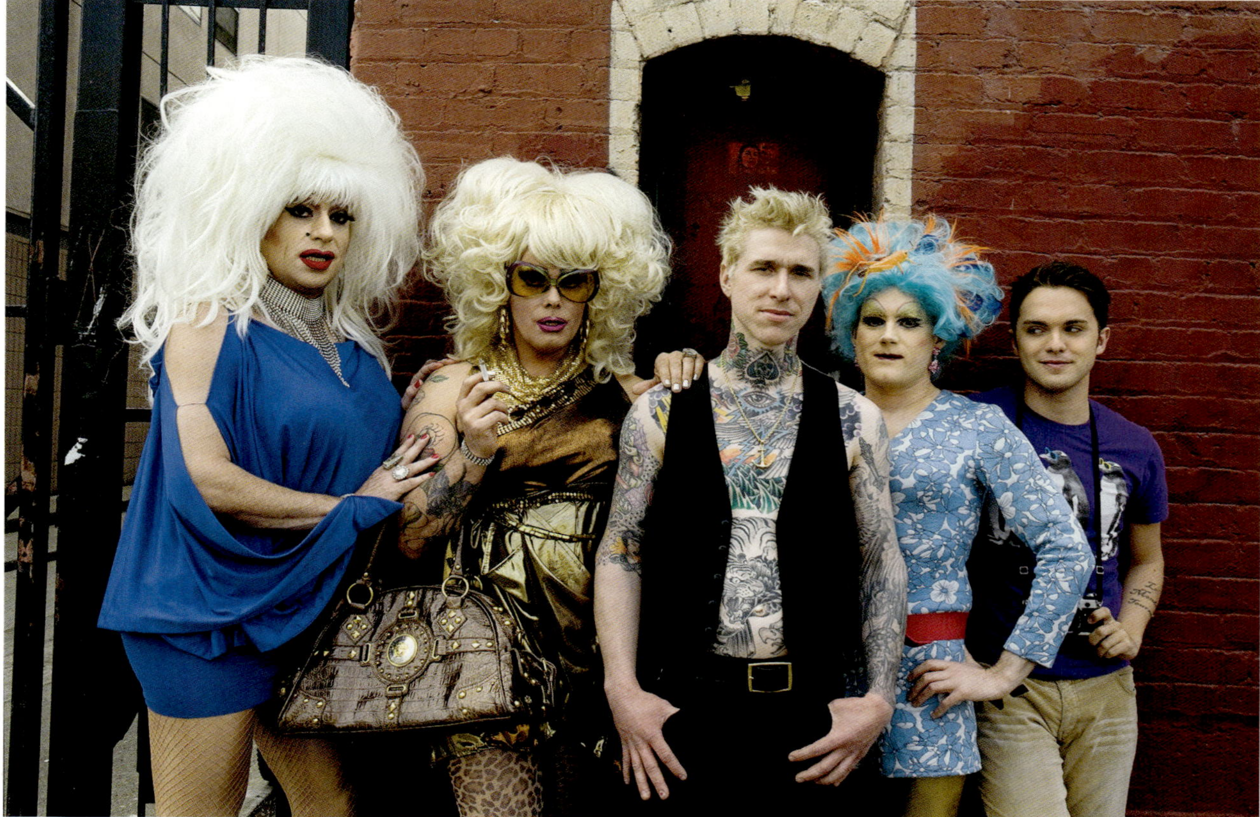

All About Evil, spring 2009. Directed by Joshua Grannell, produced by Darren Stein, Brian Benson and Debbie Brubaker.
(Top) Joshua Grannell as Peaches Christ and Cassandra Peterson as Linda;
(bottom) Heklina, Putanesca, Bama Dunne, Martiny and Thomas Dekker.

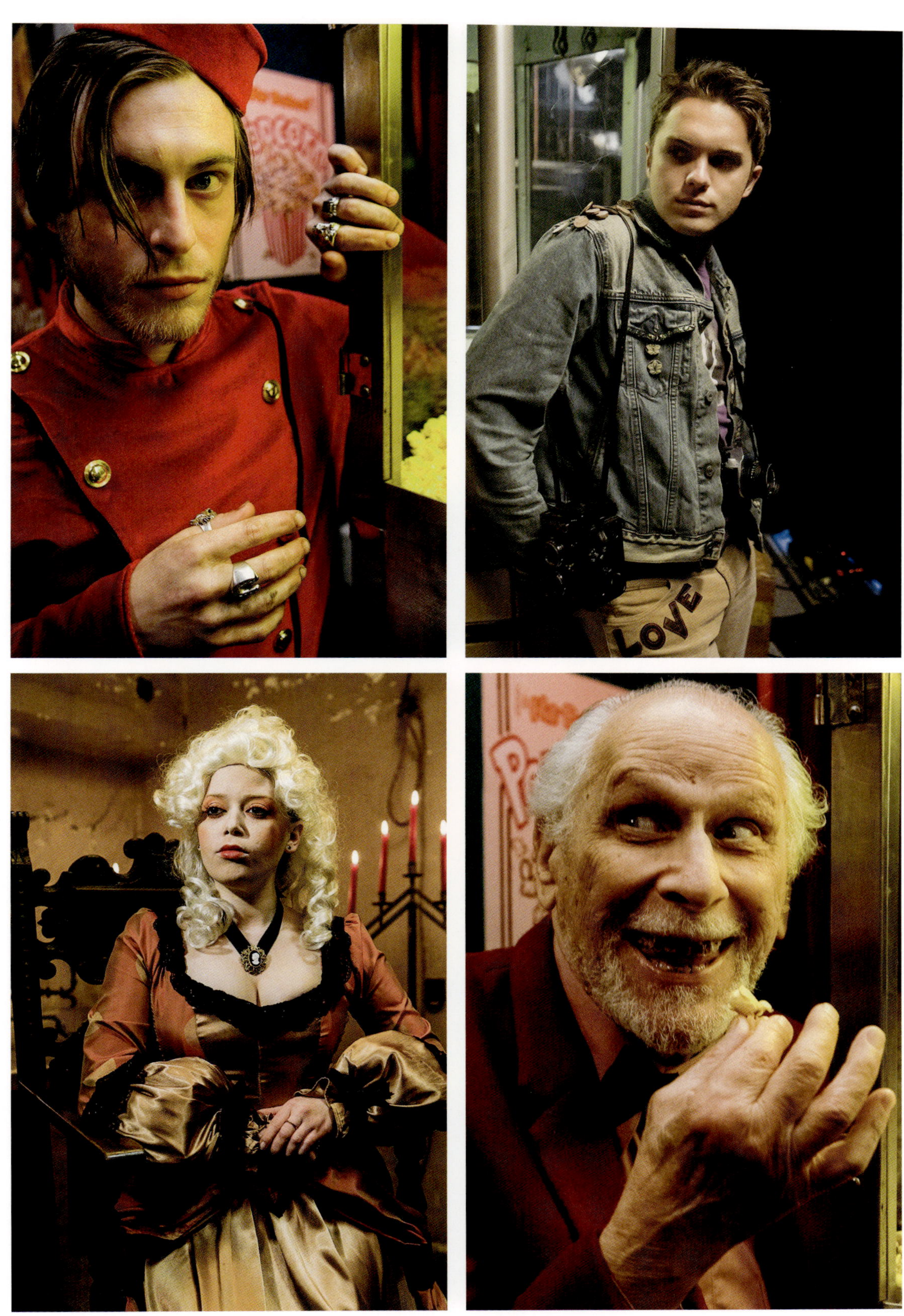

All About Evil, spring 2009. *(Clockwise from top left)* Noah Segan as Adrian; Thomas Dekker as Steven; Jack Donner as Mr. Twigs; Natasha Lyonne as Deborah Tennis.

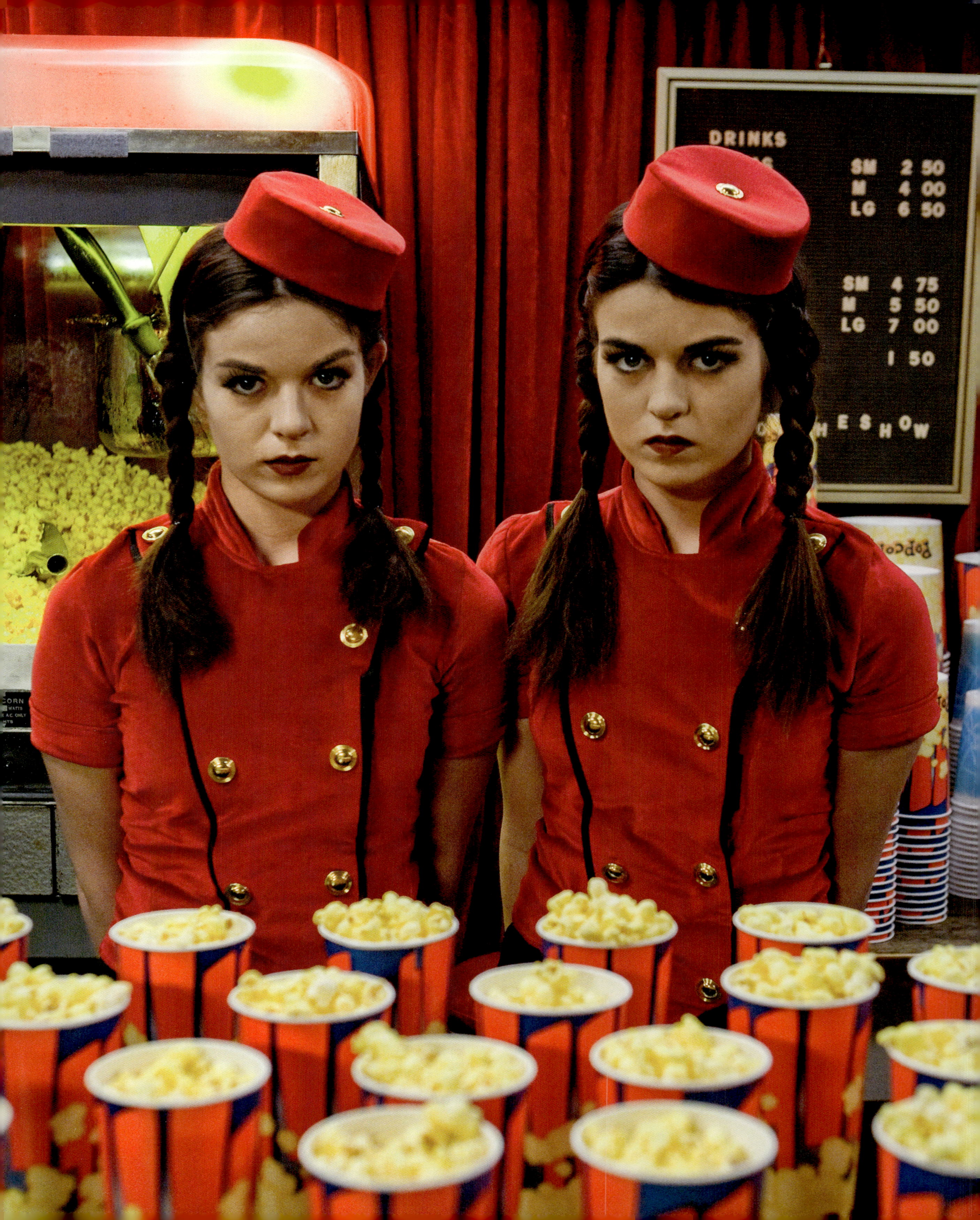
DRINKS
SM 2 50
M 4 00
LG 6 50
SM 4 75
M 5 50
LG 7 00
1 50

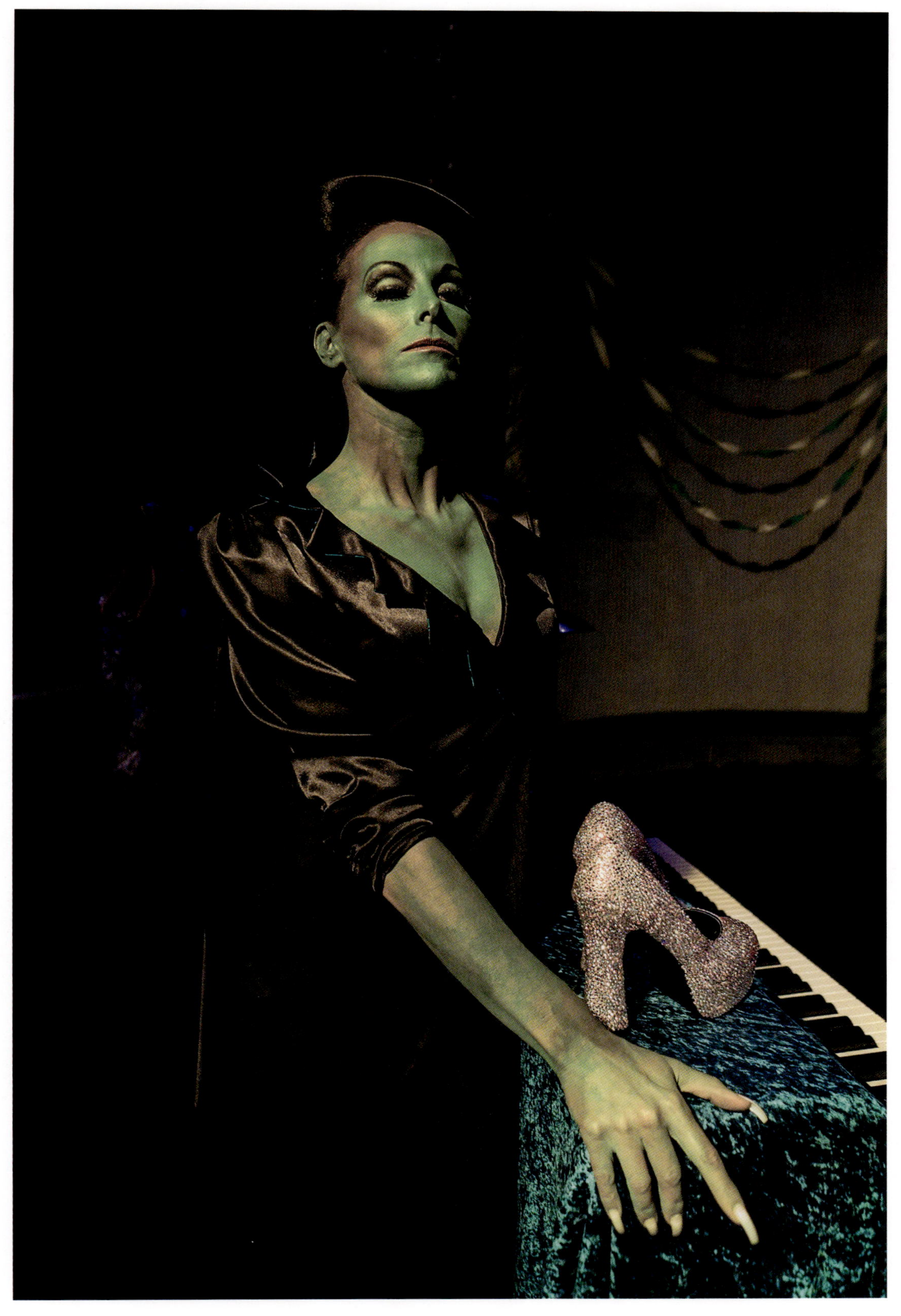

All About Evil, 2009.
(Above) Julie Caitlin Brown as Tammy Tennis; *(opposite)* Jade and Nakita Ramsey as Veda and Vera.

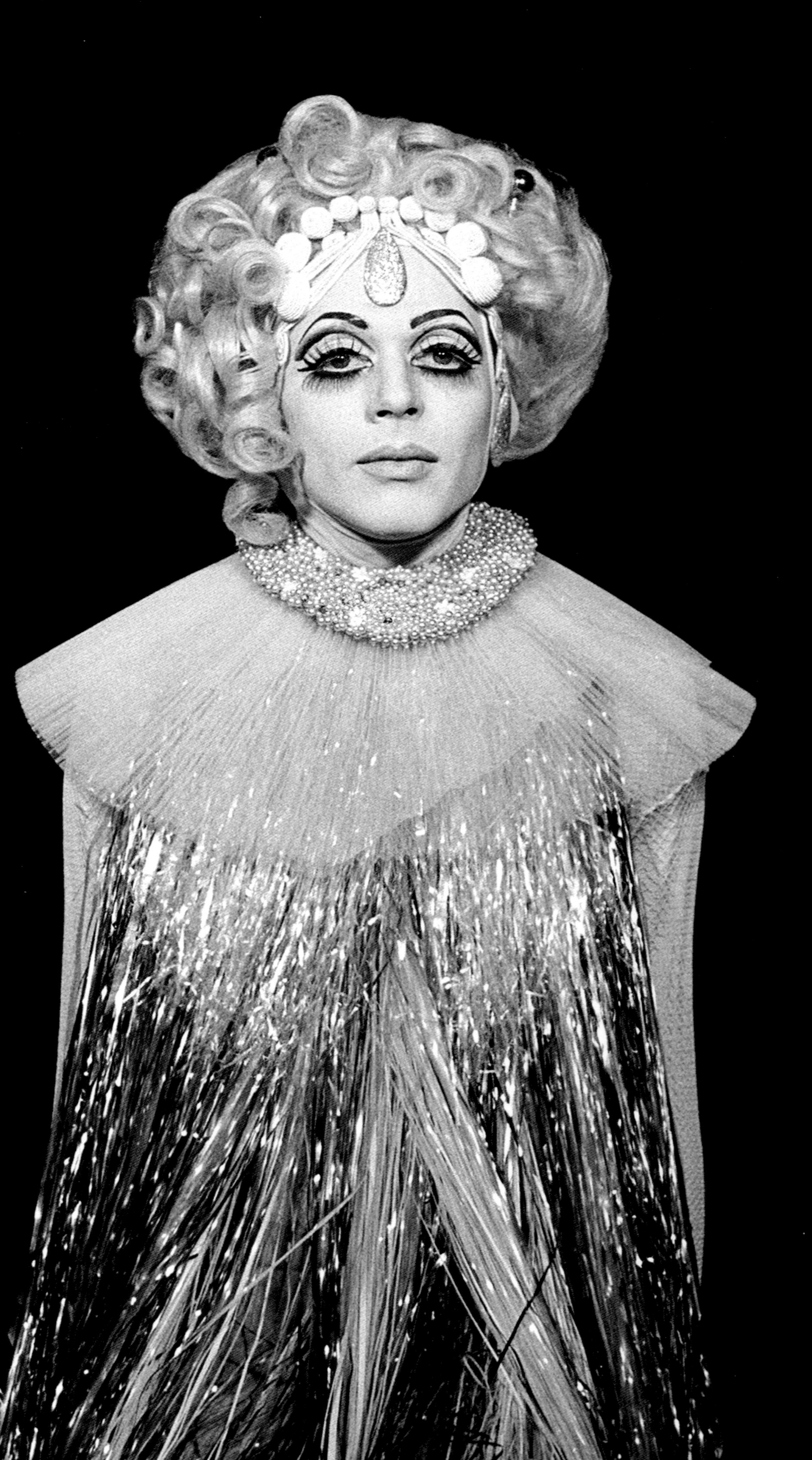

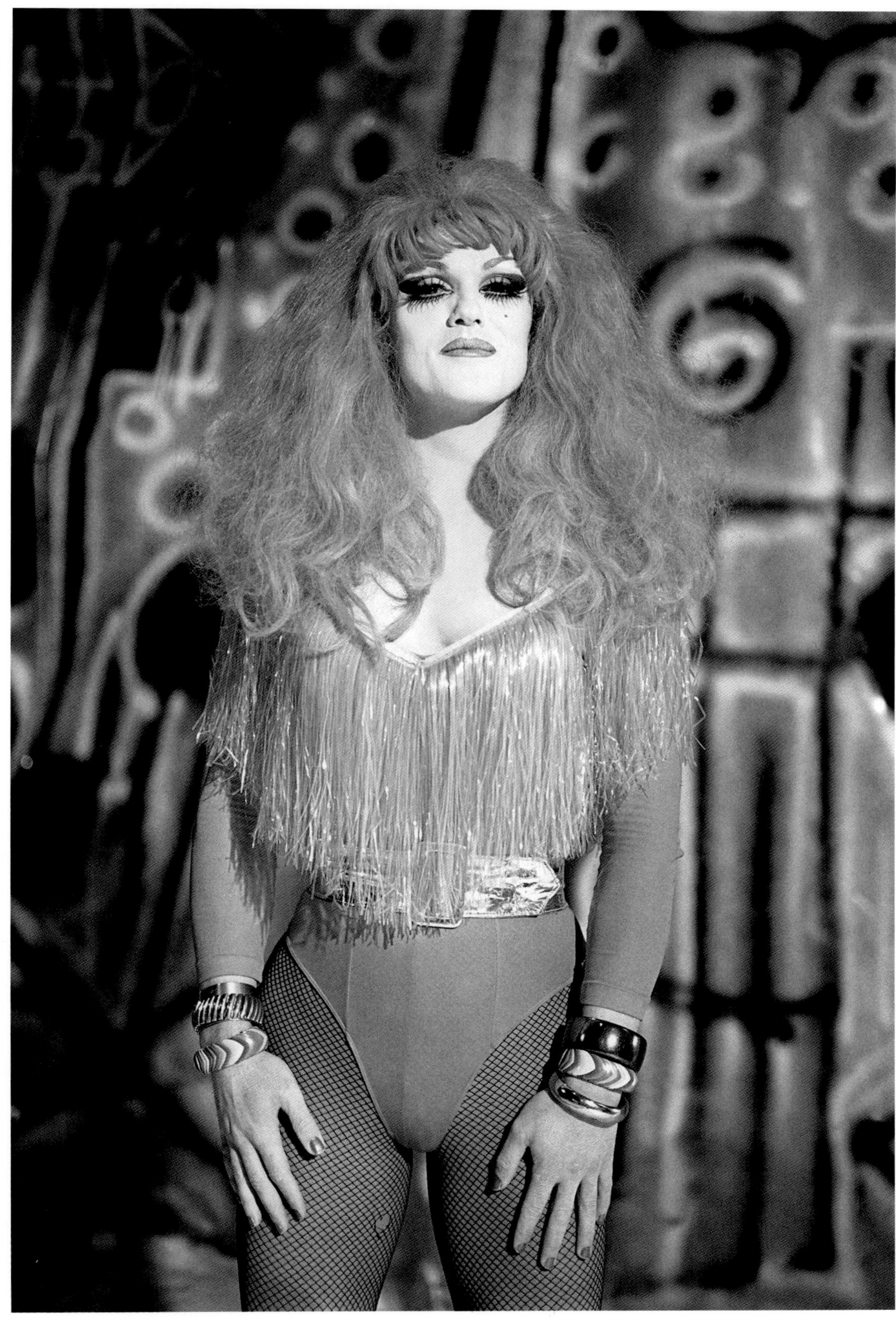

Above: Phillip R Ford's *Vegas In Space*, August 11, 1984. Doris Fish.
Opposite: Phillip R Ford's *Vegas In Space*, May 12, 1984. Tippi.

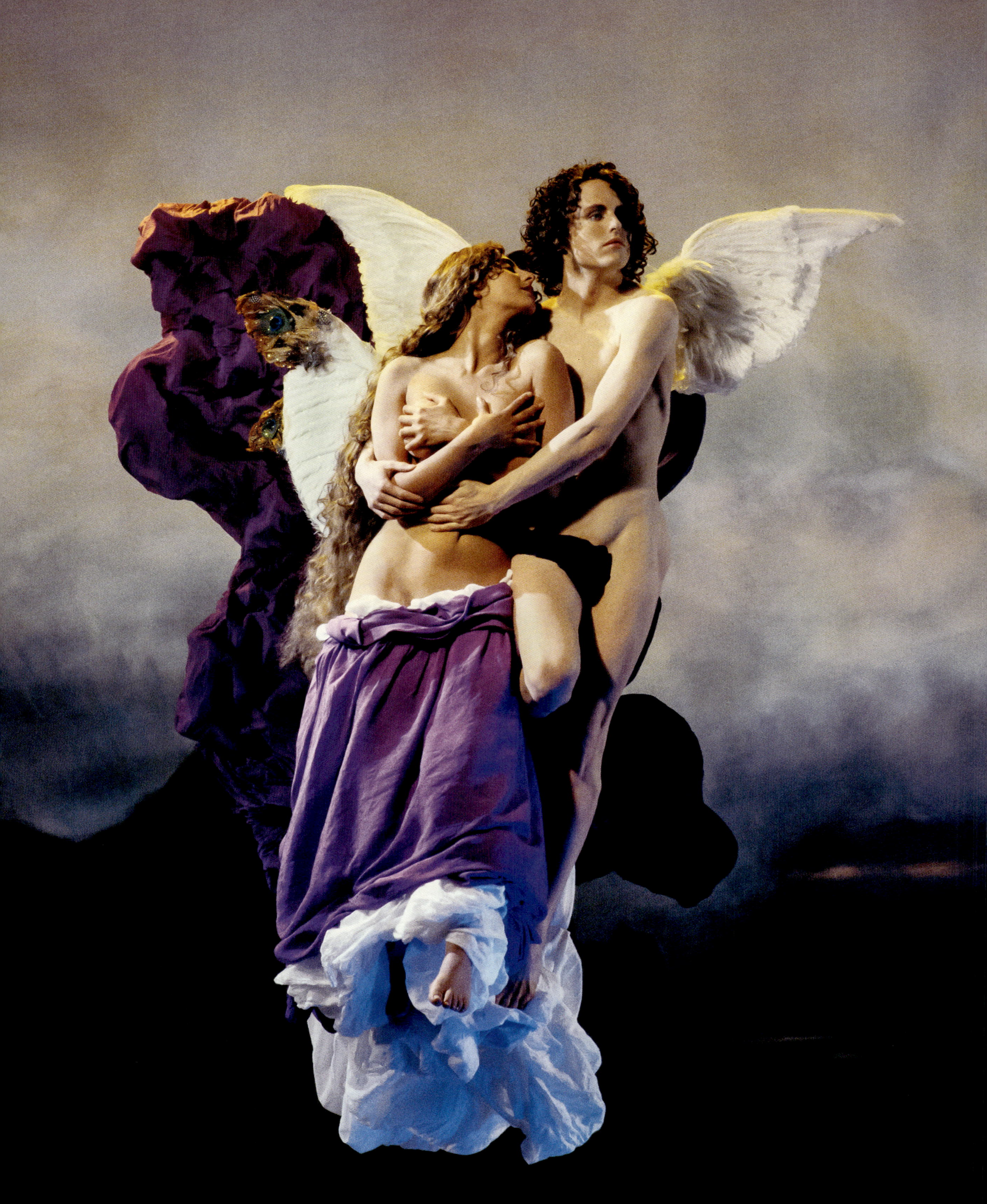

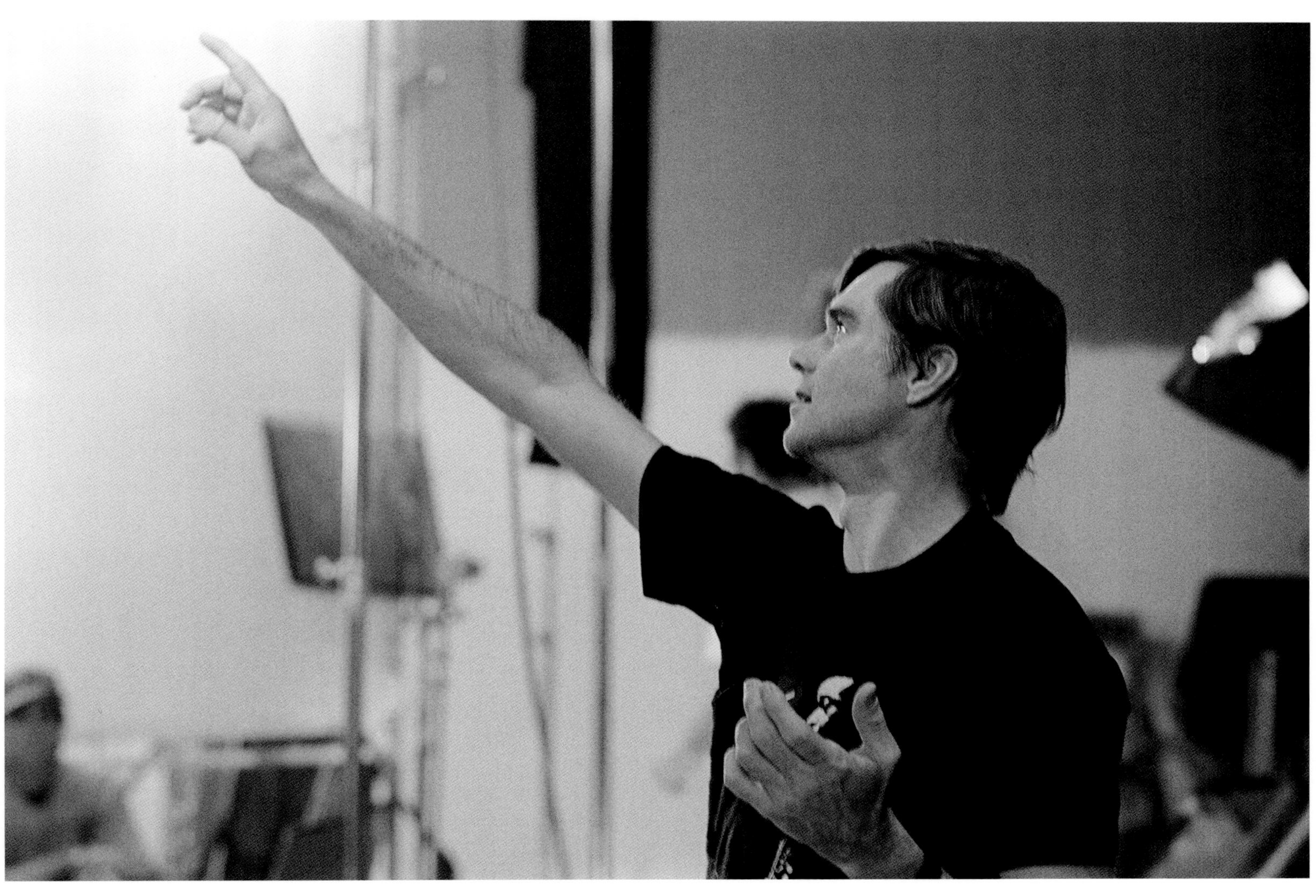

Above: Fourth Vision company logo shoot, May 4, 1993. Gus Van Sant, director.
Opposite: Re-creation of Bouguereau's painting *Abduction of Psyche* for Fourth Vision Film Production's company logo, May 4, 1993. (Director: Gus Van Sant; art director: Tom Bonauro; styling: Alexis Lecach; wings by Granite Trudeau; with Sarah Girgis and Jade Barbee.)

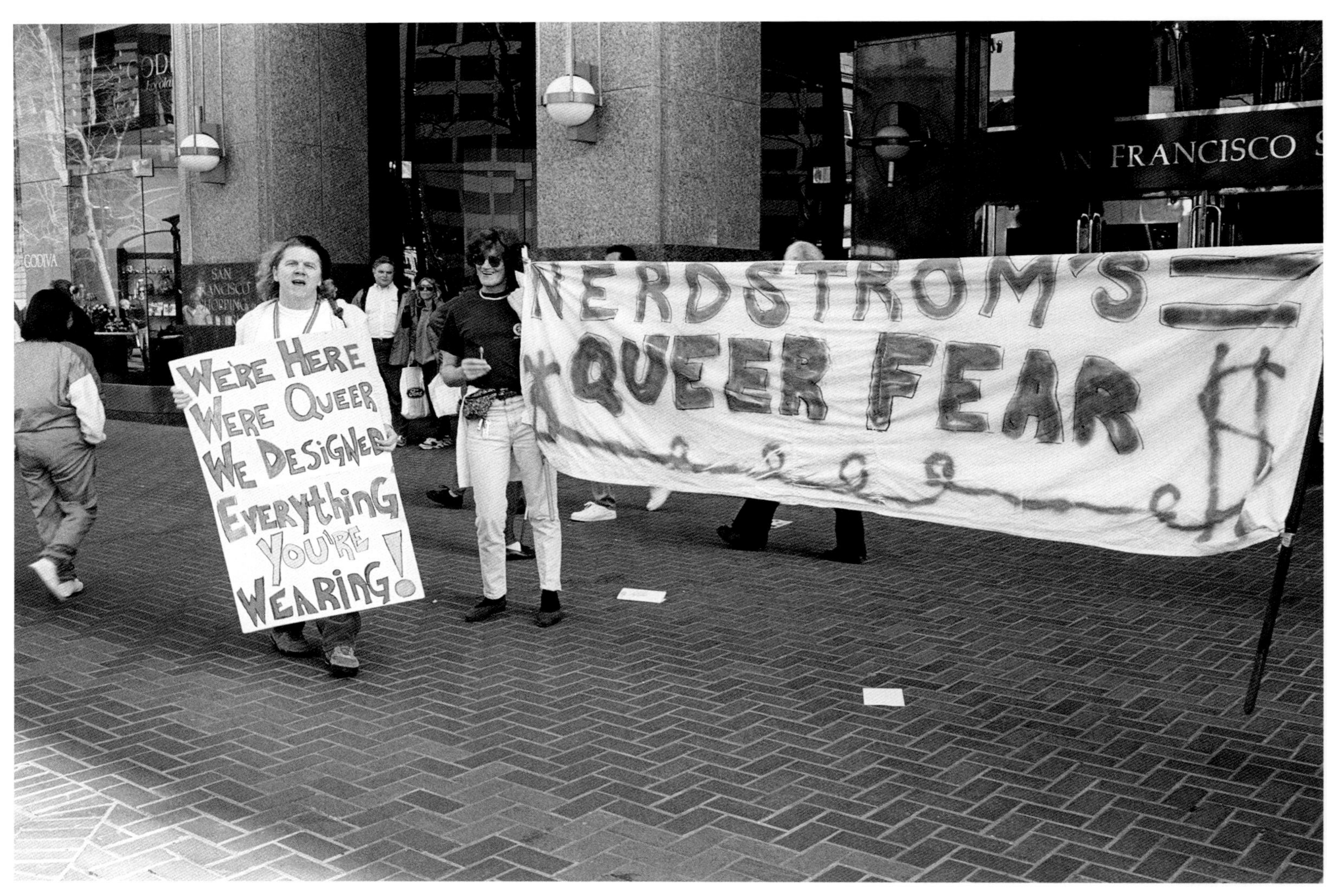

Above and opposite: Transgender Nation action against discriminatory practices at Nordstrom's make up counter, February 13, 1994.

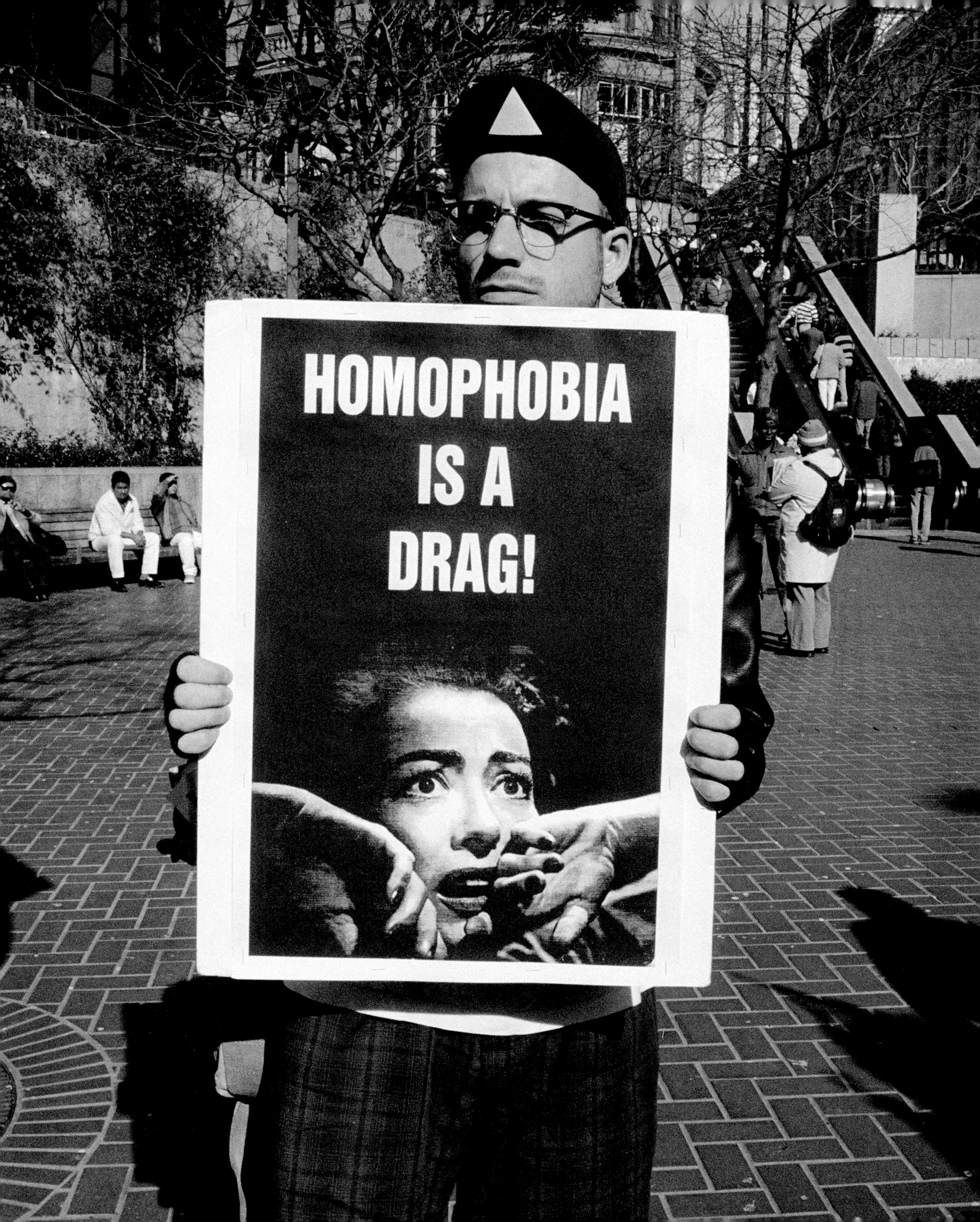
HOMOPHOBIA
IS A
DRAG!

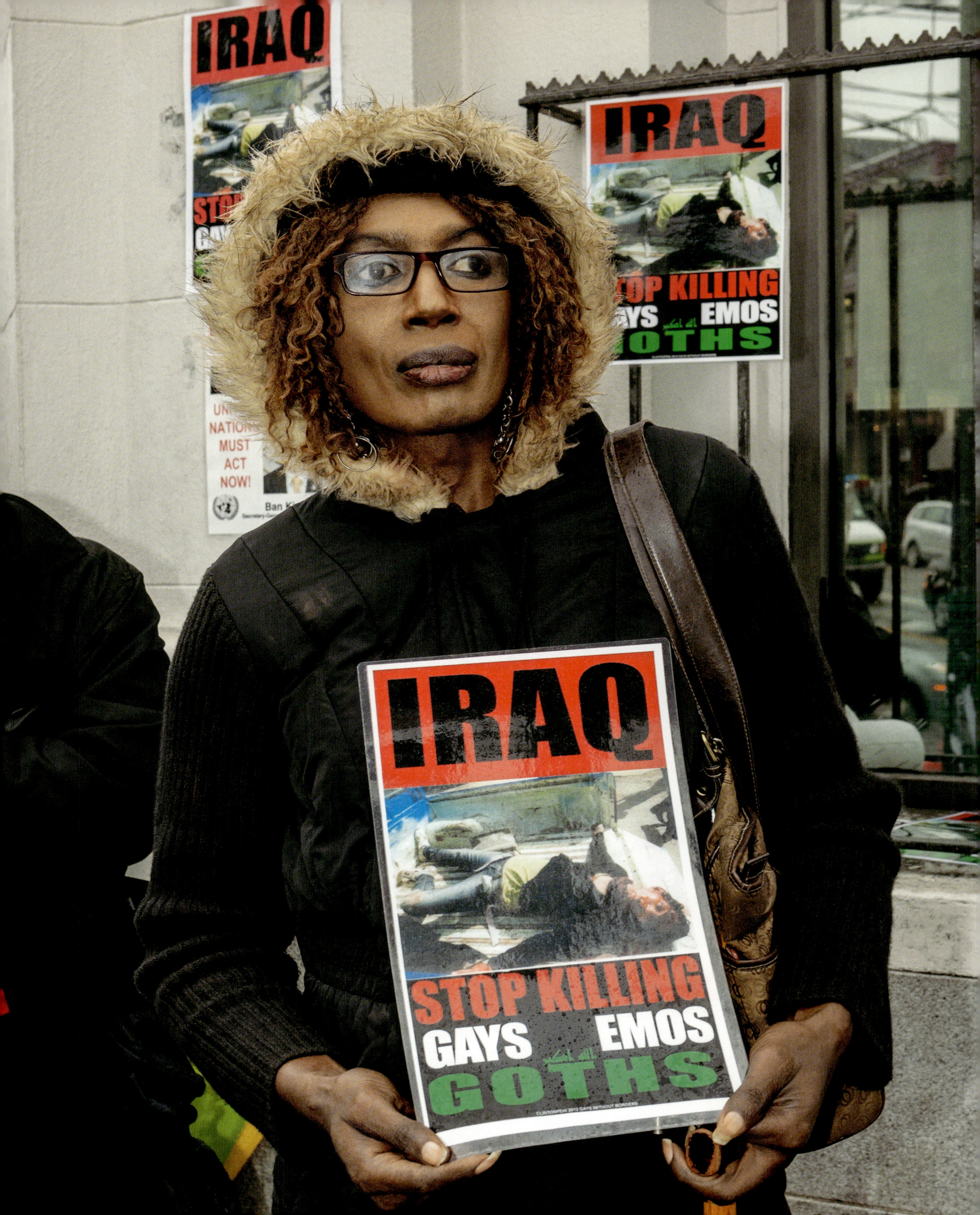
IRAQ
STOP KILLING
GAYS
EMOS
GOTHS
IRAQ
STOP KILLING
GAYS
EMOS
GOTHS
IRAQ
MUST
ACT
NOW!

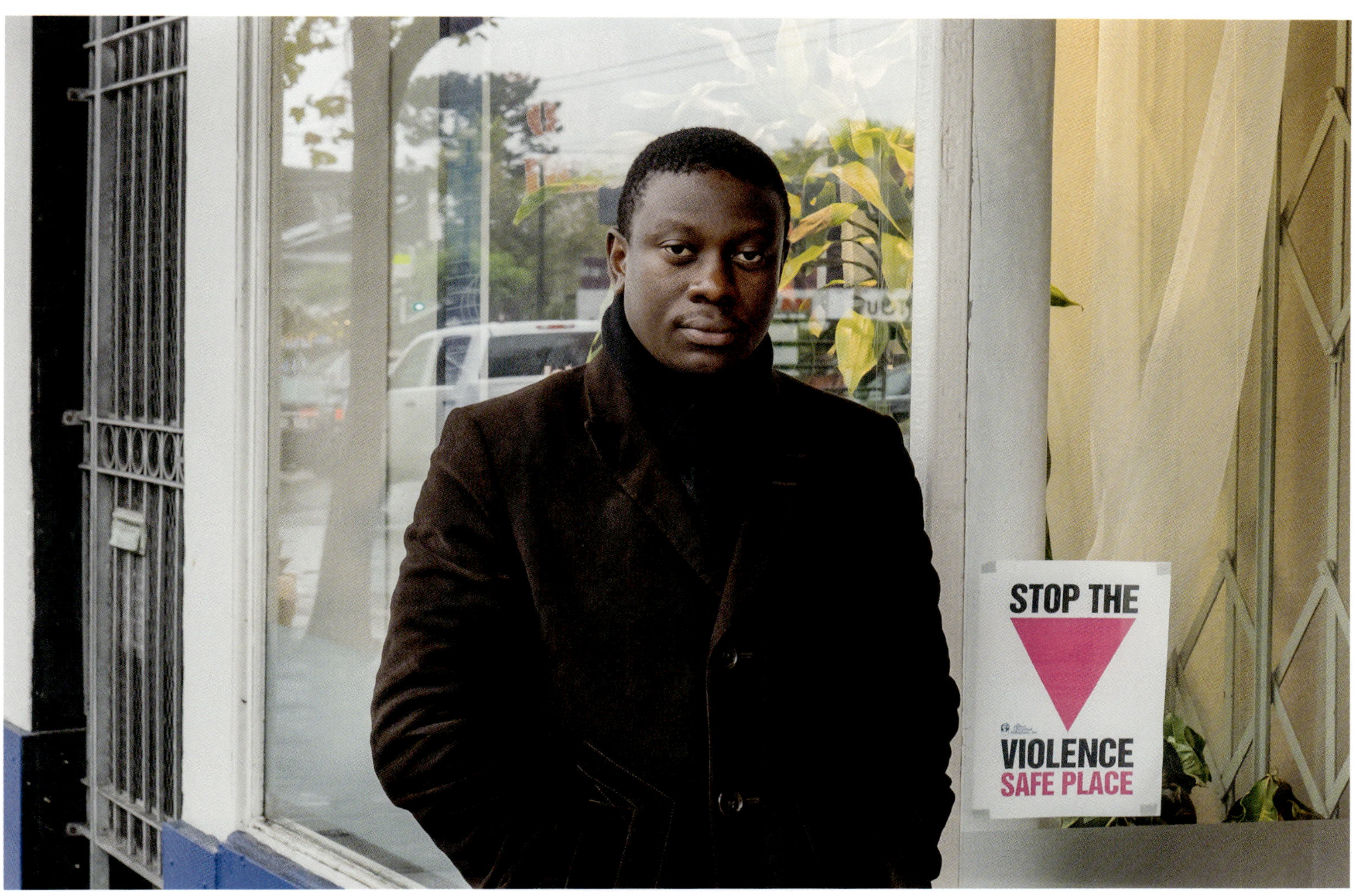

Above: Richard Lusimbo, November 19, 2016. Research and Documentation Officer of Sexual Minorities Uganda, SMUG, visiting the US for a lawsuit against anti-LGBT US missionary, Scott Lively. (The lawsuit is based on a US Alien Tort Statute [since 1980] that allows foreign citizens to seek remedies in US courts for human-rights violations committed outside the United States.)
Opposite: Demonstration against murder of LGBT people, emos and goths in Iraq, March 14, 2012. Jazzy Collins.

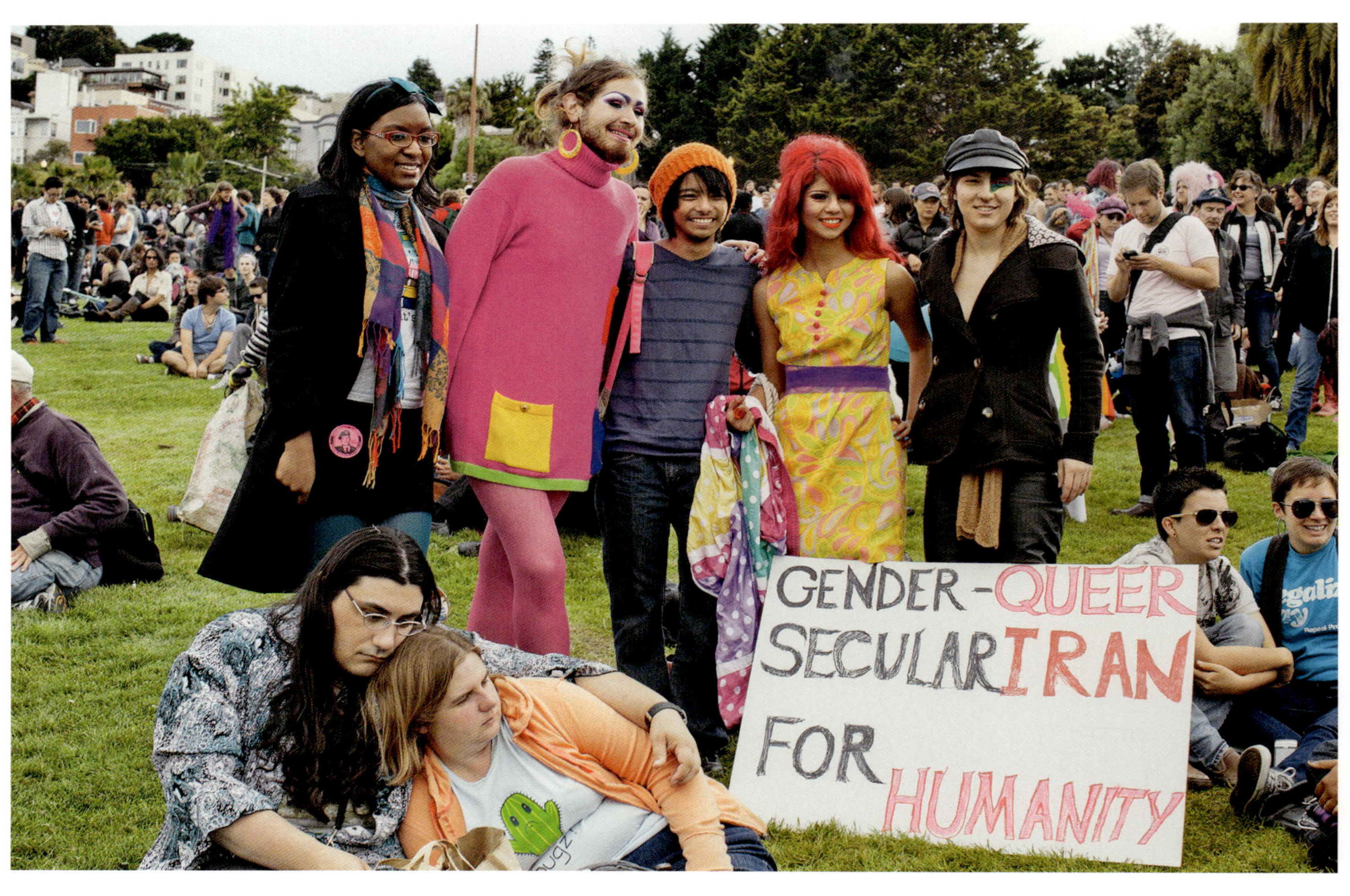

Transmarch, June 22, 2012.

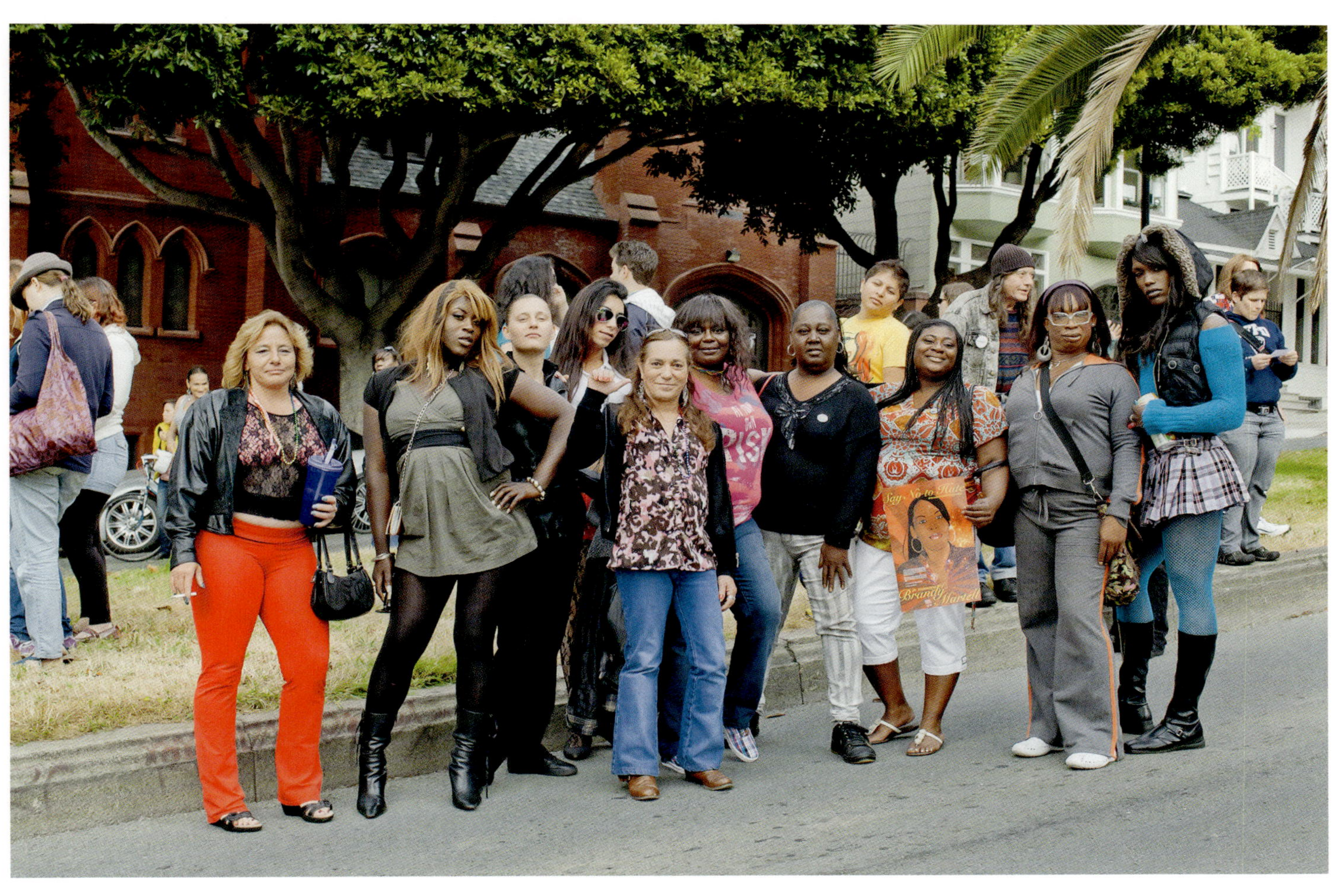

Transmarch, June 22, 2012.

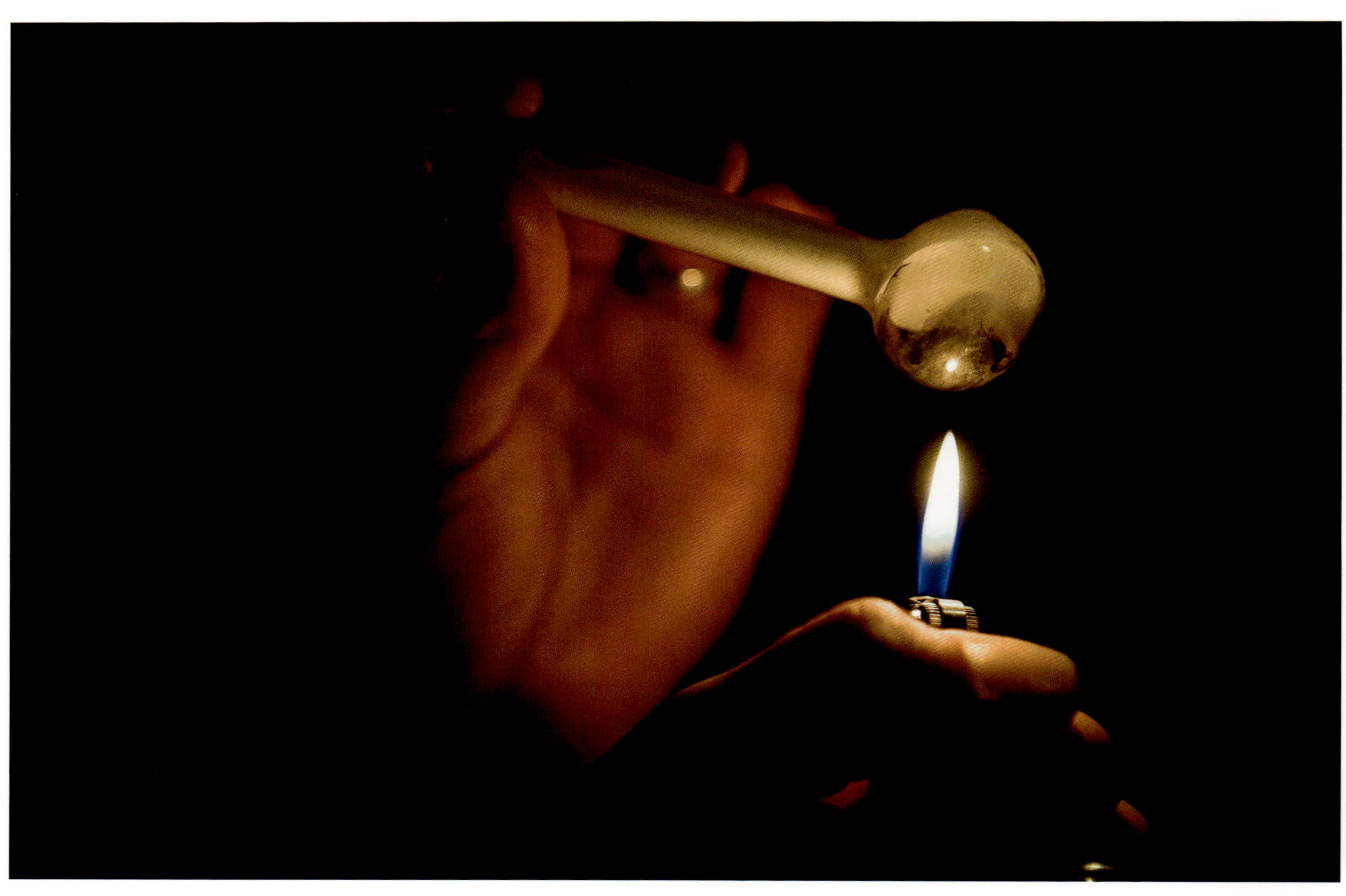

Crystal Methedrine pipe, January 11, 2009.

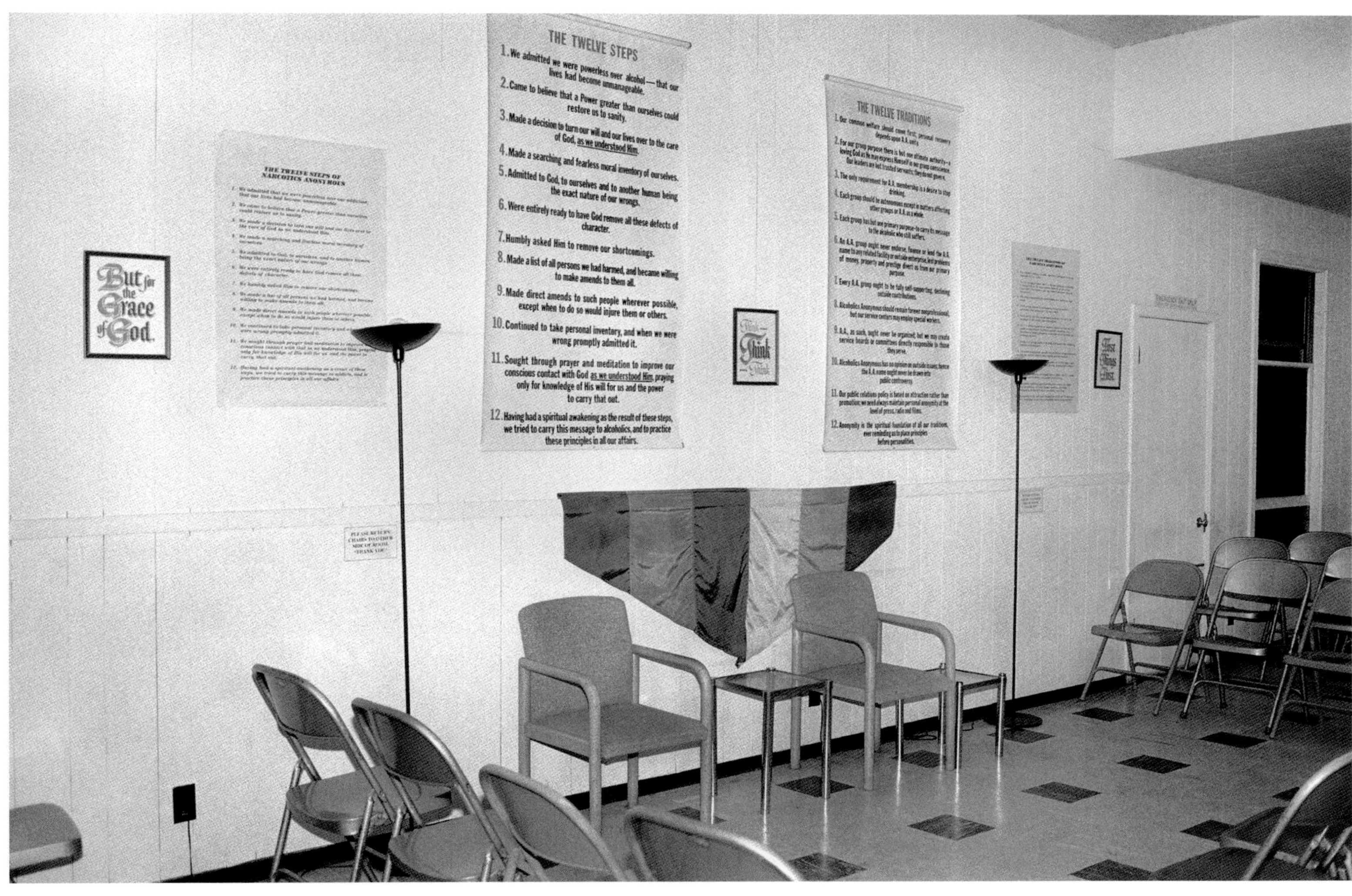

The Meeting Place, drug and alcohol recovery support hall, Castro District, November 1992.

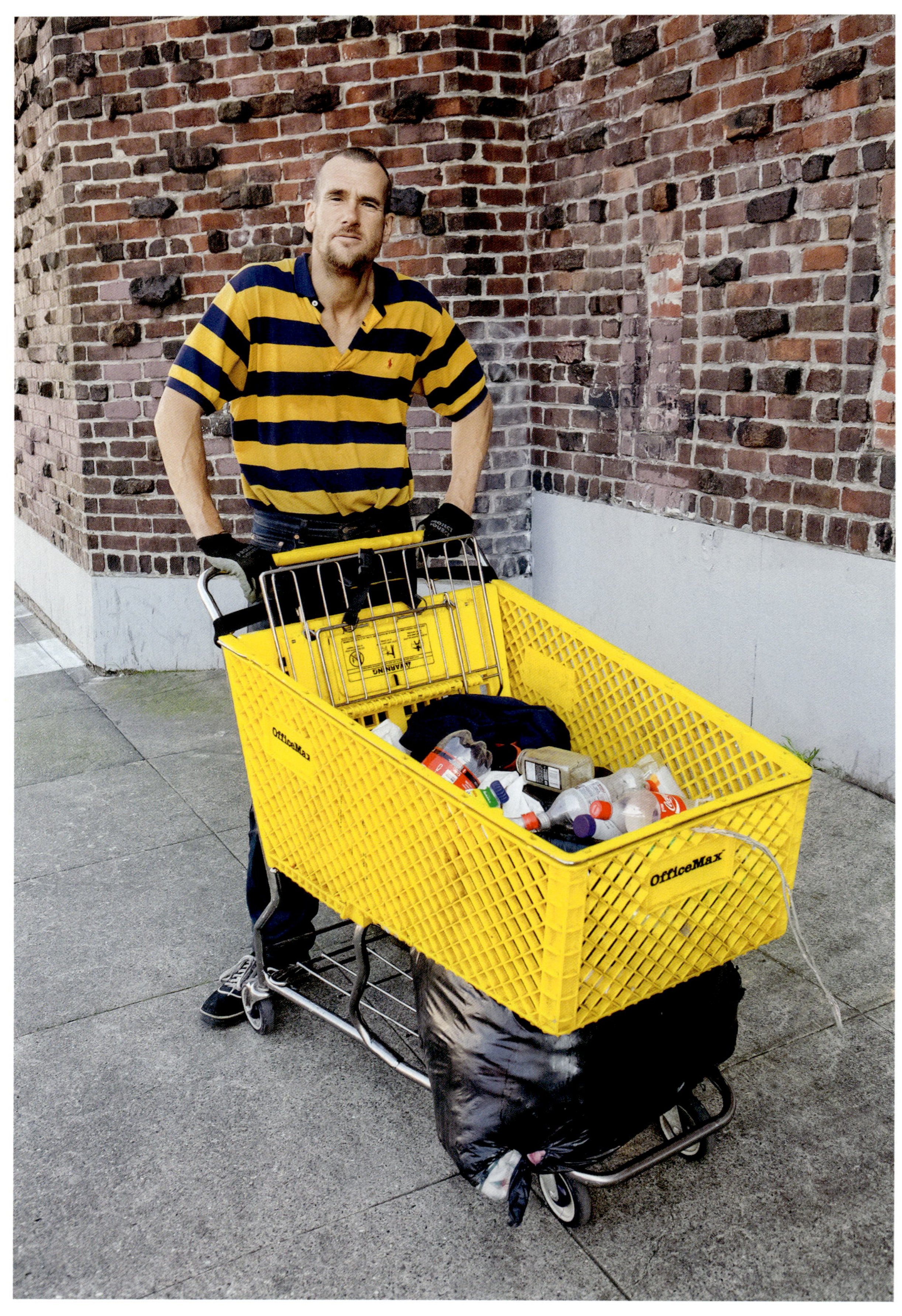

Above: Stretch, March 19, 2009.
Opposite: Artists protest displacement, October 4, 2000. Tommi Avicolli Mecca.

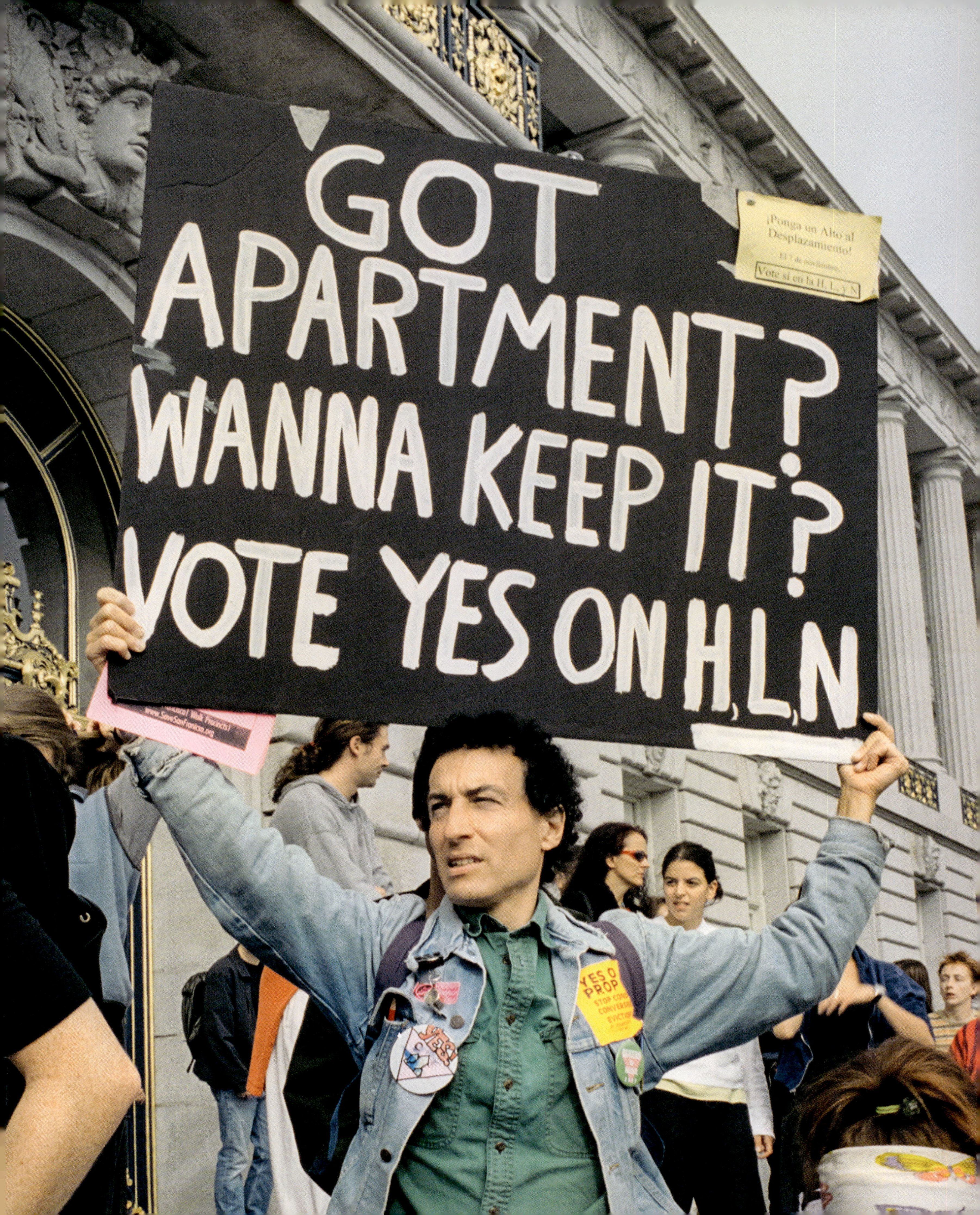
GOT
APARTMENT?
WANNA KEEP IT?
VOTE YES ON H,L,N
¡Ponga un Alto al
Desplazamiento!
Vote sí en la H, L, y N

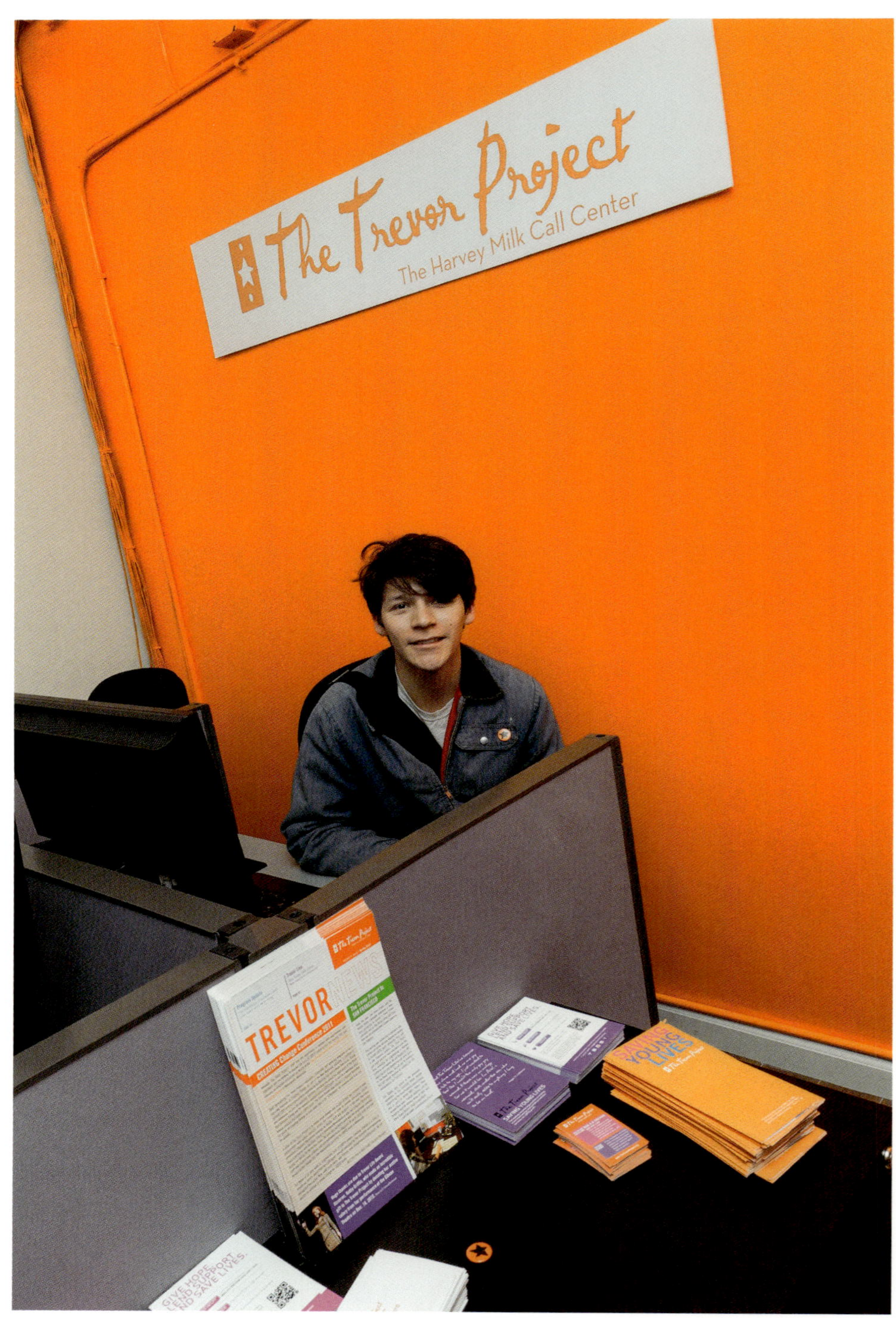

The Trevor Project suicide prevention hotline call center, May 22, 2011. Alan Guttirez.

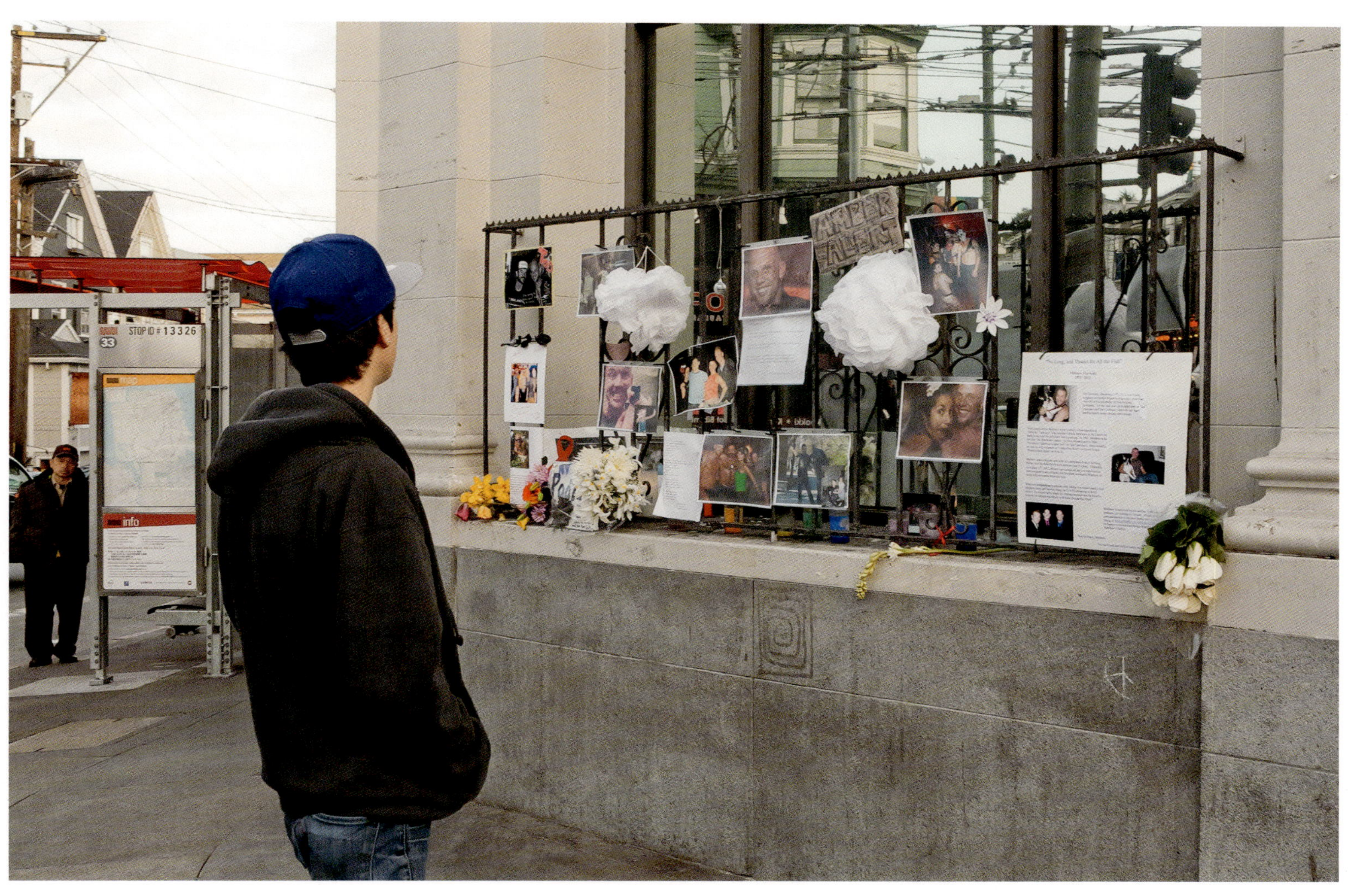

Memorial at Castro and 18th for Todd, a community member who committed suicide, January 6, 2013.

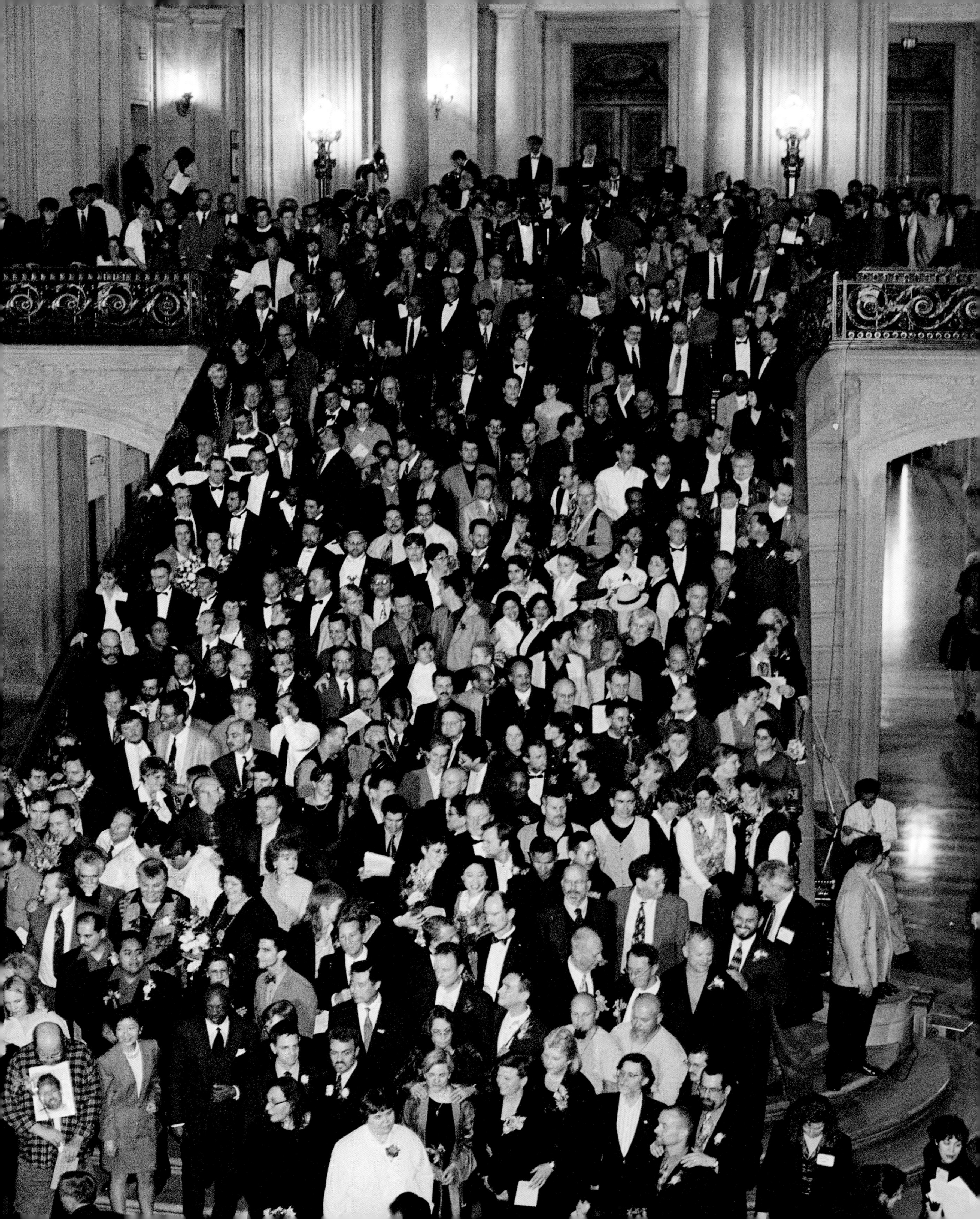

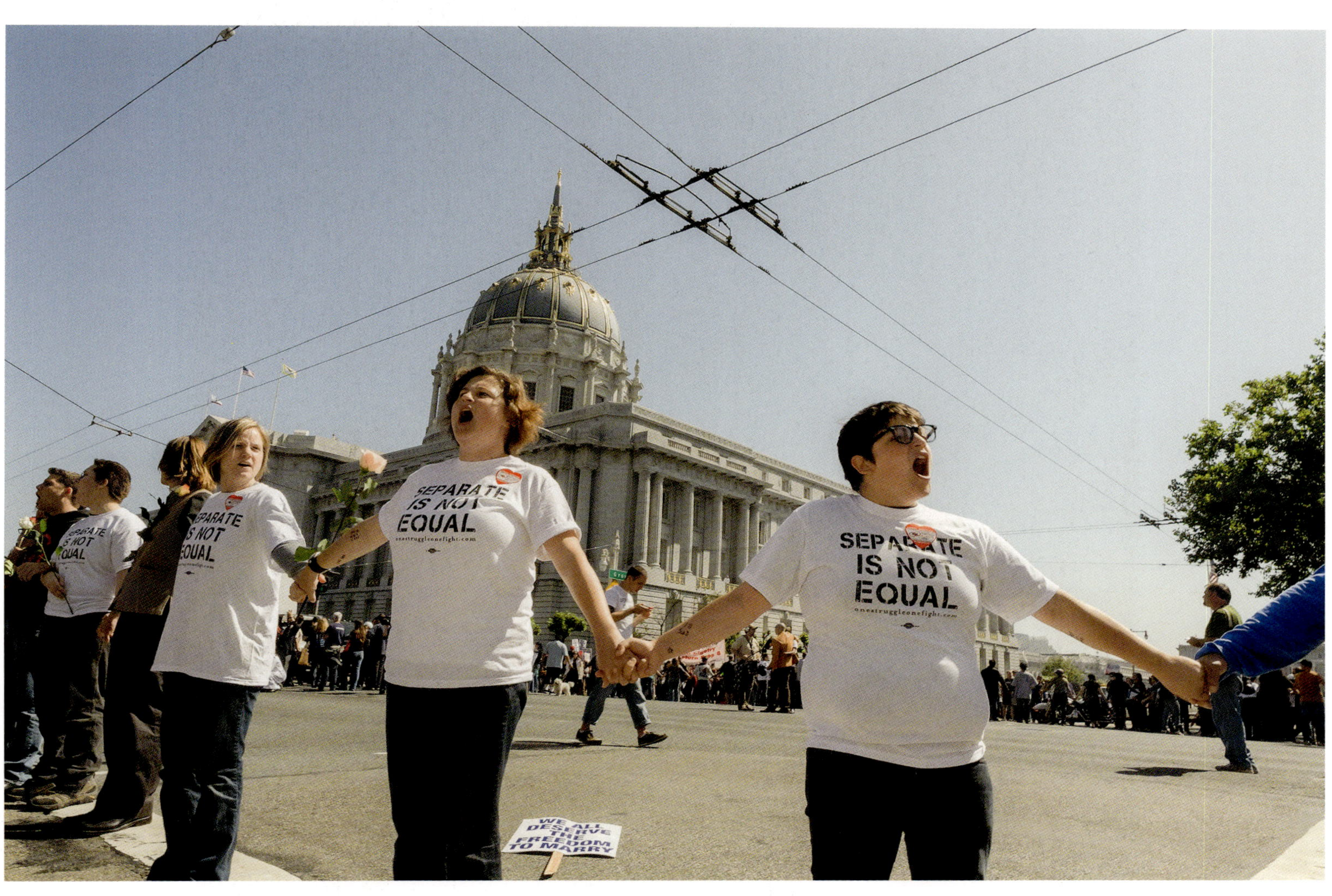

Above: Traffic stoppage political action on the day of the California Supreme Court ruling challenging Proposition 8, which sought to deny same sex marriage, May 26, 2009.
Opposite: A symbolic group same sex marriage event officiated by Mayor Willie Brown and supported by The Board of Supervisors, done primarily as a City Hall policy statement but also meant to propel actual marriage equality, March 26, 1999.

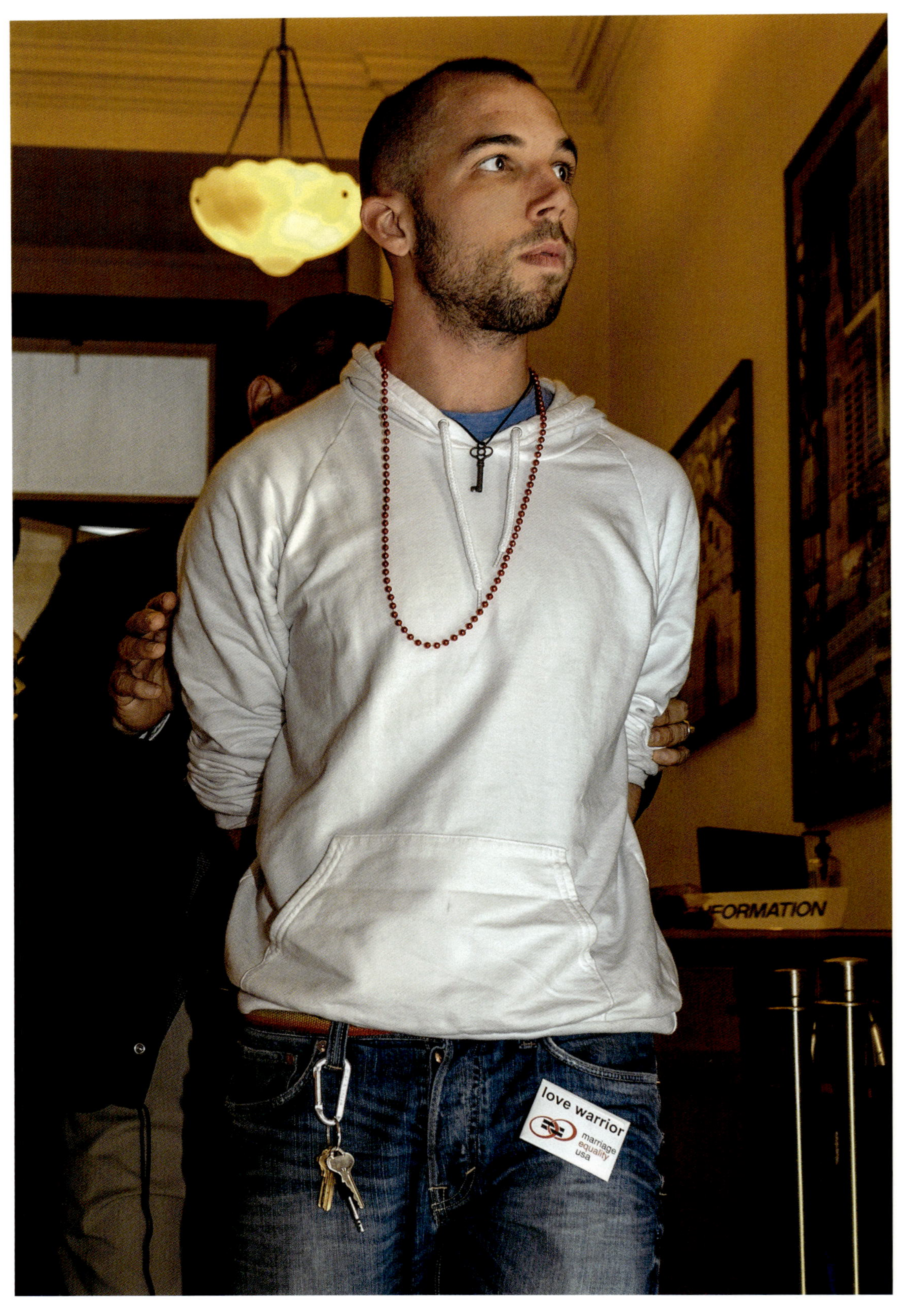

Sit-in arrests at City Hall Registrar's Office in support of same sex marriage equality, February 14, 2011. Kip Williams.

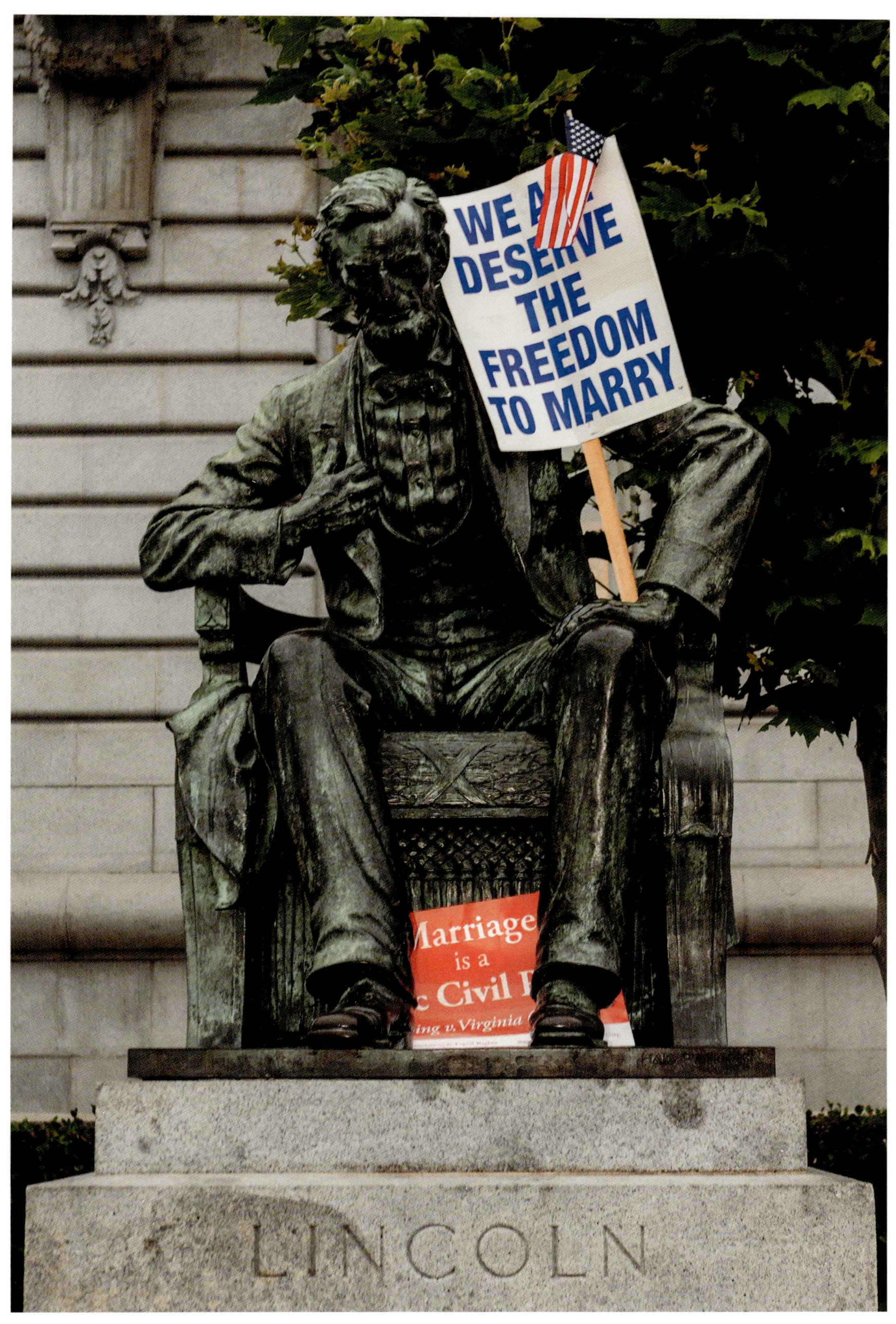

Proposition 8 Decision Rally, August 4, 2010.

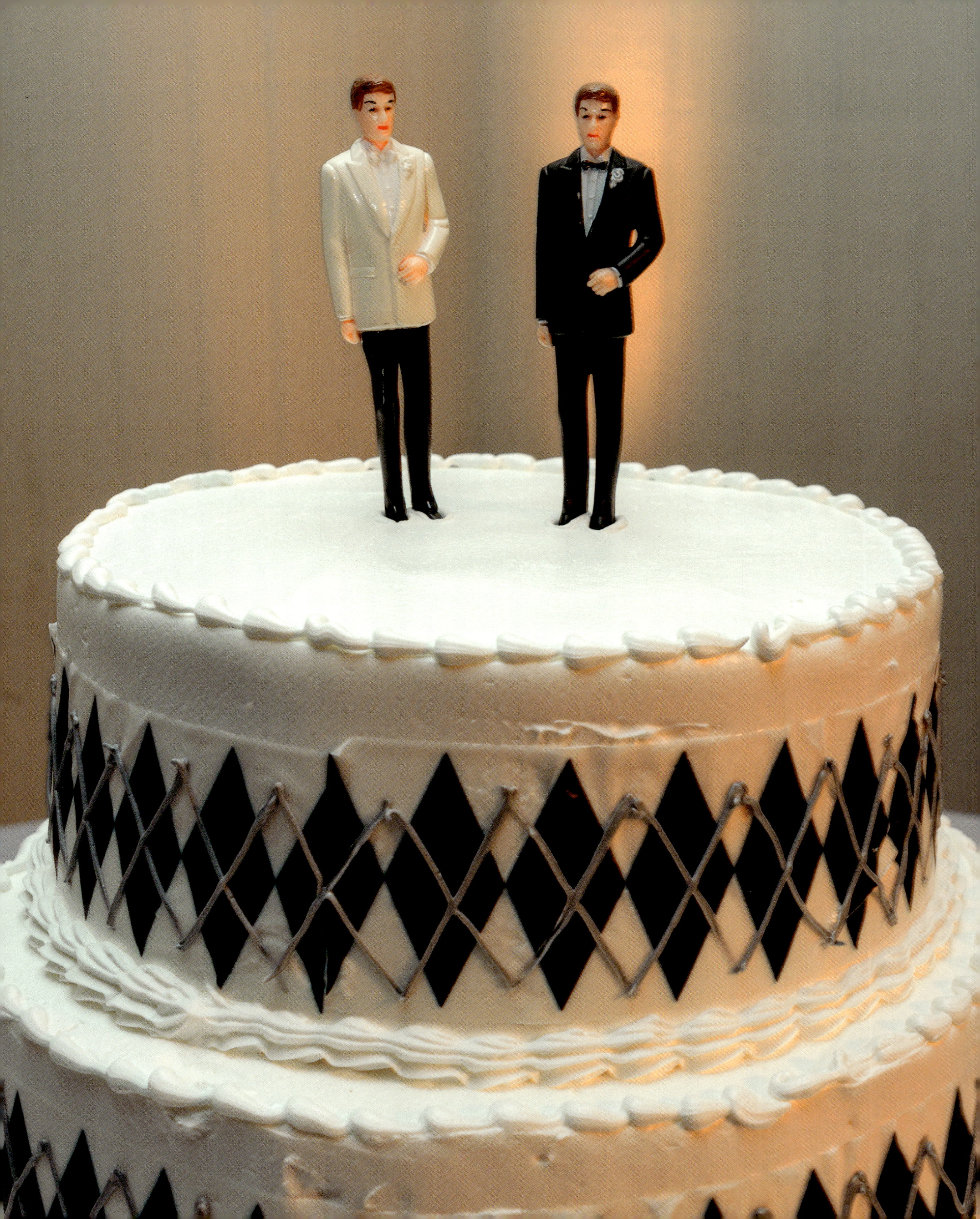

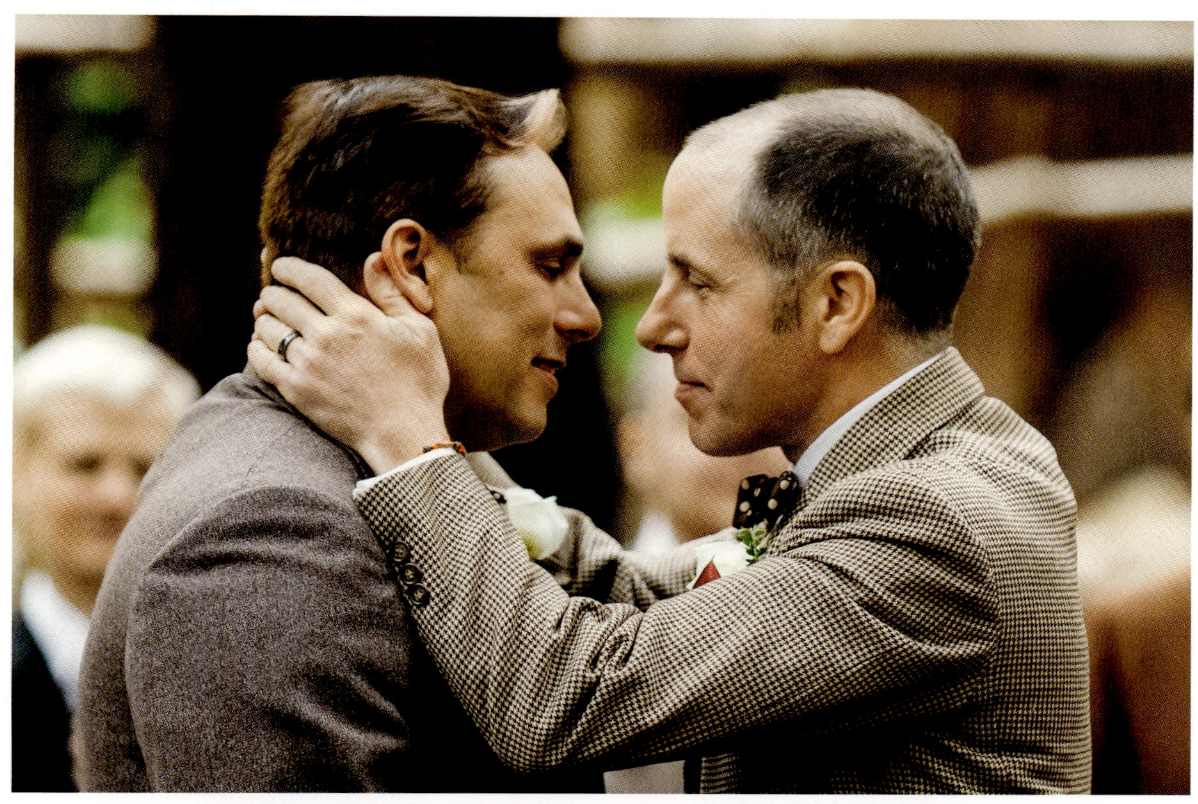

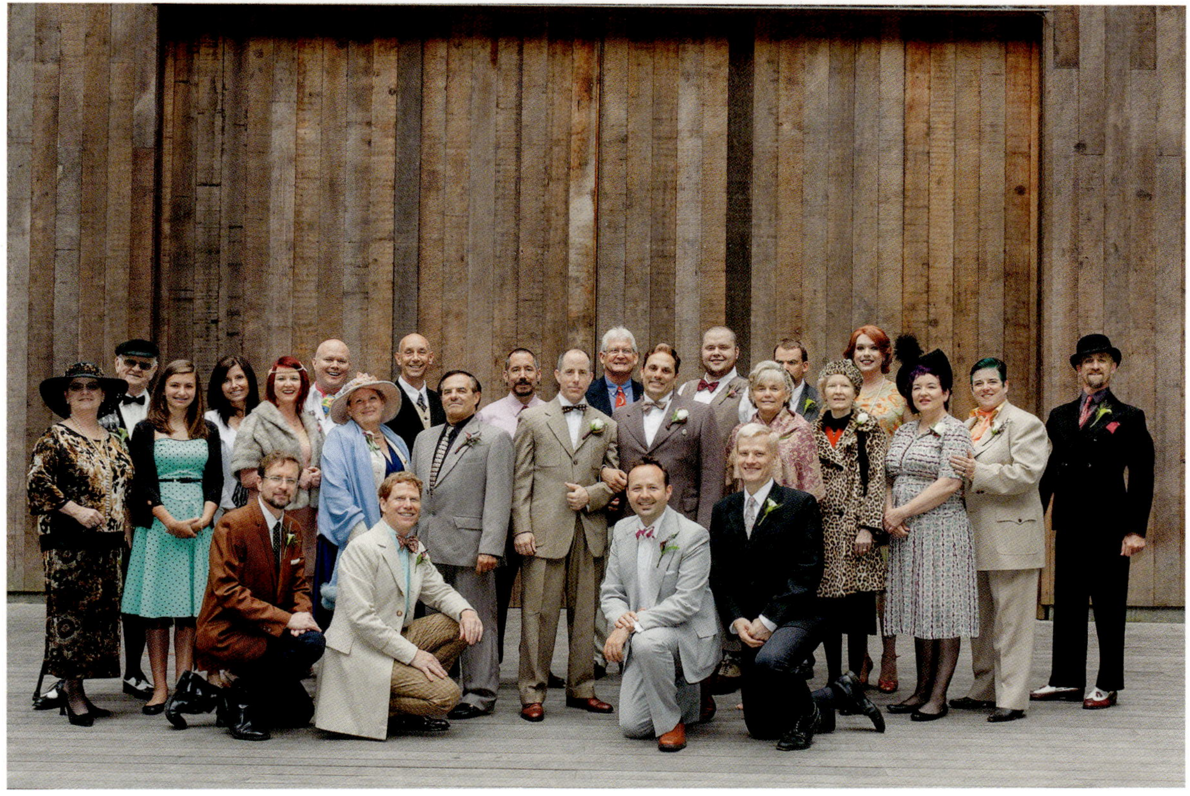

Flynn and Richard DeMarco-Board wedding, July 17, 2010.

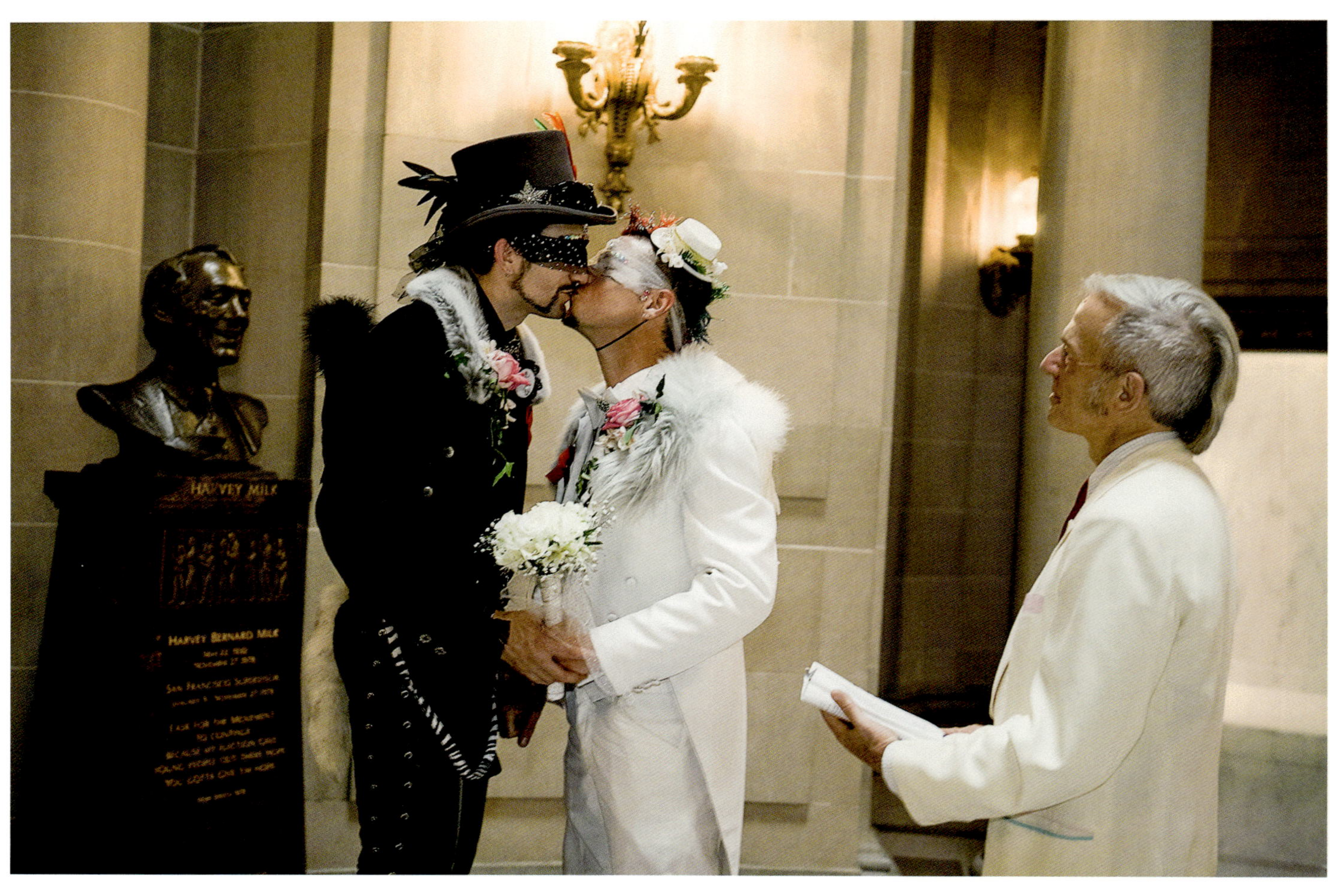

Wedding in City Hall Ceremonial Rotunda with Salamander and Spunky, and Wally Gorrell officiating, while Harvey Milk smiles on the proceedings, June 18, 2008.

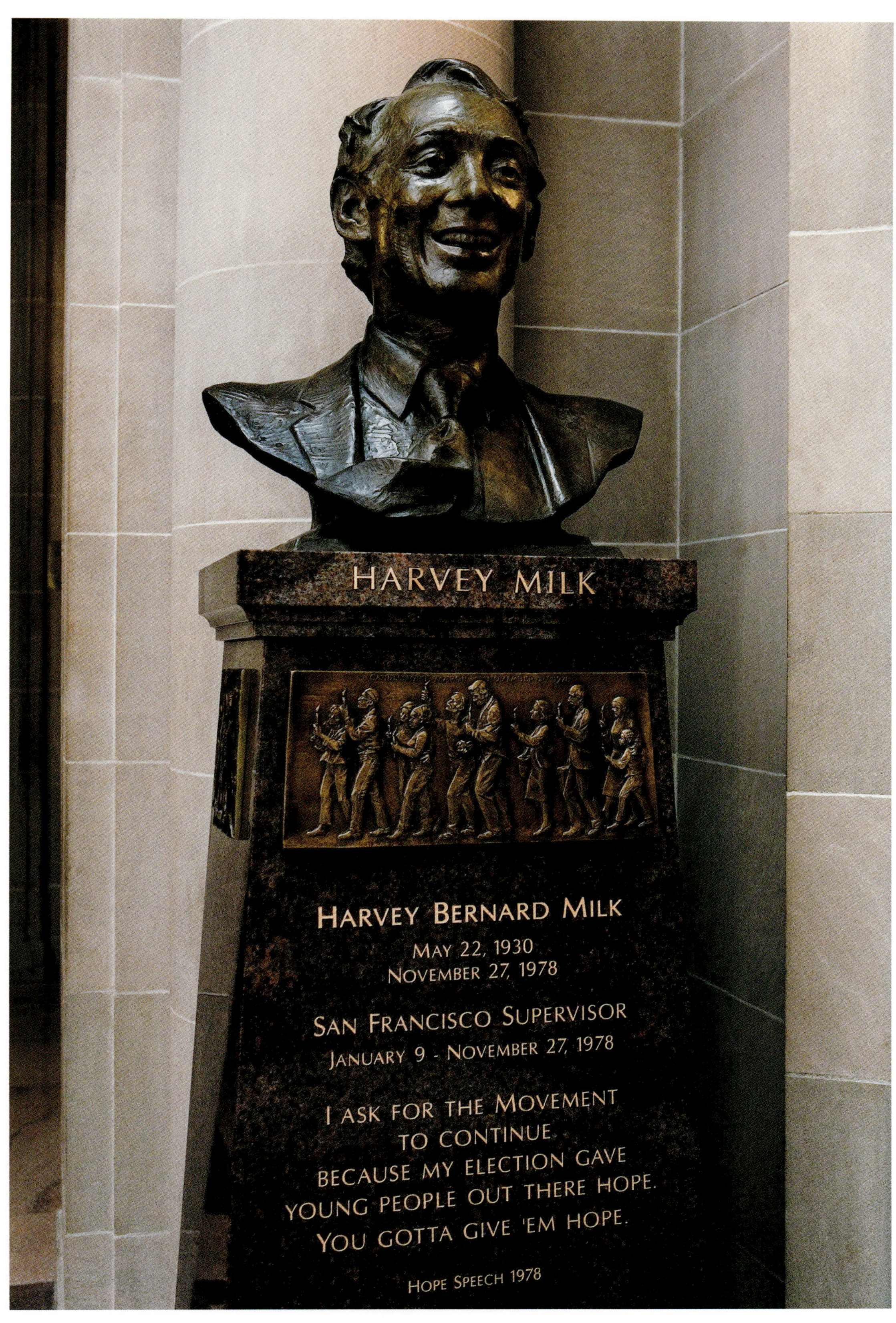

Supervisor Harvey Milk City Hall Memorial Sculpture by
Daub Firmin Hendrickson Sculpture Group, May 19, 2008.

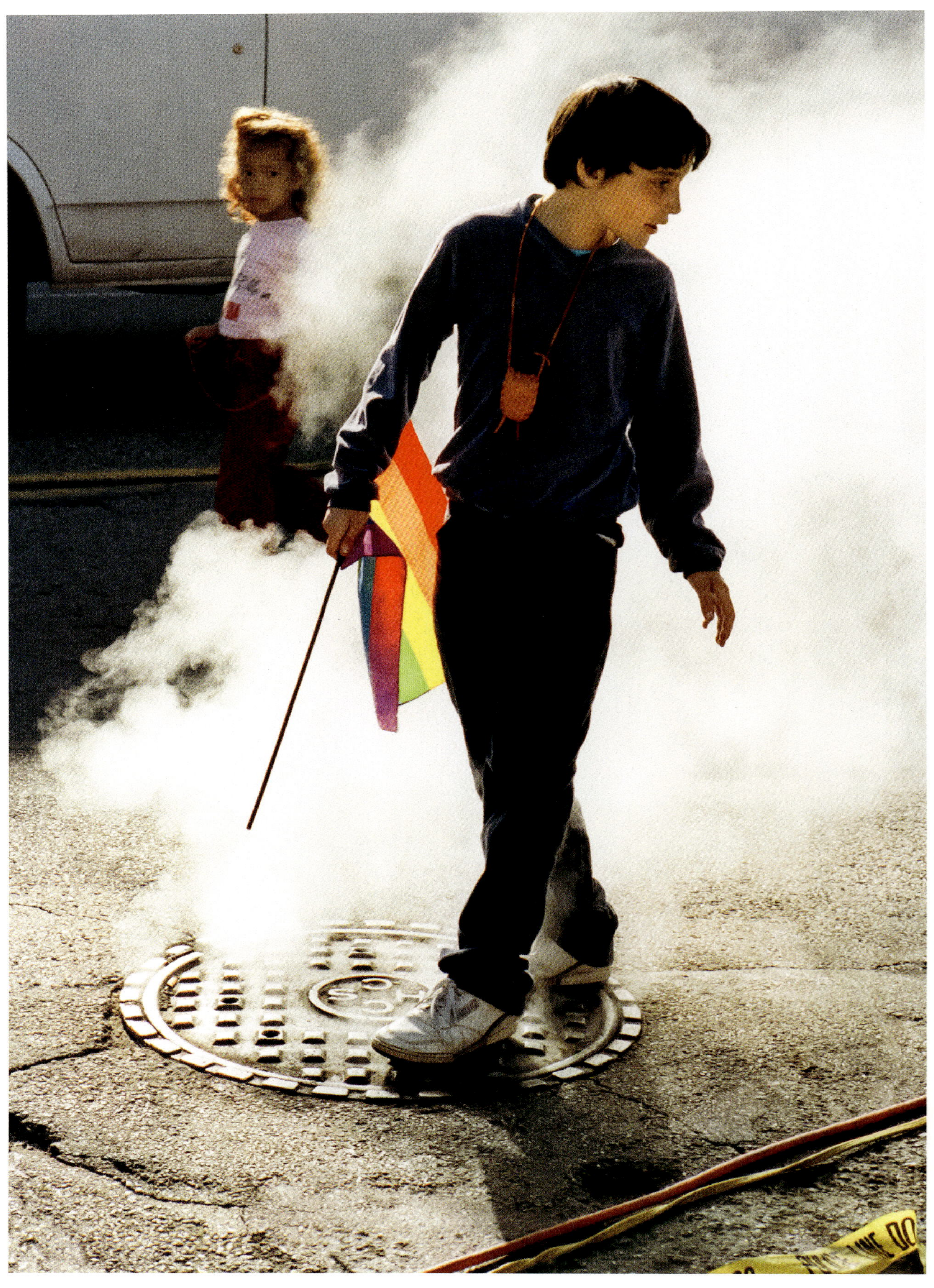

Above: SF LGBT Pride, June 26, 1988.
Opposite: Scout, Castro Street, June 20, 2015.
Overleaf: The Chuck Holmes Gay and Lesbian Bisexual Transgender Community Center Rainbow Room, July 8, 2012.

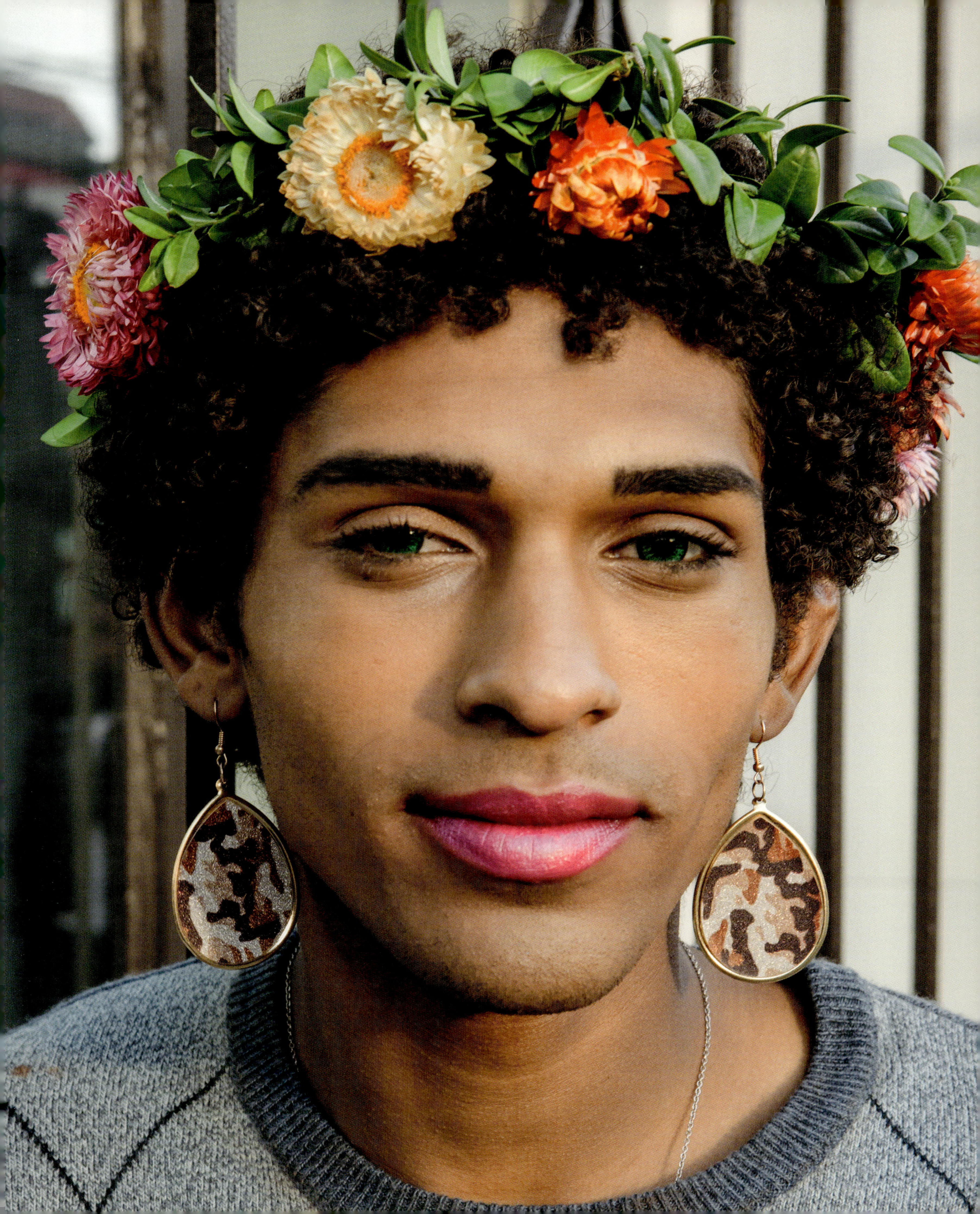

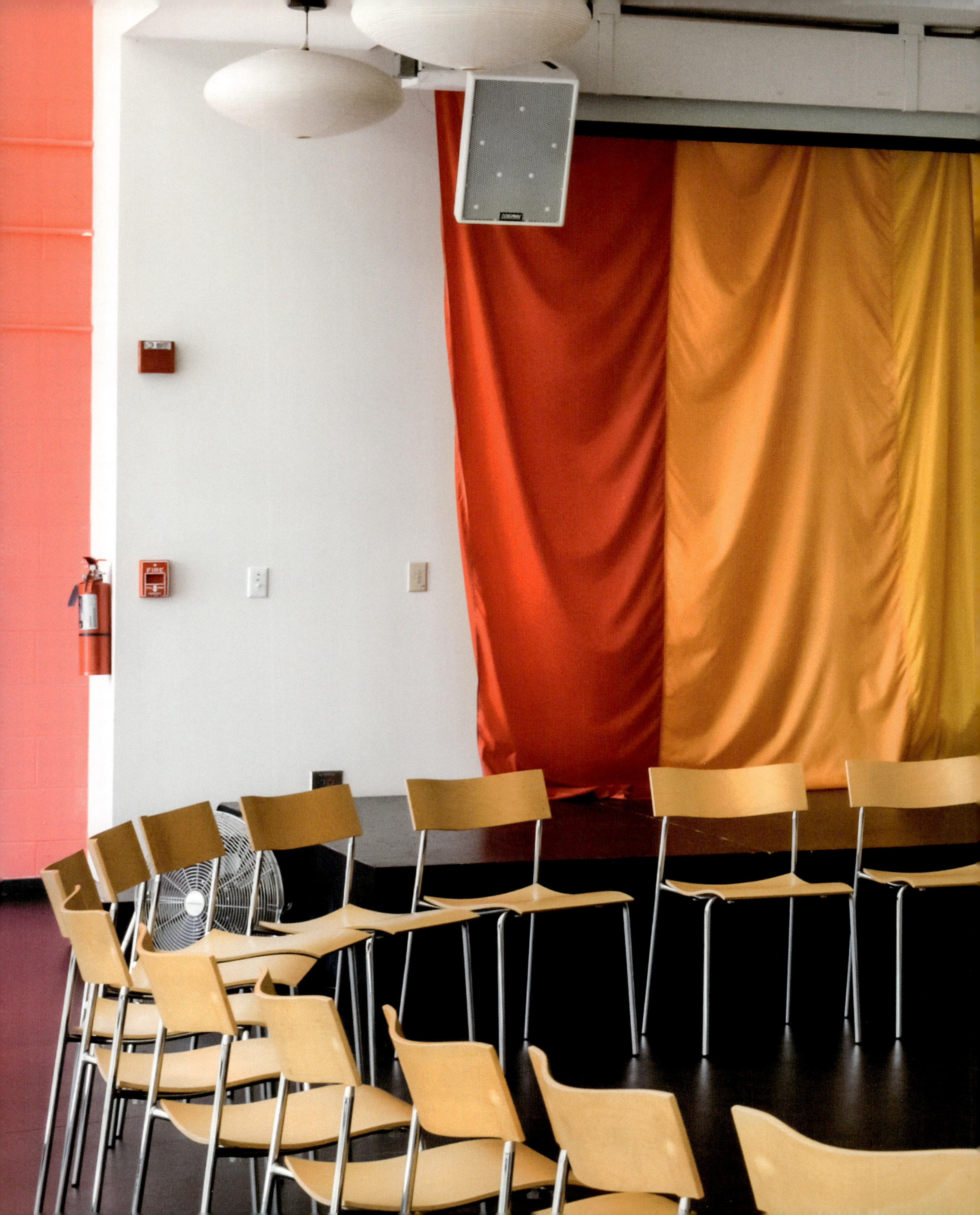
FIRE

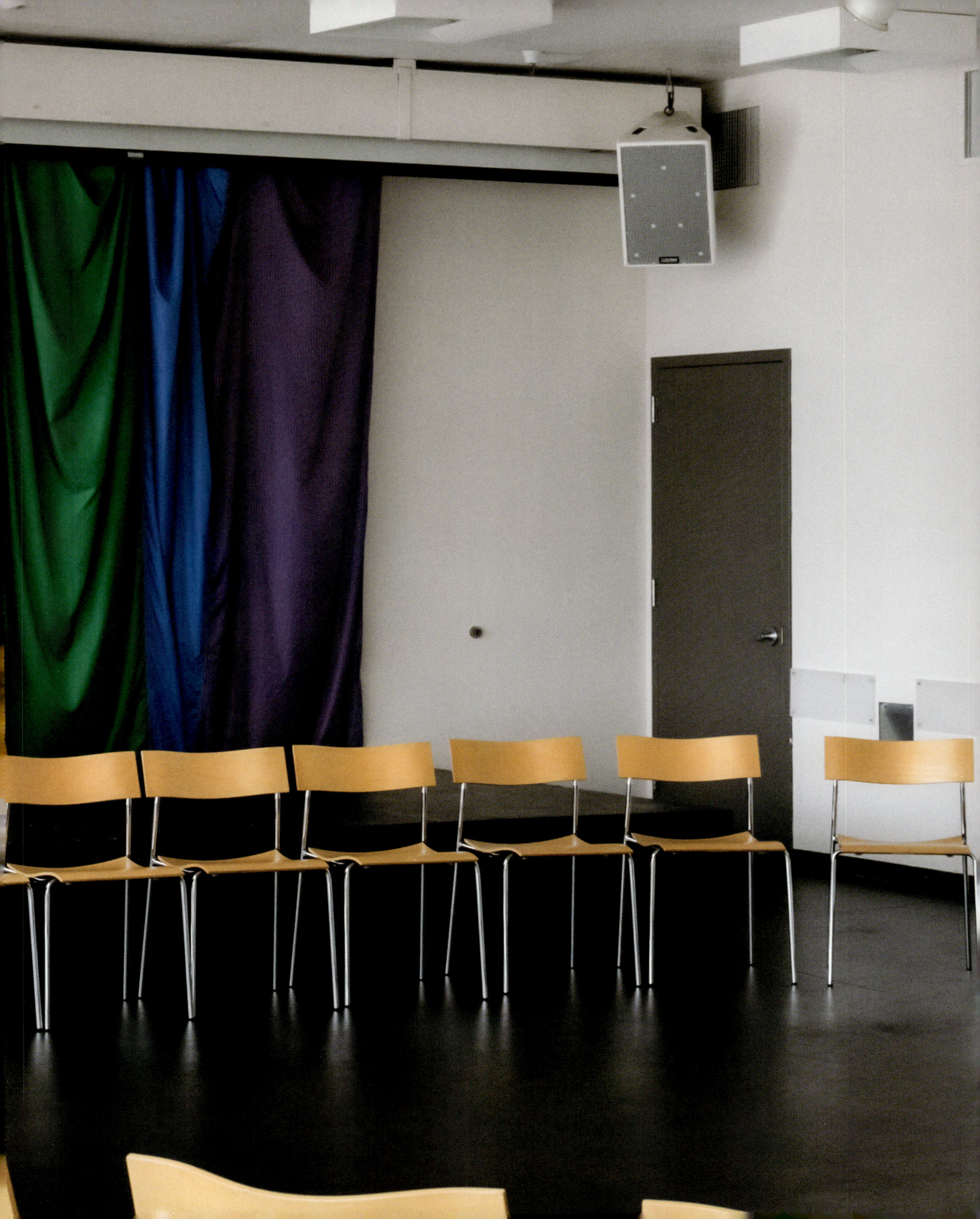

INDEX

CREDITS

Captions for Opening Pages: p.2 First version of the Rainbow Flag, 1978; p.4-5 Civic Center, 1975; p.6-7 Self-portrait in Ashbury Street darkroom, 1977; p.8-9 Castro Street Fair, August 1976; p.10 LGBT Pride Celebration, June 1990; p.12-13 LGBT Pride, "Heels on Wheels" contingent, June 1990; back jacket: Pink Triangle installation on Twin Peaks, June 25, 2006. (Appropriated as a symbol of remembrance, the pink triangle was originally the symbol assigned to identify gay and lesbian captives in the Nazi death camps during World War II.)

Captions for Front End Pages: 1. Marlon Fixico, (Cheyenne and Seminole Tribes and International Council of Two Spirit Societies), 2. Eva Konigova and Hida Viloria (Intersex rights advocates), 3. Lee Mentley (Hulah Palace 25 year reunion, 1994), 4. Laura Thomas and Rebecca Hensler (Dyke March, 1999), 5. Scorchy, 6. Samir Khalidy and Svi Howard Rosenman, 7. Del Martin and Phyliss Lyon, 1999 (co-founders of The Daughters of Bilitis), 8. Ron Fitch, 9. Alice Hoaglan (mother of gay hero of Flight 93, Mark Bingham), 10. Lenn Keller (Bay Area Lesbian History Archives, 2015), 11. Steven Maxine, 12. Hank Wilson, 13. *Milk*; Cleve Jones with actor Emile Hirsch, 14. Shar and Jack Renour, Bruckman Family, 15. Felicia "Flames" Elizondo (SF LGBT Pride 2011), 16. *Milk*; Dennis Peron and actor Ted Jan Roberts, 17. Assemblyman Tom Ammiano, 18. Matthew Madrigal and Hubert Johnson, 19. Kozmic Lady, 20. Odder, (SF LGBT Pride 2005), 21. Marilyn Monroe impersonator, 22. Reverend Cecil Williams (Randy Shilt's Memorial at Glide Memorial Church, 1994), 23. Blackberri (SF LGBT Pride 1976), 24. Jenni Olson, Tom DiMaria and Mark Finch (SF LGBT Film Festival staff, 1993). 25. Susan Stryker (SF LGBT Pride 1995), 26. Joe and Frank Capley-Alfano (Pink Triangle on Twin Peaks Ceremony, 2009), 27. John Lewis and Stuart Gaffney (marriage equality plaintiffs on the day of the US Supreme Court Decision in favor of same sex marriage, 26 June, 2015), 28. Veronica Klaus, 29. Jewelle Gomez (Dyke March 2000), 30. Joseph Amster and Rick Shelton as Emperor Norton and Countess Lola Monte, 31. *Milk* costume designer, Danny Glicker, 32. *Milk* producers, Bruce Cohen and Dan Jinks, 33. Kirk Read, 34. Viva Vinson and Cockette Pristine Condition (Hulah Palace-Cockette 25 year reunion, 1994), 35. Reverend Troy Perry (founder of Metropolitan Community Church), 36. Photographer Cathy Cade (Dyke March 1998), 37. *Milk*; Union leader Allan Baird and actor Peter Jason, 38. Willie Walker (co-founder of The LGBT Historical Society), 39. Charles Pierce and Ambisextrous (Plush Room backstage, 1981), 40. Absolute Empress XXX, Donna Sachet (SF LGBT Pride 1998), 41. Absolute Empress XXIX Anita Martini (José Sarria's 90th Birthday), 42. Jason Bishop (6th International AIDS Conference demonstration), 43. *Milk*; James Ferrera, Frank Robinson and Dustin Lance Black, 44. Sebastian, Bear and Mommy Aurelia (SF LGBT Pride 2001), 45. Kent Denning, 46. Kristin Perry and Sandy Stier, marriage equality heroes, 47. Jupiter (Supperclub performance 2010), 48. Ocean Michael Moon, Dusty Dawn and directors David Weissman and Bill Weber (Cockettes documentary, 1999).

Captions for Back End Pages: 1. Lieutenant Dan Choi (LGBT March on Washington 2009), 2. Tom Horn and Chris Nigoghossian (José Sarria's 90th Birthday), 3. Davina Kotulsky and Molly McKay (Prop 8 Decision Rally, 2010), 4. Supervisor Bevan Dufty (SF LGBT Pride 2003), 5. Joey Cain, (SF LGBT Pride 2004), 6. Zac Benfield and Jesse Sanford, 7. *Milk*; Anne Kronenberg and actress Alison Pill, 8. Empress Nicole Murray Ramirez (Queen Mother I of the Americas) and Rose Emperor XXXVIII Athens Scities, 9. Sister Dana Van Iquity, 10. Kelly Hart Rivera (Prop 8 Decision Rally, 2010), 11. Juan Crovetto, 12. Brontez Purnell, 13. Billy Powell. 14. Chuck Mobley, 15. Kate Kendall, Esq., (ED National Center for Lesbian Rights, Prop 8 Decision Rally 2010), 16. Karl Knapper (SF LGBT Pride 2005), 17. Robert Potter (Officer Emeritus, Alexander Hamilton American Legion Post 448), 18. Jordy and Marty Tackitt-Jones, 19. Anna Damiani and Senator Mark Leno (Mayor's Rainbow Flag raising, SF LGBT Pride 2007), 20. Norm Halm (Dan's assistant visiting the camera store set of *Milk*, 2008), 21. *Milk*; Stephen Spinella as Rick Stokes, 22. Paco Rios, 23. Carole Migden (Harvey Milk LGBT Democratic Club Dinner 1982), 24. Annie Sprinkle and Beth Stephens (Ecosexuals, SF LGBT Pride 2015), 25. Chuck Solomon (*Coming of Age* film event, 1986), 26. Miss Majors and friend (Transmarch 2012), 27. *Milk*; Actor Kelvin Yu and Michael Wong, 28. Adam Bouska and Jeff Parshley (No H8 campaign) with Stuart Milk (center), 29. Gina LaDavina, 30. Naomi Copperjet and JD Harp, 31. Emperor XXXVI John Weber, Empress XLIII, Cher (Pink Saturday 2008), 32. Gilbert Baker (Stonewall 25th Anniversary, 1994), 33. Alexandra Rodriguez De Ruiz (Prop 8 Decision Rally 2010), 34. Danny Celeri (SF LGBT Pride 1983), 35. Carl Linkhart (Rumipalooza at The Purple House, 2011), 36. *Milk*; Denton Smith with actor Robert Boyd Holbrook, 37. Vinc C (SF LGBT Pride 2013), 38. Jim Fouratt and Pat Brown (SF LGBT Pride 2011), 39. Gwenn Craig (Harvey Milk's Birthday Celebration, 1981), 40. James Broughton (SF LGBT Pride 1982), 41. Marilyn Pittman (KALW Radio producer and show host), 42. Shane Martin and Colton Windsor, (Human Rights Commission SF Headquarters), 43. *Milk*; Denis O'Hare as Senator John Briggs, 44. Debra Walker (Mayor's Rainbow Flag raising, SF LGBT Pride 2007), 45. Cecilia Chung and Red Jordan Arobateau (*Transgender Tuesdays* film after party 2012), 46. Eddie Hall and Steve Sirota (Godfathers to be) with Barbara Liu MacDowell, 47. Gabriel Haaland (Demonstration for Trans inclusion in US ENDA Act 2008), 48. Police Comissioners Dennis Herrera and Wayne Friday (SF LGBT Pride, 2001).

Notes from "There Is No Shelter In The Arts" by Chuck Mobley:

1. Biographical references derive from conversations and emails with the author in 2016 and significantly from an audio interview of Nicoletta by Gareth Watkins and Roger Smith for PrideNZ.com conducted on June 19, 2012.
2. See Jae Emerling, "The archive as producer," in *Photography History and Theory* (New York: Routledge , 2012).
3. See Charles T. Clotfelter, "Patterns of Enrollment and Completion" in *Economic Challenges in Higher Education*, ed. Charles T. Clotfelter, et al. (Chicago: University of Chicago Press, 1991), 31-32.
4. See Nancy M. Stuart, "Photographic Higher Education in the United States" in *The Concise Focal Encyclopedia of Photography*, ed. Nancy M. Stuart, et al. (Burlington, MA: Focal Press, 2008), 100-101.
5. "Between 1963 and 1970 over 50 million [Kodak] Instamatic cameras were produced." Stuart, 101.
6. Ibid., 102-106.
7. For a more thorough anthropological and sociological examination of how institutions coalesce and make decisions, see Mary C. Douglas, *How Institutions Think*, (Syracuse, NY: Syracuse University Press, 1986).
8. See essays in Martha Rosler, "In, Around, and Afterthoughts (On Documentary Photography)," in *Decoys and Disruptions*, (Cambridge, MA: The MIT Press, 2004); and Jae Emerling, "Documentary, or instants of truth," in *Photography History and Theory* (New York: Routledge, 2012).
9. See Vilem Flusser, *Towards a Philosophy of Photography* (1983), trans. Anthony Mathews (London: Reaktion Books, 2000).
10. See Abigail Solomon-Godeau, "Who is Speaking Thus? Some Questions about Documentary Photography," in *Photography at the Dock* (Minneapolis: University of Minnesota Press, 1991).
11. This paraphrasing, as well as the title of this essay, is derived from Vic Chesnutt, "Isadora Duncan," in *Little*, Texas Hotel Records, 1990. Also, the subtitle of this essay is an allusion to *The Life and Times of Harvey Milk* by Rob Epstein and Richard Schmiechen (1984; New York: Criterion Collection, 2011), DVD.
12. Janet Malcolm, *The Crime of Sheila McGough*, (New York: Knopf, 1999), 5.

ACKNOWLEDGEMENTS

This book would not be possible without the support of my life partner Michael Pinatelli, Jr., Tony Nourmand and the staff at Reel Art Press, Artbook/DAP, Focus Features, Inc. (*Milk*), Groundswell Films (*Milk*), Producers Bruce Cohen and Dan Jinks, and the entire staff of Milk, and Mark Hanson and Jes Espinoza at Hanson Digital.

Thank you to writers Gus Van Sant and Chuck Mobley and to all the people in the photos and to the other photographers listed. Permit me to also acknowledge all my collaborators who didn't get chosen for this book. My hope is to continue to publish theme specific books where our work together will continue to be honored and celebrated.

Thank you to all the great mentors, friends and lovers, employers and life coaches throughout my life, leading to this dream come true, including but not limited to: my parents Sal and Helen Nicoletta, siblings John Nicoletta and Lorraine Barney and our family, The Freedom Express gang, Dennis Maher, Esmé Hecht, Michael Long, Chuck Kennedy, Harvey Milk and Scott Smith, Larry Hughes and John Wahl, Roger Pielaet, Jack Love Sullivan, Dee Dee Stout, Rick Shelton, Marcus Ewert, and photographers Bill Skumurski, Crawford Barton, John Edwards, Morrie Camhi, Guy Corry and Wayne Smolen.

Thank you to Allan Baird, Alison Elangasinghe, Armando Garcia, Arthur Tress, *Bay Area Reporter*, Bern Boyle, Bill Carroll, Bob Burnside, Bob Kelley, Bryan Darling, Bus Station John, Carla McQueen, Catharine Clark Gallery, Charles Morris III, Chris Curtis, Chris Koperski, Chuck Griffin, Clyde Hall, Craig Riedel, Daniel Frontino Elash, David Bonetti, David Nemoyten, Debra St. John, Don Eckert, Ed Brett and Rick Lemos, Eddie Reynolds and Ed Jones, Elizabeta Bettinksi, Eric Smith and Mark Garrett, Eriq Chang, Fidel Lirio, Francesco D'ippolito, Gayle Rubin, Gene Brake, Gene Nevins, Gerard Koskovich, Hector Sabatés, Ian MacDonald, Jack Von Euw, et al (Bancroft Library), James Ferrera, Jason Edward Black, Jeff Dauber, Jesse Cox, Jesse Lee Stout, Jill Manton et al, (SF Art Commission), Jim Fouratt, Jim Van Buskirk, Joel Wang, John Raines, John Trudell, Jordy Jones, Kevin Fox, Kwai Lam, Laura Albert, Lauretta and Martin Dives, Lawrence Helman PR, Lee Mentley et al (Hulah Palace), Lisa Baker, Liz Bursis, Liz McGarrity, Mark Mace Gallery, Meredith Clark-Anderson, Michael Flanagan, Michael Munzell, Mike Owens, Mouci and Winston Tong, Mrs. Elva Smith, Nancy McNally, Nancy Wolff, Esq., Noah and Kris Lang and Family (Electricworks), Norm Halm, Parker Tilghman, Peggy and Joker, Peggy Sue Amison, Phil Bray, Richard Dworkin, Richard Nichols and Don Pierson, Richard Harris, Rick Castro, Rod and Michelle Funston-Carman, Rodney Phillips, Rory Bruton, Sheila Cohen and Sidney Brown (Bucheon Gallery), Stafford, Stan Maletic, The LGBT Historical Society, The Harvey Milk City Hall Memorial committee, Harvey Milk Foundation, The James Hormel Gay and Lesbian Studies Center at the SF Library, Thomas Horn and Caesar Alexzander (The Bob Ross Foundation), Tim Campbell and Steven Machado, Travis Sommerville and Robin Clark, Walker, Waiyde Palmer, Will Patterson.

Please forgive any omissions here or in the captions and bring them to my attention: dannic@charter.net or www.dannynicoletta.com

The inclusion of a person's photo in this book should never be taken as a citation of someone's sexual preference or gender identity.

Text Editor: Alison Elangasinghe
Editorial Assistant: Rory Bruton

First published 2017 by Reel Art Press, an imprint of Rare Art Press Ltd, London, UK
www.reelartpress.com

First Edition
10 9 8 7 6 5 4 3 2 1

ISBN: 978-1-909526-39-6

Pre-Press by HR Digital Solutions

This book is printed on paper Condat matt Périgord, ECF, acid free and age resistant. The Lecta Group uses only celluloses from certified or well managed forests and plantations.

Printed by Graphius, Gent

remember me

is all I ask

and if

remembered

be a task

forget me

– *Laurie Anderson*

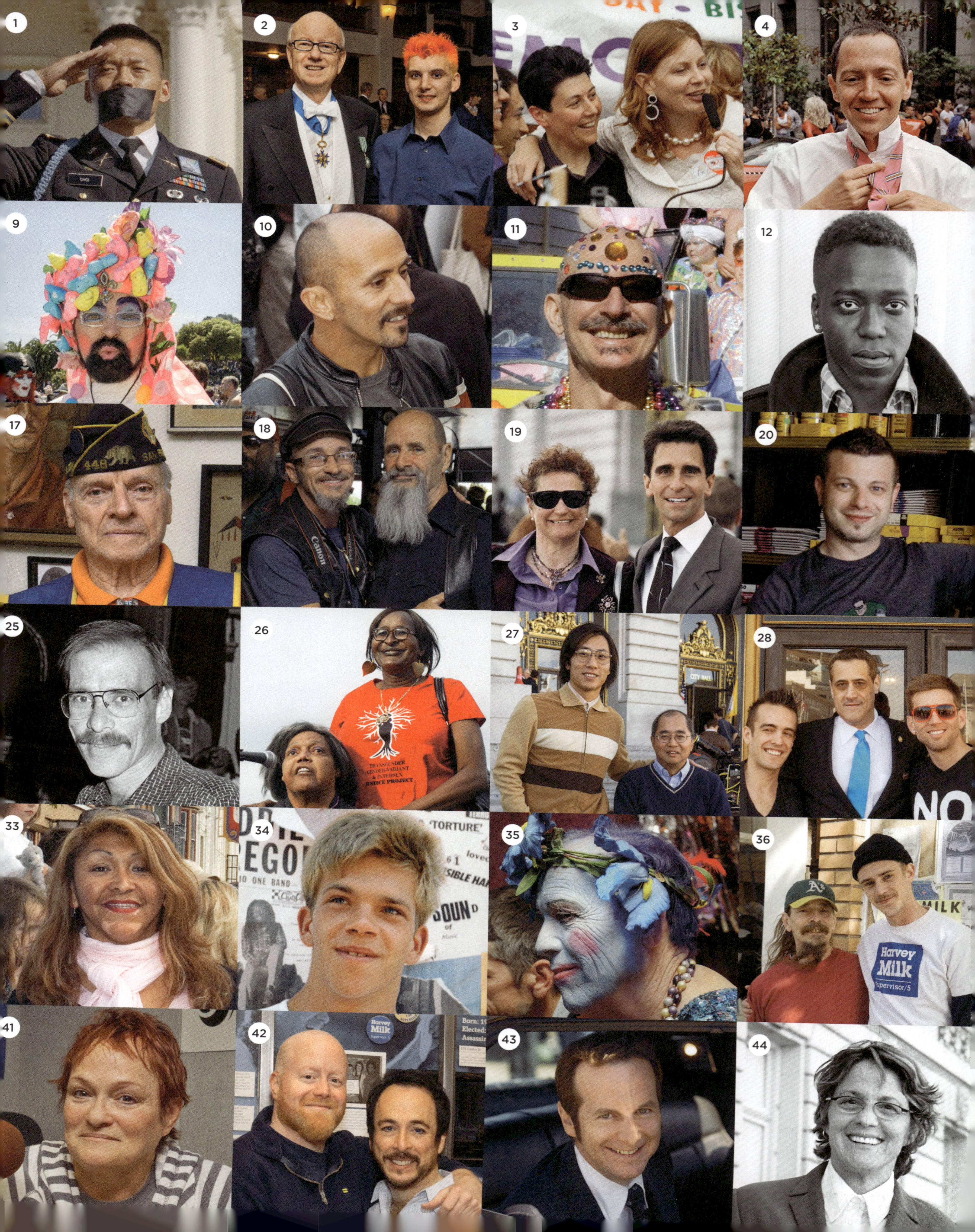
1
2
3
4
9
10
11
12
17
18
19
20
25
26
27
28
33
34
35
36
41
42
43
44
TRANSGENDER GENDER-VARIANT & INTERSEX JUSTICE PROJECT
'TORTURE'
Harvey Milk Supervisor/5